Innovative Treatment Methods in Psychopathology
edited by Karen S. Calhoun, Henry E. Adams, and Kevin M. Mitchell

The Changing School Scene: Challenge to Psychology
by Leah Gold Fein

Troubled Children: Their Families, Schools, and Treatments
by Leonore R. Love and Jaques W. Kaswan

Research Strategies in Psychotherapy
by Edward S. Bordin

The Volunteer Subject
by Robert Rosenthal and Ralph L. Rosnow

Innovations in Client-Centered Therapy
by David A. Wexler and Laura North Rice

The Rorschach: A Comprehensive System
by John E. Exner

Theory and Practice in Behavior Therapy
by Aubrey J. Yates

Principles of Psychotherapy
by Irving B. Weiner

Psychoactive Drugs and Social Judgment: Theory and Research
edited by Kenneth Hammond and C. R. B. Joyce

Clinical Methods in Psychology
edited by Irving B. Weiner

Human Resources for Troubled Children
by Werner I. Halpern and Stanley Kissel

Hyperactivity
by Dorothea M. Ross and Sheila A. Ross

Heroin Addiction: Theory, Research, and Treatment
by Jerome J. Platt and Christina Labate

Children's Rights and the Mental Health Profession
edited by Gerald P. Koocher

The Role of the Father in Child Development
edited by Michael E. Lamb

Handbook of Behavioral Assessment
edited by Anthony R. Ciminero, Karen S. Calhoun, and Henry E. Adams

Counseling and Psychotherapy: A Behavioral Approach
by E. Lakin Phillips

Dimensions of Personality
edited by Harvey London and John E. Exner, Jr.

The Mental Health Industry: A Cultural Phenomenon
by Peter A. Magaro, Robert Gripp, David McDowell, and Ivan W. Miller III

Nonverbal Communication: The State of the Art
by Robert G. Harper, Arthur N. Wiens, and Joseph D. Matarazzo

A Biodevelopmental Approach to Clinical Child Psychology
by Sebastiano Santostefano

DIMENSIONS OF PERSONALITY

DIMENSIONS OF PERSONALITY

Edited by

HARVEY LONDON

JOHN E. EXNER, Jr.

A WILEY-INTERSCIENCE PUBLICATION

JOHN WILEY & SONS, New York • Chichester • Brisbane • Toronto

Copyright © 1978 by John Wiley & Sons, Inc.

All rights reserved. Published simultaneously in Canada.

Reproduction or translation of any part of this work
beyond that permitted by Sections 107 or 108 of the
1976 United States Copyright Act without the permission
of the copyright owner is unlawful. Requests for
permission or further information should be addressed to
the Permissions Department, John Wiley & Sons, Inc.

Library of Congress Cataloging in Publication Data
Main entry under title:

Dimensions of personality.

  (Wiley series on personality processes)
  "A Wiley-Interscience publication."
  Includes bibliographies and indexes.
  1. Personality. 2. Psychology, Experimental.
3. Social psychology. I. London, Harvey.
II. Exner, John E.
BF698.D56   155.2   77-25328
ISBN 0-471-54392-6

Printed in the United States of America

10 9 8 7 6 5 4 3 2

To Gordon Allport, Raymond B. Cattell, and Henry Murray

Series Preface

This series of books is addressed to behavioral scientists interested in the nature of human personality. Its scope should prove pertinent to personality theorists and researchers as well as to clinicians concerned with applying an understanding of personality processes to the amelioration of emotional difficulties in living. To this end, the series provides a scholarly integration of theoretical formulations, empirical data, and practical recommendations.

Six major aspects of studying and learning about human personality can be designated: personality theory, personality structure and dynamics, personality development, personality assessment, personality change, and personality adjustment. In exploring these aspects of personality, the books in the series discuss a number of distinct but related subject areas: the nature and implications of various theories of personality; personality characteristics that account for consistencies and variations in human behavior; the emergence of personality processes in children and adolescents; the use of interviewing and testing procedures to evaluate individual differences in personality; efforts to modify personality styles through psychotherapy, counseling, behavior therapy, and other methods of influence; and patterns of abnormal personality functioning that impair individual competence.

Irving B. Weiner

Case Western Reserve University
Cleveland, Ohio

Preface

There is always a concurrent sense of excitement and relief for the researcher who, when poking about in the literature on a given subject matter, discovers an exhaustive, authoritative, and up-to-date review or summary of the material on which he is focusing. Thus, we enthusiastically present a volume that has as its basic goal a review of much of the contemporary thinking and research concerning the various dimensions of personality. The concept of *personality* has intrigued and baffled psychologists since the very inception of the science. Many have attempted to describe and define personality, and many more have attempted to study it so as to present empirically demonstrable evidence from which we can understand this elusive "thing." Whereas the theories of personality have usually been broad and all encompassing, the scientific evidence has evolved in bits and pieces. The work included in this volume illustrates some of the more important of those bits and pieces and, in effect, reflects the so-called uniconcept "trait" approach toward the scientific investigation of personality. There are many in the field of personality study who might dispute the usefulness of studying single dimensions of the person without also making attempts to understand those dimensions in a total context. This is by no means a new issue.

The argument about whether to approach personality by focusing on a specific attribute or by focusing on the whole of the person can be traced easily to the latter half of the nineteenth century, a time when the *mind* was the basic subject matter for psychology. By that time Wundt, by his acceptance of the "Personal Equation," had reluctantly conceded that individual differences do exist. However, it was not Wundt who provided the stimulus for the unfolding of a "personality psychology" but rather Sir Francis Galton and James McKeen Cattell. As early as 1882 Galton had established a laboratory for the study of the person and sought to develop a series of tests, both mental and physical, that would constitute a useful inventory of the human subject. In 1890 Cattell proposed a test battery that might be used to discover consistency among mental operations, the interdependence of these operations, and their variation under different stimulus conditions. It was also in 1890 that the classic work of

William James, *Principles of Psychology,* appeared. James did not use the term *personality* as we know it today but reserved its use to describe various conditions of psychopathology, following from the psychoanalytic school. He did, however, discuss the *Self,* offering a theoretical formulation of four levels of the *Self* and suggesting a hierarchical model of organization.

It would be impractical to suggest that the work of Galton, or Cattell, or James actually formed the cornerstone of what was to become the specialization of differential psychology, but it is obvious that they worked and wrote during that critical period when the *Zeitgeist* was such that individual differences were becoming a focal point of scientific preoccupation. Whatever the absolute starting point for differential psychology, it grew, haltingly at first, but ultimately developing into a massive effort by the young science of psychology to commit itself to the quest of establishing lawful theorems concerning individual features and behavioral correlates.

During the period from 1900 to 1935, the study of individual differences became one of the most lively areas of investigation (and discussion) among psychologists. And although the term *personality* as such was notably absent from much of the literature of that era, other terms having similar implications appeared quite frequently. *Characterology, psychography, typology,* and *personalistic psychology* were among the more frequent. The methodology for these investigations was generally quite orthodox for the level of sophistication that psychology had achieved by that time. A characteristic or behavior was identified for study; the range of differences among subjects with respect to this characteristic was then established; and finally attempts were made to correlate the characteristic with behavior, or to correlate two or more characteristics.

The controversy between a *trait* conceptualization of personality versus a more *holistic* framework ensued during this period, with noted psychologists from each side expressing their views with vigor. In 1921 William Stern, who was the most prominent advocate of personalistic psychology, offered strong criticism concerning the direction of differential psychology, that is, toward the study of traits as they are distributed among groups. Stern argued that although traits may exist, their manifestation varies considerably, "in constant relationship to the world outside." Stern encouraged a view of the person as an individual who might well function differently in different environmental situations. His conception of the person appears to parallel closely that of the Gestalt psychologists, and particularly that of Kurt Lewin, who offered a distinction between genotypes and phenotypes in 1927, and who in 1936 published his classic formula indicating that behavior is a function of the person interacting with the environment. The approach of Stern, Lewin, and others of that persuasion carried the strong implication that, although we might neatly identify specific dimensions of personality, the complete understanding of the person would remain elusive until such a time as we are able to understand a trait in the context of environmental conditions.

On the opposite side of the psychological coin were the many psychologists whose efforts were directed toward the study of specific traits, generally researched in isolation from other features of the person. This group of psychologists did not necessarily advocate a position different from that of Stern and Lewin, but instead they operated more in the context of an orthodox methodological tradition, with an assumption that "the whole is equal to the sum of its parts." Although some of these researchers might legitimately be classified as psychographers or typologists, most were simply trying to understand different characteristics of the person without attempting to integrate data across characteristics, or attempting to look at the context of different environmental conditions. A simple understanding of various characteristics had been the approach of Cattell when he formulated his test battery in 1890 and coined the term *mental tests*. In 1910 G.M. Whipple published a *Manual of Mental and Physical Tests* describing each test as it was purported to measure some aspect of mental capacity or trait. This test-for-traits approach was not only popular but was strongly encouraged by the more hard-core scientists of the era. For example, in 1928 H.P. Weld published his classic text, *Psychology As Science*. Weld noted that although, "traits . . . are literally innumerable . . . [it becomes important to study each for its] disposition, . . . the conditions of its variation, . . . and to examine, classify and explain [each]." Weld cautioned that a major work would be required to study traits as related to one another, but he suggested that such a study, focusing on the intervariations and interrelationships, could feasibly unfold the mysteries of the person, mainly with regard to issues of intellectual operations and temperament. Weld expressed much skepticism about the practicability of such a project, mainly because of the unique features of people, and consequently, he encouraged the major thrust of research to remain at the more simplified, trait-oriented level.

The period following the end of World War I to the early 1930s was marked by a substantial number of publications concerning traits. It is important to point out that the term *personality* was still not in vogue, generally being restricted to philosophical interpretations of the individual; many of the features (or traits) that we now subscribe to as components of personality, such as flexibility, aggressiveness, values, and so on were often itemized as elements of *temperament,* or sometimes as parts of *character.* For instance, Frank N. Freeman stated in his widely used 1926 text, *Mental Tests,* "These [non-intellectual] traits have been grouped loosely under the general head of personality. Personality is not a technical, psychological term, but it may serve as a convenience to include a number of varieties of mental traits which are not intellectual."

Most of the early trait research can be categorized under one of three broad headings commonly used between 1919 and 1935. One of these headings, *Will Temperament,* included such features as energetic versus weak, prompt versus slow, careful versus reckless, and persistence versus vacillation. A second heading, *Emotional Temperament,* included such elements as aggression, optimism, anxiety, and ambition. A third broad area was frequently defined in terms of *Moral Attitudes or Judgments* and generally focused on traits that seemed to influence interpersonal behaviors. These included the ability to make effective "ethical" discriminations (i.e., the ability to make socially desirable responses in interpersonal situations), interpersonal dominance versus submissiveness, and trustworthiness. Although most of the measures developed to investigate these various traits were quite crude by contemporary standards, many of the focal points of these investigations show interesting parallels with some of the contemporary trait research presented in this volume. For example, Shuttleworth's (1924) Ambition scale seems similar to McClelland's Need for Achievement while Moore and Gilliland (1921) developed a concept similar to Machiavellianism.

One of the products derived from the accumulation of trait studies was the attempt to combine several measures into a test battery, following the lead of Cattell and Whipple. A considerable impetus was afforded this movement by psychologists attempting to study abnormal behavior (the forerunners of the modern clinical psychologist). They often administered several measures to learn as much as possible about the person and to create a psychogram or configuration of traits. A second yield from the trait movement was an attempt to integrate, in a single measure, items that would relate to more than one trait, thus providing a broader scale of personality characteristics. One of the early efforts was R. G. Bernreuter's (1931) scale, widely used for several years. The Bernreuter Inventory attempted to combine evaluation of three basic traits in a single measure. These were introversion-extraversion (following from the Jungian typological model), dominance-submissiveness, and dependency-independency. The scale also yielded a general index of adjustment called *neuroticism.* This approach, using a single instrument to study a variety of personality characteristics, yielded numerous scales during the next 15 years, many of which focused on issues of deviance, such as the now famous Minnesota Multiphasic Personality Inventory, which was first published in 1943.

While interest in the "clinical" or abnormal aspects of personality functioning grew rapidly during the 1930s and early 1940s, so too did interest in understanding the basic framework of personality. Three major figures of that period contributed enormously to both the conceptualization of personality and to the methodological approaches that might best be used to study this elusive human phenomenon. The figures are Gordon Allport, Henry Murray, and Raymond B. Cattell. Each approached personality somewhat differently from the popular, psychoanalytic conceptualization of personality deriving from Freud.

Gordon Allport gave a broad acknowledgment to the existence of traits. He conceived of personality as a "dynamic organization" of both psychological and physical forces. It is important to remember that this era was strongly marked by the "nature-nurture" controversy, that is, the innate versus the learned (a problem first raised by Galton). Thus, Allport's famed work, *Personality: A Psychological Interpretation,* which appeared in 1937, gave careful consideration to the fact that some traits are genotypic whereas others are phenotypic. Allport also cautioned that some traits might be simply *instrumental* in significance, that is, representing a *style* of behaving but seldom being part of the nucleus of the personality structure. He viewed other traits as *motivational,* more illustrative of the personality nucleus. Following from Stern, Allport cautioned that most traits can be understood *only* when their interdependence is also understood. He suggested that some traits may be *common* (to groups) whereas others may be *individual.* Although raising some seemingly insurmountable obstacles for personality researchers (mainly because of his insistence on the interdependence of most traits), he nevertheless provided much impetus to the research movement, especially with his notions that most traits would be reasonably consistent within the individual and that many traits would be normally distributed in a large population.

Concurrent with Allport's work was the masterful contribution of Henry Murray. His *Explorations in Personality,* which has become a milestone work, was published in 1938. It contained more than 70 approaches to the study of personality features. Undoubtedly, Murray was much more influenced by the psychoanalytic movement than was Allport. He conceived of personality in terms of the dynamic or *functional mediation* that occurs between the person and his needs and the demands of the environment. He focused extensively on the need system as it relates to the *internal proceedings* of the individual and to the *external proceedings* or behaviors manifested in coping with the world. One of the important techniques developed by Murray (with Christiana Morgan) for the study of personality is the Thematic Apperception Test, published in 1935. This test has remained a very important tool for both the clinical psychologist and the personality researcher, and two of the chapters presented in this volume show extensive use of that technique.

Raymond B. Cattell's approach to personality evolved along with the gradual increase in the sophistication of measurement methods. His classic paper, *The Principal Trait Clusters for Describing Personality,* which appeared in 1945, and his first book, *The Description and Measurement of Personality* (1946), clearly signal his commitment to the factor-analytic approach. He has defined personality in a staunch empirical framework as "that which permits a prediction of what a person will do in a given situation." He has been a clear supporter of the trait approach in personality research, aspiring to establish an understanding of both the independence and interdependence of traits. Cattell suggests that the existence of traits may be inferred from a person's behavior. He has postulated that some traits will be *surface,* that is, behavior samples that fit together, whereas others will be *source* traits that reflect the underlying causes of the observed correlations among surface traits. His work has yielded numerous identifications of different traits, with six basic traits continuing to appear in most of his work.

By the late 1940s a considerable and diversified effort was obvious among personality researchers. Many studied personality along fairly traditional psychoanalytic lines, while many others used the conceptual frameworks of Allport, Murray, or Cattell. During the past 25 years, personality research has accelerated even more, and much of this newer research has been marked by a significant upswing in uniconcept dimension or trait research. Much impetus has been afforded this movement by a more sophisticated research methodology, and probably much more has occurred as a result of the variety of newer conceptualizations of personality ranging from those offered by the variety of learning theories, the research of social psychology, and the growing framework for a cognitive model of personality. This is not to suggest that the psychoanalytic model has become less important but rather that newer perspectives concerning personality have broadened the interests of more researchers. The increasing sophistication of methodology has often permitted a new look at some of the traits conceived decades ago, and much of that new look is reflected in the various chapters included in this volume.

It appears that the field is now achieving at least the beginnings of a state of maturity, and it makes sense to collect in one place the efforts of the leading trait researchers. We have culled the literature and have attempted to select not only the best known trait and trait-like variables for discussion but, in a few instances, have selected promising new traits about which a literature has begun to accumulate. For each trait, we solicited someone well qualified to discuss it. The result is the present volume. The scholar, the researcher, and the student now have in one place leading summaries of work on all the major uniconcept traits developed by experimental personality psychologists.

One outstanding fact highlighted by the collection of chapters in this book is the heterogeneity of concepts studied under the rubric of dimensions of personality or personality traits. There obviously has been no overarching plan or theory, implicit or explicit, guiding the selection of topics for trait researchers. Indeed, the editors were forced to organize the book by means of the unsophisticated tactic of simply placing the chapters in alphabetical order.

One basic issue that remains unresolved after all these years is whether the trait approach, that is, investigating personality dimensions in relative "isolation," is truly the most viable and/or productive manner of ultimately gleaning an understanding of the person. This issue, which of course was raised by Stern in the 1920s, has been resurrected most recently by Walter Mischel in his text, *Personality and Assessment,* which appeared in 1968. Mischel may have been rediscovering a rather worn wheel in his critique of personality research, or he may be making a very cogent point. Although the work in this volume is not oriented to speak directly to the Mischel argument, it does offer a sense of what has unfolded on the contemporary scene of personality research and also sheds light on what needs to be done. It will remain the judgment of the reader whether this type of personality research is the most viable and productive approach to personality, or whether some more extensive studies concerning the interdependence of traits is necessary before we can truly understand what is this thing that makes us what we are.

JOHN E. EXNER, JR.
HARVEY LONDON

Bayville, New York
Brooklyn, New York
November 1977

Acknowledgments

A number of people have helped in the preparation of this book. We would like to thank first our authors who have been extremely patient with their editors' foibles. Walter Maytham and Peter Peirce of John Wiley & Sons have been very helpful in a variety of ways. Finally, Charles Spielberger suggested the title. To these people we are grateful.

H. L.
J. E. E.

Contents

CHAPTER 1

Achievement Strivings

BERNARD WEINER

University of California, Los Angeles

The need for achievement is both more and less than a dimension of personality.[1] On the "more than" side, it is providing the foundation for a theory of motivation; it is the cornerstone of a theory of economic development; it is the target of behavioral change (psychotherapy) programs; it is shedding light on cognitive development and the relationship between thought and action; it enters into the discussion of women's liberation as well as social class and racial inequities; and it is of central importance in the writings of educators. There is perhaps no other personality structure that is associated with such a wealth of empirical, theoretical, and applied knowledge.

At the same time, the need for achievement is less than a *dimension* of personality. The cross-situational generality of achievement strivings is unknown; the stability of achievement needs is unknown; the social antecedents that give rise to a concern about achievement are unknown; the instruments for assessing this disposition are under question; and some of the most cited empirical correlates are tenuous while other reported relationships are highly suspect.

Unfortunately, I do not know the cure for the schizophrenic split conveyed in the prior two paragraphs, and I am not even certain that a disease exists. But some of the reasons for the apparent incongruities will be touched on in this chapter as the specific topics noted above are examined.

HISTORICAL DEVELOPMENTS

The starting point for the academic study of achievement motivation must be arbitrarily set. I will begin with Murray, but in so doing the earlier contributions and influential roles of Freud, Lewin, and McDougall are passed over (see Atkinson, 1964; Murray, 1959; Weiner, 1972).

1

Murray played a dual function in the history of achievement research. On the one hand, he called attention to a *need* for achievement (or an achievement attitude) by including this disposition among his list of 20 manifest psychogenic needs (Murray, 1938). According to Murray (1938), the desires and effects of achievement needs are:

To accomplish something difficult. To master, manipulate or organize physical objects, human beings, or ideas. To do this as rapidly and as independently as possible. To overcome obstacles and attain a high standard. To excel one's self. To rival and surpass others. To increase self-regard by the successful exercise of talent. (p. 164)

These desires, Murray (1938) states, are accompanied by the following actions:

To make intense, prolonged and repeated efforts to accomplish something difficult. To work with singleness of purpose towards a high and distant goal To have the determination to win. To try to do everything well. To be stimulated to excel by the presence of others, to enjoy competition. To exert will power; to overcome boredom and fatigue. (p. 164

Murray's second contribution to the study of achievement motivation was the development of an instrument, the Thematic Apperception Test (TAT), that supposedly revealed "covert and unconscious complexes" (Murray, 1938, p. 530). The TAT was almost universally adopted by subsequent investigators to assess achievement needs.

The next person of historical significance in the history of achievement motivation research is David McClelland. McClelland and his coworkers (McClelland, Atkinson, Clark & Lowell, 1953) conducted a systematic study of achievement motivation that entailed a refinement of the TAT for the measurement of achievement needs. Two questions pertinent to the legacy left by Murray are worth answering here: (1) Why was achievement chosen for study, rather than some of the other needs listed by Murray (e.g., affiliation, aggression)? and (2) Why was the TAT, rather than an objective assessment instrument, used?

Concerning the decision to study achievement needs, McClelland et al. (1953) state: "We devoted our attention to the achievement motive, primarily because there seemed to be a set of operations which had been frequently used in the laboratory for arousing it" (p. 4). Thus, methodological considerations in part dictated the concentration on achievement. In addition, McClelland was dissatisfied with the then-dominant deficit or survival theories of motivation proposed by Freud and Hull. The convergence on anxiety and food deprivation naturally leads to "stimulus offset" or reactive theories of behavior. Conversely, an emphasis on achievement needs readily generates "stimulus onset" or proactive conceptions of motivation. The theory of motivation first formulated by

McClelland was influenced by Hebb and the notion of an optimal level of stimulation (see McClelland et al., 1953). Finally, the choice to study achievement needs may have been partially dictated by personal rather than scientific considerations, such as McClelland's desire to foster social improvements as well as to contribute to the advancement of science.

As for the second question raised above concerning the use of a projective rather than an objective instrument, the selection of Murray's TAT as a medium of expression was made simply because "of our acceptance of the Freudian hypothesis that a good place to look for the effects of motivation is in fantasy" (McClelland et al., 1953, p. 107). Subsequent research indeed provided suggestive evidence that superficial verbal reports of achievement needs are not predictive of achievement-oriented behavior, whereas fantasy production is a valid index (de Charms, Morrison, Reitman, & McClelland, 1955; McClelland, 1958a; McClelland et al., 1953). But more of measurement later.

There was a bifurcation of achievement research following the publication of *The Achievement Motive* in 1953. McClelland turned from the laboratory to an analysis of economic development and the role of achievement needs in stimulating societal growth. This work culminated in 1961 with the publication of *The Achieving Society,* an awe-inspiring book that has had relatively little impact on the field of psychology while commanding much attention from other disciplines in the social sciences.

At the same time, Atkinson, who may be designated as the next figure of historical importance in achievement research, carried on with the experimental study of achievement motivation. The stage of TAT validation soon gave way to an attempt by Atkinson (1964) to construct a theory of achievement motivation. This theory was guided by the prior work of Tolman, decision theorists, and Lewin, and by the level of aspiration model proposed by Festinger and Escalona. Atkinson's achievement model, which first appeared in print in 1957, dominated research in achievement motivation for the next decade and was most fully elucidated in his fine treatise on motivation (Atkinson, 1964).

The applied versus laboratory focus respectively (and relatively) assumed by McClelland and Atkinson continued over time. However, the applied orientation of McClelland shifted from the historical analysis of economic development to a concern with behavioral change and personal development. A variety of achievement training programs were established that attempted to induce achievement strivings among the participants (see McClelland & Winter, 1969). Atkinson, on the other hand, became involved in the formulation of a rather esoteric theory of behavior, now leaning more heavily on mathematical derivations and computer simulation (Atkinson & Birch, 1970; Atkinson & Raynor, 1974).

It is difficult to assess objectively one's contribution to a field of study, and megalomania is not socially acceptable. But I would like to think that the next important juncture for research on achievement motivation occurred when achievement needs were linked with causal ascriptions, or the perceived reasons for success and failure (Feather, 1967; Weiner, Frieze, Kukla, Reed, Rest, & Rosenbaum, 1971; Weiner, 1972, 1974). This intersection with the prior conceptions of Heider (1958) and Rotter (1966) provided the avenue for a more cognitive analysis of achievement strivings and is now leading to a reexamination of basic motivational questions such as whether hedonism or information seeking is the foundation of achievement-oriented behavior.

There are three ongoing fields of investigation stemming from the historical nodes identified above. First, there are studies pertinent to Atkinson's theory of achievement motivation. Second, there are a number of active achievement change programs. And third, there is achievement-related research guided by cognitive conceptions of humans that focus on causal perceptions.

In addition to these main trends, a number of associated fields of interest are currently being examined. There are attempts to construct new measures of achievement needs; there is concern over the developmental antecedents that produce dispositions to achieve; attention is being paid to achievement striving among females, with a sudden burst of activity sparked by a hypothesized "fear of success"; and a variety of survey research is directed to the relationships between job satisfaction, success, achievement needs, and a number of demographic variables.

The Golden Age for the study of achievement needs, say, 1950 to 1965, is over. But in the face of the fickleness of psychologists the analysis of achievement concerns has continued without interruption for over 30 years and is still flourishing. This longevity is in part due to the persistent efforts of some outstanding psychologists, in part to the payoff of the work, and in part to the manifest importance of achievement strivings in this and other cultures.

With this all-too-brief historical introduction out of the way, I will now all too briefly turn to the substantive areas mentioned above. I will examine: (1) how the need for achievement is being measured and some of the controversies surrounding fantasy measurement; (2) Atkinson's theory of achievement motivation and its validity in choice situations; (3) extensions of Atkinson's theory; (4) attributional approaches to achievement needs and the perceived causes of success and failure; (5) the correlates of the need for achievement, including the cross-situational generality and stability of this disposition; (6) the developmental antecedents that produce achievement strivings; (7) the relationship between achievement needs and economic progress; (8) training programs designed to enhance achievement strivings; and (9) achievement motivation among females. I will examine current issues that have not been extensively discussed in the many pertinent books and reviews that already have been published (e.g., Atkinson, 1964; Atkinson & Feather, 1966; Birney, 1968; Byrne, 1974; Heckhausen, 1967, 1968; Weiner, 1970, 1972). But major restrictions are not possible, for this is not in the best interests of the uninitiated reader. Throughout the paper I also will look to the future and suggest areas of study that might be especially fruitful for the next generation of investigators.

THE MEASURES

Three generalizations capture the present beliefs concerning the measurement of achievement needs: (scoring system in Atkinson, 1958a)

1. The TAT is a rather poor instrument for the assessment of achievement needs.
2. The TAT is the best available instrument for the assessment of achievement needs.
3. Individuals directly involved in achievement research are more influenced by generalization no. 2 than generalization no. 1; individuals outside the area are more impressed with generalization no. 1 than with no. 2.

Generalization no. 1 is partially explainable. The principal investigators in the achievement area have been more concerned with the dynamics of behavior than with psychological structure per se (although these are obviously interrelated). Thus, relatively early in the study of achievement striving, the concern with measurement gave way to an analysis of the effects of needs on action. Atkinson's (1958a) collection represents the last *major* involvement with TAT need assessment, although in the concluding chapter of that book Reitman and Atkinson (1958) state: "Further progress in the gradual development of an instrument for assessment of total motivational structure waits upon further basic methodological research" (p. 683).

Although there were extensive studies of the properties of the TAT as a measure of achievement needs (see Atkinson, 1958a; McClelland et al., 1953), the concentration of investigators on psychodynamics rather than on structure had as one consequence the premature arrestment of the development of the TAT achievement measure. This produced a discrepancy between the subsequent immobility of operational growth and the acceleration of theoretical knowledge concerning the laws of motivation. Other areas of motivation that include the measurement of individual differences exhibit a similar theory–measurement discrepancy. For example, in the Hull–Spence conception of motivation, the Manifest Anxiety Scale used to measure drive is quite primitive when compared to the sophistication of drive theory. The personality measurement–motivational theory disparity in part accounts for the so-called "schizophrenic split" sketched in the initial two paragraphs of this review.

TAT Procedure

The scoring and administrative procedures developed by Murray were inadequate if the TAT was to be used as a research tool for the measurement of individual differences. First, a scheme had to be devised so that individuals would receive a score indicating the *magniture* of their achievement needs. And second, scoring criteria had to be clearly established so there would be between-judge agreement, or interrater reliability. These difficulties were surmounted, and a system was devised so that individuals could receive a numerical score supposedly revealing their level of achievement concerns. Furthermore, high interjudge agreement ($r \leftrightharpoons 0.90$) is readily attainable with the proposed scoring system (see Atkinson, 1958a; McClelland et al., 1953).[2]

The general assessment methodology has remained virtually unchanged since its inception. Four to six pictures are shown, typically in a group setting, with the subjects responding to four directing questions (What is happening? What led up to this situation? What is being thought? What will happen?). Four minutes of writing time are allowed for each story, and a total need achievement score is obtained for each person by summing the scores of the individual stories. Some of these procedural decisions were guided by earlier research indicating, for example, that after 20 minutes of writing, the TAT protocols do not have predictive validity, and with less time allotted for each story there is a high correlation between word productivity and the need achievement score (see Reitman & Atkinson, 1958; Ricciuti, 1954).

Scoring System

The scoring of fantasy protocols is a two-step process. On the basis of the content specified in the scoring manual (e.g., unique accomplishment, long-term achievement concern), it is first decided if a story contains achievement-related imagery. If so, then the story receives a numerical score of $+1$, and 10 other subcategories are analyzed for particular achievement imagery. Each subcategory also receives a score of $+1$ if it is represented in the fantasy production (see McClelland et al., 1953).

Procedural and Scoring Shortcomings.

There are a number of unanswered questions and weaknesses related to the administrative procedure and the rules of TAT scoring. It will be quickly apparent that these problems stem from the lack of refinement of the TAT measure. Entwisle (1972) has pointed out that there are high correlations between the major categorization (achievement-related imagery or not) and the total score. These correlations are approximately $r = 0.90$. It is doubtful the amount of time devoted to scoring the 10 subcategories is worth the effort.

There are a number of other disturbing symptoms of the lack of basic TAT research. For example, the picture sets described in Atkinson (1958a) are used today, although the scenes depicted appear quite antiquated and typically evoke laughter. One has no idea how this lack of ecological validity affects achievement imagery and, of course, the reliability and validity of the measure. Furthermore, the choice of picture sets for achievement measurement remains uncertain. Understanding of the range of picture cues that elicit achievement imagery for any given individual would certainly help to settle the issue of the generality of this disposition (this will be discussed later in the paper). The question of the "match" between the sex, age, or race of the respondent and the cues in the TAT picture also remains unsolved. And on the basis of earlier research, both negative (the boy thinks he will fail) and positive (the boy expects to succeed) imagery are scored for achievement. But conceptions of achievement motivation stress that achievement strivings are aroused by a hope of success, whereas anxiety about failure inhibits achievement behavior. The scoring procedure and the theoretical conception are therefore partially antithetical. These are not necessarily damning criticisms, nor even the worst offenses. They merely point out some of the vast number of unanswered and unexamined questions.

The Unsettling and Controversial Question of Reliability

The issue of reliability has generated a great deal of attention and controversy. The problem raised is simply this: The reported internal consistency and test--retest reliability for the TAT measure of achievement needs are quite low. Entwisle (1972) summarizes data from a number of studies indicating that the average alpha reliability is between 0.30 and 0.40. In a similar manner, she reports that "the average [test–retest] reliability for fantasy-based measures is probably around 0.30" (p. 383). Entwisle (1972) goes on to state: "The reader may find it perplexing that need achievement, a measure that seems from the overview here to have low reliability . . . is reputed to have predictive validity" (p. 386). The estimates given by Klinger (1966) are even lower. He states "test–retest correlations are generally either low or nonsignificant" (p. 300).

Individuals upholding the use of the TAT to measure achievement needs have offered two classes of defense in the face of the reliability figures presented by Entwisle and Klinger. One type of argument questions the soundness of the critics' analyses. For example, it is known that some of the TAT pictures portray scenes readily related to affiliative or power concerns. That is, the test is not "homogeneous" and often is used to assess more than one motive. Little achievement imagery is elicited by pictures highly cued for motives other than achievement, thus precluding high internal consistency if such pictures are employed in achievement assessment. Veroff, Atkinson, Feld, and Gurin (1960), for example, state: "A split-half estimate of the reliability of the present [TAT] measure is considered inappropriate because the average frequency of response is so low" (p. 5). When all the pictures in a TAT administration are highly cued for achievement, split-half reliabilities in the $r = 0.70$s have been reported (see Haber & Alpert, 1958: McClelland et al., 1953; Morgan, 1953).

The main point of this defense is that before a "box score" analysis can be accepted, with the results either confirmatory or disconfirmatory, there must be a detailed examination of the adequacy of each individual study included in the "box score." The defenders of the TAT argue that poor studies have been cited as evidence against the reliability of TAT. This counter-argument is reasonable. What is needed, then, is a clear specification of the criteria of a "good" study, a thorough search for all such studies, and a final conclusion regarding internal consistency.

Concerning test–retest reliability, McClelland et al. (1953) found that even with a test–retest correlation of only $r = 0.22$, over 70 percent of the subjects were classified identically when a dichotomous (High–Low) subject separation was used. These investigators therefore concluded: "The measure is, at present, unsuitable for purposes of precise prediction about the standing of individuals on need for Achievement, but its stability for purposes of group comparisons is fairly well established" (p. 194). Other investigators (e.g., Atkinson & O'Connor, 1963; Feld, 1967) also report high test–retest agreement using dichotomous classification. But again, a thorough analysis of all the properly conducted studies remains to be undertaken, so the citing of either positive or negative results is unconvincing.

A second type of rejoinder to the Entwisle (1972) and Klinger (1966) criticisms raises fundamental questions concerning the nature of projective measurement and "the misleading oversimplification and myths of measurement transmitted in introductory texts of psychological measurement" (Atkinson & Birch, 1974, p. 293). The TAT generally is presented as a test of "creative imagination." Thus, subjects may be reluctant to give the same general response on successive occasions. A "saw-toothed" effect has been observed in achievement imagery on the TAT, with the expression of achievement concerns waxing and waning (see McClelland et al., 1953). McClelland et al. (1953) contend:

> The test–retest unreliability of the measure may be due to the change in the subjects produced by the first administration of the test. That is, it is theoretically possible to have a test which will correlate highly with a number of other measures (high "validity") but not with itself on a second administration (low "reliability"). (pp. 193–194)

Imagine, for example, that one hears a joke and responds with a hearty laugh. When the joke is heard for the second time, little laughter might be elicited. The test-retest reliability in this case is not the proper index to assess how much one liked the joke or how adequate laughter is as an index of liking. In a similar vein,

Atkinson and Raynor (1974) state: "Instead of returning on the second occasion like the constant and unchanging block of metal presumed by traditional test theory borrowed from physics, [the subjects] might be substantially spoiled for a retest" (p. 9).

The controversial issues sketched above are far from settled. It is evident that some of the critics of the TAT have been overly harsh. It also is true that the users of the instrument will have to provide better reliability evidence. If it is decided that fantasy behavior is indeed the "best place" to look for motivational differences, then, as Reitman and Atkinson (1958) stated long ago, much more basic methodological research is needed. Because of the published criticisms of TAT measures, the burden of more definitive proof now rests on the users of the instrument.

Alternative Measures

In addition to suspicions concerning reliability, there are practical reasons to replace the TAT measure of achievement needs. A written protocol requires that the respondent be literate and fairly articulate. Furthermore, writing stories to four or six pictures is extremely wearing as well as time consuming. In addition, the TAT responses are particularly sensitive to environmental influence. Pooling subjects tested on different occasions or in different settings is likely to increase measurement error (Carney, 1966). And finally, scoring the fantasy protocols requires time, as well as training.

However, in spite of the advantages of an objective measurement instrument, in spite of the great demands for a substitute measure, in spite of the reasonably large amount of time devoted to the construction of alternative assessment instruments, and in spite of the controversy surrounding the use of fantasy measures, the TAT has not been supplanted. Entwisle (1972), borrowing from Jensen (1964), implies that this "amazing phenomenon is a task for future historians of psychology and will probably have to wait upon greater knowledge of the psychology of credulity than we now possess" (Jensen, 1964, p. 75). However, a less psychodynamic explanation is more appropriate: Simple verbal reports concerning one's beliefs about achievement desires, as well as more complex personality inventories that include achievement-related items, such as the Edwards Personal Preference Scale, have not proven valid (see, for example, de Charms et al., 1955; Hermans, 1970). Some encouraging inroads in objective testing have recently been made (e.g., Hermans, 1970; Mehrabian, 1968, 1969), but the research programs and dedication necessary for test development have not (to my present knowledge) accompanied these beginnings. Thus, these tests remain unfulfilled promises.

The instruments developed by Hermans (1970) and Mehrabian (1968) were "bootstrapped" from prior research utilizing the TAT (see Cronbach & Meehl,

1955). Many investigators found that TAT scores relate to a variety of manifestations of achievement strivings, such as level of aspiration, future orientation, recall of incompleted activities, and so on. Self-reports concerning these dependent variables then constitute "bootstrapped" test items and became the indicators of need for achievement. Notice that successful bootstrapping is possible only if the original measure (i.e., the TAT) had some validity. Furthermore, the subjects must be aware of their behaviors.

More specifically, Hermans (1970) isolated a cluster of 29 items representing behaviors that had been found empirically to relate to achievement needs. The item stems are, for example: (1) If I have not attained my goal and have not been doing my task well; (2) Working is something (see Hermans, 1970, for the entire scale). Five alternative responses follow each of the item stems. In addition to the high internal consistency of a test composed of these items, Hermans reports significant relationships between the test responses and task performance, as well as with grades in an unstructured classroom. The TAT need achievement score was only moderately related to Hermans' measure and did not predict task performance or grades.

The scale constructed by Mehrabian (1968, 1969) consists of 26 items primarily derived from Atkinson's (1957) theory of achievement motivation, as well as from empirical relationships reported in the achievement literature. The items are descriptive statements (e.g., I think I love winning more than I hate losing) which are endorsed on a rating scale. Mehrabian (1968, 1969) reports test–retest reliabilities in the $r = 0.70$s as well as successful prediction of various achievement-related behaviors (also see Cohen, Reid & Boothroyd, 1973).

ATKINSON'S THEORY OF ACHIEVEMENT MOTIVATION

As already indicated, Atkinson's (1957) theory of motivation dominated research on achievement behavior for a number of years and remains extremely influential today. In this section of this chapter I will review that theory. Following the theoretical analysis, the predictive validity of the theory in choice situations is examined.

Atkinson's Risk–Preference Model

Achievement-oriented behavior is viewed by Atkinson (1957, 1964) as a resultant of a conflict between approach and avoidance tendencies. Associated with every achievement-related action is the possibility of success, with the consequent emotion of pride, and the possibility of failure, with the consequent emotion of shame. The strengths of these anticipated emotions determine whether an individual will approach or avoid achievement-oriented activities. That is, achievement behavior is viewed as the resultant of an emotional conflict between hopes for success and fears concerning failure.

The resultant (approach minus avoidance) achievement-oriented tendency is conceptualized as:

$(Ms \times Ps \times Is) + (Maf \times Pf \times -If)$; or

$(Ms \times Ps \times Is) - (Maf \times Pf \times If)$

In this model, Ms represents the personality disposition to strive for success, or the need for achievement. Operationally, the strength of Ms generally is determined by the score on the TAT, as already indicated. The probability of success, Ps, represents the subjective likelihood that instrumental activity will lead to the goal. Thus, Ps is a goal expectancy. The probability of success has been defined operationally by presenting subjects false norms (e.g., Feather, 1961), controlling reinforcement history (e.g., Weiner & Rosenbaum, 1965), having subjects compete against varying numbers of individuals (e.g., Atkinson, 1958b), or varying the actual (and perceived) difficulty of the tasks (e.g., Atkinson & Litwin, 1960). The incentive value of success, or the potential "excitement" generated by the achievement activity, is symbolized by Is. Within Atkinson's model, Is does not have independent operational existence. Rather, Is is determined entirely by the magnitude of Ps: $Is = 1 - Ps$. Atkinson reasons that the incentive value of success is an affect often labeled "pride in accomplishment." It is postulated that the amount of pride experienced following goal attainment is inversely related to the subjective difficulty of the task. That is, one experiences more pride following success at a task perceived as difficult than after success at a task perceived as easy. Because $Is = 1 - Ps$, and Ps and Is are multiplicatively related, the greatest approach tendency is derived when $Ps = 0.50$. In that situation $Ps \times Is$ is maximum, or 0.25. As Ps increases or decreases from the level of intermediate difficulty (0.50), approach motivation decreases. The approach tendency toward a goal is therefore portrayed by a bell-shaped curve relating Ps and the strength of approach motivation. The magnitude of Ms determines the absolute level and the slope of that function. That is, the greater the need for achievement, the greater the overall motivation and relative attraction towards tasks of intermediate difficulty.

The determinants of avoidance are analogous to those of approach motivation. A personality disposition to avoid failure is symbolized by Maf. Operationally, Maf generally is determined by the score on the Mandler–Sarason Test Anxiety Questionnaire (Mandler & Sarason, 1952). This is a self-report inventory, thus creating the somewhat unusual situation of assessing approach motivation with a fantasy measure but avoidance motivation with an objective instrument.[3] Among the environmental determinants of avoidance behavior, Pf represents the subjective probability of failure and If connotes the incentive value of failure. The negative affect associated with failure is considered to be shame. Atkinson reasons that the easier the task, the greater the shame experienced given a failure.

If is therefore conceived as $- (1-Pf)$. Inasmuch as Pf and If are multiplicative, the maximum avoidance tendency is elicited when $Pf = .50$ and decreases as Pf increases or decreases from the .50 level. Hence, the tendency to avoid failure also can be plotted as a bell-shaped curve relating the strength of avoidance motivation to task difficulty. The magnitude of Maf determines the absolute level and slope of that function. That is, the greater the fear of failure, the greater the overall motivation to avoid the task and the greater the relative avoidance of intermediate difficulty tasks.

The strength of Ms relative to Maf, or the strength of hope as compared to fear, defines whether individuals will approach or avoid achievement tasks. The motive measures or individual difference variables therefore may be considered weights given to the functions that relate motivation to task probability. If $Ms >$ Maf, then greater weight is given to the approach (hope) than to the avoidance (fear) tendency, and vice versa. Furthermore, when $Ms > Maf$, resultant achievement motivation is positive and maximum when $Ps = 0.50$. Given this motive constellation or personality structure, resultant achievement motivation is positive but weak when Ps is high or low. Conversely, if $Maf > Ms$, or when fear is greater than hope, then resultant achievement motivation is negative and most inhibitory when $Pf = 0.50$ (and when $Ps = 0.50$, since $Ps + Pf = 1$). For these individuals, achievement motivation is negative but less inhibitory given tasks very easy or very difficult (high or low Ps).

Inasmuch as highly achievement-oriented individuals are most motivated by tasks of intermediate difficulty, they should select such tasks if given the opportunity and should exhibit the greatest intensity of motivation when performing activities of intermediate difficulty (such as competing against an opponent of equal skill). Conversely, individuals highly fearful of failure are theoretically expected to select easy or difficult tasks (if they must undertake achievement-oriented activities) and should exhibit the greatest intensity of performance given tasks of extreme probabilities (such as competing against an opponent of greater or lesser comparative ability). The derivations concerning task preferences have generated the most research in the achievement area and are responsible for the "risk–preference" label applied to Atkinson's model.

Empirical Evidence in Studies of Choice

This discussion is confined to choice situations testing Atkinson's theory, for task selection has been the main proving ground of the conception. Level of aspiration also involves a selection among alternative goals that vary in difficulty; therefore, relevant aspiration studies are included here under the rubric of choice. Confirmation of the predictions regarding risk–preference also provides construct validity (Cronbach & Meehl, 1955) for the instrument used to assess the need for achievement. Inasmuch as the instrument most frequently employed in these studies has been the TAT, investigations of choice also are one important testing ground for the validity of that measure.

The research questions and reported data from the many risk–preference studies may be summarized as follows:

1. Do individuals high in achievement needs exhibit a preference for tasks of intermediate difficulty?[4] Absolutely yes!

2. Do individuals low in achievement need exhibit a preference for tasks that are comparatively easy or comparatively difficult. Convincingly no!

3. Do individuals high in achievement needs exhibit a greater preference for tasks of intermediate difficulty than do individuals low in achievement needs? Most likely yes.

I have not conducted a complete search of the literature for studies that examine risk–preference in skill-related situations, and the unpublished studies must be legion. The three conclusions listed above were established on the basis of the following literature: Atkinson, Bastian, Earl, and Litwin (1960); Atkinson and Litwin (1960); Hamilton (1974); Isaacson (1964); Kukla (1972a); Mahone (1960); McClelland (1958b); Meyer (1969, reported in Heckhausen, 1968); Morris (1966); Moulton (1965); Raynor and Smith (1966); and Schneider (1971). The robustness of the data reported in these studies is enhanced by the variety of achievement measures used in the research investigations (achievement responsibility scale, "doodles," French Test of Insight, Mehrabian scale, TAT), the diversity of risk–preference domains (anagrams, career choice, connecting dots, major area of concentration in school, ring toss), and the somewhat assorted ages of the subjects (children, high school students, and college students). For a more complete review of this literature, see Meyer, Folkes, and Weiner, 1976.

Not all the research, of course, supports the three generalizations. For example, at times the different motive groups exhibit identical choice behavior, and at times individuals low in achievement need exhibit linear (easy to difficult or vice versa) task preferences. But *all* individuals seem to prefer intermediate difficulty, although this preference may be more evident among individuals highly motivated to achieve. In addition, there is an abundance of data demonstrating that the general desire for intermediate difficulty tasks increases with cognitive maturity (see Veroff, 1969).

Atkinson and Feather (1966, pp. 22, 342) acknowledge that individuals classified as highly fearful of failure have not avoided tasks of intermediate difficulty in the research investigations. They offer two explanations for this unpredicted finding. On the one hand, they contend that in the populations tested (such as college students) the subjects generally are high in need for achievement. Inasmuch as there is a paucity of subjects absolutely low in achievement needs, extreme risks should not be chosen. However, differential preference for intermediate difficulty tasks is still expected among groups differing in their relative level of achievement needs. Second, Atkinson and Feather suggest that there are sources of motivation in addition to need for achievement that promote intermediate choice. For example, "unmeasured need for Affiliation may function just like need for Achievement to overcome resistance to intermediate degree of difficulty" (Atkinson and Feather, 1966, p. 342). Notice that the arguments proposed by Atkinson and Feather explain the apparently contradictory data within the framework of Atkinson's 1957 theory; the theory is kept totally intact.

There are additional data, however, that point to another interpretation and suggest the necessity of a conceptual revision. Recent research has demonstrated that outcomes at tasks of intermediate difficulty provide actors with the most information about their efforts and/or capabilities. That is, task selection has cognitive effects pertaining to the desire for self-understanding and self-evaluation. Of course, it is quite functional and adaptive to have a realistic or veridical view of oneself.

There are logical reasons why performance at intermediate difficulty tasks provides a maximum of personal information. Selection of easy tasks typically results in success, and that outcome is perceived as being due to the ease of the task. In a similar manner, selection of a very difficult task typically results in failure, and the blame is placed on the characteristics of the task. Thus, selection of easy or difficult tasks generally confirms one's knowledge about the external world. Conversely, tasks of intermediate difficulty are just as likely to produce success as failure. Thus, performance at such tasks provides information about the efforts and abilities of the *person* undertaking the activity.

In one study supporting this line of reasoning, Weiner, Heckhausen, Meyer, and Cook (1972) presented subjects with five tasks differing in perceived difficulty level. The subjects were requested to judge "in which of these tasks was effort the most important causal determinant of performance, considering both success and failure outcomes" (Weiner et al., 1972, p. 247). The data revealed a curvilinear relationship between task difficulty and the perceived importance of effort, with greatest personal (effort) ascriptions at tasks of intermediate difficulty.

Two other investigations more directly demonstrate the informational value of intermediate difficulty choice. Meyer, Folkes, and Weiner (1976) had policemen rate their general shooting ability prior to target practice. They then presented targets of varying objective difficulty and had the policemen rate their subjective probability of success at each of the targets. Finally, it was indicated to the policemen that they could have knowledge of results or feedback from performance at *one* of these targets. The target at which the feedback was desired was then selected. Among all the policemen, feedback was chosen for the target at which the subjective probability of success was intermediate. That is, policemen perceiving themselves as poor shots requested feedback at the objectively easy (subjectively intermediate) target, whereas policemen who perceived themselves as high in shooting ability desired performance information at the objectively difficult (subjectively intermediate) target. The intermediate ability groups fell between these extremes in their choice behavior. These findings were replicated with high school students selecting feedback at a high jumping task (Meyer et al., 1976).

Thus, both the hedonic theory of Atkinson and an informational conception predict that approach motivation is maximized at tasks of intermediate difficulty. To disentangle the hedonic versus informational determinants of choice, Trope and Brickman (1975) simultaneously varied the difficulty of tasks as well as their "diagnosticity." Diagnosticity refers to the difference between the proportion of individuals designated as high versus low in ability who succeed at the task. Thus, for example, a task at which 90 percent of individuals high in ability succeed whereas 60 percent of the low-ability persons succeed has greater diagnostic value than a task accomplished by 52 percent versus 48 percent of the individuals respectively high or low in ability. However, the 52 percent to 48 percent task is more intermediate in difficulty than the 90 percent to 60 percent task. Trope and Brickman report that in this situation subjects chose to perform the tasks of greater diagnosticity rather than the tasks more intermediate in difficulty. This suggests that the preference for intermediate difficulty reported by so many investigators is attributable to the high diagnostic value of these tasks in the context in which they were studied. This investigation has been replicated (Trope, 1975).

In sum, the data from choice studies indicate that there is a general tendency to select intermediate difficulty tasks, probably because of their informational (diagnostic) value. Furthermore, intermediate preference increases with cognitive maturity and is most evident among individuals highly motivated to succeed.

These data have great significance for Atkinson's theory. First, although individuals high in achievement needs have been chiefly characterized as hope oriented, they can alternatively be described as information or feedback seeking. The latter identification shifts the emphasis from the affective to the cognitive correlates of the disposition to achieve. That is, differences in risk–preference between high and low achievement motive groups may be derived from a differential desire for self-evaluation, rather than (or in addition to) disparate emotional anticipations. Trope (1975) has presented evidence in support of this line of reasoning.

Any number of hypotheses regarding the relative importance of emotional versus cognitive sources of motivation can account for the data indicating that adults prefer intermediate difficulty, as well as the evidence indicating that there may be differences in choice behavior as a function of the level of achievement needs. Further research is badly needed to solve these important and intriguing issues, as well as to determine definitively the suggestive motive group differences in choice behavior.

THEORETICAL EXTENSIONS TO ATKINSON'S THEORY

There have been two major additions to Atkinson's theory. The theoretical revisions introduce the concepts of persisting motivational tendencies (Atkinson & Cartwright, 1964; Weiner, 1965, 1970) and future goal orientation (Atkinson & Raynor, 1974; Raynor, 1969). In addition, there have been creative attempts to place the theory within a broader behavioral framework (Atkinson & Birch, 1970; Atkinson & Raynor, 1974). Although the original theory (Atkinson, 1957) has continued to grow, the subsequent contributions have received relatively little attention, particularly when compared to the research generated by the less complex 1957 model. There seems to be a movement in motivation away from mathematical (or quasi-mathematical) models and the additions to Atkinson's early theory may be perceived as constituting a premature formalism. There is also a diminishing return from refinements to any theory and a vast array of competing phenomena to attract the attention of psychological researchers.

Persisting Motivation

As already intimated, stimulus offset models of motivation served as the foil against which achievement theory was built. Atkinson and Cartwright (1964) pointed out, however, that the model proposed by Atkinson (1957) contained some of the same deficiencies as the stimulus-bound conceptions. That is, the individual was viewed as inactive until a stimulus was presented. In achievement-oriented contexts the stimulus engages the crucial anticipatory emotions (hope of success and fear of failure) as well as a cognitive, inferential process pertaining to a goal expectancy. Yet achievement theorists had wanted to conceptualize an ever-active organism, persisting in goal-directed activities in the absence of the instigating stimulus. To capture the latter principle, it was suggested that "a goal directed tendency, once aroused, persists until it is satisfied" (Atkinson, 1964, p. 310). This so-called "inertial tendency" was added to the determinants of behavior specified in Atkinson's (1957) original model, so that the strength of motivation was conceived as:

$$(M_s \times P_s \times I_s) - (M_{af} \times P_f \times I_f) + T_{Gi}$$

where T_{Gi} symbolizes the inertial tendency toward the goal.

Now what on earth does this T_{Gi} have to do with achievement strivings, prior data in this area, or the generation of new observations? If motivation persists when a goal is not attained, then motivation will be greater following failure (nonattainment of a goal) than after success (goal attainment). That is, failure should generally augment performance. The concept of inertial motivation therefore allows the model to make contact with the vast, complex, and contradictory literature concerning the consequences of success and failure on subsequent achievement strivings.

It is inappropriate here to examine the complexities of this conceptualization (see Weiner, 1970, 1972). There is evidence suggesting that individuals highly motivated to achieve do perform better after failure than after success and that they are more likely to persist in the face of setbacks. Thus, they might be described as "tolerant of achievement frustration." On the other hand, individuals highly fearful of failure apparently react positively to encouragement or success and display decrements in performance intensity after failure. These findings resulted in a conception of inertial motivation that includes both approach and avoidance tendencies (Weiner, 1965, 1970).

Future Goal Orientation

Many achievement activities are segments within longer-term goals. For example, course grades in part determine whether one can gain admission into medical school, publication of one's research in part determines the likelihood of an academic promotion, and so on. It is intuitively reasonable to expect that performance at any immediate achievement-related activity is influenced by the future goals that are contingent upon that performance. For example, if persons want to enter medical school, then they are likely to study more in a course if the grade is included rather than excluded from their college transcript.

Raynor (1969; also see Atkinson & Raynor, 1974) has formally incorporated the impact of long-term goals on immediate action within the framework of Atkinson's model. He states that in "contingent" paths the strength of motivation to undertake an immediate activity is determined by the already discussed $Ms \times Ps \times Is$ formula, *plus* the strength of motivation associated with all the expectancies and goals in the "path." Thus, how much one studies for a course is hypothesized to be a function of the strength of motives and probability of success in that course, as well as the strength of motives and subjective probability of success of, for example, being admitted into medical school.

There is empirical evidence from both field research (classroom grades) and laboratory investigations that support this conceptual revision, although the data are not abundant and the findings for individuals low in achievement needs are ambiguous (see Atkinson & Raynor, 1974). Furthermore, the supporting research frequently reports no differences in performance between individuals high and low in achievement needs given "noncontingent" activities, that is, when the achievement tasks are not related to long-term goals. Yet Atkinson's theory was developed and substantiated from performance comparisons in such noncontingent activities, which is rather contradictory. Finally, although the results generally are as predicted, it is apparent that long-term goals are associated with multiple sources of motivation, self-concept, self-esteem, and a variety of other factors that are not captured by the concept of expectancy of success. These are problems for future researchers to disentangle. For now, however, it is reasonable to conclude that the presence of future goals augments the immediate performance of individuals high in achievement needs. These persons can be characterized as "future oriented," thus confirming an early insight about their psychological make-up (see McClelland et al., 1953, p. 253).

ATTRIBUTION THEORY AND ACHIEVEMENT STRIVINGS

The discussion of choice behavior called attention to the informational or self-evaluative aspects of task selection. It is now apparent that other manifestations of achievement motivation also are influenced by cognitive or inferential processes. Foremost among the mental events that affect achievement-related behaviors are causal attributions.

Causal Attributions

Causal attributions in achievement-related contexts refer to the perceived causes of success and failure. There are, of course, many possible reasons for a positive or a negative achievement outcome, but research has shown that four factors are perceived as most responsible for success and failure: ability, effort, task difficulty, and luck. That is, if one succeeds, then the outcome is ascribed to high ability, hard work, the ease of the task, or good luck. In a similar manner, failure generally is ascribed to low ability, lack of effort, a difficult task, or bad luck. Of these four causes, ability and effort are particularly salient. Other less used ascriptions for success and failure include the bias of a superior, mood, illness, fatigue, and so on.

The perceived causes of success and failure have been incorporated within a few basic causal dimensions (see Weiner et al., 1971; Weiner, 1972, 1974). One dimension is labeled the *locus of responsibility*. Causes are perceived as either internal (in the person) or external (in the environment). For example, ability and effort are person causes, whereas task difficulty and luck are environmental determinants of an outcome (see Rotter, 1966). A second dimension of causality has been identified as the stability or constancy of a cause. Some causes, such as ability, the ease of a task, the bias of a supervisor, and so on are typically perceived as relatively enduring or fixed. On the other hand, causes such as effort, luck, illness, mood, and so on generally are perceived as subject to momentary or periodic fluctuation. Still a third dimension of causality is the intentionality or controllability of a cause. For example, teacher or supervisor bias and effort expenditure are under volitional control, whereas luck and illness generally are not. In sum, taxonomies of causes have been developed that allow each causal factor to be placed within a multidimensional schematic framework.

The Consequences of Causal Ascriptions

It has been demonstrated that causal ascriptions and their dimensional representations are linked to specific psychological consequences. The *locus* of a causal ascription influences the affective reactions to success and failure, with perceived internal responsibility maximizing pride and shame over accomplishments. For example, one feels more pride if success is ascribed to high ability rather than to the ease of a task. In a similar manner, failure attributed to a lack of effort produces greater shame than failure ascribed to bad luck or to the skill of one's opponent (see Weiner, Russell and Lerman in press, for a detailed analysis of the relation between attributions and affect). The *stability* of a cause influences the subjective expectancy of success at a task. For example, if success is ascribed to high ability or to the ease of a task, then success is anticipated when that task is again confronted. But if success is attributed to good luck, or "superhuman" effort, then it is not assuredly expected on future occasions (see Weiner, Nierenberg, & Goldstein 1976).

In sum, causal attributions affect the incentive value and the expectancy of success and failure. Atkinson and other motivational theorists have postulated that expectancy and value are the prime determinants of action. Thus, the attributional analysis of causality and principles of self- and other-perception are directly linked with motivational theory. This union is partially depicted in Diagram 1.

Diagram 1
An attributional model of achievement strivings

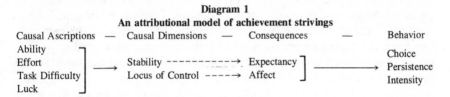

Achievement Needs and Causal Attributions

There is evidence suggesting that individuals differing in their level of achievement needs have disparate causal biases or explanations for their success and failure (see Cohen et al., 1973; Kukla, 1972a; Meyer, 1970; Weiner & Potepan, 1970; Weiner et al., 1971). Persons highly motivated to achieve ascribe success to themselves (ability and effort) to a greater extent than do individuals low in achievement needs. And given failure, persons high in achievement motivation ascribe the outcome to lack of effort, whereas those low in achievement motivation perceive lack of ability as the salient cause. Thus, in achievement-related contexts persons motivated to achieve success have a relatively high self-concept of ability (see Kukla, 1972b) and perceive that effort and outcome covary. Conversely, persons low in achievement needs have a relatively low self-concept of ability and do not strongly believe in the importance of effort as a determinant of outcome. Notice that the motive groups differ in the *locus* of causality for success and in the *stability* of their attributions for failure.

It is now possible to examine the manner in which causal ascriptions mediate the associations between achievement needs and various indexes of performance. For example, I previously indicated that individuals high in achievement needs are able to tolerate the frustration of failure. That is, they exhibit performance increments after failure and persist in their goal-related attempts. This contrasts with the behavior displayed by individuals low in achievement needs. Persons in this latter motive classification are relatively hampered by failure and are prone to cease their goal-directed activities given nonattainment of a goal.

According to attributional data, individuals high in achievement needs ascribe their failure to a lack of effort. Effort is an unstable cause that can be augmented. Thus, a high expectancy of success is maintained following failure, which results in increased intensity of performance and persistence of behavior. Conversely, individuals low in achievement needs ascribe their failure to a lack of ability. Ability is a stable characteristic that cannot be immediately modified. Thus, a low expectancy of success is produced after failure, resulting in a lowering of performance intensity and in the cessation of instrumental activity.

In one study demonstrating the influence of causal attributions on performance intensity, Weiner and Sierad (1975) experimentally severed the association between achievement needs and causal ascriptions. Subjects in an experimental condition were induced to misattribute failure to a placebo pill. The data indicated that the attribution of failure to an external source augmented the performance of individuals low in achievement needs, while causing decrements in the performance of persons highly motivated to achieve.

In sum, attribution theory provides a cognitive framework for the conceptual analysis of achievement behavior. In addition, achievement needs may be viewed as cognitive (causal) dispositions, thereby revealing another important correlate of the personalities of individuals high and low in achievement needs.

PERSONALITY CHARACTERIZATIONS

It is now time to present a general description of individuals high in achievement needs, as well as the contrasting portrait of persons low in this motivational disposition. Two difficult questions must be answered if these portrayals are to be adequate:

1. What is the generality (or extensity, or breadth) of the need for achievement?
2. Is this disposition stable, or at least *relatively* enduring?

Unfortunately, these questions have not been answered. It is not known, for example, whether a person who strives for success in a particular occupation also exhibits achievement-type behaviors on the tennis court, in his night school literature class, and so on. In the only study that focuses on this issue, Rosenstein (1952) found that chemistry majors had a significantly higher need achievement score on the TAT than physical education majors when responding to picture cues depicting laboratory situations. It certainly seems reasonable to believe that there are circumscribed avenues or outlets of achievement expression for a given individual. That is, similar genotypes may have disparate and idiosyncratic phenotypic representations. But this supposition has not been investigated.

The TAT measure of achievement needs typically includes a diverse range of picture cues that tap various achievement domains, but the sampling is completely unsystematic and is without the support of a taxonomy or a classification of situations that elicit achievement strivings (which may itself be impossible to construct). In sum, the cross-situational generality of the need for achievement remains to be determined. Research pertinent to this fundamental issue is essential to clarify whether the need for achievement is indeed a *dimension* of personality.

The stability of achievement needs has been the subject of more research than has the issue of motive generality. This is perhaps surprising, inasmuch as longitudinal studies are difficult to conduct and require a dedicated masochism. As can be anticipated, research investigations of long-term stability are therefore also few in number. The most cited data concerning motive stability come from the Fels Institute studies (see Kagan & Moss, 1959; Moss & Kagan, 1961). Kagan and Moss (1961) report low but significantly positive correlations ($r \leftrightharpoons 0.22$) between TAT scores at ages 8½ and 14½. Birney (1959) found a correlation of a slightly higher magnitude ($r \leftrightharpoons 0.29$) given equivalent-form testing over a four-month interval, and Feld (1967) reports correlations of $r \leftrightharpoons 0.38$ over a six-year period. Clearly, research of this nature is hampered because of the uncertain test–retest reliability of the TAT. It is impossible to determine the consistency of achievement needs, as inferred from fantasy productions, if test–retest reliability for such measures is low.

In addition, behavioral data from the Fels Institute studies reveal significant stability between achievement concerns at adulthood and intellectual and mechanical achievement strivings at various ages during youth ($r \leftrightharpoons 0.30$).

Studies of the stability of achievement *behaviors* circumvent the problems associated with personality measurement, although a host of other difficulties arise (such as specifying appropriate achievement behaviors at different age periods).

In sum, correlations in the magnitude of 0.25 to 0.35 are found in studies of long-term achievement stability. This indicates weak, but greater than chance, stability. There are additional complexities in some longitudinal data, but that will take us to far afield here (see Murstein, 1963; Skolnick, 1966).

The Correlates

To list all the reported correlates of achievement needs would require more space than I can afford to give; to determine which of these relationships are established definitively and which are "important" would require the space allotted for this chapter; and to understand the established correlates would require the space of this book.

The most positive and understandable empirical correlates of achievement needs have been derived from, or have been incorporated within, the theories of achievement motivation described earlier. For example, I have discussed the theory and data pertaining to the relationship between achievement needs and task preference. In a similar vein, individuals highly motivated to achieve have been characterized as "realistic" and have occupational goals that are congruent with their abilities (Mahone, 1960; Morris, 1966). As already discussed, the desire for intermediate risk may be indicative of a preference for personal feedback or knowledge about oneself. This informational explanation is consistent with the high achiever's reported preference for business occupations, where feedback (profits) is evident (McClelland, 1961, p. 55; Meyer, Walker, & Litwin, 1961). In addition, the theoretical extension to include future goal orientation makes it possible to interpret data revealing that individuals high in need for achievement are able to delay gratification (Mischel, 1961) and attain better grades in school if the grades are instrumental to long-term goals (Raynor, 1970). Inasmuch as individuals high in achievement needs are conceptualized as hope oriented, data demonstrating that they bias probabilities upward become meaningful (Feather, 1965). Finally, individuals high in achievement needs take personal responsibility for success and generally perceive themselves as high in ability. The self-attribution for success increases their pride in accomplishment and accounts for evidence that they willingly undertake achievement-oriented activities when the opportunity arises (Atkinson, 1953; Green, 1963). The self-perception of high ability in part may account for the positive self-concept among persons high in achievement needs that some investigators find (Mukherjee & Sinha, 1970).

There are a host of other reported linkages to achievement needs, although many of the relationships are tenuous and/or their theoretical meaning is unclear.

For example, it has been found that achievement needs are positively correlated with resistance to social influence, field independence, preference for particular colors (blue), aesthetic tastes, lowered recognition thresholds for success-related words, selective retention of incompleted tasks, forms of graphic expression (single and S-shaped lines), high content of serum uric acid, and so on (see the reviews cited earlier for references). Although the sampling of associations listed above increases the "relational fertility" of the need for achievement construct, the lasting significance of many of the relationships is questionable because of the absence of clear theoretical relevance. In addition, one-shot or single studies that report correlates of the need for achievement are of restricted value because of the doubt concerning the replicability of any isolated finding.

One final comment concerning the correlates of need for achievement is appropriate. Entwisle (1972) as well as others have criticized the TAT measure of need for achievement because of its failure to predict grade point average. Since the inception of work in this area investigators have cautioned against attempts to predict overdetermined behaviors, or actions that can be caused by many sources of motivation. In 1953, McClelland et al. stated "The relationship of need achievement score to college grades . . . is of dubious theoretical significance, since grades in college are affected by many unknown factors" (p. 237). And 20 years later I essentially repeated that warning:

> Grade point average is an overdetermined motivational index. One may obtain a high grade for any number of reasons, such as to receive a new car from pleased parents or to be deferred from the Army. As the extrinsic sources of motivation to undertake achievement tasks increase, the relative variance accounted for by achievement needs decrease. It therefore should be expected that need for achievement will be only weakly related to GPA. (Weiner, 1972, p. 222)

DEVELOPMENTAL ANTECEDENTS

When analyzing a personality structure, the general questions posed concern assessment (personality measurement), the influence of the disposition on thought and action (personality dynamics), antecedent conditions that produce the structure (personality development), and the method of behavioral change (psychopathology and therapy). I have thus far discussed achievement measurement and dynamics and now will examine development and change.

Social Learning

The American research tradition in developmental psychology has been to search for the experiential (social) determinants of personality, particularly focusing on early parental interactions as the prime influence of later behavior. McClelland

(1951) contended that because affective arousal is more intense during infancy, and because the younger child does not make detailed discriminations, "affective associations formed in early childhood are apt to be strong and very resistant to unlearning or forgetting" (p. 257). These points dominated the search for the antecedents of achievement needs.

Two early investigations provided the models for the great bulk of subsequent research in this area. In one of these studies, Winterbottom (1953, reported in Atkinson, 1958a) obtained TAT achievement scores for a group of boys 8 to 10 years old and also interviewed the mothers to ascertain their prior attitudes toward independence training. Winterbottom reported that the mothers of sons high in achievement needs expected earlier independence (knowing the city, dressing themselves, and so on) than did the mothers of boys scoring low in need for achievement. The second influential study, conducted by Rosen and D'Andrade (1959), related the present *behaviors* of parents to the need achievement scores of their sons, rather than relying on parental retrospective reports. The children were given tasks to complete, but the parents could interact with the children and come to their aid. Rosen and D'Andrade found that the parents of the achievement-oriented sons were more involved in the task, gave more reward and punishment, and had higher expectations than the parents of children scoring low in need for achievement. They therefore contended that achievement training (doing something well) rather than independence training (doing something by oneself) is the important antecedent of the development of achievement needs.

Unfortunately, the high expectations spawned by these initial studies have not been met. Subsequent research has produced as many nonconfirmatory as confirmatory results regarding the alleged influence of achievement and/or independence training on the development of achievement needs (see, for example, Callard, 1964; Chance, 1961). Because of the conflicting data and some additional cross-cultural discrepancies, McClelland (1961) proposed an "optimal level" theory, suggesting that independence training, if too early, would be just as inhibitory on the development of achievement needs as overly protective parental behavior. Again, however, research investigations have failed to yield clear support for this position (see, for example, Bartlett & Smith, 1966; Smith, 1969).

There are enormous complexities within the social learning research studies, and the lack of definitive results is rather predictable. For example, the encouragement of achievement and independence training is likely to be intertwined with other aspects of child rearing, such as general permissiveness or restrictiveness, beliefs about the child's competence, physical affection and reward giving, general affective climate and warmth in the home, parental expectations, and so on. All the above at one time or another have been found to relate to achievement needs by some investigators, whereas other investigators have reported no relationship between these variables and achievement needs. Finding unambiguous child-rearing correlates will probably require a conceptual foundation that guides the investigator to particular and specific antecedents. Such theoretical guidelines have been relatively absent in the child-rearing research.

There are additional problems in the child-rearing studies that require attention. For example, it has been documented that parental practices are responsive to the behavior of the child. Feld (1967) found that during adolescence the mothers of boys scoring low in achievement needs were particularly concerned about independence. In addition, across the many socialization experiments the subject populations differ in social class, culture, sex of the child, and so on. However, behaviors classified as restrictive among one social class sample may be classified as permissive in a different social class. Because there are no preestablished standards for the variable under study, inconclusive results are likely to emerge when given heterogeneous samples.

In sum, it is intuitively reasonable to believe that what takes place in the home influences the achievement dispositions of the child, but the pertinent research is plagued by a variety of problems. I suggest that it may be unwise to pursue this line of investigation at the present time.

Cognitive Development

The cognitive approach to development seeks to identify universal developmental processes rather than searching for the child-rearing antecedents that produce individual differences. In one exemplary approach, Heckhausen and Roelofsen (1962) contended that the development of achievement-related needs requires that the child be able to "direct the pleasure or the disappointment after success or failure . . . at the self, so that with success the child experiences pleasure about his competence and with failure experiences shame about his incompetence" (p. 378). Thus, Heckhausen and Roelofsen are suggesting that the development of causal ascriptions and self-attributions are a necessary antecedent to achievement strivings. They also contend that such attributional processes emerge at around three years of age. (There are related data indicating that before the age of five children are not able to use social norm information, one important cue for ability inferences; see Parsons & Ruble, 1972).

In another cognitive-developmental study of causal attributions, Weiner and Peter (1973) examined evaluative judgments of achievement actions. They found that among younger children the outcome of an activity (success or failure) most influences the evaluation of an achievement act, but with increasing cognitive development effort expenditure becomes an important evaluative determinant. Indeed, among children 10 to 12 years old, failure in spite of high effort is evaluated more highly than success in the absence of effort. Among adults the relative weighting of the outcome and effort factors again reverses, with task outcome becoming the more heavily weighted information. In sum, there apparently is a general sequence of development that influences judgments and, supposedly, achievement strivings. The precise sequence differs in an Iranian culture (see Salili, Maehr, & Gillmore, 1976).

A different cognitive analysis of achievement has been outlined by Veroff (1969). Veroff proposes three stages in the development of achievement strivings: first, an intrapersonal competition or autonomous stage; second, an interpersonal competition or social comparison stage; and last, an integration of the two prior stages. Passage from Stage 1 to Stage 2 typically takes place when the child enters school and acquires the ability to use social norm information to make comparative judgments.

Recall that Veroff (1969) also demonstrated that the preference for intermediate risk increases with cognitive maturation. It is tempting to link the ability to use social norm information and the onset of social comparison processes with the desire to select more difficult tasks. That is, the shift toward intermediate difficulty might indicate the growing importance of personal feedback and self-knowledge as motivators of choice. These motivations are best served by selecting tasks of intermediate difficulty. Still another cognitive-developmental analysis of the shift toward intermediate difficulty choice has been proposed by Nicholls (1974). Nicholls found that the postulated inverse relationship between the incentive value of success and the probability of success is not exhibited by children prior to the age of five. Therefore, very young children merely select the task with the highest expectancy of success. If one index of achievement striving is a preference for intermediate difficulty, then the emergence of achievement-like behaviors would not be possible before the development of particular cognitive abilities.

To date, only a few studies examining the cognitive-developmental determinants of achievement striving have been conducted. But the empirical findings are systematic and highly reliable. The clarity of the data is highlighted when contrasted with the often contradictory findings in the social learning area. I perceive the cognitive-developmental analysis of achievement needs as an important area with potentially great pay-off.

ECONOMIC DEVELOPMENT

One of the most interesting extensions of the study of achievement motivation has been the work of McClelland (1961) relating achievement needs to economic development. This endeavor has been summarized in many places (e.g., McClelland, 1962; Weiner, 1972) and will be only briefly introduced here.

The initial influences on McClelland's analysis of economic growth were Winterbottom's (1953) data concerning independence training and Max Weber's speculations about the Protestant Ethic. Weber contended that capitalism arose as one consequence of the Protestant reformation, for the Protestant revolt emphasized the importance of self-reliance and productivity. Furthermore, the results of one's labors could not be spent self-indulgently because of religious beliefs. Thus, profits were reinvested, resulting in further prosperity. McClelland (1961) aruged that Protestant values produced early independence training that, in turn, promoted need for achievement. This hypothesized sequence of events is shown in Diagram 2.

Diagram 2
Hypothetical relationship between
self-reliance values and economic development

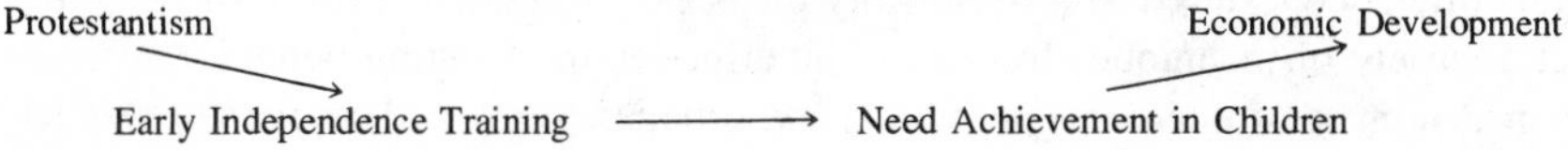

Protestantism   Economic Development

Early Independence Training   ——————→   Need Achievement in Children

The diagram above indicates four relationships that McClelland (1961) has examined: (1) Protestantism and early independence training; (2) early independence training and need for achievement; (3) need for achievement and economic growth; and (4) Protestantism and economic growth. Of these, the alleged relationship between need achievement and economic growth has produced the most extensive, novel, and controversial data.

The TAT assessment procedure devised by McClelland et al. (1953) has a unique advantage in that it is applicable to any prose material. Thus, to examine the relationship between achievement needs and economic growth, McClelland scored prose material, such as children's readers, speeches, folktales, songs, and so on for need achievement. These scores were then related to available indices of economic activity, such as the consumption of electrical power, the amount of coal imports, the number of independent artisans in a society, and so on. Data from a wide array of cultures and times, including contemporary American society, England during the Tudor period, and ancient Greece, indeed provided evidence that increments in need for achievement precede economic development, and decrements in need for achievement precede economic decline. The scope of this work is immense and really must be read to be appreciated.

ACHIEVEMENT CHANGE

One might argue that if achievement-related dispositions are formed during early childhood, and if they are relatively enduring, then attempts to modify an adult's level of achievement needs are fruitless. The only practical way to alter the achievement needs of the members of a society and, as a possible consequence, enhance the economic development of that society, would be to change child-rearing practices and then wait some time to determine if the changes were effective.

This is a somewhat pessimistic position, rather incompatible with the optimism of American environmentalism. Although McClelland originally accepted the work of Winterbottom (1953) and provided the rationale for the importance of early learning (McClelland, 1951), he subsequently disregarded this position and initiated short-term motivational change programs designed to increase the level of achievement needs of the participants (see McClelland & Winter, 1969).

The training programs generally last from four to six weeks, with the participants often sequestered in a reasonably pleasant setting. The programs make use of a variety of techniques thought to be effective in changing behavior, such as persuasion, reinforcement, individual and group therapy, and so on (see McClelland, 1965). At a general level, the training programs introduce the participants to the thoughts and actions of individuals high in achievement needs, encourage self-evaluation, and teach the benefits of realistic goal setting and instrumental planning. More specifically, the participants are taught to score the TAT for need achievement and become acquainted with the correlates of achievement needs, they are asked to consider their values about achievement, and they play a number of games where intermediate difficulty goal setting is necessary for success (see McClelland & Steele, 1972). The training programs also teach the importance of self-responsibility and having a realistic assessment of oneself. Thus, they are quite similar to "personal causation" training programs (see deCharms, 1972).

At this point in time the effectiveness of motive change training is uncertain. Positive results with underachievers (Kolb, 1965), school teachers (deCharms, 1972), and businessmen (McClelland & Winter, 1969) have been reported, but nonsupporting data are also found (see McClelland & Winter, 1969). A few years ago I summarized this research with the following, still appropriate, statement:

> [There is] hope that achievement behavior can be altered, given appropriate intervention techniques. The implications of this possibility are indeed far-reaching. Needless to say, much further evidence is needed before this hypothesis can be fully accepted. (Weiner, 1972, p. 268)

ACHIEVEMENT NEEDS AMONG FEMALES

McClelland (1958) contended that for an instrument assessing motive strength to have validity, it must reflect temporary arousal states of the organism. That is, like a thermometer, if the "motive temperature" is turned on, then the instrument should register a higher reading. Achievement motive arousal, accomplished through failure induction or "ego-involving" instructions, indeed generates high TAT need achievement scores when compared to responses given under nonarousal conditions. However, this is true only for males; females have not exhibited motive score differences in arousal versus neutral conditions. Therefore, it was believed that the TAT motive measure was not valid for females, and female subjects tended to be neglected in achievement research. Of course, many studies did include females and combined the data from both sexes, but an equally large number of research investigations either did not test females or reported systematic data for the male, but not the female, subjects.

It is uncertain why the few motive arousal studies were unsuccessful for women and why males appear to yield more systematic data than females in studies of achievement motivation. Achievement may be a more complex motivational system for females than for males because of cultural inhibitions and social norms that at one time restricted females to the home. Little has been done to substantiate these intuitively reasonable suppositions.

Another plausible explanation of the mysterious findings for the females was offered by Horner (1968). Horner postulated a motive to "avoid success," or a "fear of success" for females. She suggested that as a consequence of success the threat of social rejection or fears concerning a perceived lack of femininity are aroused in women. These fears inhibit achievement strivings. To test this notion, Horner (1968) had male and female subjects write four minute stories to this cue: "At the end of the first-term final, Anne finds herself at the top of her medical school class." Horner found much greater fear of success imagery in the female than in the male responses.

These data caused immediate excitement among many psychologists and lay people. The data meshed with the current feminist movement and were immediately incorporated into courses on the psychology of women. But the generated enthusiasm was more a symptom of an existant void and the desire for understanding rather than being a consequence of establishing a scientific truth. Subsequent research has revealed that males exhibit as much fear of success in projective imagery as females (see, for example, Brown, Jennings, & Vanik, 1974; Tresemer, 1974). Thus, the findings first reported by Horner are now very much in doubt (Zuckerman & Wheeler, 1975).

There are some additional interesting sex differences reported in the literature on achievement motivation that suggest future research directions. It has been firmly established that females generally have a lower expectancy of success than males (Crandall, 1969). Furthermore, effort and luck, rather than ability, are often perceived as the main causes of female success (see, for example, Taynor & Deaux, 1973). How such biases are formed and what can be done to alter them are questions for the future.

CONCLUSION

It is evident from this review that research on achievement motivation is still thriving. Building blocks have been provided by prior investigations, and new ideas are shaping the future. The problems have not been solved, but empirical knowledge and conceptual advances are accumulating. I see the entire achievement areas as remaining near the forefront of personality research.

GENERAL SUMMARY

Nine central problem areas within the study of achievement motivation were examined in this chapter. The areas and the general conclusions were:

1. *Measurement.* Achievement needs typically are measured with a Thematic Apperception Test (TAT). One of the main controversies surrounding the use of this instrument concerns the report that internal consistency and test–retest reliability are below acceptable standards. These criticisms have not been definitively substantiated or rejected, and test–retest reliability as currently determined may be an inappropriate index of the soundness of a projective measure. Unfortunately, alternative objective measures have not been established as valid indicators of achievement needs.

2. *Atkinson's Theory of Achievement Motivation.* Atkinson's risk-–preference model of achievement strivings was presented. The model leads to the prediction that individuals high in achievement needs will prefer tasks of intermediate difficulty, whereas persons low in achievement needs will be most attracted to tasks that are easy or difficult. Only the former prediction has been confirmed. An ''information gain'' rather than hedonic interpretation of risk-–preference accurately predicts choice behavior.

3. *Theoretical Extensions of the Theory.* Extensions of Atkinson's theory to include persisting motivational tendencies and long-term achievement goals were examined. Although these conceptual elaborations have some validity, they have not received a great deal of attention from other psychologists.

4. *Attribution Theory and Achievement Strivings.* An attributional interpretation of achievement strivings calls attention to the perceived causes of success and failure. Two dimensions of causality, locus of control and causal stability, have been identified. Locus of control influences the achievement-related affects of pride and shame, whereas causal stability affects expectancy shifts after success and failure. This theory is able to account for much of the data in the achievement area, as well as broadening the cognitive focus of current theorizing.

5. *Personality Characterization.* The thoughts and behaviors that differentiate individuals classified as high versus low in achievement needs were reviewed. At present there are not data demonstrating the generality of achievement needs, and evidence concerning the endurance of this trait is sparse.

6. *Developmental Antecedents.* At one time it was strongly believed that achievement needs are fostered by early independence or early achievement

training. However, this research is inconclusive, and the socialization practices that produce high achievement concerns have not been identified. Investigations from a cognitive-developmental perspective are a promising new direction in this area.

7. *Economic Development.* McClelland's analysis of the relationship between achievement needs and cultural growth was reviewed.

8. *Achievement Change.* Programs that attempt to enhance achievement strivings were described. The effectiveness of these change procedures is not known.

9. *Achievement Needs among Females.* There is current concern over the possibility of a "fear of success" among females. The existence and the consequences of this proposed motivational disposition remains to be established.

REFERENCES

Atkinson, J. W. The achievement motive and recall of interrupted and completed tasks. *Journal of Experimental Psychology,* 1953, *46,* 381–390.

Atkinson, J. W. Motivational determinants of risk-taking behavior. *Psychological Review,* 1957, *64,* 359–372.

Atkinson, J. W. (Ed.). *Motives in fantasy, action and society.* Princeton, N.J.: Van Nostrand, 1958.(a)

Atkinson, J. W. Towards experimental analysis of human motivation in terms of motives, expectancies, and incentives. In J. W. Atkinson (Ed.), *Motives in fantasy, action, and society.* Princeton, N.J.: Van Nostrand, 1958.(b)

Atkinson, J. W. *An introduction to motivation.* Princeton, N.J.: Van Nostrand, 1964.

Atkinson, J. W., Bastian, J. R., Earl R. W., & Litwin, G. H. The achievement motive, goal setting, and probability preferences. *Journal of Abnormal and Social Psychology,* 1960, *60,* 27–36.

Atkinson, J. W. & Birch, D. *A dynamic theory of action.* New York: John Wiley, 1970.

Atkinson, J. W. & Birch, D. The dynamics of achievement-oriented activity. In J. W. Atkinson and J. Raynor (Eds.), *Motivation and achievement.* Washington, D.C.: V. H. Winston, 1974.

Atkinson, J. W. & Cartwright, D. Some neglected variables in contemporary conceptions of decision and performance. *Psychological Reports,* 1964, 14, 575–590.

Atkinson, J. W. & Feather, N. T. (Eds.). *A theory of achievement motivation.* New York: John Wiley, 1966.

Atkinson, J. W. & Litwin, G. Achievement motive and test anxiety conceived as motive to approach success and motive to avoid failure. *Journal of Abnormal and Social Psychology,* 1960, *60,* 52–63.

Atkinson, J. W. & O'Connor, P. *Effects of ability grouping in schools related to individual differences in motivation.* Final report of Project No. 1283, Cooperative Research Program of the Office of Education, U. S. Department HEW, 1963.

Atkinson, J. W., & Raynor, J. O. (Eds.). *Motivation and achievement.* Washington, D.C.: V. H. Winston, 1974.

Bartlett, E. W., & Smith, C. P. Child-rearing practices, birth order, and the development of achievement-related motives. *Psychological Reports,* 1966, *19,* 1207–1216.

Birney, R. C. The reliability of the achievement motive. *Journal of Abnormal and Social Psychology,* 1959, 58, 266–267.

Birney, R. C. Research on the achievement motive. In E. F. Borgatta and W. W. Lambert (Eds.), *Handbook of personality theory and research.* Chicago: Rand McNally, 1968.

Brown, M., Jennings, J., & Vanik, V. The motive to avoid success: A further examination. *Journal of Research in Personality,* 1974, 8, 172–176.

Byrne, D. *An introduction to personality.* Englewood Cliffs, N.J.: Prentice-Hall, 1974.

Callard E. *Achievement motive in the four-year old and its relationship to achievement expectancies of mothers.* Unpublished doctoral dissertation, University of Michigan, 1964.

Carney, R. The effect of situational variables on the measurement of achievement motivation. *Journal of Educational and Psychological Measurement,* 1966, 26, 675–690.

Chance, J. E. Independence training and first graders' achievement. *Journal of Consulting Psychology,* 1961, 25, 228–238.

Cohen, L., Reid, I., & Boothroyd, K. Validation of the Mehrabian need for Achievement scale with college of education students. *British Journal of Educational Psychology,* 1973, 43, 269–278.

Crandall, V. C. Sex differences in expectancy of intellectual and academic reinforcement. In C. P. Smith (Ed.), *Achievement-related motives in children.* New York: Russell Sage, 1969.

Cronbach, L. J., & Meehl, P. E. Construct validity in psychological tests. *Psychological Bulletin,* 1955, 52, 281–302.

deCharms, R. Personal causation training in the schools. *Journal of Applied Social Psychology,* 1972, 2, 95–113.

deCharms, R., Morrison, H. W., Reitman, W. R. & McClelland, D. C. Behavioral correlates of directly measured and indirectly measured achievement motivation. In D. C. McClelland (Ed.), *Studies in motivation.* New York: Appleton-Century-Crofts, 1955.

Entwisle, D. R. To dispel fantasies about fantasy-based measures of achievement motivation. *Psychological Bulletin,* 1972, 77, 377–391.

Feather, N. T. The relationship of persistence at a task to expectation of success and achievement-related motives. *Journal of Abnormal and Social Psychology,* 1961, 63, 552–561.

Feather, N. T. The relationship of expectation of success to n Achievement and test anxiety. *Journal of Personality and Social Psychology,* 1965, 1, 118–126.

Feather, N. T. Valence of outcome and expectation of success in relation to task difficulty and perceived locus of control *Journal of Personality and Social Psychology,* 1967, 7, 372–386.

Feld, S. Longitudinal study of the origins of achievement strivings, *Journal of Personality and Social Psychology,* 1967, 7, 408–414.

French, E. G. Development of a measure of complex motivation. In J. W. Atkinson (Ed.), *Motives in fantasy, action, and society.* Princeton, N.J.: Van Nostrand, 1958.

Green, D. R. Volunteering and the recall of interrupted tasks. *Journal of Abnormal and Social Psychology,* 1963, 66, 397–401.

Haber, R. N., & Alpert, R. The role of situation and picture cues in projective measurement of the achievement motive. In J. W. Atkinson (Ed.), *Motives in fantasy, action, and society.* Princeton, N.J.: Van Nostrand, 1958.

Hamilton, J. O. Motivation and risk taking behavior: A test of Atkinson's theory. *Journal of Personality and Social Psychology,* 1974, 29, 856–864.

Heckhausen, H. *The anatomy of achievement motivation.* New York: Academic Press, 1967.

Heckhausen, H. Achievement motive research: Current problems and some contributions toward a central theory of motivation. In D. Levine (Ed.), *Nebraska Symposium on Motivation.* Lincoln: University of Nebraska Press, 1968.

Heckhausen, H., & Roelofsen, I. Anfange und Entwicklung der Leistungsmotivation:(I) Im Wetteifer des Kleinkindes. *Psychologisches Forschungen,* 1962, *26,* 313–397.

Heider, F. *The psychology of interpersonal relations.* New York: John Wiley, 1958.

Hermans, H. J. M. A questionnaire measure of achievement motivation. *Journal of Applied Psychology,* 1970, *54,* 353–363.

Horner, M. S. *Sex differences in achievement motivation and performance in competitive and non-competitive situations.* Unpublished doctoral dissertation, University of Michigan, 1968.

Isaacson, R. L. Relation between achievement, test anxiety, and curricular choices. *Journal of Abnormal and Social Psychology,* 1964, *68,* 447–452.

Jensen, E. R. The Rorschach technique: A reevaluation. *Acta Psychologica,* 1964, *22,* 60–77.

Kagan, J., & Moss, H. A. Stability and validity of achievement fantasy. *Journal of Abnormal and Social Psychology,* 1959, *58,* 357–364.

Klinger, E. Fantasy need achievement as a motivational construct. *Psychological Bulletin,* 1966, *66,* 291–308.

Kolb, D. Achievement motivation training of underachieving high-school boys. *Journal of Personality and Social Psychology,* 1965, *2,* 783–792.

Kukla, A. Attributional determinants of achievement-related behavior. *Journal of Personality and Social Psychology,* 1972, *21,* 166–174. (a)

Kukla, A. Foundations of an attributional theory of performance. *Psychological Review,* 1972, *79,* 454–470. (b)

Mahone, C. H. Fear of failure and unrealistic vocational aspiration. *Journal of Abnormal and Social Psychology,* 1960, *60,* 253–261.

Mandler, G., & Sarason, S. B. A study of anxiety and learning. *Journal of Abnormal and Social Psychology,* 1952, *47,* 166–173.

McClelland, D. C. *Personality.* New York: William Sloane, 1951.

McClelland, D. C. Methods of measuring human motivation. In J. W. Atkinson (Ed.), *Motives in fantasy, action, and society.* Princeton, N.J.: Van Nostrand, 1958. (a)

McClelland, D. C. Risk taking in children with high and low need for achievement. In J. W. Atkinson (Ed.), *Motives in fantasy, action, and society.* Princeton, N.J.: Van Nostrand, 1958. (b)

McClelland, D. C. *The achieving society.* Princeton, N.J.: Van Nostrand, 1961.

McClelland, D. C. Achievement drive and economic growth. *Harvard Business Review,* 1962, *40,* 99–112.

McClelland, D. C. Toward a theory of motive acquisition. *American Psychologist,* 1965, *20,* 321–333.

McClelland, D. C., Atkinson, J. W., Clark, R. W., & Lowell, E. L. *The achievement motive.* New York: Appleton-Century-Crofts, 1953.

McClelland, D. C., & Steele, R. S. *Motivation workshops.* Morristown, N.J.: General Learning Press, 1972.

McClelland, D. C., & Winter, D. G. *Motivating economic achievement.* New York: Free Press, 1969.

Mehrabian, A. Male and female scales of the tendency to achieve. *Educational and Psychological Measurement,* 1968, *28,* 493–502.

Mehrabian, A. Measures of achieving tendency. *Educational and Psychological Measurement,* 1969, *29,* 445–451.

Meyer, H. H., Walker, W. B., & Litwin, G. H. Motive patterns and risk preferences associated with entrepreneurship. *Journal of Abnormal and Social Psychology,* 1961, *63,* 570–574.

Meyer, W. U. Anspruchniveau und erlebte Selbstverantworklichkeit für Erfolg und Misserfolg. *Psychologisches Beitrage*, 1969, *11*, 328–348.

Meyer, W. U. *Selbstverantwortlichkeit und Leistungsmotivation*. Unpublished doctoral dissertation, Ruhr Universität, Bochum, Germany, 1970.

Meyer, W. U., Folkes, V., & Weiner, B. The perceived informational value and affective consequences of choice behavior and intermediate difficulty task selection. *Journal of Research in Personality* 1976, *10*, 410–423.

Mischel, W. Delay of gratification, need for achievement, and acquiescence in another culture. *Journal of Abnormal and Social Psychology*, 1961, *62*, 543–552.

Morgan, H. H. Measuring achievement motivation with "picture interpretation." *Journal of Consulting Psychology*, 1953, *17*, 289–292.

Morris, J. L. Propensity for risk taking as a determinant of vocational choice: An extension of the theory of achievement motivation. *Journal of Personality and Social Psychology*, 1966, *3*, 328–335.

Moss, H. A., & Kagan, J. Stability of achievement and recognition seeking behaviors from early childhood through adulthood. *Journal of Abnormal and Social Psychology*, 1961, *62*, 504–513.

Moulton, R. W. Effects of success and failure on level of aspiration as related to achievement motives. *Journal of Personality and Social Psychology*, 1965, *1*, 399–406.

Mukherjee, B. N., & Sinha, R. Achievement values and self-ideal discrepancies in college students. *Personality: An International Journal*, 1970, *1*, 275–301.

Murray, H. A. *Explorations in personality*. New York: Oxford University Press, 1938.

Murray, H. A. Preparations for the scaffold of a comprehensive system. In S. Koch (Ed.), *Psychology: A study of a science* (Vol. 3). New York: McGraw-Hill, 1959.

Murstein, B. I. *Theory and research in projective techniques*. New York: John Wiley, 1963.

Nicholls, J. G. *Level of aspiration in young children*. Unpublished manuscript, Victoria University of Wellington, New Zealand, 1974.

Parsons, J. E., & Ruble, D. N. Attributional processes related to the development of achievement-related affect and expectancy. *Proceedings, 80th Annual Convention, American Psychological Association*, 1972, pp. 105–106.

Raynor, J. O. Future orientation and motivation of immediate activity: An elaboration of the theory of achievement motivation. *Psychological Review*, 1969, *76*, 606–610.

Raynor, J. O. Relationships between achievement-related motives, future orientation, and academic performance. *Journal of Personality and Social Psychology*, 1970, *15*, 28–33.

Raynor, J. O., & Smith, C. P. Achievement-related motives and risk-taking in games of skill and chance. *Journal of Personality*, 1966, *34*, 176–198.

Reitman, W. R., & Atkinson, J. W. Some methodological problems in the use of thematic apperceptive measures of human motives. In J. W. Atkinson (Ed.), *Motives in fantasy, action, and society*. Princeton, N.J.: Van Nostrand, 1958.

Ricciuti, H. N. *The prediction of academic grades with a projective test of achievement motivation: I. Initial validation studies*. Princeton, N.J.: Educational Testing Service, 1954.

Rosen, B. & D'Andrade, R. C. The psychosocial origins of achievement motivation. *Sociometry*, 1959, *22*, 185–218.

Rosenstein, A. *The specificity of the achievement motive and the motivational effects of picture cues*. Unpublished doctoral dissertation, University of Michigan, 1952.

Rotter, J. B. Generalized expectancies for internal versus external control of reinforcement. *Psychological Monographs*, 1966, *80*, (1, Whole No. 609).

Salili, F., Maehr, M. L. & Gillmore, G. Achievement and morality: A cross-cultural analysis of causal attribution and evaluation. *Journal of Personality and Social Psychology* 1976, *33*, 327–337.

Schneider, K. *Leistungs- und Risikoverhalten in Abhangigkeit von situativen und uberdaurenden Komoponenten der Leistungsmotivation.* Doctoral dissertation, Ruhr University, Bochum, Germany, 1971.

Skolnick, A. Motivational imagery and behavior over twenty years. *Journal of Consulting Psychology,* 1966, *30,* 463–478.

Smith, C. P. (Ed.). *Achievement-related motives in children.* New York: Russell Sage, 1969.

Taynor, J., & Deaux, K. When women are more then men: Equity, attribution, and perceived sex differences. *Journal of Personality and Social Psychology,* 1973, *28,* 360–367.

Tresemer, D. Fear of success: Popular, but unproven. *Psychology Today,* 1974, *7,* 82–85.

Trope, Y. Seeking information about one's own ability as a determinant of choice among tasks. *Journal of Personality and Social Psychology, 1975, 32,* 1004–1013.

Trope, Y., & Brickman, P. Difficulty and diagnosticity as determinants of choice among tasks. *Journal of Personality and Social Psychology, 1975, 31* 918–926.

Veroff, J. Social comparison and the development of achievement motivation. In C. P. Smith (Ed.), *Achievement-related motives in children.* New York: Russell Sage, 1969.

Veroff, J., Atkinson, J. W., Feld, S., & Gurin, G. The use of thematic apperception to assess motivation in a nationwide interview study. *Psychological Monographs,* 1960, *74,* (12, Whole No. 499).

Weiner, B. The effects of unsatisfied achievement motivation on persistence and subsequent performance. *Journal of Personality,* 1965, *33,* 428–442.

Weiner, B. New conceptions in the study of achievement motivation. In B. A. Maher (Ed.), *Progress in experimental personality research* (Vol. 5). New York: Academic Press, 1970.

Weiner, B. *Theories of motivation: From mechanism to cognition.* Chicago: Rand McNally, 1972.

Weiner, B. (Ed.). *Achievement motivation and attribution theory.* Morristown, N.J.: General Learning Press, 1974.

Weiner, B., Frieze, I., Kukla, A., Reed, L., Rest, S., & Rosenbaum, R. M. *Perceiving the causes of success and failure.* Morristown, N.J.: General Learning Press, 1971.

Weiner, B., Heckhausen, H., Meyer, W. U., & Cook, R. E. Causal ascriptions and achievement behavior: A conceptual analysis of effort and reanalysis of locus of control. *Journal of Personality and Social Psychology,* 1972, *21,* 239–248.

Weiner, B., Nierenberg, R., & Goldstein, M. Social learning (locus of control) versus attributional (caused stability) interpretations of expectancy of success. *Journal of Personality,* 1976, *44,* 52–68.

Weiner, B., & Peter, N. A cognitive-developmental analysis of achievement and moral judgments. *Developmental Psychology,* 1973, *9,* 290–309.

Weiner, B., & Potepan, P. A. Personality correlates and affective reactions towards exams of succeeding and failing college students. *Journal of Educational Psychology,* 1970, *61,* 144–151.

Weiner, B., & Rosenbaum, R. M. Determinants of choice between achievement and nonachievement-related activities. *Journal of Experimental Research in Personality,* 1965, *1,* 114–122.

Weiner, B., Russell, D., & Lerman, D. Affective consequences of causal ascriptions. In J. H. Harvey, W. J. Ickes, and R. F. Kidd (Eds.), *New directions in attribution research,* vol. 2. Hillsdale, N.J.: Erlbaum Press (in press).

Weiner, B. & Sierad, J. Misattribution for failure and the enhancement of achievement strivings. *Journal of Personality and Social Psychology,* 1975, *31,* 415–421.

Winterbottom, M. R. *The relation of childhood training in independence to achievement motivation.* Unpublished doctoral dissertation, University of Michigan, 1953.

Zuckerman, M., & Wheeler, L. To dispel fantasies about the fantasy-based measure of fear of success. *Psychological Bulletin,* 1975, *82,* 932–946.

NOTES

1. This paper was written while the author was supported by Grant MH25687-02 from the National Institute of Mental Health. The writing of this chapter was completed in Fall, 1975.

2. The French Test of Insight (French, 1958) is a related projective instrument that also assesses need for achievement. This measure employs sentence stems, with the respondent completing a paragraph based on this lead-in. The responses are scored according to the McClelland et al. (1953) system. The French test will not be examined in this paper.

3. Heckhausen (1967) uses the TAT for both the measurement of approach and avoidance motives. His scoring system, however, has rarely been used by American investigators and is neglected here.

4. Intermediate difficulty includes some gradient around the $Ps = 0.50$ level. There has been an alternative hypothesis proposed by Heckhausen (1968) that individuals highly motivated to achieve prefer tasks with subjective probability of success near 0.30. This controversy is not discussed here (see Hamilton, 1974).

CHAPTER 2

Anxiety

DOUGLAS H. LAMB

Student Counseling Center
Illinois State University
Normal, Illinois

The primary goal of this chapter is to summarize the current status of anxiety theory and measurement with particular emphasis on one approach to the conceptualization and measurement of anxiety.[1][2] This approach, called *state*–trait anxiety theory, identifies two distinct anxiety concepts: state anxiety and trait anxiety. These concepts will be placed within a particular theoretical framework, and the measuring operations associated with state and trait anxiety will be delineated.

Although the chapter's emphasis will be on state and trait anxiety, it is important first to place these concepts in some historical perspective (1900–1960). An understanding of the current conceptualization of anxiety in terms of states and traits had its antecedents in two psychological approaches that I have called the *clinical-applied* and the *experimental* perspectives. These two perspectives will be outlined as they influenced the current interest in anxiety states and traits. More recent (1960–1975) viewpoints of anxiety will then be reviewed, and the emergence of a third perspective, the *personality-research* perspective, will be discussed. Finally, the current status of state–trait anxiety theory and measurement will be described including its application to current experimental, clinical-applied, and personality issues.

ANXIETY—THEORY AND RESEARCH: 1900–1960

The particular interest in emotional phenomena from a psychological perspective can be documented as early as 1890 when William James made a number of

---

1. The author gratefully acknowledges the encouragement, assistance, and influence of Charles Spielberger in the development of the ideas expressed in this chapter.
2. The author appreciates the assistance of Connie Pisell who was primarily responsible for typing the manuscript.

observations regarding the nature of emotional phenomena. During this period, emotional behavior was viewed as an aspect of "immediate experience" (e.g., Titchener, 1897).

In tracing the history of anxiety theory and measurement, two distinct approaches can be identified: (1) the clinical-applied perspective beginning with orthodox psychoanalytic theory and culminating in various existential viewpoints regarding the nature of anxiety, and (2) an experimental perspective emphasizing the role of learning and conditioning in the development and reduction of anxiety.

It is generally agreed that Sigmund Freud was the first individual actually to present a comprehensive view of the nature of anxiety. In his book, *The Problem of Anxiety,* Freud (1923) distinguished anxiety as an emotional state or condition in which there was a specific unpleasurable quality, and some motor discharge, and in which the individual perceived these two qualities. Freud initially believed that anxiety resulted from the inability of the ego to repress impulses, but he later regarded anxiety as a signal to the organism of impending danger. Freud indicated that this danger may be external to the organism, or, more often, that it is the result of the ego's anticipation that it will be overwhelmed by the expression of sexual and/or aggressive impulses. At any rate, Freud appeared to believe that anxiety was transitory and that it varied in intensity as a function of the particular source of perceived danger. It seems unclear whether Freud considered anxiety as a stimulus, a response, or an abstraction. His signal theory implies that anxiety is a stimulus that is responded to by the organism in some way. At other times Freud talks about anxiety responses (e.g., increased heart rate and respiration).

Since Freud's conceptualization, there have been a number of theoretical accounts of anxiety (e.g., Epstein, 1972; Lader & Marks, 1971). The majority of these conceptualizations have arisen out of direct clinical-applied settings. Representative positions on anxiety include those of Sullivan (1953, anxiety as a perceived negative evaluation by significant others); Goldstein (1939, anxiety as a catastrophic reaction); Rogers (1951, anxiety as a threat to the Self concept); and May (1950, anxiety as a threat to existence). In his review of research and theory in anxiety, Mandler (1972) concludes that the majority of the theoretical attempts to conceptualize anxiety are modifications of classic analytic theory. Mandler himself appears to prefer the term *helplessness* rather than anxiety.

In contrast to the clinical-applied perspective that viewed anxiety as resulting from perceived danger (e.g., Freud, Rogers, Goldstein), the emphasis of the experimental perspective during this period was to conceptualize anxiety either as classically conditioned (e.g., Mowrer, 1939; Pavlov, 1927), or as a drive state which motivates the organism to further behavior (e.g., Dollard & Miller, 1950; Spence & Spence, 1966; Spence & Taylor, 1953).

The first attempts to study anxiety experimentally were, not surprisingly, in laboratory settings. As part of his investigation of the digestive process, Pavlov

(1927) identified a procedure that was able to produce what he called *experimental neurosis*. In this case, he conditioned a dog to salivate in response to the presentation of a circle. To investigate the process of discrimination, he presented a situation in which the dog was required to discriminate between the original circle and an elliptical figure of similar size. As the size of the figures became more similar, the dog's discrimination failed to improve, and it responded with a number of behavioral changes (e.g., indiscriminate responding, squealing, biting, struggling to escape from the apparatus). This process, in which the dog's discrimination abilities had completely broken down, was designated by Pavlov as experimental neurosis. The behaviors exhibited were thought to be analogous to human behaviors associated with a state of anxiety.

At approximately the same time, Liddell and his colleagues were successful in developing a number of behaviors in sheep that were analogous to those observed in humans during the experience of anxiety. A detailed account of procedures used by Liddell and their application to human behavior are presented by Anderson and Liddell (1935), Liddell (1944), and Liddell and Beyne (1927).

A final example of the experimental perspective as it applied to the learning of anxiety through classical conditioning procedures is that of Watson and Rayner (1920). In this study Watson and Rayner induced fear in an 11-month-old child to a previously neutral object (a white rat) by pairing the rat with a loud sound. The behavioral disturbance of the child was very similar to that observed in individuals who have considerable anxiety. In fact, the paradigm presented by Watson and Rayner is similar to a currently popular position regarding the way phobias are generally developed. A sequel to the Watson and Rayner study is presented by Jones (1924) who deconditioned a three-year-old child of an already existing fear of rats.

A recent review of the current status of classical conditioning theory as it applies to the processes involved in behavior therapy is presented by Rizley and Reppucci (1974), who describe in considerable detail the theoretical and empirical account of Pavlovian inhibition processes as they affect such behavior modification procedures as systematic desensitization, aversion–relief conditioning, and self-control procedures.

Pavlov and Liddell used classical conditioning procedures to produce anxiety, or what they termed experimental neurosis. There have also been a number of studies that have used operant conditioning procedures for the development of experimental neurosis. One such study was conducted by Masserman (1943). In a situation in which cats were trained to lift a box lid to receive food when a sound or light occurred, a strong air blast was blown across the box as the cats began to eat. If the stimulus was very intense, a general disruption of behavior took place which Masserman interpreted as being experimental neurosis.

Although these studies provide a particular paradigm for the development of anxiety reactions, the investigators (with the exception of Masserman) were not practicing clinicians and were not generally interested in anxiety from a clinical perspective. One clinically oriented psychologist, Mowrer (1939), is credited by many for bridging the gap, as it applies to the study of anxiety, between the clinical-applied and experimental perspectives. In his 1939 article, he reinterpreted Freudian theory in terms of classical conditioning and suggested a conceptualization of anxiety as an internal response that can be learned by means of classical conditioning. In a later series of investigations Mowrer (1950, 1960) identified two processes involved in the development and reduction of anxiety. He suggested that anxiety is learned by means of classical conditioning and is reduced as a function of the instrumental procedures employed by the organism.

Dollard and Miller also reinterpreted Freudian personality theory in terms of a drive reduction model of behavior. In a now classic study of anxiety, Miller (1948) demonstrated that anxiety was learned because it had been associated with a previous neutral stimulus and had drive properties and because it motivated the learning of new instrumental behaviors to reduce the drive state. In their 1950 textbook, *Personality and Psychotherapy,* Dollard and Miller applied drive reduction theory to higher mental processes, conflict, and behavior change.

The emphasis on the acquired drive properties of anxiety reached its height during the period 1950–1965 with the work of Taylor and Spence. Taylor (1953) interpreted the general notion of drive state as incorporating ''the level of internal anxiety or emotionality.'' The conceptualization of anxiety as having drive properties has stimulated considerable research on the relationship of anxiety to performance on various learning tasks. Taylor (1951, 1953) also developed a measure of individual differences in anxiety level called the Taylor Manifest Anxiety Scale (TMAS). Based on the rationale that the level of anxiety can be ascertained by a paper-and-pencil test, Taylor constructed the TMAS from items on the Minnesota Multiphasic Personality Inventory. She assumed that individual differences in anxiety as measured by the TMAS would be indicative of individual differences in drive level (Taylor, 1951). It was further assumed that individuals who were high in anxiety tended to be chronically or consistantly anxious and thus higher in drive level in any particular situation than individuals who were lower in anxiety. Although the Taylor and Spence interpretation of the TMAS as a measure of drive is generally supported in their eye blink conditioning experiments (Spence & Spence, 1966), there have been some questions as to the generality of this interpretation. Brody (1972) summarizes the use of the TMAS as a measure of drive and includes a number of reservations that have been raised about it.

As a result of many years of research, Spence & Spence (1966) have generated several statements based on empirical evidence that bear on the relationship between anxiety level as measured by the TMAS, task complexity, and performance. These findings can be summarized as follows:

1. On simple learning tasks those Ss high in anxiety (HA) will perform better than those Ss low in anxiety (LA). This finding is consistent with Hull's drive theory in that in the easy tasks there are relatively few incorrect or competing responses. Thus, the higher drive level for the HA Ss multiplies with higher strength for the correct response and thereby facilitates performance.

2. On more complex tasks, the performance of HA Ss is generally inferior to LA Ss, particularly in earlier stages of learning, but such performance may improve and even become better than the performance of LA Ss in later stages. Consistent with drive theory, it is assumed that the correct response is initially weaker than the competing errors on more complex tasks and that high drive activates more response error tendencies, thereby leading to performance decrements.

Summaries of studies in this area can be found in Brody (1972), Levitt (1967), Spence and Spence (1966), Spielberger (1966), and Spielberger and Gorsuch (1966). In addition, Brody (1972) provides an excellent analysis of the strengths and weaknesses of this experimental body of research.

We have reviewed two perspectives on anxiety. Those individuals who were working more directly in clinical-applied settings were more interested in ways to reduce anxiety than in developing precise measuring operations. The experimental perspective, on the other hand, focused on delineating specific characteristics of anxiety and its relationship to learning.

In the next section the current status of these two perspectives will be reviewed and the emergence of a third perspective, the personality–research perspective, will be described. This third perspective has its emphasis on two major issues: (1) the role of cognitive factors in the analysis of stress and anxiety, and (2) the delineation of particular anxiety states and traits.

CONTEMPORARY VIEWS OF ANXIETY: 1960–1970

This section presents several contemporary views regarding theory and measurement in anxiety research. Many books were written on anxiety during this period. Levitt's (1967) book, *The Psychology of Anxiety,* is an excellent overview of research on anxiety during the 1950–1965 period. A second text, *Anxiety and Behavior* (Spielberger, 1966) brought together a number of noted authorities in the area of anxiety research who relate anxiety to motivation, learning, psychopathology, and cognitive functioning. Other contributions to the study of anxiety include such textbooks as *Fears and Phobias* (Marks, 1969), *Explorations in the Psychology of Stress and Anxiety* (Rourke, 1969), and *Aspects of Anxiety* (Branch, 1968).

During the 1960s considerable effort was spent differentiating anxiety as an emotional state from other affects and arousal states (e.g., Malmo, 1966). Epstein (1967) has indicated that arousal is a common component of all motivational states and describes anxiety as a state of emotional arousal following the perception of danger. Anxiety is distinguished from fear in that anxiety, unlike fear, is not typically channeled into specific avoidance behaviors. Epstein (1972, 1967) has also devoted a considerable amount of study to the relationship between anxiety and expectancy.

There were two additional research efforts during the 1960s and very early 1970s that related anxiety to other emotional behaviors. Izard (1972) suggests that anxiety involves such fundamental emotions as distress, shame, shyness, guilt, fear, and interest–excitement. Izard (1968) has developed a Differential Emotional Scale (DES) designed to identify the discrete emotions that combine to make up anxiety. Izard and Tomkins (1966) also discuss anxiety as one of eight major affects.

In a second research effort, Mandler (1972) has emphasized the instability and distress aspects of anxiety. He analyzes anxiety as helplessness that he describes as the individual's feeling of not being in control. This distress, characterized by discomfort and uneasiness, is also caused by an interruption of any well-organized behavior.

While the clinical-applied perspective in psychology continued to relate anxiety to other emotional states, the experimental perspective continued to assess the effects of anxiety on performance in various learning and performance tasks. One particular area of research that received particular attention and interest was the relationship of anxiety to verbal conditioning. Greenspoon (1955) reported a study that demonstrated verbal operant conditioning without subject awareness. Such a finding raised questions about the usefulness and necessity of developing "awareness" or "insight" in psychotherapeutic settings in order to bring about behavior change. In response to Greenspoon's findings, a number of individuals attempted to understand better the phenomena of verbal conditioning. One such program was initiated by Spielberger and Gorsuch (1966) who investigated the relationship of cognitive and motivational factors to verbal conditioning. Two studies (Gorsuch & Spielberger, 1966; Spielberger, Southhard, & Hodges, 1966) dealt with the importance of undetected awareness and uncontrolled stress as factors in verbal conditioning research. Their general findings can be summarized as follows: "Anxiety and threat influence the performance of subjects who were aware of the correct response–reinforcement contingency, but these variables had no effect on the performance of subjects who did not report a correct contingency" (Gorsuch & Spielberger, 1966, p. 344). The implication here is that awareness is necessary for individual differences in anxiety and threat to influence performance in verbal-conditioning tasks.

In addition to the clinical-applied and experimental perspectives, a third body of research was initiated during the 1960s. This approach, which I will call the personality–research perspective, emphasized the identification and measurement of (1) personality dispositions or traits, (2) factors that influence stress reactions, and (3) particular anxiety states. It was through this research perspective that a general theoretical model of anxiety emerged.

Although many individuals contributed to this personality–research perspective, the work of three particular individuals and their associates will be identified and discussed. These individuals are Raymond Cattell, Richard Lazarus, and Charles Spielberger.

The work of Cattell in the early and mid-1960s represents the first systematic attempt to identify and measure two distinct anxiety constructs: state anxiety and trait anxiety. These two constructs or factors are discussed in detail in the book, *The Meaning and Measurement of Neuroticism and Anxiety* (Cattell & Scheier, 1961). In this text Cattell and Scheier indicate that, although valuable theories of neurosis and anxiety were developed during the 1900–1945 period, these theories served only as interesting hypotheses that were not subjected to objective measurement techniques. Cattell and Scheier (1961) also indicate that during this period psychologists were primarily interested in the definition and measurement of traits (e.g., Allport, 1966, 1937; Allport & Odert, 1936) to the exclusion of states. Cattell indicates that a thorough understanding of behavioral patterns must encompass both anxiety states and traits and suggests the use of various factor-analytic approaches to isolate these two factors. Cattell (1973) and Cattell et al. (1974) have suggested that a failure to distinguish these two uniquely defined factors results in contamination with other factors such as arousal and depression.

Cattell's first analysis of mood states was published in 1947 and his most recent book, *Personality and Mood by Questionnaire* (Cattell, 1973) represents the culmination of nearly 30 years of research on states and traits. In this book he describes the Sixteen Personality Factor Questionnaire (16 PF) which he developed, in part, to measure anxiety state and anxiety trait.

There is little doubt that Cattell provided the greatest single thrust for the measurement of anxiety states and traits as two distinct factors or constructs. For a detailed historical account of the measurement of personality states and traits, see Cattell (1972, 1973) and Spielberger (1972b).

While Cattell and his colleagues were continuing the emphasis on the distinction between anxiety states and traits, there was a parallel but equally important series of investigations conducted by Lazarus and his colleagues. These investigations were concerned primarily with the concept of stress and the coping process. Lazarus (1969, 1967, 1966) discusses stress as a psychological problem and comments on various theoretical and methodological issues related to stress research. Lazarus (1966) describes stress as a stimulus and as a response. As a stimulus, stress is defined as a circumstance external to the person that makes unusual or extraordinary demands (Lazarus, 1969, p. 167). Thus, when talking about stress as a stimulus, the emphasis is on the conditions that produce stress reactions. The first category of conditions can be broadly labeled "natural" stimuli (e.g., military combat, concentration camps, and other various natural disasters such as floods, explosions, and fires). The second broad category of conditions that produce stress reactions are those that are defined externally by the experimenter in a laboratory situation. A frequently used condition of this sort is the induction of an electrical shock. Lazarus has also completed research using motion pictures and tape recordings as stress inducers. His 1966 contribution includes a detailed account of such research.

The second meaning of stress has its emphasis on response characteristics rather than on the conditions that produce stress. Lazarus (1966) indicated four main classes of reactions that have typically been used to indicate stress: (1) reports of disturbed affects, for example, fear, anxiety, anger; (2) motor behaviors, for example, tremors, increased muscular tension, speech disturbances; (3) changes in adequacy of cognitive functioning, for example, thought interruption, perception distortions; and (4) physiological changes such as in heart rate and respiration.

Although Lazarus speaks of three additional meanings of stress (physiological stress, sociological stress, and psychological stress), we are most concerned with psychological stress, the purely psychological processes used to judge a stimulus as harmful (Lazarus, 1969, p. 170). From a psychological viewpoint, Lazarus discusses the concept of *threat* as an intervening variable in psychological stress research and indicates two main properties of threat: (1) it is anticipatory, involving expectations of future harm, and (2) it is dependent on cognitive processes (Lazarus, 1966, p. 83). Lazarus spends considerable time discussing the relationship between threat and anxiety and prefers the term *threat*.

Lazarus and his colleagues place heavy emphasis on the cognitive processes that mediate between those environmental situations producing threat and the particular emotional reactions employed by individuals to reduce the threat. Great emphasis is placed on the manner in which an individual apprehends or interprets a given situation and how that interpretation relates to his mode of expressing specific coping responses. Figure 2–1 presents several theoretical concepts that are important to consider in the analysis of coping and emotion. The four dimensions characterized in Figure 2–1 (antecedent conditions, psychological mediators, modes of expression in coping, and specific coping responses) are discussed in considerable detail in seven major works: Lazarus and Averill (1972); Lazarus, Averill, and Opton (1970, 1969); Lazarus (1966, 1967, 1969); and Lazarus and Opton (1966). Although it is beyond the scope of this chapter to discuss in detail the four dimensions, a brief summary of each dimension follows.

As can be seen in Figure 2–1, the process of cognitive appraisal depends on

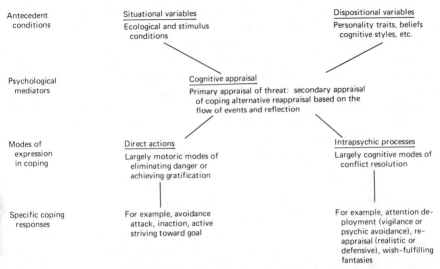

| Antecedent conditions | Situational variables Ecological and stimulus conditions | Dispositional variables Personality traits, beliefs cognitive styles, etc. |

Figure 2–1 content:

Antecedent conditions — Situational variables / Ecological and stimulus conditions — Dispositional variables / Personality traits, beliefs cognitive styles, etc.

Psychological mediators — Cognitive appraisal / Primary appraisal of threat: secondary appraisal of coping alternative reappraisal based on the flow of events and reflection

Modes of expression in coping — Direct actions / Largely motoric modes of eliminating danger or achieving gratification — Intrapsychic processes / Largely cognitive modes of conflict resolution

Specific coping responses — For example, avoidance attack, inaction, active striving toward goal — For example, attention deployment (vigilance or psychic avoidance), reappraisal (realistic or defensive), wish-fulfilling fantasies

Figure 2–1. Some theoretical distinctions relevant to the analysis of coping and emotion. From Lazarus, R. S. Averill, J. R., & Opton, E. M., Jr. *The psychology of coping: Issues of research and assessment.* Paper presented at the Conference on Coping and Adaptation, Palo Alto, Cal., March, 1969.

two classes of antecedent conditions: situational variables and dispositional variables. The first class, situational variables, are factors in the actual stimulus configuration such as the comparative power of the harm-producing condition, the counter-harm resources, the imminence of the harmful confrontation, and the degree of ambiguity in the stimulus condition. The second class of events determining appraisal consists of factors within the psychological structure of the individual, including motives, general beliefs, education, knowledge, and general anxiety or drive level.

Once the antecedent conditions are identified, various forms of cognitive appraisal take place, conceptually prior to the occurrence of any particular emotional reaction. Lazarus and Averill (1972) describe the following three kinds of appraisal processes:

Primary appraisal refers to the judgment that a situation is relevant or irrelevant, or that it will either have a beneficial or harmful outcome. Secondary appraisal is a judgment about the forms of coping available for mastering anticipated harm or for facilitating potential benefits. Reappraisal involves changes in the effects of the responses, or further reflectional about the evidence on which the original appraisals were based. (p. 242).

As the result of appraisal and reappraisal, specific modes of coping are identified, and then specific coping responses are implemented.

Lazarus and his colleagues have concluded that stress is not any one thing but rather a collective term for an area of personality study. They prefer the use of the term *threat* as a way to describe a psychological state that intervenes between the antecedent conditions prompting cognitive appraisal and the specific ways of coping. Recent research strategies for the investigation of appraisals have also been identified by Lazarus and Averill (1972) and Lazarus et al. (1970). These strategies include: (1) the evaluation of appraisal from the self-report of subjects as they undergo a threatening experience; (2) the direct manipulation of appraisal, for example, providing the subject with an interpretive framework before or during the stressful experience; (3) the indirect manipulation of appraisal by altering cognitive conditions, for example, during anticipation; and (4) the study of interaction between theoretically relevant situational and dispositional variables (Lazarus & Averill, 1972, p. 243). Examples of the use of these strategies can be seen in the studies by Lazarus and Alfert (1964); Lazarus et al. (1962); Nomikos et al. (1968); and Speisman et al. (1964). The work by Lazarus and Averill (1972) has led to a number of methodological advances in the laboratory investigations of psychological stress. Lazarus and Opton (1966) identify four such advances: (1) the continuous measurement of autonomic response patterns; (2) the intraindividual analysis of autonomic measures, for example, between and within individuals over a period of time; (3) the vicarious approach to the induction of threat with the use of films and tapes; and (4) the continuous and simultaneous measurement of the level of affective disturbance as measured by self-report, physiological, and behavioral measures of stress.

Lazarus and his colleagues have clearly been the single most influential group of individuals who have helped to delineate the relationship among antecedent conditions provoking emotional reactions, cognitive appraisals, emotional reactions themselves, and various attempts to reduce psychological threats. Lazarus' work is particularly important in the study of anxiety because it represents a major theoretical position that speaks to the relationship between threat and anxiety. Recent investigations that have focused on modifying or reducing anxiety by cognitive restructuring procedures have been greatly influenced by the work of Lazarus and his colleagues, who have also made significant methodological contributions in developing procedures to measure changes in anxiety levels. Other individuals who have made major contributions to the understanding of the relationships among anxiety, stress, and coping include Epstein (1972), Eriksen (1966), Grinker (1966), Hodges (1968), Janis (1958), Levitt (1967), Mischel (1969), Sarason (1960), and Schachter (1966).

In addition to the work of Lazarus and Cattell, there was a third emerging perspective on anxiety having its beginnings in 1964 in a series of colloquia at Vanderbilt University and George Peabody College. This series was organized and chaired by Charles Spielberger, a faculty member at Vanderbilt at the time. The paper presentations were later published in a volume entitled *Anxiety and*

Behavior (Spielberger, 1966), and Spielberger's chapter in that book represents his initial statement of a state-trait anxiety theory.

This view of anxiety has since been presented by Spielberger in a number of sources including *The State–Trait Anxiety Inventory* (Spielberger, Gorsuch, & Lushene, 1970) and in three chapters in *Anxiety: Current Trends in Theory and Research,* Volumes I and II (Spielberger, 1972b, 1972c). In these and other works, Spielberger reviews the historical developments in the study of anxiety. He maintains that the inconsistency and indiscriminate use of the term *anxiety* has arisen, in great part, because of the failure to distinguish between state and trait anxiety.

Spielberger indicates that a comprehensive view of anxiety requires clarification of the relationships among three anxiety concepts: (1) anxiety as a state, (2) anxiety as a complex process that involves stress and threat, and (3) anxiety as a personality trait. More particularly, he indicates that anxiety states must be distinguished from the stimulus conditions (stress) that arouse them and from the cognitive and behavioral measures that are learned to reduce anxiety states. Spielberger (1972b) defines state anxiety as follows:

State anxiety (A-state) is conceptualized as a transitory emotional state or condition of the human organism that is characterized by subjective, consciously perceived feelings of tension and apprehension, and heightened autonomic nervous system activity. (Spielberger et al., 1970, p. 3).

. . .it may be conceived as a complex, relatively unique emotional condition or reaction that may vary in intensity and fluctuate over time. (p. 29)

Consider the statement "Bill seems anxious." Bill is being described as anxious now, in a particular situation and at a particular moment in time. The validity of that statement may be determined by making appropriate measurements to determine whether Bill is, in fact, anxious. This is typically accomplished in at least one of three ways: (1) asking Bill how he feels or asking him to report what such feelings are, for example, by a paper-and-pencil test; (2) taking physiological measurements such as heart rate and respiration; or (3) making some observations of Bill's behavior, such as shuffling of his feet, or trembling. The relationship of these three typical ways of measuring anxiety will be discussed in much more detail later in this section. Notice that Spielberger's definition of state anxiety must involve both self-report ("subjective, consciously perceived feelings of tension and apprehension") and physiological components ("heightened autonomic nervous system activity").

The duration and intensity of particular A-state reactions are highly dependent on the stimulus conditions that arouse the A-state reactions. These conditions are often called "stress," "threat," and/or "anxiety" situations. It is important, however, to delineate the differences among these three terms. The concepts of stress and threat were introduced earlier in this chapter in the discussion of

Lazarus' position. Spielberger (1972a) has also delineated the differences between stress, threat, and anxiety. For Spielberger, the terms *stress* and *threat* are used to identify different aspects of a temporal sequence of events that result in a state anxiety reaction. Stress is identified in terms of an objective stimulus situation that may involve environmental conditions that occur naturally or that are introduced or manipulated in some laboratory situation. Examples of the first conditions would be such events as naturally occurring disasters and personal traumas. An example of the second type of stimulus condition would be use of shock as a stressor in laboratory research. Thus, stress refers to some stimulus condition external to the organism that is characterized by some degree of danger as defined by the individual himself, consensually validated by others, or established by some experimenter.

Two general classes of stressors can be identified: (1) those that pose a potential threat to self-esteem (psychological stressors) and (2) those that signal potential physical harm or danger (physical stressors). The distinction between these types of stressors and how they relate to state and trait anxiety will be discussed in considerable detail later in this chapter.

There is little doubt that there are many situations in our environment likely to be perceived as stress situations or dangerous by most persons (e.g., surgery, job interviews, impending death). Whether a particular situation is perceived as threatening by a particular person at a particular time will depend, however, on his own subjective appraisal of the situation (Spielberger, 1972b). In like manner, there may be certain situations that are generally perceived as nonstressful but that may be perceived or appraised by a particular person as potentially dangerous or harmful.

Threat refers to the individual's idiosyncratic perception of a particular situation as physically or psychologically dangerous. The particular appraisal of a situation as dangerous or threatening will be determined by a number of characteristics (Spielberger, 1972b; Lazarus, 1966) including one's belief system, skills, attitudes, aptitudes, and previous reinforcement history.

Take, for example, the situation of someone diving off a 50-foot platform. To most individuals such an objective stress situation will be appraised as threatening. Yet, for some individuals (e.g., stunt artists who dive from considerable heights for a living), that situation may not be perceived as threatening. Thus, whether the A-state reaction will be evoked depends on one's past history. Two empirical studies have dealt with the importance of assessing the individual's unique appraisal of potential stressors. Hodges and Spielberger (1966) found that the A-state reaction for individuals exposed to threat of shock was much greater for those individuals who had previously indicated a moderate to extreme fear of shock two months prior to the experiment. These individuals responded with greater heart rate elevation than did subjects who reported little or no fear of shock. In another investigation, Lamb (1973) found that it was important to identify one's proneness to experience anxiety in a speaking situation in order to accurately predict an individual's A-state reaction when exposed to a particular speaking situation.

In distinguishing anxiety from stress and threat, Spielberger (1972a) indicates that state anxiety refers to the complex emotional reaction that occurs in individuals once they interpret specific situations as personally threatening. The intensity of the A-state reaction will be proportional to the amount of threat the individual perceives in that situation, and the duration of the A-state reaction will depend on the persistence of the individual's interpretation of that situation as threatening.

Another concept that must be related to A-state, stress, and threat is anxiety as a personality trait. In contrast to the transitory fluctuating nature of A-state reactions, trait anxiety (A-trait) refers to relatively stable individual differences in anxiety proneness (Spielberger et al., 1970; Spielberger, 1966). Trait anxiety can also be conceptualized in terms of the specific tendency to perceive the world in a certain way. Trait anxiety can be defined (Spielberger et al., 1970) as follows:

> Trait anxiety (A-trait) refers to the relatively stable individual differences in anxiety proneness, that is, the differences between people in a tendency to respond to situations perceived as threatening with elevations in A-state intensity. . . . Trait anxiety . . . indicates differences in the strength of a latent disposition to manifest a certain type of reaction. (p. 3)

A-trait may also be regarded as reflecting individual differences in the frequency and intensity with which A-states have been manifested in the past, and the differences in the probability that such A-state reactions will be experienced in the future (Spielberger, 1972b). The stronger the particular trait, the more probable it is that the individual will experience an emotional state corresponding to this trait.

Spielberger indicates that whether a particular personality trait will be expressed in behavior at a given moment of time will depend on the strength of the trait and the presence of appropriate stimuli (Spielberger, 1972b, p. 32). In general, however, it is expected that those who are higher in A-trait will tend to exhibit A-state elevations more frequently than low A-trait individuals. Individuals with very high levels of A-trait are often described as "neurotically anxious."

Spielberger's theory is presented schematically in Figure 2–2. It can be seen in Figure 2–2 that any external situation or stimulus is potentially capable of eliciting or evoking an A-state reaction. If a situation is appraised as threatening, then an A-state reaction is evoked. Figure 2–2 also indicates two general ways in which A-states are reduced: specific behaviors and defense mechanisms. Such methods of reducing A-state are similar to those elaborated by Lazarus (direct and indirect expressions of coping). Spielberger's description also includes the

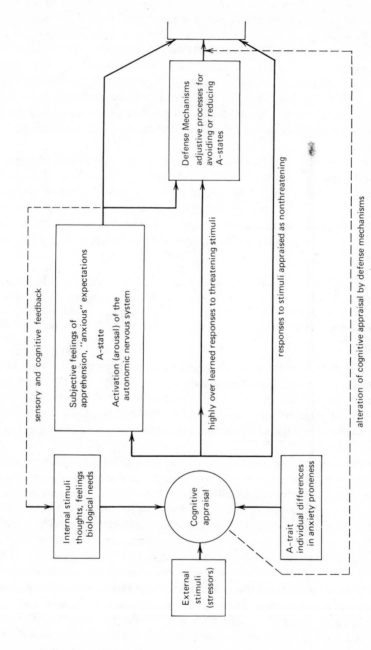

Figure 2-2. A trait–state theory of anxiety. From C. D. Spielberger (Ed.). Anxiety: Current trends in theory and research (Vol. I). New York: Academic Press, 1972.

role of sensory and cognitive feedback through which the individual is continually evaluating and reevaluating the stimulus situation.

The principal assumptions of state-trait anxiety theory can be summarized as follows (Spielberger, 1972b, p. 44):

1. In situations that are appraised by individuals as threatening, an A-state reaction will be evoked. Through sensory and cognitive feedback mechanisms, high levels of A-state will be experienced as unpleasant.

2. The intensity of an A-state reaction will be proportional to the amount of threat that the situation poses for the individual.

3. The duration of an A-state reaction will depend upon the persistence of the individual's interpretation of the situation as threatening.

4. High A-trait individuals will perceive situations or circumstances that involve failure or threats to self-esteem as more threatening than will persons who are low in A-trait.

5. Elevations in A-state have stimulus and drive properties that may be expressed directly in behavior or that may serve to initiate psychological defenses that have been effective in reducing A-state in the past.

6. Stressful situations that are encountered frequently may cause an individual to develop specific coping responses or psychological defense mechanisms which are designed to reduce or minimize A-state.

The next section describes the use of a self-report instrument, (the State–Trait Anxiety Inventory, (STAI) to measure state and trait anxiety. Before that discussion, however, it will be helpful first to review the various approaches to the measurement of anxiety.

Anxiety is typically measured by three procedures: self-report or introspective measures, physiological measures, and behavioral measures. Self-report measures assess the individual's subjective feelings by means of verbal or written reports. The most widely used self-report measures of anxiety include the STAI (Spielberger et al., 1970), the Taylor Manifest Anxiety Scale (Taylor, 1953), the 16 PF (Cattell, Eber & Tatsuoka, 1970), the Mood Adjective Checklist (Nowlis, 1965), the Multiple Affect Adjective Checklist (Zuckerman, 1960), the neuroticism scale of the Maudsley Personality Inventory (Eysenck, 1959), and the MMPI (Welch, 1952). A relatively new instrument, the Profile of Mood States (POMS) has also been developed (McNair, Lorr, & Droppleman, 1971).

Although a number of researchers (e.g., Martin & Stroufe, 1970; Krause, 1961) prefer the use of self-report measures, there are a number of difficulties with such measures (Wilde, 1972). They have been criticized because they are too idiosyncratic (having different meanings to different people), because they are subject to a variety of response sets, and because individuals are not "accurately" responding to how they feel. Although it is generally found that various self-report measures obtained in the same experimental situation tend to correlate substantially with one another, there is typically no strong relationship between self-report and other measures of anxiety taken concurrently. Maher (1966, p. 179) indicates that although correlations between self-report and physiological measures tend to be high during periods of stress, the relationship is not as great as when the measures are obtained during nonstressful circumstances.

Physiological anxiety is generally assessed by such measures as heart rate, vascular responsiveness, galvanic skin response, and palmar sweating. Several authors (Maher, 1966; Malmo, 1957) have found that physiological measures can discriminate between subjects designated as high- or low-anxious by self-report procedures when the subjects are placed in a stressful situation. Yet it has also been found that physiological measures do not always differentiate between high- and low-anxious subjects in either stressful (Katkin, 1965) or nonstressful conditions (Martin & Stroufe, 1970). Other summaries of the assessment of anxiety through physiological measures are presented by Lader and Marks (1971), McReynolds (1968), and Levitt (1967).

The third approach to the measurement of anxiety involves the use of behavioral measures. In this approach, various behaviors indicative of anxiety are judged to be present or absent. One of the most well known behavioral measures of anxiety is that developed by Paul (1966) to assess anxiety while giving a speech. Although behavioral measures of anxiety appear to be quite reliable internally, they have not always been found to be related to other measures. Lamb (1970, 1973), for example, found no systematic relationship between behaviors associated with speech anxiety and scores on various self-report and physiological measures of anxiety.

Other investigators have also found that the relationship among the three kind of measures is generally not strong. Leitenberg et al. (1971) reports a lack of any relationship between physiological and behavioral measures, whereas Schroeder and Craine (1971) report generally low correlations between behavioral and self-report measures of specific fears. In addition, Lamb (1973), Katkin (1965), and Martin (1961) reported low correlations between their physiological and self-report measures of anxiety.

Although a number of explanations can be developed to account for these discrepancies, three such explanations are mentioned here. Spielberger (1966) has suggested that comparisons among the three kinds of measures have been inappropriate because of a failure to distinguish between state and trait anxiety. He points to the widely used comparison of self-report measures of trait anxiety with physiological indices. Since physiological measures typically reflect the intensity of A-state rather than A-trait, significant relationships between these state and trait measures would not be expected. Lacey, Bateman, and Vanlehn (1953) have explained the lack of relationship between self-report and physiological measures of anxiety in terms of reponse specificity. Response specificity implies that individuals differ in the particular autonomic channel in which maximal response to stress occurs. The phenomenon of response specificity suggests that it would be helpful to obtain multiple physiological measures in stress situations as well as to identify the autonomic channel that is most likely used by a particular individual in a stress situation.

A third possible explanation for the discrepancy among the three kinds of measures of anxiety stems from a series of investigations that have delineated the various components of state anxiety. Lushene (1970) examined the relationship between three components of A-state in different kinds of stressful situations. The three components of A-state anxiety were ideational (items related to cognitive or thought processes and without obvious reference to either autonomic or motor activity), motoric (items related primarily to the muscular-skeletal system, and/or motor activity), and autonomic (items related to organ systems innervated by the autonomic nervous system). These three components are very similar to the self-report, behavioral, and physiological measures of anxiety. Whereas both physical and psychologial stressors produced increases in all components of A-state, Lushene found that the physical stressor produced a greater increase in the autonomic component of A-state than in the ideational or motoric component. This approach of isolating the separate components of A-state is encouraging in that some of the components might interact with the type of stress situation in which the individual is placed. In a similar line of research, Morris and Liebert (1973) have distinguished between a worry component and an emotionality component of anxiety. These authors have defined worry as a cognitive concern about the outcome of a future event, whereas emotionality is defined as a physiological or affective arousal elicited primarily by the stressful cues present in a particular anxiety-provoking situation (Morris & Liebert, 1973, p. 322). These authors found that worry scores were aroused in a psychological stress situation (failure–threat), whereas emotionality scores were elevated only in a physical stress (shock–threat) situation. In a later study, Morris, Spiegler, and Liebert (1974) investigated the effects of therapeutic modeling on the cognitive (worry) and emotionality components of anxiety. These authors found that although worry scores decreased significantly more for the modeling than for the control group, there were no differential changes in the emotionality component as a function of therapy intervention. They suggest that choice of therapy treatment should relate to therapeutic goals of the reduction of worry or emotionality since a particular treatment approach can have differential effects on these two components. In a final study representative of the research to separate out different components of anxiety, Blum and Wohl Z1971) trained individuals in a hypnotic trance to experience separately cognitive and somatic components of anxiety. They found the cognitive component of anxiety to be more disrupting.

THE MEASUREMENT OF STATE AND TRAIT ANXIETY

This section will provide an introduction to the measurement of state and trait anxiety by means of the State–Trait Anxiety Inventory (STAI). Although a detailed description of the development of the STAI is provided in Spielberger et al. (1970), a summary of the procedures will be briefly discussed here. As an initial step in the development of the STAI, items taken from three other currently used anxiety scales were rewritten in a way to permit each to be used as a measure of both A-state and A-trait. One hundred seventy-seven items from these three scales, correlating .25 or higher with each other, were then rewritten in a manner to reflect both A-state and A-trait. It was during this stage of the development of the STAI that key words associated with A-state or A-trait scales were identified. On the A-state scale, individuals responded to each item in terms of some intensity dimension. Intensity choices ranged from ''not at all'' to ''very much so.'' For the development of the A-trait scale, individuals were asked to respond on a frequency dimension. Since A-trait is designed to measure A-states that have been experienced frequently in the past, the A-trait measure asked individuals to respond in terms of how often they experienced the particular emotion. Answers ranged from ''almost never'' to ''almost always.''

Once the initial items were developed for the two scales, a strategy was adopted for further refinement of the A-state scale of the STAI. Spielberger (1972a) describes three aspects of that strategy: (1) state items should reflect the subject's level of anxiety at a particular moment in time, for example, mean scores for A-state should be higher in anxiety situations; (2) there should be high interitem reliability for the A-state scale since its primary emphasis is on obtaining different scores on two or more measuring occasions; and (3) the A-state scale should be easily administered so that it would not be cumbersome for repeated measures of emotional states. The first and second aspects of the strategy were accomplished by obtaining measures in different stressful situations.

First, 265 college students completed the STAI A-state scale in two hypothetical situations entitled ''exam'' and ''relax.'' Subjects were asked to imagine how they would feel in each of those two situations. As expected, it was found that A-state scores were higher in the exam situation than in the relaxed situation. These conditions were again applied to a second subject population of almost 400 undergraduates enrolled in an introductory psychology course, with the same general results.

A third validity procedure for the A-state scale involved the exposure of 197 subjects to four conditions that varied in their assumed stress-producing characteristics. Under the normal condition, subjects completed the A-state scale at the beginning of the session; then subjects again completed the scale after a 10-minute period of relaxation (relax). In the third condition, the subjects worked on a difficult I.Q. test, and measures of A-state were obtained after 10 minutes of the testing situation (exam). The final A-state measure was obtained immediately after subjects viewed a stressful movie that depicted several shop accidents (movie). The A-state means for the four measuring occasions were 37.12, 31.15, 43.35, and 55.49 respectively (Spielberger et al., 1970, p. 11). These means illustrate several characteristics of A-state measures. First, they are transitory and fluctuate according to the stress situation. Second, the intensity of the A-state reaction varies as a function of the amount of assumed stress.

The general findings using the A-state scale have been replicated several times and with different kinds of stressors. Examples of such studies and the stressor used include D'Avgelli (1974), group counseling; Endler and Shedletsky (1973), threat of shock; Auerbach (1973b), surgery; Lamb (1973), public speaking; Morgan (1973), physical activity; Saunders (1973), interview; Auerbach and Spielberger (1972), projective tests; Griffin (1972), sports competition; Lamb and Plant (1972), dental treatment; Newmark (1972), electroconvulsive therapy; O'Neil (1972), computer learning; Lushene (1970), movies; Snyder and Katahn (1970), verbal learning; McAdoo (1969), negative feedback; Nixon (1969), examination anxiety; and Taylor, Wheeler, and Altman (1968), social isolation.

The third desirable goal for the A-state measure was to have a scale that was brief and easily administered. The 20-item scale can be completed in approximately five minutes and it is suggested that the STAI A-state scale can be given on a number of occasions in which measures of A-state are appropriate. It has been found that very brief scales consisting of as few as four or five STAI A-state items may be used to provide unobtrusive yet valid measures of A-state (Hansen, & Spielberger, 1969; Spielberger, & Hansen, 1969, Spielberger, O'Neil, and & Hansen, 1972;).

Regarding the relationship between the A-state and A-trait scales, it is expected that the correlation between the scales would depend on the type and amount of stress that characterized the conditions under which the A-state is given (Spielberger et al., 1970). Correlations between the two scales appear to vary between +.44 and +.55 when given under standard instructions. It is generally found that larger correlations are obtained between the two scales under conditions of anticipated failure or threat to self-esteem.

The efforts to relate the STAI A-state scale to other measures of state anxiety are presented in Spielberger et al. (1967, 1970). The A-state and A-trait scales are presented in Tables 2–1 and 2–2.

In contrast to the test construction strategy for the A-state scale, the primary research strategy underlying the development of the A-trait scale consisted of two considerations. First, such a measure should correlate with current acceptable scales that propose also to measure trait anxiety (concurrent validity). Second, a trait measure of anxiety should reflect relatively stable differences in anxiety proneness as well as be relatively impervious to situational factors.

Table 2-1[a]   Sample Items from the STAI A-State Scale

Instructions: ". . .indicate how you feel right now, that is, at this moment."				
Sample Items:	Not At All	Some- what	Moder- ately So	Very Much So
3. I am tense	1	2	3	4
10. I feel comfortable	1	2	3	4

[a]Reproduced by special permission from *The State-Trait Anxiety Inventory* by Charles Spielberger, Richard Gorsuch, and Robert Lushene. Copyright 1970. Published by Consulting Psychologists Press Inc.

Table 2-2[a]   Sample Items from the STAI A-Trait Scale

Instructions: ". . .indicate how you generally feel".				
Sample Items:	Almost Never	Some- times	Often	Almost Always
34. I try to avoid facing a crisis or difficulty	1	2	3	4
38. I take disappointments so keenly that I can't put them out of my mind	1	2	3	4

[a]Reproduced by special permission from *The State-Trait Anxiety Inventory* by Charles Spielberger, Richard Gorsuch, and Robert Lushene. Copyright 1970. Published by Consulting Psychologists Press Inc.

Spielberger et al. (1967, 1968, 1970) report a number of studies in which a positive correlation between the STAI A-trait scale with other standard A-trait measures such as the IPAT anxiety scale, the Taylor Manifest Anxiety Scale, and the Zuckerman Affect Adjective Checklist (general) has been found. There is also a variety of evidence (e.g., Auerbach, 1973b; Johnson, 1968; Lamb, 1973; Spielberger et al., 1970) for the stability of A-trait measures across different experimental situations.

The characteristics of state and trait anxiety can be illustrated by several studies that employed these measures simultaneously. The first study (Johnson & Spielberger, 1968) investigated the effects of relaxation training and the passage of time on measures of state and trait anxiety. The three measures of A-state were systolic blood pressure, heart rate, and the "today" form of the Zuckerman Affect Adjective Checklist. The measures of A-trait were the Taylor Manifest Anxiety Scale and the Affect Adjective Checklist (general). The subjects in the study, 48 hospitalized male psychiatric patients, were exposed to a modified form of relaxation training as described by Jacobson (1938). Measures of blood pressure, heart rate, and anxiety level were made before and after the relaxation period. Similarly, the trait measures were also obtained before and after the relaxation procedure. Johnson and Spielberger (1968) reported that all three A-state measures declined significantly in response to relaxation training procedures. In contrast, scores on the A-trait measures were essentially unaffected by relaxation training. These authors interpreted these findings to mean that relaxation training reduces subjective anxiety as measured by self-report and physiological indices but has no influence on anxiety proneness (A-trait). This study provided evidence for the construct validity of both the A-state and A-trait measures in that A-state measures varied as a function of changes in stimulus conditions whereas A-trait measures remained essentially unaffected by the situational changes.

Two other studies also bear on the relationship of state and trait anxiety measures in an interview stress situation. In one study carried out by Johnson (1968), a group of psychiatric inpatients were exposed to either a stressful or nonstressful interview. The A-state and A-trait measures were the same as employed by Johnson and Spielberger (1968) and were obtained before and after the interviews. Johnson found that although the scores on all the A-state measures increased in response to the stressful interview, these measures were not affected by the nonstressful interview. As expected, the scores on the A-trait measures were influenced by neither the stress nor the nonstress interviews. In a final study, Saunders (1973) exposed high, medium, and low A-trait subjects to a standardized clinical interview. Subjects were found to differ reliably in their level of state anxiety as a function of trait anxiety.

Although there is evidence to suggest that A-trait measures do not change as a function of situational stresses and changes in A-state, there are several exceptions to this general finding. Gorsuch (1969), for example, found that A-trait scores did change as a function of stress in a classroom situation where measures were obtained at two times during the semester. Gorsuch also had his students in this study keep diaries, and he maintained A-state measures on the students. He found that increases in trait anxiety were preceded by a period of time in which there were substantial increases in A-state. Spielberger et al. (1970, p. 15) report that "increases in A-trait scores seem to depend upon whether elevations in A-state were determined primarily by external factors or resulted from psychodynamic conflicts or interpersonal stress" and suggest that one should expect to see changes in A-trait as interpersonal or psychodynamic stress changes greatly.

Such changes in A-trait as a function of changes in psychodynamic or interpersonal dimensions is generally a goal of psychotherapy. The application of A-state and A-trait measures directly to behavior change situations, however, has not been extensive. Although there is some suggestion that A-state scores do decrease after intervention, A-trait scores may increase, decrease, or remain unchanged (D'Avgelli, 1974; Kilmann & Auerbach, 1974). A more detailed review of the application of the state–trait distinction to behavior change research will be presented later in this chapter.

A number of investigators have found that it is useful to delineate specific measures of trait anxiety for particular classes of situations. In a study using both a test A-trait anxiety measure and a general A-trait measure, Sarason (1957) has reported that the degree of overlap was not sufficient to make the two trait concepts synonomous. Sarason has found that his specific "Test A-trait" measure has useful predictive value in test situations. Spielberger (1975) has indicated that he believes that A-trait actually measures a specific proneness to experience social-evaluative anxiety, a type of anxiety similar to that reported by Watson and Friend (1969).

In an effort to delineate a specific anxiety trait, Lamb (1972) conceptualized public speaking anxiety in two ways: anxiety experienced during a particular speech (Speech A-state) and individual differences in the disposition to experience A-state in speaking situations (Speech A-trait). Speech A-trait refers to relatively stable individual differences in the disposition or tendency to respond with elevations in A-state in particular speaking situations or to individual differences in the frequency and intensity with which Speech A-states have been manifested in the past and to the probability that such states will be experienced in the future.

Following the procedure used to develop the STAI, Lamb (1970) developed both Speech A-state and Speech A-trait measures. The general items for the Speech A-trait scale came from a larger pool of items from available self-report scales used in the past to assess speech anxiety. The items were selected and worded to reflect general predispositions to experience anxiety in speaking situations rather than responding to a particular speech, for example, "I am terrified at the thought of speaking before a group," or "I feel disappointed in myself after trying to address a group of people," and "I look forward to the opportunity to speak in public." In a parallel fashion, items on the Speech A-state scale were worded to reflect feelings about a particular speech, for example, "I perspired while I was speaking," "I felt self-confident while I was speaking," and "I felt that I had nothing worthwhile to say to my audience." Once the Speech A-state and A-trait measures were developed, Lamb selected students in a public-speaking class who were either high or low on the Speech A-trait measure and exposed them to an impromptu speaking situation in which measures of Speech A-state were obtained. General measures of A-trait and A-state were also obtained. Lamb found that the situation-specific Speech A-trait measure was a better predictor of elevations in Speech A-state than the general STAI A-trait measure. This is not surprising because the Speech A-trait scale was designed to predict individual differences in the disposition to experience A-state in speaking situations. The Speech A-trait scale correlated +0.67 with the Speech A-state scale. The STAI A-trait and the Speech A-trait scales were equally effective in predicting A-state in a speaking situation when a more general measure of A-state, the STAI A-state scale, was used (see Lamb, 1976).

Normative data for the STAI comes from six major sources: college freshmen, college undergraduates, high school juniors, psychiatric patients, general medical and surgical patients, and young prisoners. The specifics of these normative groups are presented in Spielberger et al. (1970). Since the development of the normative data, the STAI has been applied to a number of different subject populations. College students have been used in approximately two-thirds of the total studies using the STAI. Only recently has the STAI been used with other populations, including children and adolescents (e.g., Finch, Montgomery, & Deardorff, 1974); nonstudent normals (e.g., Bucky & Spielberger, 1973; Fehrenbach, 1972); psychiatric patient populations (e.g., Anchor, Vojtisek, & Patterson, 1973; Newmark, Ray, Frerking, & Paine, 1974); surgery, medical, and dental patients (e.g., Auerbach, 1973b; Lamb & Plant, 1972; Garrie & Garrie, 1974); and prison populations (e.g., Kling, 1972; McGuire & Megargee, 1974). Spielberger, Gonzalez-Reigosa, Martinez-Urrutia, Natalicio, and Natalicio (1971) have also developed a Spanish edition of the State–Trait Anxiety Inventory.

In summary, this section has described the development, reliability, and validity of the STAI. Although the information provided comes primarily from the test manuals, the reader is referred to the original manual sources (Spielberger et al., 1967, 1968, 1971) for more detail. Five additional sources (Cattell, 1973; Edwards, 1970; Fiske, 1971; Smith, 1974; Wilde, 1972) deal specifically with various methodological, psychometric, and conceptual issues related to the measurement of states and traits. The STAI is easily administered and professional researchers and practitioners can obtain information regarding validity, reliability, norms, and interpretation considerations directly from the manual (Spielberger et al., 1970).

ANXIETY MEASUREMENT IN EXPERIMENTAL, CLINICAL, AND PERSONALITY RESEARCH

The previous sections have presented three viewpoints in psychology (experimental, clinical-applied, and personality-research) that have been concerned with the nature and measurement of anxiety. This section reports the application of state–trait anxiety measures to these three areas of emphasis.

Within the area of experimental psychology, a number of studies have investigated the relationship of the A-state and A-trait to a variety of learning tasks. Experiments on learning in which measures of state and trait anxiety were used include studies of paired associate learning (e.g., Edmonston, 1971), prose learning (Johnson, Dunbar, & Hohn, 1971), complex verbal learning (e.g., Snyder & Katahn, 1970), verbal conditioning and locus of control (e.g., Jolley, 1972), noncontent verbal conditioning (Newmark & Dinoff, 1973), concept formation (e.g., Tennyson & Boutwell, 1973), and verbal conditioning in children (e.g., Montuori, 1971). In addition, the state–trait distinction has also been applied to studies of memory (e.g., Hodges & Spielberger, 1969), concept formation (e.g., Kilpatrick, 1972), and motor learning (e.g., Burton, 1971).

Application of the state–trait distinction to programmed instruction or computer-assisted instruction (CAI) has recently been of considerable interest to psychologists. Many of the studies with the CAI have been conducted at the Computer Assistance Instruction Center in Tallahassee, Florida, and have investigated a variety of topics from response mode (e.g., Leherissey, O'Neil & Hansen, 1973), sequence effects (e.g., Tobias, 1973), and instructional treatment (e.g., Gallagher, 1970) to the terminal review paradigm (e.g., Dunn, 1971) and learner characteristics (e.g., Rappaport, 1971). Emotional reactions to the computer have also been investigated (Hedl, 1971; Hedl, O'Neil, & Hansen 1973), and it has generally been concluded that CAI is not intrinsically anxiety provoking and that anxiety reactions are determined by both the level of the operator's A-trait and the learning materials. There is also some suggestion that computer testing procedures such as instruction, terminal familiarity, and feedback have led to significantly high levels of state anxiety and have resulted in less favorable attitudes in comparison to examiner-administered testing procedures (Hedl, O'Neil, & Hansen, 1973).

Many studies have investigated the relationship of state anxiety to performance on CAI tasks. It is generally concluded that state anxiety is more sensitive than trait anxiety in influencing such performance. Yet it has also been found that there is an interaction between levels of state and trait anxiety as it relates to performance on programmed learning tasks. O'Neil et al. (1969) found that the performance of high A-trait/low A-state students was consistently superior to that of any other group, whereas the performance of low A-trait/high A-state students was inferior to that of any other group.

More recent research has focused on two issues as they relate to anxiety and performance. Evaluating the effects of different types of feedback on performance in a CAI task, Hodges (1973) suggests that differences between high and low A-trait subjects occurs only under conditions of minimal stress and that when the level of state anxiety is increased at all, the differences between high and low trait subjects tend to be minimal or disappear.

A second issue is raised by those studies (e.g., Glover & Cravens, 1974) that have attempted to evaluate the predictions regarding the relationship between anxiety and performance from a drive theory versus a state–trait anxiety theoretical viewpoint. In general, drive theory speaks of the relationship between motivational states and performance in learning tasks whereas state–trait anxiety theory applies to a broader range of phenomena. O'Neil (1969) investigated the effects of stress on A-state and performance in a CAI task for college women with extreme A-trait (both high and low) scores. Drive theory predicted that high A-state subjects would make more errors than low A-state subjects on more difficult materials (many competing response tendencies) and make fewer errors than low A-state subjects on easier materials (fewer competing response tendencies). O'Neil reported that for the most difficult tasks there was no difference between high A-state and low A-state subjects, and, as the task became easier, the high A-state subjects made consistently more errors than the low A-state subjects. O'Neil interpreted this failure to find empirical support for drive theory as attributable to the differences in the motivational structure of men and women as they affect the relationship between drive and performance. Additional studies of the type represented by O'Neil are needed to delineate the differences among theoretical approaches to anxiety.

In an effort to isolate the relationship of anxiety to particular task, learning, and/or response variables, investigations have often been executed under somewhat artificial or contrived conditions. Recently, however, there has been an increased interest in systematically measuring anxiety in more clinical-applied settings. This section will describe the application of state–trait anxiety theory and measurement to this second major area of anxiety research: the clinical-applied viewpoint. Three types of clinical-applied issues will be discussed: (1) adjustment to naturally occurring stressors, (2) psychopathology and personality styles, and (3) behavior change efforts (e.g., psychotherapy). The first set of investigations has applied the state–trait distinction to the investigation of one's personal adjustment to a number of naturally occurring stress situations. Two such situations are adjustment to medical procedures and adjustment to academic performance.

A number of investigations have focused specifically on reactions before, during, and after surgical procedures. Spielberger, Auerbach, Wadsworth, Dunn, and Taulbee (1973) investigated emotional reactions of male patients to major surgery. STAI measures were obtained 18 to 25 hours before surgery and again three to nine days after surgery. Although it was found that mean STAI A-state scores were much higher prior to surgery than after surgery, A-trait scores remained relatively stable throughout the hospitalization period. These authors also found no difference in A-state changes as a function of high or low A-trait scores. This study indicates that anxiety level can be monitored during the course of a surgical crisis, and it found that the 24 hours immediately before the actual surgery is the period when patient anxiety is the highest. Efforts to reduce the anxiety associated with surgical stress should presumably be implemented during this period. In a related study, Auerbach (1973b) found that the magnitude of A-state decline before and after surgery was unrelated to severity or type of surgery, surgical history, or patient age. Auerbach also reported that those patients who had higher A-state levels preoperatively also experienced more worries about hospitalization, a finding that relates to Janis' (1958) observation that moderate levels of preoperative fear facilitated recovery from surgery.

Other studies conducted in medical settings include those by Haselhorst

(1970), who investigated the relationship between state–trait anxiety and out-come of heart surgery, Martinez-Urrutia (1972), who focused on pain and anxi-ety in surgical patients, and Key (1973), who investigated anxiety and stress in pregnant women. Several studies have also related surgery and dental anxiety to particular coping styles (Gentry, Foster & Hangey, 1972; Florell, 1971; DeLong, 1970).

A second general type of adjustment related to state and trait anxiety is that associated with academic achievement and performance. An overview of this topic is presented by Gaudry and Spielberger in their 1971 text, *Anxiety and Educational Achievement*. Other studies in this area include those by Martin (1970), who investigated changes in anxiety as they related to anticipated exami-nations for doctoral students, and Morris and Liebert (1970), who attempted to isolate the cognitive and emotional components of test anxiety as they related to academic test performance.

Although earlier studies (e.g., Spielberger, 1962; Spielberger, Weitz, & Denny, 1962) have found a relationship between A-trait level and academic performance, several recent studies have not found such a relationship. Stutler (1973), for example, found that the academic achievement of college women was randomly related to A-trait levels. Bassetti (1973) found no significant differences between mean trait anxiety scores of freshmen selected in either low, medium, or high academic risk populations. In addition, Allen, Lerner, and Hinrichsen (1972) found a general independence of trait anxiety and study be-haviors. Nelson (1971), on the other hand, found a more complex relationship between trait anxiety and academic achievement as measured by first semester grade point average. Nelson examined such variables as the part of the state the students came from as well as whether they were receiving financial aid from the institution. He concluded that trait anxiety was useful in predicting academic achievement for males residing out of the county who were receiving no financial assistance and for females out of the county who did receive financial aid. In a final study of this type, Kimes and Troth (1974) investigated the relationship of trait anxiety to career decisiveness. They found that students who were com-pletely undecided about a career were significantly more anxiety prone (higher A-trait) than students who had chosen careers. These authors also suggest a possible inverse relationship between trait anxiety and satisfaction with a career decision.

The second clinical-applied issue is the relationship of anxiety to psychopathology and personality styles. Beck (1971) has proposed a comprehen-sive view of psychopathological behavior that emphasizes the role of anxiety and cognition. Beck discusses cognition, affect, and the general types of psychopathological disorders. For anxiety, the cognitive appraisal is one of "danger." The affect of anxiety occurs, and the extreme reaction to this affect is typically called an *anxiety neurosis*. Beck also traces the relationship of cognition and affect for depression, mania, and the paranoid state. More recently, Beck (1972) has focused on the relationship between cognition and anxiety in the development of psychophysiological disorders. Although he acknowledges that external factors may constitute a major determinant in certain psychophysiological disorders, he indicates that the majority of such disorders develop because of the operation of cognitive factors rather than external stresses. In attempting to reduce psychophysiological and other psychopathological disorders, Beck suggests such techniques as removal from the anxiety-producing situation, restructuring one's cognitive appraisal of the situation, reeducation, and the use of drug or relaxation treatment (Beck, 1975). A discussion of anxiety, cognition, and anxiety neuroses is presented by Beck, Laude, and Bohnert (1974).

Other investigators have also related the state–trait distinction to neurosis. McLeod (1971) and Singer (1969) have investigated the relationship of state and trait anxiety to various components of the implosion technique used to reduce phobias. Dischel (1973) and Butler (1971) have related the state–trait distinction to depressive, hysteroid, and obsessive personality styles. Finally, state–trait anxiety has been related to such personality variables as aggression and hostility (Butler, 1971), locus of control (Jolly & Spielberger, 1972), social desirability (Knops, 1970), coping mechanisms (Gentry et al., 1972), and extraversion (Barton, Bartsch, & Cattell, 1974).

In addition to neurosis, the state–trait distinction has also been applied to the study of schizophrenic behaviors and processes. Patterson (1971) investigated the relationship of state anxiety to schizophrenic performance during an interview, and Anchor et al. (1973) related trait anxiety to structuring and self-disclosure in schizophrenic patients.

The final application of the state–trait distinction in the clinical-applied area has been in the assessment of behavior change procedures such as individual and group psychotherapy, behavior therapy, and somatic therapies. The findings can be summarized in four statements. First, it is generally found that state anxiety can be reduced as a function of a variety of therapeutic interventions (D'Avgelli, 1974; Kilmann & Auerbach, 1974; Newmark, 1972; Paul, 1966; Stoudenmire, 1972; Tobiason, 1971). Second, specific trait anxieties have shown changes as a function of specific interventions, for example, the reduction of specific test anxiety (Allen, 1971; Taylor, 1972). Third, there is a group of studies that report reductions in general trait anxiety as a function of some therapeutic interventions (e.g., Kilmann & Auerbach, 1974; Newmark, 1972; Paul, 1966; Percell, Berwick, & Beagle, 1974). Kilmann and Auerbach (1974) found reductions in trait anxiety for those subjects who received nondirective therapy, but they also reported increases in A-trait for subjects who received directive therapy. Control group subjects showed virtually no change in A-trait. Newmark (1972) investigated changes in A-state and A-trait anxiety as a function of electroconvulsive therapy. Although he reported that state anxiety socres decreased after ECT, he found that trait anxiety measures did not change until immediately prior to discharge, when a significant decrease occurred. This decrease of trait anxiety was significant when the discharge trait scores were compared with trait scores obtained on admission or after application of the treatment procedure. Newmark interprets these findings to suggest that trait anxiety may not be as impervious to situational change as previously suggested. Finally, there is a group of studies of behavior change (D'Avgelli, 1974; Ratzlaff, 1970; Stoudenmire, 1972) that have reported no changes in trait anxiety as a function of therapeutic interventions. Thus, it appears that although state anxiety is influenced by therapeutic interventions, trait anxiety may or may not be affected, depending on the kind of anxiety and the type of treatment approach.

The third general area in which state–trait anxiety measures have been applied is personality research, with particular emphasis on different types of stress situations. There have been a number of books written on the social and psychological factors involved in stress, and the books by Basowitz, Persky, Korchin, and Grinker (1955), Dohrenwend and Dohrenwend (1974), Gray (1971) Janis (1958), Lazarus, (1966), and McGrath (1970), represent a cross-section of viewpoints regarding the nature of stress.

In the last 10 years, the investigations of stress and anxiety have focused on the influence of different kinds of stressors on A-state reactions. As mentioned earlier in this chapter, physical stressors involve the anticipation of or confrontation with a situation characterized by physical harm, danger, pain, or discomfort. Psychological stressors involve the anticipation of confrontation with situations that are potential threats to self-esteem and that often involve fear of failure or personal evaluation.

There is considerable evidence to support the distinction between these two types of stressors. Basowitz et al. (1955) distinguished two types of anxiety that they identify as "shame anxiety" and "harm anxiety." Harm anxiety has its antecedents in physical stressors such as threat of injury or death, whereas shame anxiety is a response to psychological stressors that involve threats of failure. In a more recent study, Strahan (1974) studied the situational determinants of self-reported anxiety. Using college students and factory workers as his subject pool, Strahan asked individuals to identify stressful situations in which they experienced increases in anxiety. Two types of stressful situations were identified: those associated with social situations and those related to physical harm or discomfort. Using the S–R Inventory of Anxiousness, Endler, Hunt, and Rosenstein (1962) also supported the distinction between psychological and physical stressors. They labeled psychological stressors as "interpersonal" and physical stressors as "inanimate."   ·

Hodges and Felling (1970) developed a questionnaire describing a number of situations considered threatening by many college students. Subjects were asked to rate the degree of apprehensiveness or concern that they would experience in each of the situations. The results of an analysis indicated four distinct factors: physical danger, social and academic failure, classroom participating, and dating. The authors concluded that the social and academic failure, classroom, and dating factors could be classified as psychological stressors and that these factors were quite distinct from physical danger.

In his distinction between A-state and A-trait, Spielberger (1972a) proposes that trait anxiety scores reflect individual differences in the disposition to respond with higher levels of state anxiety in stressful situations characterized by personal failure or by some threat to self-esteem. Support for this interpretation comes from Sarason (1960) who, after reviewing the research findings with various A-trait scales, concludes that:

. . . high anxious subjects are affected more detrimentally by motivating conditions or failure reports than are subjects lower in anxiety score distribution. . . high anxious subjects have been found to be more self-deprecating, more self-preoccupied, and generally less content with themselves. (p. 401–402)

In his most recent statement of the relationship between state–trait anxiety and type of stressor, Spielberger (1972b) states:

Level of A-trait would not necessarily be expected to influence the intensity of A-state responses to all stressors but only to those which persons of high A-trait perceive as more threatening. Since high A-trait individuals have been described as more self-deprecatory, and as persons who fear failure, it may be expected that they will manifest higher levels of A-state in situations that involve psychological threats to self-esteem rather than physical danger. (p. 41)

Spielberger also indicates that psychological threats and physical dangers may differentially influence A-trait because life experiences cause people to develop different dispositions to respond to these types of stressors.

The general experimental paradigm in stress research involves obtaining measurements of A-state after exposure to a particular stressor. One such physical stressor is the application (or threat of application) of electric shock. Using the shock paradigm, Hodges (1968) and Hodges and Spielberger (1966) found that heart rate measures of A-state and self-reported A-state (as measured by the Affect Adjective Checklist) increased in response to the threat of shock and decreased after the threat was removed. Yet they found that these increases in A-state were not related to the subject's level of A-trait as assessed by the Taylor Manifest Anxiety Scale. Although in the Hodges and Spielberger study the threat of shock failed to produce differential increases in physiological and self-report measures in A-state for persons who differed in A-trait, these authors did find that individuals with much fear of shock did have greater increases in their level of A-state when threatened with shock than did subjects who reported little or no fear of shock. Katkin (1965) also found that physiological measures of A-state increased in response to stress but that these increases were not related to the subject's level of A-trait.

One naturally occurring physical stress situation is exposure to dental treatment. Lamb and Plant (1972) obtained A-state measures of patient anxiety during three phases of a dental appointment. The general findings indicated that A-state, as measured by the STAI A-state scale, increased as treatment approached and dramatically decreased after treatment. It was also found that the amount of anxiety change during the study was different for men and women. STAI A-trait measures were also obtained on the dental patients. The amount of increase in A-state did not differ for high and low A-trait patients, a finding consistent with state–trait anxiety theory.

Another naturally occurring stress, imminent surgery, has also been investigated. It has been found that A-trait differences do not predict A-state responses in situations involving this physical stress (see Auerbach, 1937b; Haselhorst, 1970; Johnson, Dabbs, & Leventhal, 1970).

In contrast to the growing evidence that physical stressors do not evoke differential A-state levels in high and low A-trait subjects, there isconsiderable evidence to support the statement that those stress situations involving threats to self-esteem do produce differential levels. Techniques employed to create such psychological stresses involve some threat to an individual's self-esteem (e.g., interview stress, public speaking, or some situation in which the person's intellectual ability, character or reputation may be questioned or evaluated). It has been observed that persons who are high in A-trait are particularly threatened in those situations in which failure is experienced or where one's personal adequacy is evaluated (Auerbach, 1973a; McAdoo, 1969; O'Neil, 1972; Spence & Spence, 1966; Spielberger & Smith, 1966).

Although the majority of the these studies primarily investigated the effects of one class of stressors on A-state reactions for individuals who differed in levels of A-trait, there have also been a number of studies (e.g., Endler & Shedletsky, 1973; Morris & Liebert, 1973) that have exposed the same subjects to both psychological and physical stressors. Measures of A-state were then obtained for individuals who differed in A-trait.

Three studies involving direct response of A-state and A-trait to the two types of stressors will be considered. Hodges (1968) was one of the first investigators who helped to delineate the relationship between different types of stressors and the level of A-trait. Applying the distinction between psychological stressors and physical stressors, Hodges defined fear of failure on a task as a psychological stressor and fear of electric shock as a physical stressor. Exposing both high and low A-trait subjects to either a failure threat or shock threat, he found that increases in A-state were greater for high A-trait subjects who experienced failure than for low A-trait subjects who experienced failure. There were no differences in A-state responses in the electric shock situation. In a second study,

Hodges and Felling (1970) found that high A-trait subjects reported higher state anxiety about situations characterized by potential failure (e.g., dating, speaking in front of a large group, classroom participation, and academic failure) than did low A-trait subjects. In this study there was no relationship between level of trait anxiety and reported state anxiety in response to physical danger.

In the last study to be considered, Lamb (1973) evaluated the effects of a psychological stressor (giving a speech) on self-report, physiological, and behavioral measures of state anxiety. The effect of this stressor on A-state measures was then compared to the A-state reponse of the same subjects after exposure to a physical stressor (blowing up a balloon until it burst). State–trait anxiety theory hypothesizes that high A-trait subjects are more prone to experience higher levels of A-state than low A-trait subjects in situations characterized by threats to self-esteem or failure but that high A-trait subjects will not respond any differently than low A-trait subjects in stress situations that do not pose such psychological threats. This prediction is consistent with Spielberger's statement that A-trait is a measure of social-evaluative anxiety. In this study it was predicted that both stressors would induce increases in A-state but that the magnitude of the increase in A-state for the psychological stressor would be greater for high A-trait subjects, whereas no differential increase in A-state for high and low A-trait subjects would be found for the physical stressor.

The experiment was divided into four periods: an initial rest period, a speech period in which individuals gave a two-minute impromptu speech, a post-speech evaluation period, and the balloon period in which individuals were required to blow up a balloon until it burst. There were four measures of A-state: the A-state scale of the STAI, a Speech A-state scale developed for the study, telemetric measures of heart rate, and ratings on a behavioral checklist made while subjects gave the two-minute speech. In addition, STAI A-trait measures were obtained in each of the four periods.

The results of the study indicated that A-state, as measured by both the STAI A-state scale and heart rate, increased in response to the stress associated with giving a speech, returned to the resting level after the speech, and then increased again when subjects were required to blow up a balloon until it burst. The A-state scores for high and low A-trait subjects are presented in Figure 2–3a. It can be seen in Figure 2–3a that those subjects with high speech A-trait scores showed a significantly greater increase in STAI A-state scores during the speech period than did the low A-trait subjects but that no differential increase in A-state scores were found for high and low A-trait subjects during the balloon period. These findings confirmed the general predicted relationship between measures of trait anxiety and changes in A-state in situations characterized by psychological and physical danger. In addition, it can be seen in Figure 2–3b that mean STAI A-trait scores remained relatively stable for all subjects despite the dramatic fluctuations in A-state as a function of experimental periods.

Concerning the heart rate data, the general hypotheses were not confirmed in

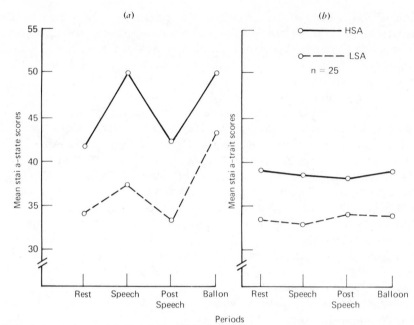

Figure 2–3.   A–State and A–Trait Scores for high and low A–Trait Subjects during four experimental periods.

that increases in heart rate were unrelated to the level of A-trait. One possible explanation for this discrepancy between self-report and physiological measures of A-state can be found in the concept of response specificity mentioned earlier in this chapter. This concept indicates that individuals may differ in the particular autonomic channel in which maximal response to stress occurs. Although heart rate was probably the autonomic channel in which maximal distress occurred for some subjects, other subjects may have expressed an increased level of A-state through a different autonomic system. The results of the behavioral measure, which was obtained during the speech period, indicated no relationship between the number of behavioral signs of anxiety and the level of A-trait.

Although the above studies generally support the usefulness of distinguishing between types of stressors, there are also a number of studies that have not substantiated the distinction between psychological and physical stressors as they relate to levels of A-state and A-trait. Morris and Liebert (1973) investigated the effects of failure and the threat of shock. These authors found that A-state scores were higher for high A-trait subjects than for low A-trait subjects in both the failure threat and threat of shock situations. Endler and Shedletsky (1973) found that, although their psychological threat and physical threat both produced A-state increases, high A-trait subjects reported greater A-state increase than did low A-trait subjects in their physical threat situation.

There may be a number of reasons for the inconsistency in this area of research. First, there may be difficulty in actually distinguishing between psychological and physical threats. Endler and Shedletsky (1973) identified a "shame factor" in their physical threat situation and suggested that this factor may have accounted for the higher levels of A-state produced by the physical threat than by the psychological threat. Other studies may not have sharply delineated the factors involved in a physical or psychological stressor. Houston, Olson, and Botkin (1972), for example, have commented on the different components that may be involved in assessing a situation as potentially physically dangerous.

A second possible explanation of the inconsistent results relates to the issue of feedback. In those studies that did find differences in response to the stress conditions (e.g., Hodges, 1968; McAdoo, 1969; O'Neil, 1969), there was either direct negative personal feedback or a strong threat to the subject's sense of personal worth in the psychological stress condition. Although such direct feedback was not present in Lamb's (1973) study, his subjects were required to make a speech while being appraised by the experimenter. In reviewing these and other studies, Lushene (1970) suggests that:

> . . . failure to confirm the hypothesis that high A-trait subjects would show greater increase in A-state under the test stress then would low A-trait subjects may suggest that ego-involvement alone may not be sufficient to induce a psychological threat in which the A-state will vary as a function of the subject's A-trait level. . . . individual negative feedback or situations in which the subject feels that he is being personally evaluated may be required for psychological threats to evoke larger A-state increases. (p. 62)

Endler and Shedletsky (1973) echo Lushene insofar as they suggest that their failure feedback (the ego threat situation) was lacking in intensity.

Another possible explanation for the inconsistent results may be in the use of particular A-state and A-trait measures. Different measures of A-state and A-trait may yield slightly different findings. In addition, physiological variables have a number of measuring problems, such as the law of initial values and individual response specificity.

It is also possible that the two types of stress situations arouse different components of A-state. In his physical stress situation Lushene (1970) found that the autonomic component of A-state increased more than the ideational or motoric components. In addition, Morris and Liebert (1973) found that the ideational component (worry) was aroused in failure threat situations whereas the motoric component tended to be elevated only in the shock threat condition. These studies suggest that it is important further to delineate the components of state anxiety that might be affected by particular stress situations.

A final possible explanation for the inconsistent results relates to the variety of coping mechanisms and reactions that are available to reduce anxiety. There is a growing body of stress research that suggests that such factors as anticipation and uncertainty (e.g., Monat, Averill, & Lazarus, 1972), personality characteristics (particular defense mechanisms) (e.g., Houston & Hodges, 1970), and beliefs regarding control over stress (e.g., Golin, 1974) do play an important role in determining the nature and magnitude of an individual's particular A-state response.

EMERGING ANXIETY THEORIES AND MEASUREMENT PROCEDURES

It seems apparent that there are several trends emerging in the study of anxiety. Four such trends will be briefly described: (1) a multifactored rather than unidimensional view of anxiety, (2) the application of anxiety theory and measurement to new target populations, (3) a renewed interest in the development of self-control and self-regulatory procedures to deal with anxiety, and (4) an increased emphasis on the interaction of the person and the situation in anxiety research.

Historically, anxiety has been conceptualized as a unitary construct. More recent research (Cattell, 1973; Spielberger, 1972b, 1972c) has suggested that anxiety is multidimensional. A new emphasis on different approaches to the measurement of A-state and A-trait and a new isolation of specific components of anxiety states supports the contention that anxiety is a multidimensional construct.

A further case for the multidimensional nature of trait anxiety is presented by Shedletsky and Endler (1974), who discuss the theoretical implications of such multidimensionality and relate these implications to their proposed interaction model of anxiety. They suggest that the construct of trait anxiety is complex and involves several dimensions other than the disposition to respond with higher levels of A-state anxiety in a stressful situation of a social nature.

A second trend concerns the application of anxiety theory and measurement to new target populations. The medical population is one such target population that has recently received considerable attention. The study by Auerbach (1973b) is illustrative of this trend. Lazarus (1975c) and Cohen and Lazarus (1973) provide a comprehensive discussion of the relationship of stress and coping to medical illnesses and surgery. These authors provide considerable evidence to suggest that individual differences in coping styles may have an important bearing on the course of recovery from surgery. Their research is encouraging in that it suggests that recovery from surgery can be facilitated when individuals are provided with particular coping procedures. Additional research is needed to specify the ways in which situational demands in medical settings may interact with one's coping dispositions.

The third emerging series of investigations has emphasized the individual's use of self-control and self-regulatory procedures to deal with anxiety. Two studies have provided information regarding personal control and its relationship to stress. Koriat, Melkman, Averill, and Lazarus (1972) investigated self-control procedures used by individuals in response to a stressful film. In particular, these authors investigated the way individuals exercised self-imposed emotional control by means of either "involving" or "detaching" themselves from the stressful situation. Physiological, self-report, and coping strategies were assessed during the experiment. After the subjects viewed the film under one of three conditions (involvement, detachment, or normal), they viewed the film several additional times with the instructions to become either involved or detached on request. The authors found that subjects could achieve control over their emotional reactions (as judged by self-report and heart rate changes) using either involvement or detachment. Regarding the types of cognitive strategies subjects used to achieve involvement or detachment, the authors found that detachment had a greater number and variety of strategies than did involvement. They found, however, that detachment was more clearly related than involvement to the use of defense mechanisms to reduce the threat. This study, then, represents one of the initial attempts to investigate particular ways (i.e., involvement versus detachment) of developing self-control as well as the ways individuals achieve such control.

Averill (1973) presents a review of the current status of the concept of personal control as it relates to stress. He found that the general assumption that control helps to reduce stress is not highly generalizable and that there is a complex relationship between stress and types of control. Types of control can sometimes increase, sometimes reduce, and sometimes have no effect on stress.

The relationship between control and stress reduction is further elaborated by Lazarus (1975b) as he discusses biofeedback research and its implications for the self-regulation of stress.

In the context of their cognitive behavior modification approach to the management of anxiety and other disruptive emotions, Meichenbaum (1975a, 1975b, 1974) and Meichenbaum and Turk (1975) present a cognitive theory of self-control. This theory (Meichenbaum, 1975b) emphasizes three stages:

. . . the client must first become an observer of his thoughts, feelings, and behaviors by means of heightened awareness. This process is facilitated by means of a conceptualization or translation process that evolves over the course of therapy. The process of self observations lays the foundation for the client to emit incompatible thoughts and behaviors which constitute the second stage of change. The third stage, which determines the persistence and generalization of treatment effects, involves the nature and content of the client's internal dialogue and image about the behavior change. Although these three stages may be viewed as occurring sequentially, they often overlap in a continual process of change. (p. 38–39)

This theory has recently been applied to the cognitive-behavioral management of anxiety, danger, and pain (Meichenbaum & Turk, 1975), as well as other emotional reactions and behavioral problems.

In summarizing the growing emphasis on self-regulatory procedures, Lazarus suggests that the best strategy for such research is to study normally functioning individuals longitudinally from one situation to another (Lazarus, 1975a, p. 34–35). Such an approach constitutes the last emerging trend in anxiety research and is exemplified by the work of Endler (1975a, 1975b) and Ekenhammar, Magnusson, and Ricklander (1974) who emphasize the interaction of the person and the situation in understanding anxiety and stress. Rather than focusing exclusively on personality traits or situational specificity, Endler (1975a, 1975b) incorporates both these categories of variables in his interaction approach to anxiety. Three additional research efforts that have emphasized both the situational and personal (trait) components of emotion and anxiety are those of Averill (1975), Epstein (1974, 1973), and Sarason, Smith, and Diener (1976).

SUMMARY

This review of anxiety theory and research has focused on developments in three major areas: clinical-applied, experimental, and personality-research. The clinical-applied perspective is best illustrated by the work of Sigmund Freud, the neo-Freudians, and the phenomenological theorists such as Rogers and May. More recent clinical approaches to the study of anxiety have focused on the relationship of anxiety to motivation, learning, psychopathology, and cognitive functioning. In addition, several research efforts have delineated anxiety from other emotional behaviors (Izard, 1972).

The experimental perspective has applied principles of learning to the study of anxiety. The works of Pavlov (1927), Mowrer (1939), Dollard and Miller (1950), and Spence and Spence (1966) describe procedures for the development and reduction of anxiety. The conceptualization of anxiety as an acquired drive stimulated considerable research in relating anxiety to performance on various learning tasks.

While the clinical-applied and experimental perspectives have continued to refine the theoretical and measurement aspects of anxiety research, a third perspective, the personality-research perspective, has emphasized the importance of personality traits, factors that influence stress reactions and particular anxiety states. Cattell is considered to have strongly contributed to the better understanding of the role of traits in determining behavior. Lazarus and his associates have contributed greatly to the understanding of stress reactions and their relationship to anxiety responses. The work of these individuals has helped to identify the ways in which individuals appraise potentially threatening events and the behaviors they engage in to reduce the magnitude of the threat. More recently, Lazarus and his colleagues have focused on developing particular coping mechanisms to assist individuals to deal more adequately with day-to-day stressors.

The focus of most of this chapter has been on the A-state and A-trait conceptualization of anxiety, and Spielberger has emphasized the importance of distinguishing one's disposition to experience anxiety (A-trait) from his/her actual anxiety response (A-state). Whereas A-state is a transitory condition of the organism, A-trait is a relatively stable measure of individual differences. In developing separate measures for state and trait anxiety, Spielberger and his associates have acquired considerable evidence that individuals who differ in their general level of A-trait also differ in the intensity of their A-state reaction to particular stressors. Two general classes of stressors (psychological and physical) have been identified, and it has been found that high and low A-trait subjects respond with different levels of A-state to these types of stressors.

Once separate measure of state and trait anxiety were developed, it became possible to apply this distinction to a variety of psychological phenomena. One area of research to which this distinction has recently been applied is that of behavior change. It has generally been acknowledged that a goal of psychotherapy is to reduce both state and trait anxiety. It has been found that a variety of therapeutic interventions can reduce both state anxiety and specific trait anxieties such as Speech A-trait and Test A-trait.

Regarding general A-trait, some studies have reported that therapeutic interventions can reduce the individual's general level of trait anxiety, although there is also a group of studies that have reported no change in trait anxiety as a function of therapeutic interventions. Thus, whereas state anxiety is influenced by therapeutic interventions, trait anxiety may or may not be effected depending on the kind of anxiety and the type of treatment approach. Further research is needed to develop therapy approaches that are more successful in reducing an individual's level of A-trait.

The final section of this chapter was devoted to a discussion of several emerging trends in the study of anxiety. These trends reflect more sophisticated attempts to assess the relative contribution of situational components and personality dispositions in determining a particular individual's anxiety response as well as to develop self-control and self-regulatory procedures to deal with anxiety.

REFERENCES

Allen, G. J. Effectiveness of study counseling and desensitization in alleviating test anxiety. *Journal of Abnormal Psychology*, 1971, *77*, 282–289.

Allen, G. J., Lerner, W. M., & Hinrichsen, J. J. Study behaviors and their relationship to test anxiety and academic performance. *Psychological Reports*, 1972, *30*, 407–410.

Allport, G. W. *Personality: A psychological interpretation.* New York: Holt, 1973.

Allport, G. W. Traits revisited. *American Psychologist,* 1966, *21,* 1–10.

Allport, G. W., & Odert, H. S. Trait names: A psycholexical study. *Psychological Monograph,* 1936, *47,* No. 211.

Anchor, K. N., Vojtisek, J. E., & Patterson, R. L. Trait anxiety, initial structure in and self-disclosure in groups of schizophrenic patients. *Psychotherapy: Theory research and practice,* 1973, *10,* 155–158.

Anderson, O. D., & Liddell, H. S. Observations on experimental neurosis in sheep. *Archives of Neurological Psychiatry,* 1935, *34,* 330–354.

Auerbach, S. M. Effects of orienting instructions, feedback information and trait anxiety on state anxiety. *Psychological Reports,* 1973, *33,* 779–786.(a)

Auerbach, S. M. Trait-state anxiety and adjustment to surgery. *Journal of Consulting and Clinical Psychology,* 1973, *40,* 264–271.(b)

Auerbach, S. M., & Spielberger, C. D. The assessment of state and trait anxiety with the Rorschach test. *Journal of Personality Assessment,* 1972, *36,* 314–335.

Averill, J. R. Personal control over aversive stimuli and its relationship to stress. *Psychological Bulletin,* 1973, *80,* 286–303.

Averill, J. R. Emotion and anxiety: Sociocultural, biological and psychological determinants. In M. Zuckerman and C. D. Spielberger (Eds.), *Emotions and anxiety: New concepts, methods and applications.* Hillsdale, N. J.: Erlbaum, 1975.

Barton, K., Bartsch, T., & Cattell, R. B. Longitudinal study of achievement related to anxiety and extraversion. *Psychological Reports,* 1974, *35,* 551–556.

Basowitz, H., Persky, H., Korchin, S. J., & Grinker, R. R. *Anxiety and stress.* New York: McGraw-Hill, 1955.

Bassetti, R. L. *Life change, trait anxiety, dogmatism and academic performance of college freshmen.* Unpublished doctoral dissertation, East Texas State University, 1973.

Beck, A. T. Cognition, affect, and psychopathology. *Archives of General Psychiatry,* 1971, *24,* 495–500.

Beck, A. T. Cognition, anxiety and psychophysiological disorders. In C. D. Spielberger (Ed.), *Anxiety: Current trends in theory and research* (Vol. II). New York: Academic Press, 1972, 343–354.

Beck, A. T. *The cognitive therapy of depression.* Unpublished manuscript, University of Pennsylvania, 1975.

Beck, A. T., Laude, R., & Bohnert, M. Ideational components of anxiety neurosis. *Archives of General Psychiatry,* 1974, *31,* 319–325.

Blum, G. S., & Wohl, B. M. An experimental analysis of the nature and operation of anxiety. *Journal of Abnormal Psychology, 1971, 78,* 1–8.

Branch, C. H. *Aspects of anxiety.* Philadelphia: Lippincott, 1968.

Brody, N. *Personality: Research and theory.* New York: Academic Press, 1972.

Bucky, S. R., & Spielberger, C. D. State and trait anxiety in voluntary withdrawal of student naval aviators from flight training. *Psychological Reports,* 1973, *33,* 351–354.

Burton, E. C. State and trait anxiety, achievement motivation and skill attainment in college women. *Research Quarterly,* 1971, *42,* 139–144.

Butler, P. E. *The relationship of depression to aggressive response intensity and state-trait anxiety.* Unpublished doctoral dissertation, University of Alabama, 1971.

Cattell, R. B. The sixteen personality factor and basic personality structure: A reply to Eysenck. *Journal of Behavioral Science,* 1972, *1,* 169–187.

Cattell, R. B. *Personality and mood by questionnaire.* San Francisco: Jossey-Bass, 1973.

Cattell, R. B., Eber, H. W., & Tatsuoka, M. M. Handbook for the sixteen personality factor questionnaire (16 PF). Champaign, Ill.: Institute for Personality and Ability Testing, 1970.

Cattell, R., & Scheier, I. H. *The meaning and measurement of neuroticism and anxiety.* New York: Ronald Press, 1961.

Cattell, R. B., Shrader, R. R., & Barton, K. The definition and measurement of anxiety as a trait and a state in the 12–17 year range. *British Journal of Social and Clinical Psychology,* 1974, *13,* 173–182.

Cohen, F., & Lazarus, R. S. Active coping processes, coping disposition, and recovery from surgery. *Psychosomatic Medicine,* 1973, *35,* 375–389.

D'Avgelli, A. R. Changes in self-reported anxiety during a small group experience. *Journal of Counseling Psychology,* 1974, *21,* 202–205.

DeLong, R. D. *Individual differences in patterns of anxiety arousal, stress relevant information and recovery from surgery.* Unpublished doctoral dissertation, University of California at Los Angeles, 1970.

Dischel, P. I. *Teacher anxiety level, personality style, and classroom teaching style: A study of the relationship among levels of trait anxiety, hysteroid, and obsession personality style and dominative and integrative teacher behavior.* Unpublished doctoral dissertation, New York University, 1973.

Dohrenwend, B. S., & Dohrenwend, B. P. (Eds.). *Stressful life events: Their nature and effects.* New York: John Wiley, 1974.

Dollard, J., & Miller, N. W. *Personality and psychotherapy.* New York: McGraw-Hill, 1950.

Dunn, T. S. The effects of various review paradigms on performance in an individualized computer-managed undergraduate course. Technical Report No. 22, Computer-Assisted Instruction Center, Florida State University, 1971.

Edmonston, L. P. *Anxiety and ability patterns in paired associate learning.* Unpublished doctoral dissertation, University of Texas at Austin, 1971.

Edwards, A. L. *The measurement of personality traits.* New York: Holt, Rinehart, and Winston, 1970.

Ekehammar, A. B., Magnusson, D., & Ricklander, L. An interactionist approach to the study of anxiety. *Scandanavian Journal of Psychology,* 1974, *15,* 4–14.

Endler, N. S. The case for person–situation interactions. *Canadian Psychological Review,* 1975, *16.*(a)

Endler, N. S. A person–situation interaction model for anxiety. In C. D. Spielberger and I. G. Sarason (Eds.), *Stress and anxiety in modern life.* Washington, D. C.: V. H. Winston, 1975.(b)

Endler, N. S., Hunt, J. M., & Rosenstein, A. J. An S–R inventory of anxiousness. *Psychological Monographs,* 1962, *76,* No. 17 (Whole No. 536), 1–33.

Endler, N. S., & Shedletsky, R. Trait versus state anxiety, authoritarianism and ego threat versus physical threat. *Canadian Journal of Behavioral Science,* 1973, *4,* 347–361.

Epstein, S. Towards a unified theory of anxiety. In B. A. Maher (Ed.), *Progress in experimental personality research* (Vol. IV). New York: Academic Press, 1967.

Epstein, S. The nature of anxiety with emphasis upon its relationship to expectancy. In C. D. Spielberger (Ed.), *Anxiety: Current trends in theory and research.* (Vol. II). New York: Academic Press, 1972, 292–338.

Epstein, S. Expectancy and magnitude of reaction to a noxious UCS. *Psychophysiology,* 1973, *10,* 100–107.

Epstein, S. *Research plan: 1967–1971.* Unpublished manuscript, University of Massachusetts, 1974.

Eriksen, C. W. Cognitive responses to internally cued anxiety. In C. D. Spielberger (Ed.), *Anxiety and behavior.* New York: Academic Press, 1966.

Eysenck, H. J. The maudsley personality inventory. London: University of London Press, 1959.

Fehrenbach, P. *Personality as a factor in reported post-retirement anxiety among professionals.* Unpublished doctoral dissertation, Duke University, 1972.

Finch, J. A., Jr., Montgomery, L. E., & Deardorff, P. A. Reliability of state–trait anxiety with emotionally disturbed children. *Journal of Abnormal Child Psychology,* 1974, *2,* 67–69.

Fiske, D. W. *Measuring the concepts of personality.* Chicago: Aldine, 1971.

Florell, J. L. *Crisis intervention in orthopedic surgery.* Unpublished doctoral dissertation, Northwestern University, 1971.

Freud, S. *The problem of anxiety.* New York: Norton, 1936. Originally published in 1923 in German under the title *Inhibition, symptom and anxiety.*

Gallagher, P. D. *An investigation of instructional treatments and learner characteristics in a computer-managed institution course.* Unpublished doctoral dissertation, Florida State University, 1970.

Garrie, E. V., & Garrie, S. A. Anxiety and atropic dermatitis. *Journal of Consulting and Clinical Psychology,* 1974, *42,* 742.

Gaudry, E., & Spielberger, C. D. *Anxiety and educational achievement.* New York: John Wiley, 1971.

Gentry, W. D., Foster, S., & Hangey, T. Denial as a determinant of anxiety and perceived health status in the coronary care unit. *Psychosomatic Medicine,* 1972, *34,* 39–44.

Glover, C. B., & Cravens, R. W. Trait anxiety stress and learning: A test of Saltz's hypothesis. *Journal of Research in Personality,* 1974, *8,* 243–253.

Goldstein, K. *The organism, a holistic approach to biology.* New York: American Book, 1939.

Golin, S. Effects of stress on the performance of normally anxious and high anxious subjects under chance and skill conditions. *Journal of Abnormal Psychology,* 1974, *83,* 466–472.

Gorsuch, R. L. *Changes in trait anxiety as a function of recent stress of anxiety.* Unpublished manuscript, George Peabody College for Teachers, 1969.

Gorsuch, R. L., & Spielberger, C. D. Anxiety, threat, and awareness in verbal conditioning. *Journal of Personality,* 1966, *34,* 336–347.

Gray, J. *The psychology of fear and stress.* New York: McGraw-Hill, 1971.

Greenspoon, J. The reinforcing effect of two spoken sounds on the frequency of two responses. *American Journal of Psychology,* 1955, *68,* 409–416.

Griffin, M. R. *An analysis of state and trait anxiety experience in sports competition by women at different age levels.* Unpublished doctoral dissertation, Louisianna State University, 1971. Dissertation Abstracts, 1972, 32–A, 3758.

Grinker, R. The psychosomatic aspects of anxiety. In C. D. Spielberger (Ed.), *Anxiety and behavior.* New York: Academic Press, 1966.

Haselhorst, J. A. *State-trait anxiety and the outcome of heart surgery.* Unpublished master's thesis, University of Illinois, 1970.

Hedl, J. J. *The affective nature of computer-based testing procedures.* Unpublished doctoral dissertation, Florida State University, 1971.

Hedl, J. J., O'Neil, H. F., & Hansen, D. N. Affective reactions toward computer-based intelligence testing. *Journal of Consulting and Clinical Psychology,* 1973, *40,* 217–222.

Hodges, W. F. Effects of ego threat and threat of pain on state anxiety. *Journal of Personality and Social Psychology,* 1968, *8,* 364–372.

Hodges, W. F. *Anxiety and the learning of conflict-relevant materials.* Paper presented at the American Psychological Association Convention. Montreal, 1973.

Hodges, W. F., & Felling, J. P. Types of stressful situations and their relation to trait anxiety and sex. *Journal of Consulting and Clinical Psychology,* 1970, *34,* 333–337.

Hodges, W. F., & Spielberger, C. D. The effects of threat of shock on heart rate for subjects who differ in manifest anxiety and fear of shock. *Psychophysiology,* 1966, *2,* 287–294.

Hodges, W. F., & Spielberger, C. D. Digit span: Indicant of trait or state anxiety. *Journal of Consulting and Clinical Psychology,* 1969, *33,* 430–434.

Houston, B. K., & Hodges, W. F. Situational denial and performance under stress. *Journal of Personality and Social Psychology,* 1970, *16,* 726–730.

Houston, B. K., Olson, M., & Botkin, A. Trait anxiety and beliefs regarding danger and threat to self esteem. *Journal of Consulting and Clinical Psychology,* 1972, *38,* 152.

Izard, C. E. *Differential emotional scale.* Unpublished test, Vanderbilt University, 1968.

Izard, C. E. Anxiety: A variable emotion of emotions. In C. D. Spielberger (Ed.), *Anxiety: Current trends in theory and research.* (Vol. I). New York: Academic Press, 1972.

Izard, C. E., & Tomkins, S. S. Affect and behavior: Anxiety as a negative affect. In C. D. Spielberger (Ed.), *Anxiety and behavior.* New York: Academic Press, 1966.

Jacobson, E. *Progressive relaxation.* Chicago: University of Chicago Press, 1938.

James, W. *The principles of psychology.* New York: Holt, 1890.

Janis, I. L. *Psychological stress.* New York: John Wiley, 1958.

Johnson, D. Effects of interview stress on measures of state and trait anxiety. *Journal of Abnormal Psychology,* 1968, *73,* 245–251.

Johnson, D. T., & Spielberger, C. D. The effects of relaxation training and the passage of time on measures of state and trait anxiety. *Journal of Clinical Psychology,* 1968, *24,* 20–23.

Johnson, E. P., Dunbar, K., & Hohn, R. L. *The effects of trait anxiety and task difficulty on prose learning.* Paper presented at the meeting of the American Educational Research Association. New York, February, 1971.

Johnson, J. E., Dabbs, J. M., & Leventhal, H. Psychological factors in the welfare of surgical patients. *Nursing Research,* 1970, *19,* 18–29.

Jolley, M. T. *The effects of locus of control and anxiety on verbal conditioning.* Unpublished master's thesis, Florida State University, 1972.

Jolley, M. T., & Spielberger, C. D. *The effects of locus of control and anxiety on verbal conditioning.* Unpublished manuscript, University of South Florida, 1972.

Jones, M. C. A behavior study of fear: The case of Peter. *Journal of Genetic Psychology,* 1924, *31,* 508–515.

Katkin, E. S. Relationship between manifest anxiety and two indices of autonomic response to stress. *Journal of Personality and Social Psychology,* 1965, *2,* 324–333.

Key, M. K. *State–trait anxiety associated with obstetric abnormalities.* Unpublished master's thesis, George Peabody College for Teachers, 1973.

Kilmann, P. R., & Auerbach, S. M. Effect of marathon group therapy on trait and state anxiety. *Journal of Consulting and Clinical Psychology,* 1974, *42,* 607–612.

Kilpatrick, D. G. Differential responsiveness of two electrodermal indices to psychological stress and performance of a complex cognitive task. *Psychophysiology,* 1972, *9,* 218–226.

Kimes, H. G., & Troth, W. A. Relationship of trait anxiety to career decisiveness. *Journal of Counseling Psychology,* 1974, *21,* 277–280.

Kling, J. K. *The effects of verbal and material reward and punishment in the verbal conditioning of primary and secondary psychopaths.* Unpublished doctoral dissertation, Florida State University, 1972.

Knops, J. *The influence of an experimentally transient increase in sensory awareness (tactile) upon self-disclosure, momentary anxiety and ratio of social desirability.* Unpublished doctoral dissertation, University of Kansas, 1970.

Koriat, A., Melkman, R., Averill, J. R., & Lazarus, R. S. The self-control of emotional reactions to a stressful film. *Journal of Personality,* 1972, *40,* 601–619.

Krause, M. S. The measurement of transitory anxiety. *Psychological Review,* 1961, *68,* 178–189.

Lacey, J., Bateman, D., & Vanlehn, R. Autonomic response specificity: An experimental study. *Psychosomatic Medicine,* 1953, *15,* 8–21.

Lader, M., & Marks, I. *Clinical anxiety.* London: Heinemann Medical Books, 1971.

Lamb, D. H. *The speech anxiety inventory (SAI):* Preliminary test manual for Form X. Illinois State University, 1970.

Lamb, D. H. Speech anxiety: Towards a theoretical conceptualization and preliminary scale development. *Speech Monographs,* 1972, *39,* 62–67.

Lamb, D. H. The effect of two stressors on state anxiety for students who differ in trait anxiety. *Journal of Research in Personality,* 1973, *7,* 116–126.

Lamb, D. H. Usefulness of situation-specific trait and state measures of anxiety. *Psychological Reports,* 1976, *38,* 188–190.

Lamb, D. H., & Plant, R. Patient anxiety in the dentist's office. *Journal of Dental Research,* 1972, *51,* 18–21.

Lazarus, R. S. *Psychological stress and the coping process.* New York: McGraw-Hill, 1966.

Lazarus, R. S. Cognitive and personality factors underlying threat and coping. In M. H. Appley, and R. Trumbull (Eds.), *Psychological stress.* New York: Appleton-Century-Crofts, 1967.

Lazarus, R. S. *Patterns of adjustment and human effectiveness.* New York: McGraw-Hill, 1969.

Lazarus, R. S. The self-regulation of emotion. In L. Levi (Ed.), *Parameters of emotion.* New York: Raven Press, 1975.(a)

Lazarus, R. S. A cognitively oriented psychologist looks at biofeedback. *American Psychologist,* 1975, *30,* 553–561.(b)

Lazarus, R. S. Psychological stress and coping in adaptation and illness. *Psychiatry in Medicine,* 1975.(c)

Lazarus, R. S., & Alfert, E. The short-circuiting of threat by experimentally altering cognitive appraisal. *Journal of Abnormal and Social Psychology,* 1964, *69,* 195–205.

Lazarus, R., & Averill, J. R. Emotion and cognition: With special reference to anxiety. In C. D. Spielberger (Ed.), *Anxiety: Current trends in theory and research* (Vol. II). New York: Academic Press, 1972.

Lazarus, R. S., Averill, J. R., & Opton, E. M. *The psychology of coping: Issues of research and assessment.* Paper presented at the Conference on Coping and Adaptation. Palo Alto, Cal., 1969.

Lazarus, R. S., Averill, J. R., & Opton, E. M. Towards a cognitive theory of emotion. In Arnold Madga (Ed.), *Third international symposium on feelings and emotiions.* New York: Academic Press, 1970.

Lazarus, R. S., & Opton, E. M. The study of psychological stress: A summary of theoretical formulation and experimental findings. In C. D. Spielberger (Ed.), *Anxiety and behavior*. New York: Academic Press, 1966.

Lazarus, R. S., Speisman, J. C., Mordkoff, A. M., & Davison, L. A. A laboratory study of psychological stress produced by a motion picture film. *Psychological Monographs*, 1962, *76*, No. 34 (Whole No. 553).

Leherissey, B. L., O'Neil, H. F., & Hansen, D. N. Effect of anxiety, response mode and subject matter familiarity on achievement in computer-assisted learning. *Journal of Educational Psychology*, 1973, *63*, 310–324.

Leitenberg, H., Agras, S., Butz, R., & Wincze, J. Relationship between heart rate and behavioral change during the treatment of phobias. *Journal of Abnormal Psychology*, 1971, *78*, 59–68.

Levitt, E. *The psychology of anxiety*. New York: Bobbs-Merrill, 1967.

Liddell, H. S. Experimental neurosis. In J. Hunt (Ed.), *Personality and the behavior disorders*. New York: Ronald Press, 1944.

Liddell, H. S., & Beyne, T. L. The development of "experimental neurasthenia" in sheep during the formation of a difficult conditioned reflex. *American Journal of Physiology*, 1927, *81*, 494.

Lushene, R. E. *The effects of physical and psychological threat on the autonomic, motoric and ideational components of state anxiety*. Unpublished doctoral dissertation, Florida State University, 1970.

Maher, B. *Principles of psychopathology*. New York: McGraw-Hill, 1966.

Malmo, R. B. Anxiety and behavioral arousal. *Psychological Review*, 1957, *64*, 276–287.

Malmo, R. B. Studies of anxiety: Some clinical origins of the activation concept. In C. D. Spielberger (Ed.), *Anxiety and behavior*. New York: Academic Press, 1966.

Mandler, G. Helplessness: Theory and research in anxiety. In C. D. Spielberger (Ed.), *Anxiety: Current trends in theory and research*. New York: Academic Press, 1972.

Marks, I. M. *Fears and phobias*. New York: Academic Press, 1969.

Martin, B. The assessment of anxiety by physiological behavior measures, *Psychological Bulletin*, 1961, *58*, 234–255.

Martin, B., & Stroufe, L. Anxiety. In C. Costello (Ed.), *Symptoms of psychopathology*. New York: John Wiley, 1970.

Martin, R. P. *The development of anxiety in persons anticipating a highly stressful event*. Unpublished doctoral dissertation, University of Texas at Austin, 1970.

Martinez-Urrutia, A. *State–trait anxiety and pain in surgery patients*. Unpublished doctoral dissertation, Florida State University, 1972.

Masserman, J. H. *Behavior and neurosis*. Chicago: University of Chicago Press, 1943.

May, R. *The meaning of anxiety*. New York: Ronald Press, 1950.

McAdoo, W. G. *The effects of success and failure feedback on A-State for subjects who differ in A-Trait*. Unpublished doctoral dissertation, Florida State University, 1969.

McGrath, J. E. *Social and psychological factors in stress*. New York: Holt, Rinehart, and Winston, 1970.

McGuire, J. S., & Megargee, E. I. Personality correlates of marijuana use among youthful offenders. *Journal of Consulting and Clinical Psychology*, 1974, *42*, 124–133.

McLeod, P. G. *Implosion therapy and its components in stress reduction*. Unpublished doctoral dissertation, University of Georgia, 1971.

McNair, D. M., Lorr, M., & Droppleman, L. F. Test manual for the profile of mood states (PMS). San Diego, California, Educational and Industrial Testing Service, 1971.

McReynolds, P. The assessment of anxiety: A survey of available techniques. In P. McReynolds (Ed.), *Advances in psychology assessment*. Palo Alto. Cal.: Science and Behavior Books, 1968.

Meichenbaum, D. *Cognitive-behavior modification*. General Learning Press, 1974.

Meichenbaum, D. *Cognitive-behavior modification: A newsletter*. University of Waterloo, 1975.(a)

Meichenbaum, D. *Toward a cognitive theory of self-control*. University of Waterloo, Research Report No. 48, 1975.(b)

Meichenbaum, D., & Turk, D. *The cognitive-behavioral management of anxiety, anger and pain*. Proceedings of the seventh Banff international conference on behavior modification, Research Press, 1975.

Miller, N. E. Studies of fear as an acquirable drive. Fear as motivation and fear-reduction as reinforcement in the learning of new responses. *Journal of Experimental Psychology*, 1948, *38*, 89–101.

Mischel, W. Continuity and change in personality. *American Psychologist*, 1969 *24*, 1012–1018.

Monat, A., Averill, J. R., & Lazarus, R. S. Anticipatory stress and coping reactions under various conditions of uncertainty. *Journal of Personality and Social Psychology*, 1972, *24*, 237–253.

Montuori, J. J. *The effects of stress and anxiety on verbal conditioning in children*. Unpublished doctoral dissertation, Florida State University, 1971.

Morgan, W. P. Influence of acute physical activity on state anxiety. *Proceedings, National College Physical Education for Men*, 1973, 113–121.

Morris, L. W., & Liebert, R. M. Relationship of cognitive and emotional components of test anxiety to physiological arousal and academic performance. *Journal of Consulting and Clinical Psychology*, 1970, *35*, 332–337.

Morris, L. W., & Liebert, R. M. Effects of negative feedback, threat of shock, and level of trait anxiety on the arousal of two components of anxiety. *Journal of Counseling Psychology*, 1973, *20*, 321–326.

Morris, L. W., Spiegler, M. D., & Liebert, R. M. Effects of a therapeutic modeling film on cognitive and emotional components of anxiety. *Journal of Clinical Psychology*, 1974, *30*, 219–223.

Mowrer, O. H. A stimulus-response analysis of anxiety and its role as a reinforcing agent. *Psychological Review*, 1939, *46*, 553–556.

Mowrer, O. H. *Learning theory and personality dynamics*. New York: Ronald Press, 1950.

Mowrer, O. H. *Learning theory and behavior*. New York: John Wiley, 1960.

Mowrer, O. H., & Viek, P. An experimental analogue of fear from a sense of helplessness. *Journal of Abnormal and Social Psychology*, 1948, *43*, 193–200.

Nelson, D. A. *Trait anxiety as an individual factor in prediction and as it correlates with other variables in predicting academic achievement*. Unpublished doctoral dissertation, University of Northern Colorado, 1971.

Newmark, C. S. The effects of electroconvulsive therapy on state and trait anxiety. *Journal of Clinical Psychology*, 1972, *28*, 413–415.

Newmark, C. S., & Dinoff, M. Noncontent verbal conditioning as a function of two types of anxiety. *Journal of Personality*, 1973, *41*, 443–455.

Newmark, C. S., Ray, J., Frerking, R. A., & Paine, R. D. Test-induced anxiety as a function of psychopathology. *Journal of Clinical Psychology*, 1974, *30*, 261–263.

Nixon, G. F. *The relationship between anxiety–trait and anxiety–state with the approach of final examinations*. Unpublished doctoral dissertation, East Texas State University, 1969.

Nomikos, M. S., Opton, E. M., Averill, J., & Lazarus, R. S. Surprise versus suspense in the production of stress reaction. *Journal of Personality and Social Psychology*, 1968, *8*, 204–208.

Nowlis, V. Research with the mood adjective checklist. In S. S. .Tomkins and C. E. Izard (Eds.), *Affect, cognition and personality*. New York: Springer, 1965.

O'Neil, H. F. *Effects of stress on state anxiety and performance in computer-assisted learning.* Unpublished doctoral dissertation, Florida State University, 1969.

O'Neil, H. F. Effects of stress on state anxiety and performance in computer assisted learning. *Journal of Educational Psychology*, 1972, *63*, 473–481.

O'Neil, H. F., Hansen, E. N., & Spielberger, C. D. *The effects of state and trait anxiety on computer-assisted learning.* Unpublished paper, Florida State University, 1969.

O'Neil, H. F., Spielberger, C. D., & Hansen, D. N. The effects of state anxiety and task difficulty on computer-assisted learning. *Journal of Educational Psychology*, 1969, *60*, 343–350.

Patterson, R. L. *The effects of censure on state anxiety and performance for good and poor premorbid schizophrenics.* Unpublished doctoral dissertation, Florida State University, 1971.

Paul, G. L. *Insight vs. desensitization in psychotherapy: An experiment in anxiety reduction.* Stanford University Press, 1966.

Pavlov, I. P. *Conditioned reflexes.* London: Oxford University Press, 1927.

Percell, L. P., Berwick, P. T., & Beigel, A. The effects of assertive training on self-concept and anxiety. *Archives of General Psychiatry*, 1974, *31*, 502–504.

Rappaport, E. *The effects of trait anxiety and dogmatism on state anxiety during computer-assisted learning.* Florida State University, 1971, Technical Report No. 33.

Ratzlaff, C. N. *Effects of relaxation on self-report measures of a basic emcounter group experience.* Unpublished doctoral dissertation, Arizona State University, 1970.

Rizley, R., & Reppucci, N. Pavlovian conditioned inhibitory processes in behavior. In B. Maher, (Ed.), *Progress in experimental personality research*. New York: Academic Press, 1974.

Rogers, C. R. *Client-centered therapy.* Boston: Houghton-Mifflin, 1951.

Rourke, B. P. *Explorations in the psychology of stress and anxiety.* Don Mills, Ontario: Longmans, Canada, 1969.

Sarason, I. G. Empirical findings and theoretical problems in the use of anxiety scales. *Psychological Bulletin*, 1960, *57*, 403–415.

Sarason, I. G. Effect of anxiety and two kinds of motivating instruction on verbal learning. *Journal of Abnormal and Social Psychology*, 1957, *54*, 166–171.

Sarason, I. G., Smith, R. E., & Diener, E. Personality research: Components of variance attributable to the person and the situation. *Journal of Personality and Social Psychology*, 1976. In press.

Saunders, T R. State anxiety as a function of trait anxiety and sex in a quasi-clinical situation. *Journal of Consulting and Clinical Psychology*, 1973, *41*, 144–147.

Schachter, S. The interaction of cognitive and physiological determinants of emotional state. In C. D. Spielberger (Ed.), *Anxiety and behavior*. New York: Academic Press, 1966.

Schroeder, H., & Craine, L. Relationship among measures of fear and anxiety for snake phobics. *Journal of Consulting and Clinical Psychology*, 1971, *36*, 443.

Shedletsky, R., & Endler, N. S. Anxiety: The state–trait model and the interaction model. *Journal of Personality*, 1974, *42*, 511–527.

Singer, M. M. *The relationship of trait and state anxiety, overall fearfulness, and suggestibility to the implosion of fear of rats.* Unpublished doctoral dissertation, Louisiana State University, 1969.

Smith, R. C. Response bias in the state–anxiety inventory: Detecting the exaggeration of stress. *Journal of Psychology*, 1974, *86*, 241–246.

Snyder, C. R., & Katahn, M. The relationship of state anxiety, feedback, and on-going self-reported affect to performance in complex verbal learning. *American Journal of Psychology,* 1970, *83,* 237–247.

Spiesman, J. C., Lazarus, R. S., & Mordkoff, A. Experimental reduction of stress based on ego-defense theory. *Journal of Abnormal and Social Psychology,* 1964, *68,* 367–380.

Spence, J. T., & Spence, K. W. The motivational components of manifest anxiety: Drive and drive stimuli. In C. D. Spielberger (Ed.), *Anxiety and behavior.* New York: Academic Press, 1966.

Spence, K. W., & Taylor, J. A. The relation of conditioned response strength to anxiety in normal, neurotic, and psychotic subjects. *Journal of Experimental Psychology,* 1953, *45,* 265–272.

Spielberger, C. D. The effects of manifest anxiety on the academic achievement of college students. *Mental Hygiene,* 1962, *46,* 420–426.

Spielberger, C. D. (Ed.). *Anxiety and Behavior.* New York: Academic Press, 1966.

Spielberger, C. D. Anxiety as an emotional state. In C. D. Spielberger (Ed.), *Anxiety: Current trends in theory and research* (Vol. I). New York: Academic Press, 1972.

Spielberger, C. D. (Ed.). *Anxiety: Current trends in theory and research.* New York: Academic Press, 1972 (Vol I).(b)

Spielberger, C. D. (Ed.). *Anxiety: Current trends in theory and research.* New York: Academic Press, 1972 (Vol. II).(c)

Spielberger, C. D. Personal communication, 1975.

Spielberger, C. D., Auerbach, S. M., Wadsworth, A. P., Dunn, T. M., & Taulbee, E. S. Emotional reactions to surgery. *Journal of Consulting and Clinical Psychology,* 1973, *40,* 33–38.

Spielberger, C. D., Gonzalez-Reigosa, R., Martinez-Urrutia, A., Natalicio, L., & Natalicio, D. Development of the Spanish edition of the state–trait anxiety inventory. *Interamerican Journal of Psychology,* 1971, *5,* 145–158.

Spielberger, C. D., O Gorsuch, R. L. *Mediating processes in verbal conditioning.* Research report, Vanderbilt University, 1966.

Spielberger, C. D., Gorsuch, R. L., & Lushene, R. E. *The state–trait anxiety inventory. Preliminary test manual for Form B.* Tallahassee, Fla.: Florida State University, 1967.

Spielberger, C. D., Gorsuch, R. L., & Lushene, R. E. *The state–trait anxiety inventory. Preliminary test manual for Form X.* Tallahassee, Fla.: Florida State University, 1968.

Spielberger, C. D., Gorsuch, R. L., & Lushene, R. E. *Manual for the state–trait anxiety inventory.* Palo Alto, Cal.: Consulting Psychologists Press, 1970.

Spielberger, C. D., O'Neil, H. F., & Hansen, D. N. Anxiety, drive theory, and computer assisted learning. In B. A. Maher (Ed.), *Progress in experimental personality research* (Vol. VI). New York: Academic Press, 1972.

Spielberger, C. D., & Smith, L. H. Anxiety (drive), stress, and serial position effects in serial-verbal learning. *Journal of Experimental Psychology,* 1966, *72,* 589–595.

Spielberger, C. D., Southard, L. D., & Hodges, W. F. Effects of awareness and threat of shock on verbal conditioning. *Journal of Experimental Psychology,* 1966, *72,* 434–438.

Spielberger, C. D., Weitz, H., & Denny, J. P. Group counseling and the academic performance of anxious college freshmen. *Journal of Counseling Psychology,* 1962, *9,* 195–204.

Stoudenmire, J. Effects of muscle relaxation training on state and trait anxiety in introverts and extraverts. *Journal of Personality and Social Psychology,* 1972, *24,* 273–275.

Strahan, R. Situational dimensions of self-reported nervousness. *Journal of Personality Assessment,* 1974, *38,* 341–352.

Stutler, D. L. *The interrelationship between academic achievement of college freshman women and measures of anxiety and ability.* Unpublished doctoral dissertation, Oregon State University, 1973.

Sullivan, H. S. *The interpersonal theory of psychiatry*. New York: Norton, 1953.

Taylor, D. A., Wheeler, L., & Altman, I. Stress reactions in socially isolated groups. *Journal of Personality and Social Psychology*, 1968, *9*, 369–376.

Taylor, F. R. *Statematic desensitization of dating anxiety*. Unpublished doctoral dissertation, Arizona State University, 1972.

Taylor, J. A. The relationship of anxiety to the conditioned eyelid response. *Journal of Experimental Psychology*, 1951, *41*, 81–92.

Taylor, J. A. A personality scale of manifest anxiety. *Journal of Abnormal and Social Psychology*, 1953, *48*, 285–290.

Tennyson, R. D., & Boutwell, R. C. Pre-task vs. within-task anxiety measures in predicting performance on a concept acquisition task. *Journal of Educational Psychology*, 1973, *65*, 88–92.

Titchener, E. B. *An outline of psychology*. New York: Macmillan, 1897.

Tobias, S. Sequence, familiarity and attribute treatment interactions in programmed instruction. *Journal of Educational Psychology*, 1973, *64*, 133–141.

Tobiason, R. V. *The relative effectiveness of individual and group desensitization in reducing student nurses' anxiety*. Unpublished doctoral dissertation, Arizona State University, 1971.

Watson, D., & Friend, R. Measurement of social-evaluative anxiety. *Journal of Consulting and Clinical Psychology*, 1969, *33*, 448–457.

Watson, J. B., & Rayner, R. Conditioned emotional reactions. *Journal of Experimental Psychology*, 1920, *3*, 1–14.

Welsh, G. An anxiety index and an internationalization ratio for the MMPI, *Journal of Consulting Psychology*, 1952, *16*, 65–72.

Wilde, G. J. Trait description and measurement by personality questionnaires. In R. B. Cattell (Ed.), *Handbook of modern personality theory*. Chicago: Aldine, 1972.

Zuckerman, M. The development of an affect adjective checklist for the measurement of anxiety. *Journal of Consulting Psychology*, 1960, *24*, 457–462.

CHAPTER 3

Authoritarianism

RONALD C. DILLEHAY
University of Kentucky

Authoritarianism as a personality syndrome received its greatest impetus in research with the publication in 1950 of *The Authoritarian Personality* (Adorno, Frenkel-Brunswik, Levinson, and Sanford) although the concept was not original with them. Its roots are in earlier attempts to understand the fascism and Nazism that developed in Germany in the 1920s and 1930s. However, Adorno and his coworkers developed the F Scale (F for fascism), which became the standard instrument operationalizing this intriguing concept. Now a formulation that stands as a classic in psychology, authoritarianism provided a link between personality and ideology, between character and prejudice. A wide variety of psychological, social, political, and economic phenomena has been studied using this construct. And even though it can be rightly argued that the F Scale is dated in some of its item content, this instrument and some others developed in the last 25 years to measure authoritarianism provide the basis for a continuing heavy volume of research.

In this chapter we will first view briefly the history of the concept and then turn to a discussion of the monumental work by Adorno and his colleagues. We will examine research relating authoritarianism to other psychological constructs, to socioeconomic status, and to behavior. In doing so, we deal with but a fraction of the hundreds of pieces of research on the topic. Those who wish to pursue the issues surrounding this landmark concept in greater depth may consult Christie and Jahoda (1954), Titus and Hollander (1957), and Kirscht and Dillehay (1967).

THE INITIAL FORMULATION OF THE CONCEPT

Adolph Hitler was appointed Chancellor of the Republic of Germany in 1933 by Hindenburg. Hitler had failed in previous attempts to gain national offices in regular elections, running on the National Socialist ticket. In 1932 he garnered 37 percent of the votes for president, a contest won by Hindenburg. By gaining a powerful public office by appointment, Hitler had already begun an odyssey that would affect the world for many years to come as a result of the atrocities of Nazi Germany under his leadership. Most of these atrocities required the complicity, cooperation, or condescension of vast numbers of the German people. The actions of the German government against the Jews in Germany, Poland, and France are well known. These actions, and more specifically, the response of the German people to them, prompted psychologists, sociologists, and other behavioral scientists to study the character of the German people, who were seen as relatively passive and accepting of their government's violent actions. How could a people, long educated in a developed and democratic country, accept the propaganda of the Nazi government, propaganda targeting the Jews as the source of economic, social, and political strife, identifying them as the evil to be overcome in the path toward healing the country's difficulties, which at the time were quite real?

We have one attempted answer to this question in *Escape from Freedom* by Erich Fromm (1941). Fromm's work provides a historical tabloid of the German character structure of that day, a character structure that he viewed as a consequence of the centuries-long joint changes in the religious experiences of individuals since the Reformation and in the alterations in economic behavior produced by the rise of capitalism as the dominant economic system. According to Fromm, changes in religious experiences brought about by Calvinism and the growth of Protestantism diminished the influence of traditional moral authority, giving greater freedom to the individual. At the same time, these religious systems provided a rationale for the insignificance and powerlessness that were widely felt as a result of changes in the economic system, which was evolving to a capitalist form. Capitalism, according to Fromm, provided the potential for strength and independence, but in setting men free, it produced a sense of isolation and fear. He felt such a historical analysis was necessary to an understanding of modern social character, but he also emphasized that once created, modern social character itself exerted a significant, autonomous influence. "The new character structure, resulting from economic and social changes and intensified by religious doctrines, became in turn an important factor in shaping further social and economic development" (Fromm, 1941, p. 101). The consequence, centuries later, in the personalities of the people of Western Europe, and particularly in the lower middle classes of Germany, was an authoritarian character structure. This character structure is typified by the idealization of authority combined with fear and submission to it in a relationship of exploitation from above. While the authoritarian needs his authorities as objects for unqualified emotional allegiance, he, too, desires the role of authority, adopting the same kind of exploitation of those below him. Fromm selected the term *authoritarian* partly because of its correspondence to the functioning of authority in Fascist social and political affairs. "By the term 'authoritarian character,' we imply that it represents the personality structure which is the human basis of Fascism" (p. 164).

It was to signal the correspondence between their own research and the conceptual analysis by Fromm, as well as the related prior work of Stagner (1936) and Maslow (1943), that Adorno and his colleagues selected authoritarianism as the integrating concept of their work.

An often-misunderstood point is worth noting at the outset: Research on authoritarianism applies less to superleaders of social and political movements than to the broad spectrum of participants in those movements, such as the lower middle class in Germany of the 1930s. Fromm, remember, was trying to account for German national character rather than explain how Hitler got to be the person he was, although Fromm did that, too (Fromm, 1941, pp. 221 ff.). Research since has applied the concept to broad populations, or at least intended that it be applied in that way.

THE BERKELEY STUDIES

When a social scientist thinks of authoritarianism, the most significant single influence that comes to mind is the work of Adorno and his colleagues, a series of investigations that was published in 1950 in a 990-page volume under the title *The Authoritarian Personality*. In contrast to Stagner, Maslow, and Fromm, Adorno and his coworkers did not study the character of the German people; they studied Americans—in San Francisco and Oakland, California, Eugene, Oregon, and other cities mostly on the West Coast of the United States. Nor did they *begin* by studying authoritarianism, although that is what they ended up studying, and in retrospect it seemed they had been on a clear course from the beginning toward unmasking this concept as the real concern of their work. These studies are sometimes referred to as the Berkeley studies, because the University of California at Berkeley was the center of the research.

Anti-Semitism was the initial focus of investigation in the Berkeley studies. The world at that time had just seen the extermination of millions of Jews (and a number of other ethnic minority groups as well) by the Nazi government. And prejudicial attitudes and behavior toward Jews were not found in Germany alone, obviously, as they had existed for centuries in many countries around the world. Could the anti-Semitism of Nazi Germany happen in the United States? Whether or not it might, it was evident that ample prejudice existed in the United States, and the American Jewish Committee established a Department of Scientific Research to support investigation of prejudice, with *The Authoritarian Personality* one of the first products of that body. "Prejudice is one of the problems of our times for which everyone has a theory but no one has an answer,'' wrote Max Horkheimer and Samuel H. Flowerman in the foreword to the Adorno et al. volume (p. v). *The Authoritarian Personality* was a monumental step toward some answers.

From the beginning the Berkeley investigators felt that dispositions deep in the fabric of personality underlay anti-Semitism. This conviction set the course of their work. The strategy they used was to identify persons who were high in anti-Semitism and individuals low in such prejudice so these two groups might be compared in terms of their personality dynamics. To accomplish this, the investigators needed to be able to measure prejudice, and somehow to conceptualize, measure, and interpret personality. Prejudice against Jews was conceptualized largely in terms of ideology about Jews; personality was viewed in these investigations from a psychoanalytic perspective.

A scale containing items about Jews was developed that would permit the assessment of anti-Semitism, and it was called the A–S Scale. The idea was to determine the extent to which people would express negative sentiment toward Jews by endorsing statements that were anti-Semitic in nature. Some sample items are as follows (Adorno et al., 1950):

> Jews seem to prefer the most luxurious, extravagant, and sensual way of living.
> One trouble with Jewish businessmen is that they stick together and connive, so that a Gentile doesn't have a fair chance in competition.
> It is wrong for Jews and Gentiles to intermarry. (p. 68–69).

Fifty-two such items comprise the total A–S Scale, each item derived from a theoretical expectation that the idea expressed was a characteristic feature of prejudice against Jews. A 10-item short form of the scale was also developed. Split-half reliabilities for both versions were .89 and above, corrected by the Spearman-Brown formula and based on several of the samples studied. It is also wroth noting at this point that all the items were written in such a way that agreement with the statement indicated prejudice. This fact—the wording of all the items in one direction, which occurred on this scale as well as the others that we will discuss shortly—has been a haunting issue in the long history of authoritarianism. Notice that in theory it *should* be possible to write items with which agreement indicates positive attitudes toward Jews. For example, ''A large number of Jews have made significant scientific and artistic contributions to mankind'' states a positive view of Jews, and agreement with this statement would indicate the opposite of anti-Semitism. But be careful of the potential meaning of some items so worded: ''Some of my best friends are Jews.'' Problems of item wording notwithstanding (we will discuss it more later), the A–S Scale played a central role in the Berkeley investigations.

With the A–S Scale the researchers could measure ideology about Jews and identify for further study those most prejudiced in their beliefs and those least prejudiced. And so they did, comparing individuals from the upper 25 percent and those from the lower 25 percent in anti-Semitism on a number of personality factors that were assessed by means of several clinical procedures, one being an in-depth and loosely structured clinical interview, another a "projective questions" technique, and a third a set of pictures forming a test based on the Thematic Apperception Test (TAT), with six pictures from the TAT and four especially prepared for the study of prejudice.

From anti-Semitism the research expanded to deal with ethnocentrism. "Scratch a person who displays anti-Semitism, and you find an ethnocentric individual" is a way of expressing what the Berkeley investigators learned in their continuing work. Consequently they broadened their investigation to examine ethnocentric ideology, using as topics for this part of the investigation Negroes, Okies, women, criminals, and other ethnic and identifiable subgroups in American society. Also included in this part of the investigation was an assessment of a kind of ethnocentrism manifested as American patriotism, a chauvinism, in fact, expressed as America First sentiment. A scale measuring ethnocentrism (the E Scale) was constructed after the fashion of the A–S Scale but referring more broadly to the groups indicated. Illustrative items from the final form of the E Scale are as follows (Adorno et al., 1950):

> Negroes have their rights, but it is best to keep them in their own districts and schools to prevent too much contact with whites.
>
> There may be a few exceptions, but in general, Jews are pretty much alike.
>
> The worst danger to real Americanism during the last 50 years has come from foreign ideas and agitators. (p. 142)

Once again, all the items of the E Scale were worded in such a way that agreement with the statement indicated ethnocentrism. In some cases scores on the E Scale were used as a substitute for responses to the A–S Scale to identify prejudiced and unprejudiced subjects for intensive follow-up study. Among the samples included in the research of the Berkeley investigators, A–S and E were correlated highly, with coefficients ranging from .63 to .75 on early forms of the scales (Adorno et al., 1950, p. 123).

As a further step in their work, based on the general theory that was guiding the investigations, Adorno and his coworkers developed a scale to study political and economic ideology. Their reason for this inclusion was a clear conviction: "That political and economic forces play a vital role in the development of ethnocentrism, in both its institutional and individual psychological forms, is no longer questioned by social scientists or even by most laymen" (p. 151). Drawing on research buttressing this assertion, these investigators developed the Politico-Economic Conservatism (PEC) Scale, using procedures similar to those earlier described for the A–S and E Scales. Levinson (Adorno et al., 1950) expressed some of the interesting guiding assumptions for the generation of this scale as follows:

> It would appear, then, that liberals tend to view social problems as symptoms of the underlying social structure, while conservatives view them as results of individual incompetence or immorality. This difference is expressed also in the evaluation of political candidates. Conservative politicians tend to base their election campaigns largely on qualities of personal character and moral standing. To be a good family man and a leading figure in the community are judged more important than to know social science or to understand the actual politico-economic problems of the community." (p. 155)

In general, PEC scores were not as highly related to the scores obtained on the other scales (A–S, E) as scores on those scales were related among themselves. The demonstrated relationships were high enough, however, to support the place of conservative ideology in the beliefs of prejudiced persons.

So where is authoritarianism in all of this? It emerged as the personality substructure for the prejudice and conservative ideology examined in the A–S, E, and PEC scales, appearing in the clinical material of the interviews, projective questions, and tests that were used to study extreme scorers on the scales. The step from antidemocratic idèology to prefascist personality was in some ways a small one: The Berkeley investigators began after all with the idea that personality underlies the consistency of beliefs and actions. In other ways the shift from a focus on what one believes to concern with the personality mechanisms that make those beliefs possible is substantial, representing a change from a descriptive to an analytic perspective, a change from a focus on phenotype to a concern with genotype. Authoritarianism was considered to be a driving force in personality toward prejudice and the acceptance of antidemocratic propaganda. It was in fact labeled "implicit antidemocratic personality trends" and "prefascism in the personality."

AUTHORITARIANISM AND THE F SCALE

When one reads the sections of *The Authoritarian Personality* that describe the development of the F Scale and the formulation of the syndrome of authoritarianism (particularly Chapter 7 of Adorno et al.), it is clear that these two consequences of the work—the scale and the concept—evolved in a union so close that a distinction in the development of the two is clearly impossible. The investigators wanted to construct a scale that would measure prejudice "without appearing to have this aim and without mentioning the name of any minority group'' (p. 222). The utility of such a scale is obvious: It could be used without evoking resistance to honest self-disclosure and hostilities toward the measuring instrument that might accompany response to a questionnaire obviously assessing prejudice. In this sense the evolution of the F Scale and its conceptualization as authoritarianism was a pratical research matter. (The authors indicate they considered using the PEC scale as an indirect measure of prejudice but rejected it because it did not correlate highly enough with ethnic prejudice, as measured by the A–S and E Scales.) We may note that accomplishment of this pragmatic purpose indicates the scale could be considered as an indirect measure of prejudice instead of a means to assess a personality syndrome, and this view was utilized by Siegel and Siegel (1957) in their research on membership and reference group influences on antidemocratic dispositions, which is discussed later. Their use of the F Scale is atypical, however.

The development of the F Scale as a measure of a personality syndrome underlying prejudice, representing a major motive force behind prejudicial sentiment, is the more trenchant aspect of the Berkeley investigations. Working within a loose but dynamic theoretical framework, which is to say a theoretical orientation that conceived of integration within the personality such that the diverse manifestations of psychological phenomena and behavior in an individual may be understood to be the consequences of underlying trends deeper within the personality, these researchers believed that the degree of prejudice in a person was a result of implicit personality dispositions. In authoritarianism they believed that they had conceptualized the personality predispositions toward anti-Semitism and general ethnic prejudice, that they had identified the personality basis of susceptibility to fascist propaganda with its emphasis on rigid conventionality, the imperiousness of authority, and the degradation of outgroups, particularly minorities.

The items of the F Scale are shown in Table 3–1. The greater the agreement with each item, the higher the authoritarianism. This is the form of the scale that evolved from the several item analyses performed to select items that would differentiate high and low scorers on both the A–S Scale and previous forms of the F Scale. The reliability of this scale over a number of groups averaged .90, with a range of .81 to .97. These items represent the operational definition of authoritarianism that has served often for the 25 years since the publication of the Berkeley investigations. When the scale is used, subjects are asked to indicate their agreement or disagreement with each item by use of the following categories: strong support, agreement; moderate support, agreement; slight support, agreement; slight opposition, disagreement; moderate opposition, disagreement; strong opposition, disagreement. In examining the items you will see that, like the A–S and E Scale items, they are all worded so that agreement indicates authoritarianism, a fact that, as we have noted and will later discuss, presents methodological problems.

Table 3–1. The California F Scale

1. Obedience and respect for authority are the most important virtues children should learn.
2. A person who has bad manners, habits, and breeding can hardly expect to get along with decent people.
3. If people would talk less and work more, everybody would be better off.
4. The businessman and the manufacturer are much more important to society than the artist and the professor.
5. Science has its place, but there are many important things that can never possibly be understood by the human mind.
6. Young people sometimes get rebellious ideas, but as they grow up they ought to get over them and settle down.
7. What this country needs most, more than laws and political programs, is a few courageous, tireless, devoted leaders in whom the people can put their faith.
8. No sane, normal, decent person could ever think of hurting a close friend or relative.
9. Nobody ever learned anything really important except through suffering.
10. What the youth needs is strict discipline, rugged determination, and the will to work and fight for family and country.
11. An insult to our honor should always be punished.
12. Sex crimes, such as rape and attacks on children, deserve more than mere imprisonment; such criminals ought to be publicly whipped, or worse.
13. There is hardly anything lower than a person who does not feel a great love, gratitude, and respect for his parents.
14. Most of our social problems would be solved if we could somehow get rid of the immoral, crooked, and feeble-minded people.
15. Homosexuals are hardly better than criminals and ought to be severely punished.
16. When a person has a problem or worry, it is best for him not to think about it, but to keep busy with more cheerful things.
17. Every person should have complete faith in some supernatural power whose decisions he obeys without question.
18. Some people are born with an urge to jump from high places.
19. People can be divided into two distinct classes: the weak and the strong.
20. Some day it will probably be shown that astrology can explain a lot of things.
21. Wars and social troubles may some day be ended by an earthquake or flood that will destroy the whole world.
22. No weakness or difficulty can hold us back if we have enough will power.
23. It is best to use some prewar authorities in Germany to keep order and prevent chaos.
24. Most people don't realize how much our lives are controlled by plots hatched in secret places.
25. Human nature being what it is, there will always be war and conflict.
26. Familiarity breeds contempt.
27. Nowadays when so many different kinds of people move around and mix together so much, a person has to protect himself especially carefully against catching an infection or disease from them.
28. Nowadays more and more people are prying into matters that should remain personal and private.
29. The wild sex life of the old Greeks and Romans was tame compared to some of the goings-on in this country, even in places where people might least expect it.
30. The true American way of life is disappearing so fast that force may be necessary to preserve it.

Source: Adorno, Frenkel-Brunswik, Levinson, and Sanford, 1950.

It is well to notice also that these items were framed on a theoretical basis to measure one or more of the variables that define the syndrome, that is, they were developed out of a coneptualization of the syndrome rather than on the basis of a statistical analysis of a very large pool of potential items. A good many of them were suggested by interview material and the responses to the TAT used in the assessment of personality of the more and less prejudiced subjects. As the authors put it, "Once a hypothesis had been formulated concerning the way in which some deep-lying trend in the personality might express itself in some opinion or attitude that was dynamically, though not logically, related to prejudice against outgroups, a preliminary sketch for an item was usually not far to 'seek' and was refined through technical procedures" (p. 225). The point here is that an economy of item selection and formulation was introduced by the conceptualization of the syndrome, and the alternative strategy of proceeding by purely statistical means of item selection was not employed. The approach used is further testimony to the way the theoretical dispositions of the investigators, the appearance of antidemocratic personality dispositions in the data (largely in the interview and clinical data), the advisability for practical purposes of an indirect measure of prejudice, and statistical analysis and refinement were highly interdependent in the development of the F Scale and the formulation of the concept.

The syndrome of authoritarianism as construed by Adorno et al. (1950) consists of nine variables which they summarize as follows:

Conventionalism: Rigid adherence to conventional, middle-class values.

Authoritarian Submission: Submissive, uncritical attitude toward idealized moral authorities of the ingroup.

Authoritarian Aggression: Tendency to be on the lookout for, and to condemn, reject, and punish people who violate conventional values.

Anti-intraception: Opposition to the subjective, the imaginative, the tender-minded.

Superstition and Stereotypy: The belief in mystical determinants of the individual's fate; the disposition to think in rigid categories.

Power and "Toughness": Preoccupation with the dominance–submission, strong--weak, leader–follower dimension; identification with power figures; overemphasis upon the conventionalized attributes of the ego; exaggerated assertion of strength and toughness.'

Destructiveness and Cynicism: Generalized hostility, vilification of the human.

Projectivity: The disposition to believe that wild and dangerous things go on in the world; the projection outwards of unconscious emotional impulses.

Sex: Exaggerated concern with sexual "goings-on." (pp. 255–257)

Theoretically, these nine variables represent a single syndrome of correlated factors. If a person displays a considerable amount of one or several of these, he or she is likely to be characterized by others as well. Departures from total consistency are expected, however, save that the overall appearance is more often than not one of general consistency across the nine areas.

Some features of these variables deserve comment. *Conventionalism* (measured by items 1, 2, 3, and 4 in Table 3–1) in the authoritarian is not owing to a rational assessment of middle class values but rather to an emotional and rigid acceptance of the standards of someone else, namely, middle class authorities. The authoritarian has not examined these values and standards; he has merely taken them on. They are not internalized, not thought through. For example, the authoritarian would have difficulty defending democracy and its principles even though he would support the label if his authorities indicate that he should. Because he lacks the substance of such standards, he can be expected to act and believe in highly inconsistent ways when confronted with conflicting authority or the situational absence of it. One is struck by the similarity of this formulation to the explanation of the response of a few prisoners of war who were supposedly brainwashed at the hands of the North Koreans: A recommendation of some investigators of these events was that military personnel be schooled in the substance of the principles for which they stand as a means of minimizing in advance the potential effects of counterpropaganda.

Authoritarian submission is measured by items 1, 5, 6, 7, 8, and 9 (Table 3–1). This variable indicates an emotional and extreme need to submit to external authority, an authority that can signal without ambiguity what is to be believed and valued, how one should behave. Not to be confused with rational respect for valid authority, authoritarian submission is rather a need for external controls that are necessary, according to the theory, because the authoritarian does not have well-developed internal standards or controls that guide behavior according to principle or reason. Thus, one view of the essence of authoritarian submission is a deficient superego or conscience.

Authoritarian aggression is measured by items 2, 10, 11, 12, 13, 14, and 15 (Table 3–1). These items were written to measure the tendency of the authoritarian to aggress against outgroups, chiefly minority groups, the weak, people who hold different values, and so on. The items presumably tap the dual aspect of authoritarian aggression: the very narrow limits of acceptance of behavior in other people and the tendency to engage in projection. In regard to the first of these, the authoritarian can be thought of as a kind of emotional cripple whose psychological dynamics require that he condemn and suppress others as he does with many of his own impulses. The element of projection serves as protection against these same impulses.

The items in the scale that were designed to measure *anti-intraception* are 3, 4, 16, and 28 in Table 3–1. The essence of this variable is an opposition to self-reflection, to introspection, and to thinking in terms of the motives and psychodynamics underlying human conduct. This aversion applies not only to oneself but to others behaving in this way as well. There is concern that if one indulges in such ephemeral matters as thoughts and feelings, they could get out of hand; it is better to be practical and concrete.

Superstition and stereotypy is measured by items 5, 17, 18, 19, 20 and 21

(Table 3–1). The tendencies to be superstitious and especially to think in stereotyped ways have an obvious connection to anti-Semitism and to prejudice in general. The prejudiced person deals in the arena of unverified assertion or half-truth; what is supposed or imagined about others takes on the mantle of reality but remains a fiction with greater affinity for fear and emotion than for cold and objective facts. Superstitions are unrestrained by the test of internal consistency, making possible a characteristic of authoritarians that seems to crop up again and again, namely the internal contradictions in their beliefs and values. Stereotyping, too, serves the separation of beliefs from verifiable reality in that the rigidified categories implied by the term neither require nor foster comparison with external fact.

Power and toughness as aspects of authoritarianism are measured by items 7, 10, 11, 19, 22, 23, 24 (Table 3–1). The toughness part of this variable is intended to refer to a façade: an assertion of toughness to overcome feelings of weakness and ineptness. As a reference to a power complex in the authoritarian, this variable points to the tendencies to admire power in others and to submit to authority, on the one hand, and to assert oneself, to dominate others, on the other. One main requirement for the authoritarian is that there be a clear leader––follower, strong–weak, superior–subordinate relationship in interpersonal affairs. The authoritarian preoccupied with power and toughness is apparently capable of satisfying himself in either position.

The variable of *destructiveness and cynicism* is measured only by items 25, 26, and 30 in Table 3–1. Whether or not these three items are an adequate measure of the variable, they do illustrate what is meant by this dimension. It is supposed to refer to "rationalized, ego-accepted, nonmoralized aggression." Whereas the *authoritarian aggression* variable refers to the tendency to condemn and attack on moral grounds, this variable implicates aggression and hostility on other bases. One such might be a rationalized tradition of violence: "Everyone else does it, why shouldn't I?" Yet other bases might be aggression rationalized by institutional requirements or expectations from other people. Thus, trivial violations of social traditions, like males wearing long hair, may need to be punished.

Projectivity is measured by items 21, 24, 27, 28, and 29 presented in Table 3–1. As a complex defense mechanism, projection can take a number of forms. It may be the perception in others of the threatening or unwanted traits in oneself; it can be the attribution to others of anxiety-arousing impulses that threaten an already precarious adjustment on the part of the authoritarian. Yet another form of this defensive personality functioning is to see in others dispositions that justify one's own feelings or beliefs. For example, a person chronically feeling weak and afraid might justify such feelings by seeing others as overpowering and hostile. In any case, the personality of the authoritarian leads him to believe that things are not right with the world.

Exaggerated concern with *sex* and in particular with deviant behavior related to sex is measured by items 12, 15, and 29 (Table 3–1). The authoritarian's preoccupations here seem to be mainly with sexual deviance, but the greater-than-normal attention to sexual topics and matters depicted in these items may belie an internal determinant, as with forsaken impulses toward sexual behavior. However, as an observational aside, we can register the impression that the variable of sex as a component of authoritarianism was included more because of the psychoanalytic orientation of the authors than because the data from the intensive study of their subjects had revealed this as a sensitive area. This observation notwithstanding, it is the case that in the engaging historical account of the paranoid style in American politics, a style with particular magnetism for the authoritarian, Hofstadter (1967) relates the attention given to sexual indulgence and prowess by those employing conspiratorial arguments against individuals and groups. Sex *does* seem to emerge frequently in such accusations. For example, Hofstadter states, "Anti-Catholicism has always been the pornography of the Puritan," with "an immense lore about libertine priests, the confessional as an opportunity for seduction, licentious convents and monasteries, and the like" (pp. 21–22).

This, then, is the syndrome of authoritarianism as defined by Adorno and his colleagues. And the F Scale measured it. As noted above, the union between the scale and the concept was remarkable, with the two seemingly emerging from both the data of the intensive study of some of their subjects and the theoretical dispositions of the investigators. The methodological and conceptual shortcomings of the Berkeley investigations were noted soon after publication of the work, and the attention they were given attests to the importance of the research. The fact that some of those issues are still debated in the literature some 25 years later signals their complexity and relevance for psychological research in general. Before we turn to a discussion of some of the criticisms, we will examine the Berkeley investigators' views of the development of authoritarian personalities.

THE MAKING OF AN AUTHORITARIAN

Fromm's study of the German character structure of the 1930s was a work of historical analysis, describing major religious, economic, and political trends over a period of several hundred years. The forces that produced the authoritarian personality of the lower middle class German had forged a cultural circumstance of relative individual freedom and an absence of personal qualities to cope with that freedom, particularly when conditions were bad economically and politically. With the deteriorated state of Germany at that time as a catalyst, the stage was set for a demagogue to arise. The anti-Semitism and persecution of Jews and other ethnic minorities were made possible by widespread authoritarian dispositions, what Fromm referred to as sadomasochism when present in pathological extreme.

Adorno and his colleagues did not search for historical determinants of authoritarianism beyond socialization. For the Berkeley investigators, authoritarianism was best understood in psychoanalytic terms: the interplay of strong biological needs and the countervailing force of cultural constraints; the development of defense mechanisms as a compensatory adjustive solution to troublesome suppressed and repressed impulses; the malajustive consequences in ideology of a failure in ego development and superego integration. What all this means, in general, is that a number of unfortunate things happen during the authoritarian's childhood, mostly having to do with parents or other authority figures, that force the authoritarian person as an adult to deal constantly with unfinished psychological business, and deal with it in a way that precludes a constructive, adjustive resolution of past and therefore present difficulties.

As part of the exposition of their work, Adorno et al. present us with extensive data and interpretation of two case histories—Larry, a person low in authoritarianism, and Mack, who exemplifies a prefascist personality—and we can borrow from Sanford's discussion of the determinants of adult personality in these two persons (see especially Chapter 20 of *The Authoritarian Personality*). Central to Mack's authoritarianism is his fear of weakness, which derives from fear of a moralistic and distant father and failure to identify with that father in a constructive resolution of Oedipal conflicts. Latent homosexuality is a prominent feature of the interpretation of Mack's personality. Mack's relation to his mother and other women in his life produce a dependency that contributes to his sense of weakness, which cannot be recognized and accepted by him, and is consequently turned into a variety of manifest personality characteristics. Some of these latter are anti-intraception, concealment of "softness," strivings for power and status, and rejection of "weak" outgroups. Some key experiences of his early childhood (e.g., his mother's illness and death when he was quite young) are considered to be primary determinants of his adult personality, and consequently his ideology. Mack's experiences of these events produced adjustive reactions that created in his adult personality most of the defining characteristics of the authoritarian (see especially p. 801).

Larry is presented as a contrasting case, although in some respects he is referred to as not exemplary of low authoritarians. He is passive and dependent, but unlike Mack he is aware of it and can act in these ways rather than having to deny them and manifest opposite tendencies of power and toughness. Moreover, Larry differs from Mack in that Larry's behavior is guided by "an internalized . . . superego" that is, however, "relatively narrow and restricting" (Adorno et al., 1950, p. 811). We need not further explore the account of Larry save to note that the psychoanalytic explanation of adult personality, used differently, is the basis for our understanding of his relative lack of authoritarianism and largely democratic view of people and events in his world.

Thus, the dynamics of the development of the authoritarian were described by the Berkeley investigators in Freudian terms, mainly in the context of family interaction as experienced by the child. In this scenario a key feature is the way the child develops control over his id-determined impulses, particularly vis-à-vis the controlling parental figures, and the way the child is induced to deal with his ambivalence toward his parents, the inevitable love and hate he experiences toward them in the development of impulse mastery. Fear of reprisal from the parent, for example, produces repression of hostile feelings on the part of the child toward the parent, but in the dynamics of personality functioning these feelings still carry psychic energy and therefore leave their mark on the thoughts and behavior of the child and the adult. Mack's dependence was transformed into assertions of power and dominance; the maladaptive feature of this transformation is in the likelihood of its being inappropriate to the logical requirements of specific situations. Mack's behavior was likely to be determined more by his needs than by situational exigencies.

Since 1950 other theoretical views of the etiology of authoritarianism have been presented, partly because more data have become available and partly in reaction to the psychoanalytic interpretation by Adorno et al. Psychoanalytic theory is objectionable to some and fetching and informative to others. Notice that it is entirely possible to leave in debate the forces that produce this personality type while recognizing its existence, with its important psychological and social consequences.

ENTER THE CRITICS

A number of questions about the material we have covered so far will have occurred to the reader, and some of these are probably issues discussed in the literature since the publication of the Berkeley research. This is not to say the field has been all controversy. A great many investigators have quite simply and naturally seized upon the availability of a scale to measure authoritarianism and set about the business of studying this syndrome in relation to psychological, social, political, or other concepts of their attachment. However, the expectable examination and reexamination of the earlier ideas and work has occurred after the fashion of scientific scrutiny, in which suspected imperfections and inadequacies are exposed and assessed, prompting refinement and further progress. A major appraisal is to be found in the volume by Christie and Jahoda (1954). Reaction to the early work falls nicely into the two categories of theory and method.

Criticisms of the theory.

One major criticism has been that the conceptualization of the authoritarian as a rightist, conservative, prefascist personality type is too limited. This criticism holds that the kind of thinking often attributed to the authoritarian—premature closure, rigidity, reverence for authorities, the absence of truly internalized standards as guides for behavior, condemnation of outgroups, and idealization of the ingroup—is not the sole province of prefascist personalities, but may characterize people of any position on a continuum of political and economic issues, from the reactionary or fascist on the extreme right to the socialist and communist on the far left. In short, authoritarian *style* may typify any given *content*. A totalitarian political system and its attendant social and economic ideas can manifest different ideological trappings. This argument is highly developed by Shils (1954), who argues the similarities of the style of belief between communism and fascism. More recently, sociopolitical events in Latin America in which military governments have instituted *leftist* social and political institutional changes in a form not unlike the traditional rightist military regimes has attracted the attention of political scientists who conceive of these leftist governments as no less authoritarian than the traditional fascist systems that stimulated the work of Adorno and his coworkers. Thus, the work of the Berkeley investigators was criticized because it dealt only with authoritarianism of the political right.

The rejoinder to this criticism can be simply put: Their work concerned the political right because they were interested in the prefascist personality. They did not undertake to study all varieties of authoritarian disposition, and they were not particularly interested in other totalitarian sociopolitical forms and their consequences. Today their focus might be different, not only because of the benefits of subsequent critical analysis of their work, but also because it is evident in the world today that anti-Semitism thrives in communist nations as well as fascist ones. It should also be noted, however, that the use of the term *antidemocratic trends* in the personality by Adorno et al. does suggest more than merely rightist extremism.

The idea of general authoritarianism—a personality style that may manifest itself in any political persuasion—has been discussed in an engaging way by Hoffer (1951), although he did not explicitly invest in the term, and it has been examined extensively by Rokeach (see the fullest early development in *The Open and Closed Mind,* 1960; Chapter 4 of this volume deals exclusively with dogmatism). There is mixed evidence that dogmatism, as general authoritarianism, is demonstrably different from authoritarianism as measured by the F Scale (see Kirscht and Dillehay, 1967, pp. 11–12; Rokeach, 1963, pp. 353–354; Rokeach, 1967). But there is no doubt that conceptually dogmatism (general authoritarianism) and authoritarianism (Berkeley investigators' variety) are different: A communist may be dogmatic but not easily seen as prefascist. A complication occurs in the Adorno et al. work because the authoritarian is at times referred to as implicitly antidemocratic, which is a much broader concept than prefascist, and in other ways the Berkeley investigators indicate that their view of authoritarianism includes various political manifestations. For example, speaking of ways to change Mack, the intensively studied authoritarian whose case was used throughout the book to illustrate the concept, Sanford (Adorno et al., 1950) notes:

He could never on his own initiative be an aggressive leader, but given strong direction from above he could pass it along to those who, in an organizational sense, were below him. He would be unlikely on his own initiative openly to attack a minority group member, not because of conscience but because of fear that he might get hurt or be disapproved of; but given the safety and influence of a crowd or the backing of someone he regarded as an authority, he could be violently aggressive. However regrettable from the democratic point of view this susceptibility to external control might be, the fact remains that it offers the best basis for preventing his antidemocratic tendencies from expressing themselves in action. The appeal should not be to his sympathy or his conscience, but to his fear and submissiveness. He must be convinced that arrayed against the overt expression of his prejudices are the law, overwhelming numbers of people, numerous conventional authorities and prestige figures. If those who stand for democracy want to win him to their side, they must do more than show him that they have high ideals and realistic plans for social improvement; they must convince him that they also have strength. Such a program, unfortunately, involves an essential paradox: in inducing him to *behave* in accordance with democratic principles, one is likely to strengthen his authoritarianism and, hence, his antidemocratic *potential*. One could not, therefore, undertake so to influence the contemporary behavior of individuals like Mack unless one exerted as much effort toward insuring that antidemocratic leadership did not gain the ascendancy in the future. (p. 816, emphasis in the original)

In short, Sanford believed that autocratic means could be used to maintain democratic behavior on the part of authoritarian personalities. Under these circumstances we would expect to find authoritarians of very different sociopolitical persuasions.

Not as apologia for the Berkeley investigators' formulation of the syndrome but rather as brief exploration of an endemic issue in personality theory and research, we can consider briefly the relationship between personality and ideology. It is this very matter that lies at the heart of the criticism just reviewed.

Personality, broadly conceived, encompasses aspects both of *style* in thought, feelings, and action, and of *content*, meaning what the thoughts, feelings, and actions are denotatively. There is no form without content; no content exists without form. It is impossible to imagine throwing a baseball (the denotative content) without a describable style. The motion is smooth or jerky, sweeping or cramped, overhand or sidearm, and so on. Analogously, a person holds his beliefs in an open or closed fashion, isolated or articulated with other beliefs and attitudes, and with strong or weak motives attached. We might argue that personality deals only with the stylistic component of psychological functioning, those highly generalized dispositions that transcend time and circumstance. Indeed, some define traits or needs in precisely this way. But authoritarianism was not so conceived, and some confusion in thinking about it has resulted.

Recall the definition of the authoritarian syndrome. The authoritarian engages in projection as a defense mechanism, is generally hostile, and thinks in rigid categories—all stylistic factors in as pure a sense as one can achieve. From here on, however, with our list of traits in the syndrome, there is not only content that serves as a vehicle for expression but specific issues relevant beyond form or style for the syndrome. Thus, the authoritarian endorses and adheres to conventional norms and is hypervigilant for transgressors, submits in uncritical ways to his or her moral authorities, believes in mystical determinants of an individual's fate, is concerned with power, strength and toughness, is opposed to sensitive and imaginative expressions of sentiment, and is unable to deal well with sexual matters, especially sexual deviancy. Content is central to each of these, not merely a convenient fiction for the analysis of style. The *what* matters a great deal. Without the content the characteristic of interest would simply not exist. Take, for example, the following: Homosexuality is evil and a sign of weakness; homosexuals should be severely punished for their unnaturalness. These are attitudes with explicit content, not merely the manifestation of a particular style of personality.

So all this is obvious, you say? Well and good, but the concept of authoritarianism and the F Scale are frequently discussed as though they were matters of style only, free of beliefs (Adorno et al. developed it to be free of ideology about specific groups), which they are not. They are laden with beliefs. The conceptualization of authoritarianism included specifically some denotative areas of special concern: It seems it was never intended that the authoritarian be distinguishable in terms of style only, at least by the Berkeley investigators. Nonetheless, the content in the definition is not sociopolitical content; it has no political referent necessarily. The proper view of the original conceptualization is that the authoritarian was about all things rigid and hostile, and in general was projective, and in addition in particular matters of content he or she was sensitive and preoccupied. The problem may be complicated, however, if the beliefs that do characterize the authoritarian as measured by the F Scale are correlated with dispositions toward rightist political ideology, even though the scale does not directly measure such inclinations and the definition of authoritarianism does not encompass them. There is evidence to suggest that this is so (e.g., Barker, 1963).

A related point of discussion concerns the PEC scale. Doesn't the correlation with such a measure of conservative political thinking indicate a one-sided view of the syndrome? Perhaps so, although what the Berkeley investigators singled out was not true conservatism—the endorsement of traditional views and old, tried principles (see Hofstadter, 1967)—but pseudoconservatism, a kind of jingoism and chauvinism putting America first, out of fears and anxieties. All things considered, perhaps our best conclusion at the moment on the kind of authoritarianism depicted by the syndrome and measured by the F Scale is Barker's statement that "the F Scale measures rightist authoritarianism (implicit prefascist tendencies) primarily, general authoritarianism somewhat, and leftist authoritarianism not at all" (1963, p. 72).

Another criticism of the concept is that there is little evidence for the separate existence of the nine variables that define it. Using factor analyses of item responses to the F Scale, investigators have not found clusters of items that parallel the theoretically derived nine variables of authoritarianism (e.g., Kerlinger & Rokeach, 1966). Other studies have shown that some clusters of items do in fact resemble the theoretical variables of the syndrome (e.g., Krug, 1961), so the picture is not clear on this point. One thing that these studies taken as a group indicate is that it is not a good idea to work independently with the separate variables of the F Scale unless one determines that there is sufficient reliability and validity for the subset of items used. In fact, the absence of statistical support for the separate nine variables of the syndrome in item analyses of the Berkeley investigators' work led them to affirm that the definitional separation was essentially heuristic.

To sum up, the F Scale is apparently best thought of as depicting authoritarianism of the political right, although one might quarrel with the sufficiency of the evidence on this point, and demur that the picture is more complicated than that simple summary statement would indicate. That the concept was developed with a focus on the sociopolitical right there can be no question, but the syndrome at the level of personality as opposed to ideology does not have explicit rightist content. Reservations about the separate identity of the nine variables of the syndrome seem well grounded, but this can be regarded as not serious—given that high reliabilities for the scale as a whole are obtained and proper relationships are found between total scale scores and other variables—unless one wishes either to make use of the theoretical subsets of items or empirically confirm the theoretical variables comprising the syndrome. In short, the syndrome may be best considered a loosely cohering set of nonindependent variables, which is about the way it was conceived in theory by the Berkeley investigators.

Criticisms of the methods.

Suppose you were going to have interviewers probe the past and present experiences of some subjects—their ideas, fears, interests, aspirations, relationships with parents and other authority figures, and so on—in depth interviews. Imagine further that some of the subjects were highly prejudiced and the remainder unprejudiced, and the purpose of the investigation was to explore personality differences between the two types. Now, would you inform your interviewers beforehand about the prejudice or lack of it in their interviewees? Would you give the interviewers as much information as you could about each subject they were to interview, with the rationale that the time and efforts of both could then be best used to obtain and clarify desired further information? Or would you send in your interviewers "blind," knowing nothing about the subjects' prejudice or scores on other instruments, with the expectation that comparable information could then be obtained from each interviewee, information uninfluenced by a prior knowledge of the subject? This is obviously a serious issue that the reader can assess according to the advantages and disadvantages of either strategy.

The Berkeley investigators felt their inverviewers should be fully informed about the interviewees they would be dealing with. In this way, they believed, the best information, tailored to each interviewee, would be obtained within the loosely structured interview schedule used by the several interviewers. The serious drawback in this strategy, of course, is that the interviewers may bias their treatment of the interview—unintentionally shading their questions so as to confirm their expectations formed on the basis of the information they already had, probing for more complete information on issues "relevant" to particular interviewees and thus biasing the amount or kind of information available, and so on. All the disadvantages have to do with unintended bias steming from the expectations of the interviewers. The one group studied that represents an exception to the problem of prior knowledge of the subjects on the part of interviewers is the group of psychiatric patients, whose interview material was taken from interview records in their clinic files; these interviews had apparently been done by clinic personnel with no explicit interest in authoritarianism or prejudice as such. The analyses of these interview data by "blind" scorers were consistent with interview data from the potentially biased material of other subjects. From the point of view of rigorous science, there is no question but that the strategy of the interview with prior knowledge is a defect in the methods of the original investigation. Therefore, the interview results do remain suspect insofar as confirmatory evidence for the theory is concerned.

Another violation of scientific canons in the interviews was that "all high-scoring subjects were interviewed by American-born Gentiles" (Adorno et al., 1950, p. 301), a condition apparently not imposed for low-scoring subjects. Thus, we have here another potential source of bias in the data depicting differences between prejudiced and nonprejudiced, authoritarian and nonauthoritarian subjects. The fact that the raters who dealt with the interview material did not know the prejudice scores of the subjects they rated does not gainsay these criticisms of potential interview bias.

But (and there is always a "but" where scholarly and competent investigators have apparently made a mistake) if one is in a stage of exploration rather than confirmation of a theory, it may be better to supply your interviewers with information and leave room for improvisation in the interview, as was done.

New, important, surprising information may then emerge.

We would note, too, that the data from the projective methods, both the questions and the Thematic Apperception Test, are not subject to the same criticism of potential bias.

The recipient of most attention as a methodological defect in the original work is the wording of the items of all the scales in a common direction, so that agreement uniformly indicates prejudice, conservatism, or authoritarianism. The problem with uniform wording is that these scales may measure not only what they are intended to measure but also a general personality set or disposition to agree or acquiesce, especially with broad generalizations of the kind found in the relatively wordy items of these scales. It would have been better if some of the items had reflected nonauthoritarian beliefs, so the authoritarian would have had to disagree with them to express his views. In fact, there were three such items included in the original set for the F Scale, but none of the three survived statistical analyses—they did not discriminate between high and low scorers on either the F or A–S Scales—and so were discarded. The scales, then, were left in the troublesome circumstance of possibly measuring not only the intended ideological or personality variable but also some undetermined amount of another, unwanted characteristic that could not be separated out readily.

If you had the assignment of correcting this shortcoming, how would you proceed? You might identify at least two ways to try it: (1) write some new items stating nonauthoritarian beliefs to put with the old F Scale items to make a balanced scale, perhaps by "reversing" some of the original items; (2) identify that portion of responses to the original items that is due to response bias or acquiescence and remove it from the scores by some statistical means. Both of these methods have been tried; neither is without its problems (see Kirscht & Dillehay, 1967, pp. 13–43). Without becoming involved here in the technicalities of the matter, let us merely note, first, that reversing items from the original scale or writing items that express nonauthoritarian dispositions is most difficult. Try, for example, reversing the following F Scale item: "Obedience and respect for authority are the most important virtues children should learn." Should it be that these are "the least important virtues" childen should learn? Or, should "disobedience and disrespect for authority" be substituted? Perhaps "autonomy and rational questioning of authority" should be used. You can see the problem. The necessity is that the reversal adequately embody a nonauthoritarian belief. "Reversed" items have generally been found to have lower reliabilities than original items, and it is not uncommon to find that respondents agree with both the original and the reversed items, a fact that unfortunately may not be simply a reflection of acquiescence response (Samelson & Yates, 1967).

The second procedure for dealing with acquiescence in the F Scale, mentioned above, requires that we have an adequate independent measure of acquiescence and statistically remove from F Scale scores that portion of them due to unwanted acquiescence. However, the measures of response bias or acquiescence are themselves not entirely satisfactory—they seem not to be measuring a consistent disposition. Unfortunately, the Dogmatism (D) Scale (see chapter 4) and some other measures of authoritarianism devised since 1950 (see Kirscht & Dillehay, 1967, pp. 29–34) are also subject to response bias interpretations or are not satisfactory psychometrically. An exception may be the scale used by Smith (1965), although it has the disadvantage of complex items that may be appropriate for highly educated subjects only.

What can we conclude about research using the F Scale and similar instruments if responses to them may have a component of acquiescence? Some investigators (e.g., Peabody, 1966) have concluded that responses are mostly due to acquiescence; others (e.g., Rorer, 1965) have argued on technical grounds that the case for scores on the F Scale and related scales being largely due to acquiescence is not sound. Rokeach (1967; see also Dillehay, 1969; Rokeach, 1963; Stanley & Martin, 1964) has argued that the problem is not a serious one and that in any case what appears to be acquiescence is in fact an aspect of authoritarianism and that we should be content to leave it there. Another cognate line of reasoning with some research support has produced similar conclusions (e.g., Gage & Chattergee, 1960; Gage, Leavitt, and Stone, 1957; Leavitt, Hax, & Roche, 1955). If we do not agree with Rokeach and others defending positively worded items, then we should recognize the need to be alert to a possible contribution of response bias in relationships between the F Scale and other factors of interest to us in research. To the extent the factor correlated with the F Scale is also subject to response bias we have a potential problem of interpretation. The problem is heightened when the correlated factor is measured by another test or scale. A reasonable view seems to be that "results based on paper-and-pencil tests are ambiguous to the extent that the tests may evoke acquiescence," but "not all the research on authoritarianism involves paper-and-pencil tests, and not all such tests are liable to acquiescence response bias" (Kirscht & Dillehay, 1967, p. 29).

AUTHORITARIANISM AND INTELLIGENCE

One of the repeatedly verified correlates of authoritarianism is intelligence: Higher intelligence is associated with lower authoritarianism. This reliable finding was reported initially by the Berkeley investigators, whose data for some of their samples show F Scale scores correlating between $-.13$ and $-.48$ with various measures of intelligence (e.g., AGCT, Otis Higher Form A) (Adorno et al., 1950, pp. 282–283). These coefficients are probably underestimates of the actual relationships since there was a restricted range of scores in intelligence in the samples on which data are presented. This restricted range would tend to reduce the correlation obtained in the analyses for purely measurement reasons. Christie (1954) concluded from early research on this relationship that the correlation in the general population would be about −.50 or slightly higher if the range of scores on intelligence and authoritarianism were not restricted. Why should such a relationship be obtained? To what can it be attributed, and what are the implications for an understanding of authoritarianism? Let us put aside these questions to consider some other regularly found relationships with authoritarianism, since these involve variables also known to be related to intelligence, namely education and socioeconomic status, and then consider these several factors together with authoritarianism.

AUTHORITARIANISM, EDUCATION, AND SOCIOECONOMIC STATUS

The same discussion in *The Authoritarian Personality* that deals with intelligence and authoritarianism treats education as a correlate of the syndrome. Although the data presented there are based on only a few samples and deal with the E Scale rather than the F Scale, the pattern is clear: More education tends to be associated with lower scores on ethnocentrism. Here again we should keep in mind that the samples obtained by the Berkeley investigators were special in that the subjects tended to be more educated than the general population and scored higher on intelligence. However, subsequent research has indicated that the relationship between education and authoritarianism is consistently negative.

Education is, of course, one of the indices of socioeconomic status or social position, along with occupational status, and, sometimes, either income or place of residence (see Bendix and Lipset, 1953; Brown, 1965; Hollingshead and Redlich, 1958). It should not be surprising, therefore, that socioeconomic status generally is associated negatively with authoritarianism, whether one uses only one or several of these indices of social status (e.g., MacKinnon and Centers, 1956; McDill, 1961; Srole, 1956).

There is a positive but far from perfect relationship between intelligence and socioeconomic status in the United States, a fact that itself is subject to a variety of interpretations. If we believe, however, that the two variables are partially independent, as the data would suggest, we may ask what happens to the relationship between either one and authoritarianism if we remove the effect of the other. For example, how much of a relationship is left between intelligence and scores on the F Scale if we remove the effect of either education or of socioeconomic status generally? On examining the literature Christie (1954) estimated that the remaining relationship would be of the order of −.20, indicating that a substantial amount of the relationship with intelligence is accounted for by educational experience or perhaps sophistication gained through education, whether formal or informal.

AUTHORITARIANISM, BREADTH OF PERSPECTIVE, AND A SOCIAL PSYCHOLOGICAL MODEL

Kelman and Barclay (1963) have argued that the F Scale is essentially a measure of a person's breadth of perspective, that it is really not a measure of authoritarianism as such.

A low scorer is a person whose psychological universe is relatively wide. He sees events in a variety of contexts. He is aware of the existence of a range of customs, values, and approaches to life. He expects differences between people and is tolerant of them. A higher scorer, by contrast, is a person who moves in very narrow circles. He sees events only in the context of his own limited frame of reference. He does not recognize the existence of a range of values and approaches, and is intolerant of differences. (p. 608).

According to Kelman and Barclay, breadth of perspective is to be understood in terms of two major etiological contributors: psychological capacity and social opportunity. The former includes authoritarianism as defined theoretically by the Berkeley investigators, that is, conventionalism, authoritarian submission, authoritarian aggression, and so on. In Kelman and Barclay's own study they use a measure of intolerance of ambiguity as a factor of authoritarianism to relate to scores on the F Scale. They mention intelligence as another aspect of psychological capacity, but they do not develop this point.

Social opportunity refers to the richness available in a person's social environment. If a person's environment is bland and homogeneous, if he is not exposed to varieties of belief and behavior, then he should have little appreciation of the fact that there may be alternative points of view about social, economic, political, and other issues, and he is likely to exhibit a rather narrow and limited personal perspective. The culprit here is social opportunity. But if there has been broad exposure to a heterogeneous environment, opportunity to see that reality is, after all, largely social reality, that is, defined by people for people, and that social reality may look different at different times and be compatible with opposing points of view, then the person's perspective is likely to be broader, he should expect differences, be less condemning of others who do differ, and so on. In our society, those who have less opportunity, relatively speaking, are those of lower socioeconomic status, the less educated, blacks, and women. Although less than totally in agreement, data from a variety of investigations generally support the assertion that F Scale scores are higher for these groups than for appropriate comparison groups (see Christie & Cook, 1958, p. 176; Kelman & Barclay, 1963; Kirscht & Dillehay, 1967, pp. 37–41). It is not true, however, that among the 1518 subjects responding to the F Scale in the Berkeley investigations women earned higher scores than men. On only one of the 30 items was the combined mean higher for women. An inspection of the means for roughly comparable groups of men and women in the sample also shows that the mean for women is not consistently higher.

The model proposed by Kelman and Barclay (1963) can be schematized as in Figure 3–1.

We can follow the lead of Kelman and Barclay in attempting to incorporate known relationships with the F Scale, and arrive at a different formulation that both clarifies the etiology of authoritarianism and yet avoids the creation of an additional construct such as breadth of perspective. This alternative formulation is a dual-factor social psychological model that makes use of psychological capacity and social opportunity as codeterminants of authoritarianism. An element that is added to psychological capacity in this new model may be referred to as anxiety or affective state. In addition, we should eliminate the variable of sex from the social opportunity factor since available data overall will not support the notion of a consistent difference between men and women in authoritarianism.

This new model is schematically represented in Figure 3–2. The solid lines indicate that psychological capacity and social opportunity are the major determinants of authoritarianism; the broken lines show the secondary relationships between psychological capacity and social opportunity, and also indicate that authoritarianism itself once developed in the personality has repercussions on psychological functioning (intelligence and affective state) and the ability to make use of one's social opportunities for personal growth (such as education).

How can we decide which model is more appropriate? By the terms of Kelman and Barclay's model we should be able to extract the contribution of authoritarianism to F Scale scores and still have left the influence of intelligence and of the social opportunity factors. By the alternate model, if authoritarianism were extracted from the F Scale scores, there would be nothing left. To do either, of course, would require an independent measure of authoritarianism, one that assessed conventionalism, superstititon and stereotypy, power and toughness, and the other variables of the syndrome. There are other measures of authoritarianism but all are, in some way, directly or indirectly, validated against the F Scale, so they will not do for our purposes. Assembling a number of independent assessment procedures for the syndrome of authoritarianism, at least one measure for each variable in the defining set, would be another possible route.

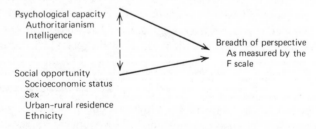

Figure 3–1.   The Kelman–Barclay model of breadth of perspective.

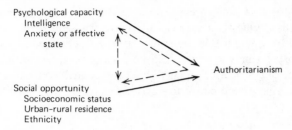

Psychological capacity
Intelligence
Anxiety or affective
state

Authoritarianism

Social opportunity
Socioeconomic status
Urban-rural residence
Ethnicity

Figure 3-2.   The social psychological model of authoritarianism.

For the moment, then, the issue is debatable, and the terms of the debate are beyond the scope of this work. My preference is, of course, for the alternative model, which accepts the conceptual and operational definitions of authoritarianism provided by Adorno et al. but looks at the etiology differently. In a rigorous, fuller development, this model would also incorporate the specific normative influences of social groups on authoritarian functioning.

Concerning the question about the relationship between intelligence and authoritarianism, it may be that some of the defining characteristics of authoritarianism directly imply a lesser intellectual capacity. For example, the disposition to think in narrow categories that are rigid and fixed may indicate a relative inability to assimilate information from the environment and, therefore, a reduced capacity to profit from experience, which is one way of considering intelligence. Levinson considers this and other possibilities (Adorno et al., 1950, Chapter 8), including the "methodological" factor of lesser discernment on the part of those with less intelligence, leading them to agree more with the items of the E or F Scale.

Thus, there was the sketch of an argument from the very beginning that lesser intelligence contributes to the development of authoritarian dispositions. The person of limited intellectual capacity may be forced to categorize in simple ways, ways that do not map very well into the actual complexities of his surroundings. We then might expect to find stereotyping, rigidity, superstition, and a tendency to deal with the relatively simple and more obvious trappings of office as the basis for allegiance, rather than the less easily discernible personal merit. Notice that this argument is wholly in terms of the capacity of the individual to process complex features of an environment.

The argument can be extended to the probable *emotional* consequences of limited intellectual ability in a complex environment, for it is likely that the maintenance of relatively nonveridical cognitive schemata would be an energy-absorbing process with attendant frustration and its consequences. So an emotional element enters that could allow the ingredient of *threat* to be added to the already established cognitive and perceptual organization, with the possibility of intensified rigidity, projection, and the like. This theoretical analysis is, of course, not the only way to explain the relationship between intelligence and authoritarianism. One might make a case for the intrusion of emotion on intellect owing to early experience in the family, which Adorno and his colleagues described in psychoanalytic terms. But the alternative argument introduced here has the virtue of considering an intellectual component to be a determinant in its own right, having a contribution to authoritarian functioning apart from affective influences.

AUTHORITARIANISM AND ATTITUDES

To speak of prejudice is to deal with attitudes of a kind. Prejudice is often regarded as not only prejudgment or bias but a disposition adverse to some individual or group; in the extreme it may be animosity or bald hostility. The concept of authoritarianism was nurtured and developed in an attempt to understand such attitudes specifically, and this personality account of prejudice has since been incorporated into general theories of the nature and development of attitudes, prejudiced ones as well as other sorts.

In an elaborate and extensive study of personality and opinions, Smith et al. (1956) identified externalization as a major source of attitudes. Externalization was defined as the outward projection of unresolved internal conflict, conflict largely unconscious (at least unrecognized by the person). This process fosters attitudes when some object or external event has a literal or metaphorical correspondence to an unresolved internal conflict, with the consequence that one's attitude toward the object or event is determined more by the internal state than by the external facts. The internal state and its affect are externalized, that is, projected onto the object or event in some significant way. Mack's attitudes toward powerful authority figures, as analyzed by Sanford in *The Authoritarian Personality* illustrate the process: These authorities were highly regarded because of Mack's failure to resolve his ambivalence toward his father, ambivalence that was unsatisfactorily dealt with in Mack's early relationship with him, producing an absence of appropriate identification with the father.

Smith and his colleagues, spending some 15 two-hour sessions with each subject, compiled extensive data on the personalities of 10 men and their attitudes toward Russia through the use of intensive interviews of several types, projective tests, standardized intelligence tests, interest tests, and other procedures. Twenty-eight investigators participated in the investigation conducted at the Harvard Psychological Clinic as one of a series of projects dealing with the personalities of normal subjects. The fullness and richness of the data can only be appreciated in the original source, but for our purposes we can note that externalization appeared in some form in each of the 10 subjects. In one subject externalization seemed to involve constructive traits or striving—rational mastery, independent self-sufficiency, and productivity—producing a positive tenor in his attitudes toward Russia: faith in the system of law, economic decentralization, Russian economic upbuilding. But the remainder of the subjects were seen as in some degree possessing traits, needs, and tensions characteristic of the authoritarian: dependence, fear, guilt, repressed aggression, inferiority feelings, and the like. Not that these men *were* authoritarians for the most part, but rather there was a relationship between such characteristics and views of Russia. In short, there was at Harvard the same kind of functional relationship between underlying personality structure and content and views of Russia that Adorno and his coworkers discovered at Berkeley. One important difference between the findings in the Harvard study and those in the Berkeley investigation is that the suppressed or repressed aspects of the personalities of the 10 subjects in the Smith et al. investigation led at times to ideology about Russia that was much more constructive in tone than was the ethnocentrism resulting from the repression, projection, and so on of the Berkeley subjects.

Daniel Katz and his colleagues (e.g., Katz, 1960; Katz, McClintock, & Sarnoff, 1957; Katz & Stotland, 1959) identified ego defensiveness as one major basis of attitude formation and a significant obstacle to attitude change. They used items from the F Scale to measure selected aspects of personality functioning in order to investigate ego defensiveness in relation to attitude change. Katz and his colleagues selected items measuring projectivity, authoritarian aggression, and destructiveness and cynicism to measure ego defensiveness, and they predicted that those high in defensiveness would not accept communications that tried to change prejudice by supplying information about the attitude object. To change prejudice in defensive individuals Katz felt one would have to provide some insight into the dynamics of prejudice, which meant interpreting prejudice as rooted in internal conflict. Their interpretation consisted of telling subjects about defensive personality functioning, chiefly about the working of defense mechanisms. Katz and his coworkers did not feel that the most defensive individuals would be receptive to this intervention, so their expectation was that those of moderate defensiveness would show most attitude change: High defensiveness indicates too great a resistance to a dynamic interpretation, while interpretation would not be relevant to the reasons for prejudice in those low in defensiveness. The results of their research generally support their predictions: Subjects of moderate defensiveness showed most attitude change in response to dynamic interpretations.

What are the effects of providing information about the attitude object *contrary* to defensively held attitudes? An experiment by Wagman (1955), which was one of the series in the Katz group, demonstrated that counterattitudinal information had a *boomerang* effect in authoritarian people, that is, they became *more* prejudiced. This boomerang presumably occurred because of the threat the information posed to the adjustive function served by the prejudiced views. On the other hand, Wagman's experiment also demonstrated that authoritative suggestion can be effective in producing either greater prejudice or less, depending upon the direction of influence in the suggestion. (Remember Sanford's comments about ways to change Mack's antidemocratic attitudes by use of autocratic influence.) Authoritative suggestion also proved somewhat effective in changing attitudes of less authoritarian subjects but only toward reduced prejudice. In this research authoritative suggestion consisted of telling the subjects how business administrators and military officers viewed the roles of blacks as supervisors or coworkers in industrial and military settings. The views of these authorities were attributed to findings by a research organization, which of course was fictitious.

The prefascist authoritarian should be especially responsive to conspiracy theories of social, political, and economic events. The essence of conspiracy theories is that they forecast imminent doom for cherished values and institutions, with the impending disaster attributed to a carefully conceived plan of action surreptitiously controlled and conditioned by a diabolical enemy. The major conspiracy theory afoot during the early 1950s in this country was the belief in an insidious and pernicious intrusion of communists into all forms of American political and social life. Hofstader (1967) called the advocacy of this type of belief the paranoid style largely because of its use of fear arousal and its affinity for anxieties that people may feel, especially about important political and social issues that are at the same time psychologically distant, ambiguous, and controversial (e.g., communism, treason, national security). Central to clinical paranoia are distrust, suspicion of others, and a sense of persecution. Hofstader is not using the term in an attempt to perform clinical diagnosis; he means rather to convey the essence of a style of expression and perception that is prevalent on the American scene and has been observed in various degrees around different issues for a number of years. In his words:

> In the paranoid style . . . the feeling of persecution is central, and it is indeed systematized in grandiose theories of conspiracy. But there is a vital difference between the paranoid spokesman in politics and the clinical paranoiac: although they both tend to be overheated, oversuspicious, overaggressive, grandiose and apocalyptic in expression, the clinical paranoid sees the hostile and conspiratorial world in which he feels himself to be living as directed specifically *against him*; whereas the spokesman of the paranoid style finds it directed against a nation, a culture, a way of life whose fate affects not himself alone but millions of others. Insofar as he does not usually see himself singled out as the individual victim of a personal conspiracy, he is somewhat more rational and much more disinterested. His sense that his political passions are unselfish and patriotic, in fact, goes far to intensify his feeling of righteousness and his moral indignation. (p. 4, emphasis in original)

Hofstadter's use of the paranoid style as essentially a nonclinical entity is reminiscent of Fromm's use of the concept of authoritarianism; for Fromm the classification "sadomasochistic" represents the clinical counterpart of authoritarianism.

The paranoid style has for centuries been used by spokesmen with respect to a vast array of issues: anti-Masonry, anti-Catholicism, Jeffersonian democracy, public education, sex education, silver versus gold as a monetary standard, communism, and fluoridation, to mention some. Opponents of fluoridation have argued that it is a communist plot designed to poison the body and weaken the will by the cumulative effects of a poison, one that in fact is used in commercial rat poison. In addition, they have argued that it is an attempt by powerful figures to force a form of medication on populations of people against their will and that it represents a step in the direction of totalitarian control. Opponents of fluoridation raise the ominous possibility of an accident in the process of adding fluoride to the drinking water supply: Great numbers of people could die by a single, mechanical mishap. Furthermore, they argue, fluoridation represents yet another small but significant step in the adulteration of food and water, a process that is destroying by degrees the integrity of our bodies for the economic gain of a few powerful, selfish interests. So goes the conspiracy argument on the issue of fluoridation. It was hotly debated in a number of communities in the 1950s; social scientists studied it as a controversial issue and public health matter.

Although the paranoid style may carry the rind of truth for many people, especially during troubled times of social, political, and economic upheaval, it should be especially effective with the authoritarian personality. It engages both the style inherent in the syndrome (anxieties, fears, internal conflicts, menacing outgroups, moral condemnation) and the content of totalitarian or antidemocratic beliefs (strong external authority is imperative to keep things in order, human beings are both weak-willed and disposed to injure others). And the paranoid style seems to be especially characteristic of pseudoconservative ideology. The Berkeley investigators felt they were measuring pseudoconservatism with the PEC scale; Hofstadter picks up this focus on pseudoconservatism and underscores it, using as illustration the Goldwater politics of the early 1960s (see especially Chapter 4 of Hofstadter).

Given that the paranoid style seems over the years to be especially associated with right-wing causes on the American scene, we can still speculate that susceptibility to the appeals of this style increases with the general stress of bad political, social, and economic times. When a nation is wracked by the internal divisions of social conflict brought on by issues such as the long and unfortunate United States involvement in Southeast Asia, people may become more responsive to this style and may indeed seem more authoritarian in their response to pressing problems. Awakened sensitivities make it possible for conspiratorial themes to leave their mark. Such themes were developed by Spiro Agnew during the Nixon administration against youth activists and opponents of the war generally. Another diabolical enemy was the press; here Agnew's major themes were the vendetta of the press against Nixon and the press' liberal bias. In short, these were conspiracies, and Agnew invented the term *radlib* to symbolically marry elements of the enemy.

That such appeals in times of national strife promote more than the change of ideas is shown in a study by Sales (1972), who examined rates of conversion to authoritarian and nonauthoritarian churches during economic good times and bad times in the United States. He studied the period 1920 to 1939 since it contains a period of economic prosperity (1920–1929) and one of depression (1930–1939). He found that conversion to authoritarian churches (the Southern Baptist Convention, the Church of Jesus Christ of Latter-Day Saints, the Seventh-day Adventist Church, and the Roman Catholic Church) increased during economic bad times and decreased during better periods. For the nonauthoritarian churches (the Presbyterian Church in the United States of America, the Congregational Christian Church, the Northern Baptist Convention, and the Protestant Episcopal Church) the findings were just the opposite: Conversion rates for these churches decreased during bad times and increased during good times. The implication is that authoritarian appeals of certain churches were more successful during periods of elevated anxiety with everyone, not just with the especially susceptible authoritarians. Sales' classification of churches as authoritarian or nonauthoritarian, it might be added, seems to be based on a careful consideration of the content and style of belief in the different denominations. The denominations do differ in terms of such matters as submission to authority, condemnation versus toleration of outgroups, and emphasis on sin and transgression (Sales, 1972, p. 422).

In considering the influence of authoritarianism on attitude formation and change it is well to keep in mind that we are not making the argument that authoritarianism is necessarily the major determinant of attitudes and attitude change. It is one such determinant. Smith and his coworkers (1956), Katz (e.g., 1960), and others have presented typologies of the functional relationship between personality and attitudes, with attention to defensive personality functioning of the sort embodied in authoritarianism. Smith et al. (1956) noted in the Berkeley investigations with respect to an understanding of ethnocentrism: "The California account of ethnocentrism is incomplete without reference to cultural and social determinants" (p. 23). We should say the same for understanding attitude formation and change in general.

AUTHORITARIANISM AND ACTION

Psychologists interested in personality typically endorse the proposition that traits have an effect upon action or behavior. We expect authoritarians, therefore, to act differently from nonauthoritarians. We further expect the differences to have psychological and social relevance. Adorno and his coworkers were clear on these points. For example, avowing that "personality is a more or less enduring organization of forces within the individual" and that "personality lies *behind* behavior and *within* the individual," they affirm that "these persisting forces of personality help to determine response in various situations, and it is thus largely to them that consistency of behavior—whether verbal or physical——is attributable" (p. 5, emphases in the original). This view of the determination of behavior by individual dispositions is widely shared though not unchallenged. If the syndrome of authoritarianism did not influence behavior, it would hold little fascination.

Disclaimers on the role of personality as a determinant of behavior are in order on at least two counts, and since these have undoubtedly occurred to the reader, they had best be recognized and put aright. First, it has long been recognized that there are profound and persistent situational determinants of behavior. For example, the social status of a transgressor crossing the street against a red light apparently determines the willingness of another pedestrian to engage in the same behavior (Lefkowitz, Blake, and Mouton, 1955). The level of shock administered by another person to someone else significantly influences the willingness of a subject to administer electric shock to an individual making errors in a learning task (Larsen, Coleman, Forbes, and Johnson, 1972). However, the recognition of significant situational influence on behavior does not indicate that personality determinants of action are to be discounted; rather, it is simply to recognize that behavior is multiply determined. The preference of the Berkeley investigators was to examine the role of personality determinants in social behavior, adhering to the position that personality structure makes for consistency in behavior across different sorts of situations. We should note, too, that individual predispositions mediate the influence of situational factors (e.g., Allport, 1968), which properly brings the study of personality into focus even for the advocate of the determination of action by situational factors. Second, as Adorno and his coworkers explicitly recognized, personality is largely the product of experience, of the learning that has taken place over a person's lifetime, which is to say the effects of many situations on the evolving personality structure. These disclaimers leave us, then, still dealing with the person—the personality content and structure—in a given situation that calls for action of some kind, posing the legitimate and natural question of the relationship between personality and behavior.

Interaction with another person: the authoritarian in the dyad.

An extremely useful research paradigm for studying interpersonal behavior is the experimental game, in which a subject is required to make choices and take action vis-à-vis another person with consequences for both of them. One of the most widely used experimental games is called the "Prisoner's Dilemma" (PD). For purposes of illustration let's consider a PD game in which persons *A* and *B* are the players. They are told that each must pick independently one of two responses, say either red (not confess) or blue (confess), and that their individual outcomes will be determined by the joint selection. The way their outcomes will be determined is shown by the matrix of Table 3–2, about which both *A* and *B* are fully instructed before they make their choices. The first entry in each cell of the matrix is the outcome for *A;* the second entry in the cell indicates *B*'s outcome.

Why such an experimental game should be labeled PD can be understood if one considers the dilemma of a person (e.g., person *A*) arrested for and being questioned about a crime allegedly committed by him and a confederate (e.g., person *B*), who is also in custody and being questioned in another room. The prisoner is told that he can help his situation by confessing guilt for both, since he will then be given a lighter sentence for turning state's evidence (assuming *B* does not confess). The dilemma that each prisoner faces is this: If he does not confess, he will get off lightly *if* his partner also does not confess. But if the partner does confess, then it is to the advantage of the first prisoner also to confess. Failure to confess when your partner has confessed produces the worst possible outcome for one's self. When the partner is trustworthy (he doesn't confess) and one is trusting (one doesn't confess either), the best joint outcome is achieved. In a true PD game players choose without knowledge of their partner's selection, and there is only one trial. Variants on this paradigm include knowledge of the other's selection before acting and play over a number of trials.

How would you expect authoritarians and nonauthoritarians to behave in the PD game? Before reading on, consider the characteristics that define individuals high and low in authoritarianism, and recognize that if *A* picks red in the matrix given above, he must count on *B* to pick red also to realize a positive outcome, for if *B* picks blue, *A* is sentenced to 20 years while *B* is sentenced to 1 year. Thus, a reponse of red by *A* is a trusting reponse, and *B* displays trustworthiness

Table 3–2.   Example of a Matrix for a Prisoner's Dilemma Game

		Person *B*	
		Red (not confess)	Blue (confess)
Person *A*	Red (not confess)	2 years, 2 years	20 years, 1 year
	Blue (confess)	1 year, 20 years	8 years, 8 years

if he also picks red. For purposes of our discussion, we may also regard the red response by B as a cooperative play and the blue response again by B as a competitive play.

Several experiments have been done examining the relationship between authoritarianism (or close variants) and play in the PD situation. In general, authoritarians tend to give competitive responses and to be untrusting and untrustworthy. An early study by Deutsch (1960) provides illustrative findings. In Deutsch's experiment the subject made his response, which was communicated to the "other player" before the latter responded. (In fact, there was no "other player" but the real subject did not know this.) The procedure was then reversed, with the real subject told what the "other player" had picked before he made his own choice. On the second trial real subjects were always confronted with a trusting (i.e. cooperative) response by the "other player." Low Authoritarians tended to make trusting choices in the first situation. In addition, those subjects with lower scores on authoritarianism were more trustworthy—they responded to trusting choices made by the "other player" by making trustworthy choices themselves. Related research partially supporting Deutsch's finding is reported by Wrightsman (1966). In another experiment Slack and Cook (1973) have shown that when a high authoritarian interacts with a low authoritarian in a PD-like game situation, the pair appears to experience more conflict and gain fewer rewards than when there are combinations of two high authoritarians or two low authoritarians. In Slack and Cook's experiment subjects not only played over many trials, but they had opportunities to change the values in the matrix so as to improve individual and joint gains.

Kelley and Stahelski (1970) have developed the argument that authoritarians exhibit behavior producing responses from others that tend to confirm the authoritarian's cognitions about people and justify his own uncooperative behavior. Furthermore, the data suggest that the authoritarian is unaware of the effect he has on others, whereas others are cognizant of their own altered actions and the reasons for them.

Research shows that if individuals are in a situation in which they can make either a cooperative response to a partner or a competitive one, two fairly distinct types emerge: those who prefer the competitive response and those who favor cooperation. Furthermore, a competitor playing opposite a cooperator over a number of trials persists in responding competitively rather than changing to the cooperative response, whereas a cooperator vis-à-vis a competitor is likely to change to the competitive response. Most interesting of all, the competitor is unaware of his influence in changing his opponent's play, but the cooperator is well aware that the competitive play of his opponent has led him to change from his preferred cooperative response to a competitive response. Kelley and Stahelski refer to this change in the behavior of the cooperator as behavioral assimilation: The behavior of the cooperator becomes like (is assimilated to) that of the competitor. So the person with the competitive disposition experiences others very differently from the way the person with the cooperative orientation does, and thus, Kelley and Stahelski argue, each has developed different expectations about the other's behavior. The competitor will tend to see all others as competitive, for if they are not that way at the outset they soon become so. The competitor does not know that he has brought this about; he simply thinks that people are competitive. The cooperator, by contrast, expects people to be varied in their inclination to cooperate and compete. He sees both kinds in his experience, even if he does assimilate his own behavior to that of the competitors.

Kelley and Stahelski describe this theoretical argument and the supporting data in the form of a triangle hypothesis, presented in Figure 3–3. When one's own orientation is highly cooperative, expectations about others' behavior range from highly cooperative to highly competitive; the more competitive one's own orientation, the more one expects others to be competitive.

The triangle hypothesis posits a relationship linking one's own behavioral disposition (cooperative or competitive) with expectations for the other's behavior (as cooperative or competitive). We know from previous research that the authoritarian tends to give competitive responses. He will thus expect that others will be competitive rather than cooperative, and he will likely be unaware of the part he plays in producing competitive behavior by others.

Can we take the above argument and generalize it to expectations by authoritarians concerning the authoritarian-like beliefs held by others, and not merely to expectations of how cooperative or competitive others will be? That is, will authoritarians tend to see others as generally authoritarian also, while nonauthoritarians will attribute a range of dispositions to others? There is some research to suggest that those who score high on the F Scale are likely to perceive others as scoring high also, whereas those who are less authoritarian are likely to see some others as high and some as low (see Kelley & Stahelski, 1970, pp. 83–85). This pattern of social perception fits the triangle hypothesis. It is interesting to note that these findings concerning the attribution of authoritarianism as a function of the degree of authoriarianism in the perceiver come out of research

Expectations as to Others' Orientation

	Cooperative				Competitive
Cooperative	X	X	X	X	X
Own					
Orientation		X	X	X	X
			X̲	X	X
				X	X
Competitive					X

Figure 3–3.   The triangle hypothesis. (From Kelley & Stahelski, 1970, p. 77. Copyright 1970 by the American Psychological Association. Reprinted by permission.)

that was aimed at the proposition that those low in authoritarianism show greater accuracy in perception of others than those high in authoritarianism. Although differential accuracy was not found, support for the triangle hypothesis was.

Data give way to argument on the question of the actual behavior of authoritarians in shaping the behavior of others on issues that correspond to the definition of the syndrome. That is, there is no evidence that authoritarians by their behavior force others who are not authoritarian to behave as though they were, to assimilate their behavior to that of the authoritarian. Nor are there data to indicate that nonauthoritarian individuals behave in a nonauthoritarian fashion with others like them on this characteristic. Trustworthiness, cooperation, and competition are not part of the authoritarian syndrome proper; trust in others, however, may be tied to destructiveness and cynicism. One might argue that the expression of beliefs (e.g., toward ethnic groups, about sexual deviancy, on the utility of considering motives behind behavior) should be less variable and less situationally determined than cooperative or competitive behavior with others, but that argument would certainly have adherents on the other side. Kelley and Stahelski's theory may be relevant for authoritarian and nonauthoritarian behavior. Authoritarians perceive others as authoritarian because others are in fact constrained to behave that way with an authoritarian, whereas nonauthoritarians, expecting some to be authoritarian in their behavior and some not, may behave in a nonauthoritarian manner until prompted or forced to do otherwise. Speculating on this matter, we might predict that the behavioral assimilation the authoritarian produces in the nonauthoritarian is more likely to be stylistic than substantive. For example, the nonauthoritarian may become more rigid in his thinking, more inclined to project defensively, and more intolerant, but he may not become more ethnocentric, more punitive toward sexual deviants, and more preoccupied with power and toughness.

Authoritarianism and harming another person.

The relationship between authoritarianism and action has been explored through the differential willingness of those high and low in this characteristic to deliver a punishing shock to another person. Milgram's laboratory demonstrations have shown that subjects will obey an authority even when such obedience means harming another person against his will (e.g., 1963, 1965). Confronted with these data we are tempted to ask whether personality factors might be important variables in such response to authority. Authoritarians would seem especially responsive to such influence.

Elms and Milgram (1966) tested the relationship between personality and obedience to authority. They used various assessment procedures—a modified form of the MMPI, a highly structured interview dealing with childhood experiences and attitudes, rating scales to assess reactions to such concepts as conscience, leader, and justice, a set of 10 hypothetical situations related to obedience, punishment, and cruel behavior, and an adaptation of the F Scale to assess authoritarianism. They compared 20 male subjects who had been obedient to authority and 20 who had been defiant. The most interesting finding for our purposes concerns authoritarianism. The obedient subjects were significantly more authoritarian; when education was held constant statistically, obedient subjects were still marginally more authoritarian than defiant subjects. Although it is an intriguing finding, some caution is in order in its interpretation because both groups were assessed for personality dispositions after they had demonstrated either obedience or defiance, and the behavior itself might conceivably have produced significant changes in personality. Elms and Milgram do not consider this possibility; their interpretation is that authoritarianism is the antecedent to obedience. But the alternative explanation is possible, and no less important, although for quite different psychological and social reasons.

That there is a difference between those high and those low in authoritarianism in willingness to deliver electric shocks to another person *without* the element of pressure from an authority was demonstrated by Epstein (1966). In an experiment subjects thought was exploring the role of punishment in learning, subjects observed another subject (the model—really an accomplice of the experimenter) elect to administer high levels of shock whenever a third subject (also an accomplice and always black) made an error in learning. The real subjects were then placed in a position to elect one of five shock levels which ranged from "very low" to "very high." The more authoritarian subjects administered significantly higher levels of electric shock. Remember that all subjects were able to pick the level of shock in the absence of pressure from authority or peer; all subjects had simply witnessed another person administer high intensities of shock in the same situation. Epstein also found that other things being equal, when the model was white he was more frequently imitated by the high authoritarians than by the low authoritarians. A third result was that the less authoritarian subjects were significantly more willing to administer high intensities of shock when the model was black. Those high in authoritarianism were apparently willing to deliver high levels of shock regardless of the skin color of the model. Epstein had in fact predicted that "high authoritarians will show less differentiation among ethnic models relative to nonauthoritarian subjects" (Epstein, 1966, p. 575), apparently because of the authoritarian's assumed generalized hostility, which would override his ethnocentric sensitivities. The authoritarian will emulate a white or a black model if doing so means aggressing against another (black) person.

AUTHORITARIANISM AND SOCIAL GROUPS

Yet another kind of "behavior" associated with authoritarianism is group membership. The behavior of interest here is manifold, at least potentially, including the act of affiliation with the group and the expression of the norms of the group explicitly through what one does and says or implicitly through public avowal of membership status. Notice, too, that a relationship between authoritarianism and group membership need not imply that authoritarians are *attracted* to the group, since a relationship could come about because of within-group socialization, (e.g., Seaman, Michel, & Dillehay, 1971), which simply means that, once in the group, members may *become* more authoritarian. Either way—through selective attraction to the group by authoritarians or the socialization of the group members to authoritarian characteristics—we might expect to observe a relationship between authoritarianism and membership in certain groups.

There is considerable variation in the relationship between an individual and a group, organization, or institution. Some membership groups are virtually total institutions for participants (e.g., prisons) whereas others involve little or no face-to-face "group" activity (e.g., political parties, professional societies). In addition, membership is sometimes by choice and sometimes not. Also, the day-by-day salience of the groups might be both an important determinant of the influence of the norms of the group on individual personality and behavior and critical to the way this influence will come about (e.g., imposition of control by the group over individual behavior versus voluntary acceptance by choice of the standards of the group). Group membership should also be distinguished from group identification, or use of the group as a reference group. A reference group, which may or may not be a membership group for an individual, typically serves one or both of two major functions: (1) normative, in which the group through its sanctioning power controls the actions of individuals for whom it serves as a relevant body, and (2) comparative, that is, group standards are used by individuals as a point of reference for perception, evaluation, beliefs, and behavior (see, for example, Kelley, 1952). Still other important distinctions could be cited.

In thinking about authoritarianism and affiliation with groups there are several questions that come to mind. Are authoritarians attracted to certain kinds of groups, namely groups with conservative ideologies and inflexible standards for the expression of those ideologies? We might expect so, because persons high on the F Scale are conservative and inflexible. Another question is what effects for the individual are there from participation in a group with authoritarian-like ideology and/or intolerance for deviation from dominant group themes? That is, does membership in such groups maintain or increase authoritarianism among its participants?

An important field experiment brings information to bear on just these questions. Siegel and Siegel (1957) seized upon an opportunity at Stanford University to examine reference group and membership group influences on antidemocratic personality characteristics. At the time of the experiment, entering freshman women were randomly assigned to a living group, and the living groups differed in their authoritarian character (i.e., their norms). Since assignment to the groups was random, one could see at the end of the first year whether living in the authoritarian groups made women more that way—a straightfoward question about membership effects. But Siegel and Siegel did more: They also asked the entering freshman women what groups they *wanted* to live in, thus gaining an expression of preference that serves as an index of each woman's reference group. This question was asked both at the beginning of the experiment and after the students had lived for a year in the groups to which they had been assigned.

At the time and place of the experiment the more authoritarian living groups were also the high status groups among freshman women, so that initially the authoritarian groups were the reference groups for all the subjects of the study. Of course, some of the subjects were assigned (by chance) to live in one of these groups for the freshman year, whereas other women were assigned to live in the nonpreferred, less authoritarian living groups.

To summarize, then, at the beginning of the year all the freshmen women preferred the high status, more authoritarian groups, and some were assigned to live in them (so the reference group and membership group for these latter women were the same). Other freshmen were assigned to the lower status groups (so their membership group was less authoritarian but their reference group was authoritarian). At the end of the year the membership groups were still the same, of course, but the reference groups of the subjects varied, since some of the women changed the group of their preference: Some subjects had at the end of the year both high authoritarian membership and reference groups, some subjects had membership groups low in authoritarianism but reference groups high in authoritarianism, and some had low authoritarian membership and reference groups. With respect to these three sets of subjects, what was the change in authoritarianism over the year? The investigators expected that the major influence on authoritarian characteristics would be the *reference* groups of their subjects; it might be predicted that those with the lower status living groups as reference groups *at the end of the year* would show a significant reduction in authoritarianism. This did happen: Women who preferred the lower status groups at the end of the year were less authoritarian than those who still preferred the higher status living groups. The authoritarianism scores also showed, however, that women who *lived* in the lower status groups were significantly less authoritarian, regardless of their reference group at the end of the year, than students who had lived in the more authoritarian groups. The membership group also influenced authoritarianism in the direction of its norms.

The Berkeley investigators had an interest in group membership and authoritarianism. Adorno and his colleagues specifically studied prison inmates and psychiatric clinic patients (Adorno, et al., 1950, the chapters by Morrow and Levinson, respectively). Prisoners produced the highest mean score on the F Scale of the numerous groups studied by the Berkeley investigators. Interest in this special group of subjects did not stem from a concern with the effects of the prison experience on authoritarianism or, obviously, from an interest in selective voluntary affiliation and its implications for the attitudes and values of the subjects. Rather, the psychoanalytic orientation of the investigators and the findings in other groups prompted special attention to prisoners. Morrow puts it this way: "If, as the foregoing chapters have indicated, failure in superego integration, inability to establish emotional relationships with others, and overcompensatory reactions to weakness and passivity are among the important sources of potentially fascist trends within the personality, should we not expect that a group of prison inmates would score particularly high on our scales?" (Adorno et al., 1950, p. 817). The prisoners' scores met these expectations. Nonetheless, the major thrust of the Adorno study of prisoners was an assessment of the differences between high and low scorers within the group, with a view toward understanding the personality dynamics of prefascist versus relatively democratic prisoners. In his conclusions Morrow notes that the degree of violence in the crimes committed by high and low scorers is not appreciably different; neither is the legal category of offense committed. What does seem to distinguish the high and low scorers is potential for meaningful and satisfying interpersonal attachments. The more democratic prisoners, seen through their interview materials, show an "apparent greater capacity to establish genuine relationships with other people; just as their criminal behavior seems to have followed upon frustration of the need for love, or upon some crisis in their love relationships, so would the establishment of new relationships offer the basis for changed behavior" (p. 890).

An obvious question of interest regarding authoritarianism is its distribution in various political groups. Groups with conservative political and social commitments should have individuals who are more authoritarian since the dynamics of the authoritarian incline him in that direction. We also know that the F Scale was developed by selecting items that correlated with ethnocentrism and anti-Semitism, and that all these were part of a set of factors that included political and economic conservatism. So both the dynamics of authoritarianism and the methods used in the construction of the measuring devices suggest a relationship with conservative political groups.

This relationship, however, does not seem to hold with respect to political group identification in the United States: There is no clear relationship between party affiliation and authoritarianism (e.g., Campbell, Converse, Miller, & Stokes, 1960; McClosky, 1958). Republicans are not more authoritarian than Democrats. Indeed, the Berkeley investigators reported similar data in their original study (e.g., Adorno et al., 1950, Table 12(V), p. 188–189). It is only when one differentiates respondents on the basis of political beliefs about specific issues or candidate ideology or some other political dimension that relationships with authoritarianism are found. When one follows such a procedure, it does appear that authoritarianism is associated with conservatism (see Kirscht & Dillehay, 1967, pp. 57 ff.). Part of the difficulty in dealing with such a relationship, of course, is that the liberal-conservative dimension in the political and social spheres is complex, and it could be argued that there is no such acceptable, general dimension of this sort that is scientifically useful. Lipset (1960), for example, has shown that working class Americans are liberal in economic terms but are not in social matters (such as civil liberties, desegration, and the like).

POSTSCRIPT

Interest in the authoritarian personality continues unabated, as gauged by the volume of theses, dissertations, and journal articles on this topic, as well as by references to the concept in scientific and popular works. The subject is inherently appealing to many behavioral scientists and laypersons alike, perhaps because it touches both the surface and the depth of the person and has implications for both antecedents and consequences of behavior. Authoritarianism also affords an explanation for behavior of diverse sorts. Moreover, attention to authoritarianism by behavioral scientists is not likely to wane in the near future, a prediction that rests on at least a three-fold recognition: The topic has many theoretical implications for psychological, social, and cultural research; instruments are at hand to assess it; authoritarianism has the ring of truth because we know people and institutions who fit the concept.

One of those areas of alluring implications due to the nature of authoritarianism is the behavior of jurors in the courtroom (e.g., Davis, Bray, & Holt, in press; Bermant, 1975); another is the relationship with psychopathology, left unsettled in the early work. From a plethora of research over the past 25 years there appears to be no clear pattern of relationship, no discernible profile of maladjustment or psychopathology associated with authoritarianism (Christie & Cook, 1958; Kirscht & Dillehay, 1967; Titus & Hollander, 1957). A complication for much of the research in this subarea is that typically paper-and-pencil tests are used to measure not only authoritarianism but psychopathology as well, with the possible intrusion of acquiescence response bias as a contaminant.

The California F Scale is still widely used as the operational definition of the authoritarian syndrome even though its items seem to be dated. Some items, for example, refer to events of 25 to 30 years ago, such as prewar authorities in Germany, which were unambiguous when the scale was developed but may have diverse referents in today's world and introduce some error in measurement. The extent of such error is not known; no one has undertaken study of the obsolescence of the instrument. Since 1950 other scales have been constructed, the best single reference to which is Robinson and Shaver (1973). Like many other available research tools, scales to measure authoritarianism seem to have been uncritically applied and callously interpreted, with by far the most serious single oversight being the matter of acquiescence response bias, although theory seems to be fashioned rather loosely in some cases, too. Advanced discussions of the problem of acquiescence can be found in Peabody (1966), Rorer (1965), Couch and Keniston (1960), and Kirscht and Dillehay (1967).

Those who claim that the topic of authoritarianism is historically dated may be confusing generic content with topical issues. Events in the world do change, and although not forgotten, the atrocities of the Nazis in the 1930s and 1940s have given way to concern about communism, to the possibility of a nuclear holocaust, to wars in Asia, to political corruption during the Nixon regime, and so on. However, the underlying personality currents probed by Fromm and by Adorno and his coworkers are neither dissipated nor resolved with the passage of time. Hofstadter's (1967) historical perspective is useful in this regard, for although the characters change and referents for the dialogue shift, the scenario remains a constant. The object of today's prejudice may differ from that of years ago, and the manifestations of prejudice might vary, but the diminution of authoritarian personality functioning is slow if not wholly doubtful.

REFERENCES

Adorno, T. W., Frenkel-Brunswik, E., Levinson, D., & Sanford, N. *The authoritarian personality.* New York: Harper & Brothers, 1950.

Allport, G. W. *The person in psychology.* Boston: Beacon Press, 1968.

Barker, E. N. Authoritarianism of the political right, center and left. *Journal of Social Issues,* 1963, *19,* 63–74.

Bendix, R., & Lipset, S. M. (Eds.). *Class, status and power.* Glencoe, Ill.: Free Press, 1953.

Bermant, G. The notion of conspiracy is not tasty to Americans. *Psychology Today,* May 1975, pp. 60–61; 63; 65–67.

Brown, R. *Social Psychology.* New York: Free Press, 1965.

Campbell, A., Converse, P. E., Miller, W. E., & Stokes, D. E. *The American voter.* New York: John Wiley, 1960.

Christie, R. Authoritarianism re-examined. In R. Christie and M. Jahoda (Eds.), *Studies in the scope and method of "The Authoritarian Personality."* Glencoe, Ill.: Free Press, 1954.

Christie, R., & Cook, P. A guide to published literature relating to the authoritarian personality through 1956. *Journal of Psychology,* 1958, *45,* 171–199.

Christie, R., & Jahoda, M. (Eds.). *Studies in the scope and method of "The Authoritarian Personality."* Glencoe, Ill.: Free Press, 1954.

Couch, A., & Keniston, K. Yeasayers and naysayers: Agreeing response set as a personality variable. *Journal of Abnormal and Social Psychology,* 1960, *60,* 151–174.

Davis, J. H., Bray, R. M., and Holt, R. W. The empirical study of decision processes in juries: A critical review. In J. L. Tapp and F. J. Levine (Eds.), *Law, justice, and the individual in society: Psychological and legal issues.* New York: Holt, Rinehart, and Winston, *in press.*

Deutsch, M. Trust, trustworthiness, and the F scale. *Journal of Abnormal and Social Psychology,* 1960, *61,* 138–141.

Dillehay, R. C. Sincerity and dogmatism: A reassessment and new data. *Psychological Review*, 1969, *76*, 422–424.

Elms, A. C. & Milgram, S. Personality characteristics associated with obedience and defiance toward authoritative command. *Journal of Experimental Research in Personality*, 1966, *1*, 282–289.

Epstein, R. Aggression toward outgroups as a function of authoritarianism and imitation of aggressive models. *Journal of Personality and Social Psychology*, 1966, *3*, 574–579.

Fromm, E. *Escape from freedom*. New York: Rinehart & Company, 1941.

Gage, N. L., & Chattergee, B. B. The psychological meaning of acquiescence set: Further evidence. *Journal of Abnormal and Social Psychology*, 1960, *60*, 280–283.

Gage, N. L., Leavitt, G. S., & Stone, G. C. The psychological meaning of acquiescent set. *Journal of Abnormal and Social Psychology*, 1957, *55*, 98–103.

Hoffer, E. *The true believer*. New York: Harper & Row, 1951.

Hofstadter, R. *The paranoid style in American politics and other essays*. New York: Vintage Books, 1967.

Hollingshead, A. B., & Redlich, F. C. *Social class and mental illness: A community study*. New York: John Wiley, 1958.

Katz, D. The functional approach to the study of attitude. *Public Opinion Quarterly*, 1960, *24*, 163–204.

Katz, D., McClintock, C., & Sarnoff, I. The measurement of ego defense as related to attitude change. *Journal of Personality*, 1957, *25*, 465–474.

Katz, D., & Stotland, E. A preliminary statement to a theory of attitude structure and change. In S. Koch (Ed.), *Psychology: a study of a science* (Vol. 3), *Formulations of the person and the social context*. New York: McGraw-Hill, 1959.

Kelley, H. H. Two functions of reference groups. In G. E. Swanson, T. M. Newcomb, & E. L. Hartley (Eds.), *Readings in social psychology* (Rev. ed.). New York: Holt, 1952.

Kelley, H. H., & Stahelski, A. J. Social interaction basis of cooperator's and competitors' beliefs about others. *Journal of Personality and Social Psychology*, 1970, *16*, 66–91.

Kelman, H. C., & Barclay, J. The F scale as a measure of breadth of perspective. *Journal of Abnormal and Social Psychology*, 1963, *67*, 608–615.

Kerlinger, F., & Rokeach, M. The factorial nature of the F and D scales. *Journal of Personality and Social Psychology*, 1966, *4*, 391–399.

Kirscht, J. P., & Dillehay, R. C. *Dimensions of authoritarianism: A review of research and theory*. Lexington: University of Kentucky Press, 1967.

Krug, R. An analysis of the F scale: I. Item factor analysis. *Journal of Social Psychology*, 1961, *53*, 285–291.

Larsen, K. S., Coleman, D., Forbes, J., & Johnson, R. Is the subject's personality or the experimental situation a better predictor of a subject's willingness to administer shock to a victim? *Journal of Personality and Social Psychology*, 1972, *22*, 287–295.

Leavitt, J. J., Hax, H., & Roche, J. H. "Authoritarianism" and agreement with things authoritative. *Journal of Psychology*, 1955, *40*, 215–221.

Lefkowitz, M., Blake, R. R., & Mouton, J. S. Status factors in pedestrian violation of traffic signals. *Journal of Abnormal and Social Psychology*, 1955, *51*, 704–705.

Lipset, S. M. *Political man*. New York: Doubleday, 1960.

MacKinnon, W. J. & Centers, R. Authoritarianism and urban stratification. *American Journal of Sociology*, 1956, *61*, 610–620.

Maslow, A. H. The authoritarian character structure. *Journal of Social Psychology*, 1943, *18*, 401–411.

McClosky, H. Conservatism and personality. *American Political Science Review*, 1958, *52*, 27–45.

McDill, E. L. Anomie, authoritarianism, prejudice, and socio-economic status: An attempt at clarification. *Social Forces*, 1961, *39*, 239–245.

Milgram, S. Behavioral study of obedience. *Journal of Abnormal and Social Psychology*, 1963, *67*, 371–378.

Milgram, S. Liberating effects of group pressure. *Journal of Personality and Social Psychology*, 1965, *1*, 127–134.

Peabody, D. Authoritarianism scales and response bias. *Psychological Bulletin*, 1966, *65*, 11–23.

Robinson, J. P., & Shaver, P. R. *Measures of social psychological attitudes* (Rev. ed.). Ann Arbor: Institute for Social Research, 1973.

Rokeach, M. *The open and closed mind*. New York: Basic Books, 1960.

Rokeach, M. The double agreement phenomenon: Three hypotheses. *Psychological Review*, 1963, *70*, 304–309.

Rokeach, M. Authoritarianism scales and response bias: Comment on Peabody's paper. *Psychological Bulletin*, 1967, *67*, 349–355.

Rorer, L. G. The great response-style myth. *Psychological Bulletin*, 1965, *63*, 129–156.

Sales, S. M. Economic threat as a determinant of conversion rates in authoritarian and nonauthoritarian churches. *Journal of Personality and Social Psychology*, 1972, *23*, 420–428.

Samelson, F., & Yates, J. F. Acquiescence and the F scale: Old assumptions and new data. *Psychological Bulletin*, 1967, *68*, 91–103.

Seaman, J. M., Michel, J. B., & Dillehay, R. C. Membership in orthodox Christian groups, adjustment, and dogmatism. *The Sociological Quarterly*, 1971, *12*, 252–259.

Shils, E. A. Authoritarianism: Right and left. In R. Christie and M. Jahoda (Eds.), *Studies in the scope and method of "The Authoritarian Personality."* Glencoe, Ill.: Free Press, 1954.

Siegel, A. E., & Siegel, S. Reference groups, membership groups, and attitude change. *Journal of Abnormal and Social Psychology*, 1957, *55*, 360–364.

Slack, B. D., & Cook, J. O. Authoritarian behavior in a conflict situation. *Journal of Personality and Social Psychology*, 1973, *25*, 130–136.

Smith, M. B. An analysis of two measures of "authoritarianism" among Peace Corps teachers. *Journal of Personality*, 1965, *33*, 513–535.

Smith, M. B., Bruner, J. S., & White, R. W. *Opinions and personality*. New York: John Wiley, 1956.

Srole, L. Social integration and certain corollaries: An exploratory study. *American Sociological Review*, 1956, *21*, 709–716.

Stagner, R. Fascist attitudes: An exploratory study. *Journal of Social Psychology*, 1936, *7*, 309–319.

Stanley, G., & Martin, J. How sincere is the dogmatist? *Psychological Review*, 1964, *71*, 331–334.

Titus, H. E., & Hollander, E. P. The California F scale in psychological research: 1950–1955. *Psychological Bulletin*, 1957, *54*, 45–64.

Wagman, M. Attitude change and authoritarian personality. *Journal of Psychology*, 1955, *40*, 3–24.

Wrightsman, L. S. Personality and attitudinal correlates of trusting and trustworthy behaviors in a two-person game. *Journal of Personality and Social Psychology*, 1966, *4*, 328–332.

CHAPTER 4

Dogmatism

HOWARD J. EHRLICH

INTRODUCTION

The cognitive theory of personality introduced by Milton Rokeach in his 1954 article, "The Nature and Meaning of Dogmatism," has grown slowly in acceptance by the psychological establishment. Although two major review articles summarizing the state of research appeared in 1969 in the *Psychological Bulletin,* the five-volume *Handbook of Social Psychology,* also appearing that year, virtually ignored the almost 1000 research reports that had by then been published. Even in 1975, the *Annual Review of Psychology* mentioned only a half-dozen references (of no especial importance) to dogmatism.

There are many reasons for this strange neglect, but to explore them all would move us into a sociology of psychology. Certainly, a major explanation is located in the theory itself. Milton Rokeach's theory—and its overwhelmingly successful confirmations—challenged the validity of the theory of *The Authoritarian Personality* (Adorno, Frenkel-Brunswik, Levinson, and Sanford, 1950) and trivialized a number of theories that were to become faddish (e.g., Leon Festinger's *Theory of Cognitive Dissonance,* 1957). In *The Open and the Closed Mind* (1960), Rokeach indicated that some psychologists could be closed-minded and that some communists could be open-minded. Worse yet, he reintroduced political beliefs as a legitimate subject for psychological inquiry at a time when college faculties were still in retreat from both McCarthyism and Christian Crusades for Anti-Communism.

Not only was Rokeach's theory in conflict with many aspects of professional psychology, even his methodology was often on a different track. His techniques, although very traditional, were often embedded within innovative study designs. Furthermore, during the 1960s social psychologists began to move away from self-report measures, and much of the work stimulated by Rokeach's theory involved the relationship of multiple measures all based on self-report.

Finally, many of the studies that actually do provide cumulative support for

129

the theory are individually trivial. The ease of administration of the Dogmatism Scale and the pressures upon American academics to publish led and continues to lead to the most banal and atheoretical research.

Rokeach's cognitive theory of personality has survived these (and other) handicaps because it is an extraordinarily creative production. It has blended elements from the psychoanalytically based theory of authoritarianism and the generally neglected personality theory of Kurt Lewin (1935). It has provided a set of hypotheses that are simply stated but by no means intuitively obvious. Most of all, its basic statements have received strong empirical support. Even when the theory of the open and closed mind is reformulated, the research it generated will remain.

BELIEFS AND DISBELIEFS

The basic unit of analysis of this theory is the *belief–disbelief system*. A belief is a statement that is accepted as true. A system of beliefs "is conceived to represent all the beliefs, sets, expectancies, or hypotheses, conscious and unconscious, that a person at a given time accepts as true of the world he lives in." (Rokeach, 1960, p. 33).

There are two tricky aspects to that statement. First, Rokeach is using the concept of "system" to refer to a *psychological* system. In a logical system all parts are related according to specified rules. By calling the belief–disbelief system a psychological system, Rokeach wants to convey the idea that the parts are related but not necessarily in keeping with the rules of logic. The "rules" here are those psychological principles that this theory attempts to organize.

The second tricky aspect is that the belief system is conceptualized as including only statements accepted as true. Since our cognitions also involve propositions that we believe to be untrue, it is necessary to introduce the conception of a disbelief system.

The disbelief system is composed of a series of subsystems rather than merely a single one, and contains all the disbeliefs, sets, expectancies, conscious and unconscious, that, to one degree or another, a person at a given time rejects as false. (Rokeach, 1960, p. 32)

Although we can talk about beliefs as propositions that are accepted and disbeliefs as propositions that are rejected, it is more fruitful to conceptualize all beliefs and disbeliefs as being located on a continuum of acceptance and rejection. As we all know, some beliefs are more strongly rejected than others.

We can also conceptualize disbelief subsystems as being located on a continuum of similarity–dissimilarity to the belief system. What this means is that all disbelief subsystems are psychologically ordered along a line in keeping with their similarity and dissimilarity to one another and to beliefs.

Now, if you think about both of these dimensions—acceptance–rejection and similarity–dissimilarity—you can anticipate their relationship. The more dissimilar the disbelief subsystems, the more they are rejected. And the greater their similarity to the belief system, the greater their acceptance.

In building a theory about the belief–disbelief system, it is useful to consider formally at least five basic questions:

What are the structural characteristics of belief systems?

How are belief systems developed?

How are belief systems modified?

How are belief systems related to other characteristics such as perception, memory, and learning?

What is the relationship between belief systems and action?

Of course, we have to ask these questions also about disbelief subsystems and about the relations between the belief and disbelief systems.

THE BASIC PROPOSITIONS

The first five propositions of the theory have now been introduced. They deal with our first question, namely, the structural characteristics of the cognitive (belief) system.

1. All beliefs are organized into two interdependent parts: a belief system and a disbelief system.
2. The belief system comprises all propositions that a person believes to be true at any given time.
3. The disbelief system is a set of systems containing all that a person believes to be false at any given time.
4. All beliefs and disbeliefs are arranged along a continuum of acceptance and rejection.
5. Disbelief subsystems are arranged along a continuum of similarity with the belief system and with one another.

   a. The greater the similarity of disbelief subsystems to the belief system, the greater their acceptance. The greater their dissimilarity, the greater their rejection.

Let us now develop Rokeach's theory further. An important structural property of the cognitive system is its degree of *differentiation*. Differentiation may be defined as the number of beliefs and disbeliefs that comprise the belief –disbelief system.

It would seem that most people know more facts, ideas, events and interpretations consistent with their belief system than with their disbelief system. . . . Similarly, people probably vary in their relative knowledge about things believed and disbelieved" (Rokeach, 1960, p. 38).

6. Belief-disbelief systems vary in their differentiation.

    a. Belief systems are more differentiated than any one of the disbelief subsystems.

    b. Disbelief subsystems relatively close to the belief system on the similarity continuum will be more highly differentiated than those further away.

Disbelief subsystems are considered to be *dedifferentiated* when a person can barely distinguish one "disbelief" from another. Rokeach offered the illustration of a major newspaper publisher writing in the 1950s about "communazis," that is of being unable to distinguish communism from Nazism. (Had he written 10 years later, Rokeach could have used the then vice-president's *radlib* label applied to those protesting the American war in Indochina.) This process of dedifferentiation apparently occurs, for all people, at the extreme end of their similarity continuum.

    c. The greater the magnitude of dissimilarity, the greater the dedifferentiation.

For some people, the total number or range of their disbelief subsystems is very narrow. That is, it may contain very few subsystems of disbelief. Thus, for some people "anarchosyndicalism" and "council communism" may be represented in their belief-disbelief system whereas for others they may be relatively meaningless political labels.

7. Disbelief systems vary in their comprehensiveness, that is, the number of disbelief subsystems represented within them.

Another structural characteristic of the cognitive system is the relative degree of *isolation* of beliefs and disbeliefs. Beliefs vary in their degree of isolation. Beliefs are said to be isolated if there is some logical connection among them that is ignored or denied by a person. There are four indicators of isolation. The coexistence of logically contradictory beliefs is the first. For example, believing in democracy and also believing in a government run by an intellectual elite or believing in value-free science while making value judgments about methodology or the outcomes of a study or the adequacy of a theory. Another indicator is the outright denial of contradiction, and third is the perception of differences or similarities as irrelevant. Finally, the fourth indicator of isolation is ignoring the relation between beliefs and disbeliefs by accentuating the differences and/or minimizing the similarities among them.

8. Belief–disbelief systems vary in the isolation of their parts.

THE CENTRAL–PERIPHERAL DIMENSION

Beliefs vary in their *centrality*—a term often used synonymously with *importance*. Centrality is defined as the number of connections, implications, and/or consequences a belief has with other beliefs. The greater the number of "connections," the greater the centrality.

Highly central beliefs are postulated to have three characteristics. First, they are *existential*. That is, they are beliefs about one's own existence and self-identity. Second, they are *shared* with others. Third, they are beliefs that have some grounding in *direct experience.*

A belief about one's self or the world (in relation to one's self) that is learned through direct experience and supported by a unanimous consensus among all of one's reference groups is the most central. Rokeach (1968) calls such beliefs Type A. They are *consensual primitive beliefs*.

> A person's primitive beliefs represents his "basic truths" about physical reality, social reality, and the nature of the self; they represent a subsystem within the total system in which the person has the heaviest of commitments. . . . "I believe this is a table," "I believe this is my mother," "I believe my name is so-and-so," are examples, respectively, of primitive beliefs about the physical world, the social world, and the self —supported by a unanimous consensus among those in a position to know. (p. 6).

Type B primitive beliefs have zero consensus. This second type, *nonconsensual primitive beliefs,* also involves existence and self-identity and is also learned by direct experience with the objects of belief. Unlike Type A beliefs, Type B beliefs do not require any reference group support. No person outside the self could disconfirm such a belief. Examples include phobias, delusions, and hallucinations. But more routine beliefs also are retained with no consensus— —beliefs held on pure faith as well as many self-enhancing and self-deprecating beliefs. For example, "I believe in a God," "I believe my body is ugly," "I am a good person."

Authority beliefs (Type C) are not considered as primitive. They presumably develop out of Type A beliefs or those experiences that lead to Type A beliefs. They lack the taken-for-granted character of both types of primitive beliefs. Type C beliefs represent "the beliefs a person has in and about the nature of authority and the people who line up with authority, on whom he depends to form a picture of the world he lives in" (Rokeach, 1960, p. 40). Authority figures are reference others who provide the individual with the source of information and with the means for validating information received. There are positive and negative authorities; those we trust and those we distrust; those dispensing what is true and those dispensing what is false about the world we live in.

To be sure, particular authorities vary from person to person, and not all of them share the same beliefs. There are, presumably, classes of reference groups that are common across all persons: family, friends, lovers, ethnic groups, religious groups, and the like.

Type D or *derived beliefs* are basically those that we accept because they derive from our trust in an authoritative source. If you believe it because you read it in a textbook or a trustworthy magazine, or a knowledgeable friend told you, then you believe not because of direct contact but because of your contact with an authority.

If we know that a person believes in a particular authority, we should be able to deduce many of his other beliefs, those which emanate or derive from the authorities he identifies with. Such derived beliefs are less important dynamically than beliefs about authority, and therefore a change of belief with respect to authority, or a direct communication from one's authority, should lead to many other changes in beliefs deriving from authority. (Rokeach, 1968, pp. 10–11).

Finally there are those *inconsequential beliefs* (Type E) within the belief system. Most of these are matters of taste. They are labeled as inconsequential because they have few connections with other beliefs and are not an integral part of one's self-beliefs. Furthermore, discarding or changing such beliefs have few consequences for other beliefs in the system.

These five categories of belief just introduced are ordered along the central-–peripheral dimension of the belief system. Type A are the most central; Type E are the most peripheral. Because of the consequence of change for the belief system, highly central beliefs are postulated to be the most resistant to change. Derived and inconsequential beliefs, those most peripheral, are easier to change. Furthermore, as it follows from the theory, a change in central beliefs will cause more changes in the belief system than a change in peripheral beliefs.

9. All beliefs are organized along a dimension of centrality.

a. There are five mutually exclusive and exhaustive categories of beliefs with primitive beliefs being the most central, derived and inconsequential beliefs being the most peripheral, and authority beliefs lying intermediate.

10. The more central beliefs are more resistant to change than those less central.

11. Changes in central beliefs entail more changes in the belief system than do changes in peripheral beliefs.

TIME PERSPECTIVE

In his original essays, Rokeach (1954, 1960) postulates *time perspective* as another dimension of belief–disbelief systems. "This refers to the person's beliefs about the past, present, and the future and the manner in which they are related to each other" (1960, p 51).

Time perspectives are postulated to vary from narrow to broad. If the past, present, and future are all represented within the belief–disbelief system, and the individual sees them as related, then we would call that person's time perspective broad. If a person overemphasizes the past, present, or future, then we would call that perspective narrow.

In view of Rokeach's later (1968) classification of central–peripheral belief types, it now does not seem appropriate to consider time perspective as an independent organizational characteristic of the belief–disbelief system. Rather, beliefs about time seem to be more appropriately construed as a form of primitive belief. They certainly involve matters of physical reality and one's self in temporal relation to the world. By not introducing a new proposition here about time perspective, I am changing the emphasis given in the original statements. However, the change is more consistent with Rokeach's subsequent theoretical statement (1968). Furthermore, from the standpoint of formal theory construction, this shift in emphasis does not change any other statements in the theory.

THE OPEN AND THE CLOSED MIND

We turn now to what is the signal contribution of Rokeach's theory: the formulation of belief–disbelief systems as varying along an open–closed continuum.

12. Belief–disbelief systems vary in the degree to which they are open to the acquisition of new beliefs and to the change of old beliefs.

What are the defining characteristics of closed-mindedness and open-mindedness?

13. A belief–disbelief system is defined as *closed* (the person is defined as dogmatic) if in its *organization*:

a. there is a high degree of rejection of all disbelief systems,
b. there is an isolation of beliefs,
c. there is an isolation between beliefs and disbeliefs,
d. there is a greater differentiation within the belief system than in the disbelief system,
e. there is little differentiation within the disbelief system.

A belief–disbelief system is *open,* then, where the rejection of disbeliefs is low; where there is a communication among beliefs and between beliefs and disbeliefs; where there is little discrepancy in the degree of differentiation between belief and disbelief systems; and where there is a relatively high degree of differentiation within the disbelief system.

The openness or closedness of the belief–disbelief system is also displayed in the structure and the content of central beliefs. With regard to the content of primitive (the most central) beliefs, Rokeach wrote:

These primitive beliefs are concerned with whether the world we live in is friendly or hostile, what the future has in store for us, the adequacy of the self, and what must be done to alleviate feelings of inadequacy. It is assumed that the more closed the system, the more will the content of such beliefs be to the effect that we live alone, isolated and helpless in a friendless world; that we live in a world wherein the future is uncertain; that the self is fundamentally unworthy and inadequate to cope alone with this friendless world; and that the way to overcome such feelings is by a self-aggrandizing and self-righteous identification with a cause, a concern with power and status, and by a compulsive self-proselytization about the justness of such a cause. (1960, p. 75).

14. A belief–disbelief system is closed if in its *content*:

a. the world is construed as fundamentally hostile,
b. people are perceived as unfriendly and rejecting,
c. the present is denied, and the past or future is emphasized,
d. the future is uncertain,
e. the self is rejected.

Beliefs about authority also distinguish the closed-minded from the open-minded. Authority beliefs are closed if in their content:

f. there are positive and negative authorities,
g. people are accepted or rejected according to the authorities they line up with,
h. there is an inability to distinguish between the content of beliefs and the authority for them,
i. there is a belief in a single cause.

In an open belief–disbelief system, the acceptance of authority is always more tentative and rational, the truth is unlikely to emanate from a single authority, and people are more likely to be accepted for themselves.

Open-minded persons, more than closed-minded persons, should be able to distinguish the quality of information from the authority of its source. The greater dependence on authority of closed-minded persons makes it more difficult for them to discriminate between the source of new beliefs and the quality of the ideas expressed.

Finally, there are some structural characteristics regarding the relations among the different types of beliefs. Rokeach writes:

> The more closed the system, the more will a change in a particular peripheral belief be determined by a prior change in the intermediate (authority) region. Further, the primitive and intermediate regions are assumed to control not only what will be represented in the peripheral region but also what will not be represented, that is, narrowed out. (1960, p. 78).

These ideas were already expressed in propositions 10 and 11: (10) more central beliefs are more resistant to change and (11) changes in central beliefs entail greater changes in the belief system than do changes in peripheral beliefs. Here, however, the variation is being proposed that if a belief–disbelief system is closed structurally, then derived (Type D) and inconsequential (Type E) beliefs will change more than in open systems as a result of changes instituted by authority. "A party-line thinker is a person," Rokeach writes, "who not only resists change but can change too easily. What he does depends on what his authorities do, and his changes and refusals to change conform with authority" (1960, p. 225).

Having formulated the general outline and major statements of his theory, Rokeach and his associates proceeded to assemble a set of questions that would index a person's level of open- or closed-mindedness. The selection of questions is dictated by the theory itself. For example, take the issue of positive and negative authority. To study this, Rokeach (1954) formulated two statements.

> In the history of mankind there have probably been just a handful of really great thinkers.
> There are a number of people I have come to hate because of the things they stand for.

People are presented with these (and other) statements and asked if they agree or disagree with them. Agreeing with the first signifies acceptance of the idea of positive authorities; agreeing with the second signifies acceptance of the idea of negative authority. Both are illustrative of parts of proposition 14, discussed above.

For those parts of the theory that were amenable to direct or indirect questioning, Rokeach compiled—after much testing—40 statements that were theoretically relevant and that satisfied rudimentary criteria of scaling. This set of items he called the Dogmatism Scale. On a pragmatic level the scale works: People respond to the items in a consistent manner, their responses are stable over time, the items are logically connected to the theory and are empirically connected to other events predicted by the theory.

The original 40-item scale is presented in Table 4–1.

Table 4–1. The Dogmatism Scale*

The following is a study of what the general public thinks and feels about a number of important social and personal questions. The best answer to each statement below is *your personal opinion*. We have tried to cover many different and opposing points of view; you may find yourself agreeing strongly with some of the statements, disagreeing just as strongly with others, and perhaps uncertain about others; whether you agree or disagree with any statement, you can be sure that many other people feel the same as you do.

Mark each statement in the left margin according to how much you agree or disagree with it. Please mark every one. Write $+1$, $+2$, $+3$, or -1, -2, -3, depending on how you feel in each case.

+1: I AGREE A LITTLE	−1: I DISAGREE A LITTLE
+2: I AGREE ON THE WHOLE	−2: I DISAGREE ON THE WHOLE
+3: I AGREE VERY MUCH	−3: I DISAGREE VERY MUCH

_____ 1. A person who thinks primarily of his own happiness is beneath contempt.

_____ 2. The main thing in life is for a person to want to do something important.

_____ 3. In a discussion I often find it necessary to repeat myself several times to make sure I am being understood.

_____ 4. Most people just don't know what's good for them.

_____ 5. In times like these, a person must be pretty selfish if he considers his own happiness primarily.

_____ 6. A man who does not believe in some great cause has not really lived.

_____ 7. I'd like it if I should find someone who would tell me how to solve my personal problems.

_____ 8. Of all the different philosophies which have existed in this world there is probably only one which is correct.

_____ 9. It is when a person devotes himself to an ideal or cause that his life becomes meaningful.

_____ 10. In this complicated world of ours the only way we can know what is going on is to rely upon leaders or experts who can be trusted.

_____ 11. There are a number of persons I have come to hate because of the things they stand for.

_____ 12. There is so much to be done and so little time to do it in.

_____ 13. It is better to be a dead hero than a live coward.

_____ 14. A group which tolerates too much difference of opinion among its own members cannot exist for long.

_____ 15. It is only natural that a person should have a much better acquaintance with ideas he believes in than with ideas he opposes.

_____ 16. While I don't like to admit this even to myself, I sometimes have the ambition to become a great man, like Einstein, or Beethoven, or Shakespeare.

_____17. Even though freedom of speech for all groups is a worthwhile goal, it is unfortunately necessary at times to restrict the freedom of certain political groups.

_____18. If a man is to accomplish his mission in life it is sometimes necessary to gamble "all or nothing at all."

_____19. Most people just don't give a damn about others.

_____20. A person who gets enthusiastic about a number of causes is likely to be a pretty "wishy-washy" sort of person.

_____21. To compromise with our political opponents is dangerous because it usually leads to the betrayal of our own side.

_____22. If given the chance I would do something that would be of great benefit to the world.

_____23. In times like these it is often necessary to be more on guard against ideas put out by certain people or groups in one's own camp than by those in the opposing camp.

_____24. In a heated discussion I generally become so absorbed in what I am going to say that I forget to listen to what the others are saying.

_____25. Once I get wound up in a heated discussion I just can't stop.

_____26. There are two kinds of people in this world: those who are on the side of truth and those who are against it.

_____27. Man on his own is a helpless and miserable creature.

_____28. The United States and Russia have just about nothing in common.

_____29. In the history of mankind there have probably been just a handful of really great thinkers.

_____30. The highest form of government is a democracy and the highest form of democracy is a government run by those who are most intelligent.

_____31. The present is all too often full of unhappiness. It is the future that counts.

_____32. Unfortunately, a good many people with whom I have discussed important social and moral problems don't really understand what is going on.

_____33. Fundamentally, the world we live in is a pretty lonely place.

_____34. It is often desirable to reserve judgment about what's going on until one has had a chance to hear the opinions of those one respects.

_____35. The worst crime a person can commit is to attack publicly the people who believe in the same thing he does.

_____36. In the long run the best way to live is to pick friends and associates whose tastes and beliefs are the same as one's own.

_____37. Most of the ideas which get published nowadays aren't worth the paper they are printed on.

_____38. It is only natural for a person to be rather fearful of the future.

_____39. My blood boils whenever a person stubbornly refuses to admit he's wrong.

_____40. When it comes to differences of opinion in religion we must be careful not to compromise with those who believe differently from the way we do.

---

*Dogmatism Scale (Form E) from THE OPEN AND CLOSED MIND: Investigations into the Nature of Belief Systems and Personality Systems, by Milton Rokeach, (c) 1960 by Basic Books, Inc., Publishers, New York.

Scoring

The original scoring procedure involved the arbitrary weighting of each item as follows: $+3 = 7$ points, $+2 = 6$, $+1 = 5$, $-1 = 3$, $-2 = 2$, and $-1 = 1$ point. Unanswered items were given a value of 4. A person's score was the sum of the points assigned each item. The highest possible score is 280; the lowest, 40. By this procedure, it is my estimate (in the absence of formal norms) that scores of 145 to 155 were average for college student populations.

A simplified scoring procedure was introduced by Rokeach and Norrell (1966), and a theoretical rationale for it appears in Ehrlich (1973). In this procedure, only the *sign* of the response is counted. That is, only whether a person agrees ($+$) or disagrees ($-$) is considered in scoring. An agree response ($+3$, $+2$, $+1$) is counted as 1; a disagree response (-1, -2, -3) is counted as 0. A score, then, is the sum of the "$+$" responses. The highest score possible is 40; the lowest is 0.

THE DEVELOPMENT OF OPEN AND
CLOSED COGNITIVE STRUCTURES

How is it that some people are open-minded and others closed-minded? Can people change, or is open- and closed-mindedness a relatively permanent cognitive structure?

These are the two critical questions to be considered in this section. The answers should be regarded as tentative since there is little research and little theory.

We can start on a firm base by dismissing one explanation that appears plausible. Being open- or closed-minded is *not* a consequence of "intelligence." In well-replicated research, no substantial relationships have been found between Dogmatism Scale scores and performance on college aptitude tests or group intelligence tests. To be sure, these tests generally measure verbal, mathematical, and sometimes spatial abilities that are relevant primarily to school performance. But knowing that these standard intellectual abilities have no major relationship with dogmatism directs us to look outside the structure of intellect for an explanation. Rokeach (1960) proposes:

All belief–disbelief systems serve two powerful and conflicting sets of motives at the same time: the need for a cognitive framework to know and to understand and the need to ward off threatening aspects of reality. To the extent that the cognitive need to know is predominant and the need to ward off threat absent, open systems should result. In the service of the cognitive need to know, external pressures and irrational internal drives will be often pushed aside, so that information received from outside will be discriminated, assessed, and acted on according to the objective requirements of the situation. But as the need to ward off threat becomes stronger, the cognitive need to know should become weaker, resulting in more closed belief systems. Under threat, information and source should become inseparable and should be evaluated arbitrarily in line with the rewards and punishments meted out by authority. (pp. 67–68)

For Rokeach, then, there is always a dynamic tension between the need to know and the need to ward off threat. Most of the time these two needs or motives operate simultaneously. And people presumably attempt to maximize them both, that is, to be as open to as many new beliefs as possible while defending against as many threatening beliefs as necessary.

Four general propositions provide a beginning.

15. Belief–disbelief systems have a characteristic level of open or closedness. (I will call this "characteristic level" the state of the cognitive system.)
16. The state of the cognitive system is established through early childhood experiences.
17. The state of the cognitive system is a joint consequence of exposure to new experiences and the degree to which such experiences threaten the content and/or the arrangement of primitive and authority beliefs.
18. The state of the cognitive system is determined in part, by the state of the affective system (especially levels of anxiety and emotional arousal).

The proposition that there is a characteristic level of open- and closed-mindedness has really been assumed throughout all the earlier discussion. I make it explicit here to emphasize two facets that may not be obvious. The first is the issue of *change*. People change. The state of the cognitive system may be established early, but it can and does change. We do not know how much change can occur from any given starting point. It is likely that extremely closed-minded persons can change less, but that is just an educated guess.

The second issue is that of *limits*. No norms have been established for the Dogmatism Scale, and we have not yet established what an optimum state of the cognitive system might be.

Two studies provide some insight on the generalization of closed-mindedness to a more comprehensive closedness in sensory perception. Kaplan and Singer (1963) hypothesized that for all sensory modalities closed-minded persons should display lower sensory acuity than the open-minded. Second, they proposed that differences in sensory acuity should occur for all persons in the following order: olfactory, gustatory, tactile, auditory, and visual. This ordering was based primarily on the presumed ease with which the different sensory inputs could be verified. The researchers argued further that closed-minded persons should be less able to evaluate sensory inputs such as smell and taste, since they were less easily verified, than inputs such as hearing and vision. Their second hypothesis, then, was that the magnitude of differences in sensory acuity between open- and closed-minded persons should follow the order indicated.

Thirteen relatively open-minded and thirteen relatively closed-minded persons, selected from a pool of 40 subjects, were administered stimulus discrimination tasks for each modality. The scoring of sensory acuity was based on the same number of tasks for each modality. Over all modalities, sensory acuity correlated −.61 with Dogmatism Scale scores, cofirming the first hypothesis. The second prediction—that the differences between high and low dogmatic groups would follow a gradient of great differences in olfactory performance to minor differences in visual performance—was also confirmed. These data strongly suggest that closed-minded persons are more dependent than the open-minded for external support in evaluating sensory inputs.

Lee and Ehrlich (1977) found, as part of a larger study, that closed-minded persons restricted their exposure to new sensory experience. Using a 160-item checklist of foods, the researchers found that the closed-minded had tasted significantly fewer foods than open-minded persons. This extraordinary level of ''sensory alienation'' exhibited in these two studies indicates that the behavioral implications of the theory may be broader than what is directly implied by its major propositions.

Can people be socialized into open- or closed-minded behaviors and cognitive patterns? Let us consider some of the ways. First of all, parents (or parent surrogates) can set themselves up as positive authorities demanding conformity. Parents are, of course, the child's first authority. Second, parents in their child-rearing practices can create a warm, loving, supportive environment or they can be rejecting, neglectful, and cold. Perhaps worse, they can be totally inconsistent in their relationship to the child. Both rejection and inconsistency seem directly related to such concomitants of closed-mindedness as anxiety, negative self-attitudes, and the rejection of others (Ehrlich, 1973). Third, parents can teach and model cognitive strategies. That is, they help their children learn how to learn and how to balance personal inquiry and authority.

Only one study at present has actually tested the correspondence in dogmatism between parents and their children. Lesser and Steininger (1975) administered the Dogmatism Scale to 167 college students and to 246 of their parents. Calculating correlations separately between parents and their same-sex and opposite-sex children, the researchers report ''low, positive, and significant [correlations] ranging from .20 to .40.'' As is commonly observed in studies of parent–child similarities, the correlations between parents were greater than those between parents and children. The authors conclude ''the more dogmatic a parent was among other parents, the more dogmatic his or her child was.''

Another way to explore the relationship between the parental family and the child's developing cognitive system is to examine selected behaviors that might indicate the child's degree of security and insecurity. In a study of highly open-minded and highly closed-minded adults, Rokeach and Kemp (1960), asked them if, as children, they had ever sucked their thumb, bit their nails, had temper tantrums, had nightmares, or walked or talked in their sleep. The underlying assumptions here were that these behaviors are indicators of anxiety and that these would have been more common in the childhood of relatively closed-minded persons. On the same basis, the researchers also asked their subjects "At what age approximately did you stop wetting the bed?" In both instances, persons of closed and open cognitive systems were strongly differentiated. Open-minded persons averaged reporting less than one indicator of anxiety and stopped bed-wetting very early. The closed-minded persons reported an average of 2.5 indicators and an average age for stopping bed-wetting as over six years of age.

In a later study, using younger persons, Hanson and Clune (1973) administered an elementary school modified form of the Dogmatism Scale to a small sample of seventh and eighth grade students. They asked the students the same questions as Rokeach and Kemp. As expected, the more closed-minded children gave significantly more affirmative response to these indicators of anxiety.

Finally, a substantial number of adult studies have shown that Dogmatism Scale scores do correlate with a variety of paper-and-pencil measures of anxiety. (Many of these appear in Rokeach, 1960, and are reviewed in Vacchiano, Strauss, & Hochman, 1969; and some of their methodological limitations are discussed in Gaensslen, May & Wolpert, 1973.)

Socialization is more than parent–child relations. People live in social organizations, and the organizational and structural characteristics of those settings are important and independent determinants of personality.

Consider, for example, what the impact of living in an unstable social network might be. Sticht and Fox (1966) compared college students who had changed their permanent residences during their life from one to three times with those who had changed from seven to 20 times. They found that persons who had experienced such extreme mobility were significantly more anxious and more closed-minded than persons of low mobility. Although a study of this design could by no means be conclusive, it is certainly provocative.

For another example of the relationship between social organization and personality, consider the relationship between being placed in an institutional setting in which you are continually being confronted with new ideas and new experiences. School and collegiate experiences, on occasion and for some people, can be such an experience. And although existing research is very difficult to evaluate, it does appear that some school periods are accompanied by significant increases in open-mindedness. The differences are not to be attributed to years of formal education. Three examples of these studies are those by Juan, Paiva, Haley, and O'Keefe (1974), Lehmann, Sinha, and Hartnett (1966), and Plant (1965).

In a comparative study of different schools, Ondrack (1975), displayed data suggesting the schools' differential impact on students. Observing nursing students from entry to graduation at three different schools, the researcher found significant changes toward open-mindedness occurring in only one school.

IMPORTANT RESEARCH

There are some consensual criteria for judging the adequancy of a scientific theory. At the very least we can require that the statements in the theory be relatively clear and consistent. Since it is a scientific theory, we can also require that some of its statements be empirically testable or imply statements that are testable. We can require, further, that the theory results in the organization of a set of otherwise isolated findings and that it leads to new findings. That is, a good theory will generate testable statements that have not been developed by other theories.

There are, of course, other general criteria, as well as some that are specific to a given domain of theory. But to comprehend a theory, you really must examine its supporting research. I have selected for illustration two different areas of research—studies dealing with the implications of closed cognitive systems for change and studies dealing with the self-beliefs and interpersonal behavior of persons as a consequence of the openness or closedness of their cognitive system.

CHANGE AND RESISTANCE TO CHANGE

A natural setting in which to study the learning and change of beliefs is the classroom. It may be one of the few times that college student samples are clearly appropriate for the research.

The first such study (Ehrlich, 1961a) compared the performance of 57 sociology students using tests taken at the beginning and the end of the course (10 weeks) and on a mail follow-up five to six months later. The sociology test consisted of 40 true–false items, half of which were statements of definition and half were empirical generalizations. The dogmatism scores of the subjects were significantly negatively related to test performance at all three time periods. The significant negative relation remained when academic aptitude scores as determined by the Ohio State Psychological Examination (OSPE) were controlled for both time periods, and it still held up with slight shrinkage when both OSPE and initial test scores were controlled. Under the controls, the average correlation for the two periods was $-.44$. In contrast, although the OSPE was significantly positively related to test performance at all three time periods, control for dogmatism reduced the OSPE–sociology test correlations to nonsignificant values.

Ehrlich (1961a) concluded: "Subjects low in dogmatism entered the sociology classroom with a higher level of learning, learned more as a result of classroom exposure, and retained this information to a significantly greater degree than the more dogmatic subjects" (p. 149).

Five years later, Ehrlich (1961b) contacted the original subjects by mail. The same results were obtained regarding dogmatism, OSPE, and test performance, with the partial correlations displaying approximately the same pattern and magnitude.

In a precise replication of Ehrlich's procedures, using 67 psychology students, a pre- and postcourse psychology test, and the School and College Ability Test (SCAT), Part 1, as a measure of academic aptitude, Costin (1965) achieved no significant correlation between dogmatism and classroom performance. The partial analyses similarly indicated that dogmatism was not related to classroom performance. In all cases, the SCAT correlated positively, and control for dogmatism had no effect on the association between the SCAT and classroom performance. Costin concluded by suggesting two hypotheses: that there was more than one kind of closed-mindedness and/or that the content of learning was the crucial variable in the differences between the two studies.

Three further studies reiterated the contradictory findings. Christensen (1963), in a partial replication without controls, reported no significant correlation between dogmatism and two postcourse measures of performance in an introductory psychology classroom. Using a different design with an introductory sociology class of 135 subjects, Frumkin (1961) compared the classroom grades of the 17 highest and 17 lowest scoring subjects on dogmatism and found that low scorers had significantly higher grades. Zagona and Zurcher (1965), also using an extreme scorers design, indicated that the 30 highest and 30 lowest subjects on dogmatism (from a pool of 517 freshmen in introductory psychology) had significantly different scores on their midterm examination, with low subjects performing at a higher level of learning. For the remaining students ($n=440$) dogmatism and examination grades correlated -0.20 ($p<0.001$).

Baker (1964) brought the classroom studies to a complete circle. Fifty-six freshmen subjects enrolled in nursing were instructed to learn the definitions of 60 psychological terms at the rate of 10 concepts a week for six weeks. The concepts were never discussed in the lectures, and at the end of the sixth week, subjects were tested on their ability to identify the definitions of 20 of the concepts. Dividing his subjects into high and low tertiles, Baker reported that high-dogmatism subjects performed significantly better than low-dogmatism subjects on this task.

During 1963 to 1965, White and Alter (1967) administered the Dogmatism Scale to 2099 students in 14 introductory psychology classes involving seven different instructors. Six of the 14 correlations between dogmatism and examination grades were significant with the average correlation being $-.18$. In an auxiliary analysis, the investigators attempted to reconcile the contradictory findings by exploring the effects of examination format on the dogmatism––learning correlations. One instructor used both true–false and multiple-choice examinations for a class of 187 students. Separate correlations were then computed between dogmatism and student performance on each type of examination. Between dogmatism and true–false scores the correlation was $-.14$, whereas the correlation for the multiple-choice items was $-.16$. Thus, these two kinds of examination format were ruled out as a source of differences.

In a subsequent study, Costin (1968) employed the same design as in his earlier study (1965), but used two measures of classroom performance—a test of psychological principles and a test of conventional misconceptions about human behavior. Costin's hypotheses were that dogmatism would be correlated positively with students' retention of psychological misconceptions but would not be related to their acquisition of basic psychological principles. The hypotheses were confirmed, with and without controls for SCAT and for precourse test performance. The zero-order correlation for dogmatism and the retention of misconceptions was .35 ($p<.01$), whereas for dogmatism and the learning of basic principles, it was $-.004$. Partial correlations reduced the coefficients only slightly. Costin's study is significant in that it suggests that closed-minded subjects may be more resistant to the charge of old beliefs than to the acquisition of new (presumably belief-congruent) beliefs.

In the most extensive of the classroom studies, Rokeach and Norrell (1966) were able to examine the relation of classroom performance to dogmatism for 798 subjects in 33 courses and for six groupings of curricular majors, four of which could be subdivided into male and female majors. The grade point averages (GPAs) for major and for all college courses were also examined. Seventeen of the 33 courses provided at least one significant negative correlation between dogmatism and course grade with or without control for sex or major. For the total analyses performed by sex and major for each course, 20 yielded low but significant negative correlations between dogmatism and classroom grades.

The number of findings were beyond chance expectancy, but the findings seemed at best to provide only moderate support for the theory especially in the light of earlier studies. Ehrlich (1971) argued that Rokeach and Norrell had failed to control for the centrality of the materials being learned. Arguing that college major could be taken as an indicator of centrality, Ehrlich reanalyzed their data by major. In classes taken in nonmajor areas, significant negative correlations between dogmatism and grades occurred only 10 percent of the time. In major area classes, significant negative correlations occurred 35 percent of the time.

Many laboratory studies have also provided evidence, although most of the laboratory research has not been very distinguished.

In an important study, Vidulich and Kaiman (1961) show how even new perceptual beliefs are mediated through authority. Thirty women, high and low in dogmatism, were individually exposed to a light stimulus in the autokinetic situation. In the first condition, each subject and a male confederate were asked to record privately on paper their judgment of the direction of apparent movement, left or right. In the second condition of additional exposures, judgments were presented verbally with the confederate speaking first and selecting, by prearrangement, a response pattern opposite to what the subject had reported in the prior condition. A status manipulation, which subdivided the high and low groups, entailed introducing the confederate as either a college professor or a high school student. Two performance criteria were used as indicators of subjects' conformity: the difference in performance in the two conditions, and the number of times subjects agreed with the confederate in the second condition. Although the two criteria yielded slightly different results, the data were consistent with theoretical expectations: There was a significant relationship between authority and dogmatism. High-dogmatism subjects conformed significantly more with the high-status than with the low-status confederate.

In a field study, Ehrlich and Bauer (1966) attempted to assess the effect of dogmatism in psychiatric hospitalization by administering the Dogmatism Scale to 254 patients on entry and exit. Length of stay was significantly associated with the open- and closed-mindedness of patients. Whereas 51 percent of low-dogmatism-quartile patients were discharged in under three weeks, only 27 percent of the high-dogmatism-quartile patients were discharged in this time. The researchers interpreted the longer hospitalization of closed-minded patients to be a consequence of their greater resistance to change.

In another hospital study, Wilkinson (1974) showed that staff resistance to changing treatment methods was a consequence, in part, of their own level of dogmatism.

In a study of dramatic context, Hallenbeck and Lundstedt (1966) proposed that adjustment to the gradual onset of blindness should vary with dogmatism. Closed-minded persons, it was hypothesized, would deny their disability and repress their affect—both indicators of a lack of acceptance of their loss. Open-minded persons, in contrast, were expected to show depression as a reaction to the disability. Both of the hypotheses were confirmed by scale and by clinical assessments of 32 blind males. Correlations of dogmatism with denial from .42 to .66, and with depression from $-.43$ to $-.52$. The closed-minded person thus appeared less willing to accept major changes of the self than the open-minded.

The response to novelty, to new belief patterns (which might be considered a way of dealing with change) has received some critical tests in the domain of esthetics. Mikol (1960) attempted two studies involving response to novel musical systems. In the first, 20 high-dogmatism and 20 low-dogmatism subjects were exposed to brief taped excerpts from Brahms and Schönberg string quartets. As predicted, subjects did not differ in their reactions, on an adjective checklist, to the conventional Brahms, but closed-minded subjects liked the nonconventional Schönberg significantly less. Checklist reactions to the composers followed the same pattern. In the second study, the number of musical samples was increased, and open and closed differences in reactions to the musical systems and composers were essentially the same. Soh (1972) reports a partial replication using music and art student samples.

Pyron (1966b) examined the art preferences of 48 students, comparing their evaluations of three media—painting, music, and literature—and three esthetics within each medium—popular, classical, and avant-garde. Comparing the evaluations of high- and low-dogmatism subjects on 12 bipolar adjective rating scales, Pyron reported that, across media, high-dogmatism subjects liked popular art significantly more than classical art and classical art significantly more than avant-garde art. Low-dogmatism subjects appeared to like all esthetics equally well.

Zagona and Kelly (1966) exposed the 44 subjects highest and lowest on dogmatism from a pool of 515 introductory psychology students to an eight-minute film in which novel jazz music was heard while the film showed lines and colors in motion. Subjects were asked to evaluate the film on an eight-point rating scale, on an adjective checklist, and on a 12-item summated rating scale. Closed-minded subjects were significantly less accepting of the film, although the checklist indicated no consistent differentiation between open- and closed-minded subjects. Eleven of the 12 items of the summated rating scale discriminated between open- and closed-minded subjects significantly and indicated that the closed-minded subjects rejected the film because of its novelty, its lack of structure, and its synthesizing demands.

Paper-and-pencil studies provide further data on the relation of novelty to dogmatism. Zagona and Zurcher (1965) compared the 30 highest and 30 lowest on dogmatism from a pool of 517 freshmen on a modified version of Mednick's Remote Associates Test (RAT). The test involves forming associations between remote cognitive elements, and it has been used as an index of creativity. The two groups were significantly differentiated, with the open-minded subjects producing more associations.

On a measure of acceptance of change, Pyron (1966a) and Pyron and Lambert (1967) reported moderate correlations between their scale and dogmatism scores. Factor analyses of their test batteries indicated that dogmatism and acceptance of change define the first factors, in both study analyses, as the highest loaded entries. Thus, consistent with theoretical expectations, the greater the closed-mindedness, the greater the rejection of change. Rubenowitz (1963), through a factor analysis of a Swedish version of the Gough-Sanford Rigidity Scale, isolated a seven-item subscale that he labeled "resistance to change in plans and opinions." Scores on this subscale were moderately correlated with scores on a Swedish-modified version of the Dogmatism Scale in keeping with theoretical expectations. To a different set of subjects, Rubenowitz administered the Edwards Personal Preference Schedule (EPPS). Scores on the change scale of that instrument correlated significantly and negatively with scores on the modified Dogmatism Scale. Vacchiano, Strauss, and Schiffman (1968) also reported a significant correlation between Dogmatism Scale scores and the need-for-change scale of the EPPS as well as between dogmatism and the Q_1 (conservatism) factor of the Sixteen Personality Factor Questionnaire. The authors interpret this finding: "In regard to their conservatism, the dogmatic subjects are confident in what they have been taught to believe, accept the tried and true despite inconsistencies, and are cautious and compromising in regard to new ideas, generally going along with tradition" (p. 84).

The only clear test of the hypothesis that more central beliefs are more resistant to change is reported in Rokeach, Reyher, and Wiseman (1968). Belief changes were induced in 29 experimental subjects through hypnotic induction. The beliefs manipulated consisted of 55 statements equally divided into five categories of belief: (Type A) primitive beliefs, unanimous consensus; (Type B) primitive beliefs, zero consensus; (Type C) authority beliefs; (Type D) derived beliefs; (Type E) inconsequential beliefs. The hypothesis that the relative order of change would be $A < B < C < D < E$ was confirmed at $p = .008$.

SELF-BELIEFS AND INTERPERSONAL BEHAVIOR

Self-beliefs

Self-beliefs are clearly integral to the theory. There were, in fact, seven self –other variables introduced in the original theory. (All these appear in or are derived from the subparts of proposition 14 discussed above.) The more closed-minded person was postulated to hold more negative beliefs about self, more contradictory beliefs about self, a need for martyrdom, and strong negative attitudes toward others. As a defense against negative self-beliefs, the more closed-minded person was postulated to be self-proselytizing—as manifested by the compulsive repetition of beliefs—and to engage in self-aggrandizing behavior—as indicated by a need for status and power and a sense of moral self-righteousness. Nine items were built into the original Dogmatism Scale to tap these variables.

In the first attempt at validating the hypothesized components of open- and closed-mindedness, Rokeach and Fruchter (1956) administered a battery of 10 scales to 207 persons. Included in the battery were the Dogmatism Scale, the Ethnocentrism Scale, and two brief ad hoc scales of paranoia and self-rejection. The correlations between Dogmatism Scale scores and the remaining three were moderately high and positive. That is, greater closed-mindedness was associated with greater ethnocentrism, paranoia, and self-rejection.

In a different mode of analysis, Kerlinger and Rokeach (1966) factor analyzed the item intercorrelations of the Authoritarianism (F) Scale and the Dogmatism Scale. They then submitted the 10 factors they obtained to a second-order factor analysis. The primary factor here comprised 19 scale items; and the majority of the dogmatism items were those explicitly concerned with self-beliefs.

In two studies, Pyron (Pyron, 1966a; Pyron & Lambert, 1967) factor analyzed the scale performances of college and high school subjects using test batteries that included the Dogmatism Scale, a 14-item measure of self-reliance, and a 15-item measure of rejection of people (eight of the items having been adopted from the Ethnocentrism Scale). In both studies dogmatism correlated positively with rejection of people and negatively with self-reliance. Both scales, moreover, loaded with dogmatism on the major factor of both analyses.

Vacchiano, Strauss, and Schiffman (1968) administered to 82 students a test battery that included the Tennessee Self-Concept Scale. The eight relevant subscales yielded a median correlation of $-.30$ with dogmatism. The researchers concluded that the "dogmatic subject lacks self-esteem, is doubtful about his own self-worth, is anxious, lacks confidence in himself, lacks either self-acceptance or self-satisfaction . . . and is dissatisfied with his behavior, his physical state, his own personal worth, and his adequacy" (p. 84).

Rubenowitz (1963), in two studies, factor analyzed a Swedish version of the Edwards Personal Preference Schedule extracting six factors. Three of these factors are relevant here. The first represented negative self-attitudes (what he termed "feeling of insufficiency"); the second represented positive self-attitudes ("self-confidence"). The third factor, sociability, will be discussed in the next section. The negative self-attitudes factor score correlated at a low but significant level with Rubenowitz's modified Dogmatism Scale in only one of two samples. The correlations of dogmatism and positive self-attitudes were not significant in either sample. Later evidence that positive self-attitudes may be independent of the level of open- or closed-mindedness—or at least only negligibly correlated—appears in Hamilton (1971), Lee and Ehrlich (1971), Ohnmacht and Muro (1967), and Pannes (1963).

Lee and Ehrlich (1971) argued that since the original Dogmatism Scale contained so many items directly related to self-beliefs and attitudes toward others, the only fair test of a relationship to these aspects would be with a version of the scale that had those items removed. Using such a scale and independent scale measures of self-beliefs, contradictory self-beliefs, beliefs about others, self-righteousness, the need for martyrdom, self-proselytization, and the need for status and power, the researchers administered their test battery to 444 undergraduate students. All the theoretical hypotheses were confirmed. Nevertheless, the correlations between the self-belief scale and the Dogmatism Scale (without the self items) were considerably lower than had been obtained in earlier studies using the full scale. This led the authors to speculate that there may be at least two types of dogmatism, only one of which is characterized by positive self-attitudes. (This speculation is discussed further in the final notes to this chapter.)

Attitudes toward others

The hypothesis that closed-minded persons will display negative attitudes toward others can be assessed by examining the performance of open- and closed-minded persons on a diverse set of measures representing differing categories of others.

In factor-analytic studies, Rokeach and Fruchter (1956), Fruchter, Rokeach, and Novak (1958), Pyron (1966) and Pyron and Lambert (1967) all reported Dogmatism and Ethnocentrism Scale scores loading on common factors. The actual correlations, where reported, are all moderately high (from .30 to .50). Rokeach (1960) reports similar levels of association in seven samples in which various measures of ethnocentrism and forms of the Dogmatism Scale were used. Similar results are reported by Roberts (1962) and Sheikh (1968).

Lee and Ehrlich (1971), using their own measure of attitudes toward others and their version of the Dogmatism Scale with self-belief items removed, reported a moderately high correlation between the two in their student sample.

Other measures of prejudice add to the substantial support for this hypothesis. Terhune (1964), using an ad hoc Nationalism Scale, found that it correlated significantly with dogmatism in an American and in a foreign student sample. Attitudes in support of the Vietnam War correlated with Dogmatism Scale scores in three independent studies (Karabenick & Wilson, 1969; Bailes & Guller, 1970; Granberg & Corrigan, 1972). Peabody (1961) provides indirect evidence indicating correlations between Dogmatism Scale scores and scores on a 20-item anti-Semitism scale in samples of English and American college students on the original and reversed versions of both scales. Rubovits and Maehr (1973) show an anti-black bias among closed-minded teachers.

The study of prejudice has always been a central concern in social psychology and in the writings of Milton Rokeach. His proposal that ''the greater the dissimilarity of beliefs and disbeliefs, the greater their rejection'' (proposition 5) led to a number of highly creative studies. Most of these have been summarized elsewhere (Ehrlich, 1973).

One study of particular importance demonstrated the relationship of perceived similarity to a social distance indicator of prejudice and the relationship of closed-mindedness to both. In this research, Rokeach (1960) studied six groups of college students. Grouping was by religion (Catholic, Episcopalian, Presbyterian, Lutheran, Methodist, and Baptist), and the groups ranged in size from 26 to 166. Subjects were presented with the following mimeographed list:

Atheist
Baptist
Catholic
Episcopalian
Jewish
Lutheran
Methodist
Mohammedan
Presbyterian

Blank lines followed the list, and the subject was asked to write the name of his or her own religion on the first line, the name of the religion most similar on the second line, with the least similar religion being written on the last line. Subjects were also administered a five-item scale of personal distance which was repeated for each of the nine religions they ranked.

Following this procedure, the social distance scores were plotted against the similarity ranks for each of the six groups. The same results, a positively accelerated curve, were obtained for every group. As religions were perceived as being increasingly dissimilar, the level of personal distance toward them increased.

One additional facet of that research was the independent analyses conducted on the effects of dogmatism. In almost every instance (47 of 48 comparisons), highly dogmatic subjects displayed greater personal distance at each level of perceived dissimilarity. The effect of closed-mindedness, then, was to increase the acceleration of the curves of rejection.

Two studies have examined attitudes toward mental patients. McCloud and Kidd (1963) and Canter (1963) both present evidence indicating that negative attitudes toward patients are highly associated with closed-mindedness. McCloud and Kidd observed that open-minded nurses and technicians treated psychiatric patients in a more effective therapeutic manner than did closed-minded personnel. The closed-minded were more likely to treat the patient as a subordinate and dependent person, whereas the behavior of the open-minded was in the direction of mutual communication and independence training. Canter (1963), in a study of student psychiatric nurses, reported correlations between dogmatism, scores on a 37-item scale of attitudes toward mental patients, and a 17-item scale measuring the nurse's attitudes toward favorable interpersonal relationships with patients (IRP). Dogmatism correlated significantly and negatively with both IRP and with attitudes toward mental patients. Hood (1974) also found that closed-minded persons are more rejecting of mental patients.

On measures of altruism—a belief in helping others, taking equalitarian actions for minorities, and treating criminals humanely—Fischer (1973) found open-mindedness moderately correlated.

In the classroom, open-minded students prefer democratic leadership and permissive teachers (Vacchiano, Schiffman, & Straus, 1968; Tosi, Quaranta, & Frumkin, 1968). Open-minded students are also more likely to approve of student demonstrations (McCarthy & Johnson, 1962).

In the larger political arena, closed-mindedness is directly related to the choice of the more conservative political candidates in both the 1964 and 1972 presidential campaigns (DiRenzo, 1968, 1971; Jones, 1973). Steffensmeier (1974), in a community study, found that adult residents who were more favorable to a "law-and-order" position were also more closed-minded.

Kirtley and Harkless (1969) administered a measure of personal distance involving 80 targets classified into eight categories: artists, scientists, left-oriented political groups and organizations, right-oriented political groups and organizations, physically deviant groups, ethnic minorities, businessmen and professionals, and clubs and service organizations. Dogmatism scores correlated significantly with the rejection of artists, scientists, leftists, physical deviants, and ethnic groups.

The data of Kirtley and Harkless, along with those cited earlier, are indicative of a major cognitive function of closed-mindedness. That is, it provides persons with the socially acceptable categories for the coding of others. The rejection of self and the rejection of others is highly correlated and probably has the same developmental basis. The studies of closed-mindedness and open-mindedness here indicate how generalized is the rejection of others and how much this rejection corresponds with the dominant norms of the society (Ehrlich, 1973).

Perhaps one extreme in the rejection of others is paranoia, and a "paranoid outlook on life" was postulated by Rokeach to be one of the distinguishing features of closed-mindedness. Rokeach and Fruchter (1956) reported a moderate correlation between Dogmatism Scale scores and their scale measure of paranoia. The only other test of the "paranoid outlook" hypothesis provides disconfirming evidence. Ehrlich and Bauer (1966) had 541 hospitalized patients rated by their psychiatrists on a nine-point scale of paranoid tendencies. In addition they compared the Dogmatism Scale scores of patients formally classified by any of the standard diagnostic categories involving paranoid characteristics with all other patients. In neither the ratings nor in formal diagnosis was there a relation between dogmatism and paranoia.

INTERPERSONAL BEHAVIOR

Although the nexus of overt acts, attitudes, and characteristics of personality is not easily established, it would be invaluable in the development of a cognitive theory of personality if precise relations to specific behaviors could be established. This section covers four general topics: perceptual accuracy, sociability and sociometric choice, self-disclosure, and interpersonal competence. The research considered in this section represents only those studies in which the basic problem involves the relation of two or more persons, and in which this relation has some bearing on self-attitudes and other attitudes.

Perceptual accuracy

Four studies provide consistent data concerning the relationship between open- and closed-mindedness and the accuracy of perceiving the attitudes of the other. Brumbaugh, Hoedt, and Beisel (1966) tested the hypothesis that open-minded more than closed-minded persons would display greater accuracy in their perceptions of the interpersonal needs of others. Their subjects were students and supervising teachers scoring relatively high and low on the Dogmatism Scale. The measure of perceptual accuracy was the relation between the subject's prediction and the actual performance of the other on Schutz's (1958) FIRO–B Scale of interpersonal needs (measuring the degree of expressed or wanted inclusion, control, and affection). Predictions were elicited after the subjects had worked together for eight weeks. For neither the student teachers nor the supervising teachers was open and closed-mindedness significantly related to the accurate perception of the needs of the other.

Still in a school setting, and using well-acquainted subjects, Croft (1965) found that open- and closed-minded school principals did not differ in the accuracy of their perception of the teachers' and school superintendents' response to their administrative attitudes.

In a laboratory study, Hunt and Lin (1967) had student judges listen to recordings of two different male speakers reading the *same* prose passage. For one speaker, the passage had been previously determined by the experimenters to be self-descriptive; for the other speaker it had been determined to be quite opposite to his own self-descriptions. On the basis of listening to the recorded passages, judges were asked to predict the responses of the speakers to an 18-pair adjective checklist. Accuracy scores were determined by having the speakers rate themselves on the checklist and by comparing judge–speaker ratings. Accuracy of judgment was found to be independent of both dogmatism and whether the speaker performed in or out of character.

Sawatzky and Zingle (1969) gauged the responses of 131 students to six films of personal interviews. The students were asked to predict how the persons interviewed would behave in specified situations and asked to describe that person on an adjective checklist. The accuracy of responses was established with other data the researchers had for the persons filmed. The correlation between Dogmatism Scale scores and the accuracy of the students' interpersonal judgments was not significant.

Another set of studies deals with the perception of one's own and other persons' levels of dogmatism. Burke (1966) provides data indicating that open- and closed-minded student subjects are equally inaccurate in their perception of the dogmatism level of fellow students. Kemp (1964) has complementary data demonstrating that people are inaccurate in perceiving their own level of dogmatism, regardless of how closed- or open-minded they are. Thus, open- and closed-minded persons appear equally inaccurate in their perception of dogmatism both in themselves and in others.

Basically, these data suggest that the degree of accuracy of person perception is independent of the dogmatism of the perceiver.

Sociability and Sociometric Choice

An indirect test of the hypothesized relation between dogmatism and attitudes toward others would be the demonstration of the lower sociability of closed-minded persons. The relevant evidence, however, is inconclusive. Rubenowitz's (1963) sociability factor, cited above, yielded a significant but low correlation with open-mindedness, and that in only one of his two samples. Plant, Telford, and Thomas (1965) found a significant difference between open-minded and closed-minded students on the sociability scale of the California Psychological Inventory. Day (1966), however, found no significant correlation between Dogmatism Scale scores and responses to a scale of introversion–extroversion.

Sociometric measurements—the actual choosing of or preference for other persons—do show some variation with the state of the cognitive system. Byrne and Blaylock (1963) administered the Dogmatism Scale to 36 married couples and obtained significant correlation of spouse scores. Lesser and Steininger (1975) also observed moderately high correlations between marriage partners. Stefflre and Leafgren (1964) investigated the relation between dogmatism and sociometric choice in a class of 40 counselor trainees who had worked together for a five-month period. Each pair of subjects was grouped into those making mutual choices, those making mutual rejections, and those in which only one chose the other. Mean differences in Dogmatism Scale scores were tested for each group comparison. Only one comparison was significant: Sets of persons making mutual choices displayed significantly smaller differences in dogmatism than sets of persons in which only one chose the other.

In the most intensive study of the relationship of open- and closed-mindedness to interpersonal relations, Rosenfeld and Nauman (1969) studied the interaction patterns in two units of a freshman women's dormitory over a 10-week period. Their findings provide some new insights.

1. People were more satisfied with their interactions with persons similar to themselves in dogmatism than with persons who were quite different.

2. Over time, people initiated fewer contacts with closed-minded persons, and the closed-minded became more negatively evaluated by unit residents.

3. Contacts between closed-minded persons and others were typically initiated by the closed-minded.

It does appear from the sociometric data that the mutuality of levels of open- and closed-mindedness is an important factor in interpersonal choice.

Self-disclosure

Altman and Haythorn (1965), in a design to be discussed below, demonstrated open- and closed-mindedness to be unrelated to self-disclosing behavior in isolated and normal encounters and in dyads homogeneous and heterogeneous in dogmatism level. Similar findings using various measures of self-disclosure are reported in Altman and Taylor (1973), Field (1975), and Worthy, Gary, and Kahn (1969). The willingness or unwillingness of persons to disclose their self-attitudes and personal experiences thus appears to be independent of their open- or closed-mindedness.

Interpersonal effectiveness

Three studies of the ability of persons in a dyad to solve mutual problems help to elaborate the theory of open- and closed-mindedness. Altman and Haythorn, in four reports (Altman & Haythorn, 1965, 1967; Haythorn, Altman, & Myers, 1966; Haythorn & Altman, 1967), provide unique but limited data on interpersonal relationships. Thirty-six Navy recruits were run in dyads, half under isolated conditions and half under control conditions. Each pair was selected to meet specific composition criteria on need affiliation, need achievement, need dominance, and dogmatism.

One-third of the subjects were homogeneously high on the Dogmatism Scale, one-third homogeneously low, and one-third were heterogeneous. Isolated pairs lived and worked in a small room for 10 days with minimal outside contact. Controls followed the same schedule but in regular Naval facilities. During the study period, groups worked on three tasks—two group tasks and a one-man perceptual monitoring task. Several types of analyses were performed to determine the effects of group composition and of isolation. (The analysis of self-disclosure was discussed above.)

Our major concern here is the researchers' analysis of task performance. Their data indicate that under the control, nonstress conditions, the dogmatism composition of a dyad had no relationship to task performance. Under conditions of stress (isolation), the task performance of dyads heterogeneous in dogmatism was impaired whereas the task performance of homogeneous dyads was enhanced.

Ehrlich and Bauer (1966) provide evidence indicating no difference in behavior as a function of the homogeneity or heterogeneity of the dogmatism levels of members of a dyad. Using patient–therapist pairs, they demonstrated the dogmatism level of the patient to be a better predictor of 14 psychiatric variables than the correlation of patient–therapist levels. Since the patient–therapist pair is not an equal-status relation, and since the hospital situation is presumably stressful only for the patient, their data are not inconsistent with the Altman and Haythorn findings.

Druckman (1967) compared the performance of high and low dogmatic persons in playing the roles of union and management representative in a simulated bargaining game. He found that regardless of role, closed-minded subjects resolved fewer issues, were more resistant to compromise, and were more likely to view compromise as defeat. Druckman's data also provide no comparability with the two preceding reports.

No final statement on the relation of open- and closed-mindedness to interpersonal effectiveness appears warranted as yet.

SOME FINAL NOTES

I have attempted to present concisely the major statements of Milton Rokeach's theory of cognitive structure and to elaborate on those statements through a relatively detailed reporting of the research relating to selected critical aspects of the theory. In this section, I want to add some notes about what I did not include as well as some notes about where we need to go.

There are at least five areas of theory and research that I either passed over lightly or did not cover. First, there is a considerable amount of work on the relation of open- and closed-mindedness to problem solving and to concept attainment strategies. Rokeach's (1960) original presentation is still the best source for those materials, although the Rokeach and Norrell (1966) report contains the best theoretical discussion of the issues.

Second, I did not review the research on time perspective, and my theoretical commentary was, as I indicated, a departure from the original theory. Again, Rokeach (1960) is still the best source for understanding the postulated role of time perspective within the framework of his theory. The most comprehensive research review and theoretical statement on the subject of time perspective is Clifton's (1971) unpublished dissertation.

Third, I did not present a formal discussion of the writing and research concerning the principle of belief congruence. The principle of belief congruence is a direct implication from the major statements of the theory of open- and closed-mindedness. Basically, the principle asserts that our acceptance or rejection of beliefs *and* the people who hold them is a consequence of the degree to which their beliefs are similar to ours in content and in centrality. Rokeach (1968) presents his basic arguments; Ehrlich (1973) offers a reformulation.

Fourth, I have not attempted any detailed review of the extensive literature on the structure and content of primitive and authority beliefs. Quite obviously, a substantial part of psychological research is devoted to such inquiry—although very little of it is placed within the context of this theory.

Finally, I have not considered many of the methodological problems associated with research in this area. Most of them are general to the study of personality. One specific problem, having to do with the Dogmatism Scale itself, I do want to discuss briefly in these final notes.

Assuming that a single instrument designed to measure dogmatism is convenient and necessary, the present scale requires substantial revision. Many of its words and idioms are showing their age. Its exclusive use of male pronouns and male examples is no longer acceptable. Its more directly political items are also outdated (and may even require a theoretical change). But even if all these item changes were made, several problems still remain. The scale is used to measure 24 theoretical dimensions simultaneously—and all in 40 items. Certainly each of these 24 requires independent instrument development and independent study. Instrument and operational research takes a long time to complete. Until then, we shall have to rely on an omnibus scale, although a better version of the present one, it is hoped.

No one as yet has attempted to compile norms for Dogmatism Scale performance. As a consequence, the criterion groups in many studies are simply not comparable. The absence of norms is particularly difficult for psychological research since most psychologists do not use formal sampling techniques in their research in areas such as this. Although the principles of cognitive structure may be the same in all populations, a study of closed-mindedness in opportunistic samples of college students (who may be clustered in a narrow range of scale performance) may lead to misleading results. Having a set of norms as a reference point would probably facilitate better research.

One form of instrument research that has been common here and in other domains of personality study has been the direct factor analysis of scale items. Virtually all the factor-analytic studies of the Dogmatism Scale have concluded that the scale is multidimensional and that some dimensions are more highly intercorrelated than others. Only a few studies have seriously attempted to test hypotheses or explore new problems of theoretical concern. Instead of building correlation matrixes of items or scales, most of that research should be concerned with building clusters of people. Only one such factor-analytic study using the Dogmatism Scale has been reported (Jay, 1969), and it was not very conclusive.

This technique of inverse factor analysis, the Q-technique, is not the only way to "type" people. The failure of researchers, however, to explore various typological procedures is critical especially since there have been many subtle indications in the literature that there may be more than one type of closed-mindedness. In addition, there have been occasional suggestions (although none in print) that persons scoring extremely low on the Dogmatism Scale may manifest an entirely different syndrome—not merely the opposite extreme of high scorers.

On the issue of "types," Dorothy Lee and I, in our continuing research program, have isolated persons high on dogmatism who appear to have strong positive self-attitudes, as well as highly dogmatic persons with the expected negative self-attitudes. These findings, which still require replication, will obviously call for some theoretical revision. At present, my guess is that Rokeach's conception of authority beliefs (Type C) may be too limited. The critical issue may be *beliefs about verification*. For some persons, there may be a relative emphasis placed on authority as compared with a personal test for validating information received. Thus, closed-minded persons whose verification beliefs require reference to authority may have negative self-attitudes. Closed-minded persons whose verification beliefs require some mode of personal test may have positive self-attitudes.

My final note. Work in this area as in most other established domains has taken on a very routine and plodding quality. People throw the Dogmatism Scale into all kinds of test batteries, and many of the well-confirmed statements of theory keep being retested, often in the same way. What is needed is an attempt to test the limits of the theory, to generate those outrageous hypotheses that can potentially open new territory for exploration. In addition, the theory should be worked on as a theory. In two decades there have been no major reformulations. To treat it as a party line would be to violate the very spirit of the theory of the open and closed mind.

EDITORS SUMMARY

The basic principles of Rokeach's cognitive theory of personality are introduced. The theory depends heavily on a conception of a belief system (all propositions that a person believes to be true at any given time) and a disbelief system (a set of systems containing all that a person believes to be false at any given time). All beliefs and disbeliefs are arranged along a continuum of acceptance and rejection. Furthermore, disbelief subsystems can be more or less similar with the belief system and with one another. There are a number of other postulates in Rokeach's theory. Perhaps most provocative is the postulate that belief–disbelief systems vary in the degree to which they are open to the acquisition of new beliefs and to the change of old beliefs. This postulate formalizes Rokeach's notion of the open and closed mind. Rokeach expands upon this notion with respect to its implications for *organization* of the belief–disbelief system, for *structure and content* of beliefs lying along the dimension of centrality, and with respect to *change*.

Operationally, Rokeach uses the theory to generate a set of questions that will index a person's level of open- or closed-mindedness. The questions are collectively called the Dogmatism Scale and have been used in many studies.

In studying change and resistance to change, it has been found that dogmatic people are more closed to change, whereas nondogmatic people are more open to change. Of course this conclusion is very general and subject to many qualifications.

With respect to attitudes toward the self, investigators have found that dogmatic people have more negative attitudes than nondogmatic people. Furthermore, closed-minded people are more likely to reject others who do not fit into the dominant norms of society.

In the realm of interpersonal behavior, researchers have explored a variety of topics. One conclusion that may be drawn is that accuracy of person perception is independent of the dogmatism of the perceiver. Another is that mutuality of levels of open- and closed-mindedness is an important factor in interpersonal choice. Third, the willingness of people to disclose themselves appears to be independent of their level of open-mindedness. Finally, there is an inconclusive relation between the level of open-mindedness and interpersonal effectiveness.

REFERENCES

Adorno, T. W., Frenkel-Brunswik, E., Levinson, D. J., & Sanford, R. N. *The authoritarian personality*. New York: Harper, 1950.

Altman, I., and Haythorn, W. Interpersonal exchange in isolation. *Sociometry*, 1965, *28*, 411–426.

Altman, I., and Haythorn W. The ecology of isolated groups. *Behavioral Science*, 1967, *12*, 169–182.

Altman, I., and Taylor, D. A. *Social penetration*. New York: Holt, Rinehart and Winston, 1973.

Bailes, D. W., and Guller, I. B. Dogmatism and attitudes toward the Vietnam war. *Sociometry*, 1970, *33*, 140–146.

Baker, S. R. A study of the relationship of dogmatism to the retention of psychological concepts: A research note. *Journal of Human Relations*, 1964, *12*, 311–313.

Brumbaugh, R., Hoedt, C., and Biesel, W. Teacher dogmatism and perpetual accuracy. *Journal of Teacher Education*, 1966, *17*, 332–335.

Burke, W. W. Social perception as a function of dogmatism. *Perceptual and Motor Skills*, 1966, *23*, 863–868.

Byrne, D., and Blaylock, B. Similarity and assumed similarity of attitudes between husbands and wives. *Journal of Abnormal and Social Psychology*, 1963, *67*, 636–640.

Canter, F. M. The relationship between authoritarian attitudes, attitudes toward mental patients and effectiveness of clinical work with mental patients. *Journal of Clinical Psychology,* 1963, *19,* 124–127.

Christensen, C. M. A note on "Dogmatism and Learning." *Journal of Abnormal and Social Psychology,* 1963, *66,* 75–76.

Clifton, A. K. A theory of time perspective and a test of crucial hypotheses. Unpublished doctoral dissertation, University of Iowa, 1971.

Costin, F. Dogmatism and learning: A follow-up of contradictory findings. *Journal of Educational Research,* 1965, *59,* 186–188.

Costin, F. Dogmatism and the retention of psychological misconceptions. *Educational and Psychological Measurement,* 1968, *28,* 529–534.

Croft, J. C. Dogmatism and perceptions of leader behavior. *Educational Administration Quarterly,* 1965, *1,* 60–71.

Day, H., Looking time as a function of stimulus variables and individual differences. *Perceptual and Motor Skills,* 1966, *22,* 423–428.

DiRenzo, G. J. Dogmatism and presidential preferences in the 1964 elections. *Psychological Reports,* 1968, *22,* 1197–1202.

DiRenzo, G. J. Dogmatism and presidential preferences: A 1968 replication. *Psychological Reports,* 1971, *29,* 109–110.

Druckman, D. Dogmatism, prenegotiation experience, and simulated group representation as determinants of dyadic behavior in a bargaining situation. *Journal of Personality and Social Psychology,* 1967, *6,* 279–290.

Ehrlich, H. J. Dogmatism and learning. *Journal of Abnormal and Social Psychology,* 1961, *62,* 148–149. (a)

Ehrlich, H. J. Dogmatism and learning: A five-year follow-up. *Psychological Reports,* 1961, *9,* 283–286. (b)

Ehrlich, H. J. Dogmatism and classroom grades: Reappraisal of the Rokeach–Norrell studies of academic performance. *Psychological Reports,* 1971, *29,* 1133–1134.

Ehrlich, H. J. *The social psychology of prejudice.* New York: John Wiley, 1973.

Ehrlich, H. J., and Bauer, M. L. The correlates of dogmatism and flexibility in psychiatric hospitalization. *Journal of Consulting Psychology,* 1966, *30,* 253–259.

Festinger, L. *A theory of cognitive dissonance.* Evanston: Row, Peterson, 1957.

Field, T. F. Relationship of dogmatism to self-disclosure. *Psychological Reports,* 1975, *36,* 594.

Fischer, E. H. Consistency among humanitarian and helping attitudes. *Social Forces,* 1973, *52,* 159–168.

Fruchter, B., Rokeach, M., and Novak, E. G. A factorial study of dogmatism, opinionation, and related scales. *Psychological Reports,* 1958, *4,* 19–22.

Frumkin, R. M. Dogmatism, social class, values and academic achievement in sociology. *Journal of Educational Sociology,* 1961, *34,* 398–403.

Gaensslen, H., May, F., and Wolpert, F. Relation between dogmatism and anxiety. *Psychological Reports,* 1973, *33,* 955–958.

Granberg, D., and Corrigan, G. Authoritarianism, dogmatism and orientations toward the Vietnam war. *Sociometry,* 1972, *35,* 468–476.

Hallenbeck, P. N., and Lundstedt, S. Some relations between dogmatism, denial and depression. *Journal of Social Psychology,* 1966, *70,* 53–58.

Hamilton, D. L. A comparative study of five methods of assessing self-esteem, dominance, and dogmatism. *Educational and Psychological Measurement,* 1971, *31,* 441–452.

Hanson, D. J., and Clune, M. Dogmatism and anxiety in relation to childhood experience. *Journal of Social Psychology,* 1973, *91,* 157–158.

Haythorn, W. W., and Altman, I., Personality factors in isolated environments. In Appley, M. H. and R. Trumbull, (Eds.), *Psychological stress,* New York: Appleton-Century-Crofts, 1967.

Haythorn, W. W., Altman, I., and Myers, T. I. Emotional symptomatology and subjective stress in isolated pairs of men. *Journal of Experimental Research in Personality,* 1966, *1,* 290–305.

Hood, R. W. Dogmatism and opinions about mental illness. *Psychological Reports,* 1973, *32,* 1283–1290.

Hood, R. W. Cognitive and affective rejection of mentally ill persons as a function of dogmatism. *Psychological Reports,* 1974, *35,* 543–549.

Hunt, R. G., and Lin, T. K., Accuracy of judgments of personal attributes. *Journal of Personality and Social Psychology,* 1967, *6,* 450–453.

Jay, R. L. Q-technique factor analysis of the Rokeach dogmatism scale. *Educational and Psychological Measurement,* 1969, *29,* 453–459.

Jones, J. M. Dogmatism and political preferences. *Psychological Reports,* 1973, *33,* 640.

Juan, I. R., Paiva, R. E. A., Haley, H. B., and O'Keefe, R. D. High and low levels of dogmatism in relation to personality characteristics of medical students: A follow-up study. *Psychological Reports,* 1974, *34,* 303–315.

Kaplan, M. F., and Singer, E. Dogmatism and sensory alienation: An empirical investigation. *Journal of Consulting Psychology,* 1963, *27,* 486–491.

Karabenick, S. A., and Wilson, W. R. Dogmatism among war hawks and peace doves. *Psychological Reports,* 1969, *25,* 419–422.

Kemp, C. G. Self-perception in relation to open-closed belief systems. *Journal of General Psychology,* 1964, *70,* 341–344.

Kerlinger, F., and Rokeach, M. The factorial nature of the F and D scales. *Journal of Personality and Social Psychology,* 1966, *4,* 391–399.

Kilpatrick, D. G., Cauthen, N. R., Sandman, C. A., and Quattlebaum, L. F. Dogmatism and personal sexual attitudes. *Psychological Reports,* 1968, *23,* 1105–1106.

Kirtley, D., and Harkless, R. Some personality and attitudinal correlates of dogmatism. *Psychological Reports,* 1969, *24,* 851–854.

Lee, D. E., and Ehrlich, H. J. Sensory alienation and interpersonal constraints as correlates of cognitive structure, *Psychological Reports,* 1977, 40, 840–842.

Lee, D. E., and Ehrlich, H. J. Sensory alienation and interpersonal constraints as a consequence of cognitive structure, *Psychological Reports,* in press.

Lehmann, I. J., Sinha, K., and Hartnett, R. T. Changes in attitudes and values associated with college attendance. *Journal of Educational Psychology,* 1966, *57,* 89–98.

Lesser, H., and Steininger, M. Family patterns in dogmatism. *Journal of Social Psychology,* 1975, *126,* 155–156.

Lewin, K. A dynamic theory of personality. New York: McGraw-Hill, 1935.

McCarthy, J., and Johnson, R. C. Interpretation of the "city hall riots" as a function of general dogmatism. *Psychological Reports,* 1962, *11,* 243–245.

McCloud, K., and Kidd, A. H., Rokeach's Dogmatism Scale in the selection of psychiatric nursing personnel. *Psychological Reports,* 1963, *13,* 241–242.

Mikol, B. The enjoyment of new musical systems. In M. Rokeach, *The open and closed mind.* New York: Basic Books, 1960.

Ohnmacht, F. W., and Muro, J. J. Self-acceptance: Some anxiety and cognitive style relationships. *Journal of Psychology*, 1967, *67*, 235–239.

Ondrack, D. A. Socialization in professional schools: a comparative study. *Administrative Science Quarterly*, 1975, *20*, 97–103.

Pannes, E. D. The relationship between self-acceptance and dogmatism in junior-senior high school students. *Journal of Educational Sociology*, 1963, *36*, 419–426.

Peabody, D. Attitude content and agreement set in scales of authoritarianism, dogmatism, anti-Semitism, and economic conservatism. *Journal of Abnormal and Social Psychology*, 1961, *63*, 1–11.

Plant, W. T. Longitudinal changes in intolerance and authoritarianism for subjects differing in amount of college education over four years. *Genetic Psychology Monographs*, 1965, *72*, 247–287.

Plant, W. T., Telford, C. W., and Thomas, J. A. Some personality differences between dogmatic and nondogmatic groups. *Journal of Social Psychology*, 1965, *67*, 67–75.

Pyron, B. A factor-analytic study of simplicity–complexity of social ordering. *Perceptual and Motor Skills*, 1966, *22*, 259–272. (a)

Pyron, B. Rejection of avant-garde art and the need for simple order. *Journal of Psychology*, 1966, *63*, 159–178. (b)

Pyron, B., and Kafer, J. Recall of nonsense and additudinal rigidity. *Journal of Personality and Social Psychology*, 1967, *5*, 463–466.

Pyron, B., and Lambert, P. The generality of simplicity–complexity of social perception in a high school population. *Journal of Psychology*, 1967, *66*, 265–273.

Roberts, A. H. Intra-test variability as a measure of generalized response set. *Psychological Reports*, 1962, *11*, 793–799.

Rokeach, M. The nature and meaning of dogmatism. *Psychological Review*, 1954, *61*, 194–204.

Rokeach, M. *The open and closed mind*. New York: Basic Books, 1960.

Rokeach, M. *Beliefs, attitudes and values*. San Francisco: Jossey-Bass, 1968.

Rokeach, M., and Fruchter, B. A factorial study of dogmatism and related concepts. *Journal of Abnormal and Social Psychology*, 1956, *53*, 356–360.

Rokeach, M., and Kemp, C. G. Open and closed systems in relation to anxiety and childhood experience. In M. Rokeach, *The open and closed mind*. New York: Basic Books, 1960.

Rokeach, M., and Norrell, G. *The nature of analysis and synthesis and some conditions in the classroom which facilitate or retard these cognitive processes*. Final Report of Cooperative Research Branch Project No. 879, 1966, Michigan State University.

Rokeach, M., Reyher, J., and Wiseman, R. An experimental analysis of the organization of belief systems. In M. Rokeach, *Beliefs, attitudes and values*. San Francisco: Jossey-Bass, 1968.

Rosenfeld, H. M., and Nauman, D. Effects of dogmatism on the development of informal relationships among women. *Journal of Personality*, 1969, *37*, 497–511.

Rubenowitz, S. *Emotional flexibility–rigidity as a comprehensive dimension of mind*. Stockholm: Almquist & Wiksell, 1963.

Rubovits, P. C., and Maehr, M. L. Pygmalion black and white. *Journal of Personality and Social Psychology*, 1973, *25*, 210–218.

Sawatzky, D. D., and Zingle, H. W. Accurate interpersonal perception and open-mindedness. *Perceptual and Motor Skills*, 1969, *29*, 395–400.

Schutz, W. C. *FIRO; a 3-dimensional theory of human behavior*. New York: Rinehart, 1958.

Sheikh, A. A. Stereotype in interpersonal perception and inter-correlation between some attitude measures. *Journal of Social Psychology,* 1968, *76,* 175–179.

Soh, K. C. Dogmatism, training and enjoyment of Western classical music. *Psychologia,* 1972, *15,* 59–64.

Steffensmeier, D. J. Levels of dogmatism and attitudes toward law and order. *Psychological Reports,* 1974, *34,* 151–153.

Stefflre, B., and Leafgren, F. Mirror, mirror on the wall . . . A study of preferences for counselors. *Personnel Guidance Journal,* 1964, *42,* 459–462.

Sticht, T., and Fox, W. Geographical mobility and dogmatism, anxiety and age. *Journal of Social Psychology,* 1966, *68,* 171–174.

Terhune, K. W., Nationalism among foreign and American students: An exploratory study. *Journal of Conflict Resolution,* 1964, *8,* 256–270.

Tosi, D. J., Quaranta, J. J., and Frumkin, R. M. Dogmatism and student teacher perceptions and ideal classroom leadership. *Perceptual and Motor Skills,* 1968, *27,* 750.

Vacchiano, R. B., Strauss, P. S., and Hochman, D. The open and the closed mind: a review of dogmatism. *Psychological Bulletin,* 1969, *71,* 261–273.

Vacchiano, R. B., Strauss, P. S., and Schiffman, D. C. Personality correlates of dogmatism. *Journal of Consulting and Clinical Psychology,* 1968, *32,* 83–85.

Vidulich, R. N., and Kaiman, I. P. The effects of information source status and dogmatism upon conformity behavior. *Journal of Abnormal and Social Psychology,* 1961, *63,* 639–642.

White, B. J., and Alter, R. D. Dogmatism and examination performance. *Journal of Educational Psychology,* 1967, *58,* 285–289.

Wilkinson, G. S. Social psychological dimensions of resistance to psychiatric innovations. *Psychological Reports,* 1974, *34,* 1083–1085.

Worthy, M., Gary, A. L., and Kahn, G. M. Self-disclosure as an exchange process. *Journal of Personality and Social Psychology,* 1969, *13,* 59–64.

Zagona, S. V., and Kelly, M. A. The resistance of the closed mind to a novel and complex audio-visual experience. *Journal of Social Psychology,* 1966, *70,* 123–131.

Zagona, S. V., and Zurcher, L. A. Participation, interaction, and role behavior in groups selected from the extremes of the open-closed cognitive continuum. *Journal of Psychology,* 1964, *58,* 255–264.

Zagona, S. V., and Zurcher, L. A. The relationship of verbal ability and other cognitive variables to the open-closed cognitive dimension. *Journal of Psychology,* 1965, *60,* 213–219.

CHAPTER 5

Field Dependence

DONALD R. GOODENOUGH

Educational Testing Service
Princeton, New Jersey

This chapter is concerned with a dimension of individual differences in cognitive functioning, proposed by H. A. Witkin and defined with increasing precision by Witkin and many others over a period of work now spanning some 30 years (e.g., Witkin & Berry, 1975; Witkin, Dyk, Faterson, Goodenough, & Karp, 1962/1974; Witkin & Goodenough, 1976; Witkin, Lewis, Hertzman, Machover, Meissner, & Wapner, 1954/1972).[1] The dimension reflects the degree to which people function autonomously of the world around them. People at one extreme of the dimension are likely to have internal frames of reference available to them that they use in articulating incoming information. People located at this extreme are said to be *field independent*. People at the opposite extreme are likely to use external frames of reference and are less active in processing incoming information. They are said to be *field dependent*. (The historical development of this definition has recently been discussed in detail by Witkin and Goodenough, 1976.[2])

The theme of this chapter is contained in a set of four major, interrelated propositions concerning the nature and origins of field dependence. These propositions will be stated now and elaborated in the sections to follow.

A central proposition of field-dependence theory is that people are self-consistent in mode of field approach across a wide variety of situations. There is an abundance of data in support of this proposition. For example, it has been demonstrated that people who are field independent in one perceptual situation tend to be field independent in many other perceptual and problem-solving situations as well. The expression of field independence in perceptual and intellectual tasks may be described in terms of a restructuring ability. The stimulus world around us is almost always organized into a field of objects. Correspondingly, our perception of the world is almost never an accurate representation of the stimuli that reach our receptors but is better described as a reproduction "of the

165

objects which those stimuli suggest'' (Hilgard, 1948, p. 332). This reproduction involves a preperceptual organization or structuring of the stimulus elements. Our dimension concerns the extent to which these cognitive reproductions are restructured to meet the requirements of a particular situation. For people at the field-independent end of the continuum, restructuring is commonly found. A cognitive Gestalt may be analyzed into its component parts, and/or cognitive elements may be arranged into a new organization. In contrast, for people at the field-dependent end of the continuum, the Gestalt tends to be accepted as given.

A major thrust of the work on self-consistency in recent years has been directed at the role of field dependence in social-interpersonal behavior. As we shall see, it seems clear from this work that people who are oriented toward external fields in perceptual-intellectual functioning also tend to be oriented toward external (interpersonal) fields in social situations. In social behavior, it has been said of field-independent people that they have a sense of separate identity; that they maintain a set of internalized values and standards that regulate their interpersonal behavior apart from the requirements of the immediate social framework. In contrast, field-dependent people pay more attention to, and often get along better with, others.

The field-dependence dimension thus appears to cut across the traditional boundaries between the areas of cognition and personality. It is only superficially paradoxical, therefore, to find a chapter on what may be described as a dimension of cognitive functioning located in a book on dimensions of personality.

A second, central proposition of field-dependence theory involves the conceptualization of the field-dependence construct as a cognitive style dimension. Cognitive styles are concerned with the form rather than the content of cognitive activity. They are pervasive, stable dimensions of individual differences in the processes of perception, thinking, problem solving, learning and so on. They are primarily concerned with how we deal with information about the world rather than with how much or how well we do so. There may be some situations in which a particular style leads to better performance, but other styles are more effective in other situations. Thus, cognitive styles are bipolar in nature. This bipolarity is particularly noteworthy. Intelligence and most other ability measures are unipolar. To have more of the ability is better than to have less of it. In contrast, for cognitive style dimensions, each pole has adaptive value under some specified conditions.

The evidence suggests that the field-dependence dimension may have this kind of bipolarity. A relatively field-independent mode of functioning is more adaptive in certain situations. For example, there are many perceptual and intellectual tasks in which restructuring leads to relatively successful behavior. There are many other situations, however, in which a relatively field-dependent mode of functioning may be more adaptive. In many social situations, for example, it seems reasonable to expect that an orientation toward other people may lead to relatively successful interpersonal behavior.

A third major proposition of field-dependence theory involves the origins of the cognitive styles in ontogenetic development. The evidence indicates that the individual moves from a state of relative field dependence to a state of greater field independence during the course of development from childhood to young adulthood. Within this developmental framework, it has been proposed that socialization factors have an important effect on the extent to which a field-independent mode of functioning emerges. The evidence suggests that child-rearing practices that encourage autonomous functioning foster the development of relatively field-independent adults. In contrast, rearing practices that strongly impose parental authority on the behavior of the child or that inhibit his separation from parental control foster the development of relatively field-dependent adults.

A fourth major proposition concerns the origins of the cognitive styles in cultural evolution. Nomadic subsistence-level hunting and gathering cultures tend to have "loose" societies in which there is little social structure beyond the family unit. The relatively isolated existence of the hunting band places a premium on self-reliance. In addition, the ability to perceive hidden cues may be particularly required in the search for food and for negotiating a safe return to camp. Thus, it is proposed that the cognitive restructuring involved in field-independent functioning is particularly adaptive under these ecological and economic conditions. Sedentary, agricultural-pastoral cultures, in contrast, are more often characterized by "tight" societies with elaborate social structures in which authorities enforce strict adherence to social norms. In these settings, the ability to get along with others involved in field-dependent functioning may be at a premium. In this conception, man's historical development from a hunter –gatherer to a farmer–herder was accompanied by a change from relative field independence to relative field dependence. Furthermore, the shift in cognitive styles may be understood as a natural consequence of the cultural evolution in socialization practices from the relatively permissive child rearing that tends to be found among hunting-gathering societies to the relatively strict child rearing that tends to be found among agricultural-pastoral societies.

Before turning to a more detailed discussion of these propositions, it is useful to consider how the concepts of field dependence and field independence emerged in the early research of Witkin and his associates.[3]

HISTORICAL ORIGINS OF THE FIELD-DEPENDENCE AND FIELD-INDEPENDENCE CONCEPTS

Perception of the upright in space

The concepts of field dependence and field independence originated in classical laboratory experiments concerned with the relative importance of inner versus visual field cues to the perception of the upright in space. The question of how we tell which way is up has long been of interest in the history of physiology and psychology. Ordinarily, the location of the upright is automatically and accurately perceived by everyone. However, marked inaccuracy sometimes does occur, and these cases are dramatic and important for perceptual theory. As a consequence, research attention early focused on the determinants of perception of the upright, and the nature of some inaccuracies is now fairly well understood.

One factor that may produce perceptual errors is cue conflict. Two sets of cues are normally available to tell us which way is up. One set includes straight (or nearly straight) lines in the visual field that usually correspond to the true horizontal and vertical directions. In addition to these cues from the visual field, inner frames of reference are also available, arising from gravitational effects on the vestibular and kinesthetic senses. Either one of these cue sets, operating alone, is adequate for reasonably accurate location of the perceptual upright. Most often they are both available, providing congruent, redundant information for locating the vertical and horizontal dimensions of space. However, there are occasions when inner cues and cues from the visual field yield conflicting information, and large errors of judgment may result, depending on how the cue conflict is resolved in perception. In airplanes, for example, cloud layers may produce prominent, nearly straight lines in the visual field that are tilted with respect to the invisible horizon. For the pilot of a plane in level flight, these misleading field cues conflict with the valid inner cues to the location of the upright, and inaccuracies will result if the perceptual conflict is resolved in favor of the cues from the visual field. To cite another aeronautical example, the vector resulting from gravitational and centrifugal forces is displaced from the upright in a banked and turning plane. Under these conditions, the inner cues may be misleading. They may conflict with valid field cues to the location of the upright, and errors of judgment will result if the perceptual conflict is resolved in their favor.

"Real world" examples of this sort are dramatic and are of obvious importance to the safety of air crew and passengers. However, conflict resolution in perception of the upright is much more effectively studied by producing examples of disorientation in the laboratory.

One laboratory situation developed to study how cue conflicts are resolved is called the Tilting-Room–Tilting-Chair Test (Witkin, 1949). In this test the subject is seated in a chair that is projected into a room. The entire room can be tilted to the right or left around the subject. The chair can also be tilted, independently of the room, and the subject's task is to move his chair until he is seated in an upright position. To the extent that the perceptual conflict is resolved in favor of the inner cues, the subject will correctly align himself with the objective vertical. However, if the upright is located by reference to the visual field, he will align himself with the axes of the tilted room. This situation is analogous to the aeronautical example in which a pilot attempts to keep his plane in a level attitude while flying between tilted cloud layers in the absence of instrument assistance.

Another device that was developed to study cue conflict, called the Rotating-Room Test, is illustrated in Figure 5–1. This situation is similar to the Tilting-Room–Tilting-Chair Test, except that the subject and the room in which he sits are rotated around a circular track as in a merry-go-round. The room is located in an upright position, but the combination of gravitational and centrifugal forces displaces the inner cues, as in the banking airplane. Here again, the subject's task is to align himself with the objective upright. In contrast with the Tilting-Room –Tilting-Chair Test, however, the subject will correctly orient himself if cues from the visual field predominate, but he will align himself with the tilted force vector to the extent that inner cues predominate in the resolution of the perceptual conflict. Thus, reliance on inner cues will lead to inaccurate perception of the upright.

Much simpler laboratory devices have also proven effective in studying perception of the upright. In the earliest situations mirrors were used to tilt the visual

Figure 1. The Rotating-Room Test.
(After Witkin, 1952) From Witkin et al., PERSONALITY THROUGH PERCEPTION. Copyright © 1954, Harper & Row, Publishers, Inc. Reprinted by permission.

field and thereby create a conflict between inner and field cues (e.g., Asch & Witkin, 1948a). Subsequently, the Rod-and-Frame Test, illustrated in Figure 5–2, has commonly been employed for this purpose. In this test, the subject is seated in a dark room in which the only visible objects are a luminous square frame surrounding a luminous rod. The frame is tilted clockwise or counterclockwise with respect to the upright, providing a visual field with erroneous cues as to the location of the vertical and horizontal axes of space in conflict with the valid inner cues. The subject's task is to align the rod (rather than his body) to the upright. To the extent that the perceptual conflict is resolved in favor of the inner cues, the rod will be adjusted to the gravitational vertical. In contrast, to the extent that the upright is apprehended by reference to visual cues, the rod is aligned with the axes of the frame.

Figure 2.   The Rod-and-Frame Test.
The subject is tilted to the right and the frame is tilted to the left. (After Witkin and Asch, 1948b) From Witkin et al., PERSONALITY THROUGH PERCEPTION. Copyright © 1954, Harper & Row, Publishers, Inc. Reprinted by permission.

Early studies using laboratory devices of this sort were aimed at determining which cues are most important in the perception of the upright. In several studies it was found that inner cues were more important than cues from the visual field (Gibson & Mowrer, 1938; Mach, 1875). However, just the opposite conclusion was reached in another study (Wertheimer, 1912). In the attempt to resolve this discrepancy, Witkin and Asch did a series of similar studies, and, as sometimes happens in research, the reconciliation attempt led to new insights about the nature of perception of the upright (Asch & Witkin, 1948a, 1948b; Witkin & Asch, 1948a, 1948b). Two novel features of this series are noteworthy. A relatively large number of subjects was used, and attention was directed to individual differences. These features made it possible for Witkin and Asch to arrive at the dramatic conclusion that the relative importance of inner versus visual field cues depends on the person involved. For some people, the upright is apprehended by reference to cues from the visual field, whereas for other people, inner cues predominate. For most people, however, perception of the upright under conditions of cue conflict involves some compromise resolution. Scores on the tests of upright perception are typically calculated in terms of degrees of error from the objective upright and produce distributions of individual performance that vary continuously from near perfect alignment with the upright to many degrees of error. Most people are located in the midrange of these distributions. Earlier studies had followed the then-common practice in perceptual experiments of using only a few subjects, and they evidently emphasized inner cues or cues from the visual field depending on the type of subject they happened to employ.

Witkin and his colleagues subsequently demonstrated individual consistency across situations in the degree to which inner versus visual field cues were relied on (Witkin et al., 1954/1972). People who tended to rely on inner cues in adjusting the rod to the upright in the Rod-and-Frame Test, for example, also tended to rely on inner cues when aligning themselves to the upright in the Tilting-Room–Tilting-Chair Test and in the Rotating-Room Test. Hence, using one or more of the laboratory situations, people could be graded in terms of the degree to which they depended on the external visual field in their perception of the upright in general. At one end of this dimension people were said to be dependent on the field (or simply field dependent) whereas people at the other end were said to be field independent.

The early work by Witkin and his colleagues showed the existence of an individual difference dimension in the use of inner versus visual field cues in the perception of the upright. A host of questions remained, however, as to the nature of this dimension and the extent to which it might be identified in other situations. These issues quickly attracted attention. Before examining the substance of this work, it is worth considering some of the reasons why the field-dependence construct has become so popular over the years.

THE GROWTH OF INTEREST IN FIELD DEPENDENCE AND FIELD INDEPENDENCE

There is no doubt that the field-dependence construct can be counted among the most stimulating concepts to emerge in the recent history of research on individual differences. Bibliographies of articles relating to field dependence now number nearly 2000 items (Witkin, Cox, & Friedman, 1976; Witkin, Cox, Friedman, Hrshikesan, & Siegel, 1974; Witkin, Oltman, Cox, Ehrlichman, Hamm, & Ringler, 1973). No dimension could achieve such notice without touching on the concerns of specialists in a variety of fields, and only a general, pervasive dimension could hope to accomplish this. Field dependence is a term that can be found in the literature of domains such as physiological psychology, intelligence, social psychology, learning and memory, personality defenses, perception, child development, anthropology, guidance, auto safety, psychotherapy, psychosomatic medicine, and many others. Furthermore, the possibility of viewing some of the phenomena in each of these domains within a single conceptual framework has appealed to many scholars involved in attempts at integration of diverse findings. One major reason for its popularity, then, was the quickly emerging evidence that the field-dependence construct was very general in nature.

A second reason is very practical but no less important. The field-dependence concept emerged from classical laboratory studies of perception, as we have seen, and research on field dependence in perceptual functioning has continued to occupy the attention of many investigators. As a consequence, there are now available a variety of standardized, reliable measures of perceptual field dependence that may be used as marker or "tracer" variables for the more general dimension. The accessibility of these tests makes it easy to do research on the field-dependence concept (Oltman, 1968; Witkin, Oltman, Raskin, & Karp, 1971).

Another feature of the field-dependence construct that has attracted considerable interest involves its conceptualization as a cognitive style dimension. The stylistic nature of the field-dependence dimension emerged early in the history of research on perception of the upright. As noted, under ordinary conditions either inner cues or cues from the visual field may be used to perceive the location of the upright with considerable accuracy. Field-dependent and field-independent people do not differ in how accurately they perceive the upright but only in how they arrive at their percept. To be sure, there are some situations in which reliance on inner cues does lead to better performance: the pilot flying between tilted cloud layers and the laboratory analogue of this situation, the Tilting-Room–Tilting-Chair Test, are examples. In these cases field-independent people are more accurate. But there are other situations in which reliance on cues from the visual field leads to better performance; the banking aircraft and the laboratory analogue of this situation, the Rotating Room Test, are examples. In these cases field-dependent people are more accurate. Thus, within the area of perceptual orientation to the upright in space, the bipolar nature of the field-dependence dimension was soon apparent. Since cognitive style variables are defined as bipolar dimensions concerned primarily with how rather than how well we deal with information about the world, it seemed appropriate to talk about field-dependent and field-independent cognitive styles. The stylistic feature of the field-dependence construct undoubtedly contributes to its popularity by appealing to the view that each of us can make a contribution to society by ''doing his own thing'' in his own way.

Perhaps another reason why the field-dependence dimension has attracted attention is its salience in ordinary interpersonal encounters. It is common to hear comments from researchers after their first contact with extremely field-dependent and field-independent subjects to the effect that the contrasting groups are noticeably different in personal characteristics. In fact, there is considerable evidence that field dependence is a salient personal characteristic even to people who are naïve with respect to the field-dependence construct and without any professional training in personality assessment. A number of studies have found that people who are similar to each other in degree of field dependence get along better with each other than people who are dissimilar in degree of field dependence. For example, a study of college students found that roommates who chose to continue living together were more similar in extent of field dependence than roommates who chose to separate (Wong, 1976). Other studies of groups of people who are working toward some common goal have suggested the same conclusion. Thus, patient–therapist pairings in which both parties are field dependent or both are field independent tend to like each other better, and the patients tend to stay in therapy longer than in pairings where one party is field dependent and the other party is field independent (Folman, 1973; Greene, 1972). Similar match–mismatch effects have been observed in some studies of teacher–student interactions, but the evidence is not as consistent on this point (DiStefano, 1969; James, 1973). There is nothing surprising about the finding that people with similar personalities get along better than people with dissimilar personalities. However, the fact that matching on the basis of degree of field dependence produces detectable effects of this sort must mean that field-dependent people are different from field-independent people in some way that stands out against the background of other personal characteristics that could have produced their own match–mismatch effects. Results of this sort lend credence to the view that the field-dependence construct has significant psychological reality in interpersonal behavior.

The presence of match–mismatch effects tells us that field-dependent people are different from field-independent people in some way but tells us nothing about what the difference may be. We turn now to a detailed consideration of the nature of these differences.

THE APPLICATION OF THE FIELD-DEPENDENCE CONCEPT
TO FURTHER PERCEPTUAL AND INTELLECTUAL PHENOMENA

It is obvious that field-dependent performance in tests of the location of the upright involves a reliance on the external field and that field-independent performance involves a degree of autonomy from the field. In the early history of research on field dependence, it was not evident, however, that individual differences in extent of field dependence could be described in terms of a general dimension of autonomous functioning. It seemed possible, for example, that field-dependent people were simply insensitive to vestibular cues, or that visual stimuli were dominant in their perception. A number of hypotheses about the nature of the field-dependence dimension were explored to pursue such possibilities (Witkin et al., 1954/1972, 1962/1974), and it was only gradually that the current view emerged. The process of refinement in definition continues, but the evidence now available supports the hypothesis that a rather general dimension of autonomous functioning is involved.

Early indications of widespread self-consistency in cognitive styles came from studies relating the field-dependence measures to performance in other perceptual and intellectual tasks. These studies suggested that field-dependent people tend to accept perceptual fields as given, in a variety of situations. In contrast, field-independent people achieve a greater degree of autonomy from the field by a process of cognitive restructuring. The range of perceptual-intellectual tasks requiring restructuring that have been related to field dependence is illustrated in the sections to follow.

The Capacity to Overcome Embedding Contexts in Perceptual Functioning

One of the first indications that cognitive restructuring is closely linked to field independence came from studies of the relationship between measures of perception of the upright in space and the ability to locate camouflaged figures. In his classical study of disembedding, Gottschaldt (1926) was able to show that simple figures were difficult to find when their elements were initially seen as part of another figure-ground organization. This principle is illustrated in Figure 5–3.

In Figure 5–3, the problem is to locate a square, like the one shown as 5–3a, that is hidden in the picture of the coffeepot shown as 5–3b. The solution is marked by the shaded lines in 5–3c. As the reader may discover for himself, the several parts of the square in 5–3b are difficult to imagine as belonging to the

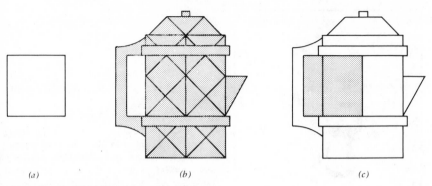

(a)   *(b)*   *(c)*

Figure 3.   An Embedded Square.
Find the square shown in Figure 3a camouflaged in the coffeepot shown in 3b. The solution is shaded in Figure 3c.

same (square) figure. Instead, the right half of the square is immediately perceived as a section of the coffeepot, and the left half is seen as part of the background seen through the opening between the pot and the pot handle. To find the camouflaged square, it is necessary to restructure this perceptual field.

Using modifications of figures originally developed by Gottschaldt, Witkin developed an Embedded Figures Test to examine the hypothesis that field-dependent people have greater difficulty than field-independent people in overcoming embedding contexts (Witkin, 1950).[4] As would be expected on the basis of the restructuring hypothesis, field-independent people did better than field-dependent people on the Embedded Figures Test (Witkin et al., 1954/1972). In fact, the relationship between the Embedded Figures Test and tests of perception of the upright like the Rod-and-Frame Test is now so well established that the Embedded Figures Test is commonly used as a measure of field dependence (Witkin et al., 1971).

Restructuring and Other Perceptual Phenomena

Field dependence in perception of the upright has also been related to the speed with which perceptual closure is achieved. A typical test of closure speed requires a subject to identify a mutilated figure. For difficult problems of this type the display is initially seen as an ambiguous, disorganized field that must be restructured in the process of imposing an integrated figural organization. A sample item of this type is shown in Figure 5–4.

At least for difficult tests of closure speed, most studies show a relation with measures of field independence, as would be expected on the basis of the restructuring hypothesis (e.g., Goodman, 1962; Messick & French, 1975).

Restructuring has also been studied extensively in connection with the well-

Figure 4.   A Mutilated Figure.
Try to identify the object shown in the picture by using your imagination to fill in the missing parts. The object is a hammer head. (From *Gestalt Completion Test–CS–1*, copyright © 1962 by Educational Testing Service. All rights reserved.) Reproduced by permission.

known phenomenon of perceptual constancy. We tend to see objects as relatively stable features of our world despite the fact that the actual stimuli that reach us from an object may vary enormously as a function of lighting conditions, distance from us, viewing angle, and so on. Although our immediate perception is subject to these constancy effects, it is possible and sometimes useful to become aware of the properties of the actual retinal image cast by an object. An artist, for example, may need to do so in order to paint a canvas that looks undistorted to a viewer. The act of imagining the retinal image must require a restructuring of the immediate perception of objects and has therefore been studied in relation to field dependence. Although not all studies have produced consistent results, the available evidence tends to confirm the hypothesis that field-independent people are more accurate than field-dependent people at estimating parameters of the retinal image when required to do so (e.g., Gardner, Jackson, & Messick, 1960; Perez, 1955).

The classical perceptual phenomena of reversible perspective provide still other examples of perceptual restructuring. Certain figures can be seen in more than one perspective. As the viewer continues to inspect the figure, these two perspectives spontaneously alternate in perception. Individual differences in the rate of spontaneous alternation have been noted in figures of this sort, but they are not related to measures of field independence (Thurstone, 1944). However, the ability to modify the spontaneous rate of alternation either by speeding up or slowing down the natural rate has been related to field independence in most studies (Haronian & Sugerman, 1966; Jackson, 1955; Newbigging, 1954; Sewell, 1973). Here again, field-independent viewers are able to overcome the immediate perceptual events that dominate the cognitive functioning of field-dependent people.

Restructuring in Problem Solving

The field-dependence dimension may also be identified in problem-solving situations that seem to require restructuring. One of the most widely studied of these situations involves spatial visualization. In problems of this type the subject is typically asked questions about a display, the answers to which require him to imagine the display or himself in an orientation or perspective other than the one immediately present in perception. Many studies have found tests of spatial visualization to be related to field-independence measures (e.g., Witkin et al., 1962/1974).

Some of the best illustrations of restructuring problems come from the work of Piaget (e.g., Piaget & Inhelder, 1962). As one example, conservation of weight is studied in children by using plasticine balls, one of which is molded into a "long stick" or a "large pancake" as the subject watches. The experimenter then asks whether the ball weighs the same as the stick or pancake. The problem is difficult for children because the ball "looks" smaller in immediate perception. Thus, intuitively, it seems reasonable to suppose that the ball weighs less. To answer the question correctly, this impression must be discarded and the problem elements restructured. As might be expected, field-independent subjects appear to be more accurate than field-dependent subjects on conservation problems (Pascual-Leone, 1969).

Another problem type that may be used to study restructuring in problem solving was developed by Duncker (1945) in his classical work on functional fixity. In one example, the subject is required to construct a shelf. He has available for the job a limited set of objects, including pieces of wood nailed together and a pair of pliers. To construct the shelf he must first use the pliers to remove the nail, and then he must use the pliers as a shelf support. The problem requires that the pliers be taken out of their usual functional context and reconsidered in the unconventional support application. As might be expected, field-independent people have been found to solve problems of this type much more effectively than field-dependent people (Glucksberg, 1956; Witkin et al., 1962/1974).

Restructuring in Concept Attainment

Some of the most interesting work on the cognitive correlates of field dependence is to be found in the literature on concept attainment. It is particularly interesting because the study of learning styles has been a major focus of attention in the area of concept attainment. In concept attainment problems, the subject is given a series of items and is told for each item whether it is an exemplar of the concept. The problem is to learn how to pick exemplars from nonexemplars of the concept. Hypothesis testing about the attributes that define the concept readily occurs in the process of learning and can be observed by a variety of techniques. One can therefore determine whether a hypothesis-testing approach is being employed by a particular individual. In addition, procedures can be used that favor or even force such an approach in order to examine the sequence of hypotheses as they are adopted and discarded in the process of search for the relevant concept. The opportunity to examine problem-solving strategies as they are revealed in the hypothesis sequence has been exploited by many investigators.

The literature suggests two important conclusions with respect to differences between field-dependent and field-independent people in how they go about learning concepts. First, field-independent people tend to use a hypothesis-testing approach, and field-dependent people use an intuitive approach. When hypothesis-testing *is* employed by field-dependent people, their hypotheses are dominated by the salient cues available for use in hypothesis construction. Both of these conclusions seem consistent with the restructuring hypothesis.

The history of research on concept attainment has featured two prominent types of theory about the learning process involved. One theory type assigns a passive, receptive, intuitive role to the learner, and to the other type an active participant role in which some common element of the stimuli illustrating the concept (exemplars) serves as the basis of a hypothesis about the nature of the concept. These theory types were emphasized, for example, by Woodworth (1938):

According to the "composite photograph" theory, the features common to a class of objects summate their impressions on the observer [O] who thus gradually acquires a picture in which the common features stand out strongly while the variable characteristics are washed out. The . . . [O] plays a passive or receptive role, simply letting himself be impressed by the objects. The other theory assigns to O the more active role characteristic of trial and error behavior. The concept is supposed to originate as a hypothesis, which O proceeds to test by trying it on fresh specimens of the class. (p. 801)

From these descriptions it seems reasonable to suggest that the composite photograph approach reflects a field-dependent orientation, whereas a hypothesis testing approach requires a process of perceptual restructuring and would therefore be more common among field-independent people.

The composite photograph type of learning process is characterized by continuity in the course of concept attainment. Each trial adds an increment to what is learned, producing a gradual decrease in errors until the criterion for success is achieved. However, the hypothesis-testing approach is characterized by discontinuity. Performance does not improve until the correct hypothesis is hit on, at which point the criterion is suddenly attained. If field-independent people tend to use a hypothesis-testing approach to concept learning, then discontinuity should be more characteristic of field-independent than of field-dependent subjects. This hypothesis was suggested, tested, and confirmed by Nebelkopf and Dreyer(1973). These authors found no significant change in accuracy from trial to trial until a sudden improvement to criterion among field-independent subjects. In contrast, field-dependent subjects were characterized by a gradual improvement, as expected. It is interesting to notice that there was no difference between field-dependent and field-independent subjects in this study in the number of trials required to learn the concepts. Neither of the two approaches mentioned is better in this respect. Thus, field dependence made a difference in how concepts were learned but not in how rapidly they were learned.

In most concept attainment studies the subject is required to guess at the concept after each trial and/or after the set of hypotheses is carefully listed from which the concept is to be drawn. Thus, the subject is implicitly directed to adopt a hypothesis-testing approach. It is clear in these cases that field-dependent people are able to adopt a hypothesis-testing approach when required to do so. However, the evidence suggests that when field-dependent people use such an approach, they tend to ignore nonsalient attributes of the stimuli in constructing their hypotheses.

It has repeatedly been found that field-independent subjects tend to sample more fully from a set of attributes that might be relevant to the concept definition (e.g., Kirschenbaum, 1968; Shapson, 1973). In addition, the hypothesis-testing strategy, different for field-dependent and field-independent subjects, can be understood in terms of preference for salient cues.

Two hypothesis-testing strategies, called *wholist* and *partist*, have been distinguished in "receptive" concept attainment problems in which the sequence of items is determined by the experimenter (Bruner, Goodnow, & Austin, 1956). In the wholist strategy, the first exemplar produces the hypothesis that the values present for all attributes that define the stimulus set are relevant for the concept definition. When given the second exemplar, any attribute that changes in value is eliminated in a revised hypothesis, and so on, until the correct hypothesis is achieved. In the partist strategy only some of the attributes are used in constructing the initial hypothesis. When disconfirmed by a subsequent exemplar, a new hypothesis is constructed that includes the common values of both exemplars. If field-dependent subjects tend to ignore nonsalient attributes, then a wholist strategy should be less common among them than among field-independent subjects. Just this result has been obtained in several studies (e.g., Kirschenbaum, 1968; Shapson, 1973).

Another source of evidence on the role of cue salience is provided by studies of the effectiveness of aids to cue usability. Cue naming and experimenter prompts appear not to be more effective for field-dependent than for field-independent subjects (Davis & Klausmeier, 1970). However, significant results have been reported in another study involving a more elaborate aid in the form of cue cards made available to the subject throughout the trials. Each card showed one cue corresponding to one of the possible concept definitions. The introduction of this aid changed the strategy of field-dependent subjects from partist to wholist and virtually eliminated errors (Shapson, 1973). This study suggests that under some conditions at least, field-dependent people are able to sample fully from sets of cues if the cues are provided in discrete form. It is easy to suppose that the presence of the separate elements of a stimulus configuration may help to minimize the effects of cue salience.

The evidence on correlates of field dependence in concept learning appears to be interpretable in terms of two simple constructs describing the communality involved. First, field-independent people seem more likely to use a hypothesis-testing approach to concept attainment whereas field-dependent people tend to behave according to a composite photograph model of learning. Second, when field-dependent people adopt a hypothesis-testing approach, their hypotheses appear dominated by the salient cues. In contrast, field-independent people more fully sample from the set of possible cues in forming their hypotheses. Both of these conclusions fit field-dependence theory.

A "real world" illustration of cue salience effects

Our examples of restructuring in perceptual and intellectual tasks have come from the laboratory or from paper-and-pencil testing. However, research on practical applications has recently begun to appear in the literature. An example from this literature suggests that restructuring has consequences in our daily lives as well.

Many automobile accidents occur in heavy throughway traffic, particularly for commuters moving between suburban homes and urban centers. Under these conditions high speeds and inadequate spacing between cars are commonly found, with the result that a sudden deceleration by one car sometimes leads to rear-end collisions involving many cars in the line of traffic. If the driver focuses all his attention on the car immediately ahead of him and if that car suddenly stops without warning, then it may simply be impossible to avoid an accident. In most cases, however, the driver of the car ahead applies his brakes in response to a deceleration of the cars ahead of him in the line of traffic. Fortunately, it is usually possible to see and respond to events at least several cars ahead in line. This type of "defensive" driving no doubt avoids accidents.

The car immediately in front is the one that will be hit if an accident occurs, and it is certainly a more salient visual object than the cars farther ahead in line. It has been hypothesized, therefore, that field-dependent drivers focus more attention on the car immediately in front and consequently may be more prone to accidents in crowded high-speed traffic (Goodenough, 1976a; Olson, 1974).

Olson conducted an ingenious series of experiments to explore this possibility. The studies involved lines of three cars, driven over a test field, with the first car in line accelerating and decelerating, and the second and third cars following the leader to simulate traffic conditions. Reaction times were measured for the subjects of the experiments, who always drove the third car in line. One experiment was conducted under conditions in which the subject's view of the lead car was blocked. In a second experiment, however, the lead car was visible as in normal traffic. The results of the study dramatically confirmed the hypothesized relation between field dependence and driver behavior. Little difference was found in reaction times between field-dependent and field-independent drivers when the car just ahead was the only car visible. Under normal conditions, field-independent drivers showed a marked reduction in reaction times, showing that they made use of the less salient lead-car cues in the situation. For field-dependent drivers, however, reaction times were little different, whether or not the lead car was visible.

Although no work has been done on specific driver behaviors under actual road conditions, several studies have reported that field-dependent drivers tend to be involved in more accidents than field-independent drivers (e.g., Harano, 1970; Williams, 1971). These findings suggest that detailed analyses of field-dependent and field-independent driver behavior may eventually lead to a clearer understanding of highway accidents, and, perhaps, more effective instructional programs or aids for safer driving.

The relationships among restructuring factors

If field dependence is as pervasive a characteristic of perceptual and intellectual functioning as the examples above suggest, then it would not be surprising to find a similar construct emerging from a variety of approaches to individual differences in cognition. Indeed, relationships among many of the behaviors considered here have been noted repeatedly in the factor-analytic literature. Although it seems clear, for example, that the capacity to overcome embedding contexts, closure speed, and perhaps two spatial-visualization dimensions may be distinguished as separate, specific factors (French, Ekstrom, & Price, 1963), it is generally recognized that these factors are interrelated, indicating a more general, higher-order dimension of individual functioning that has often been referred to as a visualization dimenson (e.g., Horn & Cattell, 1966; Messick & French, 1975; Pawlik, 1966; Royce, 1972; Vernon, 1972a).

Because of the large number of subjects required in comprehensive factor-analytic studies, most of the work in this area has been limited to group administered tests. There have been several factor-analytic studies on tests of field dependence in the perception of the upright (e.g., Bergman & Englebrektson, 1973; Goodenough & Karp, 1961; Karp, 1963; Pascual-Leone, 1969). Unfortunately, the extra time required to administer laboratory tests is usually purchased at the cost of a reduction in the number of subjects and/or a reduction in the size of the test battery.

As a consequence of the limitations on the data now available, a detailed factor-analytic description of the structure of the relationships between laboratory tests of upright perception and paper-and-pencil tests is not yet possible. However, the evidence clearly indicates that measures of perception of the upright belong in the general cluster with measures of overcoming embeddedness, closure speed, and spatial visualization. In factor-analytic terms, the field-dependence dimension may be located at the apex of a hierarchical, pyramidal factor structure in which a number of more specific cognitive dimensions such as overcoming embeddedness, closure speed, and spatial visualization are nested.

The history of research on field dependence is strikingly different from the history of factor-analytic research. As we have seen, the field-dependence construct began with classical laboratory experiments on the contributions of different cues to the location of the upright in space. In contrast, research on factor structure developed as part of the paper-and-pencil testing tradition. Despite these differences, the evidence suggests that a similar dimension of cognitive functioning has been emerging from both fields.[5] We turn now to the expression of this dimension in social-interpersonal functioning.

FIELD DEPENDENCE AND INTERPERSONAL BEHAVIOR

We have traced the field-dependence dimension across a variety of classical perceptual and intellectual situations. Of course, cognitive systems are operative whether the external field comprises inanimate objects or other people. In fact, people are obviously among the most if not *the* most significant objects in the world around us. Thus, if field dependence is a relatively general dimension of cognitive functioning, it should not be surprising to find implications of the field-dependence concept for behavior in social situations. If the field-dependent cognitive style involves a reliance on the external stimulus field, then people ought to play a particularly significant role for the field-dependent person. In contrast, field-independent people should function with a greater degree of separateness from the immediate social context in which they find themselves. The evidence from a wide variety of sources tends to confirm these expectations.

The effects of ambiguity in social situations

If field-dependent people rely on other people for guidance, then we might expect that their behavior would be more affected than the behavior of field-independent people in ambiguous social situations. This possibility was early suggested by a set of observations on the effects of different instructions given to subjects entering a sensory deprivation experiment (Culver, Cohen, Silverman & Shmavonian, 1964). For some subjects the experimenter gave relatively specific directions concerning what was going to happen to them during their stay in an isolation chamber, whereas for other subjects the instructions were ambiguous and the experimenter was relatively noncommittal and silent throughout. For field-dependent subjects heart rates tended to be higher in the noncommunicative than in the informative condition, suggesting the possibility that they were less relaxed when they did not know what was going to happen to them. These results were only marginally significant, but they served to stimulate further research on the behavior of field-dependent subjects under conditions in which their roles were not well defined.

One approach to the study of ambiguity effects has emerged from research on verbal conditioning in conversation. In ordinary dialogue the listener often signals that he is attending to and understands the speaker's message by interjecting comments like "um hmm" or "yeah" during pauses in the speaker's talk. The effects of these comments on field-dependent and field-independent subjects have been studied by comparing interviews during which the interviewer systematically emits such comments with interviews during which the interviewer keeps silent. In one interesting study using this technique, each subject was asked to talk about a topic of interest to her, and the number of words she spoke was recorded (Gates, 1971). For field-dependent subjects the word output was found to be much lower with a silent interviewer than with a responsive interviewer. In contrast, the word output of field-independent subjects was little affected by the interviewer's behavior. At the conclusion of the experiment, the subjects' feelings about the interview were examined in detail, and the reactions of field-dependent and field-independent people were found to be quite different. For example, the field-dependent subjects who had been confronted by the silent interviewer more often agreed with the statements, "I think I might have done a little better during the interview if the interviewer had told me at times just how I was doing," and "It would have been easier during the interview if the interviewer had simply asked me questions rather than made me think up things to talk about." In contrast, the field-independent subjects more often agreed with the statements, "I don't think it made much difference one way or the other that the interviewer didn't tell me how I was doing during the interview," and "It really didn't make much difference to me that I had to think things up to talk about during the interview. Things came to mind fairly easily without my being asked specific questions by the interviewer." It is clear from these data that the field-dependent subjects were particularly affected by the lack of guidance from the interviewer.

It is interesting to note here that the desire for conversational guidance expressed by field-dependent subjects may actually be met by sensitive interviewers who are free to conduct the best interview they can. A study of verbal interactions between patients and their doctors during the first few psychotherapy sessions may be cited in this connection (Witkin, Lewis & Weil, 1968). It was found in this study that the mean length of the comments made by field-dependent patients was much shorter (39 words per comment) than for field-independent patients (158 words per comment). An unpublished analysis of the transcripts from this study (cited in Witkin, Moore, Goodenough, & Cox, 1977) suggests that the shorter comments of the field-dependent patients may be owing to the fact that the questions asked of them by their therapists tend to be more specific in form (e.g., they can be answered by a yes or no) than the questions asked by the same therapists of their field-independent patients. Thus, the type of interview procedure adopted by the therapists seemed well designed to provide the guidance field-dependent people say they find most comfortable.

Research in naturalistic psychotherapeutic and educational settings has produced many valuable insights into the importance of other people in reducing ambiguity for field-dependent people. For example, the evidence suggests that therapists more often assign their field-dependent patients to supportive therapy in which a well-defined structure is provided for the therapeutic process. In contrast, field-independent patients are more often given modifying therapy in which the patient himself plays a role in deciding the content and progress of the process (Greene, 1972; Karp, Kissin, & Hustmyer, 1970). Moreover, there is evidence that field-dependent patients drop out of unstructured therapy more often than do field-independent patients (e.g., Koff, 1972). Research on classroom structure, recently reviewed in detail (Witkin et al., 1977), suggests that information from others may play an equally important role in the educational setting.

The effect of other people's opinions

The evidence clearly suggests that field-dependent people are particularly likely to take information from other people into account in defining their own attitudes and opinions. This tendency has been observed in a variety of laboratory situations. The first study to explore the effect of the opinion of others in relation to field dependence was conducted by Linton (1955). One of the techniques she used was adopted from the work of Sherif (1935) on social factors in the autokinetic effect. In this technique, the subject is seated in a dark room in which the only visible stimulus is a point of light. Although the light is actually stationary, it usually gives the appearance of movement when inspected for a period of time, and the subject's task is to judge the extent of this apparent movement. Under control conditions these judgments are made while the subject is alone. Under experimental conditions, however, the subject is paired with another person who ostensibly is a fellow subject but who actually is a confederate of the experimenter. The confederate publically announces his judgment before the real subject. Thus, the real subject has the confederate's opinion available to him when he makes his judgment, as well as his own impression of the extent of movement. In general, under these experimental conditions subjects' judgments tend to shift in the direction of the confederates' judgments. The conforming tendency is more pronounced in some people than in others, however. The autokinetic situation is therefore useful in studying conforming behavior in relation to field dependence. Using this technique, Linton found that the judgment of the confederate had a much greater influence on field-dependent than on field-independent subjects.

Following the lead provided by this early work, a number of studies have been done in recent years on the extent to which field-dependent and field-independent people are affected by the opinions of others. The majority of this work has supported the hypothesized relationship with field dependence when judgments are exchanged during direct interpersonal interactions[6] (e.g., Balance, 1967; Boschi & Loprieno, 1968; Paeth, 1973).

In the Sherif-type situation described above, the confederates announce their opinion before the subject's judgment is required, but there is no discussion among group members concerning the judgment. Another type of situation that has been used to study interpersonal influence involves the resolution of opinion conflict by a process of conversational interaction. For example, one study of conflict resolution among field-dependent and field-independent people involved attempts to compromise intial differences in opinions about moral issues (Oltman, Goodenough, Witkin, Freedman, & Friedman, 1975). In this study, pairs of college students were selected on the basis that they were strangers to each other and disagreed with each other on how they would handle each problem in a set of moral dilemmas. Each problem described a situation in which either one of two courses of action was possible. As an example, one problem required the subject to assume the role of a physician who must choose between a 14-year-old girl and a 40-year-old man who is a prominent surgeon with a family. Both are critically ill with a kidney ailment, and time is available for only one on a dialysis machine used to treat the ailment. The issue is: Which of the two is to be saved and which allowed to die? One member of each subject pair solved this problem in an initial individual test session by choosing the girl, while the other member solved it by choosing the surgeon. They were then asked to try to resolve their difference during a discussion session by finding some set of conditions under which both members could agree to one or the other of the alternatives. Three types of partnerships were studied: (a) both members were field dependent; (b) both were independent; and (c) one member was field dependent and one member field independent. In partnerships with one member field dependent and one member field independent, agreements were more often reached by an accommodation in the view of the field-dependent partner than by accommodation on the part of the field-independent partner. Furthermore, the results showed clearly that when both members were field dependent, the initial conflicts ended in disagreements less frequently (5 percent) than when only one member was field dependent (18 percent) or than when both members were field independent (35 percent). Thus, field-independent people were often unwilling or unable to modify their positions on the issues to reach an agreement with their partners as required.

It should be noted that all the situations cited above involve the subject in a difficult judgment about which additional information from others might prove profitable. The tendency among field-dependent people to use the extra information appears quite reasonable in such cases. It is interesting to consider whether field-dependent people also rely on information from others when they believe this information will not be profitable. This point was examined in a study involving experimental manipulation of the subject's confidence in his own judgment relative to the judgment of another person (Mausner & Graham, 1970). A Sherif-type technique was used in this study of judgments about the rate of flicker of a flashing light. The subjects were run in two-person groups. In an initial series of trials, each subject served as the experimenter's assistant, recording the judgment of his fellow subject. In each pair one subject was told that he was right on the majority of the trials, and his partner was told that he was wrong on the majority of trials. Thus, one of the subjects in each pair was led to believe that he was more accurate than his partner, whereas the other subject was led to believe that he was less accurate. The effect of these contrasting conditions was then examined in a second series of trials in which the two subjects were run concurrently. In this series the subjects were led to believe that they were in communication with each other, each ostensibly receiving his partner's judgment of flicker rate as an aid but actually fed false information about the partner's judgment before he made his own. Extent of field dependence was then examined in relation to the influence of the partner's judgment. The results showed that for field-independent subjects there was relatively little difference between those who had been led to believe that they were more accurate than their partners and those who had been led to believe that they were less accurate. Among field-dependent subjects, in contrast, there was a clear difference. The field-dependent subjects who were told they were wrong and had a more accurate partner showed large shifts toward their partner's judgment. However, the field-dependent subjects who were told they were right and their partners were wrong in the initial series, showed a small shift toward their partner's judgment.

The work of Mausner and Graham makes two important points. It seems clear that the field-independent people were so individualistic that their strategies were virtually unaffected by evidence about the relative competence of their partners. In contrast, the field-dependent people took the evidence about themselves and their partner into account in a reasonable way. In addition, the study emphasizes situational determinants of the relationship between field dependence and interpersonal influence. Field-dependent people tend to rely on others only when the others may have something to offer. In fact, in the data of Mausner and Graham, field-dependent people were less influenced by others than were field-independent people when the evidence suggested that the opinion of others would add nothing to their own effectiveness.

It seems clear from these studies that field-dependent people give some weight to potentially useful information provided by others in ambiguous situations, as they rely in a similar way on the external visual field in perceiving the upright in space. However, there is little evidence to suggest that field-dependent people rely on others in unambiguous situations or when others are not likely sources of disambiguating information.

Attention to social stimuli

In view of the particularly important role other people appear to play as a source of information for field-dependent people, it would not be surprising to find that they are more attentive to others than are field-independent people. Indeed, the evidence supports this view.

A number of studies have examined what people look at in their environment as a function of extent of field dependence. Most of these studies have concluded that field-dependent subjects spend more of their time looking at people and less time looking at inanimate objects than do field-independent subjects. One recent example on this point involved college students who were observed while working on difficult anagram problems (Nevill, 1974). Field-dependent subjects showed longer durations of eye contact with the experimenter than did field-independent subjects. These studies quite directly support the hypothesis that field dependence involves an orientation toward significant people in the surrounding field.

Another kind of evidence that may be cited in support of the social orientation hypothesis concerns the use of interpersonal space. Field-dependent subjects simply prefer to be closer to other people than do field-independent subjects. In one study, for example, subjects were required to give prepared talks on several topics to the experimenter, and the physical distance between the subject and the experimenter was measured during the presentations (Justice, 1969). Field-dependent speakers literally chose to stand closer to their listeners than did field-independent speakers. In another study of interperson distance, field-dependent subjects showed more speech disturbances when seated five feet away from their conversational partners than when seated only two feet away. In contrast, interperson distance had less of an effect on field-independent subjects (Greene, 1973). These data suggest that field-dependent people not only approach their conversational partners more closely than do field-independent people but may feel more uncomfortable (more speech disturbance) when required to keep their distance.

In addition to these indications that field-dependent people literally attend more to others, the relationship between field dependence and social orientation has a number of less direct implications that have been examined. For example, in one study, subjects were required to speak the first word that came to their minds at periodic metronome beats (Goldberger & Bendich, 1972). These words were then coded into social and nonsocial categories. As expected, field-dependent subjects produced more social words than did field-independent subjects, suggesting the greater importance of such material for them.

Another interesting example involves the use of social cues in concept attainment (Ruble & Nakamura, 1972). In this study children were given three concept attainment problems to learn. Each problem consisted of a number of trials on which the subject tried to learn which of three figures, differing from one another on several attributes, was correct. For the first problem the smallest figure was the correct one. In addition, the experimenter provided a redundant social cue by always leaning toward and looking at the correct figure. For the second problem, only the social cue, and for the third problem, only the size cue, was correct. There were no differences noted between field-dependent and field-independent subjects in how rapidly they learned to identify correct figures on the first problem. However, field-dependent children learned more effectively than field-independent children on the second problem, where only the social cue was relevant. In contrast, field-independent children did better on the third problem where size was the only relevant cue. The greater attentiveness to social cues on the part of field-dependent children helped or hindered their performance in a predictable way in this study.

Perhaps the commonest sign of social orientation in everyday life is our memory for the names and faces of people we have met. This sign has not been neglected by researchers. In one very elaborate study, a large number of Air Force captains spent a period of time together at an assessment center (Crutchfield, Woodworth, & Albrecht, 1958). These subjects were then given photographs of some of these officers mixed up with photographs of strangers. As expected, the field-dependent officers were better able to identify the photos of the men they had previously met than were field-independent officers. Another study found evidence relating field dependence to recognition of names (Oltman et al., 1975). The study of conflict resolution, cited earlier, involved female students who were drawn from a large city college and who were assigned conversational partners with whom they were previously unacquainted. To determine acquaintanceship relations each subject was given a list of the names of all other subjects in the pool and asked to check the names she recognized. As expected, the field-dependent students knew more people and were known by more people than the field-independent students.[7]

Communication about oneself

The evidence cited in the previous sections suggests that field-dependent people are particularly likely to seek information from others to define their own roles and that they are likely to be more affected when such information is not forthcoming. There is also considerable evidence that the commerce in information is not one-way for them. Not only are they receivers of information from other people, but they are also particularly likely to tell others about themselves. In contrast, field-independent people tend to be more noncommunicative about themselves. The tendency toward self-disclosure has been examined in several studies by variants of a questionnaire that was originally developed by Jourard (Jourard, 1971; Jourard & Lasakow, 1958). This self-report measure consists of a number of items asking subjects to indicate how much they have disclosed about themselves in various topic areas to various people in their lives. Most of these studies have found that field-dependent people report more self-disclosing than do field-independent people (e.g., Berry & Annis, 1974; Sousa-Poza, Rohrberg, & Shulman, 1973).

Self-disclosing comments have also been observed directly in the conversations of field-dependent and field-independent people in several studies. In one study, for example, transcripts of patients' talk in psychotherapy were subjected to a clause-by-clause count of the number of self-disclosing statements (Sousa-Poza & Rohrberg, 1976). The results indicated a much greater flow of self-related information to the therapists from field-dependent than from field-independent patients. In another study, subjects were asked to talk about any topic of interest to them, and word counts of statements involving self-referred feelings were examined (Gates, 1971). It was found that field-dependent subjects talked more about their own feelings during a spontaneous baseline period than did field-independent subjects, although this difference disappeared when verbal reinforcement was administered for such comments.

These findings suggest that field-dependent people are more open and field-independent people more reserved in their communication with others.

Popularity

The greater social orientation of field-dependent and the more impersonal, autonomous orientation of field-independent people has sometimes been evident in self-ratings and in ratings by others. In one early study (Pemberton, 1952), for example, field-dependent subjects more often than field-independent subjects described themselves as "socially outgoing" and "dependent on the good opinion of others." In contrast, field-independent subjects more often described themselves as "not sensitive to social undercurrents" and "logical and theoretical." None of these self-descriptions seem to be very derogatory. However, the lack of social sensitivity among field-independent people is sometimes described by others in more negative terms. For example, among Air Force captains who served as subjects in the study cited earlier (Crutchfield et al., 1958), the most field-independent men were rated as "cold and distant with others" and "unaware of their own stimulus value." If field-independent people are perceived in such terms, it would not be surprising to find them unpopular among their peers.

The evidence on popularity in relation to field dependence appears to lead to a different conclusion in childhood than it does in adulthood. For children, the data suggest that sex plays an important role as a moderator of the relationship between field dependence and popularity. Iscoe and Carden (1961) have reported that among 11-year-olds field-dependent girls tend to be chosen over field-independent girls for class officer. However, field-independent rather than field-dependent boys tend to be so chosen. A similar result among kindergarten children for choices of a playmate (but not for choices of a work companion) has been reported by Dreyer, McIntire, and Dreyer (1973). It is interesting to note here that in our culture the male sex role would seem to involve more autonomous functioning than the female sex role. Moreover, females tend to be slightly more field dependent than males (e.g., Witkin et al., 1962/1974). It is possible, therefore, that the preferences shown by these children is a function of sex-role stereotypes. Among older children and adults, the weight of the evidence suggests that field-dependent females are more popular than, and field-dependent males at least as popular as, field-independent people among their peers (e.g., Dingman, 1971; Joshi, 1968; Oltman et al., 1975; Vernon, 1972b; Victor, 1973; Wong, 1976). By adolescence, then, there is an overall tendency for field-dependent people to be more popular.

Field dependence and the need for approval

The fact that some studies have shown field-dependent adults to be relatively popular can easily be misunderstood. The evidence does not suggest that field-dependent people are out to win love and friendship to a greater extent than is true for field-independent people. That field-dependent people are particularly attentive to and open with others may make them relatively popular, but the attentiveness may be owing to a search for information rather than to a need for approval from others.

The conclusion that field dependence is not much related to the effects of social approval has been drawn from most operant conditioning studies (e.g., Paclisanu, 1970; Steinfeld, 1973). In the study by Steinfeld, for example, children were asked to play a "marble-in-the-hole" game, commonly used to measure reinforcement effects. The game is played on a board with two holes into which the child can drop marbles. The experiment begins with a baseline period during which the child's preference for one hole or the other is determined. Marble dropping in the nonpreferred hole is then reinforced, and the percentage of marbles dropped into this hole is computed. In this study, three types of reinforcement were compared. In one type, material reinforcements were given in the form of token rewards redeemable for toys. A second type involved social rewards in the form of praise from the experimenter. Finally, an abstract reinforcement was employed in the form of a flashing light that served as a cue for self-reward. As expected, field-independent children learned better than field-dependent children with abstract reinforcement. However, no difference was observed between field-dependent and field-independent children either with material or social rewards. These results suggest that field-independent people function more effectively in the absence of external rewards, in keeping with their greater autonomy. Although field-dependent people rely more on external rewards, they seem to perform effectively whether the rewards are material or social in nature. Approval is not a uniquely effective reward.

The conclusion that field-dependent people do not do things merely to please people can also be drawn from a variety of other sources. Studies of volunteering behavior are interesting in this regard because it seems reasonable to suppose that complying with a request to help would gain approval. There is little evidence of a relationship between field dependence and the tendency to volunteer, however (e.g., Soat, 1974; Webb, 1972). In the study by Soat, for example, the experimenter approached college undergraduates, appealing for donations of their time to help him on his dissertation. The amount of time volunteered by field-dependent and field-independent people did not differ significantly. Other studies have shown that field-independent people are just as suggestible as field-dependent people except when the suggestion is disambiguating. For example, most studies have found no relationship between field dependence and hypnotizability (e.g., Morgan, 1972; Palmer & Field, 1971) or placebo responsiveness (e.g., Freund, Krupp, Goodenough, & Preston, 1972; Halm, 1967). In situations of this sort, where the subject needs no information from other people to define his role, there is little evidence that field-independent people are any less influenced by social pressures or less often do things to gain favor than field-dependent people.

The term *field dependence* seems appropriate as a description of the cluster of behaviors we have been discussing, but the concept of social dependence has often implied a need for approval. Thus, the concepts of field dependence and social dependence should be carefully distinguished to avoid a misunderstanding concerning the nature of field-dependent social behavior.

Career differentiation

There is a recent, rapidly growing literature on academic and vocational interests, attitudes, choices, and achievement. This literature is interesting and important to examine for several reasons. First, it provides another illustration of the potential for the practical application of information about field-dependent and field-independent cognitive styles. In addition, it serves to emphasize the view that field-dependent people do well in some situations, whereas field-independent people do well in others. We have considered the evidence suggesting that field-independent people tend to function effectively in certain perceptual and intellectual tasks. They do well, for example, in tasks that require restructuring. We have also considered the evidence suggesting that field-dependent people tend to function effectively in certain interpersonal situations. For example, they tend to be more open in exchanging information with others; they may resolve interpersonal conflicts with relative ease; and they may be better liked. In view of their contrasting strengths and weaknesses, it might be expected that people with a relatively field-independent cognitive style would tend to be interested in, choose, and achieve more in academic and vocational areas in which their cognitive skills are called for but which are relatively impersonal. In contrast, it might be expected that people with a relatively field-dependent cognitive style would more often prefer and show achievement in areas involving dealing with other people for which restructuring competence does not particularly matter. The weight of the evidence, now emerging, tends to support these views, suggesting the possibility that the field-dependence dimension may have an application to problems of career guidance (e.g., Witkin et al., 1977).

The relationship between extent of field dependence and standard measures of occupational interests has been examined in many studies (e.g., Clar, 1971; Levy, 1969; Pierson, 1965). These studies suggest that field-independent people are particularly interested in mathematical and scientific occupations such as physics, architecture, and engineering; in health professions such as medicine and dentistry; and in certain practical occupations such as carpentry, farming, and mechanics. On the other hand, field-dependent people more often show interests in the helping humanitarian occupations such as social worker, minister, and rehabilitation counselor; in certain teaching areas such as elementary school teaching and social sciences; and in certain business occupations such as selling, advertising, and personnel. The clusters of occupations preferred by people at each extreme of the field-dependence dimension seem strikingly in keeping with the kinds of cognitive styles they have.

The actual academic and vocational choices made by field-dependent and field-independent people show a similar picture (e.g., Barrett & Thornton, 1967; DeRussy & Futch, 1971; Holtzman, Swartz, & Thorpe, 1971; MacKinnon, 1962; Osipow, 1969). Relatively field-independent students are likely to be found in such academic departments as the physical sciences, mathematics, art, experimental psychology, engineering, and architecture. Similarly, field-independent people are likely to be found in occupations such as engineering, architecture, aviation, and mathematics or science teaching. In contrast, field-dependent students are more often found in such academic areas as social work, elementary school teaching, clinical psychology, and nursing. They tend to be found in occupations such as social studies teaching, social work, and writing.

It is important to note that the field-dependence dimension is not related to overall academic achievement, at least at the college level. This point has been checked repeatedly (e.g., Anderson, 1971; Glass, 1967; Witkin et al., 1977). The study by Witkin et al. provides a comprehensive example. Practically an entire entering class of almost 1600 college freshmen were given tests of field dependence in this study, and the test scores were examined in relation to the grade point averages subsequently achieved during their college stay. The correlation observed between extent of field dependence and college grades was almost nil (0.04).

Although grade averages show little relation to field dependence, the mix of courses whose grades contribute to this average is obviously different for students with field-dependent and field-independent cognitive styles. Unfortunately, the data on the relationships with grades in specific courses are not yet very extensive. Field-independent students appear to gain higher grades in mathematics, sciences, engineering, and architecture, as might be expected, but the evidence is as yet meager for other areas. This evidence has recently been reviewed in detail (Witkin et al., 1977).

Success in the occupations chosen by people with field-dependent and field-independent cognitive styles has been examined in a few studies. Two of these are particularly interesting. In one study of student nurses, the best psychiatric nurses were found to be relatively field dependent, whereas the best surgical nurses were found to be field independent (Quinlan & Blatt, 1972). In another study, most architects selected by their peers as outstandingly creative in their profession were found to be markedly field independent, whereas most writers selected on a similar basis were found to be markedly field dependent (MacKinnon, 1962).

In both of these studies, the types of jobs at which field-independent and field-dependent people excel seem consistent with the cognitive styles at each extreme. Surgical nursing and architecture are relatively impersonal occupations that may not require much involvement with people for successful performance. However, both may emphasize competence at cognitive restructuring. On the other hand, psychiatric nurses and creative writers are necessarily concerned with interpersonal behavior. Restructuring skill may not be as important as the ability to get along and effectively communicate with other people. Although information on occupational achievement is not yet very extensive, it seems to be consistent with what we know about academic and occupational interests and choices. Furthermore, in more general terms it suggests that the strengths and weaknesses of field-dependent and field-independent people, first noted in more experimental, laboratory situations, are meaningfully expressed in the real world of career performance.

ONTOGENETIC DEVELOPMENT IN EXTENT OF FIELD INDEPENDENCE

Age changes

It is a feature of all theories of development that children function less autonomously than adults, and it is not surprising to find a change from a state of field dependence toward greater field independence during the course of development. Figure 5–5 summarizes the results of two longitudinal studies of development in Rod-and-Frame Test performance among boys (Witkin, Goodenough, & Karp, 1967).

In one study (represented by the dashed line in Figure 5–5), the boys were initially tested at 8 years of age and retested at 13. In the other study (represented by the solid line in Figure 5–5), the boys were first seen as 10-year-olds, and were retested when 14, 17, and 24 years of age. The data from these two studies fit together quite well, showing a continuous decrease in the effect of the visual field from 8 to about 17 years of age, with little change thereafter.

Standard tests of field dependence for use with young children have only

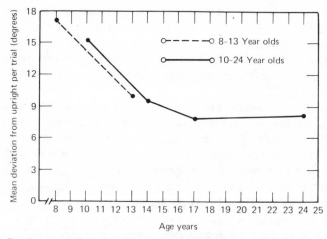

Figure 5.   Developmental Curve for Males on the Rod-and-Frame Test.
(After Witkin et al., 1967) Copyright © 1967 by the American Psychological Association. Reprinted by permission.

recently become available. Consequently, developmental data from children younger than 8 years old are not very extensive. There is no doubt, however, that changes toward increasing field independence begin earlier in life (e.g., Goodenough & Eagle, 1963).

Although field dependence decreases quite dramatically with age, the individual differences in extent of field dependence that are observable in adulthood appear to be established to a significant extent by the early school years at the latest. For example, for the boys of age 10 whose data are shown in Figure 5–5, Rod-and-Frame Test scores are correlated substantially with retest scores at 14 (r = .71), at 17 (r = .72), and at 24 (r = .66). Thus, a boy who is relatively field dependent with respect to his peers at 10 is likely to be relatively field dependent with respect to his peers in adulthood, despite the fact that his level of field independence increases in absolute terms.

Although standard tests of field dependence cannot be given to very young children, there is some evidence that the course of later development may be predicted with some accuracy from behavior at earlier ages. For example, in one study, ratings of 2½-year-old children on degree of autonomous play and attention-seeking behavior were related to performance on tests of field dependence subsequently administered to these children when they were 6 years of age (Wender, Pedersen, & Waldrop, 1967).

The correlations in these studies are far from perfect. Furthermore, the subjects grew up under relatively stable environmental conditions. Thus, an individual's position in his peer group is obviously nowhere near completely predictable from one age to another. However, it is evident that the factors responsible for the differences among adults in extent of field dependence are at work at an early age.

Socialization Practices and the Development of Field Independence

There is now a large body of evidence that socialization factors play an important role in the development of field independence. In the most general terms, the evidence supports the common sense hypothesis that when socialization practices encourage separation from parental control, then development proceeds toward greater field independence. However, when the course of development is either governed by a tightly organized, strictly enforced set of rules and prescriptions for behavior, or when parental nurturing and protective functions inhibit separation, then greater field dependence ensues.

The earliest studies of socialization and field independence were based on interviews with mothers of 10-year-old boys concerning child-rearing attitudes and practices in their families (Dyk & Witkin, 1965; Witkin et al., 1962/1974). These exploratory studies were intended to identify gross features of family experiences as possible correlates of development toward field independence. It was found that the interviewer could predict with some accuracy which were the mothers of the field-dependent and field-independent children on the basis of a cluster of indicators. Several of these indicators suggested that the mothers of field-dependent children tended to inhibit separation from her. For example, some mothers' physical care of the child seemed to continue long after the usual time reported by other mothers; they seemed to limit the child's activities through anxieties for or ties to the child, and they did not permit the child to assume responsibilities for himself. For other mothers of field-dependent children, strict training practices that stressed conformity to adult norms seemed the most salient characteristic of child rearing. In all types of families, maternal involvement with the field-dependent child seemed intense.

The hypotheses suggested by these early studies have now been examined in many studies using a variety of approaches. Some have examined child-rearing attitudes and practices as reported by the parents of field-dependent and field-independent children, as in the early studies. Others have examined reports of these practices given by the children themselves (usually in retrospective accounts collected after the children are mature). Others have observed parent-child interactions under the assumption that enduring modes of interacting with children will be evident even in relatively trivial and artificial laboratory situations. Still others have compared children from different cultural or subcultural groups that differ in relevant socialization practices. The picture that emerges from these studies, is somewhat complicated by the fact that maternal and paternal roles obviously differ from each other and may be different for sons and daughters. Furthermore, parental and sex roles obviously vary from culture to culture and may do so even among subcultures. However, the weight of the evidence from each of these sources appears to converge on the conclusion that socialization practices that encourage separation tend to contribute to the development of field independence.

The most common methods of assessing parental behavior have used field-dependent and field-independent subjects as sources of information concerning their own childhood experiences. The information that may be obtained in this way is necessarily lacking in detail, but it is also relatively easy to collect since all the required information is contributed by one family member. Because of data collection economy this approach has often been used in field studies of nonwestern cultural groups, and the results are particularly interesting because similar conclusions have been drawn for a variety of cultures.

It has usually been found in these studies that field-independent people report that their parents were relatively permissive. In contrast, field-dependent people often report an emphasis on parental authority in their families. For example, Dawson (1967) found that ratings of parental strictness were related to measures of field dependence in Temne and Mende tribesmen of West Africa. Berry(1966) found the same relationships with the Temne and with Eskimos. Similar results have been reported for females of a rural Zulu tribe (but not for males or for Zulu urban dwellers) (Baran, 1971), for Mexican boys (but not Mexican girls) (Mebane & Johnson, 1970), for Canadian boys (Jones, 1975), and for Chinese children (Dawson, Young, & Choi, 1974).

A number of studies have followed the approach of Witkin et al. (1962/1974) in collecting data about child rearing from the mothers of field-dependent and field-independent children. Several of these studies have assessed *general* parental attitudes concerning child-rearing practices; these studies have typically produced only marginal support for the hypothesized relationships between parental attitudes and field dependence of children in the family (e.g., Domash, 1973; Hauk, 1967). However, most studies that have asked mothers how they actually raised their children have confirmed the exploratory studies by Witkin et al. (1962/1974). This work is particularly interesting because it has provided greater detail and refinement in the description of parent–child interactions that are related to the course of development in field independence.

One of the early studies on this point employed an interview with mothers of field-dependent and field-independent 10-year-old boys and girls who were matched for intelligence (Seder, 1957). The interview was designed to elicit answers to a number of specific questions about how mothers were raising their children. Among the many detailed findings reported by Seder, several may be cited here as illustrations. For example, during childhood, field-dependent children (particularly boys) were found to share their parents' bedroom and even their bed more often than field-independent children. Field-dependent parents were more often found to punish harshly acts of disrespect for, or aggression against, parental authority, whereas parents of field-independent children more often tolerated disrespect but punished babyish or passive behavior in their children. Mothers of field-dependent children often intervened to settle disputes with peers, but field-independent children were encouraged to fight their own battles. Although no difference was found in the age at which toilet training began, mothers reported that punishment for failure was harsher and training completed earlier for field-dependent than for field-independent children. Standards were more often set by the parents of field-dependent children, whereas field-independent children were more often allowed to participate in setting their standards. In view of these and many other maternal responses, Seder concluded that "parents of field-independent children are more permissive, democratic, and encouraging to independent behavior" (p. 117). Similar conclusions have been drawn in most subsequent studies using mothers' descriptions of how they raised their children (e.g., Jones, 1975).

Observations of actual parental behavior toward field-dependent and field-independent children were more often allowed to participate in setting their the interpretation of results with respect to socialization practices is not always easy. The most comprehensive work of this genre has been that of Busse (1969) who studied fifth-grade Negro boys and their parents. The boys were given a battery of cognitive tests, the scores from which were factor analyzed. One of the factors isolated in the analysis was called "flexible thinking" and was defined by high scores on the Embedded Figures Test, a Closure Speed Test, and an insight problems test, among others. The flexible thinking factor scores may be taken as a measure of the field-independence construct as defined in this chapter. Each boy was seen in a session with his father and in a separate session with his mother; in both the parent was asked to teach the son to do a set of experimental tasks. Observations of parental behavior were then related to the flexible thinking scores of their sons. Contrary to expectations, no significant relation was found between parents' asking their son to try the task on his own and the son's level of field independence. However, mothers who attempted to dominate and directly control the behavior of the child during the task did have more field-dependent sons. A curvilinear relationship was found for frequency of parental manipulation of task material, a variable chosen to assess nonverbal help-giving behavior. For both parents, either very much or very little manipulation was present in the teaching of the field-dependent boys, whereas parents of field-independent children engaged in a moderate amount of manipulative teaching behavior. Several other observational studies have also not confirmed the simple hypothesis that field-dependent children receive more help from their parents than field-independent children (Johnston, 1974; Sholtz, 1973).

Turning now to the extensive set of studies involving comparisons between cultural groups, the evidence seems quite clear that field-dependent children tend to be found in cultural settings in which family and social authority demand conformity to a tightly defined set of customs and traditions regulating the behavior of the individual. One of the most comprehensive of these studies was conducted by Witkin and an international team of colleagues (Witkin, Price-Williams, Bertini, Christiansen, Oltman, Ramirez, & van Meel, 1974). The design of the study involved two contrasting villages in each of three countries (Mexico, Holland, and Italy). One of the villages was selected because it represented a subculture in which strict conformity to family, social, religious, and political authority was a salient characteristic, and the other village was selected because pressures for conformity were relatively low. For example, the more conforming villages were characterized by an extended family structure in which the grandparents exercised great authority. The father typically had a much revered role but little responsibility for the early child-rearing activities. A premium was placed on parental authority, and there were many taboos strictly enforced by parental, religious, and political forces. In the less conforming villages the extended family structure was less evident, and the father assumed a more active role in child rearing. There was much more tolerance of deviant behavior and less encompassing religious and political authority.

Within each of these villages approximately 100 children were given a battery of cognitive tests to measure extent of field dependence. Because the villages were relatively small, it was possible to test a representative sample of the children living in the village, thus avoiding the thorny sampling problem common in cross-cultural research. The results of the study are therefore particularly noteworthy. As expected, it was found that the average child living in the more conforming village of each country is more field dependent than the average child in the less conforming village.

Similar findings have been reported in most cross-cultural studies. To cite a few examples, Israeli residents of Middle Eastern origin have been compared with Israeli residents of Western origin (e.g., Preale, Amir, & Sharan, 1970); Temne tribesmen of Sierra Leone have been compared with the Mende tribesmen of Sierra Leone (e.g., Dawson, 1967); Mexican children have been compared with American children (e.g., Holtzman, Diaz-Guerrero, & Swartz, 1975); and Tsimshian Indians have been compared with Cree Indians of Canada (Berry & Annis, 1974). In each comparison the first-named group was characterized by insistence on adherence to authority and by strict socialization practices to achieve that goal, and the second-named group was characterized by more permissiveness and pride in their children's individual autonomy. In each case the stricter group was found to be more field dependent, as expected.

Obviously, any particular approach to so complex a question is fraught with unique problems of interpretation. It is comforting, therefore, when the same conclusion emerges from a variety of approaches. The conclusion that development toward greater field independence is to be found in settings that encourage separate functioning in children is comfortable in this sense.

The paternal role in the development of field independence

There is an extensive body of literature suggesting that the father plays an important role in the development of field independence. There are several bases for expecting that fathers who actively participate with the mother in child rearing may have more field-independent children than fathers who are less involved. One view involving sex role modeling has been particularly important in the history of research on fathers' roles. Many studies have been stimulated by an interest in sex differences in extent of field dependence. As noted earlier, in Western and in many other cultures the male sex role would seem to involve more autonomous functioning than the female sex role, and it has been found that males tend to be slightly more field independent than females. One explanation of this difference assumes that parents serve as models that their children may emulate. Since girls typically identify more with their mothers and boys with their fathers, the difference in parental roles may produce girls who, like their mothers, tend to be more field dependent and boys who, like their fathers, tend to be more field independent (e.g., Bieri, 1960; Lynn, 1969). As a corollary of the modeling view, it may be hypothesized that children who identify more with their father will develop in a more field-independent fashion. This hypothesis has focused attention on the father's role in child rearing and, more specifically, on the possibility that fathers who participate more actively in the child-rearing process, because they provide a more accessible, salient model, will produce children, and particularly boys, who are relatively field independent.

A second basis for assigning importance to the father assumes that an active participation by him facilitates separation from the mother. It seems clear in Western cultures, at least, that more field-dependent children tend to be found in families where the mother is very nurturing and protective whereas mothers who permit separation from them tend to have field-independent children. It seems reasonable to suppose that the presence of the father as a factor in child rearing may loosen the mother–child bond and provide the opportunity for more autonomous development. Here again, it may be true that a father's participation is greater for sons than for daughters, and his presence may therefore be more important for his sons. Thus, both the sex role modeling view and the facilitation of separation view would lead to similar predictions.

The evidence that the father's role is critical can be found in the earliest studies of child-rearing practices. For example, mothers of field-dependent children more often than mothers of field-independent children have expressed dissatisfaction with the help in family life they were getting from their husbands (Dyk & Witkin, 1965; Witkin et al., 1962/1974). On the basis of parental interviews, Seder (1957) also concluded that fathers of field-dependent children are relatively inactive in child rearing and "do not counteract the 'overprotecting,' restrictive influence of the mothers."

Similar findings have been reported in most subsequent studies. For example, fathers of field-independent boys more often express feelings of powerfulness than do fathers of field-dependent boys (Busse, 1969), and ratings of fathers' vs. mothers' dominance has been related to field independence among boys from West India and Hong Kong (Dawson et al., 1974). Cross-cultural comparisons have also tended to support the view that relatively field-dependent cultural groups tend to assign less active child-rearing roles to the father. For example, Orthodox Jewish families, in which the father's role in the physical and emotional care of the child is minimal, appear to have more field-dependent sons than do either non-orthodox Jewish families or non-Jewish controls (e.g., Dershowitz, 1971; Meizlik, 1973).

In another interesting study of polygamous families from Sierra Leone, the greater the number of wives in the family, the more field dependent the sons were found to be (Dawson, 1967). In interpreting this result, the author of the study suggested that the more wives there are, the more limited is the father's relationship with any one of his sons and the more dominant is the mother's role in child rearing.

The studies that have been cited above suggest that the more important the paternal role relative to the maternal role in intact family units, the more field independent are the children likely to be. Another source of evidence on the father's role in the family comes from studies of families with fathers who were totally absent for varying periods of time during the development of their children. These studies generally indicate that when the mother is left with the sole child-rearing responsibility, the child is likely to be more field dependent (e.g., Barclay & Cusumano, 1967). This conclusion appears to hold for daughters as well as for sons, for temporary father absences due to forces beyond his control as well as due to divorce and desertion, and appears to be less extreme if the absence occurs before the age of 6 than after (Louden, 1973; Wohlford & Liberman, 1970).

There is little doubt about the fact that mothers tend to have field-dependent children if their husbands are absent. This fact whets the appetite for information about what happens to children when the mother is absent and the father is the sole parent in residence, or when the child is abandoned or orphaned by both parents. Unfortunately, it has been possible to locate only one such study in the literature. This study compared 7- to 9-year-old children who were institutionalized by court order for parental abuse or neglect, with matched children raised normally at home with both parents (Baumberger, 1960). Some evidence was found that the abandoned children were more field independent than normal controls. This result suggests that the absence of father alone and the absence of both parents produce opposite effects on children. Such a pattern is difficult to understand in terms of the father's role as a model for field independence. The more viable view would seem to be that the father is important in intact families because his parental participation facilitates separation from the mother.

THE DEVELOPMENT OF FIELD DEPENDENCE IN CULTURAL EVOLUTION

The contrast between hunting and farming cultures

From archeological evidence we know that man was a hunter and a gatherer in the beginning. In his search for food he typically led a nomadic existence, following the game that provided his principal existence. His possessions were few, limited by his capacity to carry material. He traveled in relatively small bands, limited by the capacity of the local environment to sustain his needs. Beginning perhaps 8000 years ago, man learned to plant and cultivate crops and to domesticate animals. Obviously, the change from a hunting and gathering economy to a farming and herding economy was accompanied by dramatic changes in how men lived. As agricultural methods developed, people stopped wandering in search of food and began a more sedentary existence. It was possible, therefore, to accumulate wealth. The seasonal nature of farming led people to store food for times of scarcity. The availability of food supplies made it possible and perhaps even economical for people to collect in larger groups. People began to live in villages (e.g., Lee & Devore, 1968; Lomax & Berkowitz, 1972).

There is a limit to what can be learned from archeological evidence about the structure of society for early man, but we can study hunting-gathering and farming-herding subsistence level cultures in existence today and learn something about the social forms compatible with these contrasting types of economies. Anthropologists tell us that migratory hunting and gathering groups are characterized by relatively "loose" social structures in which there are only minimal differences among social roles, and little permanent political authority. Socialization practices emphasize self-reliance and autonomous functioning. In contrast, food-accumulating cultures, including agriculturalists and pastoralists, are characterized by relatively "tight" social structures in which many different social roles exist, and elaborate social organizations can be identified with many rules governing the relationships among the role holders. These structures often include aristocracies and theocracies that exert social pressure toward adherence to the rules and to the authorities who administer them. Socialization practices emphasize obedience and responsibility (e.g., Barry, Child, & Bacon, 1959; Berry, 1971; Witkin & Berry, 1975).

From the relationship between social structure, socialization practices, and extent of field dependence considered in the preceding section, and in view of the differences between hunting-gathering and agricultural-pastoral cultures described above, it may be expected that field independence is greater among the members of hunting-gathering groups. This expectation has been confirmed by most studies.

The earliest cross-cultural comparison of field dependence between a hunting group and an agricultural group was reported by Berry (1966) working with the Eskimo of Baffin Island, Canada, and the Temne of Sierra Leone, West Africa. The traditional Eskimo is a hunter. The principal food supply is provided by caribou and seal, which he hunts by boat in the summer and from the ice in the winter. The arctic environment is harsh and almost barren of vegetation. The men must travel great distances on the sea and along the coast on hunting trips in search of game. The camps are family-sized and are scattered widely along the coast. In contrast, the traditional Temne are farmers. Their major crop is rice, but they also cultivate groundnuts and peppers. Meat is caught in traps hidden in fences around the rice fields, and few people hunt. They have a single rice crop each year and ration the food supply from the harvest for use throughout the year. The traditional Temne live in a village whose population may number in the hundreds. Their farms are located near the village, and they rarely leave the well-trodden interconnecting paths through the bush. Like the Eskimo, the Temne is faced with a harsh environment with extremes of temperature, humidity, and rainfall, and like the Eskimo, the traditional Temne has only a subsistence level economy. Thus, the Eskimo and the Temne provide a clear contrast between a migratory hunting and a sedentary agricultural economy.

The contrast between the social structure of the traditional Temne and Eskimo cultures is equally clear. The Eskimos have very little social organization beyond the family. There is no permanent political authority. At one time the Eskimo were polygamous, but more recently they have one wife each. Within the family, the father apparently exercises little authority over his wife. In the Temne culture, on the other hand, there is an elaborate social structure with a high degree of social stratification involving religious and political authority (Dawson, 1969). An intricate network of tribal values is maintained by a set of harsh social sanctions. For example, deviation from the group norm may be punished by a "swear," involving public confession of wrongdoing. A person who offers an unauthorized opinion may be accused of witchcraft and punished accordingly. Individuality is strictly discouraged. The family is polygamous. The wives are responsible for most of the routine work and are tightly controlled by their husbands and by tribal values, with infractions of marital laws punishable by severe penalties (Berry, 1966; Dawson, 1967).

The socialization practices of the Eskimo and Temne seem well designed to produce adults who are adapted to their respective cultures. Eskimo children are educated in the family. The boys are taught to hunt by their fathers, who provide close contact during extensive hunting expeditions while the girls learn homemaking skills from their mothers. Child rearing is extremely permissive (Berry, 1966). For example, according to Butt (1950) "Children are scarcely ever subjected to blows or even to scolding or cross words, and they do practically as they wish, even to the extent of ordering about their parents and getting their own way in everything" (quoted by Berry, 1966, p. 214).

Child-rearing practices among the Temne are very different. The youngest child in the family is carried on the back of the mother while she works and is treated with affection until the age of weaning at about 2 to 2½ years of age. Beginning at that age, the child is strictly prohibited, by harsh discipline and frequent beatings, from expressing individuality. The mother, rather than the father, plays the dominant role in raising the child. In traditional Temne cultures, formal education is provided by a separate society for boys (Poro) and for girls (Bundu). The activities of these societies are secret. In addition, education is provided for some children by religious schools. The early content of the training in these schools is described by Berry (1966) as follows: ". . . the main concern . . . is learning religious texts and prayers, and becoming familiar with the rules of the classroom—sitting still, paying attention and responding to questions" (p. 208).

From these descriptions it seems clear that the Temne and Eskimo lie at opposite extremes of a number of dimensions that are thought to be relevant to the development of field independence. It was partly on these bases that Berry selected his groups for study, and on these bases his finding that the Eskimo tend to be dramatically more field independent than the Temne is not surprising.

Since Berry's work, a number of additional studies have compared migratory hunting-gathering groups and sedentary agricultural-pastoral groups in extent of field dependence. For example, the Arunta aborigines, migratory game hunters of the central Australian semidesert lands, have been found to be more field independent than the African Temne (Dawson, 1969). Another interesting study compared two groups living in Hong Kong, the Tanka and the Hakka (Dawson, 1970). The Tanka are called boat people because the family lives on a boat and spends much of its time fishing at sea. As expected, the Tanka tend to be more field independent than the agricultural Hakka. Still another study compared two Amerindian tribes, the Algonkian Cree of northeastern Canada and the Tsimshian of northwestern Canada (Berry & Annis, 1974). The traditional Cree live in migratory family bands whose economy is based on winter hunting and summer fishing. In contrast, food supplies for the traditional Tsimshian Indians consist of salmon and shellfish readily caught in nearby coastal waters. This study is particularly interesting because the Tsimshian tribe represents a sedentary food accumulation economy although it is not agricultural in the usual sense. Despite this variation, the Tsimshian were found to be more field dependent than the Cree. The results of these and other cross-cultural studies have recently been reviewed by Witkin and Berry (1975).

Many anthropologists have argued persuasively that the contrasts in social organization between "loose" and "tight," and in socialization practices between permissive and strict, may be seen as plausible adaptive consequences of the ecological and economic differences between migratory hunting-gathering and sedentary agricultural-pastoral life styles (e.g., Barry et al., 1959; Berry, 1966; Witkin & Berry, 1975). While man wandered in family-sized hunting bands, it was unnecessary and perhaps even maladaptive to have many diverse social roles, and most members of the society more or less had the capacity to occupy many or all the roles that existed. With the increase in the size of the band made possible by the development of agriculture, it is easy to see how the development of more elaborate rules for interpersonal behavior may be encouraged. Given the possibility for the accumulation of wealth, which a sedentary existence allows, it is also easy to imagine how social stratification may have emerged. With the accumulation of wealth, moreover, some people were freed from the job of providing food, making possible a proliferation of roles, some of which only selected individuals could perform. The emergence of role diversity, we may imagine, also contributed to the development of traditions and customs concerning the relationships among the various role holders in society. The necessity to generate and hoard food supplies for group survival from one harvest to another may have further encouraged the development of social mechanisms for control over the behavior of group members. Thus the types of social structure that characterize migratory hunting and sedentary agricultural groups may be tuned in broad outline to the requirements of life in each case.

Many psychologists who have considered the cross-cultural data on field dependence have also argued persuasively that field-dependent and field-independent modes of functioning may be similarly viewed in terms of their adaptive significance in these contrasting ecological settings (e.g., Berry, 1966, 1971; Berry & Annis, 1974; Dawson, 1969; Witkin & Berry, 1975). In the case of migratory hunting-gathering groups, it seems reasonable to suppose that autonomous functioning is well adapted to the requirements of existence. Not only does the hunter lead a relatively isolated life, but the activities involved in his search for game may place a premium on field-independent, cognitive restructuring skills, particularly in the relatively homogeneous environmental field that often characterizes the hunter's world. In the view of Witkin and Berry (1975), for example, "The ecological demands placed upon persons pursuing a hunting and gathering subsistence economic life style require the ability to extract key information from the surrounding context for the location of game and the ability to integrate these bits of information into a continuously fluctuating awareness of the hunter's location in space for the eventual safe return home" (p. 16).

The requirements of life in subsistence-level sedentary agricultural-pastoral cultures present a contrasting picture in which it has been proposed that field-dependent modes of functioning may be more adaptive. Adherence to group norms may become more valuable to group survival than autonomous individual functioning. Social sensitivity and attentiveness to others may become more adaptive than cognitive restructuring skills. Within the framework of field-dependence theory, both field-dependent and field-independent cognitive styles have adaptive value in the contrasting ecological-cultural contexts in which they tend to occur.

If we accept the view that culture evolves from relatively field-independent hunting-fishing peoples to relatively field-dependent agricultural peoples, then it is interesting to speculate about what processes might have been responsible for the change in extent of field dependence. It is possible, of course, that genetic factors may in part have been involved (e.g., Vandenberg, 1962). However, it is unnecessary to postulate a genetic mechanism. As we have seen, the evidence suggests that child-rearing practices that encourage separate functioning are related to the development of greater field independence within modern cultural groups. These practices are similar to the features of socialization that appear typical of hunting-gathering cultures. In contrast, the evidence suggests that child-rearing practices that encourage adherence to authority are related to the development of greater field dependence. These practices are similar to the features of socialization that appear to be typical of agricultural cultures. It is possible to suppose, therefore, that socialization practices that foster field dependence were adopted as one aspect of the evolution of cultural forms to meet the emerging adaptive requirements of the agricultural economy in which man found himself.

AN OVERVIEW

The literature on field dependence is so voluminous that any chapter-length treatment of the subject must be very selective. Two competing temptations inevitably arise in such cases. On the one hand, it is tempting to introduce the reader to all the relevant topics, and on the other, it is tempting to discuss the material within each topic in some depth. This chapter reflects a compromise resolution of this selection dilemma. Many topics of relevance to personality functioning have not been included. For example, there are bodies of literature on field dependence/independence in relation to shame and guilt, hostility expression, empathy, role definition, nature of personality defenses and controls, impulsivity, forms of pathology, and responsiveness to psychotherapy. These topics might interest the reader and were therefore omitted reluctantly. Even with a relatively limited selection of topics, however, it was possible to include only a few studies to illustrate what seems to be the current consensus of the evidence on key issues. This kind of selection runs the risk of conveying an exaggerated impression of the consensus and, therefore, was also undertaken with reluctance. Fortunately, more exhaustive and critical reviews of most of the topics covered here have recently appeared (Goodenough, 1976b; Witkin & Berry, 1975; Witkin et al., 1977; Witkin & Goodenough, 1976), and the reader who is interested in greater detail may refer to these works. The fact that the theory of field dependence rests on such a wide variety of data sources provides additional insurance against the risk that changing conclusions about a few issues will dramatically change the conceptual framework. Indeed, a major goal of conceptualizations of cognitive style is to provide an integrated view of phenomena in diverse areas of investigation. To see how the theory of field dependence attempts to meet this goal, the reader must be acquainted with the theory's application to different areas of behavioral science. The selection of topics for discussion here was designed in the hope of providing this kind of acquaintanceship.

The concepts of field dependence and field independence have been traced through the areas of perceptual, problem-solving, and social-interpersonal functioning to identify the nature of the dimension of individual difference that is involved. Some implications of the theory for questions of ontogenetic development in the process of cultural evolution have also been examined. These topics were chosen in the attempt to illustrate the range of phenomena that may be understood within the framework of field-dependence theory, to place the theory in the broad perspective of the behavioral sciences, and to emphasize the stylistic character of the field-dependence dimension.

The cognitive style view of field dependence and field independence is so central a feature of the theory that special emphasis seems warranted. As we have seen, the bipolar nature of the field-dependence dimension was evident in the early studies on perception of the vertical and horizontal axes of space. Reliance on inner cues may lead to more accurate location of the upright in some situations but less accurate location in other situations. As the outline of the broader dimension of autonomous functioning became apparent in subsequent research, the bipolar feature reemerged. This expression of the field-independent style as the ability to restructure cognitive fields may lead to particularly effective performance in certain perceptual and problem-solving situations, but the expression of the field-independent style as a separation from other people may lead to particularly ineffective performance in certain social situations. The bipolar feature of the field-dependence dimension seems evident in the study of origins as well. A field-independent cognitive style is apparently more adaptive to life in a nomadic subsistence-level hunting-gathering culture, but less adaptive to life in a sedentary subsistence-level agricultural culture.

Field-dependence theory may also be described as bipolar in another sense —the treatment of ontogenetic and cultural-evolutionary development. Common theories of man's development suppose that evolutionary change and ontogenetic change proceed in the same general direction. Such theories may be described as unipolar in character. As we have seen, field-dependence theory is not unipolar in this sense. Ontogenetic development proceeds from a state of relative field dependence to a state of relative field independence. In contrast, the theory suggests that evolution proceeded in the opposite direction, from a state of relative field independence to a state of relative field dependence, at least through much of the history of man's cultural development. By assigning adaptive value to the attributes at each extreme of individual difference dimensions, cognitive style theories can easily handle developmental series that go in opposite directions under different sets of adaptive demands.

REFERENCES

Anderson, D. L. Cognitive styles and perceived liberalism-conservatism among protestant ministers (Doctoral dissertation, University of Texas at Austin, 1971). *Dissertation Abstracts International,* 1972, *32,* 6023B-6024B. (University Microfilms No. 72-11, 302)

Asch, S. E., & Witkin, H. A. Studies in space orientation: I. Perception of the upright with displaced visual fields. *Journal of Experimental Psychology,* 1948, *38,* 325-337. (a)

Asch, S. E., & Witkin, H. A. Studies in space orientation: II. Perception of the upright with displaced visual fields and with body tilted. *Journal of Experimental Psychology*, 1948, *38*, 455–477. (b)

Balance, W. D. G. Acquiescence: Acquiescent response style, social conformity, authoritarianism, and visual field dependency (Doctoral dissertation, University of Alabama, 1967). *Dissertation Abstracts International*, 1968, *28*, 3458B. (University Microfilms No. 68-1027)

Baran, S. *Development and validation of a TAT-type projective test for use among Bantu-speaking people* (CSIR Special Report No. PERS 138). Johannesburg, South Africa: National Institute for Personnel Research Council for Scientific and Industrial Research, 1971.

Barclay, A., & Cusumano, D. R. Father absence, cross-sex identity, and field-dependent behavior in male adolescents. *Child Development*, 1967, *38*, 243–250.

Barrett, G. V., & Thornton, C. L. Cognitive style differences between engineers and college students. *Perceptual and Motor Skills*, 1967, *25*, 789–793.

Barry, H., Child, I. L., & Bacon, M. K. Relation of child training to subsistence economy. *American Anthropologist*, 1959, *61*, 51–63.

Baumberger, T. S. Identification differences between accepted and rejected children at one critical stage of ego development (Doctoral dissertation, University of Oklahoma, 1960). *Dissertation Abstracts International*, 1961, *21*, 2780. (University Microfilms No. 60-5526)

Beijk-Docter, M. A., & Elshout, J. J. Veldafhankelijkheid en geheugen met betrekking tot sociaal relevant en sociaal niet-relevant materiaal. *Nederlands Tijdschrift Voor de Psychologie en Haar Grensgebieden*, 1969, *24*, 267–279.

Bergman, H., & Engelbrektson, K. An examination of factor structure of rod-and-frame test and embedded-figures test. *Perceptual and Motor Skills*, 1973, *37*, 939–947.

Berry, J. W. Temne and Eskimo perceptual skills. *International Journal of Psychology*, 1966, *1*, 207–229.

Berry, J. W. Ecological and cultural factors in spatial perceptual development. *Canadian Journal of Behavioural Science*, 1971, *3*, 324–336.

Berry, J. W., & Annis, R. C. Ecology, culture and psychological differentiation. *International Journal of Psychology*, 1974, *9*, 173–193.

Bieri, J. Parental identification, acceptance of authority, and within-sex differences in cognitive behavior. *Journal of Abnormal and Social Psychology*, 1960, *60*, 76–79.

Boschi, F., & Loprieno, M. Stile conoscitivo e resistenza alle pressioni di gruppo. *Rivista di Psicologia*, 1968, *62*, 207–225.

Bruner, J. S., Goodnow, J. J., & Austin, G. A. *A study of thinking*. New York: John Wiley, 1956.

Busse, T. V. Child-rearing antecedents of flexible thinking. *Developmental Psychology*, 1969, *1*, 585–591.

Butt, A. *The social organization of the eastern and central Eskimos*. Unpublished doctoral dissertation, Institute of Social Anthropology, Oxford University, 1950.

Cattell, R. B. Is field independence an expression of the general personality source trait of independence, U.I. 19? *Perceptual and Motor Skills*, 1969, *28*, 865–866.

Clar, P. N. The relationship of psychological differentiation to client behavior in vocational choice counseling (Doctoral dissertation, University of Michigan, 1971). *Dissertation Abstracts International*, 1971, *32*, 1837B. (University Microfilms No. 71-23, 723)

Crutchfield, R. S., Woodworth, D. G., & Albrecht, R. E. *Perceptual performance and the effective person* (WADC-TN-58-60). Lackland Air Force Base, Texas: Personnel Laboratory, Wright Air Development Center, Air Research and Development Command, April 1958. (ASTIA No. AD-151 039)

Culver, C. M., Cohen, S. I., Silverman, A. J., & Shmavonian, B. M. Cognitive structuring, field dependence–independence, and the psychophysiological response to perceptual isolation. In J. Wortis (Ed.), *Recent advances in biological psychiatry*. (Vol. VI). New York: Plenum Press, 1964.

Davis, J. K., & Klausmeier, H. J. Cognitive style and concept identification as a function of complexity and training procedures. *Journal of Educational Psychology*, 1970, *61*, 423–430.

Dawson, J. L. M. Cultural and physiological influences upon spatial-perceptual processes in West Africa—Part I. *International Journal of Psychology*, 1967, *2*, 115–128.

Dawson, J. L. M. Theoretical and research bases of bio-social psychology. *University of Hong Kong, Supplement to the Gazette*, 1969, *16*, 1–10.

Dawson, J. L. M. Psychological research in Hong Kong. *International Journal of Psychology*, 1970, *5*, 63–70.

Dawson, J. L. M., Young, B. M., & Choi, P. P. C. Developmental influences in pictorial depth perception among Hong Kong Chinese children. *Journal of Cross-Cultural Psychology*, 1974, *5*, 3–22.

Dershowitz, Z. Jewish subcultural patterns and psychological differentiation. *International Journal of Psychology*, 1971, *6*, 223–231.

DeRussy, E. A., & Futch, E. Field dependence–independence as related to college curricula. *Perceptual and Motor Skills*, 1971, *33*, 1235–1237.

Dingman, R. L. A study of cognitive style differences as a factor of communications in school counseling (Doctoral dissertation, Wayne State University, 1971). *Dissertation Abstracts International*, 1972, *32*, 6756A. (University Microfilms No. 72-14, 544)

DiStefano, J. J. Interpersonal perceptions of field independent and field dependent teachers and students (Doctoral dissertation, Cornell University, 1969). *Dissertation Abstracts International*, 1970, *31*, 463A-464A. (University Microfilms No. 70-11, 225)

Domash, L. G. Selected maternal attitudes as related to sex, sex-role preference and level of psychological differentiation of the five-year-old child (Doctoral dissertation, New York University, 1973). *Dissertation Abstracts International*, 1973, *34*, 2925B. (University Microfilms No. 73-30,059)

Dreyer, A. S., McIntire, W. G., & Dreyer, C. A. Sociometric status and cognitive style in kindergarten children. *Perceptual and Motor Skills*, 1973, *37*, 407–412.

Duncker, K. On problem solving. *Psychological Monographs*, 1945, *58*(5, Whole No. 270) (translated by L. S. Lees).

Dyk, R. B., & Witkin, H. A. Family experiences related to the development of differentiation in children. *Child Development*, 1965, *30*, 21–55.

Eagle, M., Goldberger, L., & Breitman, M. Field dependence and memory for social vs. neutral and relevant vs. irrelevant incidental stimuli. *Perceptual and Motor Skills*, 1969, *29*, 903–910.

Fitzgibbons, D. J., & Goldberger, L. Task and social orientation: A study of field dependence, "arousal," and memory for incidental material. *Perceptual and Motor Skills*, 1971, *32*, 167–174.

Folman, R. Z. Therapist–patient perceptual style, interpersonal attraction, initial interview behavior, and premature termination (Doctoral dissertation, Boston University, 1973). *Dissertation Abstracts International*, 1973, *34*, 1746B. (University Microfilms No. 73-23, 482)

French, J. W., Ekstrom, R. B., & Price, L. A. *Kit of reference tests for cognitive factors*. Princeton, N. J.: Educational Testing Service, 1963.

Freund, J., Krupp, G., Goodenough, D., & Preston, L. W. The doctor–patient relationship and drug effect. *Clinical Pharmacology and Therapeutics*, 1972, *13*, 172–180.

Gardner, R. W., Jackson, D. N., & Messick, S. J. Personality organization in cognitive controls and intellectual abilities. *Psychological Issues*, 1960, *2*(4, Whole No. 8).

Gates, D. W. Verbal conditioning, transfer and operant level "speech style" as functions of cognitive style (Doctoral dissertation, City University of New York, 1971). *Dissertation Abstracts International*, 1971, *32*, 3634B. (University Microfilms No. 71-30, 719)

Gibson, J. J., & Mowrer, O. H. Determinants of the perceived vertical and horizontal. *Psychological Review*, 1938, *45*, 300–323.

Glass, G. G. Rate of reading: A correlation and treatment study. *Journal of Reading*, 1967, *11*, 168–178.

Glucksberg, S. *Perception and problem-solving*. Unpublished bachelor's thesis, City University of New York, 1956.

Goldberger, L., & Bendich, S. Field dependence and social responsiveness as determinants of spontaneously produced words. *Perceptual and Motor Skills*, 1972, *34*, 883–886.

Goodenough, D. R. Individual differences in field dependence as a factor in auto safety. *Human Factors*, 1976, *18*, 53–62. (a)

Goodenough, D. R. The role of individual differences in field dependence as a factor in learning and memory. *Psychological Bulletin*, 1976, *83*, 675–694. (b)

Goodenough, D. R., & Eagle, C. J. A modification of the embedded-figures test for use with young children. *Journal of Genetic Psychology*, 1963, *103*, 67–74.

Goodenough, D. R., & Karp, S. A. Field dependence and intellectual functioning. *Journal of Abnormal and Social Psychology*, 1961, *63*, 241–246.

Goodman, B. Field dependence and the closure factors. Cited by H. A. Witkin, R. B. Dyk, H. F. Faterson, D. R. Goodenough, and S. A. Karp. *Psychological Differentiation*. Potomac, Md.: Erlbaum, 1974. (Originally published, 1962.)

Gottschaldt, L. Über den einfluss der erfährung auf die wahrnehmung von figuren 1: Über den einfluss gehäufter einprägung von figuren auf ihre sichtbarkeit in umfassenden konfigurationen. *Psychologische Forschungen*, 1926, *8*, 261–317.

Greene, L. R. Effects of field independence, physical proximity and evaluative feedback on affective reactions and compliance in a dyadic interaction (Doctoral dissertation, Yale University, 1973). *Dissertation Abstracts International*, 1973, *34*, 2284B-2285B. (University Microfilms No. 73-26,285)

Greene, M. A. Client perception of the relationship as a function of worker–client cognitive styles (Doctoral dissertation, Columbia University, 1972). *Dissertation Abstracts International*, 1972, *33*, 3030A-3031A. (University Microfilms No. 72-31,213)

Guilford, J. P. *The nature of human intelligence*. New York: McGraw-Hill, 1967.

Halm, J. The relationship of field articulation and affective placebo reaction (Doctoral dissertation, Yeshiva University, 1967). *Dissertation Abstracts International*, 1968, *28*, 4283B. (University Microfilms No. 68-5575)

Harano, R. M. Relationship of field dependence and motor-vehicle-accident involvement. *Perceptual and Motor Skills*, 1970, *31*, 272–274.

Haronian, F., & Sugerman, A. A. Field independence and resistance to reversal of perspective. *Perceptual and Motor Skills*, 1966, *22*, 543–546.

Hauk, M. W. Effects of maternal attitudes, field-dependence and curiosity on weight and volume conservation in children (Doctoral dissertation, Catholic University of America, 1967). *Dissertation Abstracts*, 1967, *28*, 2642B. (University Microfilms No. 67-15,463.)

Hilgard, E. R. *Theories of learning*. New York: Appleton-Century-Crofts, 1948.

Holtzman, W. H., Diaz-Guerrero, R., & Swartz, J. D. *Personality development in two cultures: A cross-cultural longitudinal study of school children in Mexico and the United States*. Austin, Texas: University of Texas Press, 1975.

Holtzman, W. H., Swartz, J. D., & Thorpe, J. S. Artists, architects, and engineers—three contrasting modes of visual experience and their psychological correlates. *Journal of Personality*, 1971, *39*, 432–449.

Horn, J. L., & Cattell, R. B. Refinement and test of the theory of fluid and crystallized general intelligences. *Journal of Educational Psychology*, 1966, *57*, 253–270.

Iscoe, I., & Carden, J. A. Field dependence, manifest anxiety, and sociometric status in children. *Journal of Consulting Psychology*, 1961, *25*, 184.

Jackson, D. N. Stability in resistance to field forces (Doctoral dissertation, Purdue University, 1955). *Dissertation Abstracts International*, 1955, *15*(868). (University Microfilms No. 11,633)

James, C. D. R. *A cognitive style approach to teacher-pupil interaction and the academic performance of black children*. Unpublished master's thesis, Rutgers University, 1973.

Johnston, P. K. Relationship between perceptual style, achievement, and childrearing practices in elementary-school boys and girls (Doctoral dissertation, University of Southern California, 1974). *Dissertation Abstracts International*, 1974, *34*, 5169B-5170B. (University Microfilms No. 74-9070)

Jones, P. A. Socialization practices and the development of spatial ability. In J. L. M. Dawson and W. J. Lonner (Eds.), *Readings in cross-cultural psychology*. Hong Kong: Hong Kong University Press, 1975.

Joshi, R. T. *The relationship between individual differences in perception and some personality correlates*. Unpublished master's thesis, University of London, 1968.

Jourard, S. M. *Self-disclosure: An experimental analysis of the transparent self*. New York: John Wiley, 1971.

Jourard, S. M., & Lasakow, P. Some factors in self-disclosure. *Journal of Abnormal and Social Psychology*, 1958, *56*, 91–98.

Justice, M. T. Field dependency, intimacy of topic and interperson distance (Doctoral dissertation, University of Florida, 1969). *Dissertation Abstracts International*, 1970, *31*, 395B–396B. (University Microfilms No. 70–12,243)

Karp, S. A. Field dependence and overcoming embeddedness. *Journal of Consulting Psychology*, 1963, *27*, 294–302.

Karp, S. A., Kissin, B., & Hustmyer, F. E. Field dependence as a predictor of alcoholic therapy dropouts. *Journal of Nervous and Mental Disease*, 1970, *150*, 77–83.

Kirschenbaum, J. Analytic-global cognitive style and concept attainment strategies (Doctoral dissertation, Claremont Graduate School, 1968). *Dissertation Abstracts International*, 1969, *29*, 4868B–4869B. (University Microfilms No. 68–18,276)

Koff, J. H. W. Field dependence and psychotherapy expectancies, presenting symptoms, defensive style, and length of stay in psychotherapy (Doctoral dissertation, George Washington University, 1972). *Dissertation Abstracts International*, 1972, *32*, 7312B. (University Microfilms No. 72–18,590)

Lee, R. B., & De Vore, I. (Eds.), *Man the hunter*. Chicago: Aldine, 1968.

Levy, S. *Field independence–field dependence and occupational interests*. Unpublished master's thesis, Cornell University, 1969.

Linton, H. B. Dependence on external influence: Correlates in perception, attitudes, and judgment. *Journal of Abnormal and Social Psychology*, 1955, *51*, 502–507.

Lomax, A., & Berkowitz, N. The evolutionary taxonomy of culture. *Science*, 1972, *177*, 228–239.

Louden, K. H. *Field dependence in college students as related to father absence during the latency period*. Unpublished doctoral dissertation, Fuller Theological Seminary, 1973.

Lynn, D. B. Curvilinear relation between cognitive functioning and distance of child from parent of the same sex. *Psychological Review*, 1969, *76*, 236–240.

Mach, E. *Grundlinien der Lehre von der Bewegungsempfindungen*. Leipzig: Wilhelm Engelmann, 1875.

MacKinnon, D. W. The personality correlates of creativity: A study of American architects. In G. Nielson (Ed.), *Proceedings of the XIV International Congress of Applied Psychology* (Vol. 2). *Personality research*. Copenhagen, Denmark: Munksgaard, 1962.

Mausner, B., & Graham, J. Field dependence and prior reinforcement as determinants of social interaction in judgment. *Journal of Personality and Social Psychology*, 1970, *16*, 486–493.

Mebane, D., & Johnson, D. L. A comparison of the performance of Mexican boys and girls on Witkin's cognitive tasks. *Inter-American Journal of Psychology*, 1970, *4*, 227–239.

Meizlik, F. *The effect of sex and cultural variables on field independence/dependence in a Jewish subculture*. Unpublished master's thesis, City University of New York, 1973.

Messick, S., & Damarin, F. Cognitive styles and memory for faces. *Journal of Abnormal and Social Psychology*, 1964, *69*, 313–318.

Messick, S., & French, J. W. Dimensions of cognitive closure. *Multivariate Behavioral Research*, 1975, *10*, 3–16.

Morgan, A. H. Hypnotizability and "cognitive styles": A search for relationships. *Journal of Personality*, 1972, *40*, 503–509.

Nebelkopf, E. B., & Dreyer, A. S. Continuous-discontinuous concept attainment as a function of individual differences in cognitive style. *Perceptual and Motor Skills*, 1973, *36*, 655–662.

Nevill, D. Experimental manipulation of dependency motivation and its effects on eye contact and measures of field dependency. *Journal of Personality and Social Psychology*, 1974, *29*, 72–79.

Newbigging, P. L. The relationship between reversible perspective and embedded figures. *Canadian Journal of Psychology*, 1954, *8*, 204–208.

Olson, P. L. Aspects of driving performance as a function of field dependence. *Journal of Applied Psychology*, 1974, *59*, 192–196.

Oltman, P. K. A portable rod-and-frame apparatus. *Perceptual and Motor Skills*, 1968, *26*, 503–506.

Oltman, P. K., Goodenough, D. R., Witkin, H. A., Freedman, N., & Friedman, F. Psychological differentiation as a factor in conflict resolution. *Journal of Personality and Social Psychology*, 1975, *32*, 730–736.

Osipow, S. H. Cognitive styles and educational-vocational preferences and selection. *Journal of Counseling Psychology*, 1969, *16*, 534–546.

Paclisanu, M. I. Interacting effects of field dependence, stimulus deprivation and two types of reinforcement upon problem-solving in elementary school children (Doctoral dissertation, Temple University, 1970). *Dissertation Abstracts International*, 1970, *31*, 2290B–2291B. (University Microfilms No. 70–19,763)

Paeth, C. A. A Likert scaling of student value statements, field independence–field dependence, and experimentally induced change (Doctoral dissertation, Oregon State University, 1973). *Dissertation Abstracts International*, 1973, *34*, 2288B–2289B. (University Microfilms No. 73–25,368)

Palmer, R. D., & Field, P. B. Cognitive factors in hypnotic susceptibility. *Journal of Consulting and Clinical Psychology*, 1971, *37*, 165.

Pascual-Leone, J. *Cognitive development and cognitive style: A general psychological integration.* Unpublished doctoral dissertation, University of Geneva, 1969.

Pawlik, K. Concepts in human cognition and aptitudes. In R. B. Cattell (Ed.), *Handbook of multivariate experimental psychology.* Chicago: Rand McNally, 1966.

Pemberton, C. L. The closure factors related to temperament. *Journal of Personality, 1952, 21,* 159–175.

Perez, P. P. Experimental instructions and stimulus content as variables in the size constancy perception of schizophrenics and normals (Doctoral dissertation, New York University, 1955). *Dissertation Abstracts, 1958, 18,* 2214–2215. (University Microfilms No. 24,888)

Piaget, J., & Inhelder, B. *Le développement des quantités chez l'enfant. Conservation et atomisme.* Neuchatel & Paris: Delachaux & Niestle, 1962.

Pierson, J. S. Cognitive styles and measured vocational interests of college men (Doctoral dissertation, University of Texas at Austin, 1965). *Dissertation Abstracts, 1965, 26,* 875–876. (University Microfilms No. 65–8082)

Preale, I., Amir, Y., & Sharan, S. Perceptual articulation and task effectiveness in several Israel subcultures. *Journal of Personality and Social Psychology, 1970, 15,* 190–195.

Quinlan, D. M., & Blatt, S. J. Field articulation and performance under stress: Differential predictions in surgical and psychiatric nursing training. *Journal of Consulting and Clinical Psychology, 1972, 39,* 517.

Royce, J. R. *The conceptual framework for a multi-factor theory of individuality.* (Papers in Progress 012C 72) Edmonton: University of Alberta, Center for Advanced Study in Theoretical Psychology, 1972.

Ruble, D. N., & Nakamura, C. Y. Task orientation versus social orientation in young children and their attention to relevant social cues. *Child Development, 1972, 43,* 471–480.

Seder, J. A. *The origin of differences in extent of independence in children: Developmental factors in perceptual field dependence.* Unpublished bachelor's thesis, Radcliffe College, 1957.

Sewell, B. L. Ability and preference for analyzing under ambiguous and analytical instructions (Doctoral dissertation, George Washington University, 1973). *Dissertation Abstracts International, 1973, 34,* 2318B. (University Microfilms No. 73–25,095)

Shapson, S. M. *Hypothesis testing and cognitive style in children.* Unpublished doctoral dissertation, York University, 1973.

Sherif, M. A study of some social factors in perception. *Archives of Psychology,* New York, 1935, No. *187.*

Sholtz, D. The development of sex differences in field independence (Doctoral dissertation, Boston University, 1972). *Dissertation Abstracts International, 1973, 33,* 6066B–6067B. (University Microfilms No. 73–14,180)

Soat, D. M. Cognitive style, self-concept, and expressed willingness to help others (Doctoral dissertation, Marquette University, 1974). *Dissertation Abstracts International, 1974, 35,* 2063A–2064A. (University Microfilms No. 74–22,305)

Sousa-Poza, J. F., & Rohrberg, R. Communicational and interactional aspects of self-disclosure in psychotherapy: Differences related to cognitive style. *Psychiatry, 1976, 39,* 81–91.

Sousa-Poza, J. F., Rohrberg, R., & Shulman, E. Field dependence and self-disclosure. *Perceptual and Motor Skills, 1973, 36,* 735–738.

Steinfeld, S. L. Level of differentiation and age as predictors of reinforcer effectiveness (Doctoral dissertation, Hofstra University, 1973). *Dissertation Abstracts International, 1973, 34,* 2912B–2913B. (University Microfilms No. 73–25,324)

Thurstone, L. L. *A factorial study of perception.* Chicago: University of Chicago Press, 1944.

Vandenberg, S. G. The hereditary abilities study: Hereditary components in a psychological test battery. *American Journal of Human Genetics,* 1962, *14,* 220–237.

Vernon, P. E. The distinctiveness of field independence. *Journal of Personality,* 1972,*40,* 366–391. (a)

Vernon, P. E. Sex differences in personality structure at age 14. *Canadian Journal of Behavioral Sciences,* 1972, *4,* 283–297. (b)

Victor, J. B. *Peer judgments of teaching competence as a function of field-independence and dogmatism.* Paper presented at the meeting of the Eastern Psychological Association, Washington, D. C., May 1973.

Webb, D. The effect of ordering and contrast of feedback and perceptual style on liking of an evaluative source (Doctoral dissertation, University of Cincinnati, 1972). *Dissertation Abstracts International,* 1973,*33,* 3966B. (University Microfilms No. 73–3825)

Wender, P. H., Pedersen, F. A., & Waldrop, M. F. A longitudinal study of early social behavior and cognitive development. *American Journal of Orthopsychiatry,* 1967,*37,* 691–696.

Wertheimer, M. Experimentelle Studien über das Sehen von Bewegung. *Zeitschrift für Psychologie,* 1912,*61,* 161–265.

Williams, J. R. A study of the relationships between three-dimensional spatial relations ability and driving performance: A comparison of performance on the three-dimensional embedded figures test and on-the-job driving performance of telephone company drivers (Doctoral dissertation, New York University, 1971). *Dissertation Abstracts International,* 1972,*32,* 5628A. (University Microfilms No. 72-11,484)

Witkin, H. A. Perception of body position and of the position of the visual field. *Psychological Monographs,* 1949, *63* (7 Whole No. 302).

Witkin, H. A. Individual differences in ease of perception of embedded figures. *Journal of Personality,* 1950, *19,* 1–15.

Witkin, H. A. Further studies of perception of the upright when the direction of the force acting on the body is changed. *Journal of Experimental Psychology,* 1952,*43,* 9–20.

Witkin, H. A., & Asch, S. E. Studies in space orientation. III. Perception of the upright in the absence of a visual field. *Journal of Experimental Psychology,* 1948,*38,* 603–614. (a)

Witkin, H. A., & Asch, S. E. Studies in space orientation. IV. Further experiments on perception of the upright with displaced visual fields. *Journal of Experimental Psychology,* 1948, *38,* 762–782. (b)

Witkin, H. A., & Berry, J. W. Psychological differentiation in cross-cultural perspective. *Journal of Cross-Cultural Psychology,* 1975, *6,* 4–87.

Witkin, H. A., Cox, P. W., & Friedman, F. *Supplement No. 2, Field-dependence-independence and psychological differentiation: Bibliography with index.* Research Bulletin 76–28. Princeton, N. J.: Educational Testing Service, 1976.

Witkin, H. A., Cox, P. W., Friedman, F., Hrishikesan, A. G., & Siegel, K. N. *Supplement No. 1, Field-dependence-independence and psychological differentiation: Bibliography with index.* Research Bulletin 74–42. Princeton, N. J.: Educational Testing Service, 1974.

Witkin, H. A., Dyk, R. B., Faterson, H. F., Goodenough, D. R., & Karp, S. A. *Psychological differentiation.* Potomac, Md.: Erlbaum, 1974. (Originally published, 1962.)

Witkin, H. A., & Goodenough, D. R. *Field dependence revisted.* Research Bulletin 76–39. Princeton, N.J.: Educational Testing Service, 1976.

Witkin, H. A., Goodenough, D. R., & Karp, S. A. Stability of cognitive style from childhood to young adulthood. *Journal of Personality and Social Psychology,* 1967, *7,* 291–300.

Witkin, H. A., Lewis, H. B., Hertzman, M., Machover, K., Meissner, P. B., & Wapner, S. *Personality through perception.* Westport, Conn.: Greenwood Press, 1972. (Originally published, 1954.)

Witkin, H. A., Lewis, H. B., & Weil, E. Affective reactions and patient–therapist interactions among more differentiated and less differentiated patients early in therapy. *Journal of Nervous and Mental Disease,* 1968, *146,* 193–208.

Witkin, H. A., Moore, C. A., Goodenough, D. R., & Cox, P. W. Field-dependent and field-independent cognitive styles and their educational implications. *Review of Educational Research,* 1977, *47,* 1–64.

Witkin, H. A., Oltman, P. K., Cox, P. W., Ehrlichman, E., Hamm, R. M., & Ringler, R. W. *Field-dependence-independence and psychological differentiation: A bibliography through 1972 with index.* Research Bulletin 73–62. Princeton, N. J.: Educational Testing Service, 1973.

Witkin, H. A., Oltman, P. K., Raskin, E., & Karp, S. A. *A manual for the embedded figures tests.* Palo Alto, Cal.: Consulting Psychologists Press, 1971.

Witkin, H. A., Price-Williams, D., Bertini, M., Christiansen, B., Oltman, P. K., Ramirez, M., & van Meel, J. Social conformity and psychological differentiation. *International Journal of Psychology,* 1974, *9,* 11–29.

Wohlford, P., & Liberman, D. Effect of father absence on personal time, field independence, and anxiety. *Proceedings of the 78th Annual Convention of the American Psychological Association,* 1970, *5,* 263–264.

Wong, K. L. Psychological differentiation as a determinant of friendship choice. (Doctoral dissertation, City University of New York, 1976.) *Dissertation Abstracts International,* 1977, *37,* 3639B. (University Microfilms No. 76–30,278.)

Woodworth, R. S. *Experimental psychology.* New York: Holt, 1938.

NOTES

1 The preparation of this review was aided by support of U. S. Public Health Service Grant MH-21989. The author is indebted to Dr. H. A. Witkin for many helpful comments on earlier drafts of this manuscript and for his continuous support throughout its preparation.

2 During the history of research on this dimension, the theory of field dependence has undergone a process of enlargement and refinement as new findings have become available. As part of this process the terms field dependence and field independence have been used in several different ways in the literature. As we shall see, the terms were originally used to describe individual differences in the relative importance of inner versus visual-field cues to the location of the upright in space. The terms were subsequently used to refer to extremes of a broader perceptual dimension involving the capacity to overcome embedding contexts in perception (Witkin et al., 1962/1974). Most recently, the terms have been used to refer to the more general dimension of separateness from the external world, as defined above.

3 The field–dependence dimension has been treated in a larger context of differentiation theory (e.g., Witkin et al., 1962/1974), but the differentiation construct is unnecessary for the discussion to follow and will not be considered in this chapter.

4 The capacity to overcome embedding contexts has also been called Closure Flexibility (Thurstone, 1944) and Convergent Production of Figural Transformations (Guilford, 1967).

5   It is interesting to note the apparent convergence in definition during the historical development of Cattell's general temperament factor (U.I. 19), now called ''Independence,'' and the historical development of the field-independence construct as described herein (Cattell, 1969).

6   There is a voluminous literature on field dependence and attitude changes following written statements attributed to authoritative sources. The evidence from this literature suggests little if any relationship with impersonal influence effects of this sort.

7   The idea that field-dependent people will show a better memory than field-independent people for social material has been examined in many laboratory studies. In some cases the hypothesis has been clearly confirmed (e.g., Eagle, Goldberger, & Breitman, 1969; Messick & Damarin, 1964) but other studies have failed to find the expected results (e.g., Beijk-Docter & Elshout, 1969; Fitzgibbons & Goldberger, 1971). Although the reason for the discrepancy is unclear at this time, it may be true that memory consequences are not as pronounced with laboratory stimuli of social relevance as they are for social stimuli arising from actual interpersonal interaction.

CHAPTER 6

Introversion/Extroversion

GLENN WILSON Ph.D.

Institute of Psychiatry (Maudsley Hospital)
University of London, England.

INTRODUCTION*

Although C. G. Jung, the famous mystic psychiatrist, is often credited with the discovery (invention?) of introversion–extroversion, the terms were familiar to European psychologists at least a century earlier. English dictionaries from Dr. Johnson's (1755) onward contained reference to the terms *extrovert* and *introvert,* and they were defined in ways very similar to current usage. Extroversion was typically defined as a "turning outward of the mind" onto people and objects in the external world; introversion as "inner directedness" and a preference for abstract ideas rather than concrete objects. Today we have broadened the scope of these terms so that extroversion also refers to impulsive, sociable tendencies, and introversion includes controlled and responsible behavior.

Interest in a related distinction goes back as far as the second century A.D. The Greek physicians Hippocrates and Galen described four major temperamental types: the melancholic, choleric, sanguine, and phlegmatic, and nominated four "humors" (rather like hormones) that were supposed to be responsible for them. Their physiological theory is, of course, now regarded as somewhat quaint, but the descriptive scheme is still used. It was an oversimplification in that people cannot be neatly pigeonholed into four categories, but that problem was solved in the nineteenth century when Wilhelm Wundt pointed out that the four-way classification could be accommodated by two independent and continuous variables of emotional response: *strength* of emotions and *speed of*

This contribution is based largely on a chapter by the author entitled Introversion/Extroversion in T. Blass (Ed.), *Personality variables in social behavior*. Hillsdale, N.J.: Lawrence Erlbaum Associates, 1977. It is reprinted with the permission of the Editor and Publishers.
*I am grateful to Hans Eysenck and David Nias for carefully reading and commenting on the manuscript.

change. Studies using the statistical technique of factor analysis have repeatedly confirmed the broad descriptive usefulness of such a two-dimensional scheme, although different researchers have applied different names. What Wundt described as speed of change is now usually called introversion–extroversion (although R. B. Cattell prefers "invia–exvia"), and his strength factor is now variously called instability, emotionality, neuroticism (Eysenck), and anxiety (Cattell).

Figure 6–1 shows how these two major dimensions of personality relate to the old Greek typology. The advantage of the dimensional system over the categorical system is that an individual can be described more flexibly by assigning him a point anywhere within the space formed by the two factors. Most people congre-

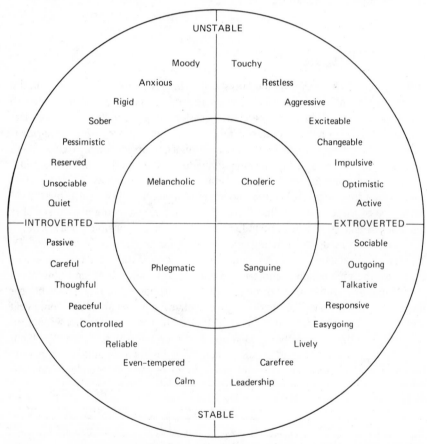

Figure 6–1.   Two major dimensions of personality revealed by factor analysis compared with the four Greek categories (Eysenck, 1973a).

gate in the middle range on these dimensions with fewer numbers falling toward the extremes. In the conventions of factor analysis the two factors are drawn at right angles to indicate that they are independent (i.e., a position on one does not predict a position on the other). This question of the structure or patterning of personality traits will be taken up again later.

DESCRIPTION AND MEASUREMENT

Measurement of introversion–extroversion is normally achieved by questionnaire. Among the more famous self-report measures are the social introversion scale of the Minnesota Multiphasic Personality Inventory (MMPI) and the introversion–extroversion measure of the Eysenck Personality Inventory (EPI). Examples of the kinds of items used in the latter are given in Table 6–1. The picture of the extrovert and introvert given by the EPI is as follows:

Table 6-1 Items of the kind used to measure introversion–extroversion in the Eysenck personality Inventory [a]

Do you often long for excitement?	E
Are you usually carefree?	E
Do you stop and think things over before doing anything?	I
Would you do almost anything for a dare?	E
Do you often do things on the spur of the moment?	E
Generally, do you prefer reading to meeting people?	I
Do you prefer to have few but special friends?	I
When people shout at you do you shout back?	E
Do other people think of you as very lively?	E
Are you mostly quiet when you are with people?	I
If there is something you want to know about, would you rather look it up in a book than talk to someone about it?	I
Do you like the kind of work that you need to pay close attention to?	I
Do you hate being with a crowd who play jokes on one another?	I
Do you like doing things in which you have to act quickly?	E
Are you slow and unhurried in the way you move?	I
Do you like talking to people so much that you never miss a chance of talking to a stranger?	E
Would you be unhappy if you could not see lots of people most of the time?	E
Do you find it hard to enjoy yourself at a lively party?	I
Would you say that you were fairly self-confident?	E
Do you like playing pranks on others?	E

[a] To score for extroversion, give 1 point for each "E" item answered "yes" and each "I" item answered "no." High scores then indicate extroversion and low scores introversion. A properly standardized self-scoring scale may be found in Eysenck and Wilson (1976) and in Eysenck and Eysenck (1964).

The typical extrovert is sociable, likes parties, has many friends, needs to have people to talk to, and does not like reading or studying by himself. He craves excitement, takes chances, often sticks his neck out, acts on the spur of the moment, and is generally an impulsive individual. He is fond of practical jokes, always has a ready answer, and generally likes change; he is carefree, easygoing, optimistic, and likes to "laugh and be merry." He prefers to keep moving and doing things, tends to be aggressive and loses his temper quickly; altogether his feelings are not kept under tight control, and he is not always a reliable person.

The typical introvert is a quiet, retiring sort of person, introspective, fond of books rather than people; he is reserved and distant except to intimate friends. He tends to plan ahead, "looks before he leaps," and distrusts the impulse of the moment. He does not like excitement, takes matters of everyday life with proper seriousness, and likes a well-ordered mode of life. He keeps his feelings under close control, seldom behaves in an aggressive manner, and does not lose his temper easily. He is reliable, somewhat pessimistic and places great value on ethical standards. (Eysenck & Eysenck, 1964.)

These descriptions of the characteristic introvert and extrovert do not conform exactly to the traditional or Jungian definitions, but they are fairly close. Differences in detail must be put down to the fact that the earlier descriptions were based on uncontrolled observation and intuitive theorizing, whereas Eysenck's dimensions are established empirically by means of factor analysis, a mathematical technique for classifying attributes on the basis of the relative strengths of relationships (intercorrelations) among them.

Apart from questionnaires and other rating techniques, indirect or "objective" measures of extroversion–introversion are sometimes used. These depend on a high established correlation between the questionnaire measure and some other kind of behavior or physiological response. For example, there have been several reports that introversion is related to the amount of saliva that an individual will produce in his mouth when a standard amount of lemon juice is placed on his tongue. The results of one such study are shown in Figure 6–2. As we will see, this finding is of considerable theoretical interest, but the relationship is also apparently so strong (correlation around 0.7) that the "lemon-drop test" has been employed in other studies as an "objective" measure of introversion––extroversion. Another piece of behavior that has sometimes been used as an extroversion measure, even though the actual correlation is rather low, is the color/form ratio on a test such as the Rorschach inkblots. Apparently there is a tendency for extroverts to respond more to the color of a visual display and introverts to the form, and this may may be used as an I–E index. These are just two randomly selected examples of the many perceptual, motor, physiological, and other kinds of behavior that correlate with questionnaire measures of extroversion and that may therefore be used as measures of that dimension themselves, with varying degrees of precision loss.

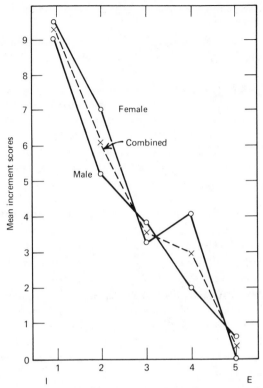

Figure 6–2. Mean salivation increments of five groups of male and female subjects, ordered according to degree of introversion, after placing four drops of lemon juice on tongue. Reprinted with permission of author and publisher from: Eysenck, Sybil B. G., and Eysenck, H. J. Salivary response to lemon juice as a measure of introversion. PERCEPTUAL AND MOTOR SKILLS, 1967, 24, 1047–1053.

EXTROVERSION IN ITS TEMPERAMENTAL CONTEXT

The E dimension is one of three dimensions of personality that Eysenck considers to be of prime importance (apart from intelligence). The other two are *neuroticism* (N, also called instability or emotionality) and *psychoticism* (P, for which the name "toughmindedness" is sometimes preferred). These three personality dimensions are conceived as independent from one another and are thought to provide a good summary of the varieties of normal and abnormal personality. Two of these dimensions, extroversion and neuroticism, are shown in Figure 6-1. The placement of various trait-descriptive adjectives in relation to them illustrates how individuals can fall in any position between the extremes on either dimension. Thus, with respect to the E dimension, most people are actually ambiverted rather than extreme extroverts or introverts, and they may be more or less stable or neurotic regardless of their position on E. The third dimension, psychoticism, refers to behavior that is bizarre, impersonal, hostile, and antisocial; it may be thought of as coming straight out of the diagram from the cross in the center as well as reflected back through the other side of the paper. This complicates the situation geographically since an individual person can be located anywhere in the three-dimensional space according to his coordinates on the three dimensions. It is necessary to understand this model of personality to fully appreciate the modern concept of extroversion because it is partly defined in terms of its relationship to (and independence from) other major personality factors.

It is often said that factor analysis is a dubious technique because different workers using it tend to come up with different solutions. Cattell, for example, is known to have identified 16 personality dimensions using factor analysis. How can this be reconciled with Eysenck's view that there are only three? In fact, the apparent dispute between Cattell and Eysenck is largely unreal; the only difference is that they are dealing at different levels of generality. Cattell's 16 factors are not independent of one another, and because they are intercorrelated they can themselves be factor analyzed. When this is done, second-order factors are produced that are very similar to Eysenck's major dimensions. Naming factors is always arbitrary, however, and Cattell prefers the label exvia–invia to extroversion–introversion.

Whether one deals at a primary factor level (as does Cattell) or the second-order level (as Eysenck usually does) is a matter of preference and depends on one's purpose. The primary factors give a more detailed picture of the personality; on the other hand, their reliability and separability are questionable (Eysenck, 1972a), and they may be of less theoretical interest, being more difficult to pin to biological substrata. It will be clear, however, that both factor analysts are agreed upon a hierarchical model of personality such as that illustrated for the extroversion dimension in Figure 6–3. In this diagram, primary factors have been called *traits* and second-order factors *types*, but use of the term *type* should not be taken to imply that people must be categorized as either extrovert or introvert; remember, most people are more or less ambiverted.

IS EXTROVERSION UNITARY?

In a review of the literature concerning the status of E as a dimension of personality, Carrigan (1960) concluded that on the basis of research reported up to that time the unidimensionality of extroversion–introversion had not been unequivocably demonstrated. On the positive side, she found that repeated analyses of the

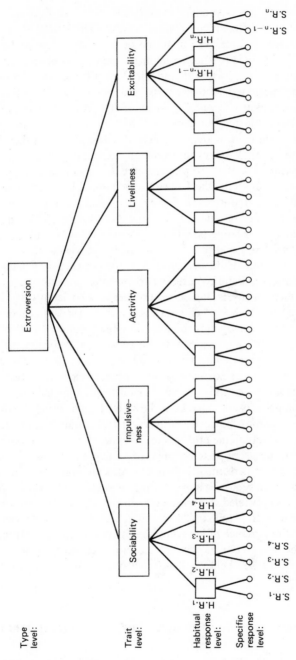

Figure 6–3. Diagrammatic representation of hierarchical organization of personality. (From Eysenck, 1970a)

Type level:

Trait level:

Habitual response level:

Specific response level:

223

same questionnaire would produce a fairly reliable E dimension, and that E factors derived from different questionnaires were intercorrelated to a reasonable degree. The problem comes in linking up questionnaire-measured E with extroversion factors derived from different media. Rating studies provide E factors that fit in fairly well, but it is more difficult to identify an extroversion factor in objective and projective personality tests, and they do not link up with a very high degree of certainty. Eysenck's answer is that projective tests are not valid anyway, and that objective behavior tests are only likely to correlate with E questionnaires when there is some theoretical reason to expect that they might (e.g., the lemon test). It is not reasonable to expect any randomly assembled selection of performance tests to produce an extroversion factor.

There is a sense in which the E factor as measured by questionnaires is not unitary. Inspection of the items in Table 6–1 reveals that a large proportion of them could be classified into those that deal with aspects of *sociability* (e.g., Do you prefer reading to meeting people? Do you find it hard to enjoy yourself at a lively party?) and those that refer to forms of *impulsiveness* (Do you stop and think things over before doing anything? When people shout at you do you shout back?). The partial separability of these two main components of extroversion is confirmed by factor analysis, the correlation between sociability and impulsiveness subfactors being around .5 (Eysenck & Eysenck, 1963). In accordance with Figure 6–1, impulsiveness tends to be an unstable (neurotic) form of extroversion, whereas sociability is associated with stability or "adjustment." Overall, extroversion is fairly independent of neuroticism. It may be possible to identify several other subfactors of extroversion at the primary factor level (e.g., activity, liveliness, excitability, optimism), but sociability and impulsiveness emerge as the clearest components and have been the most studied. It is sometimes found that known correlations between extroversion and certain other behaviors are attributable exclusively to the effect of one or other of these two subfactors. For example, it may be ascribed to impulsiveness that extroverts generally show faster deterioration of performance than introverts on monotonous tasks such as keeping watch for infrequent signals. A recent study by Thackray, Jones, and Touchstone (1974) revealed that increasing attention lapses of extroverts relative to introverts on a reaction time task were a function of their impulsivity, not their sociability. The importance of studying impulsiveness separately from sociability will also be seen when theories of the biological basis of personality are considered. Gray (1972) believes that impulsiveness and not extroversion is a personality "primary."

EXTROVERSION AND THE CLASSIFICATION OF ABNORMAL BEHAVIOR

Eysenck (1957, 1970a) has shown how his three-dimensional system of personality description can be extended to accommodate many forms of psychiatric disorder. He first demonstrated that, as hypothesized by Jung (1923), neurotics could be classified according to whether they are introverted or extroverted. Anxious, phobic, obsessional, compulsive, and depressive neurotics were found to be generally introverted according to their performance on questionnaire and objective test measures; hysterics and psychopaths were found to be relatively extroverted (Figure 6–4). It has been customary to call introverted neuroses *dysthymic* and the extroverted neurotics *hysterical,* although a wide range of antisocial behavior is also characteristic of the latter group.

Since developing an interest in a third major dimension of personality,

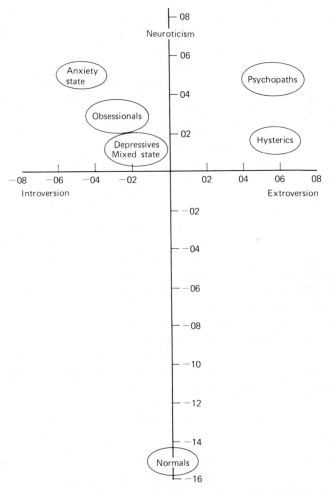

Figure 6–4. Position of one normal and six neurotic groups in two-dimensional framework determined by canonical variate analysis of objective test performances. (From Eysenck, 1970a.)

psychoticism, Eysenck's dimensional diagnostic system has naturally become more elaborate. The addition of the third dimension was necessitated by the discovery that neurotic and psychotic illnesses did not represent increasing degrees of the same disease process but were actually qualitatively different disorders. This finding was established by factor analysis and discriminant function analysis of symptom patterns and objective test performance, and was further confirmed by differential heritability studies (e.g., children of neurotic parents are predisposed to develop neuroses but not psychoses). Diagnostic groups high on the psychoticism factor are schizophrenia, manic depression, psychotic or endogenous depression, paranoia, and psychopathy (hence also criminality). In relation to the extroversion dimension, schizophrenia (particularly the "process" kind) and psychotic depression are often found to be introverted, whereas mania, manic-depressive psychosis, paranoia, and psychopathy tend to be extroverted. There is some question regarding the consistency of these relationships,but the unreliability of psychiatric diagnosis may be responsible for this.

The notion that traditional psychiatric groups can be specified by locating them within Eysenck's three-dimensional (ENP) space has been supported by factor-analytic studies of the basic MMPI scales (e.g., Wakefield, Yom, Bradley, Doughtie, & Cox, 1974). Typically these show a factor of neuroticism loading on hypochondriasis, depression, and hysteria, a factor of psychoticism loading on paranoia, schizophrenia, and mania, and a factor of extroversion loading on social introversion (negatively), psychopathy, and mania. Furthermore, it is doubtful that the MMPI provides any further information than is obtainable from scores on the three factors.

This dimensional view of psychiatric disorder implies that abnormal behavior is continuous with normal behavior and usually represents an extreme position on one or more of the three dimensions, particularly N and P. This approach seems appropriate to describe a great deal of abnormal behavior, but it has limitations. Some disorders, such as epilepsy and homosexuality, simply do not fit the structure at all. Either they are better conceived within the traditional medical model, or they refer to deviant habits so specific that they are not well accommodated by Eysenck's primary dimensions. Other disorders, perhaps including schizophrenia, may be located within the dimensional system but are determined at least in part by a specific gene disorder. Here is not the place for a detailed discussion of the problems of classification, diagnosis, and origins of psychiatric disorder; suffice to note that different neuroses and psychoses may be partly differentiated on the basis of their position on the introversion–extroversion continuum.

An interesting application of the Eysenck diagnostic system concerns a case of epidemic overbreathing in a North of England school reported by Moss and McEvedy (1966). It began with one or two girls complaining of dizziness and fainting, and by late morning "they were going down like ninepins." Eighty-five of the most severely affected girls were taken to hospital by ambulance, and the school was closed. Twice it was reopened and the same thing happened again. Attempts to find a physical cause proved negative, but since this behavior appeared classically "hysterical," Moss and McEvedy decided to compare the personalities of the girls who were affected with those who were not. True to expectation, the girls who had been susceptible to the epidemic (about one-third of the school) were very much higher in both neuroticism and extroversion than those who were not affected. The investigators concluded that the epidemic was hysterical, the population having been rendered vulnerable by a previous outbreak of polio in the area. Personality scores have been similarly shown to differentiate psychogenic back pains from those traced to a physical cause.

THE ORIGINS OF EXTROVERSION

If it can be conceded that introversion–extroversion is a consistent and identifiable dimension of personality, the next question arising is that of its origins. As usually turns out to be the case, variations along the extroversion dimension have both hereditary and environmental antecedents. Attention is now focused on assessing the relative contribution of these two groups of determinants and their precise nature.

Shields (1976) has reviewed the evidence for the partial inheritance of extroversion. Several studies have compared the similarity of identical (monozygotic) and fraternal (dizygotic) twins on questionnaire measures of extroversion. DZ twins show much less concordance than MZ twins, typically correlations of about .2 compared with .5. The former correlation coefficient is fairly consistent with that found for normal siblings and for parent/child correlations; it is the MZ twins who show the unusually high similarity. Furthermore, it does not seem to matter whether, or at what age, the identical twins separated from each other. In fact, in one study Shields found that identical twins were actually *more* alike when they had been raised *apart* than when they had been raised together. This finding held for both extroversion and neuroticism. It seems that sometimes identical twins raised together will react against each other in such a way as to maximize their differences (e.g., a tendency for one to take the lead), and this effect may be sufficient to override any similarities owing to the environment.

Such findings indicate that heredity plays a major part in determining extroversion scores. Although quantitative estimates of the proportion of variance due to heredity and environment differ from study to study, on average they indicate that about half to two-thirds is contributed by genetic factors. Additionally, there is some evidence that extroversion may be slightly higher in heritability than the other major personality dimensions, although this is by no means a consistent finding. Studies that have broken extroversion down into subfactors such as sociability, impulsivity, and activity (e.g., Buss, Plamin, & Willerman, 1973) have generally indicated that these components are roughly equal as regards the proportion of their variance that is due to heredity. Thus, the hypothesis that sociability may be more open to environmental influence than impulsiveness (Eysenck & Eysenck, 1963) does not appear to be supported.

For readers not familiar with the concept of heritability, it may be useful to note that an attribute can be strongly influenced by the genes without necessarily implying a close similarity between parents and children. The actual correlations between parents and children on personality variables are quite low (around 0.2), and the use of midparent scores (based on an average of the two parents) does not improve prediction of the child's characteristics very much. This is partly because the genes determine *differences* from parents as well as similarities, in the same way that they determine differences between siblings. Parents who have more than one child usually observe that their offspring display stable differences in temperamental characteristics that were apparent virtually from the moment of birth. These parents will insist that they did not treat their children differently, and they are probably right; such differences are in large part innate. Heritability coefficients are based on the gradient of recession of intrafamily correlations with diminishing degrees of relationship, and parents are not as closely related to their children as identical twins are to each other.

It is useful to distinguish between personality genotypes and phenotypes. The genotype of extroversion refers to positions on the dimension that are programmed by the genes and that give the best prediction of extroversion scores at the moment of conception. Extroversion as observed and measured in adulthood, however, is always phenotypic; it reflects observational error and changes due to the environment as well as the genotypic foundation. Short of microscopic examination of the chromosomes, a measure of pure genotypic extroversion is virtually impossible. Perhaps physiological measures and laboratory performance measures that come closer to the genotype than a questionnaire can be found, and a combination of various measures might come even closer, but the phenotypic measure always remains an approximation to the genotype.

Given that half or more of the variance in extroversion is due to the genes, what contributes the rest? Presumably there are various environmental influences that affect extroversion, but in the present state of knowledge we cannot say for sure what aspects of the environment are effective in this respect. Perhaps growing up in the city makes one more sociable than would a rural background. Perhaps authoritarian parents make one less impulsive. Perhaps certain dietary deficiencies make one less lively and active. We really do not know.

THEORIES OF EXTROVERSION

The most highly developed theory of extroversion is that of Eysenck (1967). Briefly, he postulates that variations in introversion–extroversion reflect individual differences in the functioning of the reticular activation system. This structure is thought by neurophysiologists to be responsible for producing nonspecific arousal in the cerebral cortex in response to external stimulation, and Eysenck hypothesizes that introverts are more highly aroused than extroverts given standard conditions of stimulation. Somewhat paradoxically, this results in the introvert showing more restrained or "inhibited" behavior because the cortex is exercising control over the more primitive, impulsive, lower brain centers. The arousal concept is used to explain most of the differences between extroverts and introverts that have been observed in the laboratory and in real life. For example, introverts are supposed to acquire conditioned responses more rapidly than extroverts because their higher arousal facilitates the formation of connections. The difference in conditionability in turn accounts for the different types of abnormal behavior to which introverts and extroverts are prone. Emotional (high N) introverts develop dysthymic symptoms because of their overready conditioning to normally neutral stimuli. The hysterical and psychopathic behavior of the emotional extrovert is said to result from a failure of the conditioning that constitutes the normal socialization process in childhood. Eysenck thus uses the concept of extroversion as a link in a causal chain that goes all the way from genetic and biological processes at the most "reductive" end through to complex social behaviors such as mental disorder, criminality, and attitudes at the other.

Two other theories of extroversion, which are to a greater or lesser extent derivative of Eysenck's, are also worth considering. Gray (1972, 1973) starts out from physiological evidence that points to the separation of reward and punishment systems in the brain. Approach behavior is apparently controlled by the medial forebrain bundle and lateral hypothalamus whereas an inhibitory function is attributed to mechanisms in the medial septal and hippocampal areas. Gray suggests that introverts and extroverts differ in their relative sensitivities to threats of punishment and promises of reward. Introverts, he says, are more sensitive to punishment, and extroverts are more oriented toward the pursuit of rewards. At the physiological level this means that introverts have a more reactive septo-hippocampal "stop system," and extroverts are more reactive in the medial forebrain bundle and lateral hypothalamic areas (the "go system"). Neuroticism, according to Gray, is an additive function of the reward and punishment systems, high N people being absolutely sensitive to both. Thus, the neurological substrates in Gray's theory run diagonally in relation to Eysenck's two major dimensions of personality (Figure 6–5). The trait names "anxiety" and "impulsiveness" would correspond to his elemental dimensions.

Gray notes that the two major clusters of neuroses discussed by Eysenck (the dysthymic and the hysteric/antisocial groups) then fall directly on the continua corresponding to their postulated neural bases. He also claims that the effects of frontal leucotomy are consistent with his theory. This operation involves severing the orbital frontal cortex from the rest of the septo-hippocampal stop system

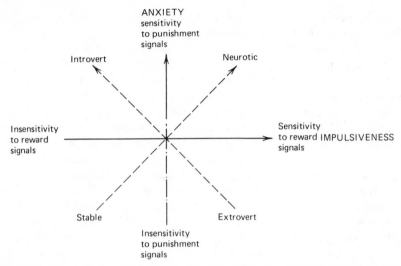

Figure 6–5.   Gray's theory of neuroticism and introversion as derived variables based upon fundamental dimensions of sensitivity to reward signals (impulsiveness) and sensitivity to punishment signals (anxiety). (Adapted from Cartwright, 1974.)

and is believed to be most effective with the typically dysthymic symptoms such as obsessions, agoraphobia, anxiety, and depression. According to Gray, Eysenck's theory would need to suppose that the frontal cortex was a part of two separate mechanisms to account for this effect, interference with one reducing neuroticism and interference with the other causing a shift away from introversion toward extroversion. Clearly this would not be very parsimonious. However, although there is strong evidence that lobotomy shifts people in the direction of extroversion (e.g., Petrie, 1952), it is still an open question whether there is any reduction in neuroticism following the operation.

The difficulty in choosing between the Eysenck and Gray theories is that they make similar predictions in many areas. In fact, Gray's theory is derivable from that of Eysenck. Eysenck would say that introverts are more sensitive to punishment because a stimulus of standard intensity has a greater effect on them. Thus, their pain threshold is lower and punishment of any kind is experienced as more severe. By corollary, extroverts are reward seekers because they require more intense reward before any impression is made. Nevertheless, there are some points at which the predictions derived from the two theories are distinguishable, particularly with respect to the relation between personality and conditioning. These issues will be considered below.

Finally, we consider the theory of Claridge (1967), which is best understood by studying the spatial model shown in Figure 6–6. Claridge assumes two independent though interacting causal mechanisms: a *tonic arousal system*, responsible for maintaining the individual's gross level of arousal (derived from both interoceptive and exteroceptive sources) and an *arousal modulating system* which exerts inhibitory control over the tonic arousal system as well as filtering, by inhibition and facilitation, the sensory input into both systems. The two main sources of personality variation are postulated to be the overall level of excitability and the degree of equilibrium maintained between the two arousal systems. The behavioral continuum of dysthymia–hysteria is assumed to represent an equilibrium between the two systems but with varying levels of excitability. In the dysthymic, high tonic arousal is matched by efficient modulating inhibition; in the hysteric, both tonic arousal and arousal modulation are low. The psychotic (active versus retarded) continuum involves a functional dissociation between the two systems, which may occur in either of two directions. If modulation is weak, the tonic system is released from inhibitory control (leading to an increase in general arousal), and filtering is inadequate (resulting in a loss of directed atten-

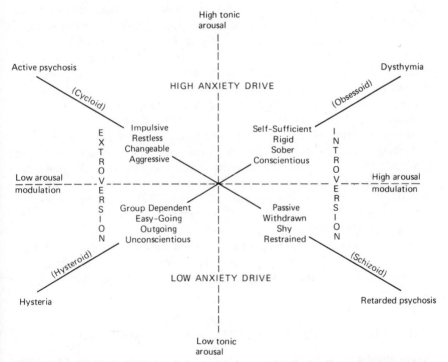

Figure 6–6. Claridge's (1967) descriptive model of personality. Broken lines refer to two underlying causal mechanisms determining two behavior continua of neuroticism and psychoticism. Extroversion is identified with low arousal modulation and introversion is postulated to reflect high arousal modulation (i.e., strong filtering and control processes).

tion). If modulation is excessive, there is strong inhibitory control and a severe narrowing of attention.

Figure 6–6 also shows the behavioral traits expected to be shown by individuals falling at different points along the two continua. Extroversion is seen as referring jointly to the impulsive, changeable cyclothyme and to the carefree, sociable hysteroid. Similarly, introversion in Claridge's model is a general term applied to the obsessoid and schizoid types. In relation to the causal processes, extroversion is viewed as low arousal modulation (regardless of the degree of tonic arousal) whereas introversion is thought to reflect the strong inhibitory control and sensory filtering characteristic of high arousal modulation.

It is not possible here to go into the details of experiments that led Claridge to formulate this model. Partly it grew out of an attempt to reconcile the typologies of Hippocrates, Kretschmer, Jung, and Eysenck, but more importantly it was inspired by the serendipitous finding that different groups of psychotics showed a crossover in performance on two tests: sedation threshold (later given as a prime measure of tonic arousal) and the spiral aftereffect (suggested as an operationalization of arousal modulation). These two tests will be described later on. With respect to the nature of extroversion, Claridge's theory differs from Eysenck's in a number of important ways. Whereas Eysenck sees the high arousal of the introvert as arising from the brain stem reticular system, Claridge thinks of it in terms of strong control processes directed back against the upcoming alertness signals, and in the focusing of sensory attention. Thus, the mechanism that he proposes as basic to extroversion–introversion is somewhat more cortical and "sophisticated," in fact more like an earlier version of Eysenck's theory that was expressed in terms of the Pavlovian concept of cortical excitation–inhibition balance. Another major way in which Claridge's model elaborates on that of Eysenck is that it includes the different types of psychoses within the same two-dimensional system as extroversion–introversion and neuroticism. This leads to a number of interesting new predictions such as the positioning of different psychoses in relation to the E and N dimensions. As we have already seen, these positions are generally in accord with Claridge's model; for example, there is some evidence that manic patients are more extroverted than schizophrenics. Eysenck's P dimension is, of course, not connected with Claridge's psychotic continuum since it identifies similarities among psychotic conditions rather than differences.

EXPERIMENTAL STUDIES OF EXTRAVERSION–INTROVERSION

Psychophysiological Studies

Gale (1973) has reviewed more than a dozen studies of the relationship between extroversion and EEG arousal. (The EEG consists of moment-to-moment voltage fluctuations across two points on the scalp; low amplitude and high frequency are generally thought to indicate high arousal). Some of the studies show extroverts to be *less* aroused than introverts (consistent with the Eysenck theory), some show them to be *more* aroused (not really consistent with any theory), and still others indicate that they are equally aroused. Gale points out that the EEG is not a fixed and immutable characteristic of an individual like his eye color, so it is reasonable to suppose that there are certain conditions under which introverts will be more aroused and other conditions that would produce higher arousal in extroverts. In the typical EEG experiment subjects are instructed simply to sit and relax and not think about anything. Since this is impossible, what the subject *does* think about probably has an important influence on his EEG. In a post hoc reconciliation of the contradictory results, Gale suggests that extroverts appear as more highly aroused when the experimental procedure is either very interesting or excruciatingly boring; otherwise introverts show higher arousal. Apparently, some tasks may be so lonely and tedious that they become (paradoxically) stressful and arousing to the sensation-hungry extrovert. Anyway, there is at present no evidence that people at one end or other of the extroversion––introversion dimension show uniformly higher EEG arousal across various experimental situations.

Extroversion has also been studied in relation to other psychophysiological variables such as electrodermal reactivity (GSR) and cortical evoked potentials (both of which have been frequently put forward as measures of arousal). Again, the results are apparently situation specific; some experiments have yielded evidence for higher arousal in introverts than extroverts, whereas others have found no difference. Rust (1974) concludes again that introverts find some situations more arousing than extroverts and vice versa. An alternative or supplementary possibility is that extroverts, when put into a situation that is boring to them, contrive to raise their level of arousal by imagination, fidgeting, or whatever means they can find, thus confounding any attempt to demonstrate in such a direct way that they are chronically less aroused than introverts.

Pharmacological Studies

Many drugs are reputed to affect arousal. Some, such as amphetamine, are classified as stimulants or "uppers"; others are described as depressants or "downers." If introverts are chronically more aroused than extroverts, we would expect them to be more difficult to sedate with a drug such as sodium amatyl. Indeed, this is what has been found. Sedation threshold, which may be measured by EEG changes, slurring of speech, or loss of facility on cognitive tasks such as adding digits, is significantly higher in dysthymic patients (introverted neurotics) than hysterics (extroverted neurotics). Some typical results are shown in Figure 6–7.

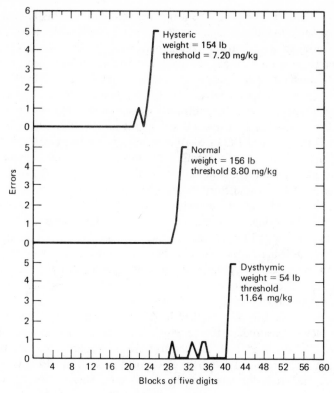

Figure 6–7. Typical sedation threshold curves of extroverted and introverted neurotics: one subject from each group. (From Claridge and Herrington, 1963.)

There is also some evidence that depressant drugs have an extroverting effect on behavior, whereas stimulants have an introverting effect. Thus, Laverty (1958) found that injections of sodium amatyl resulted in a significant shift in the extrovert direction on a questionnaire measure, as well as in behavior changes consistent with a shift toward extroversion (e.g., increased talkativeness, sociability, and excitability). Many other studies have shown that stimulant and depressant drugs affect performance on laboratory tests in a manner predictable from the differing performance of introverts and extroverts on them. For example, Gupta (1974a) conducted a study of drug effects and personality in relation to the kinesthetic figural aftereffect (KFAE) (a kind of contrast effect observed in judgments of width). He reported the following results: (1) extroverts showed greater KFAEs than introverts, (2) the depressant drug phenobarbitone led to greater KFAEs for all subjects, (3) the stimulant dexedrine led to reduced KFAEs in extroverts only (the introverts were presumably not affected because their arousal was already at maximum). Thus, the depressant caused introverts to behave more like extroverts on this particular laboratory task, whereas the stimulant caused the extroverts to act more like introverts.

Other studies that compare the effects of drugs and personality on various laboratory tasks have been reviewed by Eysenck (1967); in general they support the notion that introverts, particularly anxious introverts, are higher in arousal than extroverts. Many drug studies are also compatible with the Gray theory since the drugs investigated seem to shift personalities along Gray's anxiety dimension; tranquillizers, for example, seem to have this effect. Other drugs, such as amphetamine, seem to affect introversion–extroversion only.[1]

Studies on Sensitivity to Stimuli

One fairly direct consequence of Eysenck's arousal theory is that introverts would be more sensitive to stimuli at all levels of intensity. The lemon drop test cited earlier provides one demonstration of this. Introverts salivate more than extroverts in response to drops of lemon juice placed on their tongue. A complication not mentioned earlier, however, is that if the lemon juice is swallowed completely rather than left sitting on the back of the tongue, the extroverts apparently produce *more* saliva. The only way to account for this paradox, it seems, is to invoke the Pavlovian concept of protective inhibition. This is the idea that if stimulation is too intense, a defensive inhibitory mechanism is brought into play that radically reduces the nervous system's response to impinging stimuli. The reversal in the association between extraversion and the lemon drop test would be accounted for if this protective mechanism appears earlier (i.e., at a lower stimulus intensity) for introverts (Figure 6–8). At the moment this must be regarded as an ad hoc hypothesis only; further research specifically designed to test it is called for.

Studies reprinted in Eysenck (1971b) indicate that in general introverts do have lower sensory thresholds (i.e., greater sensitivity to barely detectable stimuli) as well as lower pain thresholds (less tolerance of painful stimuli) than extroverts. This is consistent with Eysenck's arousal theory of introversion, especially since amphetamine has independently been shown to reduce pain tolerance. However, these findings are also consistent with Gray's theory because, relative to stable people, neurotics are also intolerant of pain. Thus, among psychiatric patients it is the dysthymics who are least tolerant of pain, whereas prefrontal leucotomy results in an increase in pain tolerance.

Closely related to sensitivity differences is the question of preferred levels of sensory stimulation. Eysenck has produced the model shown in Figure 6–9 to predict the relationship between level of stimulation and pleasantness of affect. The thick line shows that medium levels of stimulation are preferred by people in general; both very high levels of stimulation (pain) and very low levels (sensory

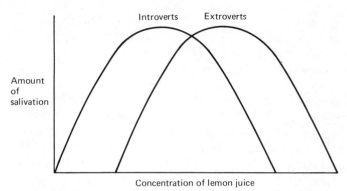

Figure 6–8. Hypothesis to account for contradictory findings on the lemon drop test. At low stimulus concentrations, introverts salivate more than extroverts. With intense stimuli the reverse may be true. The downturn in each curve is assumed to reflect the onset of "protective inhibition."

deprivation) are aversive. The curve for introverts is shifted to the left and that for extroverts displaced to the right. This would mean that introverts should tolerate sensory deprivation better than extroverts and pain less well. The letters O.L. refer to optimum level; A and B are two arbitrarily chosen points along the stimulus continuum at which marked differences in pleasantness would be expected between extroverts and introverts (differences in opposite directions).

As we have seen, the difference in pain threshold between extroverts and introverts is consistent with that theory. However, results in the area of sensory deprivation are much more contradictory (in many ways reminiscent of the EEG studies). In one fairly representative study, Tranel (1962) compared the reactions of introverts and extroverts to four hours of sensory deprivation. He found that the extroverts were less likely to quit before the prescribed time period was up. On the other hand, they were more inclined to violate the experimental instructions, to engage in reverie, to fall asleep, and to move about while awake. The introverts were more obedient to the instructions and attended more closely to the experimental situation; probably as a result they found it more uncomfortable and tended to opt out sooner. This is similar to the conclusion Gale (1973) came to in connection with the EEG studies. Apparently, extroverts are better able in boring situations to keep up their level of arousal by fantasy, physical movement, and attention to extraneous factors. Such a conclusion is supported by a study by Hill (1975) in which extroverts were found to build variety into a monotonous task. There is little that an introvert can do, however, about excessively high levels of stimulation (except for withdrawing from the situation or trusting to protective inhibition). Ludvigh and Happ (1974) studied the pleasantness–unpleasantness of various intensities of light and sound in groups of extroverts and introverts. Their results confirmed the theoretical prediction that extroverts would prefer higher levels of stimulation than introverts. However, the differences appeared

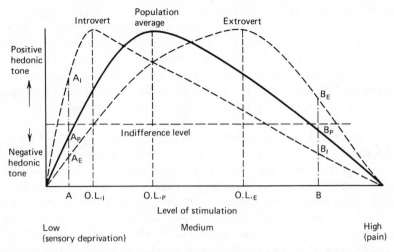

Figure 6–9. Relation of hedonic tone to level of sensory stimulation, showing relative displacement of extroverted and introverted subjects from population mean. (From Eysenck, 1971b.)

only at the high intensity end. Extroverts accepted higher levels of light and sound before describing them as aversive, but there were no differences in the liking/disliking for very low stimuli (the deprivation threshold). The model depicted in Figure 6–9 is fairly well substantiated at the high stimulation end, then, but findings with respect to hedonic tone are complex and contradictory at the low (deprivation) end.

On the other hand, there are some less direct studies that do seem to verify the model at both the high and low ends. If subjects in a sensory deprivation situation are asked to judge the amount of time that has passed, they are inclined to underestimate. It is thought that this is because we normally estimate time on the basis of the number and variety of things that have happened to us during the period. Reed and Kenna (1964) hypothesized that if extroverts are more dependent on external events, their error in estimation would be greater. This they confirmed by comparing groups of extroverts and introverts on a task of judging the length of a 15-minute period. What is more, the differences occurred only under sensory deprivation conditions; there was no difference between extroverts and introverts under normal conditions. Another fairly ingenious demonstration of "stimulus hunger" in extroverts was provided by Weisen (1965). He showed that extroverts would expend considerable effort in order to obtain a "reward" of loud jazz music and bright lights; introverts, by contrast, would work to avoid these same stimuli.

Perhaps the most interesting of all the studies in this area is one by Holmes (1967) using the pupillary response. When a bright light source was shone onto the subjects' eyes, introverts were found to show faster pupillary contraction (as though trying to protect themselves from the strong stimulus). In a dark adaptation situation, however, the extroverts showed faster pupillary dilation (as though trying to enhance stimuli in this perceptual deprivation condition). This finding is particularly impressive since, if the speed of pupillary response was the critical factor, one personality type or the other should be quicker at both constriction *and* dilation. As it is, the study suggests that the pupillary response is aiding in the homeostatic optimization of stimulus intensity and that the optimal intensity is higher for extroverts than introverts.

On vigilance performance tasks (i.e., keeping watch for irregular signals) introverts have generally been found to perform better than extroverts. This is especially true when subjects are required to maintain the vigil for a long period of time; extroverts may be as good or even better in the short term. Increasing the rate of signal presentation, increasing the background noise (e.g., turning on a radio), or providing social stimulation is likely to improve the performance of the extrovert, thus reducing his progressive disadvantage relative to the introvert. No doubt this is because these are all arousing conditions that may offset the characteristic low arousal of the extrovert (presumably the introverts are already at an optimum level of arousal). Frith (1967) has shown this explanation diagramatically (Figure 6–10) and has provided supplementary results concerning the interaction between noise and extroversion in determining another kind of performance, critical flicker fusion. Notice that, as with the lemon drop test (Figure 6–8), an inverted U-shaped relationship is postulated between arousal and performance. Such a relationship is now well established, even if the Pavlovian explanation of transmarginal (protective) inhibition is not universally accepted by personality theorists.

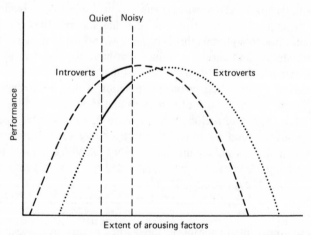

Figure 6–10. Hypothesized relationship between the extent of arousing factors, personality, and performance (From Frith, 1967.)

Studies in Perceptual Phenomena

Visual constancy refers to a perceptual mechanism that enables us to see colors, shapes, and so on veridically (i.e., as they "really are") despite great variations in the conditions of viewing. Since extroverts are supposed to be more outer directed and concerned with objects, we might expect them to show greater constancy than introverts. Several experiments have borne out this expectation, although it seems likely that under an appropriate instructional set extroverts would be equally capable of attending to direct sensations rather than meaningful objects and thus break down or control the extent of their constancies. Therefore, it is doubtful that the personality difference in constancy is of far-reaching theoretical importance.

Another perceptual test that has been related to extroversion–introversion is the kinesthetic figural after-effect that was mentioned above in connection with drug studies. This is the tendency to judge a wooden black by touch as wider after experience with a narrow "anchor" and vice versa (a kind of successive contrast phenomenon). Some experiments have indicated that extroverts are more susceptible to this aftereffect (e.g., Gupta, 1974), but others have suggested that the difference may be partly artifactual. Similarly, studies with the Archimedes Spiral Test have demonstrated that the illusion of counterrotation after a rotating spiral is stopped persists longer for introverts than for extroverts. However, Levy and Lang (1966) suggest that the duration of spiral aftereffect may simply reflect a response latency rather than differences in the amount of aftereffect actually experienced. That is, the extroverts may press their button sooner because they are impulsive, whereas the cautious introverts hang back until they are certain of a change in their perception. As with many of the other findings in the area of perception, the results might be explained by saying that extroverts take a casual and straightforward attitude toward the experimental task whereas introverts concentrate hard in an effort to please the experimenter, giving studied, introspective responses, some of which go beyond the obvious. Thus, results are often explainable directly from the known trait characteristics of extroverts and introverts without the need to resort to reductive theories and concepts such as arousal or inhibition.

For the sake of completeness, here are listed a number of other perceptual tests that have been shown to differentiate introverts from extroverts (for documentation see Eysenck, 1971b):

Rate of Fluctuation of Reversible Figures Such as the Necker Cube and Alternation Behavior in Choice-of-Viewing Situations

Extroverts show greater fluctuation and alternation, as though they more quickly become satiated, fatigued, or bored. It is not clear whether this satiation is peripheral (e.g., occurring at the level of the retina) or central (i.e., at the "psychological" or overall brain level). It could, in fact, be both.

Visual Masking

Visual masking is the tendency for a stimulus to block perception of another stimulus presented just previously. It occurs at a greater interstimulus interval (i.e., more markedly) with extroverts than with introverts.

Critical flicker fusion

Critical flicker fusion, the point at which a flickering light is perceived as continuous, occurs sooner (i.e., at a slower flicker rate) for extroverts. This is consistent with the difference in visual masking and could be taken as evidence for the notion that extroverts are less aroused, especially since there is a tendency for depressant and stimulant drugs to affect those visual phenomena in parallel fashion.

Sharpening

When subjects are asked to describe from memory some drawings of stick figures engaged in various activities, the extroverts are more given to exaggeration and simplification. For example, a drawing normally described as "two men fighting a duel" might evoke the response "one man running his sword through and killing his opponent." This tendency to express the activity in stronger, more violent form is reminiscent of the "sharpening" of recall found in studies of the rumor mechanism.

Time Perception

We have already noted that extroverts are inclined to underestimate the passage of time in a sensory deprivation situation. There is some evidence that they may also do it under normal conditions. In a rather clever study by Lynn (1961) subjects were asked to match an interval of 15 seconds. They were then given nine further trials in which their last judgment was given as a new standard. With this method the judgment of extroverts and introverts was seen to diverge progressively, with extroverts underestimating and introverts overestimating. At the end of the tenth trial the average produced by introverts was 18.2 seconds; that for extroverts was 10.2 seconds.

Field Dependence

There have been several studies using tests such as the Rod and Frame Test and the Embedded Figures Test that indicate that extroverts are more dependent on external cues when making perceptual judgments. This finding is, of course, consistent with the traditional definition of extroversion as "outer directedness."

Perceptual Defense

There is a tendency for introverts to behave more defensively (e.g., to inhibit the reporting of taboo words). But there are complications to this general finding; moderator variables such as neuroticism and situational stress also seem to be important in determining whether this relationship will emerge.

Esthetic Preferences

In general, extroverts like modern, brightly colored paintings; introverts prefer subdued colors. There is some disagreement as to whether extroverts prefer simplicity or complexity in visual stimuli, but one recent study of preferences for polygons varying in complexity found that extroverts preferred greater complexity than introverts (Bartol & Martin, 1974).

Motor Performance

One of the complications in studying the correlates of extroversion is the need to consider "moderator" variables. The effect of extroversion may not be apparent until some other factor such as neuroticism or intelligence is taken into account. Thus, for example, studies of expressive movements such as handwriting and the expansiveness of "doodles" suggest that when extroverts are high in neuroticism they may display overt behavior opposite to that otherwise typical of their personality type. Taft (1967) found that neurotic extroverts were the smallest writers whereas stable extroverts used the largest script. Introverts were intermediate in writing size regardless of their neuroticism level. If extroversion alone had been considered, no significant relationship would have been detected.

Extroversion has also been shown to be related to the noncontent aspects of speech. Ramsay (1968) studied differences between extroverts and introverts on a variety of verbal tasks ranging from reading a short passage of prose to conducting a conversation with the experimenter. He found that introverts tended to allow longer silences between utterances as though they were weighing their words more before talking. Apparently the introvert is more heedful of the maxim "be sure brain is engaged before putting mouth into gear." This difference was independent of sex, intelligence, and neuroticism.

As regards major body movements, few differences between extroverts and introverts have been reliably established. Yates (1973) reviews the evidence relating to psychomotor functions such as control movements, persistence, and body-sway suggestibility, and concludes that although neuroticism is quite important, extroversion has less relevance in determining performance as measured by crude output. There are, however, a couple of qualitative differences between extroverts and introverts that have been fairly reliably identified. First, where there is a choice between speed and accuracy in performance, extroverts tend to sacrifice accuracy for speed, giving faster performance with a lot of errors, whereas introverts are more likely to drop behind time in order to preserve accuracy. This difference is illustrated most clearly in a study by Frith (1971), who studied differences between extroverts and introverts on a tracking task in which subjects had to pursue a target light around a triangular course while trying to keep a hand stylus in photoelectric contact with it. By photographing the position of the subject's stylus at short intervals it was possible to identify distinctly different strategies for the two personality groups (Figure 6–11). The extroverts would literally cut corners in order to match the angular velocity of the target, whereas introverts would fall behind in attempting to match the target position. Overall, the two groups performed equally well in terms of time-on-target. Their performance was equally good but arrived at by different strategies.

Second, there is a tendency for extroverts to begin faster (and often better) on a task, but introverts tend to catch up and surpass the performance of extroverts after a certain amount of time. Apparently this is because the extroverts are more susceptible to boredom and fatigue. For example, Wilson, Tunstall, and Eysenck (1971) studied performance on a tapping task in which subjects had to tap on a Morse key fast enough to maintain a rate of five taps per second for a one-minute period. Extroverts began better than introverts, but by the end of the minute they were showing signs of fatigue and missing so many taps that the introverts' tap output was superior. This kind of crossover has also been noted in cognitive tasks such as vigilance and verbal memory.

Classical Conditioning

An early hypothesis derived from Eysenck's theory was that introverts (having higher cortical arousal) would acquire classically conditioned responses more

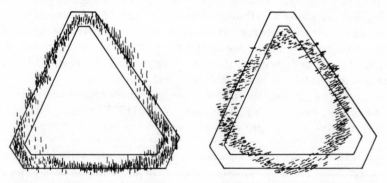

Figure 6–11.   Pursuit rotor strategies typical of introverts (left) and extroverts (right). Introverts fall behind attempting to match the target position whereas extroverts cut corners to match target speed. (From Frith, 1971.)

readily than extroverts. The first experiments conducted at the Maudsley Hospital by Franks, using the eyeblink and GSR responses, seemed to confirm this expectation (correlations of around .48 between conditioning and introversion were obtained for both normal and neurotic subjects). Franks' studies showed also that the neuroticism dimension was not related to conditionability as some other theorists had supposed. Later studies from various parts of the world, however, produced inconsistent results with respect to the relationship between extroversion and conditioning; some found introverts to be more readily conditioned, some found no difference, and others found extroverts more conditionable. Clearly, the hypothesis of a simple relationship between introversion and conditionability could not be sustained.

Eysenck (1965) then theorized that introverts would display greater conditionability only under certain experimental conditions—in particular, conditions not so highly arousing that protective inhibition is likely to occur (recall the discussion of the lemon drop test). A review of the literature up to that point suggested that the discrepancies reported therein could be accounted for along these lines. Eysenck and Levey (1972) reported a study in which experimental parameters thought to affect the personality/conditioning relationship were systematically varied. Figures 6–12 and 6–13 illustrate the results of this study in which, again, the eyeblink reponse was used. When reinforcement was partial and weak, and the interstimulus interval short, the introverts conditioned much more readily (correlation of .40); these were the low arousal conditions thought to favor introverts. However, with 100 percent reinforcement, a strong UCS, and long CS–UCS interval (high arousal conditions), the extroverts showed faster conditioning. Collapsing results over all experimental conditions would have obscured these marked differences between extroverts and introverts. This in-

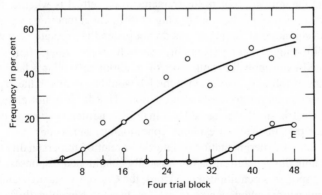

Figure 6–12.   Rate of eyelid conditioning for introverts and extroverts under conditions of partial reinforcement, weak UCS, and short CS–UCS interval. (From Eysenck and Levey, 1972.)

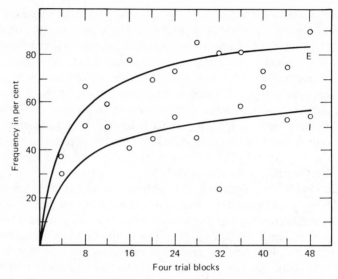

Figure 6–13. Rate of eyelid conditioning for extroverts and introverts under conditions of 100 per cent reinforcement, strong UCS, and long CS-UCS interval. (From Eysenck & Levey, 1972.)

teraction supports Eysenck's arousal theory because meaningful and significant results are found when experimental parameters are selected on the basis of the theory. When extroversion was broken down into the components of impulsivity and sociability (discussed earlier), it was found that impulsivity alone was responsible for the correlations between extroversion and conditioning. In this respect the results were not fully consistent with Eysenck's theory, so the issue cannot be regarded as closed yet.

A second theoretical problem that remains to be settled is whether there is a general factor underlying the conditioning of different autonomic responses. For example, eyeblink conditioning scores do not generally correlate very well with GSR conditioning scores. Presumably, though, if the interaction found by Eysenck and Levey applied to both types of conditioning (so far is has been done only with the eyeblink response), then the job would be to match the experimental parameters so as not to mask a correlation. That is, it is not obvious what strength of electric shock (the usual UCS in GSR conditioning) is equivalent to a particular air puff intensity in eyeblink conditioning, and so on.

Another line of experimentation of interest in relation to personality theory is that concerning the generalization of classically conditioned responses. When an emotional response is conditioned to a word, the CR may generalize along either of two dimensions: phonetically (e.g., cat–hat) or semantically (e.g., cat––animal). In normal adults the semantic dimension usually predominates, but the

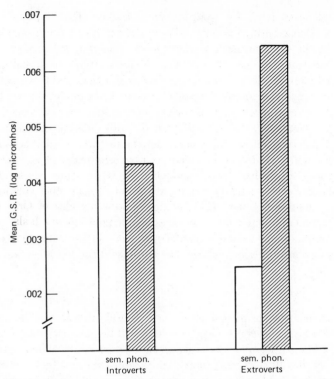

Figure 6–14. Generalization of conditioned GSRs along semantic and phonetic dimensions for introverts and extroverts. (From Schalling, Levander, & Wredenmark, 1975.)

phonetic dimension is likely to be dominant in children or in adults whose alertness is impaired (e.g., by alcohol or tiredness). If, as Eysenck thinks, extroverts are generally lower in cortical arousal than introverts, then we might expect them to show a relatively greater amount of phonetic generalization. This hypothesis was confirmed in a recent study by Schalling, Levander, and Wredenmark (1975). Figure 6–14 shows GSR scores in the generalization phase of their experiment. The extroverts show a striking preponderance of phonetic generalization, whereas there is hardly any difference for the introverts. This finding is clearly consistent with the prediction based on Eysenck's arousal theory.

Verbal Conditioning

Verbal conditioning is an instrumental procedure in which, typically, the subject is presented with a series of cards each containing a past tense verb and a selection of pronouns: I, we, you, he, she, and they. The subject's task is to make up a sentence using the verb and a pronoun of his choice. Conditioning is achieved by the experimenter's saying "good" following any sentence starting with the personal pronouns "I" or "we." Holmes (1967) found that introverts conditioned more readily than extroverts in this situation, and he suggested that this greater sensitivity to environmental contingencies might account for their learning the rules and restraints of society more readily than extroverts.

However, Gupta (1974b) showed that, as with classical conditioning, the experimental parameters are important in determining what kind of person conditions most readily. He found that when positive reinforcement was used (e.g., saying "good" rather than "bad") and when the experimenter was an attractive female, the extroverts actually conditioned faster. Under other conditions the introverts conditioned faster. This finding supports the idea of Gray that extroverts respond more favorably to rewards than to punishments. It also provides further confirmation of what has been demonstrated in any other contexts—that extroverts respond better to sociable than to isolated conditions.

Memory

The area of memory has proved particularly fruitful in relation to the investigation of personality. Several studies have indicated that extroverts are superior to introverts on verbal learning tasks such as paired associates and digit span, but it is significant that all such tasks inolve fairly short-term recall tests. Recently it has become clear that long-term memory processes need to be distinguished from those involved in short-term memory. One of the most influential theories in this area is that of Walker (1958), who hypothesized that any perceptual event sets up a perseverative trace that fades gradually over time. If motivation or arousal is sufficient, it will be transferred to permanent memory through a process called *consolidation*, While consolidation is taking place, retrieval is temporarily inhibited to protect the trace against disruption. High arousal therefore facilitates consolidation but at the same time makes immediate recall more difficult. Such an interaction between arousal at the time of learning and the amount of time elapsing before recall is tested has been experimentally demonstrated on several occasions (e.g., Kleinsmith & Kaplan, 1963). When verbal learning takes place under conditions of high arousal, immediate recall is poor but long-term recall is relatively good. Learning under low arousal generally follows a reverse pattern, starting off well but deteriorating over time.

These facts suggested a means of testing Eysenck's theory that introverts are more highly aroused than extroverts. Extroverts ought to be superior to introverts when memory is tested shortly after learning, but introverts should be superior when it comes to long-term recall. This is precisely what was found by Howarth and Eysenck (1968) using recall intervals varying from immediate to a 24-hour delay. The predicted crossover occurred after about five minutes (Figure 6–15). These results are strikingly similar to those of Kleinsmith and Kaplan and suggest that a single mechanism may apply to both. Presumably the lower arousal in extroverts produces weaker consolidation that interferes with recall less at short-term intervals but does not favor long-term recall. This finding has now been replicated at least twice, and there is some evidence that it applies also to reminiscence phenomena in the learning of motor skills such as the pursuit rotor (Eysenck, 1973b).

Another well-established finding concerning the relationship between arousal and memory is the Yerkes–Dodson Law. This law incorporates two very well established findings: (1) There is an inverted-U function relating performance to motivation, with optimal performance being obtained at medium levels of drive; (2) high levels of motivation are likely to facilitate performance on simple tasks but impair complex functions. McLaughlin and Eysenck (1967) reasoned that chronic drive differences between personality types might be shown to parallel

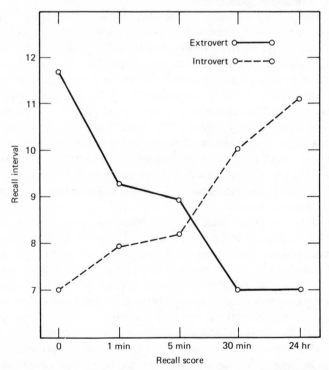

Figure 6–15. Recall scores of five groups of extroverts and five groups of introverts after different recall intervals. Introverts show reminiscence as recall interval increases; extroverts show forgetting. (From Howarth & Eysenck, 1968.)

other motivational conditions in producing these two Yerkes–Dodson effects. Stable extroverts were assumed to be lowest in drive and neurotic introverts (having both high autonomic activation and high cortical arousal according to Eysenck's theory) would be expected to be highest in drive. Neurotic extroverts and stable introverts were assumed to be intermediate in terms of drive level. Two paired-associates learning tasks were used, one constructed to be easy and the other comparatively difficult. Overall, extroverts performed significantly better than introverts, which is in line with expectation since testing immediately followed learning. But more interesting, the hypothesis concerning an interaction between personality type and list difficulty was also supported. Examination of Figure 6–16 reveals that with the difficult list the optimum point on the inverted-U function is shifted toward the low arousal side in terms of personality types. In other words, the results of McLaughlin and Eysenck's experiment could be neatly accounted for by supposing that the stable extroverts were too low in arousal to give optimal performance when the learning task was easy but asserted their superiority when the difficulty of the task pushed the other groups into the area of super-optimal arousal.

M. W. Eysenck (1974) adopted the original tack of studying interactions between extroversion–introversion (assumed to be a measure of trait arousal) and Thayer's Activation–Deactivation Adjective Checklist (which he took as an indication of transient state arousal) in determining fluency in a word association task. As had been found in previous studies, extroverts produced associates more fluently (despite equivalence in vocabularies). Of the two main subfactors of extroversion, sociability was the better predictor of fluency ($r = .63$) but impulsivity was also significantly related ($.39$). More interesting, however, was the finding of a significant interaction between extroversion and activation. High activation was found to enhance performance for extroverts but reduce it for introverts. This fits with the idea that introverts generally tend toward overarousal for the optimum performance of certain tasks, whereas extroverts are inclined to be underaroused.

The robustness of this finding has since been confirmed under several other experimental conditions, including a paradigm that involved the use of controlled new learning which ensured equivalent storage of learned material before the testing of retrieval (M. W. Eysenck, 1975a). Again, transient activation and extroversion produced a highly significant interaction effect on memory retrieval. Extroverts responded more quickly under high activation than under low activation, whereas the reverse was true for introverts. As might have been predicted from the Yerkes–Dodson Law, the two slowest groups were the low-activated extroverts and the high-activated introverts (those theoretically lowest and highest in arousal). Presumably these groups were below and above optimal arousal respectively for performance on this particular task.

In another ingenious study by M. W. Eysenck (1975b), the nature of extrovert–introvert differences in recall were further specified. This time he used

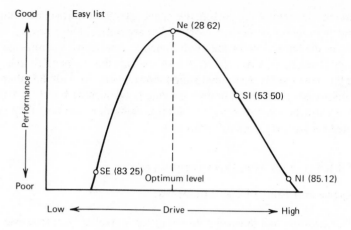

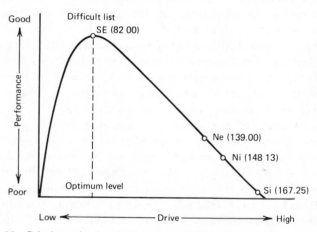

Figure 6–16. Paired-associate learning for easy and difficult lists of four personality type groups. (From McLaughlin and Eysenck, 1967.)

association tasks that varied in terms of the amount of memory search that would have to be called upon. He found that the extroverts produced faster associations than introverts particularly on tasks that demanded a great deal of memory search (e.g., those requiring very remote associates). When a relatively short search process was involved, the difference between extroverts and introverts was attenuated. At the extreme, a speed-of-recognition task (which is known to draw hardly at all on the retrieval mechanism) did not differentiate extroverts and introverts at all.

The main conclusions to draw from this series of experiments by Eysenck the younger are: (1) Transient activation levels appear to affect memory by means of the same mechanism as the personality characteristic of introversion (the unifying concept probably being best described as arousal); (2) high arousal, whether inherent in the subject or in the environmental conditions, operates on the retrieval mechanism and has the effect of biasing the memory search process toward the most readily accessible stored information. As with the other experiments discussed in this section they provide good support for H. J. Eysenck's theory of extraversion–introversion, and it is difficult to see how they could be accounted for by Gray's modification.

SOME SOCIAL AND APPLIED CORRELATES

Intelligence and Educational Attainment

Overall, extroverts and introverts do not differ in intelligence. However, recent work has shown that intellectual performance may be broken down into at least three independent components: speed, accuracy, and persistence. When this is done, it is found that the extroverts tend to be faster but less accurate and less persistent (e.g., Brierley, 1961). In addition and consistent with findings in other types of performance (e.g., learning and psychomotor functions), the extroverts start well but slip back progressively relative to introverts. When these interactions are collapsed (e.g., across different types of subjects or different components of intelligence), the differences are usually obscured.

Mohan and Kumar (1973) conducted a quantitative analysis of the performance of introverts and extroverts on the Standard Progressive Matrices I.Q. test. The performance of 100 students (50 male and 50 female) was examined in terms of items done correctly, wrongly, abandoned, and not attempted, as a function of difficulty level and time spent on the test. The extroverts began with an edge over the introverts but showed a greater performance decrement, allowing the introverts to draw ahead by the end of the test (Figure 6–17). In terms of overall I.Q. scores the two personality types came out as about equal. Once again we find an interaction between personality and another variable which is readily obscured by averaging performance or taking crude total scores.

If introverts are superior at long-term verbal memory, we might expect them to show higher achievement in an educational setting (after all, short-term recall is not generally very useful for examination purposes). Generally speaking this is found to be so. Introverts do better at school and achieve higher university grades, although extroverts are sometimes rated better by their teachers at the primary school level. The advantage of introverts becomes progressively clear into the university years. This may be because there is less variance in intelligence, and personality differences therefore become relatively more important (Eysenck, 1974).

In a recent survey of Birmingham University students, Wankowski (1973) found that introverts had obtained better grades at secondary school and were

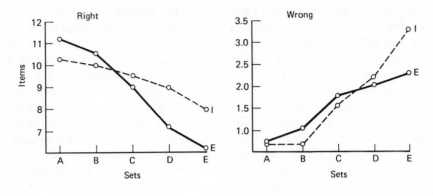

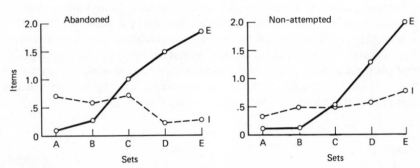

Figure 6–17. Analysis of performance of introverts and extroverts on the Standard Progressive Matrices. (From Mohan & Kumar, 1973.)

more likely to obtain a good degree at university. He concluded that "generally high neuroticism and extroversion combine to inhibit academic achievement." Stable introverts were most likely to obtain good honors degrees, neurotic extroverts least. Wankowski also found that personality was related to choice of subject. Introverts preferred theoretical subjects, whereas extroverts chose practical and "people-oriented" areas of study. Sociologists tended to congregate in the neurotic extrovert (psychopathic?) quadrant. Finally, temperament was linked with reasons for withdrawal from university. Students who withdrew for academic reasons (exam failure) tended to be neurotic extroverts; those who withdrew for medical and psychiatric reasons tended to be neurotic introverts.

Although introverts show better overall academic achievement, there are certain teaching methods and conditions of learning that seem to be advantageous to extroverts. Leith (1974) studied the interactions between personality and different teaching methods in determining achievement on a genetics course. Over 200 students who had no previous knowledge of the material to be learned were involved in the study. Two teaching strategies were compared: *Discovery learning* stressed individuality, personal interaction, flexibility and spontaneity in teaching, tolerance of uncertainty and error making, and concern with global effects rather than precise detail. The other approach, *reception learning,* emphasized obedience, regularity, standardization, attentiveness, formality, and direct instruction. These two teaching methods were equally effective overall, but there was a clear tendency for the extroverts to benefit more from the informal discovery learning and for introverts to learn better from the formal reception approach. This interaction was observed when achievement was tested one week after the learning period and was even more marked when subjects were retested without warning a month later (Figure 6–18).

In another experiment using social psychology students, Leith (1974) considered the question of whether introverts and extroverts would learn better by themselves, paired with another person of the opposite personality type, or paired with someone of the same personality. Results showed that overall the introverts learned slightly better, but their advantage was seen only when they were working individually. In the two paired conditions the extroverts were about as good. There was also an indication that the introverts were more debilitated when paired with an extrovert than when they were working with another of their own kind. For both introverts and extroverts, working in homogeneous pairs produced the highest achievement scores (Table 6–2).

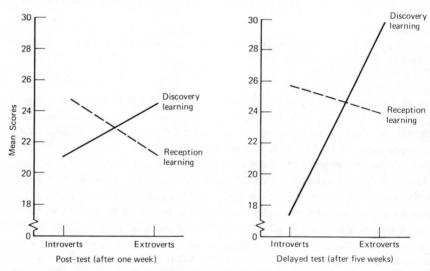

Figure 6–18. Interactions of strategies of instruction (direct vs. discovery) with extroversion on two occasions of testing achievement and problem solving. (From Leith, 1974.)

Table 6-2   Achievements of 85 Social Psychology students learning in
Homogeneous or Heterogeneous Personality Pairs or as Individuals

Personality	Methods		
	Homogeneous Pairs	Heterogeneous Pairs	Individuals
Introverts	32.2	27.3	30.0
Extroverts	30.6	27.7	25.4
Significance of differences (1-tailed)	N.S.	N.S.	$p < 0.01$
Homogeneous versus heterogeneous pairs:	$p < 0.01$		
Homogeneous pairs versus individuals:	$p < 0.025$		

Source: Leith, 1974

The results of these studies by Leith may be accounted for by saying that the extroverts are more easily bored by formal and isolated learning conditions. Apparently they need a greater amount of stimulation to maintain their interest and attention (presumably because of their lower arousal), and this may be provided either by novelty and variation in the method of instruction or by social contact with fellow students. Given these conditions, they may even respond better than introverts, who are likely to feel overwhelmed by excessive uncertainty and noisy companionship. The introverts, however, do better when conditions are structured and quiet. Thus, introverts are not intrinsically better students than extroverts; it may simply be that our current teaching methods happen to favor introverts.

Another important interacting variable is no doubt the degree of interest that the two personality types have in the task or material to be learned. Nias and Hardy (1971), for example, showed that introverts experience greater difficulty in learning to swim than extroverts. It is reasonable to suppose that the same would apply to many other outdoor, practical, and social skills that have greater intrinsic appeal to extroverts.

Industrial and Vocational Applications

Eysenck (1971b) reprints and discusses a number of papers showing that extroversion is linked with vocational preferences and various aspects of industrial performance. In general, extroverts display greater ''social intelligence,'' that is, ability to relate to other people, to take a personal interest in them and their problems, and to anticipate their reactions. So they tend to gravitate toward and often excel in jobs that involve dealing with other people (e.g., sales and personnel work, nursing, teaching). On the other hand, the ability of the introvert to resist boredom and persist with a task for a long period of time is also valuable in certain occupational contexts. Introverts are also more reliable and conscientious, they are more punctual, absent less often, and stay longer a a job (having less need for novelty). While on the job, the extroverts very probably waste more time talking to their work mates, drinking coffee, and generally seeking diversion from the routine. Personality tests are of limited usefulness as selection devices in education and industry, however, because they are readily faked. If extroversion were to be used in this way, it would have to be measured covertly, and the ethical acceptability of this is doubtful.

As regards vocational interests, introverts tend to prefer theoretical and scientific occupations such as architecture, journalism, and the teaching of mathematics, whereas extroverts are apparently happier with people oriented jobs such as social work and selling life insurance (Table 6–3). But again, although this is of some theoretical interest, it has little practical application because specialized interest scales are more directly relevant for vocational guidance purposes.

Social Behavior

Extroversion is implicated in many other forms of social behavior; we will consider just a few examples. Extroverts tend to be more suggestible than introverts. They are more inclined to change their judgments under the influence of prestige suggestions (Sinha & Ojha, 1963) and to change their evaluation of paintings after discovering the name (and thus the reputation) of the artist (Mohan & Mohan, 1965). On the other hand, when an extrovert is paired with an introvert and they are asked to discuss a topic on which it has been previously established that they disagree, the introvert is more likely to change his opinion as a result of the interaction (Carment & Miles, 1965). It is not quite clear why this should be so. It may be because the extrovert does most of the talking (this was observed to be the case), or it may reflect the toughmindedness of extroverts (a kind of dogmatism and assertiveness) that has been established independently in the area of social attitudes (Eysenck, 1961).

Extroverts take more risks than introverts; therefore, they do more gambling. (This, of course, is in line with Gray's view of extroverts as reward seekers who are inclined to disregard the possible unpleasant consequences of their behavior.) They enjoy sexual and aggressive humor (preferably fairly explicit), whereas introverts prefer more cognitive styles of humor such as puns and incongruity jokes. As regards sexual behavior, extroverts have intercourse more frequently, in more different ways, and with more different partners than introverts. They are more permissive in their attitudes, confess to higher levels of libido, and are less prone to nervousness and inhibition (Wilson & Nias, 1975).

Table 6-3 Correlations between Scales of the Strong Vocational Interest Blank and the Maudsley Personality Inventory

Strong Area	Strong scale	Extraversion M	Extraversion F	Neuroticism M	Neuroticism F
I	Artist	$-.29^b$	$-.40^b$	.12	.05
	Psychologist (Rev.)	$-.08$	$-.27^b$	.05	.03
	Architect	$-.37^b$	$-.50^b$	$-.01$	.03
	Physician (Rev.)	$-.11$	$-.46^b$	$-.01$	$-.03$
	Dentist	$-.30^b$	$-.54^b$	$-.17$	$-.05$
II	Mathematician	$-.27^b$	$-.47^b$	$-.15$	$-.04$
	Physicist	$-.38^b$	$-.48^b$	$-.15$	.03
	Engineer	$-.38^b$	$-.38^b$	$-.18$	$-.02$
	Chemist	$-.36^b$	$-.49^b$	$-.12$	$-.03$
III	Production Mgr.	$-.29^b$	$-.02$	$-.19^a$	$-.19^a$
IV	Math. Phys. Sci. Tchr.	$-.26^b$	$-.31^b$	$-.18$	$-.23^a$
	Indust. Arts Tchr.	$-.23^a$	$-.18$	$-.09$	$-.14$
	Voc. Agricul. Tchr.	$-.12$	$-.09$	$-.14$	$-.32^a$
V	Personnel Director	$-.32^b$	$.21^a$	$-.02$	$-.18$
	Public Admin.	.15	.15	.02	$-.27^b$
	Soc. Sci. H. S. Tchr.	.14	.14	.00	$-.21^a$
	City School Supt.	$.21^a$	.14	$-.11$	$-.14$
	Social Worker	$.26^b$	.07	.13	$-.12$
	Minister	$.21^a$	.07	.17	$-.11$
VI	Musician (Perform)	$-.09$	$-.22^a$	$-.19^a$	$-.03$
VII	C.P.A.	$-.08$	$-.15$	$-.10$	$-.04$
VIII	Senior C.P.A.	$-.14$	.04	$-.22^a$	$-.22^a$
	Accountant	$-.21^a$	.01	$-.35^b$	$-.25^a$
	Office Manager	$-.12$	.13	$-.19^a$	$-.22^a$
	Banker	$-.32^b$	.13	$-.29^b$	$-.21^a$
	Pharmacist	$-.21^a$	.06	$-.06$	$-.11$
IX	Sales Manager	.18	$.43^b$	$-.08$	$-.22^a$
	Real Estate Sales	$-.03$	$.27^b$	$-.08$	$-.02$
	Life Insurance Sales	$.24^a$	$.33^a$	.07	.00
X	Advertising Man	.06	.05	.05	.06
	Lawyer	.00	$-.02$	.05	.06
	Author-Journalist	$-.24^a$	$-.27^b$	.10	.14
XI	Pres. Mfg. Concern	$-.24^a$	$-.01$	$-.08$	$-.06$
	Interest Maturity	.05	.11	$-.11$	$-.21^a$
	Occupational Level	$-.13$	$-.26^b$	$-.09$	.08
	Masculinity	$-.13$	$-.04$	$-.18$	$-.13$

$^a p < 0.05$
$^b p < 0.01$

Source: Bendig, 1963.

Crime and antisocial behavior

From a variety of different lines of reasoning we would expect a greater amount of antisocial behavior from extroverts than introverts. In Eysenck's theory this would be because extroverts are less susceptible to the kinds of conditioning that constitute the socialization process. According to Gray, extroverts would be more prone to crime and antisocial behavior because they would be pursuing rewards without fear of consequences. We would also expect a link between extroversion and delinquency because extroverts are by definition impatient and impulsive compared to the more reliable, responsible, and controlled introverts. For whatever reason, it has been found to be the case that extroverts have more accidents and violations on the road, break institutional rules of all kinds, and find their way to prison more often than introverts (Eysenck, 1971b). In addition, unmarried mothers and venereal disease patients are more extroverted than average. Extroversion, however, is not the only personality predictor of delinquent and antisocial behavior, nor is it the best predictor. The relationships just listed are usually stronger when high levels of neuroticism are also involved, and the psychoticism factor is an even better predictor. Most of the current research on the temperamental basis of criminality and antisocial behavior is now concentrated on the P dimension, although, as we have said, neuroticism and extroversion are also positively correlated with these kinds of behavior.

Psychotherapy

The usefulness of the extroversion variable as part of a dimensional system of psychodiagnostics was discussed earlier. Does the concept have any relevance to the therapeutic process? Stern and Grosz (1966) studied the frequency of patients' verbalizations in group therapy in relation to their personality scores. The main findings were that (1) extroverts interacted more with other patients in general, and (2) patients tended to interact with others of a similar degree of introversion–extroversion. That is, extroverts interacted more with other extroverts, whereas introverts likewise preferred their own kind. This latter finding was contrasted with findings for the internal-external control dimension where patients tended to interact with *dissimilar* others. In a group situation, then, the interaction patterns are partly determined by the personalities of the individuals concerned, and one of the important dimensions is apparently extroversion. However, since nobody is clear as to precisely what benefits patients in group therapy, if indeed anything does, the relevance of this finding to the prediction of therapeutic outcome is rather obscure.

Di Loreto (1971) compared the effectiveness of three types of treatment on extroverts and introverts. The sample consisted of 100 students admitting a high level of social and general anxiety and seeking treatment for it. The three types of treatment compared were: *systematic desensitization,* in which the patient is helped to relax while visualizing a graded series of anxiety-provoking situations; *client-centered therapy,* in which the patient is encouraged to disclose his feelings in the presence of a warm and empathetic therapist who merely clarifies what is said; and *rational-emotive therapy,* in which the patient is confronted with his irrational and maladaptive behavior patterns and urged to change. Their effects were evaluated in terms of patient and therapist ratings of interpersonal and general anxiety and defensiveness, before and after the various treatments. The design included both placebo and no-contact control conditions. Overall, systematic desensitization was the most effective therapy for it produced positive changes in both extroverts and introverts. Client-centred therapy was really effective only with extroverts, and rational-emotive therapy seemed to work only with introverts. This study gives a clear indication that the time has come to go beyond the simple question of whether psychotherapy works and to ask what kind of treatment is most effective with particular kinds of patients. Introversion–extroversion is obviously one variable that must be considered in this connection.

Conclusion

It is hoped that enough has been said to establish the importance of introversion–extraversion as a major dimension of individual differences. Like intelligence, it is a truly psychological concept, slotting in between phenomena at the biological and social levels and providing an explanatory link between them. In fact, the chain of causation runs all the way from genetics through anatomical structures and physiological processes such as the reticular formation and cortical arousal to variations in extroversion measured by laboratory tests and questionnaires, thence to a wide range of social behavior such as neurosis, crime, accident proneness, drug taking, sexual behavior, and educational attainment. This causal chain is illustrated in Figure 6–19. At each successive stage the genotypic level of introversion–extraversion is probably further modified by environmental influences, so that by the time the level of social behavior is reached the link with heredity might seem tenuous. Even so, the evidence is now quite strong that biological factors cannot be ignored at any point in the chain.

The most highly developed theory of extroversion is that of Eysenck, which is built on the contributions of such unlikely collaborators as Hippocrates, Wundt, Jung, and Pavlov. Eysenck's theory is the best supported of the available alternatives, but then it is also the one that has stimulated the greatest amount of experimentation. Certain findings appear to fit better the modification of Eysenck's theory produced by Gray, but it is too soon to tell whether this version will have the power to explain as many experimental phenomena as Eysenck's original theory. Findings in the area of verbal learning and memory, in particu-

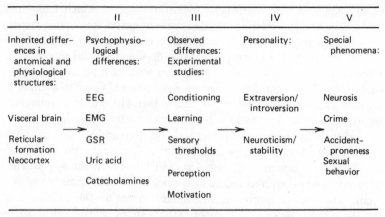

I	II	III	IV	V
Inherited differ- ences in antomical and physiological structures:	Psychophysio- logical differences:	Observed differences: Experimental studies:	Personality:	Special phenomena:
	EEG	Conditioning	Extraversion/ introversion	Neurosis
Visceral brain	EMG	Learning		Crime
Reticular formation Neocortex	GSR Uric acid Catecholamines	Sensory thresholds Perception Motivation	Neuroticism/ stability	Accident- proneness Sexual behavior

Figure 6–19.   Stages of personality description and interpretation. (From Eysenck, 1972b.)

lar, appear to provide good support for Eysenck's arousal theory and it is difficult to see how Gray's theory could accommodate them. On the other hand, Gray's theory does very well with verbal conditioning phenomena and it is a strength of his view that no general factor of conditionability is required (the existence of such a general factor is increasingly being called into question).

Whatever the future may show, personality study may be regarded as having reached a healthy state now that we have two and more theories to choose between that are formulated at the same level of scientific discourse. It is not easy to devise experiments to decide between Eysenck's theory and that of, say, Freud. The theories of both Eysenck and Gray lend themselves to experimental testing, and whatever the outcome of the experiments provoked by them, the cumulative development of scientific knowledge about personality is assured.

REFERENCES

Bartol, C. R., & Martin, R. B. Preference for complexity as a function of neuroticism, extraversion, and amplitude of orienting response. *Perceptual and Motor Skills,* 1974, *38,* 1155–1160.

Bendig, A. W. The relation of temperamental traits of social extraversion and emotionality to vocational interests. *Journal of General Psychology,* 1963, *69,* 311–318.

Brierley, M., The speed and accuracy characteristics of neurotics. *British Journal of Psychology,* 1961, *52,* 273–280.

Buss, A. M. Plamin, R., & Willerman, L. The inheritance of temperaments. *Journal of Personality,* 1973, *41,* 513–524.

Carment, D. W., & Miles, C. C. Persuasiveness and persuasibility as related to intelligence and extraversion. *British Journal of Social Psychology,* 1965, *4,* 1–7.

Cameron, J. S. Specrt, P. G., & Wendt, G. R. Effects of amphetamine on moods, emotions and motivations. *Journal of Psychology,* 1965, *61,* 93–121.

Carrigan, P. M. Extraversion–introversion as a dimension of personality. *Psychological Bulletin,* 1960, *57,* 329–60.

Cartwright, D. S. *Introduction to personality*. Chicago: Rand McNally, 1974.

Claridge, G. S. *Personality and arousal*. Oxford: Pergamon, 1967.

Claridge, G. S., & Herrington, R. N. Excitation–inhibition and the theory of neurosis: A study of the sedation threshold. In H. J. Eysenck (Ed.), *Experiments with drugs*. New York: Pergamon, 1963.

Di Loreto, A. O. *Comparative psychotherapy: An experimental analysis*. Chicago: Aldine, 1971.

Eysenck, H. J. *The Dynamics of Anxiety and Hysteria*. London: Routledge and Kegan Paul, 1957.

Eysenck, H. J. Classification and the problem of diagnosis. In H. J. Eysenck (Ed.), *Handbook of Abnormal Psychology*. London: Pitman, 1960.

Eysenck, H. J. Personality and social attitudes. *Journal of Social Psychology*, 1961, *53*, 243–343.

Eysenck, H. J. Extraversion and the acquisition of eyeblink and GSR conditioned responses. *Psychological Bulletin*, 1965, *63*, 258–270.

Eysenck, H. J. *The Biological basis of personality*. Springfield, Ill.: Thomas, 1967.

Eysenck, H. J. *The structure of human personality*. London: Methuen, 1970. (a)

Eysenck, H. J. A dimensional system of psychodiagnostics. In A. R. Mahrer (Ed.), *New approaches to personality classification*. New York: Columbia University Press, 1970. (b)

Eysenck, H. J. *Readings in extraversion-introversion I: Basic processes*. London: Staples, 1971. (a)

Eysenck H. J. *Readings in extraversion-introversion II: Fields of application*. London: Staples, 1971. (b)

Eysenck, H. J. Primaries or second-order factors: A critical consideration of Cattell's 16PF battery. *British Journal of Social and Clinical Psychology*, 1972, *11*, 265–269. (a)

Eysenck, H. J. Human typology, higher nervous activity and factor analysis. In V. D. Nebylitsyn and J. A. Gray (Eds.), *Biological bases of individual behavior*. New York: Academic Press, 1972. (b)

Eysenck, H. J. *Eysenck on Extraversion*. London: Crosby, Lockwood, Staples, 1973. (a)

Eysenck H. J. Personality. Learning and "anxiety." In H. J. Eysenck (Ed.), *Handbook of Abnormal Psychology* (2nd ed.). London: Pitman, 1973. (b)

Eysenck, H. J. Personality and learning: The experimental approach. *Proceedings, Association of Educational Psychologists Conference, 1974.*

Eysenck, H. J., & Eysenck, S. B. G. *Manual of the Eysenck Personality Inventory*. London: University of London Press, 1964.

Eysenck, H. J., & Levey, A. Conditioning, introversion-extraversion and the strength of the nervous system. In V. D. Neblitsyn and J. A. Gray (Eds.), *Biological bases of individual behavior*. New York: Academic Press, 1972.

Eysenck, H. J., & Wilson, G. D. *Know your own personality*. New York: Penguin, 1976.

Eysenck, M. W. Extraversion, arousal and retrieval from semantic memory. *Journal of Personality*, 1974, *42*, 319–331.

Eysenck, M. W. Individual differences in speed of retrieval from semantic memory. *Journal of Research in Personality*, 1975. (a)

Eysenck, M. W. Extraversion, arousal and speed of retrieval from secondary storage. *Journal of Personality*, 1975. (b)

Eysenck, S. B. G., & Eysenck, H. J. On the dual nature of extraversion. *British Journal of Social and Clinical Psychology*, 1963, *2*, 46–55.

Eysenck, S. B. G., & Eysenck, H. J. Salivary response to lemon juice as a measure of introversion. *Perceptual Motor Skills*, 1967, *24*, 1047–1053.

Frith, C. D. The interaction of noise and personality with critical flicker fusion performance. *British Journal of Psychology*, 1967, *58*, 127–131.

Frith, C. D. Strategies in rotary pursuit tracking. *British Journal of Psychology,* 1971, *62,* 187–197.

Gale, A. The psychophysiology of individual differences: Studies of extraversion and the EEG. In P. Kline (Ed.), *New Approaches in Psychological Measurement.* London: John Wiley, 1973.

Gray, J. A. The psychophysiological nature of introversion-extraversion: A modification of Eysenck's theory. In V. D. Neblitsyn & J. A. Gray (Eds.), *Biological bases of individual behaviour.* New York: Academic Press, 1972.

Gray, J. A. Causal theories of personality and how to test them. In M. P. Royce (Ed.), *Multivariate analysis and psychological theory.* London: Academic Press, 1973.

Gupta, B. S. Stimulant and depressant drugs on Kinaesthetic figural aftereffects. *Psychopharmacologia,* 1974, *36,* 275–280. (a)

Gupta, B. S. *Extraversion and reinforcement in verbal operant conditioning.* Unpublished study, Guru Nanak University, Amritsar, India, 1974. (b)

Heimstra, N. W. Effects of amphetamine sulfate (Benzedrine) on the behavior of paired rats in a competitive situation. *Psychological Record,* 1962, *12,* 25–34.

Hill A. B. Extraversion and variety seeking in a monotonous task. *British Journal of Psychology,* 1975, *66,* 9–13.

Holmes, D. S. Pupillary response, conditioning and personality. *Journal of Personality and Social Psychology,* 1967, *5,* 98–103.

Howarth, E., & Eysenck, H. J. Extraversion, arousal, and paried associate recall. *Journal of Experimental Research in Personality,* 1968, *3,* 114–116.

Jung, C. G. *Psychological types.* New York: Harcourt Brace, 1923.

Kleinsmith, L. J., & Kaplan, S. Paired associate learning as a function of arousal and interpolated interval. *Journal of Experimental Psychology,* 1963, *65,* 190–193.

Laverty, S. G. Sodium amytal and extraversion. *Journal of Neurology, Neurosurgery and Psychiatry,* 1958, *21,* 50–54.

Leith, G. O. M. Individual differences in learning: Interactions of personality and teaching methods. *Proceedings, Association of Educational Psychologists Conference, 1974.*

Levy, P., & Lang, P. J. Activation control and the spiral after-movement. *Journal of Personality and Social Psychology,* 1966, *3,* 105–112.

Ludvigh, E. J., & Happ, D. Extraversion and preferred level of sensory stimulation. *British Journal of Psychology,* 1974, *65,* 359–365.

Lynn, R. Introversion–extraversion differences in judgments of time. *Journal of Abnormal and Social Psychology,* 1961, *63,* 457–458.

McLaughlin, & Eysenck, H. J. Extraversion, neuroticism and paired assocates learning. *Journal of Experimental Research in Personality,* 1967, *2,* 128–132.

Mohan, J., and Mohan, V. Personality and variability in esthetic evaluation. *Psychological Studies,* 1965, *10,* 57–60.

Mohan, V., and Kumar, D. *Qualitative analysis of the performance of introverts and extroverts on the Standard Progressive Matrices.* Paper read at Diamond Jubilee Session of Indian Science Congress, Jan. 1973, Chandigarh, India.

Moss, P. D., and McEvedy C. P. An epidemic of overbreathing among schoolgirls. *British Medical Journal,* 1966, Nov. 26, 1295–1300.

Nias, D. K. B., and Hardy, C. A. Predicters of success in learning to swim. *British Journal of Physical Education,* 1971, *2,* 25–27.

Petrie A., *Personality and the frontal lobes.* London: Routledge and Kegan Paul, 1952.

Ramsay, R. W. Speech patterns and personality. *Language and Speech,* 1968, *11,* 54–63.

Reed, G. F., and Kenna, J. C. Personality and time estimation in sensory deprivation. *Perceptual and Motor Skills,* 1964, *18,* 182.

Rust, J. *Genetic factors in psychophysiology.* Unpublished doctoral dissertation, University of London, 1974.

Schalling, D., Levander, S. E., and Wredenmark, G. *Semantic generalization as reflecting cortical functions in extrovert and introvert subjects.* Unpublished paper, University of Stockholm, 1975.

Shields, J. Heredity and environment. In H. J. Eysenck and G. D. Wilson (Eds.), *A textbook of human psychology.* Baltimore: University Park Press, 1976.

Sinha, A. K. P. and Ojha, H. An experimental study of the operation of prestige suggestions in extroverts and introverts. *Journal Social Psychology,* 1963, *61,* 29–34.

Stern, H., & Grosz, H. J. Verbal interactions in group psychotherapy between patients with similar and dissimilar personalities. *Journal of Psychosomatic Research,* 1963, *7,* 11–14.

Taft, R. Extraversion, neuroticism and expressive behavior: An application of Wallach's moderator effect to handwriting analysis. *Journal of Personality,* 1967, *35,* 570–584.

Thackray, R. I., Jones, K. N., and Touchstone, R. N. Personality and physiological correlates of performance decrement on a monotonous task requiring sustained attention. *British Journal of Psychology,* 1974, *65,* 351–358.

Tranel, N. Effects of perceptual isolation on introverts and extraverts. *Journal of Psychiatric Research,* 1962, *1,* 185–192.

Wakefield J. A. , Yom, B. L., Bradley, P. E., Doughtie, E. B., and Cox, J. A., Eysenck's personality dimensions: A model for the MMPI. *British Journal of Social and Clinical Psychology,* 1974, *13,* 413–420.

Walker, E. L. Action decrement and its relation to learning. *Psychological Review,* 1958, *65,* 129–142.

Wankowski, J. A. *Temperament, motivation and academic achievement.* University of Birmingham Educational Survey and Counselling Unit, 1973.

Weisen, A. *Differential reinforcing effects of onset and offset of stimulation on the operant behavior of normals, neurotics, and psychopaths.* Unpublished doctoral dissertation, University of Florida, 1965.

Wilson, G. D., and Nias, D. K. B. Sexual Types. *New Behavior,* 1975, *2,* 330–332.

Wilson, G. D., Tunstall, O. A., and Eysenck, H. J. Individual differences in tapping performance as a function of time on the task. *Perceptual and Motor Skills,* 1971, *33,* 375–378.

Yates, A. Abnormalities of psychomotor functions. In H. J. Eysenck (Ed.), *Handbook of Abnormal Psychology,* 2nd ed. London: Pitman, 1973.

NOTES

1 Unfortunately some results also have been reported that seem to run counter to the hypothesis that amphetamine is introverting. In terms of effects on mood, it has been reported that college students given normal clinical dosage felt more optimistic, friendly, energetic, talkative, decisive, egotistic, keyed up, and lightheaded than placebo controls (Cameron, Specht, & Wendt, 1965); all of these seem typically extrovert characteristics. As regards behavior, amphetamine tends to increase activity and has even been found to make rats more sociable (Heimstra, 1962). Clearly, this particular stimulant has a variety of effects on behavior and experience, not all of which are consistent with a shift toward greater introversion.

CHAPTER 7

Locus of Control

E. JERRY PHARES
Kansas State University

AN INTRODUCTION TO LOCUS OF CONTROL

If we consulted a random sample of people on how best to influence other people's behavior it is almost certain that the answers would in some way deal with rewards and punishments.[1] Although some might emphasize one over the other, the role of reinforcement would likely be paramount. Such an emphasis is not limited to laypeople. It may well be true that the most ubiquitous concept in psychology is some version of reinforcement. Indeed, the presumed power of reinforcement could be the central dynamism behind the polarized reactions to the 1971 publication of Skinner's controversial book, *Beyond Freedom and Dignity*. The many cries of outrage following Skinner's social prescriptions testifies to the seriousness with which people take their reinforcement. The crucial issue of who will control the technocrats who dispense the reinforcements that control society has repeatedly been voiced (and inadequately answered) and underscores again the practical and theoretical concerns that are catalyzed by the concept of reinforcement.

So strong is our reinforcement orientation that it may come as a shock to observe someone whose behavior seems to violate our notions about the effects of rewards and punishments. Imagine, if you will, a 23-year-old unmarried army veteran who was referred for psychotherapy. He possessed few social skills and even fewer friends. Therapy took the form of increasing the patient's expectations for gratification in the general social-sexual and education–employment life areas. This was deemed more useful in this case than the tedious search for unconscious forces that presumably might have been generating neurotic defenses. Indeed, this patient was not so much neurotic as he was socially undereducated. Therefore, the focus of therapy became the development of techniques by which the patient could find employment, enhance his education, become comfortable and successful with girls, and so on. Suggestions and discussions

263

about these specific techniques filled many therapeutic hours. Very often the patient was successful in his efforts. Curiously, however, none of these successes appeared to have any effect on his behavior. Normally, we assume that a behavior will be increased in potential when it leads to success. For this individual, however, reinforcement carried no implications for the future.

For a while, the failure to build this patient's repertory of behaviors by increasing his expectancies for their success based on past successes was quite puzzling. Everyone "knows" that reinforcement increases behavior potential. But not so in this case. Only gradually did the reasons for this anomolous situation emerge: The patient did not perceive any causal connection between his behavior and any ensuing outcomes! He did not attribute these outcomes to his own behavior, but rather, he saw as being crucial such things as luck or other factors over which he had no control.

What this patient was asserting through his apprently "irrational" behavior was simply that notions emphasizing the "stamping in" of behaviors through reinforcement are incomplete. Reinforcement may be necessary to increase behavior potential, but it is not sufficient. The individual must also believe that there is a causal relationship between what one does and what follows.

Through this case, a real one, the groundwork for a whole series of studies on a concept was laid. Sometimes referred to as *locus of control* or as *internal versus external control* (I–E), the concept was first outlined by Rotter (1966) and defined as follows:

When a reinforcement is perceived by the subject as following some action of his own but not being entirely contingent upon his action, then, in our culture, it is typically perceived as the result of luck, chance, fate, as under the control of powerful others, or as unpredictable because of the great complexity of the forces surrounding him. When the event is interpreted in this way by an individual we have labeled this a belief in *external control*. If the person perceives that the event is contingent upon his own behavior or his own relatively permanent characteristics, we have termed this a belief in *internal control*. (p. 1)

Since 1966 an astonishing volume of research on this concept has appeared. By 1969 over 300 studies were cited by Throop and MacDonald (1971). At the present time, it is likely that more than 1000 studies have appeared. Several reviews, bibliographies, and analyses of the concept have been published (Joe, 1971; Lefcourt, 1966a, 1972; Phares, 1973; Prociuk and Lussier, 1975; Rotter, 1966, 1975; Throop and MacDonald, 1971). Books setting forth the theoretical background and general literature related to internal versus external control have recently been completed (Lefcourt, 1976; Phares, 1976.)

Locus of control is not a typological concept. It is not the case that people are either internally or externally controlled. Locus of control is a continuum, and people can be ordered along that continuum. For the sake of convenience, we will refer to internals and externals, but it should be emphasized that the behavior of an individual in any given situation is determined by many converging factors. To classify one as internal or external is a typological error that ignores these factors, oversimplifies the predictive process, and will surely lead to disappointing results. We will have more to say about this later.

Rotter's (1966) description of the external individual not only fits the patient described earlier, it also aptly fits many other individuals who live and work in our society. These individuals have been variously depicted as powerless, fatalistic, alienated, or normless. Regardless of terminology, however, all live in a world that does not seem able to come to grips with overcrowding, overpopulation, pollution, unresponsive government, the generation gap, campus disorders, ghetto riots, police riots, and so on. In any event, the enormous popularity of the I–E concept is not simply a function of its theoretical origins or the scale that was developed to measure it. I–E touches vibrant social phenomena that have been and still are very much alive in society.

SOME THEORETICAL BACKGROUND

A major shortcoming of much empirical I–E research is its lack of theoretical foundation, which has sometimes led to failures in prediction, disappointment in the amount of variance accounted for by I–E, or difficulty generalizing from one study to the next. Therefore, to better understand the research and issues that will be described later in this chapter, let us now briefly examine social learning theory (Rotter, 1954; Rotter, Chance, and Phares, 1972)—the framework from which locus of control developed.

In the most rudimentary sense, any behavior is determined by (1) the individual's expectancy that the behavior in question will lead to a reinforcement, and (2) the value of that reinforcement. The magnitude of the expectancy and the value of the reinforcement are conditioned in part by the nature of the specific situation to which we are predicting. Therefore, prediction of behavior involves three variables: expectancies, reinforcements, and the psychological situation.

Of particular import for locus of control are expectancies. Ignoring reinforcements for the moment, suppose we wish to determine the extent of a student's expectancy that he will be admitted to graduate study. At least three factors will contribute to this expectancy. First, specific experiences in applying previously will be important. Second, it is necessary to know how much previous experience of this specific nature the student has had. Third, what experiences has the student encountered in other situations that he sees as similar? We may postulate that the more specific experience the student has in applying for graduate study, the less important will be experiences generalized from other related experiences. We may also postulate that, in the absence of any specific experience, generalized expectancies will account for nearly all the variance. These relationships are stated by Rotter (1954, p. 166):

$$Es_1 = f(E'_{s1} \, \& \, \frac{GE}{Ns_1})$$

In this formula, Es_1 refers to the expectancy of successfully applying to graduate school, E'_{s1} refers to expectancies based on specific experience in the same situation previously, Ns_1 refers to amount of prior experience in that same situation, and GE refers to expectancies generalized from past situations that the student regards as similar. This formula clearly suggests the importance of broad, general personality factors, but it also suggests the great importance of specific situational variables as well.

The notion of generalized expectancy (GE) refers to the probability of the occurrence of related reinforcements (in this case, reinforcements related to successful application to graduate school). However, social learning theory deals with another kind of GE: It incorporates generalized expectancies that a given manner of categorizing situations will prove useful. People are constantly faced with the need to solve problems. Most human situations, regardless of the needs they engage, present problems. By categorizing situations, the individual can better cope with the problems involved. From this perspective, locus of control represents a generalized expectancy or belief as to the optimum way in which one feels the relationship between one's behavior and the subsequent occurrence of reward and punishment should be viewed.

Therefore, in determining how confident the student is that applying to graduate school will be successful, we must consider not only his generalized expectancy for the attainment of the goal (GEr). Also of significance are his generalized expectancies about how this situation should be construed from the point of view of problem solving $(GEps)$. Thus, whether institutions can be trusted or whether the world is capricious are just two potential ways of construing the nature of problem situations. The relationships among these various expectancy notions have been schematized as follows (Rotter, et al., 1972, p. 41):

$$E_{s_1} = \frac{f(E' \, \& \, GE_r \, \& \, GE_{ps_1} \, \& \, GE_{ps_2} \dots GE_{ps_n})}{f(N_{s_1})}$$

From this discussion, then, it should be obvious that I–E is only one entry in a very complex formula for the prediction of behavior. It is important that in our quest for greater understanding of the I–E concept we not lose sight of the other determinants of behavior that in many (if not most) situations may be of even greater saliency. The expectancy that a given behavior will be successful in a specific situation depends on the frequency with which the person has been rewarded in this situation before, the frequency of achievement of similar rewards in the past, and the nature of a variety of generalized expectancies involving such things as I–E, trust, and many others. The introduction of problem-solving generalized expectancies increases the complexity of prediction, but it seems necessary given the enormous richness of human behavior.

Finally, it is important to emphasize the role of the psychological situation. Although space does not permit an extended discussion, the psychological situation exerts a pronounced effect on reinforcement values and expectancies (both specific and generalized). The value of a given reinforcement may be adversely affected in a specific situation because of certain punishments that might ensue from its attainment there but not elsewhere. Similarly, expectancies are not invariant across situations. Even generalized expectancies (both of a reinforcement and problem-solving nature) may differ in their effects depending on the person's previous experience in specific situations. Also, some situations permit alternative behaviors that other situations may not. Surely, then, an analysis of the situation is essential before we set about predicting a specific behavior.

LOCUS OF CONTROL AS A CHARACTERISTIC OF THE SITUATION

The previous section distinguished between specific and generalized expectancies. Before dealing in detail with generalized problem-solving expectancies for locus of control, let us examine locus of control from a more situationally specific point of view.

Some situations are so clear and explicit in their meaning that internals are going to behave in an external fashion or externals in an internal fashion. The relative importance of generalized and specific locus of control expectancies depends on the situation but, as a rule of thumb, the greater the individual's experience in a specific situation, the less important will be the role of I–E *generalized* expectancies.

Effects on Expectancies and Learning

The first locus of control studies did not deal with generalized internal-external expectancies at all. They were studies of the differential roles of skill and chance factors in affecting expectancies for task success. As noted by Phares (1976), the goal of these early studies was twofold. First, it was hoped that more could be learned about the exact manner in which reinforcement operates. Second, it seemed plausible that skill–chance research would help to determine the feasibility of pursuing the skill–chance distinction at the level of individual differences. That is, it was anticipated that the behavior of subjects in specific skill or chance situations would ultimately turn out to be analogous to that of people who were internally or externally controlled in the generalized sense.

Three studies are generally representative of ths work. Phares (1957) asked subjects to perform two perceptual judgment tasks. Some subjects were told that the task was so difficult that success was largely a matter of chance. Others were instructed that success was entirely a matter of personal skill or ability. Over a series of trials, subjects were asked to state an expectancy or confidence level prior to each trial. In essence, the results demonstrated that changes in expectancy following success or failure were greater under skill conditions than under chance conditions.

A second study by Phares (1962) confirmed the hypothesis that when escape from a painful stimulus is possible as a result of the subject's efforts, greater learning will ensue than when escape is completely outside the subject's control. In essence, the subject's recognition thresholds for nonsense syllables were significantly reduced when knowledge of those syllables was instrumental in reducing the magnitude of electric shock received.

The third study (Rotter, Liverant, & Crowne, 1961) manipulated the subject's skill or chance categorizations of tasks through the intrinsic nature of the task rather than by instructions, as was largely true of the previous two studies. Using an ESP task as a chance situation and a hand steadiness task as a skill situation, the investigators were able to support two conclusions. First, in the skill task positive and negative reinforcements lead to greater changes in expectancies for success than in the chance situation. Second, resistance to extinction of expectancies is greater for a 50 percent reinforcement schedule than for a 100 percent schedule—but only under chance conditions. Under skill conditions the 100 percent schedule is more effective in retarding the effects of extinction.

The foregoing studies suggest several things. When individuals feel they do not control the occurrence of reinforcement, they generalize significantly less from prior experience and do not use increasing experience in the present task in the formulation of expectancies or strategies. In brief, tasks controlled by chance seem to result in less learning. Furthermore, as suggested by Rotter (1966), these results from skill–chance studies have very important implications for many experimental studies of learning. Much of the data in learning studies has been collected in situations that were probably perceived by subjects as being under experimenter control. If nothing else, the study by Rotter et al. (1961), should lead us to question (and perhaps reinterpret) learning data from studies in which subjects may have perceived some subtle experimenter control.

Other Effects of the Situation

The expectancy changes outlined thus far are not the only consequences of perceived lack of control. Nor are they the most extreme. For example, the sense of personal helplessness that enveloped prisoners in Nazi concentration camps has been vividly described by Bettelheim (1960). Even research at the animal level has sharply emphasized the deleterious emotional and physical reactions that follow from aversive stimuli that the organism can neither control nor predict (Brady, Porter, Conrad, & Mason, 1958; Seligman, Maier, & Solomon, 1971).

Of course, many situations appear to be similar in that they all seem to involve lack of control or inability to predict. However, we do not know that they are precisely equivalent in their effects on human behavior. For example, are chance, complex, unpredictable, authoritarian, unstable, or helpless situations all alike? Probably not. To authoritarianism the individual may react with anger or aggression. To extreme complexity the reaction may be bewilderment. In fact, lack of control does not always lead to inability to predict, particularly if the would-be controller is very regular (rather than irregular) in exerting the control.

Lazarus (1966) has contended that anxiety in threatening situations is intimately associated with degree of personal control, and research is generally supportive of his contention. Subjects report less stress when they believe they can terminate an electric shock (Corah & Boffa, 1970), even when that belief is incorrect (Geer, Davison, & Gatchel, 1970). Preference is greater for predictable shock over unpredictable shock (D'Amato & Gumenik, 1960) as is degree of discomfort experienced for predictable shock (Houston, 1972; Staub, Tursky, & Schwartz, 1971). Glass and Singer (1972) have investigated the effects of noise as it relates to urban stress and note that predictable aversive and distractive events disrupt people's performance less than do unpredictable ones.

The conclusion appears to be that learning and performance are reduced and anxiety and stress levels are increased when aversive stimuli are either unpredictable or uncontrollable. The previous work on differential expectancy changes as a function of skill and chance situations suggested that under chance conditions the individual is unable to generalize expectancies or experience from the past to the future. Aversive-stress research reinforces this observation by suggesting that lack of personal control or ability to predict is especially debilitating because it prevents the individual from developing expectancies for successful coping. As a result, anxiety mounts.

To illustrate the wide-ranging effects of lack of control or predictability, two additional concepts may be noted. First, there is reactance (Brehm, 1972)—a phenomenon in which, among other things, goals the individual is prevented from achieving assume greater value than they had before. For example, Hammock and Brehm (1966) found that when children are led to expect they may choose between candy and toys but are later not allowed to do so, their chosen alternative becomes more attractive while an alternative forced upon them becomes less attractive.

A second phenomenon, cognitive dissonance (Festinger, 1957), describes a situation in which the individual behaves in a manner that is discrepant from his beliefs, experiences an unpleasant feeling state, and then changes his beliefs to accord with his behavior. However, Cooper (1971) presents evidence to show that cognitive dissonance will not occur unless the individual feels personally responsible or voluntarily chooses to behave in opposition to his beliefs.

Stability and Locus of Control

Weiner (1972) has introduced the notion of causal stability to complement locus of control. He argues that subjects utilize not only an internal-external dimension to explain their performance but also a stable-unstable dimension. Indeed, he contends that much research has confounded locus of control with stability. He employs four factors as determinants of perceived achievement: ability (internal-stable), effort (internal-unstable), task difficulty (external-stable), and luck (external-unstable). He further asserts that the causal stability dimension influences expectancy for success and that the locus of control dimension influences affective responses to success and failure. His analysis is couched in an attributional, Expectancy × Value theoretical framework.

At the present time there does not appear to be a convincing body of data supporting the utility of adding the stability dimension. Most locus of control research would subsume ability and effort under internal control, while task difficulty could be either internal or external depending on where the control of task difficulty really lies.

In general, Weiner's work is most relevant to laboratory studies of the determinants of expectancy changes. The actual I–E literature deals with generalized I–E beliefs and their relationship to many life areas, including coping behavior, resistance to influence, and the like. The I–E literature also encompasses the study of needs other than achievement or the desire to do well. Thus, even should the addition of stability find support in laboratory studies of expectancy changes, it is not at all clear that similar demonstrations of utility will be forthcoming in the broader, personality applications of locus of control.

The findings in this section on locus of control as a characteristic of the situation are, of course, interesting by their very nature. However, they suggest something else as well. They give us confidence that what we have learned about situations will apply to the personality level also. That is, we can approach the measurement of individual differences in beliefs about locus of control with greater assurance. These situational findings provide important clues as to the effects that broad beliefs in internal or external control may promote.

In predicting human behavior these situational studies are also important in a more theoretical sense. As emphasized earlier, we cannot hope to predict or understand behavior by exclusive reliance on broad, generalized personality characteristics. We must also know a great deal about the situation. These situational studies (at least in the realm of locus of control) tell us something about the E'_{s1} factor in the social learning theory formula given earlier. We can now turn our attention to the companion personality (GE) aspects of locus of control.

THE MEASUREMENT OF LOCUS OF CONTROL

To determine the effects that locus of control beliefs have on behavior, we must first devise a way of measuring such beliefs. We need a device that will distinguish among people who hold differing expectations regarding their general capacity to exert an influence on the world around them. The most widely used measure of locus of control is the scale introduced and described by Rotter (1966). Phares (1976) has analyzed the Rotter I–E Scale in some detail (along with other measures of locus of control).

The I–E Scale evolved out of early work by Phares (1955), but subsequent scale development was carried out by the late Shephard Liverant, J. B. Rotter, Melvin Seeman, Douglas Crowne, and William James. The present version of the I–E Scale (Rotter, 1966) consists of 23 forced-choice I–E items, along with six filler items to help disguise the nature of the test. The items that follow are drawn from some earlier versions of the I–E Scale and illustrate the general flavor of the scale. (Readers interested in carrying out research using the I–E Scale should consult Rotter [1966]).)

I more strongly believe that:
1. a. Many people can be described as victims of circumstances.
   b. What happens to other people is pretty much of their own making.
2. a. Much of what happens to me is probably a matter of luck.
   b. I control my own fate.
3. a. The world is so complicated that I just cannot figure things out.
   b. The world is really complicated all right, but I can usually work things out by effort and persistence.
4. a. It is silly to think one can really change another's basic attitudes.
   b. When I am right I can convince others.
5. a. Most students would be amazed at how much grades are determined by capricious events.
   b. The marks I get in class are completely my own responsibility.

Originally, the intent was to build a test consisting of subscales that would measure I–E beliefs in several need areas such as recognition, love and affection, dominance, and so on. For a variety of reasons, these efforts were abandoned. In particular, the subscales were not independent, and social desirability effects were too strong. The resulting 23 items showed evidence of validity in that endorsement of internal alternatives was related to information seeking in a hospital setting (Seeman and Evans, 1962) and to trials to extinction (Rotter et al., 1961). Only those items were retained that did not show substantial correlations with social desirability measures. Items that contributed to lack of acceptable internal consistency or that contained alternatives endorsed more than 85 percent of the time were also eliminated.

Reliability

The test–retest reliability of the scale was reported by Rotter (1966) to range from 0.49 to 0.83 depending on the time period and particular population. Hersch and Scheibe (1967) report highly similar results. Kiehlbauch (1967), over time periods of three, six, and nine month intervals, reported reliability coefficients of 0.75, 0.39, and 0.26, respectively. Clearly, the size of reliability coefficients will be closely tied to the length and nature of the time periods involved. These periods may provide subjects with experiences that could alter I–E beliefs.

Social Desirability

Most studies of the social desirability characteristics of the I–E Scale report minimal effects (e.g., Rotter, 1966; Strickland, 1965; Tolor, 1967). Nonetheless, occasional studies do report significant relationships. However, it is important to recognize that social desirability is not an entity that scales either possess or do not possess. Rather, social desirability estimates for a scale will vary depending on the nature of the testing situation and the needs or goals that influence the subjects at that particular time. Surely, the I–E Scale is not completely devoid of social desirability effects (no scale is), but across a wide band of situations it does not appear reasonable to conclude that the utility of the I–E Scale is seriously compromised.

Intelligence

With respect to intelligence, most research fails to find a substantial relationship to beliefs concerning locus of control (Hersch and Scheibe, 1967; Kiehlbauch, 1967; Rotter, 1966).

Sex Differences

Most of the early research on sex differences in I–E scores failed to support the presence of such differences. However, more recent work (McGinnies, Nordholm, Ward, & Bhanthumnavia, 1974; Parsons & Schneider, 1974) finds small differences in favor of greater externality in women. Whether the difference between early research and more recent studies reflects shifts in cultural role expectations in men and women is hard to assess at this time. Recent research by Hochreich (1975a) does, however, indicate the presence of sex-role stereotypes as regards locus of control. When subjects were asked to answer the I–E Scale as a "supermale" would, scores shifted in the internal direction. When the instructions involved a set as "superfemale," comparable shifts in the external direction ensued. At the same time, no evidence was adduced to suggest that the wish to present oneself as either very masculine or very feminine is a significant determinant of I–E scores. Parenthetically, it might be noted that, regardless of whether there are sex differences in I–E scores, sex very often does affect the magnitude of the relationship between I–E scores and other behavioral measures, particularly achievement and defensiveness.

Social Class, Ethnic, and National Differences

In the realm of ethnic and social class differences there do appear to be significant effects of I–E. In general, it is probable that such differences can be reduced most often to explanations involving access to socioeconomic power and mobility. Many studies indicate greater internality among whites than blacks (e.g., Battle & Rotter, 1963; Zytkoskee, Strickland, & Watson, 1971). Such data very likely reflect differences in socioeconomic status and are simply another example of the fact that middle class children are more internal than lower class children (Gruen & Ottinger, 1969). Other work reports cross-cultural effects and compares I–E scores among wide varieties of groups ranging from Anglo-Americans, American- and Hong Kong-born Chinese (Hsieh, Shybut, & Lotsof, 1969) to Anglo, Spanish, American Indian groups and Mexican-Americans (Garza & Ames, 1974; Jessor, Graves, Hanson, & Jessor, 1968), and groups from the United States, Denmark, West Germany, and Japan (Parsons, Schneider, & Hansen, 1970; Schneider and Parsons, 1970). Such data can be particularly informative in that they may provide some insight into the cultural and familial antecedents of locus of control beliefs.

Typical I–E Scores

Many people, when they first encounter the I–E notion, immediately want to know what the typical or average I–E score is. This is a very difficult question to answer since such scores vary widely depending on the population being considered and the point in time involved. We have already noted differences among racial, cultural, and socioeconomic groups. It is instructive to note, however, that among college students I–E scores have generally shifted in the external direction in recent years. As noted elsewhere (Phares, 1976), such changes have been of the order of three to four points and are probably attributable to changes in sociopolitical awareness. This point will be discussed later in this chapter.

Additional Conceptions and Misconceptions

The foregoing are some of the chief characteristics of the Rotter I–E Scale. However, over the past few years the volume of studies employing the I–E Scale has been so enormous that a variety of misconceptions have developed. These misconceptions are associated both with the manner in which I–E is conceptualized and with the means by which it is measured. All these misconceptions have been discussed elsewhere in more detail (Phares, 1976; Rotter, 1975). We can briefly touch on them here since doing so may help to clarify the following sections on correlates, functions, and antecedents of I–E.

First of all, the I–E Scale is an *additive* scale. Some items relate to school, others to work, interpersonal relations, or politics. The scale samples a wide array of human endeavors and *adds* responses. As a result of sampling a *variety* of situations, we can categorize the I–E Scale as a measure of *generalized* expectancies. This means that the scale should relate to behavior across a very broad band of situations. Consequently, the I–E Scale will show modest but significant correlations with many behaviors. However, should our only goal be the prediction of behavior in a single, narrow class of situations, then we would be better advised to discard the I–E Scale and develop a scale that measures locus of control exclusively in the one area that interests us. In this vein, it is important to note that the measures of internal consistency reported by Rotter (1966) were from 0.65 to 0.79. It is the generalized, additive nature of the scale that ensures the noncomparability of items and thereby reduces the internal consistency estimates. A so-called power test that samples locus of control in a single life area would be expected to produce higher levels of internal consistency.

Recently, considerable discussion has centered around whether the I–E Scale is unidimensional or multidimensional. The discussion often implies that the scale was intended to be unidimensional but through factor analysis has been unmasked as multidimensional. However, from the very beginning the generalized nature of the scale opened the possibility that subscales might be developed. Many locus of control subscales might conceivably be developed that would be useful in that they could be designed to predict to certain specific types of situations. For those specific situations, such subscales should lead to more precise predictions than a traditional I–E scale that would be serviceable across a range of situations but would do a lesser job in any specific situation than would a subscale designed specifically for that situation.

A large number of factor analyses of the I–E Scale have appeared. Their results vary in reporting from two to five or more factors. Such variability can be accounted for by differing factor methods, different populations used (college students, for example, may have examined minutely the issues of control in our society whereas others may not have), and time at which they were carried out (e.g., Gurin, Gurin, Lao, & Beattie, 1969; Mirels, 1970). Subscales have also been identified by adding new items to the I–E Scale or otherwise altering its format (e.g., Collins, 1974; Gurin et al., 1969; Levenson, 1973a, 1973b).

At any rate, the simple production of additional factor analyses will be useful only insofar as they lead to the development of better calibrated, more predictive scales. Distinguishing between beliefs in powerful others and chance may be highly useful and may increase our understanding of an external locus of control (Levenson, 1973a, 1973b). But hoping that factor analysis will reveal the "true nature" of locus of control is fallacious when we recall that the conditions mentioned above can all affect the results of the factor analysis. We will develop later the notion that there are at least two "kinds" of externals (defensive and congruent). We will show that such distinctions are useful and can add to the predictive potential of the I–E Scale.

At the level of conceptualization of I–E, several misconceptions have impeded research. The first is the failure to consider other social learning theory variables besides I–E in the prediction of behavior. For example, action taking may be associated with internal control but only when the goal of the action taking is regarded by the individual as valuable. When Gore and Rotter (1963) found that internal southern black college students were very likely to become actively involved in civil rights activities, this came as no surprise. But the value of the goal was shared by most subjects in the study. If another study fails to relate internality to petition signing to find jobs for South Vietnam refugees, is this surprising? No, because there may not be agreement on the desirability of doing so by all subjects. In short, the reinforcing qualities of the goal to which the activity leads must be clearly demonstrable before we can predict that an internal subject will resort to greater activity to reach that goal than will an external.

Another conceptual problem is that of specificity versus generality. As noted earlier, a score on the I–E Scale allows us to describe a person's I–E status over a broad range of situations. But the broader we make the range, the less predictive to any specific situation will be the score. Most of us show a pattern of I–E beliefs that is not homogeneous across all situations. In some situations we may be quite internal but in others much less so. If all we wish to deal with is affectionate behavior, then we would do well to devise an I–E Scale that contained only love and affection items. Whether to develop a broad or narrow I–E Scale is not a question that can be answered independent of one's predictive goals. For example, clinical psychologists may want to predict their patient's behavior in future situations that are quite vague and unknown. To do that, a broad, generalized scale would undoubtedly be more useful than one that deals exclusively with love and affection situations.

We will discuss later the relationship between I–E and adjustment. However, for the moment it is well to heed the warning that not everything internal is good nor is everything external bad (Rotter, 1975). In some cases it may be good to be internally oriented, for example, in the achievement of valued goals. In other cases, a strong internal orientation may lead to overpowering feelings of guilt when one's behavior goes wrong. In any event, issues of values are involved here.

We have now completed our discussion of the theoretical and measurement aspects of locus of control. We have, of course, been selective in our coverage. In particular, we have not dealt with several other measures of locus of control because of space considerations. Nowicki and Duke (1974a) have developed an adult scale that might be especially suitable for noncollege samples; they have also published a scale for preschool and primary grade children (Nowicki and Duke, 1974b). A children's scale (IAR) has been developed by Crandall, Katkovsky, and Crandall (1965) and is widely used; the scale measures locus of control separately for success and failure situations. The Nowicki and Strickland (1973) scale and the Bialer (1961) scale are also appropriate for children. Mischel, Zeiss, and Zeiss (1974) have produced some preliminary evidence for the utility of a preschool I–E scale.

Projective or unobtrusive measures of I–E have been developed by Dies (1968), Adams-Webber (1969), and Battle and Rotter (1963). More limited and specific measures have also been offered (Gurin et al., 1969; Lao, 1970; Jessor et al., 1968; Stephens and Delys, 1973; and Gruen, Korte, and Baum, 1974).

In succeeding sections we will examine a variety of evidence regarding the behavioral correlates of I–E scales. In large part, these studies have used the Rotter I–E Scale, and thus they can be viewed as evidence for the construct validity of that scale.

RELATIONSHIP BETWEEN I–E AND ENVIRONMENTAL CONTROL

An internal orientation seems to imply an active and controlling approach to life. By definition, an internal is one who approaches situations with a more directive and alert posture than externals. Indeed, the most straightforward evidence of the validity of the I–E Scale would seem to follow this definition. Although there are many important determinants of coping behavior other than one's locus of control beliefs, evidence of the importance of I–E has been widely and consistently forthcoming.

Health and Body Care

One of the most important aspects of the environment is one's own body and its well-being. Strickland (1974) has recently commented on the significant and dramatic implications that locus of control offers for both physical and emotional well-being. It was Seeman and Evans (1962) who noted that in a tuberculosis hospital internal patients possessed more information about their physical condition, were more demanding of such information from both physicians and nurses, and were generally less satisfied about the extent of information they were receiving.

Both Straits and Sechrest (1963) and James, Woodruff, and Werner (1965) found that smokers tend to be somewhat more external than nonsmokers. The latter study also revealed that smokers who were convinced by the Surgeon General's evidence and altered their smoking behavior tended to be more internal than those who were unconvinced. These findings suggest a modest but reliable relationship between internality and a tendency to take active steps to guard one's health. As Strickland's (1974) review points out, I–E appears to be related similarly to prophylactic dental behavior, use of seat belts in autos, preventive medical shots, participation in physical fitness activity, ability to influence postoperative care, and patient behavior in a variety of kidney, diabetic, and cardiovascular conditions.

The role of I–E in the control over self has also been observed in weight reduction programs (Balch & Ross, 1975). Furthermore, Lundy (1972) and MacDonald (1970) have demonstrated that external females are less likely to practice effective birth control than are internals. As we observed earlier, there are many complex, general, and specific determinants of all the foregoing behaviors. I–E, therefore, could hardly be regarded as the essential predictor. Given this complexity of multidetermined behavior, the fact that a general, nonspecific personality variable such as locus of control can show significant relationships is indeed quite impressive.

Cognitive Control

Several of the studies in health-related areas indicate that internals possess greater information regarding their personal situation. Of course, such knowledge places them in a superior position to control or change their lives. Seeman (1963) observed the same phenomenon in a reformatory, where he found prisoners with an internal belief system to be more knowledgeable about reformatory policies and rules, parole regulations, and long-range economic facts that could affect their lives. A question arises as to specifically how it is that the internal is able to acquire such information even though Seeman and Evans (1962) provided some hints.

Davis and Phares (1967) found that when subjects believe they are going to attempt to change another's attitudes (in this case, attitudes about the Vietnam conflict), internals actively seek more information about the other person in order to be better equipped to wield influence. In further work, Phares (1968) found that internals are superior to externals in the utilization of information in solving a problem even when both groups have learned the information equally. Lefcourt and colleagues (Lefcourt & Wine, 1969; Lefcourt, Lewis, & Silverman, 1968) have also concluded that internals, more than externals, will pay attention to potentially information-relevant cues and will avoid task-irrelevant thoughts. It has also been found that internals are more adept at discovering the rule involved in a problem-solving task (DuCette & Wolk, 1973) and are superior in the realm of incidental learning (Wolk & DuCette, 1974). Taken as a whole, the preceding research clearly supports the conclusion that internals more actively seek, acquire, utilize, and process information that is relevant to their manipulation and control over the environment.

Along with these tendencies (and perhaps because of them), internals generally appear more competent and personally effective than externals. Evidence of the foregoing occurs across a wide range of data, but we will save till later that data dealing specifically with issues of adjustment. Phares, Ritchie, and Davis (1968) reported that when subjects were given threatening feedback regarding their personality, internals were somewhat more disturbed by that feedback than were externals. At the same time, the internals were significantly more likely to express a willingness to take remedial action to deal with their personality problems.

In another approach, Phares (1965) found that internal experimenters were more persuasive and effective in inducing attitude change in their subjects than were external experimenters. This evidence is consistent with that of Hersch and Scheibe (1967), who note that internals describe themselves as more active, striving, achieving, powerful, independent, and effective. Finally, Tseng (1970) found that internal vocational rehabilitation clients were rated by their instructors as more proficient and as possessing better personal qualities than were external clients.

Needs and Power

It is interesting to speculate on the possibility that internals are motivated by *needs* for personal control and efficacy or what might be roughly depicted as power. In other words, perhaps the internal's superior information seeking, learning, and utilization of information is mediated not only by expectancy considerations (with respect to both success and locus of control) but also by needs.

Rotter and Mulry (1965) used decision time as an indirect measure of the value of a reinforcement. They asked subjects to perform a difficult perceptual matching task described to some as involving skill and to others as being entirely a matter of chance. They found that internals took longer to decide on their responses when the instructions involved skill, whereas externals took longer in the chance condition (although the bulk of the difference was a function of the internals in the skill condition). If one accepts decision time as a measure of need to do well (valuing the reinforcement), then Rotter and Mulry's results are supportive of the notion that internals are motivated to do well in skill situations and externals by a desire to succeed under chance conditions. Julian and Katz (1968) have presented data that is consistent with that of Rotter and Mulry. Similarly, Watson and Baumal (1967) report that internals make more errors under chance conditions whereas externals are more error prone under skill conditions. These authors argue that such errors are determined by anxiety produced by tasks that are not congruent with subjects' generalized expectancies for control of reinforcement. Hrycenko and Minton (1974) found that, in males, satisfaction with a power position (high or low) is determined by both the degree of power possessed and locus of control orientation. Internals are more oriented toward high power and externals toward low power.

Preference for certain kinds of activities is also relevant here. Schneider (1972) found not only that internals prefer skill activities whereas chance activities are preferred by externals but that sex of the subject and the active-passive nature of the activities are important determinants of preferences.

The foregoing work supports the view that I–E contains a motivational element. However, a word of caution. The preceding work has probably not adequately controlled for expectancy for success. In a later section we will argue that externals' preference for nonskill tasks or activities is mediated by their low expectancies for success on skill tasks. Therefore, the external's preference for nonskill activities may be less than real; rather, it may really be a desire to avoid failure on skill activities.

INFLUENCE, CONFORMITY, AND ATTITUDE CHANGE

We noted in the previous section that internals were active and controlling individuals. Resistance to others who seek to influence them would seem to be an obvious corollary since to do otherwise would result in relinquishing one's sense of personal efficacy and control. In any event, acceptance by an internal of the control of another will most certainly be thoughtful and analytic rather than blind and unthinking.

Conformity and Influence

Research by Crowne and Liverant (1963) suggests that internals are better able to resist group pressures than are externals, at least when tested in an Asch-like conformity situation. Similarly, Tolor (1971) found that when a stationary light was suggested to be moving, externals were more likely to acquiesce and see the moving light.

Subtle influence is regarded by many as an especially corrosive form of influence since it tends to rob one of freedom of choice. Gore (1962) focused on this kind of influence by exerting either subtle influence, overt influence, or no influence in a situation in which subjects were asked to generate stories of specified length in response to TAT cards. In neither the no-influence nor the overt-influence conditions did internals and externals differ in the length of stories produced. Under subtle influence conditions, however, internals (unlike externals) became negativistic and actually produced shorter stories rather than the longer ones being subtly requested. Biondo and MacDonald (1971) found conformity in externals and resistance by internals to high influence. Internals did not, however, manifest reactance to a low influence condition as was the case for Gore's subtle influence.

Verbal Conditioning

Operant conditioning of verbal responses represents another excellent arena in which to observe the differential responsiveness of internals and externals since it is a situation in which one person, through dispensing reinforcements (usually unobtrusive), tries to influence the verbal behavior of another. Furthermore, since verbal conditioning paradigms can be construed as occasions for the operation of subtle influence, it is interesting from this vantage point to note the differential behavior of internals and externals.

Getter (1966) found that those who conditioned well tended to be external. This finding is expected, given the postulated greater suggestibility and conformity of externals. However, Getter also found a group of so-called "latent conditioners." These were subjects who showed little evidence of conditioning during training trials but manifested conditioning during extinction trials when there was no reinforcement. These subjects were predominantly internal in orientation. Strickland (1970) supports these results although evidence from somewhat different experimental arrangements is not supportive (Lichtenstein & Craine, 1969). Still other verbal conditioning work by Doctor (1971), requiring subjects to construct sentences, does suggest the greater resistance of internals to subtle influence and externals' greater compliance and responsivity.

Jolley and Spielberger (1973) report that only those subjects who were aware of the reinforcement nature of the situation showed evidence of verbal conditioning and that I–E did not affect the performance of unaware subjects. Among the subjects who were aware, high-anxiety externals were more responsive than were high-anxiety internals but, in the case of low anxiety, the I–E results reversed themselves. Recent work by Alegre and Murray (1974) showed that among aware subjects, verbal conditioning is greatest in externals, less in mid-range subjects, and least in internals. Furthermore, externals seemed to intend to cooperate with the experimental demands of the situation.

All in all, then, verbal conditioning work supports the contention that externals are more susceptible to social influence than are internals.

Attitude Change

The greater persuasibility of externals is also reflected in studies of attitude change. Ritchie and Phares (1969) found that externals changed more in response to a high-prestige source than they did to a low-prestige source. They also responded more to a high-prestige source than did internals. Internals manifested similar attitude change across both low- and high-prestige sources. Thus, externals seem differentially responsive to amount of prestige. These results are supported by the research of Ryckman, Rodda, and Sherman (1972) and by that of McGinnies and Ward (1974), although the latter work suggests caution in generalizing from subjects of one nationality to another. Sherman (1973) found that internals show greater attitude change after they have written counter-attitudinal messages, whereas externals revealed the greatest change after reading a persuasive message. Finally, a study by Snyder and Larson (1972) indicates that greater acceptance of interpretations about one's personality is related to an external locus of control.

The general conclusion from the work cited appears to be that externals are more readily persuasible, conforming, and accepting of information from others. Those effects seem enhanced in the presence of prestige. Internals, on the other hand, seem to react negatively to subtle attempts to influence them. The reasons for such differences probably reside in expectancy, values, or a combination of both. That is, externals may be more susceptible simply because of their relatively low expectancy for the success of their own *unaided* efforts or perhaps because of a disbelief in their *unaided* ability to control outcomes. Similarly, internals may have greater confidence in their own competence. From the standpoint of values, it is possible that internals prefer personal control and abhor manipulation by others. Future research that deals systematically with both expectancy and values simultaneously can best deal with this question.

SOCIAL ACTIVISM

Some years ago Gore and Rotter (1963) and Strickland (1965) showed that in southern black college students an increasing commitment to social action in the area of civil rights was associated with an internal locus of control.

But times change. Phares (1976) has observed that much of the later work in civil rights suggests a greater proclivity for social action by externals. Lao (1970) found expected evidence for greater competence in academics by internal blacks. But in the realm of sociopolitical events, external blacks predominated. Silvern and Nakamura (1971), Thomas (1970), and others find similar results. Whatever the cause, research in this area is inconsistent; some indicate internals as being more action oriented, and some reveal externals as being more action oriented.

What is clear, however, is that most of this research has failed adequately to conceptualize the interplay between I–E and reinforcement values (Phares, 1976; Rotter, 1975). Before one predicts that internals will be more active, one must make sure that internals as a group place a high value on the "cause" or goal toward which the action is directed. Similarly, before one rules out action taking by externals, one must be certain that the importance of the issue involved does not overpower the locus of control, such that both internals *and* externals are active.

Because of the greater politicizing of the country in the last decade, it is quite likely that I–E scores have changed somewhat in their meaning (and this may have affected the factor structure of the I–E Scale as noted earlier). In any case, we must recognize that social activism is probably motivated by different considerations as times change, and we must be careful to incorporate these considerations (values and expectations) into our thinking as we attempt to relate locus of control to social activism.

HELPING AND THE ATTRIBUTION OF RESPONSIBILITY

Social action can be viewed as a kind of helping behavior. Although research on social action is conflicting vis-a-vis I–E, evidence of a more direct nature suggests that internals are more likely to offer assistance to others. In laboratory studies involving tests of skilled performance, subjects low in fatalism (internals) were observed more often to help another subject in difficulty than were external or subjects high in fatalism (Midlarsky, 1971; Midlarsky & Midlarsky, 1973). The factors that stimulate greater helping in internals are not clear. It could be the greater competence and self-confidence of the internal. In the Midlarsky experiments such factors seem especially reasonable. Although greater altruism in internals is a possibility, research to be discussed below would seem to argue against such an explanation. Certainly the determinants of helping behavior are complex and may be highly tied to the specific helping situation in question.

The concept of assimilative projection, the tendency of people to attribute their own self-perceptions to others, would suggest that internals ought to be less helping of others. Thus, if internals tend to regard other people as more responsible for their own situation than do externals, then they should be less helping than externals. Both Phares and Wilson (1972) and Sosis (1974) have found support for the notion of greater responsibility attributed to others by internals. Perhaps holding another responsible for an event is also to predetermine to a degree whether one will help that other person, be kind to him, and so on, although, admittedly, the Midlarsky studies argue otherwise.

In any event, utilizing the foregoing analysis, Phares and Lamiell (1974) studied the ratings subjects made of several case histories. Subjects were asked to rate these case histories along several general dimensions. Internals were observed to be less prone to sanction help, sympathy, or financial aid. Although such lessened altruism (presumably because of greater attributed responsibility to others for their plight) would seem to contradict the work of Midlarsky, perhaps such variables as the face-to-face nature of the helping situation and the degree to which it engages the internal's achievement orientation are important.

LOCUS OF CONTROL AND ACHIEVEMENT

School Achievement

The relationships bewteen locus of control and achievement are limited, although many people seem to expect nearly a one-to-one relationship between them. In children, internals show greater school achievement than do externals (Coleman, Campbell, Hobson, McPartland, Mood, Weinfeld, & York, 1966; Crandall, Katkovsky, & Preston, 1962; McGhee & Crandall, 1968; e.g.). Very often, IAR (Crandall et al., 1965) has been used as the measure of locus of control.

However, as we move nearer to college-age subjects, the relationship declines or else proves to be inconsistent and elusive (Phares, 1976). Several reasons are possible. First, in the case of college students, school is a highly structured and very familiar experience. Such things as study habits or other specific academic experiences may be much more important in college than locus of control, whereas the reverse may be true in primary and secondary school, which are perhaps more ambiguous or uncertain situations for students (Rotter, 1975). Furthermore, college samples are much more homogeneous as regards both ability and internality. This should significantly lessen the correlation between grades and I–E.

Need for Achievement

When we move to the relationships between I–E and measures of *need* for achievement, the picture is even less clear. At best, relationships are modest. Although people high in need for achievement (n Ach) are very likely to be internally oriented, there is no reason to expect all low n Ach people to be external. Nor should all internals be expected to be uniformly high in achievement motivation. In addition, most measures of n Ach (particularly projective ones) are amalgams of expectancies, behaviors, and needs. This failure to differentiate makes predictions to I–E difficult and confusing. Furthermore, recent work, to be discussed later, has identified "defensive externals." These persons are internals who espouse external attitudes as a defense against anticipated failure. Such persons may be quite achievement oriented, but their defensive statement of external beliefs will lower any relationships between n Ach and I–E.

Relationships in this area are also often clouded by sex differences. Relationships often appear for males but not for females—perhaps because of cultural differences in the expectations for achievement aroused early in boys and girls. It is perhaps such considerations that are responsible for the finding that, in women, fear of success is associated with an external locus of control (Midgley & Abrams, 1974).

Another facet of achievement is the attribution of responsibility for success and failure. If one consistently attributes his performance outcomes to external forces, then he is denied the experiences of pride and satisfaction that are so necessary to sustain achievement efforts over time (Karabenick, 1972). Unwillingness to assume responsibility for personal failures should also impede achievement (Phares, Wilson, & Klyver, 1971; Davis & Davis, 1972; Krovetz, 1974).

The capacity to forgo smaller, immediate rewards for large, delayed rewards seems to be an essential attribute of the achieving personality. In general, research has been supportive of the hypothesis that internals (especially among school-age children) are significantly more capable of delaying rewards (Bialer, 1961; Strickland, 1972, 1973). The size of the relationship is often mediated by the nature of the population, the experimenter, and the specific experimental method employed. However, as Lefcourt (1972) has pointed out, the research in this area has more often than not been conducted in somewhat trivial, circumscribed experimental situations.

ADJUSTMENT, ANXIETY, AND PATHOLOGY

We observed earlier that the concept of locus of control owes its origins to attempts to understand the behavior of a patient in therapy (Phares, 1976). Thus, it is surely no accident that a persistent focus of I–E research has been in the areas of adjustment, anxiety, and, more recently, defensiveness.

Adjustment

The observation has been made that locus of control beliefs are related to physical well-being (Strickland, 1974). The same relationship appears to hold for psychological well-being, or adjustment. Perhaps the more active, striving, and self-reliant qualities of internals lead to greater success and are responsible for this latter relationship. Or perhaps the simple belief the internal has in his own personal control leads to better personal adjustment and less anxiety. Because most of the evidence is strictly correlational, as with many of the other findings presented in this chapter, it is very difficult to disentangle cause from effect.

The number of studies supporting the view that externality is associated with maladjustment and anxiety is so large that we cannot deal with them individually here. They are reviewed at greater length elsewhere (Joe, 1971; Phares, 1976, Strickland, 1974; see also Hersch & Scheibe, 1967; Strassberg, 1973). Nearly all this research suggests that the relationships between I–E and maladjustment or anxiety are linear. The earliest hypotheses about the nature of locus of control suggested a curvilinear relationship. It was felt that *extreme* internals, for example, could be so obsessed with personal responsibility that extreme guilt and remorse would produce maladjstument. And extreme externals would become such social misfits that they would surely be maladjusted. The failure to verify these curvilinear relationships may stem from the adjustment measures used, the populations used (often inherently better adjusted than the population at large), or the nature of the adjustment criteria employed. It is also well to recall our earlier caution about regarding internals as the "good guys." As Felton and Kahana (1974) found in an elderly population, circumstances can easily result in a correlation between high morale and feelings of external control. Wolk and Kurtz (1975) also comment on the potential for the situation to mediate the relationship between I–E and adjustment.

Schizophrenia

Beyond the preceding relationships, external beliefs often seem to characterize a variety of psychiatric groups. For example, Cromwell, Rosenthal, Shakow, and Zahn (1961) found a sample of male schizophrenics to be more external than normal control subjects. Harrow and Ferrante (1969) and others have confirmed a similar relationship. Furthermore, within a schizophrenic population, process schizophrenics (having a poorer premorbid adjustment pattern) were found to be more external than reactive schizophrenics (whose adjustment problems had a more recent history) (Lottman & DeWolfe, 1972). The specific role of I–E in schizophrenia and its cause–effect relationships are yet to be determined.

Depression

In the case of depression one might also expect to find locus of control implicated. In a sense, encountering failures or other negative outcomes should lead internals, who harbor strong feelings of personal responsibility, to get depressed

(Phares, 1972). On the other hand, the external's powerlessness and low expectancies for personal control might also produce a depressed reaction. This latter view is compatible with Seligman's (1975) position that regards depression as a kind of passivity with a corresponding negative cognitive set regarding the effects of the individual's behavior. Hiroto's (1974) work is supportive here in suggesting that external beliefs, chance conditions, and inescapable pretreatment learning all retard the development of escape behavior. Other work has found a correlation between externality and depressive self-report (Calhoun, Cheney, & Dawes, 1974; Naditch, Gargen, & Michael, 1975; Warehime & Foulds, 1971).

Thus far it is impossible to disentangle the variables and assert with confidence that depression relates to an external orientation and is unrelated to internal beliefs. A variety of factors could be obscuring relationships here, including the potentially pessimistic wording of external items (Lamont, 1972), possible relationships between internality and social desirability, and the possible difference between assuming responsibility for failures and successes. In addition, the presence of defensive externals, to be discussed below, (who are basically internally oriented) in a sample may seriously inflate the relationship between externality and depression.

Alcoholics and Narcotics Users

Since an external orientation seems to so often accompany indices of maladjustment, one might expect that alcoholics or heavy drinkers will be externally oriented. Nowicki and Hopper (1974) and Palmer (1971) have reported such findings. However, both Goss and Morosko (1970) and Gozali and Sloan (1971) found the reverse relationship. Phares (1976) attempted to resolve this apparent contradiction by pointing out that chronic alcoholics often have a history of institutitonalization and participation in treatment programs that reinforce the verbalization of confidence, self-control, and personal responsibility. Recent work by Naditch (1975) with noninstitutionalized drinkers would seem to reinforce such an analysis.

In the case of narcotics users, Berzins and Ross (1973) found that users are more internally oriented than are nonusers. However, there is a question as to whether the sample of users (hospitalized Lexington USPHS patients) was adequately matched with nonusers (University of Kentucky students). Strassberg and Robinson (1974) found that within a user population the expression of external attitudes was associated with greater maladjustment.

DEFENSIVENESS

Much of the work presented above clearly indicates that externals more readily admit to maladjustment. In contrast, internals manifest a more repressing or forgetting approach. For example, Efran (1963) noted that internals are more likely than externals to forget failure, and Lipp, Kolstoe, James, and Randall (1968) reported that handicapped internals showed higher recognition thresholds for threatening stimuli than did similar externals. Phares et al. (1968) found that when subjects were given threatening feedback regarding their personality, internals were less likely to recall the unfavorable feedback than were externals. All this research taken together indicates that externals have less need to repress unfavorable or threatening information. Internals thus seem to use the defense of repression.

In a kind of parallel to Byrne's work (e.g., 1964) on repression-sensitization, externals may be more open about their pathology or anxieties and will thus be more likely regarded as maladjusted. Obviously, however, in the final analysis, we have no universally accepted body of data that proves that those who openly contemplate their anxieties are more maladjusted than those who repress. A case can be made for either side. And in the final analysis adjustment is a value judgment whose ultimate definition cannot be provided by psychology or psychiatry.

Phares et al. (1968) observed that, although some behavior of internals seemed to be disrupted by failure, those same internals professed a greater willingness than externals to take steps to resolve their personality problems. Thus, the immediate maladjusted reactions of internals may turn out, in the long run, to be a kind of facilitative anxiety that ultimately leads to greater, more successful coping efforts (and thus to a lessening in anxiety).

This consideration, along with data that suggest inferior coping–mastery behavior in externals, may mean that externals will confront failure more often. How does one mitigate the personal effects of such failure? One technique is the devaluation of the goals that one fails to achieve. The potential for such a "sour grapes" approach led Phares (1971) to predict that externals will manifest greater evidence of such devaluation of goals following failure than will internals. Using intelligence subtests as tasks, Phares was able to verify his hypothesis. Along the same lines, Phares and Lamiell (1974) found that externals, anticipating failure, will choose to perform tasks that offer a built-in rationalization for subsequent failure.

Attribution of responsibility, discussed earlier, is an excellent technique externals can use to lessen the impact of failure. For example, Phares et al. (1971) gave both internals and externals failure experiences under two conditions—one where environmental distractions were present and one where they were not. As expected, externals, following failure in the nondistractive condition, blamed environmental factors more than did internals. Under distractive conditions there were no differences between the two groups. In a more elaborate study, Davis and Davis (1972) found that after failure internals resorted to blaming themselves more than did externals. Following success, there was no difference in the two groups in assuming personal responsibility. The study of Gilmor and Minton (1974), while somewhat equivocal, is less supportive.

Weiss and Sherman (1973) assumed that internals will see failure as owing to their own behavior. They therefore hypothesized that internals will work harder following failure than will externals. Their results supported this prediction and suggested also that externals reduce their original expectancy for success after they have failed. Recent work by Lamiell and Phares (1975) is also supportive here.

Defensive Externality

Almost from the inception of the concept of locus of control, it was hypothesized that for some individuals the statement of external beliefs serves a defensive function (Phares, 1973, 1976; Rotter, 1966). Hersch and Scheibe (1967) commented on the greater heterogeneity that has always seemed to characterize externals although more recently Parsons and Schneider (1974), in cross-cultural work, have found the expected evidence of passivity and fatalism in externals. But of course, most work in America on externals has used college students who, in many ways, seem quite achievement oriented.

Davis (1970) tried to distinguish "defensive" from "congruent" externals by means of an action-taking questionnaire. Congruent externals in a college population were defined as having high external scores and also as being unwilling to take action to improve their academic standing. This definition reflects the classical picture of the passive, nonachievement-oriented external. Defensive externals, on the other hand, were defined not only in terms of high external scores but also in terms of a willingness to sign up for remedial study techniques. The latter behavior is at variance with the usual passive orientation of the external. As she expected, Davis found that defensive externals placed a higher value on academic goals and manifested a greater discrepancy between the value of these goals and the expectation of their attainment (an expression of maladjustment possibly resulting from excessively high goals) than did congruent externals. She also noted that defensive externals and internals engaged in more information-seeking behavior than did congruent externals.

Another method of separating defensive and congruent externals has been utilized by Hochreich (1968), who used the Interpersonal Trust Scale (Rotter, 1967) in conjunction with I–E. Thus, subjects high in externality and low in trust could be construed as people who use blame projection as a technique for coping with failure. Such a characteristic defense is consonant with a distrustful attitude toward others. Congruent or passive externals, on the other hand, are those who express both high trust and high externality.

Hochreich (1974) found that male defensive externals under failure conditions attributed less responsibility to story heroes than did either true externals or internals—a finding accentuated when heroes failed in achievement situations. These results did not, however, occur with female subjects. Furthermore, in the case of males, defensive externals were more likely than congruent externals or internals to describe themselves unfavorably by means of an adjective checklist. An additional study by Hochreich (1975b) used a questionnaire to assess blame projection in subjects following failure. Again, defensive externals were more likely than congruent externals or internals to direct blame for their failure to factors other than themselves.

Another approach to the identification of defensive externals is a postulated tendency for defensive externals to endorse failure items on the I–E scale in preference to success items. Such hypothesized tendencies were not observed in a study of adults (Rotter, 1966) but do seem to be operative in the case of children (Crandall et al. 1965; Mischel et al. 1974).

Levenson's (1973a, 1973b) Internal, Powerful Others, and Chance scales have also proved useful here. For example, Prociuk and Breen (1975) used these scales and found that defensive externals were academically superior to congruent externals. This finding may help to account for the results discussed earlier, which showed little achievement differences between internal and external college students. The presence of large numbers of defensive externals may easily have attenuated differences.

An essential aspect of the defensive externality concept is the assumption that the external responses of defensive externals reflect a desire to escape responsibility for anticipated failure. It is quite probable that a significant portion of college student externals are, in fact, defensive externals. Were they really congruent externals, attendance in college and the pursuit of achievement goals would seem to contradict the passivity normally seen in such externals. Data from several investigators suggest that college student externals do possess rather low generalized expectancies (Nelson & Phares, 1971; Phares & Lamiell, 1974; Strassberg, 1973). Thus, their external scores could be serving a defensive function in the sense of being prompted by a desire to rationalize anticipated failure. The previously cited work with college samples is also entirely consistent with this interpretation (Davis & Davis, 1972; Phares, 1971; Phares & Lamiell, 1974; Phares et al., 1971).

Evidence from several sources suggests the potentially defensive role that externality may play even though that research does not specifically differentiate between congruent and defensive externals. For example, research indicates an association between externality and a preference for success on chance-related tasks (Julian & Katz, 1968; Rotter & Mulry, 1965; Schneider, 1972). Although usually these studies are interpreted in a straightforward fashion, it is possible that these chance preferences reflect not a preference for chance activities but rather reflect a low expectancy for success on skill tasks, thus leading externals to choose chance tasks rather than to risk failing on a skill task. This possibility gains more force when we consider that most of these studies of preference value have not really adequately matched (or otherwise controlled) internals and externals as regards their expectancies for success.

More recently, Phares and Lamiell (1974) reported a greater preference on the part of external college students to perform on poorly constructed intelligence tests as compared to internals. In this fashion, an external can explain away failure as being owing to a poor test. At the same time, he can accept the label of "intelligence test" should he later succeed.

This research, then, suggests the hypothesis that in college student externals (many of whom may be defensive externals), choosing chance tasks or poorly constructed intelligence tests may stem less from the value of these tasks than from a fear of doing poorly on skill tasks or well-constructed intelligence tests.

Recent work by Lamiell and Phares (1975) attempted to investigate these latter possibilities. Male college students were given descriptions of four so-called intelligence tests that varied in the extent to which ability or factors beyond the subject's control determined one's score. Subjects were asked on which test it was most important for them to succeed. Careful instructions also led them to expect either a 0.85, 0.50, or 0.15 probability of succeeding on the skilled version of the test. It was found that when probability of success was low, external subjects in particular tended to choose the nonskill test in preference to the noncontrollable task. However, their preference for the skilled test tended to increase when probability of success was high. Internals, on the other hand, tended to be less influenced by the probability of success factor. Such data seem consistent with the view that externals' chance preferences really stem from lowered expectancies for success on skilled tasks.

It is not meant to imply that the beliefs of all externals are defensive in nature. Indeed, as we will see later, many externals, such as ghetto inhabitants and lower socioeconomic groups, very likely contain a heavy proportion of people whose external locus of control beliefs are veridical rather than defensive. However, it does appear feasible to regard the external college group as containing many defensive externals.

The goal in all of this is not to determine who is *really* maladjusted or threatened. Rather, the goal is to better predict and understand behavior in various groups. We can do this by searching for variables or techniques that will enhance the utility of I–E (for example, through moderator variables such as trust and powerful other scales, and techniques such as action-taking questionnaires, etc.) and by carefully examining the role played by expectancies for success and reinforcement values. The quest is not for labels but for understanding.

SOME ANTECEDENTS OF LOCUS OF CONTROL

In this section we will examine some of the social and familial determinants of locus of control. In general, research in this area is sparse, inconclusive, and heavily correlational in nature. This is unfortunate since an understanding of how

I–E beliefs develop is important for our successful use of the locus of control concept. Although solid research here is difficult and time consuming to execute, it is hoped that future research efforts will show more focus in the area of antecedents.

Family

By and large, parents who exhibit warm, protective, positive, and nurturant child-rearing practices spawn children who develop an internal locus of control. Obviously, these are broad and rather vague characterizations that have stemmed basically from correlations between paper-and-pencil measures of both I–E in the child and parental child-rearing practices (e.g., Chance, 1965; Davis & Phares, 1969; Nowicki & Segal, in press). Consistency of parental reinforcement, discipline, and standards also seem linked to the development of internality, especially in boys (Davis & Phares, 1969; Levenson, 1973b; MacDonald, 1971a). Earlier born children tend to be somewhat more internal, but the effects are often small, sex-linked, and variable in their manifestation (Chance, 1965; Crandall, et al., 1965; MacDonald, 1971b; Marks, 1973).

Social Factors

With respect to social antecedents, the research clearly suggests a relationship between social class and locus of control. The lower one goes down the socioeconomic scale, the more one finds evidence of external beliefs. Of course, those ethnic and minority groups that possess little access to social or economic power and mobility are going to be overrepresented in the external group. Work by Battle and Rotter (1963), Lefcourt and Ladwig (1966), Zytkoskee, Strickland, and Watson (1971), along with many others, reports greater internality in whites as compared to black samples. The general role of culture has been examined by Hsieh et al. (1969), Jessor et al. (1968), and Parsons et al. (1970).

Little in the preceding research tells us in detail what the specific mechanisms are that mediate the relationship between I–E and social class, race, or ethnic background. Is it direct teaching in the family or peer group, veridical experiences as a minority member in the larger society, so-called national character factors, or what? Only more extensive research can answer these questions.

FACTORS LEADING TO CHANGES IN LOCUS OF CONTROL

So many seemingly desirable outcomes are associated with locus of control, sometimes with internality, perhaps sometimes with externality, that knowledge of the conditions that change I–E beliefs becomes very important. Therefore, in this section we will be concerned with I–E not as a variable that affects behavior but as a variable that is itself influenced by the person's experiences or surroundings. Again, we must be careful not to overgeneralize from this discussion and thereby regard everything internal as good and everything external as bad. There are surely many situations where this will be reversed.

Age Factors

Growth in the extent of belief in internal control may be expected with increasing age. Research by Penk (1969) and Crandall et al. (1965) supports the view that, as the child develops, he becomes a more effective human being and thus increases his belief in internal control. However, there are many complications. Events in the life of the individual that lead to a fear of loss of control might easily result in changes in an external direction. For example, fear of loss of parental support as one leaves high school (Crandall et al, 1965) may temporarily retard internal beliefs. Similarly, the plight of many aging poor or else those whose physical deterioration makes them dependent on others would likely lead to an increase in externality.

Little data exist in regard to these questions, and what do exist are complex. For example, Wolk and Kurtz (1975) observe that the internal scores of their elderly sample are much higher than might be expected. This finding could result from many factors, including the general affluence and health of the sample. It could also indicate that this sample reached adulthood in a more "internal" era as compared to today's adolescents and young adults who are assaulted by a world that pushes them toward alienation. Certainly what is important is not age itself but what age reflects in the way of present circumstances, prior learning, and so on.

Experience in a Reformatory

The element of present circumstances is particularly evident in the research of Kiehlbauch (1967), who found that the I–E scores of reformatory inmates over time showed a curvilinear shape. Using a cross-sectional approach, he noted that newly admitted inmates were relatively more external than inmates about half-way through their sentence. Inmates about to be released showed a reversion to a more external level. A logical interpretation here is that a new inmate is still unsure about the institution, its rules and power sources, thus leading to feelings of external control. By the midpoint of his sentence the inmate "knows his way around" and expresses stronger feelings of internal control. As he is about to be released, old fears assail him—can he find a job, will his wife accept him, and so on? Interestingly, a work release sample who functioned in jobs outside the reformatory for several months prior to release did not show the reversion to externality. Presumably, their work gave them a better sense of control through experiences in the community.

The Generality and Stability of Changes

Both Schneider (1971) and Phares (1976) have commented on the marked increase in external scores over the past decade. This increase has been particularly obvious in college student populations, whose sensitivities to events such as the Vietnam conflict, Watergate, nuclear bombs, and so on are well known.

Are these changes stable or transitory? Longitudinal research yet to be done can best answer such a question. However, it is true that several studies report changes in I–E scores that seem to be largely a function of transitory, specific experiences. Whether these effects are long-term is highly uncertain. Gorman (1968) found evidence of increases in externality in some political supporters of Eugene McCarthy following their disappointment in actions of the Democratic National Convention. McArthur (1970) reports increases in externality in students following their experience with the draft lottery. Eisenman (1972) notes a similar phenomenon following a specific experience in an experiment.

Training and Experience

There has been some research to assess the effects of training programs on I–E socres. Using the Origin–Pawn notion, which has strong similarity to the concept of locus of control, deCharms (1972) tried to enhance the growth of feelings of personal causation in black elementary school teachers and their pupils. Using a highly structured series of training exercises, deCharms found that feelings of enhanced personal causation positively affected the behavior of both teachers and pupils, particularly in increasing certain facets the latter's academic performance. Supporting evidence has also been offered by Tyre and Maisto (1974).

In related work, Nowicki and Barnes (1973) found that a highly structured camp experience enhanced the internal control beliefs of a group of inner city adolescents. Both Levens (1968) and Gottesfeld and Dozier (1966) have shown how community organizational experience can affect internal beliefs.

Effects of Therapy

A large number of recent studies have attempted to show how therapeutic experiences of one sort or another can affect I–E scores. Lefcourt (1966b) very early recognized that psychotherapy can positively influence internal locus of control scores (Dua, 1970; Gillis & Jessor, 1970; Smith, 1970) and that internals are better therapeutic risks (Kilman & Howell, 1974).

Much recent research has been designed to determine which form of therapy is better for internals and which for externals. Abramowitz, Abramowitz, Roback, and Jackson (1974) found that internals responded better to a nondirective approach, whereas the reverse held for externals. Work by Friedman and Dies (1974) suggests that internals will respond better when therapy involves relatively greater client control, whereas externals prefer greater structure and control by the therapist. A similar inference could be made from a study by Kilman, Albert, and Sotile (1975).

Helweg (1971) observed that students and patients who preferred the directive approach of Ellis over the nondirective approach of Rogers were more dogmatic and also more external. Jacobsen (1971) found similar results, although Wilson (1973) feels that such results may be partly determined by biased presentations of therapy descriptions to potential patients.

Certainly the preceding work represents an encouraging trend toward research designed to investigate patient and therapist (or technique) matching to determine the optimum combination for improvement. Such research is important in helping better to understand the phenomenon of therapy; the research also points out again the ubiquitous role of locus of control. Even in an area as apparently remote as weight reduction, research has revealed that an internal locus of control increases the potential for successful loss of weight (Balch & Ross, 1975) and that successful weight loss, in turn, tends to enhance one's internal locus of control (Jeffrey, 1974).

CONCLUSIONS

In the preceding pages, we presented the origins, theoretical context, measurement, and correlates of locus of control. Because the research effort and output have been so prodigious over the past few years, our bibliography is lengthy. But even so, it is only a representative sample of the much larger number of studies that have been published.

Although some may dismiss I–E as a fad, such a label does little to explain this burgeoning volume of research. Most behavior is complexly determined, and research activity is no exception. However, a prime factor in research on I–E seems to be the simple recognition that individual differences in interpretation of reinforcement are bound to be highly important contributors to behavior. That statement subsumes such factors as relevance. Indeed, relevance may only be a code word for the fact that many individuals in our society respond to events or reinforcements as if they themselves were controlled by others, by fate, or by a technological and bureaucratic world that is enormously complex. It may be such modern sociopolitical situations, along with the alienated people they have produced, that have in part forced us to rethink some of our simplistic notions of the role of reinforcement, thereby enhancing our awareness of individual differences in learning and behavior.

Our survey of the I–E literature has revealed the typical internal to be one who actively comes to grips with the world. Compared to the external, the internal is resistant to social pressure and dedicated to the pursuit of excellence. Although the external may appear more maladjusted, we must be wary of thinking in terms of labels. In the final analysis, adjustment cannot be defined apart from values and must be examined in the light of the situational constraints on the individual.

Although we know something about how people both develop their locus of control orientations and change them, our information is incomplete. In view of the pervasive effects exerted on behavior by locus of control, it is obvious that one of the most important and challenging areas for future research lies in the search for antecedents and for methods of altering I–E beliefs.

More sensitive scales will probably be developed. Some are under construction, and others have been recently produced. It is hoped such scales will offer the possibility of multidimensional measurement. However, the utilization of a theoretical framework and an awareness of the conceptual problems involved will undoubtedly be helpful (Phares, 1976; Rotter, 1975).

The concept of locus of control began with speculations about the unusual behavior of a patient in psychotherapy. Both the improvement of that patient and the force of accumulated research on locus of control have taught us that I–E can be a useful tool. But locus of control also offers us insight into what is possible in the way of human behavior. Such an awareness helps to provide the potential for change in the human situation.

REFERENCES

Abramowitz, C. V., Abramowitz, S. I., Roback, H. B., & Jackson, C. Differential effectiveness of directive and nondirective group therapies as a function of client internal-external control. *Journal of Consulting and Clinical Psychology,* 1974, *42,* 849–853.

Adams-Webber, J. Generalized expectancies concerning the locus of control of reinforcements and the perception of moral sanctions. *British Journal of Social and Clinical Psychology,* 1969, *8,* 340–343.

Alegre, C., & Murray, E. J. Locus of control, behavioral intention, and verbal conditioning. *Journal of Personality,* 1974, *42,* 668–681.

Balch, P., & Ross, A. W. Predicting success in weight reduction as a function of locus of control: A unidimensional and multidimensional approach. *Journal of Consulting and Clinical Psychology,* 1975, *43,* 119.

Battle, E., & Rotter, J. B. Children's feelings of personal control as related to social class and ethnic groups. *Journal of Personality,* 1963, *31,* 482–490.

Berzins, J. I., & Ross, W. F. Locus of control among opiate addicts. *Journal of Consulting and Clinical Psychology,* 1973, *40,* 84–91.

Bettelheim, B. *The informed heart.* New York: Free Press, 1960.

Bialer, I. Conceptualization of success and failure in mentally retarded and normal children. *Journal of Personality,* 1961, *29,* 303–320.

Biondo, J., & MacDonald, A. P. Internal-external locus of control and response to influence attempts. *Journal of Personality,* 1971, *39,* 407–419.

Brady, J. V., Porter, R. W., Conrad, D. G., & Mason, J. W. Avoidance behavior and the development of gastroduodenal ulcers. *Journal of Experimental Analysis of Behavior, 1958, 1,* 69–72.

Brehm, J. W. *Responses to loss of freedom: A theory of psychological reactance.* Morristown, N.J.: General Learning Press, 1972.

Byrne, D. The Repression–Sensitization Scale: Rationale, reliability and validity. In B. A. Maher (Ed.), *Progress in experimental personality research.* New York: Academic Press, 1964.

Calhoun, L. G., Cheney, T., & Dawes, A. S. Locus of control, self-reported depression, and perceived causes of depression. *Journal of Consulting and Clinical Psychology, 1974,42,* 736.

Chance, J. E. *Internal control of reinforcements and the school learning process.* Paper read at the Biennial Meeting of the Society for Research in Child Development, Minneapolis, April 1965.

Coleman, J. S., Campbell, E. Q., Hobson, C. J., McPartland, J., Mood, A. M., Weinfeld, F. D., & York, R. L. *Equality of educational opportunity.* Superintendent of Documents Catalog No. FS 5.238:38001, U. S. Government Printing Office, Washington, D.C., 1966.

Collins, B. E. Four separate components of the Rotter I–E Scale: Belief in a difficult world, a just world, a predictable world, and a politically responsive world. *Journal of Personality and Social Psychology, 1974, 29,* 381–391.

Cooper, J. Personal responsibility and dissonance: The role of foreseen consequences. *Journal of Personality and Social Psychology, 1971, 18,* 354–363.

Corah, N. L., & Boffa, J. Perceived control, self-observation, and response to aversive stimulation. *Journal of Personality and Social Psychology, 1970, 16,* 1–4.

Crandall, V. C., Katkovsky, W., & Crandall, V. J. Children's beliefs in their control of reinforcements in intellectual-academic achievement situations. *Child Development, 1965, 36,* 91–109.

Crandall, V. J., Katkovsky, W., & Preston, A. Motivational and ability determinants of children's intellectual achievement behaviors. *Child Development,* 1962, *33,* 643–661.

Cromwell, R. L., Rosenthal, D., Shakow, D., & Zahn, T. P. Reaction time, locus of control, choice behavior, and descriptions of parental behavior in schizophrenic and normal subjects. *Journal of Personality,* 1961, *29,* 363–379.

Crowne, D. P., & Liverant, S. Conformity under varying conditions of personal commitment. *Journal of Abnormal and Social Psychology, 1963, 66,* 547–555.

D'Amato, M. E., & Gumenik, W. E. Some effects of immediate versus randomly delayed shock on an instrumental response and cognitive processes. *Journal of Abnormal and Social Psychology,* 1960, *60,* 64–67.

Davis, D. E. *Internal-external control and defensiveness.* Unpublished doctoral dissertation, Kansas State University, 1970.

Davis, W. L., & Davis, D. E. Internal-external control and attribution of responsibility for success and failure. *Journal of Personality,* 1972, *40,* 123–136.

Davis, W. L., & Phares, E. J. Internal-external control as a determinant of information-seeking in a social influence situation. *Journal of Personality, 1967, 35,* 547–561.

Davis, W. L., & Phares, E. J. Parental antecedents of internal-external control of reinforcement. *Psychological Reports,* 1969, *24,* 427–436.

deCharms, R. Personal causation training in the schools. *Journal of Applied Social Psychology,* 1972, *2,* 95–113.

Dies, R. R. Development of a projective measure of perceived locus of control. *Journal of Projective Techniques and Personality Assessment, 1968, 32,* 487–490.

Doctor, R. M. Locus of control of reinforcement and responsiveness to social influence. *Journal of Personality,* 1971, *39,* 542–551.

Dua, P. S. Comparison of the effects of behaviorally oriented action and psychotherapy reeducation on intraversion-extraversion, emotionality, and internal-external control. *Journal of Counseling Psychology,* 1970, *17,* 567–572.

DuCette, J., & Wolk, S. Locus of control and extreme behavior. *Journal of Consulting and Clinical Psychology,* 1972, *39,* 253–258.

DuCette, J., & Wolk, S. Cognitive and motivational correlates of generalized expectancies for control. *Journal of Personality and Social Psychology,* 1973, *26,* 420–426.

Efran, J. S. *Some personality determinants of memory for success and failure.* Unpublished doctoral dissertation, Ohio State University, 1963.

Eisenman, R. Experience in experiments and change in internal-external control scores. *Journal of Consulting and Clinical Psychology,* 1972, *39,* 434–435.

Felton, B., & Kahana, E. Adjustment and situationally bound locus of control among institutionalized aged. *Journal of Gerontology,* 1974, *29,* 295–301.

Festinger, L. *A theory of cognitive dissonance.* Stanford, Cal.: Stanford University Press, 1957.

Friedman, M. L., & Dies, R. R. Reactions of internal and external test anxious students to counseling and behavior therapies. *Journal of Consulting and Clinical Psychology,* 1974, *42,* 921.

Garza, R. T., & Ames, R. E. A comparison of Anglo- and Mexican-American college students on locus of control. *Journal of Consulting and Clinical Psychology,* 1974, *42,* 919.

Geer, J. H., Davison, G. C., & Gatchel, R. I. Reduction in stress in humans through nonveridical perceived control of aversive stimulation. *Journal of Personality and Social Psychology,* 1970, *16,* 731–738.

Getter, H. A personality determinant of verbal conditioning. *Journal of Personality,* 1966, *34,* 397–405.

Gillis, J. S., & Jessor, R. Effects of brief psychotherapy on belief in internal control: An exploratory study. *Psychotherapy: Theory, Research, and Practice,* 1970, *7,* 135–137.

Gilmore, T. M., & Minton, H. L. Internal versus external attribution of task performance as a function of locus of control, initial confidence and success–failure outcome. *Journal of Personality,* 1974, *42,* 159–174.

Glass, D. C., & Singer, J. E. *Urban stress: Experiments on noise and social stressors.* New York: Academic Press, 1972.

Gore, P. *Individual differences in the prediction of subject compliance to experimenter bias.* Unpublished doctoral dissertation, Ohio State University, 1962.

Gore, P., & Rotter, J. B. A personality correlate of social action. *Journal of Personality,* 1963, *31,* 58–64.

Gorman, B. S. An observation of altered locus of control following political disappointment. *Psychological Reports,* 1968, *23,* 1094.

Goss, A., & Morosko, I. E. Relations between a dimension of internal-external control and the MMPI with an alcoholic population. *Journal of Consulting and Clinical Psychology,* 1970, *34,* 189–192.

Gottesfeld, H., & Dozier, G. Changes in feelings of powerlessness in a community action program. *Psychological Reports,* 1966, *19,* 978.

Gozali, J., & Sloan, J. Control orientation as a personality dimension among alcoholics. *Quarterly Journal of Studies on Alcohol,* 1971, *32,* 159–161.

Gruen, G. E., Korte, J. R., & Baum, J. R. Group measure of locus of control. *Developmental Psychology*, 1974, *10*, 683–686.

Gruen, G. E., & Ottinger, D. R. Skill and chance orientations as determiners of problem-solving in lower- and middle-class children. *Psychological Reports*, 1969, *24*, 207–214.

Gurin, P., Gurin, G., Lao, R., & Beattie, M. Internal-external control in the motivational dynamics of Negro youth. *Journal of Social Issues*, 1969, *25*, 29–53.

Hammock, T., & Brehm, J. W. The attractiveness of choice alternatives when freedom to choose is eliminated by a social agent. *Journal of Personality*, 1966, *34*, 546–554.

Harrow, M., & Ferrante, A. Locus of control in psychiatric patients. *Journal of Consulting and Clinical Psychology*, 1969, *33*, 582–589.

Helweg, G. C. *The relationship between selected personality characteristics and predictions of directive and non-directive psychotherapeutic approaches.* (Doctoral dissertation, University of Maryland). Dissertation Abstracts International, 1971, Ann Arbor, Michigan: University Microfilms, 1971. No. 71-26,965.

Hersch, P. D., & Scheibe, K. E. On the reliability and validity of internal-external control as a personality dimension. *Journal of Consulting Psychology*, 1967, *31*, 609–613.

Hiroto, D. S. Learned helplessness and locus of control. *Journal of Experimental Psychology*, 1974, *102*(2), 187–193.

Hochreich, D. J. *Refined analysis of internal-external control and behavior in a laboratory situation.* Unpublished doctoral dissertation, University of Connecticut, 1968.

Hochreich, D. J. Defensive externality and attribution of responsibility. *Journal of Personality*, 1974, *42*, 543–557.

Hochreich, D. J. Sex-role stereotypes for internal-external control and interpersonal trust. *Journal of Consulting and Clinical Psychology*, 1975, *43*, 273. (a)

Hochreich, D. J. Defensive externality and blame projection following failure. *Journal of Personality and Social Psychology*, 1975, *32*, 540–546. (b)

Houston, B. K. Control over stress, locus of control, and response to stress. *Journal of Personality and Social Psychology,* 1972, *21*, 249–255.

Hrycenko, I., & Minton, H. L. Internal-external control, power position, and satisfaction in task-oriented groups. *Journal of Personality and Social Psychology*, 1974, *30*, 871–878.

Hsieh, T. T., Shybut, J., & Lotsof, E. J. Internal versus external control and ethnic group membership. *Journal of Consulting and Clinical Psychology*, 1969, *33*, 122–124.

Jacobsen, R. A. *Personality correlates of choice of therapist.* (Doctoral dissertation, Columbia University). Dissertation Abstracts International, 1971, Ann Arbor, Michigan: University Microfilms, 1971. No. 71-6193.

James, W. H., Woodruff, A. B., & Werner, W. Effect of internal and external control upon changes in smoking behavior. *Journal of Consulting Psychology*, 1965, *29*, 127–129.

Jeffrey, D. B. A comparison of the effects of external control and self-control on the modification and maintenance of weight. *Journal of Abnormal Psychology*, 1974, *83*, 404–410.

Jessor, R., Graves, T. D., Hanson, R. C., & Jessor, S. *Society, personality, and deviant behavior.* New York: Holt, Rinehart and Winston, 1968.

Joe, V. C. A review of the internal-external control construct as a personality variable. *Psychological Reports*, 1971, *28*, 619–640.

Jolley, M. T., & Spielberger, C. D. The effects of locus of control and anxiety on verbal conditioning. *Journal of Personality*, 1973, *41*, 443–456.

Julian, J. W., & Katz, S. B. Internal versus external control and the value of reinforcement. *Journal of Personality and Social Psychology*, 1968, *8*, 89–94.

Karabenick, S. A. Valence of success and failure as a function of achievement motives and locus of control. *Journal of Personality and Social Psychology,* 1972, *21,* 101–110.

Kiehlbauch, J. B. *Selected changes over time in internal-external control expectancies in a reformatory population.* Unpublished doctoral dissertation, Kansas State University, 1967.

Kilman, P. R., Albert, B. M., & Sotile, W. M. The relationship between locus of control, structure of therapy, and outcome. *Journal of Consulting and Clinical Psychology,* 1975, *43,* 588.

Kilman, P. R., & Howell, R. J. The effects of structure of marathon group therapy and locus of control on therapeutic outcome. *Journal of Consulting and Clinical Psychology,* 1974, *42,* 912.

Krovetz, M. L. Explaining success or failure as a function of one's locus of control. *Journal of Personality,* 1974, *42,* 175–189.

Lamiell, J. T., & Phares, E. J. *Locus of control, probability of success, and defensiveness.* Paper read at annual meetings of the Midwestern Psychological Association, Chicago, May, 1975.

Lamont, J. Depression, locus of control, and mood response set. *Journal of Clinical Psychology,* 1972, *28,* 342–345.

Lao, R. C. Internal-external control and competent and innovative behavior among Negro college students. *Journal of Personality and Social Psychology,* 1970, *14,* 263–270.

Lazarus, R. S. *Psychological stress and the coping process.* New York: McGraw-Hill, 1966.

Lefcourt, H. M. Internal versus external control of reinforcement: A review. *Psychological Bulletin,* 1966, *65,* 206–220. (a)

Lefcourt, H. M. Belief in personal control: Research and implications. *Journal of Individual Psychology,* 1966, *22,* 185–195. (b)

Lefcourt, H. M. Recent developments in the study of locus of control. In B. A. Maher (Ed.), *Progress in experimental personality research* (Vol. 6). New York: Academic Press, 1972.

Lefcourt, H. M. *Locus of Control.* Hillsdale, N.J.: Lawrence Erlbaum Associates, 1976.

Lefcourt, H. M., & Ladwig, G. W. Alienation in Negro and white reformatory inmates. *Journal of Social Psychology,* 1966, *68,* 153–157.

Lefcourt, H. M., Lewis, L., & Silverman, I. W. Internal versus external control of reinforcement and attention in a decision making task. *Journal of Personality,* 1968, *36,* 663–682.

Lefcourt, H. M., & Wine, J. Internal versus external control of reinforcement and the deployment of attention in experimental situations. *Canadian Journal of Behavioral Science,* 1969, *1,* 167–181.

Levens, H. Organizational affiliation and powerlessness: A case study of the welfare poor. *Social Problems,* 1968, *16,* 18–32.

Levenson, H. Perceived parental antecedents of internal, powerful others, and chance locus of control orientations. *Developmental Psychology,* 1973, *9,* 268–274. (a)

Levenson, H. Multidimensional locus of control in psychiatric patients. *Journal of Consulting and Clinical Psychology,* 1973, *41,* 397–404. (b)

Lichtenstein, E., & Craine, W. H. The importance of subjective evaluation of reinforcement in verbal conditioning. *Journal of Experimental Research in Personality,* 1969, *3,* 214–220.

Lipp, L., Kolstoe, R., James, W., & Randall, H. Denial of disability and internal control of reinforcement: A study using a perceptual defense paradigm. *Journal of Consulting and Clinical Psychology,* 1968, *32,* 72–75.

Lottman, T. J., & DeWolfe, A. S. Internal versus external control in reactive and process schizophrenia. *Journal of Consulting and Clinical Psychology,* 1972, *39,* 344.

Lundy, J. R. Some personality correlates of contraceptive use among unmarried female college students. *Journal of Psychology,* 1972, *80,* 9–14.

MacDonald, A. P. Internal-external locus of control and the practice of birth control. *Psychological Reports*, 1970, *27*, 206.

MacDonald, A. P. Internal-external locus of control: Parental antecedents. *Journal of Consulting and Clinical Psychology*, 1971, *37*, 141–147. (a)

MacDonald, A. P. Birth order and personality. *Journal of Consulting and Clinical Psychology*, 1971, *36*, 171–176. (b)

Marks, E. Sex, birth order, and beliefs about personal power. *Developmental Psychology*, 1973, *6*, 184.

McArthur, L. A. Luck is alive and well in New Haven. *Journal of Personality and Social Psychology*, 1970, *16*, 316–318.

McGhee, P. E., & Crandall, V. C. Beliefs in internal-external control of reinforcement and academic performance. *Child Development*, 1968, *39*, 91–102.

McGinnies, E., Nordholm, L. A., Ward, C. D., & Bhanthumnavin, D. L. Sex and cultural differences in perceived locus of control among students in five countries. *Journal of Consulting and Clinical Psychology*, 1974, *42*, 451–455.

McGinnies, E., & Ward, C. D. Persuasability as a function of source credibility and locus of control: Five cross cultural experiments. *Journal of Personality*, 1974, *42*, 360–371.

Midgley, N., & Abrams, M. S. Fear of success and locus of control in young women. *Journal of Consulting and Clinical Psychology*, 1974, *42*, 737.

Midlarsky, E. Aiding under stress: The effects of competence, dependency, visibility, and fatalism. *Journal of Personality*, 1971, *39*, 132–149.

Midlarsky, E., & Midlarsky, M. Some determinants of aiding under experimentally induced stress. *Journal of Personality*, 1973, *41*, 305–327.

Mirels, H. L. Dimensions of internal versus external control. *Journal of Consulting and Clinical Psychology*, 1970, *34*, 226–228.

Mischel, W., Zeiss, R., & Zeiss, A. Internal-external control and persistence: Validation and implications of the Stanford Preschool Internal-External Scale. *Journal of Personality and Social Psychology*, 1974, *29*, 265–278.

Naditch, M. P. Locus of control and drinking behavior in a sample of men in army basic training. *Journal of Consulting and Clinical Psychology*, 1975, *43*, 96.

Naditch, M. P., Gargen, M. A., & Michael, L. B. Denial, anxiety, locus of control, and the discrepancy between aspirations and achievements as components of depression. *Journal of Abnormal Psychology*, 1975, *84*, 1–9.

Nelson, P. C., & Phares, E. J. Anxiety, discrepancy between need value and expectancy, and internal-external control. *Psychological Reports*, 1971, *28*, 663–668.

Nowicki, S., & Barnes, J. Effects of a structured camp experience on locus of control orientation. *Journal of Genetic Psychology*, 1973, *122*, 247–252.

Nowicki, S., & Duke, M. P. A locus of control scale for college as well as noncollege adults. *Journal of Personality Assessment*, 1974, *38*, 136–137. (a)

Nowicki, S., & Duke, M. P. A preschool and primary internal-external control scale. *Developmental Psychology*, 1974, *10*, 874–880. (b)

Nowicki, S., & Hopper, A. Locus of control correlates in an alcoholic population. *Journal of Consulting and Clinical Psychology*, 1974, *42*, 735.

Nowicki, S., & Segal, W. Perceived parental characteristics, locus of control orientation, and behavioral correlates of locus of control. *Developmental Psychology*, 1974, *10*, 33–37.

Nowicki, S., & Strickland, B. A locus of control scale for children. *Journal of Consulting and Clinical Psychology*, 1973, *40*, 148–154.

Palmer, R. D. Parental perception and perceived locus of control in psychopathology. *Journal of Personality*, 1971, *39*, 420–431.

Parsons, O. A., & Schneider, J. M. Locus of control in university students from eastern and western societies. *Journal of Consulting and Clinical Psychology*, 1974, *42*, 456–461.

Parsons, O. A., Schneider, J. M., & Hansen, A. S. Internal-external locus of control and national stereotypes in Denmark and the United States. *Journal of Consulting and Clinical Psychology*, 1970, *35*, 30–37.

Penk, W. E. Age changes and correlates of internal-external locus of control scale. *Psychological Reports*, 1969, *25*, 856.

Phares, E. J. *Changes in expectancy in skill and chance situations*. Unpublished doctoral dissertation, Ohio State University, 1955.

Phares, E. J. Expectancy changes in skill and chance situations. *Journal of Abnormal and Social Psychology*, 1957, *54*, 339–342.

Phares, E. J. Perceptual threshold decrements as a function of skill and chance expectancies. *Journal of Psychology*, 1962, *53*, 399–407.

Phares, E. J. Internal-external control as a determinant of amount of social influence exerted. *Journal of Personality and Social Psychology*, 1965, *2*, 642–647.

Phares, E. J. Differential utilization of information as a function of internal-external control. *Journal of Personality*, 1968, *36*, 649–662.

Phares, E. J. Internal-external control and the reduction of reinforcement value after failure. *Journal of Consulting and Clinical Psychology*, 1971, *37*, 386–390.

Phares, E. J. A social learning theory approach to psychopathology. In J. B. Rotter, J. Chance, & E. J. Phares (Eds.), *Applications of a social learning theory of personality*. New York: Holt, Rinehart and Winston, 1972.

Phares, E. J. *Locus of control: A personality determinant of behavior*. Morristown, N.J.: General Learning Press, 1973.

Phares, E. J. *Locus of control in personality*. Morristown, N.J.: General Learning Press, 1976.

Phares, E. J., & Lamiell, J. T. Relationship of internal-external control to defensive preferences. *Journal of Consulting and Clinical Psychology*, 1974, *42*, 872–878.

Phares, E. J., & Lamiell, J. T. Internal-external control, interpersonal judgments of others in need, and attribution of responsibility. *Journal of Personality*, 1975, *43*, 23–38.

Phares, E. J., Ritchie, D. E., & Davis, W. L. Internal-external control and reaction to threat. *Journal of Personality and Social Psychology*, 1968, *10*, 402–405.

Phares, E. J., & Wilson, K. G. Responsibility attribution: Role of outcome severity, situational ambiguity, and internal-external control. *Journal of Personality*, 1972, *40*, 392–406.

Phares, E. J., Wilson, K. G., & Klyver, N. W. Internal-external control and the attribution of blame under neutral and distractive conditions. *Journal of Personality and Social Psychology*, 1971, *18*, 285–288.

Prociuk, T. J., & Breen, L. J. Defensive externality and its relation to academic performance. *Journal of Personality and Social Psychology*, 1975, *31*, 549–556.

Prociuk, T. J., & Lussier, R. J. Internal-external locus of control: An analysis and bibliography of two years of research (1973–1974). *Psychological Reports*, 1975, *37*, 1323–1337.

Ritchie, E., & Phares, E. J. Attitude change as a function of internal-external control and communicator status. *Journal of Personality*, 1969, *37*, 429–443.

Rotter, J. B. *Social learning and clinical psychology*. Englewood Cliffs, N.J.: Prentice-Hall, 1954.

Rotter, J. B. Generalized expectancies for internal versus external control of reinforcement. *Psychological Monographs*, 1966, *80* (Whole No. 609).

Rotter, J. B. A new scale for the measurement of interpersonal trust. *Journal of Personality*, 1967, *35*, 651–665.

Rotter, J. B. Some problems and misconceptions related to the construct of internal versus external control of reinforcement. *Journal of Consulting and Clinical Psychology*, 1975, *43*, 56–67.

Rotter, J. B., Chance, J. E., & Phares, E. J. (Eds.). *Applications of a social learning theory of personality*. New York: Holt, Rinehart and Winston, 1972.

Rotter, J. B., Liverant, S., & Crowne, D. P. The growth and extinction of expectancies in chance controlled and skilled tasks. *Journal of Psychology*, 1961, *52*, 161–177.

Rotter, J. B., & Mulry, R. C. Internal versus external control of reinforcement and decision time. *Journal of Personality and Social Psychology*, 1965, *2*, 598–604.

Ryckman, R. M., Rodda, W. C., & Sherman, M. F. Locus of control and expertise relevance as determinants of changes in opinion about student activism. *Journal of Social Psychology*, 1972, *88*, 107–114.

Schneider, J. M. College students' belief in personal control, 1966–1970. *Journal of Individual Psychology*, 1971, *27*, 188.

Schneider, J. M. Relationship between locus of control and activity preferences: Effects of masculinity, activity, and skill. *Journal of Consulting and Clinical Psychology*, 1972, *38*, 225–230.

Schneider, J. M., & Parsons, O. A. Categories on the Locus of Control Scale and cross-cultural comparisons in Denmark and the United States. *Journal of Cross-Cultural Psychology*, 1970, *1*, 131–138.

Seeman, M. Alienation and social learning in a reformatory. *American Journal of Sociology*, 1963, *69*, 270–284.

Seeman, M., & Evans, J. W. Alienation and learning in a hospital setting. *American Sociological Review*, 1962, *27*, 772–783.

Seligman, M. E. P. *Helplessness: On depression, development, and death*. San Francisco: Freeman, 1975.

Seligman, M. E. P., Maier, S. F., & Solomon, R. L. Unpredictable and uncontrollable aversive events. In F. R. Brush (Ed.), *Aversive conditioning and learning*. New York: Academic Press, 1971.

Sherman, S. J. Internal-external control and its relationship to attitude change under different social influence techniques. *Journal of Personality and Social Psychology*, 1973, *23*, 23–29.

Silvern, L. E., & Nakamura, C. Y. Powerlessness, social-political action, social-political views: Their interrelation among college students. *Journal of Social Issues*, 1971, *27*, 137–157.

Skinner, B. F. *Beyond freedom and dignity*. New York: Knopf, 1971.

Smith, R. E. Changes in locus of control as a function of life crisis resolution. *Journal of Abnormal Psychology*, 1970, *3*, 328–332.

Snyder, C. R., & Larson, G. R. A further look at student acceptance of general personality interpretations. *Journal of Consulting and Clinical Psychology*, 1972, *38*, 384–388.

Sosis, R. H. Internal-external control and the perception of responsibility of another for an accident. *Journal of Personality and Social Psychology*, 1974, *30*, 393–399.

Staub, E., Tursky, B., & Schwartz, G. E. Self-control and predictability: Their effects on reactions to aversive stimulation. *Journal of Personality and Social Psychology*, 1971, *18*, 157–162.

Stephens, M. W., & Delys, P. A locus of control measure for preschool children. *Developmental Psychology*, 1973, *9*, 55–65.

Straits, B. C., & Sechrest, L. Further support of some findings about characteristics of smokers and non-smokers. *Journal of Consulting Psychology*, 1963, *27*, 282.

Strassberg, D. S. Relationships among locus of control, anxiety, and valued-goal expectations. *Journal of Consulting and Clinical Psychology*, 1973, *41*, 319.

Strassberg, D. S., & Robinson, J. S. Relationship between locus of control and other personality measures in drug users. *Journal of Consulting and Clinical Psychology*, 1974, *42*, 744–745.

Strickland, B. R. The prediction of social action from a dimension of internal-external control. *Journal of Social Psychology*, 1965, *66*, 353–358.

Strickland, B. R. Individual differences in verbal conditioning, extinction and awareness. *Journal of Personality*, 1970, *38*, 364–378.

Strickland, B. R. Delay of gratification as a function of race of the experimenter. *Journal of Personality and Social Psychology*, 1972, *22*, 108–112.

Strickland, B. R. Delay of gratification and internal locus of control in children. *Journal of Consulting and Clinical Psychology*, 1973, *40*, 338.

Strickland, B. R. *Locus of control and health related behaviors.* Paper presented at the XV Interamerican Congress of Psychology, Bogota, Colombia, Dec., 1974.

Thomas, L. E. The I–E Scale, ideological bias, and political participation. *Journal of Personality*, 1970, *38*, 273–286.

Throop, W. F., & MacDonald, A. P. Internal-external locus of control: A bibliography. *Psychological Reports*, 1971, *28*, 175–190 (Monograph Suppl. 1–V28).

Tolor, A. An evaluation of the Maryland Parent Attitude Survey. *Journal of Psychology*, 1967, *67*, 69–74.

Tolor, A. Are the alienated more suggestible? *Journal of Clinical Psychology*, 1971, *27*, 441–442.

Tseng, M. S. Locus of control as a determinant of job proficiency, employability, and training satisfaction of vocational rehabilitation clients. *Journal of Counseling Psychology*, 1970, *17*, 487–491.

Tyre, T. E., & Maisto, S. A. *The modification of external control perception in the pre-adolescent.* Paper presented at the annual meeting of the American Psychological Association, New Orleans, August, 1974.

Wareheim, R. G., & Foulds, M. F. Perceived locus of control and personal adjustment. *Journal of Consulting and Clinical Psychology*, 1971, *37*, 250–252.

Watson, D., & Baumal, E. Effects of locus of control and expectation of future control upon present performance. *Journal of Personality and Social Psychology*, 1967, *6*, 212–215.

Weiner, B. *Theories of motivation.* Chicago: Markham, 1972.

Weiss, H., & Sherman, J. Internal-external control as a predictor of task effort and satisfaction subsequent to failure. *Journal of Applied Psychology*, 1973, *57*, 132–136.

Wilson, K. G. *Therapist choice as related to selected personality characteristics in a college sample.* Unpublished doctoral dissertation, Kansas State University, 1973.

Wolk, S., & DuCette, J. Intentional performance and incidental learning as a function of task dimensions. *Journal of Personality and Social Psychology*, 1974, *29*, 90–101.

Wolk, S., & Kurtz, J. Positive adjustment and involvement during aging and expectancy for internal control. *Journal of Consulting and Clinical Psychology*, 1975, *43*, 173–178.

Zytkoskee, A., Strickland, B. R., & Watson, J. Delay of gratification and internal versus external control among adolescents of low socioeconomic status. *Developmental Psychology*, 1971, *4*, 93–98.

NOTES

1   The preparation of this chapter was supported in part by grant GS-32265X from the National Science Foundation.

CHAPTER 8

Machiavellianism *

FLORENCE L. GEIS

University of Delaware

The original description of Machiavellianism was, of course, _The Prince_ by Niccolo Machiavelli, first published in sixteenth century Italy. This was the era of the infamous Medici family, of Caesar and Lucrezia Borgia and the Sforzas, a Renaissance era of developing nation–states, competition between states and between their respective princes, would-be princes, and former princes. It was an era of developing affluence for the few, with a reputation for intrigue and corruption. There is dispute among scholars as to whether Machiavelli was a cynic, a patriot, or both. What concerns us here is not Machiavelli's character but his ideas. Taken at face value, his writings consist of short essays advising a prince on how to stay in power, given the weak and corruptible nature of friends and enemies alike. The gist of Machiavelli's advice is that the prince should maintain the public _appearance_ of praising all the conventional virtues of the day, and in fact should practice them whenever he could with maximum publicity and minimum cost. But the prince should be prepared to take any action, virtuous or otherwise, that might be required to achieve his goals. Basically, Machiavelli was talking about priorities—and the management of public support.

Richard Christie, a social psychologist at Columbia University, invented the idea of treating Machiavellianism as an individual differences variable. From this viewpoint we are all princes or would-be princes of our own human estate. All of us have goals, and we all strive in various ways to get what we want. We may want an extra week to hand in a term paper; we may want an independent income; we may want prestige and influence to pull the strings in some group.

This chapter was prepared especially for London, H., and Exner, J. (Eds.), _Dimensions of Personality_, New York: Wiley, 1978. Most of the material is based on _Studies in Machiavellianism_ by R. Christie and F. L. Geis (New York: Academic Press, 1970), which contains the original, more complete descriptions of the work, although some material from more recent research has also been included. A preliminary version of this chapter was read by Dr. Joyce Walstedt, whose helpful comments have benefited the present version immeasurably.

Obviously, there may be strings to pull in groups of any size, from the two-person group of student and professor, to local campus groups, to larger economic, political or professional organizations. Christie's initial question was: Do contemporary string-pullers practice Machiavellian tactics? Are those who have achieved power positions in contemporary institutions more likely than the powerless to agree with Machiavelli?

Construction of the Mach Scales

Christie (1970a) and his associates culled from the writings of Machiavelli a list of 71 statements describing human nature and tactics for dealing with people. Some of the items were then reversed in wording. For example, Machiavelli's advice that one must be ready to defy any moral precept to achieve one's ends was reversed to read, "One should take action only when sure it is morally right." Items worded in the original Machiavellian direction are scored for agreement, so greater agreement with Machiavelli yields higher scores. For items that are reversed in wording, the scoring is also reversed, so that greater *dis*agreement yields higher scores. Thus, scores on all the items can be summed to give a total score that theoretically indicates overall agreement with Machiavelli. The device of reversing some of the items ensures that no person taking the test will achieve either a very high score, or a very low score simply by agreeing or disagreeing with questionnaire statements indiscriminately, regardless of content.

Colleagues in a fortuitously captive population, which included some power wielders in the social science establishment of the day, were asked to respond to the statements on a 1 to 7 scale, from strong disagreement to strong agreement, and were later interviewed informally for their interpretation of what each statement meant. Those colleagues Christie and his coworkers believed to be more effective manipulators agreed with Machiavelli more than did those they considered less effective. The interview responses were used to edit the items and clarify ambiguities.

The obvious question at this point was: Could this batch of statements be considered a *scale*? Would the items, as a group, discriminate between persons who actually agreed with Machiavelli and those who disagreed? Another form of the question is: Is Machiavellianism a consistent individual differences dimension? That is, are people who might agree with one of Machiavelli's precepts also likely to agree with most of the others? To gather information about how the set of items might work, they were administered to 1196 college undergraduates at three different colleges in different parts of the United States. Ideally, of course, this test population should have been a random sample of United States adults, or a random sample of the world population, or even a random sample of English-speaking college students. But random samples are expensive, and the research did not have grant support at this stage.

The students responded to the items on a 1 to 7 scale, again from strong disagreement to strong agreement. Item analysis revealed that 50 of the 71 items discriminated significantly in all three of the different populations. The item analysis consisted of an item-whole correlation (*phi* coefficient) analysis. This analysis answers the question: Do people who score higher than average on this particular item also score higher than average on the scale as a whole? In other words, do people who agree more with Machiavelli on this particular topic also take the Machiavellian attitude on other topics, in general? The finding that so many of the original items did discriminate significantly suggested that Machiavellianism might indeed be a consistent and scaleable individual differences variable.

The next step was to reduce the scale to a more usable length for research purposes. Twenty items, 10 Machiavellian-worded and ten reverse-worded, were selected from the 50 discriminating items on the basis of having high item–whole correlations and representing a diversity of overt content. This version of the scale was called Mach IV, and it is included at the end of this chapter. This is the version (along with Mach V, to be described next) that has been used in most of the research. The mean item–whole correlation of these 20 items was .38.

At the time the Mach Scale was being developed, psychologists were beginning to notice that a major factor in personality, attitude and opinion questionnaires was social desirability. When presented with a series of statements and asked to indicate their agreement, most people tend to claim the socially desirable alternative and disclaim the unflattering options (Edwards, 1957; Crowne & Marlowe, 1960). Since advocating expedience, duplicity, and guile in interpersonal relations is generally considered socially undesirable in our culture, this could be a problem for the Mach Scale. To cope with it, Christie constructed a forced-choice version of the Mach Scale (Mach V) which ingeniously reduces the influence of social desirability. The first step was to obtain social desirability ratings for the 20 Mach IV items and for a large set of other items known to be uncorrelated with Mach. The raters' task was to answer on a 1 to 5 scale how desirable their parents and best friends would consider a "true" or "agree" response to the item in question. The social desirability ratings were obtained independently from students at elite and nonelite colleges in case the social desirability of particular opinions might vary with social class. Then, each Mach item was paired with one of the unrelated items that matched it in social desirability in both of the judging samples. If people were asked to choose one of the two items in each pair, the researcher would simply have to count the number of positively worded Mach items chosen and the number of reverse-worded Mach items rejected.

Unfortunately, such a scale is frustrating to answer. The person is repeatedly faced with claiming one of two equally reprehensible attitudes, or with rejecting one of two equally attractive ones. To make answering the scale more palatable, a third item was added to each pair. This third item was selected for being far removed from the matched pair in social desirability. Thus, when the Mach-and-matched pair were both undesirable, the third "buffer" item was high in social desirability, and when the Mach-and-matched pair were high in desirability, the buffer was low. Now the instructions are to mark which of the three items you agree with most, and which you agree with least, and leave the other blank. Thus, for each set of three items, the person answering always has the opportunity of either claiming something nice (and disclaiming one of two equally nasty attitudes), or of disclaiming a nasty statement (and claiming one of two equally nice ones). In addition to making the forced-choice Mach V Scale easier to answer, the addition of the items loaded for social desirability or undesirability makes the scale extremely tricky for the uninitiated to figure out or fake.

There are two important facts about the development of the Mach Scale that are unique. First, it is surprising that advice to princes based on the personal observations of an Italian gentleman of the Renaissance remains coherent and discriminating in an alien culture 400 years later. The second factor is Christie's sagacity in selecting and editing the items.

Correlations with Other Scales and Variables

Correlational studies between Mach scores and other scales and variables will not be discussed at length in this chapter. For more information see Christie (1970b, 1970c). However, to forestall misconceptions, it might be noted that the Mach Scale does not correlate with I.Q., social class, political ideology, authoritarianism, need for achievement, or sensation seeking.

The Mach Scale, and especially the Likert-format Mach IV, does show a noderate negative correlation with social desirability. Thus, the Mach Scale will correlate with any scale in which willingness to attribute undesirable characteristics to self or others is a major factor, such as scales of manifest hostility and some anxiety scales. (On the other hand, researchers who have worked with high and low Mach subjects in the laboratory, although admittedly lacking in clinical training, have never mentioned high Machs as being notably anxious or hostile.) Scales measuring other negative attitudes, such as anomia, external locus of control, and suspiciousness, also correlate moderately with Mach scores. However, the Mach Scale also correlated negatively with test-taking defensiveness, as measured by the MMPI Lie and K Scales. It is possible that high scorers on the Mach Scale answer questionnaires as they think life is, whereas low scorers answer as they think it ought to be.

Consistently, the Mach Scale correlated negatively with faith in human nature and with belief that most people are trustworthy, altruistic, independent, or strong of will. These are, of course, the beliefs that Machiavelli explicitly rejected.

In the remainder of this chapter persons who score high on the Mach Scale will be called high Machs; those who score low will be called low Machs. "High" means "above the median," in the top 50 percent of scores in the particular group tested at that time; "low" means in the lower 50 percent of scores. Actual median scores vary from one study to another.

THE MACHIAVEL AND THE CON GAME: CONSTRUCT VALIDITY

We now have a scale that sorts people out on a conceptual dimension. We call the dimension *Machiavellianism* because that is where the idea—and the items—came from. But does this concept, this hypothetical construct, have any validity? Does the scale actually measure what its name claims that it measures? Do people who score high on the Mach Scale behave in ways we would call "Machiavellian" in situations other than answering a questionnaire? In short, can the Mach Scale predict behavior?

The kind of behavior that seems most central to the idea of Machiavellianism is manipulation of other people. Unfortunately, "manipulation" has a negative connotation for many people. These same people, however, usually endorse "interpersonal competence," "ability to handle others effectively," and "leadership." Although subtle conceptual distinctions can be made to differentiate these terms, all of them describe what high Machs do. As a (high Mach) subject explained in a postexperimental interview, " 'handling people effectively' is what you or your friends do; 'manipulation' is done by other people."

In the early stages of research no one knew exactly what kind or quality of "manipulation" to expect or look for. Rather than jump to conclusions, studies were designed to clarify the meaning of the concept. With "manipulation" as a central definition, "Machiavellianism" can be analyzed into three components, each independently observable:

(1) belief that people are manipulatable;
(2) willingness to practice or attempt manipulation;
(3) skill or ability in manipulation.

If the construct of *Machiavellianism* has any validity, these three components ought to be related. That is, in order to be called "Machiavellian," a person would have to believe that people are manipulatable, be willing to try to manipulate them, and show considerable skill in the art.

A face-valid interpretation of the Mach Scale is that it measures the belief component, the extent to which the person answering it believes that people in general are manipulatable. If one agrees that, "It is wise to flatter important people," it seems reasonable to assume that one believes that important people can be influenced by flattery—that important people are manipulatable. It should be noted that all the Mach Scale items are worded impersonally. The person responding is not claiming that he or she practices flattery, or even endorsing the use of flattery by others; rather the person is simply claiming a belief that flattery works.

In Search of the Machiavel

Logically, one might believe that flattery works but never use it. To be called *Machiavellian*, however, one must believe that flattery works and also be willing to use it when the occasion arises. Specifically, high Machs, who according to their Mach scores believe that people are manipulatable, should be willing to practice manipulation given an appropriate opportunity.

Notice that the idea of *Machiavellianism* was conceived and the Mach Scales were constructed on the hypothesis that people who actually practiced manipulation would score higher on the scales. Since it is difficult to identify ''manipulation'' unequivocally in the real world, we are now going to turn that original hypothesis around and ask: Are people who score higher on the Mach Scale also more willing to practice manipulation in a laboratory situation designed so that ''manipulation'' will be identifiable and measurable? This was the hypothesis tested in the Machiavel study (Geis, Christie, & Nelson, 1970).

A situation was needed in which some measurable manipulation would be seen by the subject as warranted but not required. Pilot testing suggested that high Machs were highly inquisitive about the various procedures we tried out. In fact, they seemed downright suspicious. It was clear that a laboratory situation was needed in which manipulation would be so obviously legitimate that few subjects would question it. The problem was finally solved by having the subject play the role of ''experimenter'' in a social psychology study involving deception.

Method

Mach Scales, identified only as ''Opinion Inventory,'' were given in introductory psychology and sociology classes, and the students were also asked to volunteer for additional research projects. No connection between the questionnaires and the later experiment was mentioned.

Only male students were recruited for this study. The early stages of Mach research were done in an era when women in general were not taken seriously. Since little was known about the construct at the time, the question of its relevance for women seemed even more obscure. More recent research, described later in this chapter, has studied subjects of both sexes.

When the subject arrived at the laboratory, he was informed that the research was designed to study an important personality trait—field dependence and independence. He would take the Embedded Figures Test that was designed to measure this trait. And, since norms for the test from a group of Harvard students were available, he would be given his percentile score for each test item as he went along. A second purpose of the study, it was explained, was to find if college students like himself could be trained to administer the test. For this reason he would be given the test by the subject ahead of him, and he, in his turn, would administer the test to the next scheduled subject. Subjects were told that the entire session would be observed through a one-way mirror. The two other "subjects" were actually stooges who alternated in the previous-subject and next-subject roles. They had been trained to perform each of the roles according to a standardized routine.

The subject was taken to the experimental room and introduced to the first stooge who gave him a 10-item adaptation of Witkin's (1950) Embedded Figures Test. Whatever the subject's performance on the items, the stooge reported to him a predetermined series of percentile scores clustering around 70, except for the ninth item on which a score of 30 was reported. In taking the test the subject learned that percentile scores depended upon speed and that the items required concentration.

When the subject completed the test, the experimenter returned and said,

Thank you both very much. At this point, Mr. _____ (naïve subject), I owe you some further explanation. In addition to our interest in your performance on the Embedded Figures Test, and in training students to administer the test, we are also very much interested in the kind of situation in which one person has absolute power over the rewards and punishments of another person. I'm sure you can think of many situations that are like this. Usually, of course, the power is used fairly and in accord with the rules. Sometimes, however, in such situations, the person who has the power may use it arbitrarily, or for his own private purposes. Now, we are interested in the motivations and in the personal reactions and feelings of both people in this kind of situation. Therefore . . the student who is giving the test is asked to use his power arbitrarily. Mr. _____ (stooge), what did you do?

The stooge confessed making a couple of comments and lying about the low percentile score, then added, "I don't think I'd like to do this kind of thing very much." This was to reassure the subjects that not manipulating, or not liking it, was also possible and acceptable in this situation.

After a brief discussion to ensure that the subject understood the nature of the deception practiced on him, both "subjects" completed a short questionnaire. At this point the subject believed that he was through being "a subject" in the experiment; he had been deceived (mildly), and now it was his turn to be experimenter. After teaching the subject the correct procedure for administering the Embedded Figures Test, the experimenter said,

Once you've been assigned to the experimental condition you remain in it, so we are asking you to use your power arbitrarily—to confuse or distract the subject who will be taking the test. Now precisely how you go about doing this, and how much of it you do, is up to your imagination—and your conscience. Obviously, we want you to be in the position of having absolute power to use as *you* choose to use it. Some people find this very uncongenial—as apparently the man who tested you did, and they do very little. Other people find it a great deal of fun. What you do is up to you.

Any questions by the subject were answered as briefly as possible, usually by a "yes" or "no," and always followed by the standard assertion, "What you do is up to you." By the end of the study the experimenters had learned that subjects who asked at this time whether they could do this or that specific behavior while administering the test were usually high Machs, whereas those who asked whether they *had* to do anything at all were usually lows Unfortunately, no formal records of these questions were kept.

While the subject was administering the test to the second stooge, the first stooge observed his behavior through the one-way mirror and sound system connecting the experimental room to an adjoining observation room. The subjects' behaviors were judged as "manipulative" or "not manipulative" by the observer. Those judged manipulative were coded into categories on a prepared rating sheet. Behaviors that could not be categorized were quoted, paraphrased, or described briefly.

A serious and formal atmosphere was maintained throughout the entire session. Subjects were addressed as "Mr. Jones." The importance of the Embedded Figures Test was emphasized; the adaptation of it was genuinely difficult and did require concentration. The same serious tone was maintained in delivering the ambiguously worded permission to the naive subject to manipulate the "next subject." Thus, although manipulation was clearly permitted, the implications were by no means trivial. In fact, after listening attentively to the permission to manipulate, one low Mach subject said, "Oh, I wouldn't do anything like that." And he didn't.

Twenty-seven male subjects participated—14 who had scored above the median for males on both forms of the Mach Scale (105 on Mach IV and 112 on Mach V) and 13 who had scored below the median on both forms.

Results

If agreement with Machiavelli goes with willingness to manipulate others, then high Machs should engage in more manipulative behaviors than low Machs while administering the test to their subject. Table 8–1 shows that they did. The "total number of manipulations" was the number of false scores reported to the stooge plus the number of all other manipulative behaviors recorded by the

Table 8-1   Amount and Variety of Manipulation of a Peer Performed
by High- and Low-Mach Subjects

	Group means			
	High Mach ($n = 14$)	Low Mach ($n = 13$)	t	$p <$
Total number of manipulations	15.43	7.08	2.88	.005
Variety of manipulations	6.43	3.08	3.38	.005
Induced manipulations				
Magnitude of lies told	117.86	70.77	2.42	.025
Number of verbal distractions	1.86	.62	2.30	.025
Innovative manipulations				
Verbal distractions				
Number	5.93	1.69	3.31	.005
Variety	3.57	1.15	3.93	.0005
Nonverbal distractions				
Number	3.21	1.54	.77	.25
Variety	.93	.46	.98	.20

Source: Geis, Christie & Nelson, 1970, p. 87.

observer. High Machs performed an average of 15 manipulative acts while they tested the stooge, compared to an average of 7 such behaviors by lows. (All differences mentioned here and throughout this chapter are statistically significant unless otherwise specified.)

High Machs practiced a greater variety of manipulations as well as a greater number of them. A total of 16 different types of manipulation were identified: one falsification of percentile scores, 11 classifications of verbal content, and four types of nonverbal distraction. Some examples are: "compliment on stooge's test performance;" "fortuitously repeating testing instructions;" "accusing stooge of confusion, making a mistake, doing the test wrong, looking too long, etc.;" "giving false instructions or test rules;" "nondiscursive sounds, such as whistling, humming, coughing, throat-clearing;" and "manipulation of objects, such as clicking pencil or pen clip, repeatedly moving ash tray, fortuitously lighting matches, intentionally knocking over divider board on table separating subject and experimenter, etc." High Machs used an average of six of these 16 categories; lows averaged three.

High Machs used the manipulations demonstrated by the stooge in the first half of the session more than lows used them, but the biggest difference between high and low Machs was in the number and variety of original, innovative manipulations. The highs averaged six "originals" each, whereas the lows averaged two. The average high Machs invented four different kinds of distracting comment; the average low Mach fabricated only one.

It is obvious that high and low Machs differed statistically when given an open-ended invitation to manipulate a supposed peer. But the statistics scarcely convey the imaginative interpretation of the situation by some of the highs. For example, the list of manipulations performed by one high includes, among other things:

(Grinning at stooge before first trial) rubs hands together in stereotyped gesture of relish; bends over double, unties shoe, shakes foot, reties shoe; jingles contents of pocket noisily, pulls out Chapstick and applies it while staring absentmindedly at ceiling (acting bored that stooge is taking so long to solve the test item); whistles a tune; slaps leg and straightens up noisily and abruptly in chair; taps pencil rhythmically on table; hums; reaches around table divider board and carefully knocks it over (this produces a loud crash and sends papers on table flying in all directions); after 10-second dead silence apologizes profusely to stooge for "distracting" him; erases vigorously on blank margin of score sheet (divider board prevents stooge from seeing that all of his scores are not being erased); comments to stooge, with serious frown at one-way vision mirror, "I feel like I'm on TV, don't you?" (followed by delighted, confiding grin at mirror as soon as stooge returns his attention to test booklet) . . . dismantles own ballpoint pen behind divider board, uses spring to shoot it, parts flying, across the room; jumps from chair, dashes across room to retrieve pen parts saying, "Sorry, I'm a little nervous." (Geis *et al.*, 1970, p. 92)

Clearly, high scorers on the Mach Scale were more willing to practice manipulation than low scorers.

An Eyeball Test of Honesty.   High Machs' behavior in an earlier study by Exline, Thibaut, Hickey, and Gumpert (1970) can also be seen as willingness to manipulate. In this study a confederate posing as the subject's partner implicated the subject in cheating on the experimental task when the experimenter was unexpectedly called out of the room. (A $10 prize had been offered for the best team performance in the study.) After completing the task the pair were interviewed by the experimenter, ostensibly to learn what "problem-solving techniques" the two had developed. As the interview progressed, the experimenter displayed first impatience, then suspicion. Finally, the experimenter accused the pair of cheating and demanded an explanation. More than low Machs, high Mach subjects (both sexes) looked the experimenter in the eye while denying cheating.

Looking an accuser in the eye while protesting innocence can be seen as an attempt to manipulate credibility. Subjects found themselves caught in a difficult situation; manipulation was defensive. In the Machiavel study, described above, the subject was on the offensive. In these two different situations, then, people who claimed on the Mach Scales to believe that manipulation is possible also practiced it.

The Con Game

Does practice make perfect? There was no way to tell in either study above whether the high Machs' manipulations would have been effective or not, since the target of manipulation was a stooge in one study and the experimenter in the other.

High Machs ought to be willing to manipulate, but they also ought to show skill in the art. If a high Mach score indicates acceptance of Machiavellian attitudes—a belief that people are manipulatable, if belief implies practice, as the Machiavel results indicate, and if practice leads to skill, then high scorers should be more skillful at manipulating others than low scorers. Obviously, the measure of skill is success.

Successful manipulation seems generally to mean getting someone to do something they would not have done otherwise, without the use of force. In the simplest case the manipulator derives direct benefit at the other's expense. Some manipulation is socially acceptable. For example, when parents induce their children to adopt conventional manners, it is generally seen as being for the children's own good. Nevertheless, in the immediate context, the child incurs a cost of giving up some pleasure or accepting some discipline, and the parent is seen as reaping a benefit of "satisfaction." In general, then, successful manipulation is a process in which the manipulator gets more of some kind of reward than he or she would have gotten without manipulating, and in which someone else gets less, at least within the immediate context.

One way to measure success is to hold a contest and see who wins (Geis, 1970a). A contest was needed in which all subjects would be willing and eager to manipulate—so that losing would reflect lack of skill rather than reluctance to try. Since the Machiavel study showed that low Machs were reluctant to manipulate in a realistic appearing situation, a game was used for this study. The three players in the game are the potential manipulators of one another. The game consists essentially of bargaining for shares of the total payoff, 100 points per game. These points can be won by a single player; they can be divided between two players; or they can be distributed among all three. The points can be divided in any proportions agreed to by the players–for example, 50–50–0, 60–40–0, 33–33–34, and so on. A player's score over a series of games is determined by his ability to manipulate opponents relative to their ability to manipulate him.

Method

As in the previous study, potential subjects were pretested on the Mach Scales in their psychology or sociology classes. Again, only male subjects were recruited.

When the subjects arrived at the laboratory, they were told that the purpose of the experiment was to study "the results of decision making." The game was described as a simulation of typical decision situations. They were told that success in the game, as in actual decisions, would depend on three factors: (1) luck or chance, which would be represented in the game by dice tossing; (2) relevant resources, represented by the hand of power cards assigned them for each game (they were advised that the three players would always be unequal in resources: sometimes they would have more resources than the others, sometimes less); and (3) skill in decision making, represented in the game by the bargaining provisions.

Three players and a male research assistant were seated around a playing board on a small table (see Figure 8–1). To begin the game, the assistant gave each player a hand of power cards, much like ordinary playing cards. One player was given a hand of low-value cards (player A in Figure 8–1); another was given a middle-value hand (player B); and the third was assigned the high-power position (player C). At his turn, a player tossed the dice and advanced his marker the number of spaces equal to the higher of his two die values multiplied by whichever of his power cards he chose to play at that turn. For example, if player A in Figure 8–1 tossed the dice and threw a two and a five, he would use the five to multiply his power card value for that turn. If he then decided to play a six from his hand, he would advance $(5)(6) = 30$ spaces around the board. The player or coalition of players first to reach the end of the path received the 100 points for that game.

Three rules were introduced to make winning over a series of games a direct reflection of success at manipulating one's fellow players:

1. *Subjects could form coalitions*. Any player could propose a coalition to any other player at any time in the game. Coalition partners played as a single unit. At the turn of a coalition, only one toss of the dice was made, but each member played one of his own power cards. Then both moved forward, together, the number of spaces equal to their higher die value multiplied by the *sum* of the power cards they played for that turn. For example, suppose A and B were in coalition and their dice toss yielded a five as their higher die value; if A played a six from his hand and B played a three, they would both advance $(5) (6 + 3) = 45$ spaces on the board. Since the power cards were actually prearranged so that any two players in coalition could beat the third one, every player had a chance to be a member of a winning coalition in every game. As a result, one way to win was to talk one of the other players into a coalition with you rather then permitting them to ally with each other, thus leaving you out.

2. A second rule was that *each coalition had to include an agreement between the partners* as to how they would divide the 100 points if their coalition should win. The fact that players differed in power position created strong pressures to divide the points unevenly. Most players felt that the partner with the stronger hand deserved more points. But how many more? The crucial issue was whether

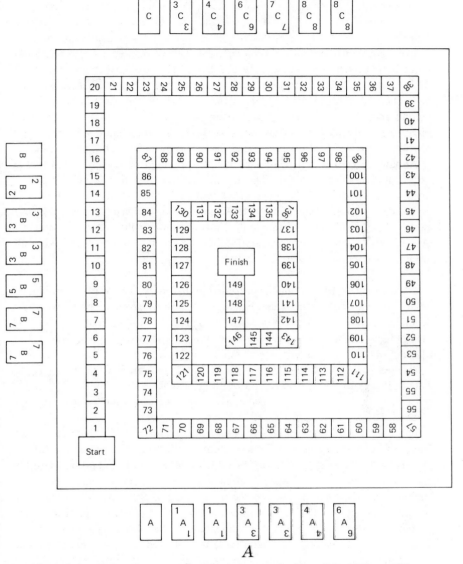

Figure 8–1. The Con Game: game board and power cards. (From Geis, 1970a, p. 109)

to split 55–45, or 60–40—or maybe 70–30? The result of this rule was that a second way to accumulate more points over the series of games was to succeed in talking coalition partners into giving more of the points rather than less.

3. The final rule was that *coalitions could be made or broken at will* at any time in the game. When a coalition was formed after play had begun between two players at different positions on the path, the two markers were moved to the point halfway between where they had been. This meant that a player could advance on the board simply by forming a coalition with an opponent who had been ahead of him. Naturally, this tactic usually cost the player who had been behind an unfavorable point-split agreement. But if he were skillful he could then, in his advantageous board position, break his agreement and form a new coalition with the third player, giving himself a more favorable point-split.

Another tactic involving breaking coalitions would be to withhold a few of one's highest power cards during play in coalition, meanwhile on any pretext urging one's partner to play his highest card each time. Then, one or two turns before the end, one would simply break the coalition and use one's hoarded high cards to beat the deserted partner to the Finish box to win the entire 100 points for oneself. This strategy was particularly effective when games were played in the ambiguous condition, described next.

Ambiguity. A further hunch was tested in this study. This was that ambiguity would give high Machs an extra advantage. If there are no clear criteria by which to judge whether an offer or request is "reasonable" or "justified," the skillful manipulator might be able to secure advantages that would not be granted or tolerated if such criteria were clear. For example, if no one knows what anyone "deserves" and if everyone knows that no one knows, knowledge of the general state of ignorance might be used for bluffing or other tactics. Ambiguity, in this sense, can be thought of as a protective screen of obscurity for manipulative tactics.

This idea was tested by having the triads play half their games with their cards laid out face up on the table in front of them, as illustrated in Figure 1, so that all players could see exactly what power cards each of them had at all times during play. In this unambiguous condition each player's power position was public knowledge in the triad, and so was the rough share of points he "deserved" as a coalition partner, his desirability as a partner, and the basis of his bargaining actions. To create an ambiguous playing situation, the players held their cards in their hands, like playing cards, and were not allowed to show them to anyone else at the table. However, they were explicitly instructed that they could *tell* fellow players anything they wished to tell them. Thus, the ambiguous condition eliminated public knowledge of power positions. In effect, it eliminated the "objective" criteria for judging the worth of offers and demands.

Each subject played six games in all, once in each power position in each of the two ambiguity conditions. Subjects participated in groups of nine or 12, so that three or four triads at separate game tables were playing simultaneously. After each game all the players changed tables to face two new opponents in their next game. A triad always had one high Mach, one middle, and one low. In all, 66 subjects participated, 22 high Machs, 22 middles, and 22 lows. The high Machs had total Mach scores of 108 and higher; the middles had scores of 97 to 107; and the lows had scores of 96 and below.

The game turned out to be challenging. Bargaining for coalition partners and point-splits was intense. After the session, a number of subjects usually asked to return to play another tournament. Some suggested that the experimenter might sell the game; others asked the experimenter to give them the game so they could sell it.

Results

Since there were three players in each game, and 100 points to be won, the expected or average value of the game was 33⅓ points. If Machiavellianism had no effect on the outcome of the game and coalitions were formed randomly, the average player could expect to be a member of a winning coalition two times in every three games, and he could expect to average 50 points per coalition (since the number of times he would get more than 50 would be balanced, in our random game tournament, by the number of times he would get less than 50). Thus, he would average 100 points over every three games, or 33⅓ points per game.

However, winning was not random, as shown in Table 8–2. The high Machs averaged 47 points per game, more than they could have obtained by chance. The middle Machs, managing 31 points per game, just about held their own. The low Machs, with 22 points per game, lost noticeably. The correlation between total number of points won over all six games and the subject's total Mach score

Table 8-2   Machiavellianism and Success in the Con Game
(22 Ss per Mach group)

Mach group	Mean game score	Game score minus 33.33[a]	t	p <
High	47.32	13.99	5.56	.001
Middle	31.11	−2.22	−.97	.20
Low	21.58	−11.75	3.58	.001

[a]The expected value per game, per subject.

Source: Geis, 1970a, p. 118.

was .71. This approximates the correlation of .73 between scores on Mach IV and Mach V in this sample.

Ambiguity was indeed an advantage to the high Machs, as can be seen in Figure 8–2. Although they also won in the unambiguous games, they won even more when bargaining conditions were ambiguous, and they did so specifically at the expense of the low Machs rather than the middles. In the ambiguous games the high Machs averaged 53 points per game, the middles again broke even with 31 points, but the lows managed only 17 points per game. The high Machs' winning margin of 36 points per game over the lows under cover of ambiguity was about double their winning margin of 15 points in the unambiguous games.

High Machs won in this bargaining game, and low Machs lost. The implication of this finding is that the theoretically defined ability component of Machiavellianism is associated with the belief component measured by the Mach Scales. People who believe that manipulation is possible are also successful manipulators. Combining the results of this study and the previous one, it appears that Mach scores predict both the willingness and the ability to manipulate others. The evidence for construct validity is positive.

Winning in the game appeared to satisfy the rough criteria of "successful manipulation": securing more of the rewards than chance or an equal distribution would have provided—at someone else's expense. The instructions and description of the game initially given the subjects created an individualistic orientation. Each player was to try to win as many points for himself as he could. Yet the structure of the game was such that to win the player had to get opponents to

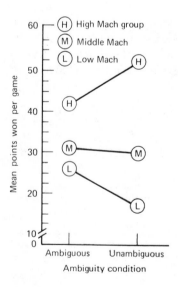

Figure 8–2. Machiavellianism, success in the Con Game, and ambiguity (22 subjects per Mach group). (From Geis, 1970a, p. 120)

cooperate in forming coalitions and agreeing on prize divisions. To the extent that a player won more than the average, he had to get his opponents to cooperate with him rather than with the third player in the group, and further, to agree to give him a little more of the prize, at their own expense.

Ambiguity in the bargaining situation doubled the high Machs' margin of success as manipulators. In the unambiguous games the players' publicly visible power cards served as "objective" criteria of about how much each might "reasonably" expect in a coalition. A high Mach in the low-power position might parlay his share up to 40 points, or 45, or even 50, but he could not seriously demand 70. In the ambiguous games these "objective" criteria were concealed; players had only one another's statements and demeanor to rely on. Evidently high Machs know how to make their proposals sound reasonable and justified.

Can the results of a game be generalized to other situations? The Con Game was designed to simulate competition of interests in a small group. Everyone wanted something that not everyone could get, and who got what was determined by negotiation. The tentative conclusion is that high Machs have an ability to manipulate others that they turned on in these games and that they could similarly apply to any situation they chose. Some further evidence supporting this conclusion will be considered next.

First, recall that in the preceding Machiavel study high Machs were willing to practice manipulation in a more realistic-appearing situation, one in which the subject believed he was administering an important psychological test to another subject. If high Machs are willing to manipulate in a more serious situation, it seems likely that the ability demonstrated in the Con Game might be applied in other, more serious contexts.

Cracker-Pushing.   High Machs' skill in con artistry may begin at an early age. Braginski (1970) studied the ability of fifth grade high and low Machs (both sexes) to persuade a middle Mach child to eat bitter crackers. The experimenter introduced herself as a representative of a cracker company testing out some new health crackers. Actually the crackers had been flavored with quinine by the experimenter. The child was asked to eat one cracker and then was given a drink of water and a piece of candy. The experimenter then explained that the cracker company wanted children to eat as many crackers as possible but that she was having a hard time getting children to eat them. She asked the subject to help her out by persuading the next child to eat as many crackers as possible, and she promised five cents for every cracker the subject could get the next child to eat. The experimenter called in the next child and left the two alone with the crackers.

Each pair of children had been matched for age, sex, IQ, degree of acquaintance, and social class of parents. The children had been classified as high, middle, or low Mach on Braginski's "Kiddie Mach" version of the Mach Scale.

High and low Mach children served as persuaders, middle Mach children as targets.

The results were clear. The average young high Mach in the study induced his or her target child to stomach six of the bitter crackers; the low Mach children got their targets to eat only three of them. This situation clearly fits the definition of manipulation. The persuader benefited (five cents a cracker plus possible psychic satisfaction) at the direct expense of another.

The Semireal World of the College Classroom. In Braginski's study the situation was realistic but not serious. Another study (Geis, 1968) bears on high Machs' ability to manipulate when the stakes are of greater consequence. The subjects were 276 students in a personality course. Although some students view college courses as a sort of game, they are usually considered more serious than the laboratory situations described so far, in that grades are at stake. In this study one-fourth of the course grade was based on a research project students worked on all semester in four-person teams. At the first meeting of the team members, after 20 minutes to get acquainted and begin discussing project ideas, each team was asked to name a leader. If leaders were selected randomly, about one-quarter of the teams might have been expected by chance to select their highest Mach member as leader. In fact, in teams with high Machs available, the highest Mach member was almost twice as likely to become leader as chance could account for. In 43 percent of these teams, the highest Mach member became leader.

In these teams one did not assume authority by individual fiat. Basically, leadership was negotiated. Once again the high Machs succeeded by mobilizing the agreement and support of others.

High Machs got themselves named as leader, but were they effective? If high Machs have an ability to manipulate others, they should be more effective in getting their team's resources applied to the group project. This idea was tested by comparing each team's project grade against an independent estimate of the team's resources. At the end of the semester each team's project was read anonymously by 24 fellow class members, each of whom compared it against the project of another, different team. The number of times a team's paper was called superior to the comparison paper, divided by the 24 comparisons, yielded a percentage score for each team. This percentage score was the team's project grade for the course.

The average of the four team members' course exam grades was used as an independent estimate of the team's relevant resources. Course examinations were, of course, taken individually. Presumably, a student's average represents a combination of intellectual ability and motivation. The question then becomes: How well did each team get its available ability, motivation, and time mobilized for the group project? The answer is that teams with high Mach leaders did better on their team project than they had done individually on the exams, whereas teams with low Mach leaders got lower grades on their projects than the average of their members' exam grades.

Presumably, the high Mach leaders manipulated their fellow group members into more effective team work on the project. And, to be sure, these high Mach leaders benefited in terms of their own project grades, but the other team members, who might be classified as the "victims" of manipulation, also benefited—in the end—from the superior project grades.

Taken together, these studies support the construct validity of Machiavellianism. The attitudinal, volitional, and ability components all hang together. At this point the tentative conclusion is that high Machs are more willing to manipulate others and are more successful at it.

The initial predictions about Machiavellianism were confirmed but confirmed, literally, in a blaze of ambiguity. *How* do high Machs manipulate other people? By what tactics do they achieve their success? What do they do that low Machs don't do, or do differently? What are the psychological mechanisms that account for these differences? Would high Machs win in any kind of situation? Although there are no final answers, there are some hints and hypotheses.

HOW HIGH MACHS WIN: STRATEGIES, TACTICS, AND OTHER DYNAMICS

The first thing that has to be said about high Machs is that they *have* strategies for winning. At least, after winning in the Con Game, they claimed they had on a post-session questionnaire. One high Mach wrote, "I learned to make any coalition, however extravagant, at the start of the game. . . . However, I held onto my high coefficients [power cards] in anticipation of going on my own at the finish." Another high Mach described his strategy as, "Use your opponents' greed." Low Machs tended to report that they had not used any strategies. One answered, "No—it wasn't possible because our opponents in every game were different people."

Con Game Tactics

Limits-Testing

Records of the bargaining in the Con Game triads provided some further hints (Geis, 1970b). One emergent hypothesis was that high Machs might be limits testers. In the earlier Machiavel study the high Machs had been more active than lows in manipulating their subject. But in the Con Game, the high Machs were not significantly more active: They did not propose more coalitions or specific point-splits, accept more proposals from another player, or break more coalitions. A major difference between the two studies was that in the Machiavel testing situation the victim had no recourse. He could not get out of the situation, and he had no means of retaliating against the test administrator. In the Con Game, both recourse and retaliation were available. If "manipulation" became obvious or obnoxious, the potential victim and the third party witness could retaliate by making a deal with each other. A frequency of manipulation that would be significant by statistical test might also look significantly excessive to fellow players. High Machs evidently know how to manipulate without being obvious—when the situation requires it. Apparently, they tune their tactics to the limits of the situation.

Initiating and Controlling Structure

Another hypothesis about tactics was that the high Machs were somehow in control in their triads. Both the middle and low Machs seemed to prefer the high as a partner. For example, in one game the first coalition offer in the game was an offer by the low Mach to the middle for a 50–50 split. The middle ignored the low. Then the high offered the middle exactly the same deal, and the middle accepted it. Since this game was in the ambiguous condition, the middle's decision could not have been based on relative power positions. Then the low offered the high 60 points, and the high accepted. Then the middle offered 85 to either of them. After the high rejected the offer, the low did also. This game was typical. Both middle and low Mach players made more offers to the high than they made to each other. (The middle and low Machs did not receive fewer offers, overall, because the relatively large number of offers they received from the high Mach compensated for the relatively few they received from each other.) The same pattern of preferring the high Mach appeared in all the other transactions of the game. Middle Machs accepted more of the offers made to them by high Machs (46 percent) than they accepted from lows (38 percent). And, once a middle Mach had a coalition with the high, the middle did not break it. Middle Machs did break coalitions, but the ones they broke were those with low Machs, not those with highs. Low Machs showed the same kind of discrimination against the middle Machs in favor of the highs.

The data showed the middle and low Machs preferring the high over each other. But what caused these preferences? Evidently the high Machs were doing something not captured by the frequency counts that made them more attractive as partners. The emergent hypothesis was that "attractiveness as a partner" is simply an alternative description of being psychologically in control.

There is some additional support for this hypothesis. In a later laboratory study (Geis, Krupat, & Berger, 1970), groups of five subjects differing in Mach scores held a short group discussion on a topic on which they initially disagreed. After the discussion, they were privately asked their own opinion on the topic, and they also rated each other on a number of dimensions, including "leadership." The high Machs in the groups were unanimously seen as the leaders, and the low Machs were the ones whose opinions were influenced by the discussion. These laboratory findings of high Machs taking control were later supported in the field study mentioned earlier in which high Machs took over the leadership in classroom research teams.

Although high Machs have consistently appeared to be in control in these and other studies, they score in the *external* direction on Rotter's (1966) Internal versus External Locus of Control Scale, compared to low Machs who claim to believe in internal control. The present interpretation of this finding is that the external items on the Locus of Control Scale present a probabilistic view of social life, acknowledging that one's fate may often be influenced by chance or luck, whereas the internal items depict persons as captains of their own destiny. As noted earlier, it is possible that the high Machs are being realistic, whereas lows are answering as they feel life ought to be.

Legislature: The Locus of Cognitive Focus

One way high Machs may succeed in their manipulations is by paying attention to winning. They keep their mind's eye focused on what has to be done to win; low Machs are more liable to be distracted. It's not that low Machs are not interested in winning; they are. It's that they get involved with other elements in the situation that are irrelevant to winning.

This hypothesis grew out of watching subjects play the Con Game. All the players appeared to be highly involved in the game. On a questionnaire after the game, high and low Machs both claimed they had been trying to win as hard as they could. A subjective impression, however, was that the high Machs had been involved in the *game;* lows seemed, somehow, more involved with other *players.* A little speculative generalizing led to the new hypothesis that high Machs maintain a cognitive focus on their goal, whereas lows are liable to be distracted.

To test this hypothesis (Geis, Weinheimer, & Berger, 1970), a situation was needed in which all subjects would strive to achieve some goal, *and* a potential distraction could be either present or absent. If the hypothesis is correct, low Machs should lose when the distraction is present and should not lose when there is no distraction.

Again, a game was used to avoid any reluctance about manipulating on the part of low Machs. Coleman's (1965) Legislature Game was revised for the study. Subjects participate in groups of seven. Each subject plays the role of a congressman. Winning depends on getting Congress (the group of seven players) to pass certain bills and defeat certain others. Thus, the game consists basically of lining up voting support in the group on assigned issues.

The potential for distraction was the content of the issues. Each group of subjects played two rounds of the game. In one round all the issues were salient and meaningful (e.g., raising the minimum drinking age, instituting universal military conscription, etc.). These "emotional" issues were selected for eliciting strong disagreement among students at the time. In the other legislative session, all the issues were matters of utter indifference to the subjects (e.g., issuing a new postage stamp, relocating the bureau of documents, etc.). The idea was that when meaningful issues had to be discussed in making deals to exchange voting support, the low Machs might get involved in the merits of the issues at the expense of efficiency in lining up allies, but they wouldn't have any such potential distraction in the trivial issues game. If high Machs somehow maintain a cognitive focus on the goal, the content of the issues should make little difference to them.

Method

The procedures for the emotional issues game and the trivial issues game were identical. First, the subject was assigned a set of five issues with payoff positions. Two were high payoff issues, each worth 50,000 constituency votes. One would pay off if Congress passed it, the other if Congress defeated it. Two were low payoff issues, worth 30,000 votes each. Again, payoffs depended upon getting Congress to pass one and defeat the other. The fifth issue for each subject was a pork barrel item worth 20,000 votes if Congress passed it.

The game began with an opening session of Congress. The seven subjects were seated in a circle, and each in turn had the option of making an opening statement. Most subjects used this opportunity to make position statements on their issues, buttressed with more or less elaborate supporting arguments. These statements provided a subject's first indication that others also had a payoff position on some of his issues. Depending on the whims and strategies of others in the group, a subject might have learned that he had both allies and enemies on four of his five payoff issues.

In fact, every issue except the pork barrel items had been assigned to four different players in the group. Two held the high payoff positions, one for passage, the other for defeat. Two others held the opposing low payoff positions on the same issue. Thus, for each of his 50,000- and 30,000-vote issues, a subject had one ally in the group and two enemies. More important, there were three players who were neutral and had no payoff position on the issue. These details were not explained to the subjects.

After the opening statements, Congress "recessed" for a 10-minute "cloakroom bargaining session." During this period subjects were free to move about the room as they wished, talk to whichever of the other subjects they could corner, and make whatever arrangements they could to line up voting support on their payoff issues. In general, efficient use of this bargaining period consisted in locating the three players in the group who were neutral on one's payoff issues before one's opponents got to them, and lining up their votes, usually in return for a promise to support them on one of their issues. Since three different players were neutral on each of one's four contested issues, the activity during the bargaining sessions was both lively and intense.

After the log-rolling period, Congress reconvened. The seven players were again seated in a circle, and each in turn proposed an issue for vote. The player who proposed an issue was allowed a brief argument for or against the bill, and then one equally brief rebuttal was permitted. Then the group voted on the issue. Vote was by show of hands, and no abstentions were allowed, so all subjects could see just how everyone voted on every issue.

Subjects were scheduled on the basis of Mach scores obtained earlier in the semester. The Mach Scale distribution of male student's scores was divided into sextiles (the median was 103.5), and at least one subject from each sextile was scheduled for each group. A total of 54 subjects participated, 29 low Machs and 25 highs.

Results

Payoffs were described to subjects in multiples of 10,000 to approximate numbers of constituency votes a legislator might find meaningful. To simplify discussion all payoffs were divided by 10,000. The average value of this game was 9.86 points (one of two 5-point issues, plus one of two 3-point issues, plus most of the 2-point port barrel issues).

In the trivial issues games, the low Machs did just as well as the highs. In fact, the directional difference (not statistically significant) was in favor of the lows; they averaged 10.21 points per game, compared to 9.32 for highs, as shown in Figure 8–3. Since the game was designed so that equitable and mutually advantageous bargains were easy to find and make, the high Machs had no advantage over lows in the trivial issues game.

However, these same low Machs lost to the highs when salient issues had to be discussed. In the emotional issues games, the high Machs averaged 11.24 points per game, while the lows managed only 8.86. This finding supports the hypothesis that low Machs can be distracted by irrelevant affect. When meaningful issues had to be discussed in bargaining, the low Machs evidently got involved in the content of the issues at the expense of efficiency in lining up the crucial alliances. The results suggest that a significant advantage of high Machs is that they are able to keep their mind's eye on their goal and do not get distracted by aspects of the situation that are irrelevant to winning.

It might be supposed that the low Machs lost in the emotional issues game because they refused to lobby against their convictions. This was not the case. In fact, the low Machs lost to the highs most dramatically on precisely those issues on which they privately supported their payoff position. All seven of the emotional issues had been selected on the basis of eliciting virtually unanimous

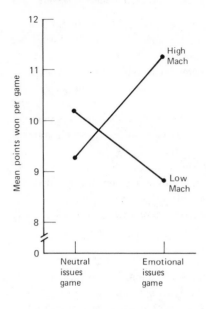

Figure 8-3. Mean Legislature score by Mach of subject and type of issues used in the game ($n = 25$ high Machs, 29 lows). (From Geis, Weinheimer & Berger, 1970, p. 221)

opposition in the entire student population. Each player had a high payoff position on two issues. On one he held the popular *anti* position, on the other the unpopular *pro* position. The high Machs won nearly every one of their popular, high payoff issues. They averaged 4.20 points out of the possible 5.00. In contrast, the low Machs won their popular high payoff issue only about half the time, averaging 2.41 points. Clearly, conscience was not the cause of the low Machs' undoing.

It cannot be argued that the low Machs did not understand the game. They did just as well as the highs on high value issues in the trivial issues game. And in the introductory part of the game, when players had a chance to make a statement to the group, the low Machs mentioned their high payoff issues more often than their low value issues. In this introductory period the high Machs mentioned their popular issues, regardless of payoff value. Apparently they believed that successful politicians "tell 'em what they want to hear."

Again in this study, the Machiavellianism of the person interacted with the characteristics of the situation. In the Con Game the high Machs won more in the ambiguous condition. The Legislature study showed that their ability to win can be attributed, at least in part, to a psychological mechanism that might be called "cognitive focus," but this mechanism can produce a difference in outcome only if the situation contains some emotionally involving element irrelevant to outcome.

Persuasiveness: A Debating Contest

The Con Game and the leadership studies mentioned earlier suggested that high Machs might be more persuasive than lows. High Machs might be more able to make demands, assertions, or arguments sound credible and convincing. This idea was tested by Novielli (1968). Four subjects of the same sex participated in each session. Two subjects debated each other on a topic assigned by the experimenter while the other two listened, serving as judges. Debates between high and low Machs were judged by high-low pairs. The winner was determined by summing the independent ratings of the two subject-judges.

However, the Legislature study had shown that high Machs were more likely to win when lows were distracted by irrelevant affect. Defending one's own convictions against attack by an opponent should be more affectively ego involving than defending a position contrary to private belief. To test this idea, each pair debated twice. The topic assigned them each time was one on which they actually disagreed. In one debate, both were assigned to defend their own personal beliefs. In the other, both were assigned the position contrary to their own convictions.

The high Machs won these debating contests but only when both subjects were defending their true convictions. High Machs won in 22 out of 32 "sincere" debates but won only 17 of 32 "insincere" ones. The moral of this story seems to be that low Machs can be as persuasive as highs—provided they don't believe what they're saying. Or, only a high Mach can make the truth sound convincing.

If high Machs are the persuaders, lows are the persuadables. In the group discussion study mentioned earlier, the low Machs changed their opinion on the topic after the discussion, but the highs did not. In a questionnaire study (Harris, 1970), both high and low Machs reported attitude change after reading alleged scientific data contradicting their previous beliefs, but low Machs also reported change after reading alleged poll data showing that most educated people disagreed with them. The highs showed no opinion change in this social influence condition.

Social Facilitation: Arousal Interpreted

The idea that low Machs can be distracted from their goal by irrelevant affect was pushed one step further. Geis and Hopstock (1976) proposed that the affect which distracts low Machs might be attributable to the arousal produced by the presence of other people.

Social facilitation theory (Zajonc, 1965) proposes (1) that people are aroused by the mere presence of other people, and (2) that arousal enhances dominant responses. A dominant response is whatever act is already well learned and familiar to the person in the particular situation. For example, in a word association test the dominant response to "bacon" is "eggs."

From the two basic propositions of the theory one can deduce that people ought to do better on simple performance tasks in a group than they would do alone. In a simple performance task such as canceling all the vowels on this page of print, the correct response is easy—a series of pencil strokes—and the discrimination between vowels and consonants is already well learned and familiar. The number of vowels you cancel in a given period depends on how "activated" or aroused you are while you do it. According to social facilitation theory, you will be more aroused and therefore will cancel more vowels in the presence of others than you will alone. On the other hand, exactly the opposite would be true in a learning task. If you were asked to memorize the names of 10 strangers in a photograph, you should do better alone than in the presence of others. In a learning task the correct responses are not initially dominant. Whatever responses are initially dominant are probably not correct. If the presence of others enhances these incorrect responses, you would obviously do less well. There is a fair amount of research supporting this theory.

The question, of course, was whether these well-known arousal effects would be more distracting for low Machs than for highs.

Method

High and low Mach subjects, half men and half women, did two equivalent forms of a learning task, once alone and once in the presence of two observers. Each subject also did two equivalent forms of a performance task, once alone and once in the presence of observers.

Learning was measured with a paired associates task. The subject first saw a series of 10 portrait photographs of 10 different unfamiliar persons. Under each photograph was a nonsense syllable. The subject's job was to learn which syllable went with each face. After seeing the 10 photos with their syllables, the subject was shown the same 10 faces in the same order but without the syllables, and asked to write down the syllable that went with each one as it was shown. This entire procedure was then repeated, and the number of correct syllable identifications on the second test trial was taken as the subject's learning score. In the alone condition the subject did the task seated alone in the experimental room with the door closed. In the social condition the male experimenter and a female observer watched the subject attentively.

The performance task was vowel cancellation. The subject was given a page of printed material and asked to cancel as many vowels as possible in a three-minute period. Again, the subject did the task once seated alone in a room with the door closed, and also did the alternate form (a different page) with the experimenter and observer watching attentively.

Results

The presence of observers interfered with low Machs' learning more than with that of the highs, as shown in Figure 8–4. The same low Mach subjects who learned seven of the 10 face–syllable pairs working alone learned only five of 10 when they were observed. High Mach subjects learned six out of 10 in both conditions.

However, we cannot conclude that the low Machs were simply more aroused by the presence of others than the highs were. If that were the case, then the low Machs should also show a greater arousal effect on the performance task. In fact, as shown in Figure 8–5, it was the high Machs who tended to show a greater performance increase in the social condition. The low Machs canceled 15 more vowels in the group condition than they did in privacy, but the highs canceled 31 more. Although the high Machs' degree of increase over the lows' reached only borderline statistical significance, the fact that it was approximately twice the size of the lows' makes it impossible to ignore.

Both high and low Machs showed the effects of arousal in the presence of observers. Low Machs showed a decrease in learning, and highs showed an increase in performance.

Obviously, the low Machs were debilitated relative to highs in the social condition on both tasks. Obviously, there was something about the arousal produced by the social conditions that distracted the low Machs from the tasks.

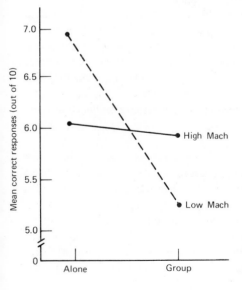

Figure 8–4. Paired associates learning scores, alone versus group, for high and low Mach subjects (n = 24 subjects per plotted mean). (From Geis and Hopstock, 1976)

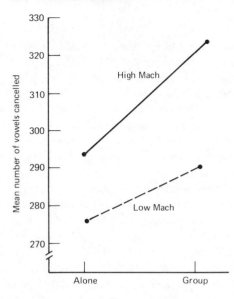

Figure 8-5. Vowel cancellation performance scores, alone versus group, for high and low subjects ($n = 24$ subjects per plotted mean). (From Geis and Hopstock, 1976)

The present hypothesis is that arousal not only facilitates the subject's dominant responses on the specific task assigned by the experimenter but also facilitates the subjects' dominant interpretation of the situation as a whole.

Arousal is a nonspecific state of physiological activation. A shot of adrenalin produces arousal, but arousal is a physiological concomitant of all emotional states. Schachter and his associates (1964) gave subjects a shot of adrenalin and produced euphoria, anger, or amusement, depending on the situation in which the subjects found themselves. In effect, given a state of physiological arousal, we interpret which emotion we are feeling by reference to the cognitive cues provided by the situation. The present speculation is that high and low Machs differ in their dominant interpretation of being attentively observed by others. The data suggest that high Machs interpreted their socially produced arousal as greater interest in the task, whereas lows interpreted the same arousal as apprehension about being evaluated.

This interpretation, although sophisticated and plausible, has yet to be tested directly. If it is correct, the low Machs' interpretation of arousal under observation as evaluation apprehension can be seen as another example of their tendency to be distracted from the task at hand by some irrelevant affect, as proposed in the Legislature study. The present study differs from the previous one in that this time there is evidence that high Machs are equally aroused. The difference appears to be that high Machs' dominant interpretation of arousal leads them to concentrate more on the task, whereas the lows' interpretation of the same arousal distracts them from the task.

The data also provide some other hints about how and when high Machs win and lows lose.

The Face-to-Face Hypothesis.   In their survey of Mach research, Geis and Christie (1970) proposed that high Machs have an advantage over lows in face-to-face situations. This study provided a direct test of that hypothesis. High and low Machs did not differ from each other in the alone conditions on either task. It was specifically in the social conditions, face-to-face with the observing experimenters, that high Machs did better than lows.

Learning versus Performance.   In most of the previous Mach research the tasks given the subjects had required both learning and performance in uspecifiable proportions. It was impossible to tell whether the high Machs' advantage was due to the learning component of the situation, to the performance element, to both, or to neither. The present data suggest that high Machs have the advantage in social situations in both learning and performance.

Learning Alone versus Together.   At the beginning of the chapter you were told that there is no difference in I.Q. between high and low Machs. Scholastic Aptitude scores for the Con Game subjects showed no Mach differences, and Christie (1970b) reported no Mach differences in six other samples using six different I.Q. measures. In the present study the high Machs' advantage over lows in the learning task was specific to the social condition. High and low Machs did equally well at memorizing the paired associates in privacy. Obviously, most I.Q. tests are taken in privacy. It may also be wise for low Machs to decline invitations to group-study sessions. However, most of our life outside of laboratories and classroom exams is social.

Taken together, these studies suggest that high Machs win by keeping their mind on the goal. Low Machs lose by getting distracted from the goal by affective involvement with elements in the situation irrelevant to winning. High Machs may interpret socially generated arousal as greater interest in the task, whereas lows interpret the same arousal as apprehension about being evaluated. The high Machs' advantage is specific to social situations, but it involves both learning and performance. Their success in interpersonal manipulation increases when the situation is more ambiguous or when it contains potentially distracting irrelevant affect. High Machs keep tabs on the situation by testing the limits; they control the group, possibly by their greater persuasiveness in presenting their own position.

In view of high Machs' effectiveness in getting the job done and in getting the credit for it, Christie (1970c) was surprised to find that high Machs in a national sample survey did not have better jobs or higher salaries than low Machs. Nor had the highs achieved greater upward mobility from their parents' social status.

One possibility is that low Machs gravitate toward jobs in which they can succeed, jobs in which advancement depends on objectively definable performance, whereas high Machs gravitate toward jobs in which the criteria for success are more ambiguous. Another possibility is that low Machs succeed by dint of long hours and hard work whereas highs achieve the same degree of success with less arduous labor but greater expertise in securing recognition.

PEOPLE AS PERSONS: THE SECRET LIFE OF THE LOW MACH

So far, the difference between high and low Machs has been conceptualized as "distraction" from the task at hand on the part of low Machs. The task at hand, of course, was the task assigned by the experimenter. The behavior that was measured was task-relevant behavior. But how did the subjects experience the entire situation in which they were doing the tasks? The first hint was provided by the low Mach subject in the Con Game who explained that he had not been able to use any strategies because his opponents in every game were different people. The present hypothesis is that while high Machs concentrate on the task, low Machs attend to the person. From this point of view it might be said that high Machs are distracted from wholehearted focus on the immediate person and conversation by their underlying preoccupation with some private, external goal.

The Eye of the Beholder

When two people have a conversation, how much of each of them gets through to the other, and what kinds of things get through? Presumably, of course, this depends on the openness and perceptiveness of the one in absorbing information, as well as on the characteristics the other possesses or reveals. From the way the high Machs had won so deftly in bargaining, it might have been supposed that they must be astute judges of other people. On the other hand, they had appeared to be strategy oriented not person oriented; it was the low Machs who had seemed to focus more on others as persons.

Fortunately, there was a body of research on "person perception" that suggested a solution. Two different kinds of accuracy in perceiving the characteristics of others had been identified (Cronbach, 1955). One was called "stereotype accuracy," a sort of overall accurate conception of what people in general are like. For example, if you were asked to guess three items of information, for example, degree of political liberalism, age, and preference for city versus country living, for three different people, and you made smaller errors in your guesses over all three items for all three people than someone else doing the same guessing task, you would have higher stereotype accuracy than the other person.

Notice that you would not need to be exactly accurate for any of the target people on any of the guessing items. Stereotype accuracy depends on the average amount of error over all the guesses: the smaller the average error, the greater the stereotype accuracy.

The other kind of accuracy in judging people was called "differential accuracy." This is the ability to tell how one person differs from another. Can you guess, for example, that Joe has a stronger preference for country living than Susan has? Differential accuracy seems to represent a sensitivity to particular other persons.

The hypothesis that seemed most likely to explain the previous Mach results was that high Machs would show stereotype accuracy and lows would show differential accuracy. The data (Geis and Levy, 1970) were collected at the conclusion of each of the sessions of Legislature, described above. The subjects had all been unacquainted before the session. They had all had two hours of highly involving interaction with one another in the course of playing the Legislature games. After the last game, the seven subjects were seated in a circle and given a copy of the Mach IV Scale with the reminder that this was a questionnaire they had all taken earlier in the semester. They were then asked to pick out the one other player in the group they thought they could size up most accurately and try to guess his answers to the items.

Results

The guessed Mach Scale responses were scored in the same way the initial Mach Scales had been scored. The Mach score derived from the guesses for a particular target person was then compared against that person's actual Mach score.

Overall Accuracy.   The high Machs as a group were amazingly accurate. Their guesses for their target persons averaged 108. Their target persons' actual Mach scores averaged 109. Since Mach scores can range from 40 to 160, and the standard deviation in this sample was 17, an average error of one point is very small. It is also very small compared to the low Mach's average error of 14 points. Low Mach judges' guesses for their target persons yielded an average Mach score of 93, but their target persons' actual scores averaged 107.

Obviously, the low Machs underestimated the Machiavellianism of others. If low Machs see other people's Machiavellian behavior as less Machiavellian than it really is, this would help to account for the way the high Machs manage to succeed in their manipulations in bargaining contests.

Perceiving Individual Differences.   Since low Machs had seemed to focus on particular other persons in previous studies, it had been expected that they would be more sensitive to the individual characteristics of their target persons. Since the subjects in this study made guesses for only one target person, it was not possible to tell whether the subject could differentiate accurately between one target person and another. However, it was possible to separate subjects who chose high Mach target persons from those who chose lows, and compare the Mach scores attributed to these two different kinds of target persons. These comparisons are shown in Figure 8–6. The high Machs did not differentiate at all between high and low Mach target persons. Low Machs did. Low Machs who chose a high Mach target predicted Mach scores averaging 98, whereas those who chose a low Mach predicted scores averaging 86. Although the low Machs underestimated Mach scores in general, they did differentiate accurately between high and low Mach others.

Assuming Similarity. Low Machs saw their target person as being much more similar to themselves than he actually was. The answers they guessed were much more like the answers they themselves had given initially than the target person's actual answers warranted. In the person perception literature, this has been called the tendency to ''assume similarity.'' This is usually seen as an error tendency, a distortion of accuracy. However, this particular distortion can also be seen as a cognitive translation of feelings of empathy. If low Machs do in fact

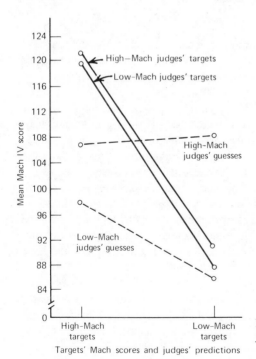

Figure 8–6. Targets' Mach scores and judges' predictions. (From Geis and Levy, 1970, p. 216)

open themselves up to others, if they put themselves emotionally in the other's place, it would not be surprising to find that they somehow feel close to others with whom they have interacted. These feelings of psychological closeness may have been translated into guesses of attitudinal similarity on the Mach Scale. Since they had maintained no psychological distance, they had no perspective to judge others' differences from themselves.

High and Low Machs as Target Persons.   High Machs were overchosen as target persons. Recall that subjects were instructed to choose "the one person in the group you think you can size up best." Recall also that the subjects had no idea which of them was a high Mach and which was a low; they had never heard of "Machiavellianism." They had only the two hours of playing Legislature together as a basis for selecting their target person. The high Machs must have appeared transparent, open, and easily predictable. In fact, they turned out to be less predictable. Subjects who chose high Mach target persons misjudged their Mach scores by an average of 18 points; low Mach targets' Mach scores were misjudged by only 7 points.

The curious paradox is that although subjects chose high Machs as "easiest to predict," in fact the lows were the easiest. Evidently there was something about the way the low Machs had related to others in the preceding interactions that gave others an accurate impression of where they stood on the Mach dimension. High Machs had managed to convey the impression that they were predictable, but in fact they had given others little basis for accuracy in judging them.

As shown in Figure 6, the greatest accuracy was achieved when both judge and target person were low Machs. This may have been owing partly to the low Mach judges' tendency to assume similarity (with target persons who, by chance, were actually similar), but assumptions of similarity cannot be the whole explanation since the low Mach judges also correctly differentiated between high and low Mach target persons. It appears that low Machs may·be more effective at both giving and receiving person-specific information, especially when paired with another low Mach.

Overall, this study showed that Machiavellianism is related to accuracy in judging the characteristics of another person. High Machs seem to have an accurate conception of what others in general are like. The low Machs' ability to place another person (relatively) higher or lower on the Mach scale suggested that they must attend to particular characteristics of particular other people with whom are interacting. Their tendency to assume similarity might be interpreted as a consequence of feelings of openness, closeness, or empathy in their previous interactions with the person. High Machs are seen by others, especially low Machs, as less Machiavellian than they really are. They are seen as more predictable; in fact, they are less predictable. The greatest accuracy in person perception occurred when both judge and target were low Machs.

Encountering: What Low Machs Do

Low Machs get carried away with each other when they interact. High Machs stand off from others, maintaining psychological distance and keeping their minds on the situation as a whole in terms of their own private goals.

At about the same time that the Legislature and Eye of the Beholder studies were being done, Durkin (1970) was developing a theory of "encountering." An encounter, in this theory, is a special kind of interaction between people. In an encounter the participants open themselves up to each other; they respond to what is happening between them at the moment and may get carried away in the process in directions they never anticipated. The encounter process is spontaneous and unpremeditated. Encounters may be friendly or hostile; they may be creative or banal. What makes a particular interaction an encounter is not *what* is said or done but how it all comes about. Durkin contrasted the encounter process with a different kind of interpersonal process he called a "cognitive exchange." In cognitive exchanges people talk about a topic or work at a task. The goal of the exchange is predefined, and the conversation or action is directed toward that goal. The participants are not open to each other as persons, or to following in any direction the process may take; rather, everything is filtered for its relevance to the predefined goals of the participants. In a cognitive exchange, the goals are brought into the situation individually by the participants; in an encounter, the goals emerge and develop spontaneously in the process of the moment.

Most interpersonal situations contain elements of both encountering and cognitive exchanging, but there are situations in which one predominates over the other. An example of a cognitive exchange is a well-run committee meeting. The committee's business is brought up, one item at a time. Each item is dealt with as required, and the group members stay on the (predefined) topic. Another example of a cognitive exchange is a small discussion seminar in college. The participants all focus on a predefined topic and exchange information and opinions about the topic. An encounter, on the other hand, might occur when two friends meet for a quick beer after work and get so involved in their conversation that two hours slip by before they know it. Notice that phrase, "before I knew it." It is a phrase aptly used by people who have been involved in some kind of encounter in attempting to explain the situation, later, to someone else. According to Durkin, the encounter process is basically a noncognitive action process. It is a process by which people move psychologically. Cognitive exchanges are cognitive processes. Few committee meetings or college seminars go two hours overtime without anyone noticing, however important and interesting the meetings or seminars may be.

Durkin's hypothesis was that low Machs are encounter prone, and high Machs are encounter blind. This would explain how low Machs get carried away in interpersonal situations, and before they know it, the prize has been secured by someone else. It would also explain how low Machs are open to others as persons.

How can this encounter process be measured? One way is to find a situation in which the experimenter can measure how much two people are responding to each other directly and personally, as distinguished from the way they would respond to anyone in general who happened to be in the situation with them. To do this, Durkin used a subjects-by-subjects design. This is a simple experimental design, but since it is not widely used in psychology, let's begin with an example.

The basic idea is that combinations of persons are observed rather than combinations of situational variables. For example, suppose four friends, Ann, Betty, Chuck, and Dan, decide to enter a dancing contest. During the contest each of the women will have one turn dancing with each of the men. Ann and Dan hit it off together beautifully; the judges give them a score of 75. But when Ann dances with Chuck, that team gets a score of only 25. Similarly, Dan and Betty just can't get together and also make only a 25. Does this mean that Ann and Dan are simply better dancers, and Betty and Chuck are less skillful? If that were true, then when Betty and Chuck dance together they should get a very low score indeed, but in fact it turns out that Betty and Chuck as a team are just as good as Ann and Dan. Obviously, all four are equally skillful as dancers. Ann's average dance skill over "partners in general" is 50; so is Betty's, and so are Chuck's and Dan's. What makes the difference in this group is who dances with whom. This situation is shown in the lefthand side of Figure 7. The dance scores of each of the four pairs are shown in the four cells at the top and are diagrammed below. Those who are familiar with statistics will recognize the crossed lines as the familiar interaction effect. The results that are obtained cannot be explained by either variable (in this example, by either person) alone; rather, the results depend on a particular combination. In this example, you cannot predict a team's dance score by knowing the individual skills of the two partners separately; you have to know who danced with whom. Each member responded to who his or her partner was, in particular.

A numerical interaction score can be calculated from these four team scores. The interaction score represents in numbers how much difference it makes to the participants to be paired with one or the other of the two possible partners.

A situation with no encountering is shown in the right half of Figure 8–7. Another group of four friends, Judy, Karen, Lenny and Monty, also come to the dancing contest, and each of them also dances with each of the opposite-sex partners in their group. But in this group it turns out that Judy is simply a better dancer than Karen, and Monty is a better dancer than Lenny. The dancing score of each of the four pairs can be predicted simply from knowing the individual dancing ability of the two partners separately. These four people are not responding to each other personally. Nothing develops between them that makes their

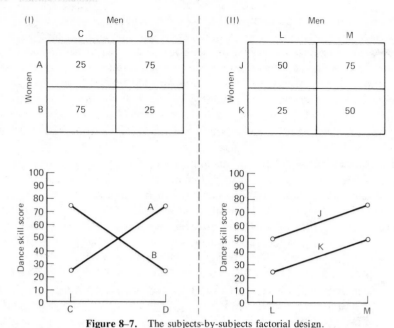

Figure 8–7.   The subjects-by-subjects factorial design.

(I) All subjects-by-subjects interaction, teams AC, AD, BC, and BD dance skill scores. (II) No subjects-by-subjects interaction, teams JL, JM, KL, and KM dance skill scores.

(I) Calculation of interaction score				(II) Calculation of interaction score			
=	(AD − AC)	−	(BD − BC)	=	(JM − JL)	−	(KM − KL)
=	(75 − 25)	−	(25 − 75)	=	(75 − 50)	−	(50 − 25)
=	50	−	(−50)	=	25	−	25
=	50	+	50	=		0	
=		100					

(From Durkin, 1970, p. 264)

dance scores either more or less than could have been predicted on the basis of the skills each of them brought individually to the team. The parallel lines of the graph of these scores show no interaction, only main effects of differences in skill level. When the numerical interaction score for this group is calculated, it turns out to be zero.

Method

Instead of dancing contests, this study used the ball and spiral game shown in Figure 8–8. The two players hold the apparatus between them by the handles at either side so that together they can tilt it to any angle. To begin the trial the experimenter places a tennis ball at the bottom of the spiral ramp. The task of the

The ball and spiral in play

Figure 8–8. The ball and spiral in play. (From Durkin, 1970, p. 265)

two players is to tilt the spiral continuously around so that the ball rolls up the ramp and eventually into the goal cup at the top. This is a relational task. A tilt by one partner has an effect only in relation to the action on the apparatus at the same moment by the other partner.

Four subjects, two men and two women, were scheduled together. The study was run in adjoining experimental rooms with two experimenters and two ball and spiral devices. When the subjects arrived, the two men were taken to one room and the two women to the other for 15 minutes of practice. Then each man was randomly paired with one of the women, and the two opposite-sex teams each played 10 trials. A trial began when the experimenter placed the ball at the base of the ramp and ended either when the team got the ball all the way up the ramp and into the goal cup at the top or when the ball fell off the ramp. The team's score for the trial was the number of quarter turns up and around the ramp the team had rolled the ball before it fell off. Scores could range from one to 17. After the first set of 10 trials, the women switched partners and played 20 trials with the other man. Then partners were switched again, and the two original opposite-sex teams played a final set of 10 trials. This counterbalancing was designed to compensate for any practice or fatigue effects that had not been eliminated in the initial practice trials.

Twenty-three groups (92 subjects) participated in this study. The Mach scores of the four members of each group were averaged. The groups were then classified as high Mach or low Mach on the basis of a median split of the distribution of these group-average Mach scores (95.50), giving 11 high Mach groups and 12 low Mach groups.

Results

The prediction was that the low Mach groups would show the interaction effect as in Figure 8–7, that pairs of low Machs would do either better or worse together than could have been predicted from their individual skills separately. The high Mach groups were expected to show less interaction, indicating that the high Mach subjects were treating their two partners alike and doing as well with each as individual skill levels would permit. This prediction was tested by calculating an interaction score for each foursome. First, the woman whose average team scores with her two male partners differed most from each other was identified. This woman was called A in the low Mach groups and J in the high Mach groups. Then the man who did best with this woman was identified and called D in the low Mach groups and M in the high Mach groups. This procedure ensured that all interaction scores would be positive and that they could range from zero upward. The interaction score for each group was calculated as shown in Figure 8–7. The results are shown in Figure 8–9. The average interaction score for the low Mach groups was 2.38, about twice as large as the high Machs' average interaction score of 1.01.

The average skill score of the high Mach teams was 12.69, not significantly higher than the low Machs' average score of 11.64. There was no relation at all between the average skill of a group and the interaction score of that group. The correlation between interaction score and skill level was .03.

Teams of two low Machs did better or worse together than their separate skills could account for. The two low Machs together became engrossed in the interaction that developed between them and got carried away into either much better or much worse performance than skill alone could have produced. This kind of process occurred less in high Mach teams. Apparently high Machs played the situation, the game, from their own individual perspective and were not influenced into unexpected performance levels by their particular partners. The predefined goal for the subjects, of course, was rolling the ball up the spiral ramp. The measure of success in achieving this goal was the total (or average) skill score of the team. High Mach teams concentrated on the predefined goal. Their performance could be predicted from the individual skills of the members involved.

Durkin theorizes that (1) cognitive exchanges are reciprocal individual effects, predictable from the goals of the individuals prior to the exchange, whereas encounters are mutual group system effects that are unrelated to predefined individual goals (as the interaction scores were uncorrelated with skill scores in this study). The two other characteristics that distinguish encounters from cognitive exchanges have already been mentioned: (2) Cognitive exchanges are (ob-

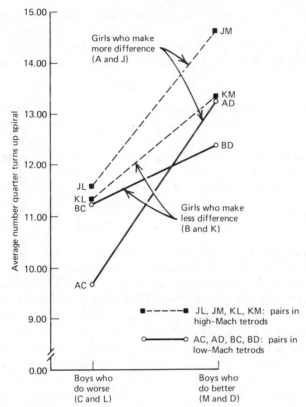

Figure 8–9.   Subjects-by-subjects interaction in low Mach versus high Mach groups. (From Durkin, 1970, p. 269)

viously) cognitive, whereas encounters are noncognitive. Two people engaged in a cognitive exchange do what they do because of what they know; the exchange process is guided by individual memory of predefined goals. Two people engaged in an encounter do what they do because of what they are; they are open to whatever the interaction between them at the moment happens to be. (3) Cognitive exchanges are convergent whereas encounters are divergent. In a cognitive exchange the group process converges on the private goals of the participants. In encounters the group process diverges from private goals; participants respond spontaneously to the event of the moment and get carried away in directions irrelevant to prior goals.

Durkin interprets these results as indicating that low Machs respond to others more openly, more personally, more spontaneously. Low Machs are more apt to be carried away—before they know it—in whatever direction the other is going.

High Machs maintain more individual (cognitive) control; they filter out the "distractions" of different partners or momentary events and maintain their own goal-directed paths. High Machs can be seen as being distracted from encountering by their preoccupation with maintaining cognitive focus on the task.

And on to Romance

High Machs may be better strategists, but low Machs may have the advantage in romance. In the previous studies high Machs have been selectively preferred and chosen over lows in a variety of situations. In the Con Game, lows preferred highs as coalition partners; in the group discussion and the classroom project studies, all subjects chose high Machs as leaders; and in the Eye of the Beholder they chose highs as target persons. But in all of these situations the choice of high Machs was task related. What happens if there is no external, predefined task? Suppose subjects found themselves interacting together with no objective other than the experience itself?

Novgorodoff (1974) studied groups of 12 subjects. Each group had six men and six women, three high Machs and three lows of both sexes. Each group met for three hours divided between two sessions a week apart. The purpose of the study, subjects were told, was to try out some sensitivity training procedures for groups. During the sessions the group members were in fact guided through a series of increasingly unstructured interpersonal sensitivity exercises. The exercises were designed so that every member interacted with every opposite-sex person several times in each session. At the end of each session, subjects completed a short questionnaire containing, among other things, a three-item scale of romantic attraction on which they rated all the opposite-sex members of their group.

All men, both high Machs and lows, expressed greater romantic preference for low Mach women, as shown in Figure 8-10. Consistent with previous findings, it was the low Mach men who discriminated most. If low Mach women are more sought after by more men, they are likely to have more first-choice romantic relationships. And the men they prefer are the low Mach men. High Mach women preferred high Mach men. These findings suggest that low Machs of both sexes might have more first-choice romantic partnerships. The major problem with this conclusion, of course, is that having a romantic preference is one thing; establishing the relationship is another. The low Machs' advantage of being the first choice of those they prefer may be only an unrealized potentiality if high Machs are quicker to translate interest into action.

Cheating and Dissonance

High Machs' strength, their attention to cognitive definitions, is also their weakness. You can fool a high Mach with facts. Low Machs are influenced more by

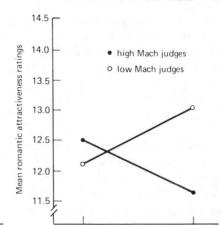

Figure 8–10.   Machiavellianism and romantic attraction. (From Novgorodoff, 1974)

persons than by facts. In the previous studies, low Machs have consistently discriminated between others who actually differed in Machiavellianism without the aid of any explicit cues that might have alerted subjects to expect differences. High Machs have also discriminated in some studies, but less frequently, less strongly, and in The Eye of the Beholder study less accurately.

To Cheat or Not To Cheat?

What would happen if subjects were given explicit but false cognitive cues about a target person? This was the first step in a study by Bogart, Geis, Levy, and Zimbardo (1970) designed to test a dissonance theory prediction. The test required that subjects perform some counterattitudinal act with either high or low external justification for doing it. The counterattitudinal act was cheating in an experiment. Although classroom cheating reputedly occurs, all evidence indicates that subjects do not ordinarily cheat in psychological experiments. The high and low justifications were created by having the subject urged to cheat by an attractive, competent, prestigious (alleged) partner versus being urged to cheat by an unattractive, incompetent, low status (alleged) partner.

Method.   Subjects were told that the purpose of the study was to compare the problem-solving performance of teams of workers with similar or different personalities under various conditions. All true subjects (all males in this study) had previously taken a "personality test" (including the Mach Scales). The other "subject" arrived shortly (actually a confederate of the experimenter) and was given the same explanation. The subjects were then told that since they would be working as a team each would be given some information about his partner, as well as the promised results of his own personality test. The two subjects were taken to separate rooms to receive this private information from the experimenter.

All naïve subjects received the same favorable interpretation of their personality test results. They were shown a profile indicating that they were well above average in intelligence, responsibility, lack of neurotic symptoms, and so on. This was to prevent any identification, later, with the incompetent partner. They were then given some "basic information" about their partner. Half of the subjects were given the high status partner description, and half were given the low status partner description. The high status description informed the subject that his partner was a graduate law student, that he had graduated *cum laude* and Phi Beta Kappa, and that his hobbies were amateur photography and football. In addition, the experimenter mentioned that the partner had scored "very well" on the same personality test as the subject. Subjects given the low status description learned that their partner was a freshman majoring in metal shop in the school of education, that he had no honors, no hobbies, and no interests. In addition, the experimenter mentioned that the partner had "done poorly" on the personality test and had "some weaknesses in some areas of psychological functioning." The confederate, of course, never knew which description the subject had received.

The two subjects were then brought together to begin work as a team on a human-relations problems test. This test, actually fabricated by the experimenter, was described as a new psychological test that was going to be used extensively in industry and was thought to be quite valid. It was emphasized that it was a test of knowledge, not a test of opinion. It was presented in multiple-choice format. The first nine problems were relatively easy; a "rational" solution was always included among the answer alternatives. The second nine problems were ambiguous and more difficult. The problems in the final set were impossible; no reasonable solution was among the answer alternatives.

As the two subjects were finishing the easy problems, the phone on the experimenter's desk rang. (The following procedure was adapted from Exline et al., 1970.) From the experimenter's conversation the subjects could infer that someone was demanding her immediate presence elsewhere. At first she protested over the phone that she was in the middle of running an experiment and could not leave. Finally, she agreed to go. In some apparent consternation she explained to the two subjects that she had to go up to the next floor in the building. She asked them to continue working on the test, to time themselves, and when they were finished to bring their test papers up to her at a specified room number on the floor above.

After the experimenter left the two subjects worked in silence on the increasingly difficult problems. Gradually the confederate began to give distress signals. He scratched his head, showed a "frustration" facial grimace, and shifted in his chair. Finally he broke his pencil and went up to the experimenter's desk to get another. While he was there, he picked up a paper from her desk and said, as if half to himself, half to the naïve subject, "Here's the answer key." He paused a moment. Then he said, "I'm going to use it; I don't want our team to look stupid." He returned to his desk, looked at the key, and copied down an answer. Then, offering the page to the subject, said, "You wanna look?" If the naïve subject accepted the key, the two completed the test, handing the key back and forth. If the subject refused, the confederate continued cheating alone until the second-to-last problem, then said, "You better look," again offering the key. If the subject refused again, the confederate waited till the final problem, again offered the key, and said, "You gotta look; you'll never get this one." Throughout this sequence, the confederate first suggested, then urged, cheating by the naïve subject, and set the example but never forced the naïve subject to cheat.

Results. There was no difference in cheating, overall, between high and low Mach subjects. (The median Mach score in this sample was 104.2) Half of the high Machs cheated, and about half of the lows did, also. However, there was a Mach difference in discriminating between partners. In this situation the high Machs discriminated overwhelmingly, and lows did not. In general, high Machs cheated with the high-status partner and refused to cheat with the low-status partner. For low Machs, cheating was not systematically influenced by partner description. These results are shown in Table 8–3.

In this situation the subjects had two sources of information about their partner. One source was the cognitive, descriptive information about their partner provided before the session by the experimenter. The other source of "information" about their partner was being in his physical presence during the test-taking

Table 8-3 Number of Subjects Who Complied (Cheated) and
Refused to Comply, by Mach and Dissonance Condition

	High Machs			Low Machs		
	Cheated	Refused to cheat	Total	Cheated	Refused to cheat	Total
Low Status Partner	5	13	18	6	8	14
High Status Partner	11	3	14	7	7	14
Total	16	16	32	13	15	28
	$\chi^2 = 6.22, p < .02.$			$\chi^2 < 1.00$, n.s.		

Source: Bogart, Geis, Levy & Zimbardo, 1970, p. 245.

session, observing his cheating, and hearing him suggest and urge the mutual cheating.

High Machs' behavior was based on the cognitive description of the partner provided initially by the experimenter. They decided whether or not to cheat on the basis of private knowledge about their partner brought into the session with them. The high Machs' decisions can be seen as rational. The attractive partner was allegedly well-adjusted, competent, and intelligent. If problems arose (e.g., if the experimenter had returned and caught them), this attractive partner could reasonably be assumed competent to handle the situation. On the other hand, the alleged characteristics of the unattractive partner provided little justification for engaging in a risky cheating venture with him.

Recall, though, that both the attractive and unattractive partner descriptions were in fact false. The actual person who served as the confederate was the same person, regardless of the description given the subject. The low Machs' actions with their partner were not influenced by the false descriptions. They evidently cheated or refused to cheat depending on how they felt about the particular person serving with them in the experiment.

In four different studies and in completely different situations, high Machs have attended to explicit cognitive cues about the situation (including other persons in the situation with them) and have ignored or been insensitive to personal, individual characteristics of other persons. In these same four studies, without being given any explicit cues and in spite of false cues, low Machs have responded differently to others who were actually different.(1) In the Con Game players were given no hint that partners differed in Mach score, and low Machs preferred high Machs over middle Machs as partners, whereas highs did not discriminate between middles and lows. (2) In the Eye of the Beholder study, low Machs guessed their high Mach target persons as being higher in Machiavellianism than low Mach target persons, and again, in spite of the actual difference, high Mach subjects made no discrimination. (3) In the ball and spiral study on encountering, low Machs were influenced away from their individual skill level on the task by the particular partner they were paired with at the moment, but high Machs played according to skill with all partners. (4) Finally, in the cheating study low Machs ignored the false cognitive descriptions of a partner, but high Machs used the descriptions to decide whether or not to cheat as urged.

No Dissonance for High Machs

Dissonance is the uncomfortable state of having inconsistent cognitions. In the cheating study just described dissonance was created by knowing one had cheated with poor justification. In general, psychologists have been interested in dissonance because it produces "irrational" attitude change. If people are persuaded to do something they do not believe in, this creates the unpleasant dissonance of the inconsistent cognitions, "I don't believe in X," and "I just did

X." One way dissonance can be reduced is by changing one of the cognitions. Since it is very difficult to change a cognition representing an overt act (e.g., few people can convince themselves they did not cheat when in fact they did), the only cognition that can be changed is the one representing the initial belief. In the cheating experiment, the subject would have to change his belief from "I don't believe in cheating in experiments" to "I do believe in cheating in experiments." The psychological processes involved are difficult for many of us to acknowledge. First, we allow ourselves to be talked into doing something we do not believe in. Although this first step is irrational, it is understandable. But then we compound the irrationality by changing our initial belief to be consistent with the irrational behavior.

In the present study, the unattractive-partner description produced the high dissonance condition. The unattractiveness of the partner provided no rational justification for cheating as he urged. The attractive-partner description produced the low dissonance condition. Although the subject was still doing something he privately did not believe in, he had a seemingly rational justification for his behavior: He had cheated because a high status, attractive teammate wanted him to. The dissonance prediction, then, was that subjects who cheated with the unattractive partner should describe themselves as less moral afterward, whereas subjects who cheated with the attractive partner would show less change in how moral they claimed to be. Since it seemed a little too obvious to ask subjects, "How much do you believe in cheating in experiments?" the Mach IV Scale was used as a measure of the subject's endorsement of conventional morality in general. After the cheating session the subject was asked to take the "Personality Test" again. Subjects who had cheated with low justification were expected to show an increase in Mach IV score compared to those who cheated with greater justification.

Results. Low Machs showed the predicted dissonance effect, but high Machs did not. As shown in Figure 8–11, the low Machs who cheated with the unattractive partner scored about eight points higher on the Mach IV Scale than they had two weeks earlier, while the lows who cheated with the attractive partner went down a little in Mach score (as if they were saying to themselves, "Yes, I *do* believe in honesty and morality; I just cheated because that nice partner wanted me to"). On the other hand, high Machs did not change in Mach score after cheating. The few who had finally been persuaded to cheat with the unattractive partner did not raise their Mach score by describing themselves as less moral than they had previously. Their apparent decrease in Mach score was not statistically significant.

Dissonance is usually described as a cognitive phenomenon, and high Machs are the ones who attend to cognitions. Yet the high Machs showed no dissonance effects. In fact, dissonance operates *on* cognitions, but the force that operates

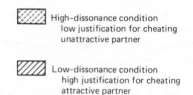

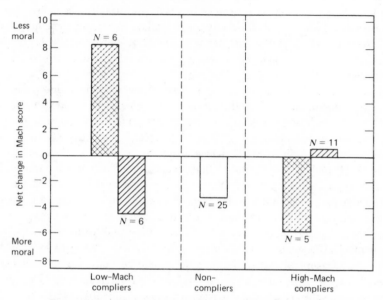

Figure 8–11.   Mach IV change after cheating or refusing to cheat.

High versus low dissonance for low Mach compliers, $t = 4.35, p < .01$; for high Mach compliers, $t = 2.10, p < .10$. High versus low Mach compliers: in the high dissonance condition, $t = 4.05, p < .01$; in the low dissonance condition, $t = 1.95, p < .10$. (From Bogart, Geis, Levy & Zimbardo, 1970, p. 247)

may not be cognitive. A purely cognitive response to the dissonance dilemma would not produce attitude change. The purely cognitive response would be to cognize having acted irrationally, to acknowledge the discrepancy between belief and behavior. This is apparently what high Machs did. The force that moves low Machs into dissonance-reducing attitude change is less describable. It may be a commitment to consistency, fear of losing face, or something else. Whatever it is, it appears to be reliable. In three other dissonance studies in which Mach scores of subjects were known (Bogart, 1971; Epstein, 1969; Feiler, 1970), high Machs have shown no dissonance-reducing attitude change; in every case the lows did.

The two parts of this study together illustrate the different psychological processes influencing the behavior of high and low Machs. In the face-to-face cheating session, the high Machs used their cognitions to guide their behavior, complying differentially depending on the information they had about their partner; but the low Machs' overt behavior (cheating or not cheating) in the face-to-face action situation was not influenced by their prior cognitions about their partners. In the second part of the session the subject's private cognitions about himself were measured. The high Machs' cognitions were not influenced by their behavior in the cheating session, but low Machs changed their cognitions to fit their behavior. It appears that high Machs use their cognitions to guide their behavior but do not allow their behavior to influence their cognitions. Low Machs, on the other hand, did not use the false cognitive cues to guide their behavior, but then they did allow their behavior, in light of these cues, to influence their own subsequent cognitions about themselves. High Machs act by what they know, lows by what they feel. For high Machs, actions follow cognitions; for lows, cognitions follow actions.

CONCLUSIONS

The conclusion that high Machs think first and act accordingly whereas lows act "before they know it" and cognize later fits the results of all the Mach studies. High Machs win when manipulation can influence the outcome because they keep their mind on the task and act on the basis of planned strategies aimed at the goal. Low Machs lose because they find themselves responding before they know it in ways irrelevant to the goal of winning. When high Machs use their talents for private goals seen as illegitimate by others, they are called "manipulators." The same talents applied to approved goals are described as "interpersonal competence" or "effective leadership."

Low Machs are more open to others, more personal, more in touch with others as individuals. Encountering, according to Durkin, is a noncognitive action process. Low Machs move psychologically with their partners. In contrast, high Mach maintain psychological perspective and deal with others impersonally. High Machs attend to the cognitive definition of the situation and to their own individual strategy for dealing with "others in general" in ways that are highly effective, in general, for achieving the cognitively defined goals. Life for high Machs may be a series of achievements, for low Machs a series of experiences.

This is not to suggest that high Machs are more interested in achievement or that lows are more interested in experience. Quite the contrary. Low Machs *have* experiences; they think and worry and strive for achievements. They have to, precisely because they are distracted so easily away from tasks and into encountering. High Machs, on the other hand, do not have to puzzle over how to succeed at tasks. Rather, they seem especially interested in the encounter process. They also claim they do it and enjoy it. And, of course, it is entirely possible that high Machs do "let themselves go" in encountering in situations other than when they are serving as subjects in experiments. However, there have been no systematic observations to date in which what high Machs did could clearly be interpreted as encountering. The kinds of situations in which they might do this, and the extent to which they might do it, remain open questions.

SUMMARY

"Machiavellianism" as measured by the Mach Scales is a consistent and reliable individual differences variable. The cognitive or attitudinal component is a belief that people are weak and manipulatable. Scores on the Mach Scales also predict the theoretically implied volitional component, a willingness to attempt manipulation when the situation warrants it. The Scales can also be considered an ability measure: High Machs are more successful in manipulating others to get what they want.

Situational Variables Influencing the Mach Effect

In some situations high and low Machs behave differently; in other situations there is no Mach effect. Situational characteristics that produce Mach differences have been termed latitude for improvisation, irrelevant affect, and face-to-face contact (Geis & Christie, 1970).

Latitude for Improvisation. High Machs win when interpersonal manipulation can influence the outcome. The more unstructured or ambiguous the situation is, the more outcome can be influenced by improvisations, the more they win. High Machs doubled their winning margin over lows in the ambiguous condition in the Con Game compared to the unambiguous condition in which power positions were laid out on the table for all to see. On the other hand, high Machs do not win when the situation only requires choosing among a set of predefined alternatives (e.g., Christie & Boehm, 1970; Christie, Gergen, & Marlowe, 1970). High Machs also did not win in the ball and spiral game, which requires moment-to-moment improvisation. But ball and spiral improvisations are relational and depend on coordination between the partners; unilateral improvisation is disastrous. The improvisations required by the ball and spiral game are also noncognitive in nature. The high Mach improvisational forte seems to require a base of other people's cognitions on which to operate.

Irrelevant Affect. When the situation contains some potentially involving element irrelevant to winning, low Machs can get distracted from the task goal. High Machs ignore the distractions and concentrate on winning. In the Legislature study the low Machs lost to the highs when relevant issues that were meaningful to the subjects had to be discussed in bargaining for voting support, but the same lows did not lose when the issue content was trivial. Similarly, in the debating study high Machs won over low Mach opponents when both subjects were defending their private convictions on a meaningful issue, but highs did not win significantly when both were defending insincere positions. When the affect that is irrelevant to the task is focused on other persons in the situation, high Machs win at the task but low Machs have a more personal experience.

Face-to-Face Contact.   High Machs win when the task must be done in a face-to-face situation; they do not win at tasks done in privacy. This hypothesis was first inferred from a comparison of situations in which high Machs had won with others in which they had not. It was subsequently tested in the social facilitation study in which subjects worked at the same tasks once alone and once in the presence of two attentively observing experimenters. High and low Machs did ot differ in either learning or performance in the alone conditions, but highs did better than lows in the social conditions.

There are two reasons for the importance of the face-to-face variable in producing Mach effects. One reason is that one of the ways high Machs succeed is by manipulating other people's cognitions and commitments, and others are more accessible to such manipulations in face-to-face situations. The second reason for the importance of the face-to-face variable is that others who are physically present are a prime source of distracting involvement for low Machs.

Characteristics of High and Low Machs

When face-to-face situations provide latitude for improvisation and contain potential affective distractions, high and low Machs often differ in behavior. High Machs are "cool"—objective, unflustered, in control. Low Machs are "warm"—empathizing, involved, distractible. The behavioral differences can be seen as a difference in focus of attention—a focus on cognitions versus persons—a difference in response to social pressure, and a difference in social control.

High Machs Attend to Cognitions; Low Machs Attend to Persons.   High Machs operate on the situation as a whole in terms of the cognitive cues available. They concentrate on the task and their own private goal. For high Machs, actions follow cognitions. Low Machs attend to other persons as individuals and see things from the other's point of view. They can get carried away in interpersonal interactions in directions that may have little to do with the task or goal they started out with. For low Machs, cognitions follow actions.

High Machs attend to the situation as a whole and change their strategy when the situation changes. They manipulated visibly and statistically more than low

Machs in the Machiavel test-administering situation when the victim had no recourse, but not in the Con Game when potential victims could retaliate. One result of their sensitivity to the limits of the situation is that they never appear to be obvious manipulators—when such an appearance might work to their disadvantage. In fact, it is often the low Machs who appear unreasonable.

Persons make more difference than cognitions to low Machs but not to highs. Changing partners in the ball and spiral game did not change the situation for high Machs; they played as skillfully as they could with both persons alike. Similarly, they did not differentiate between high and low Mach target persons in guessing Mach scores. But changing the explicit, cognitive description of a partner in the dissonance study, from a law student to an incompetent freshman, did change the situation for them. In each of these studies low Machs responded differently to persons who actually differed. They did better or worse with different partners in the ball and spiral game than skills could account for; they guessed high Mach target persons as more Machiavellian than lows. But the actually false descriptions of their partner in the dissonance study had no influence on whether they cheated with him or not.

In attending to the explicit, cognitive cues relevant to winning, high Machs do not allow ethical, ideological, or interpersonal concerns to distract them from task-relevant strategy. On the other hand, they do not appear cold or unconcerned with others. On the contrary, they appear quite aware of others' concerns. But rather than taking others' concerns as their own, they use them to their own advantage—for example, to strike a bargain ensuring themselves the lion's share of the payoff. High Machs are the ones who get others to help them win in such a way that the others feel grateful for the opportunity.

There are two ways of viewing the orientation to cognitions characteristic of high Machs compared to the orientation to persons of lows. One is to see the low Mach as being distracted from winning at the task by getting involved with other persons or other affective concerns in the situation. The consequence, of course, is that the high Machs win. Another way of looking at the same difference is to see the highs as being so preoccupied with the task that they close themselves off from the open, spontaneous interactions with other persons that most people seem to value. One consequence is that low Machs seem to be better at guessing the characteristics of others as individuals. Another is that lows may have the advantage in choice of romantic partnerships. Other consequences can only be speculated about, since there is little previous work in psychology on differences between cognitive and empathic relationships. We need measures of the quality, the "feel" of experience in interpersonal relationships, rather than relying on the cognitive residue of the experience after the fact.

High Machs Resist Social Influence; Low Machs Accept Social Influence. In general, a high Mach will not do or say or believe something just because someone else wants him to; a low Mach is more likely to go along with another's wishes. In the dissonance study high Machs cheated or refused according to what they believed about their partner, not according to the wishes he expressed; they cheated when they perceived some rational justification for it. Low Machs cheated because their partner wanted them to, regardless of justification. High Machs can be persuaded to take an action they do not believe in, as low Machs can, also. But the high Machs do not then follow the dissonance pattern of changing their beliefs to "justify" their action. It is low Machs who produce the dissonance results.

High Machs as well as lows change their beliefs when they are given more rational justification. The difference is that low Machs can also be persuaded by sheer social pressure.

High Machs Control the Group; Lows Accept the Structure Defined by Others.   In the Con Game the fact that the high Machs were sought as partners was interpreted as evidence of their dominance in the triads. And they were rated higher in leadership in the group discussion study. Presumably the behaviors fellow participants described as "providing leadership" could be classified as initiating and controlling the group structure during the discussion. Leadership in the student research teams was clearly assumed by high Machs in the classroom project study, and teams with high Mach leaders got more of their resources applied to the project. Either the groups' efforts were being mobilized by their acknowledged leaders or by some other factor mysteriously correlated with having a high Mach leader. In the debating contests the high Machs were more persuasive when both opponents were defending personal convictions. Persuasiveness in selling one's own ideas would seem an obvious asset in exercising social control. On the other hand, Oksenberg (1970) had subjects work at a tedious task, and gave participants the opportunity between trials to send notes to each other suggesting ways to organize the group to work more efficiently at the task. High Machs did not become leaders in this situation. It is possible that high Machs take over only when they are motivated to do so.

REFERENCES

Bogart, K. Machiavellianism and individual differences in response to cognitive inconsistency. *Journal of Social Psychology*, 1971, *85*, 111–119.

Bogart, K., Geis, F. L., Levy, M., & Zimbardo, P. No dissonance for Machiavellians. In R. Christie and F. L. Geis, *Studies in Machiavellianism*. New York: Academic Press, 1970.

Braginski, D. D. Machiavellianism and manipulative interpersonal behavior in children. *Journal of Experimental Social Psychology*, 1970, *6*, 77–99.

Christie, R. Scale Construction. In R. Christie and F. L. Geis, *Studies in Machiavellianism*. New York: Academic Press, 1970.(a)

Christie, R. Relationships between Machiavellianism and measures of ability, opinion, and personality. In R. Christie and F. L. Geis, *Studies in Machiavellianism*. New York: Academic Press, 1970.(b)

Christie, R. Social correlates of Machiavellianism. In R. Christie and F. L. Geis, *Studies in Machiavellianism*. New York: Academic Press, 1970.(c)

Christie, R., & Boehm, V. Machiavellians meet Miss Rheingold. In R. Christie and F. L. Geis, *Studies in Machiavellianism*. New York: Academic Press, 1970.

Christie, R., & Geis, F. L. *Studies in Machiavellianism*. New York: Academic Press, 1970.

Christie, R., Gergen, K. J., & Marlowe, D. The penny-dollar caper. In R. Christie and F. L. Geis, *Studies in Machiavellianism*. New York: Academic Press, 1970.

Coleman, J. Personal communication, 1965.

Cronbach, L. J. Processes affecting scores on "understanding of others" and "assumed similarity." *Psychological bulletin.* 1955, *52,* 177–193.

Crowne, D. P., & Marlowe, D. A new scale of social desirability independent of psychopathology. *Journal of Consulting Psychology,* 1960, *24,* 349–354.

Durkin, J. E. Encountering: What low Machs do. In R. Christie and F. L. Geis, *Studies in Machiavellianism*. New York: Academic Press, 1970.

Edwards, A. L. *The social desirability variable in personality assessment and research.* New York: Dryden Press, 1957.

Epstein, G. F. Machiavelli and the devil's advocate. *Journal of Personality and Social Psychology,* 1969, *11, 38*–41.

Exline, R. V., Thibaut, J., Hickey, C. B., & Gumpert, P. Visual interaction in relation to Machiavellianism and an unethical act. In R. Christie and F. L. Geis, *Studies in Machiavellianism*. New York: Academic Press, 1970.

Feiler, J. Machiavellianism, dissonance, and attitude change. In R. Christie and F. L. Geis, *Studies in Machiavellianism*. New York: Academic Press, 1970, p. 391. (Abstract).

Geis, F. L. Machiavellianism in a semireal world. *Proceedings of the 76th Annual Convention of the American Psychological Association,* 1968, *3,* 407–408.

Geis, F. L. The con game. In R. Christie and F. L. Geis, *Studies in Machiavellianism*. New York: Academic Press, 1970.(a)

Geis, F. L. Bargaining tactics in the con game. In R. Christie and F. L. Geis, *Studies in Machiavellianism*. New York: Academic Press, 1970.(b)

Geis, F. L., & Christie, R. Overview of experimental research. In R. Christie and F. L. Geis, *Studies in Machiavellianism*. New York: Academic Press, 1970.

Geis, F. L., Christie, R., & Nelson, C. In search of the Machiavel. In R. Christie and F. L. Geis, *Studies in Machiavellianism*. New York: Academic Press, 1970.

Geis, F. L., & Hopstock, P. Machiavellianism and social facilitation. Submitted for publication, 1976.

Geis, F. L., Krupat, E., & Berger, D. Taking over in group discussion. In R. Christie and F. L. Geis, *Studies in Machiavellianism*. New York: Academic Press, 1970, p. 392. (Abstract).

Geis, F. L. & Levy, M. The eye of the beholder. In R. Christie and F. L. Geis, *Studies in Machiavellianism*. New York: Academic Press, 1970.

Geis, F. L., Weinheimer, S., & Berger, D. Playing legislature: cool heads and hot issues. In R. Christie and F. L. Geis, *Studies in Machiavellianism*. New York: Academic Press, 1970.

Harris, T. M. Machiavellianism, judgment independence and attitudes toward teammate in a cooperative judgment task. In R. Christie and F. L. Geis, *Studies in Machiavellianiasm.* New York: Academic Press, 1970, p. 393. (Abstract).

Novgorodoff, B. D. *Boy meets girl: Machiavellianism and romantic attraction.* Unpublished master's thesis, University of Delaware, 1974.

Novielli, J. *Who persuades whom. Unpublished master's thesis, University of Delaware, 1968*

Oksenberg, L. Machiavellianism and organization in five-man task-oriented groups. In R. Christie and F. L. Geis, *Studies in Machiavellianism.* New York: Academic Press, 1970, p. 397. (Abstract)

Rotter, J. B. Generalized expectancies for internal versus external control of reinforcement. *Psychological Monographs.* 1966, *80* (Whole No. 609).

Schachter, S. The interaction of cognitive and physiological determinants of emotional state. In L. Berkowitz (Ed.), *Advances in experimental social psychology.* New York: Academic Press, 1964.

Witkin, H. A. Individual differences in ease of perception of embedded figures. *Journal of Personality,* 1950, *19,* 1–15.

Zajonc, R. B. Social facilitation. *Science,* 1965, *149,* 269–274.

APPENDIX A

PERSONALITY INVENTORY ANSWER SHEET

INVENTORY I

	Disagree						Agree
1.	1	2	3	4	5	6	7
2.	1	2	3	4	5	6	7
3.	1	2	3	4	5	6	7
4.	1	2	3	4	5	6	7
5.	1	2	3	4	5	6	7
6.	1	2	3	4	5	6	7
7.	1	2	3	4	5	6	7
8.	1	2	3	4	5	6	7
9.	1	2	3	4	5	6	7
10.	1	2	3	4	5	6	7
11.	1	2	3	4	5	6	7
12.	1	2	3	4	5	6	7
13.	1	2	3	4	5	6	7
14.	1	2	3	4	5	6	7
15.	1	2	3	4	5	6	7
16.	1	2	3	4	5	6	7
17.	1	2	3	4	5	6	7
18.	1	2	3	4	5	6	7
19.	1	2	3	4	5	6	7
20.	1	2	3	4	5	6	7

INVENTORY II

	A	B	C
1.	A_____	B_____	C_____
2.	A_____	B_____	C_____
3.	A_____	B_____	C_____
4.	A_____	B_____	C_____
5.	A_____	B_____	C_____
6.	A_____	B_____	C_____
7.	A_____	B_____	C_____
8.	A_____	B_____	C_____
9.	A_____	B_____	C_____
10.	A_____	B_____	C_____
11.	A_____	B_____	C_____
12.	A_____	B_____	C_____
13.	A_____	B_____	C_____
14.	A_____	B_____	C_____
15.	A_____	B_____	C_____
16.	A_____	B_____	C_____
17.	A_____	B_____	C_____
18.	A_____	B_____	C_____
19.	A_____	B_____	C_____
20.	A_____	B_____	C_____

Total, I _____

Total, II _____

Sum (I + II) _____

Mean _____ (Sum of I + II, divided by 2. Round up to nearest whole number if necessary)

Mean + 20 _____ This is your final SCORE.

APPENDIX B

PERSONALITY INVENTORY I

Listed below are a number of statements. Each represents a commonly held opinion and there are no right or wrong answers. You will probably disagree with some items and agree with others. We are interested in the extent to which you agree or disagree with such matters of opinion.

Read each statement carefully. Then indicate the extent to which you agree or disagree by circling the appropriate number on the answer sheet. The numbers and their meaning are indicated below:

If you *agree strongly*	Circle 7
If you *agree moderately*	Circle 6
If you *agree slightly*	Circle 5
No Opinion	Circle 4
If you *disagree slightly*	Circle 3
If you *disagree moderately*	Circle 2
If you *disagree strongly*	Circle 1

First impressions are usually best in such matters. Read statement, decide if you agree or disagree and the strength of your opinion, and then circle the appropriate number on the answer sheet. *Give your opinion on every statement.*

If you find that the numbers to be used in answering do not adequately indicate your own opinion, circle the one that is *closest* to the way you feel.

The statements follow.

1. Never tell anyone the real reason you did something unless it is useful to do so.
2. The best way to handle people is to tell them what they want to hear.
3. One should take action only when sure it is morally right.
4. Most people are basically good and kind.
5. It is safest to assume that all people have a vicious streak and it will come out when they are given a chance.
6. Honesty is the best policy in all cases.
7. There is no excuse for lying to someone else.
8. Generally speaking, people won't work hard unless they're forced to do so.
9. All in all, it is better to be humble and honest than to be important and dishonest.

10. When you ask someone to do something for you, it is best to give the real reasons for wanting it rather than giving reasons which carry more weight.
11. Most people who get ahead in the world lead clean, moral lives.
12. Anyone who completely trusts anyone else is asking for trouble.
13. The biggest difference between most criminals and other people is that the criminals are stupid enough to get caught.
14. Most people are brave.
15. It is wise to flatter important people.
16. It is possible to be good in all respects.
17. Barnum was wrong when he said that there's a sucker born every minute.
18. It is hard to get ahead without cutting corners here and there.
19. People suffering from incurable diseases should have the choice of being put painlessly to death.
20. Most people forget more easily the death of their parents than the loss of their property.

APPENDIX C

PERSONALITY INVENTORY II

You will find 20 groups of statements listed below. Each group is composed of three statements. Each statement refers to a way of thinking about people or things in general. They reflect opinions and not matters of fact—there are no "right" or "wrong" answers.

Please read each of the three statements in each group. Then decide *first* which of the statements is *most true* or comes *the closest* to describing your own beliefs. Mark a plus (+) in the space on the answer sheet.

Then decide which of the remaining two statements is *most false* or is *the farthest* from your own beliefs. Place a zero (0) in the space on the answer sheet.

Here is an example:

_____	A.	It is easy to persuade people but hard to keep them persuaded.
___+___	B.	Theories that run counter to common sense are a waste of time.
___0___	C.	It is only common sense to go along with what other people are doing and not be too different.

In this case, statement B would be the one you *believe in most strongly* and A and C would be ones that are not as characteristic of your opinion. *Statement C* would be the one you *believe in least strongly* and is least characteristic of your beliefs.

You will find some of the choices easy to make; others will be quite difficult. Do not fail to make a choice no matter how hard it may be. You will mark *two* statements in each group of three—the one that comes the closest to your own beliefs with a + and the one farthest from your beliefs with a 0. The remaining statements should be left unmarked.

Please do not omit any groups of statements.

1. A. It takes more imagination to be a successful criminal than a successful business manager.
   B. The phrase, "the road to hell is paved with good intentions" contains a lot of truth.
   C. Most people forget more easily the death of their parents than the loss of their property.
2. A. Men are more concerned with the car they drive than with the clothes their wives wear.
   B. It is very important that imagination and creativity in children be cultivated.
   C. People suffering from incurable diseases should have the choice of being put painlessly to death.
3. A. Never tell anyone the real reason you did something unless it is useful to do so.
   B. The well-being of the individual is the goal that should be worked for before anything else.
   C. Once a truly intelligent person makes up his mind about the answer to a problem he rarely continues to think about it.
4. A. People are getting so lazy and self-indulgent that it is bad for our country.
   B. The best way to handle people is to tell them what they want to hear.
   C. It would be a good thing if people were kinder to others less fortunate than themselves.
5. A. Most people are basically good and kind.
   B. The best criterion for a wife or husband is compatibility—other characteristics are nice but not essential.
   C. Only after a person has gotten what he wants from life should he concern himself with the injustices in the world.
6. A. Most people who get ahead in the world lead clean, moral lives.
   B. Any man worth his salt shouldn't be blamed for putting his career above his family.
   C. People would be better off if they were concerned less with how to do things and more with what to do.

7. A.   A good teacher is one who points out unanswered questions rather than gives explicit answers.
   B.   When you ask someone to do something for you, it is best to give the real reasons for wanting it rather than giving reasons which might carry more weight.
   C.   A person's job is the best single guide as to the sort of person he is.

8. A.   The construction of such monumental works as the Egyptian pyramids was worth the enslavement of the workers who built them.
   B.   Once a way of handling problems has been worked out, it is best to stick with it.
   C.   One should take action only when sure that it is morally right.

9. A.   The world would be a much better place to live in if people would let the future take care of itself and concern themselves only with enjoying the present.
   B.   It is wise to flatter important people.
   C.   Once a decision has been made, it is best to keep changing it as new circumstances arise.

10. A.   It is a good policy to act as if you are doing the things you do because you have no other choice.
    B.   The biggest difference between most criminals and other people is that criminals are stupid enough to get caught.
    C.   Even the most hardened and vicious criminal has a spark of decency somewhere within him.

11. A.   All in all, it is better to be humble and honest than to be important and dishonest.
    B.   A person who is able and willing to work hard has a good chance of succeeding in whatever he wants to do.
    C.   If a thing does not help us in our daily lives, it isn't very important.

12. A.   A person shouldn't be punished for breaking a law which he thinks is unreasonable.
    B.   Too many criminals are not punished for their crimes.
    C.   There is no excuse for lying to someone else.

13. A.   Generally speaking, people won't work hard unless they're forced to do so.
    B.   Every person is entitled to a second chance, even after he commits a serious mistake.
    C.   People who can't make up their minds aren't worth bothering about.

14. A.   A man's first responsibility is to his wife, not his mother.
    B.   Most people are brave.
    C.   It's best to pick friends who are intellectually stimulating rather than those it is comfortable to be around.

15. A.   There are very few people in the world worth concerning oneself about.
    B.   It is hard to get ahead without cutting corners here and there.

    C. A capable person motivated for his own gain is more useful to society than a well-meaning but ineffective one.

16. A. It is best to give others the impression that you can change your mind easily.

    B. It is a good working policy to keep on good terms with everyone.

    C. Honesty is the best policy in all cases.

17. A. It is possible to be good in all respects.

    B. To help oneself is good; to help others, even better.

    C. War and threats of war are unchangeable facts of human life.

18. A. Barnum was probably right when he said that there's at least one sucker born every minute.

    B. Life is pretty dull unless one deliberately stirs up some excitement.

    C. Most people would be better off if they controlled their emotions.

19. A. Sensitivity to the feelings of others is worth more than poise in social situations.

    B. The ideal society is one where everybody knows his place and accepts it.

    C. It is safest to assume that all people have a vicious streak and it will come out when they are given a chance.

20. A. People who talk about abstract problems usually don't know what they are talking about.

    B. Anyone who completely trusts anyone else is asking for trouble.

    C. It is essential for the functioning of a democracy that everyone vote.

APPENDIX D

SCORING KEY FOR PERSONALITY INVENTORY I AND II

Inventory I

Write the item score to the right of each item, as follows:
Reverse score Items No. 3, 4, 6, 7, 9, 10, 11, 14, 16, and 17:

If Response Marked Is		Item Score Is
1	....	7
2	....	6
3	....	5
4	....	4
5	....	3
6	....	2
7	....	1

For all remaining items in Inventory I, the score is the response number marked. Write these also to the right of each item.

Add up the 20 item scores.

Inventory II

Look up the score for each item in the table below. Your score for each item is shown in the column that matches your choices of + and 0 for that item. First score items no. 4, 5, 10, 11, 20, using the item scores on the first row in the table, as indicated. Then score items 8, 9, 12, 15, 16, using the second row, and so on. Write each item score to the right of the item on the answer sheet. When you have scored all the items, add up the 20 scores.

Item No.	A+ B CO	A+ BO C	A B+ CO	A BO C+	AO B+ C	AO B C+
4, 5, 10, 11, 20	3	1	5	3	7	5
8, 9, 12, 15, 16	5	3	7	1	5	3
1, 2, 6, 17	1	3	3	5	5	7
3, 13, 18	7	5	5	3	3	1
14, 19	3	5	1	7	3	5
7	5	7	3	5	1	3

Compute your total Mach Score: Add your score on Inventory I plus your score on Inventory II; then divide this sum by 2; then add 20.

Interpretation of Mach Scores

Are you a high Mach or a low Mach? That depends on the group of people you are in. If most of the others are higher than you, then you are a low Mach; if most of the others are lower, then you are a high. Mach scores are relative. Average Mach scores vary from one group of people to another and may also vary from one decade to another. Mach scores in large undergraduate psychology classes at the University of Delaware averaged about 98 from 1972 to 1977.

CHAPTER 9

The Need for Approval

JIM MILLHAM
University of Houston, Houston, Texas

and

LEONARD I. JACOBSON
University of Miami, Coral Gables, Florida

SOCIAL DESIRABILITY RESEARCH

The impetus for the work on approval motivation was provided by Edwards' research on social desirability (SD). In 1957 Edwards published an influential monograph, *The Social Desirability Variable in Personality Assessment and Research,* in which two distinct but related aspects of the social desirability variable were identified.

In the first approach, social desirability was viewed as a property of self-descriptive test items. In one study cited, Edwards (1953) correlated judges' ratings of the social desirability values of self-descriptive items with their probability of endorsement by subjects. The correlation of 0.87 obtained indicated that the more favorable the SD rating of a self-descriptive item, the greater was the probability of its endorsement for a given population under standard conditions. From these and other studies cited by Edwards, it seemed reasonable to conclude that the responses of individuals to traditional self-descriptive personality items could be predicted relatively accurately from the social desirability scale value of the items *apart from other factors.*

In the second approach, social desirability was viewed as a differential tendency of subjects to endorse socially desirable items. In this individual differences approach, the differential tendency of individuals to give socially desirable responses when confronted with a given item pool was measured. To implement this approach, an initial pool of 150 self-descriptive statements was drawn from items from the F, L, and K scales of the MMPI and from the Taylor Manifest

Anxiety Scale, the latter scale drawn also from MMPI items. A variety of items was employed to ensure heterogeneity of content.

For 79 of the 150 statements there was perfect agreement by 10 judges as to their social desirability value. This 79-item scale was then administered to a large group of subjects, and a final set of 39 items was chosen that showed the greatest differentiation between high and low scorers on the longer scale. This shorter 39-item scale became the Edwards Social Desirability Scale (ESD). High scores on this instrument measured the tendency of subjects to respond to self descriptive personality items in a socially desirable manner for statements of varied content. Low scores indicated a tendency to respond in a socially undesirable manner.

The relationships obtained when the Edwards Scale was correlated with traditional personality scales were quite impressive. For example, the correlations between many MMPI Scales and the SD Scale were great enough to suggest to Edwards and Walker (1961) that the SD Scale could be used as a short form of the MMPI. Although this contention has been hotly disputed (e.g., Dicken & Wiggins, 1964), the correlations remain of sufficient importance to this day to require—at the least—a thorough revision of formulations concerning the MMPI with regard to both its theory and its practice. Table 9–1 reproduces some of the relationships presented by Edwards concerning SD and the scales of the MMPI. Impressive correlations for SD and non-MMPI based scales were reported also.

The implications of these findings have been clearly stated by a number of

Table 9-1. Correlations Between the SD Scale and MMPI Scales

MMPI Scale	SD Scale 79 Items[a]	SD Scale 39 Items[b]
L	0.24	0.14
F	−0.82	−0.63
K	0.69	0.81
F-K	−	0.90
Hs	−0.70	−0.52
D	−0.69	−0.61
Hy	−0.38	0.08
Pd	−0.57	−0.50
Mf	−0.21	−0.36
Pa	−0.60	−0.09
Pt	−0.86	−0.85
Sc	−0.91	−0.77
Ma	−0.50	−0.13

[a]Fordyce (1956): N = 97 VA Neuropsychiatric Patients.
[b]Merrill and Heather (1956): N = 155 counseling center males.
Source: Abridged from Edwards, 1957.

investigators (Crowne & Marlowe, 1964; Edwards, 1970; Heilbrun, 1964). Crowne and Marlowe (1964) stated:

> From the magnitude of these correlations it is apparent that the systematic variance remaining after the correlations with the SD scale have been accounted for is small indeed. Evidently, then, there is little left in personality testing but social desirability. Since the SD scale relates so highly to the MMPI and to a wide array of personality tests, the logical extension of the social-desirability hypothesis would be that the SD scale is a kind of abbreviated universal personality test, from which an individual's scores on most other personality instruments could be predicted with impressive accuracy. (p. 15)

Heilbrun (1964) reached a similar conclusion concerning the relationship of SD to psychopathology.

> Psychopathology represents a deviation from socially desirable standards of behavior and its corollary, the greater the psychopathology, the greater the deviation. . . . the dimensions of psychological health and social desirability are in large measure one and the same.

THE MARLOWE–CROWNE SOCIAL DESIRABILITY SCALE (M–CSD)

The belief that social desirability and psychopathology were synonymous or highly related proved to be a popular one. However, the conception was not without its critics. An alternative explanation was provided by Crowne and Marlowe (1960). These authors suggested that the correlations obtained by Edwards were inflated by the procedure of using MMPI items as an indicator of social desirability. The argument is a persuasive one. The MMPI is a method of diagnosing psychopathology with items selected on the basis of their value in discriminating among clinically pathological groups. Therefore, it is not surprising that scores on the Edwards Scale, which is composed entirely of MMPI items, should correlate highly with other items from the same test, or even with other tests of psychopathology.

That the Edwards Scale confounds social desirability and psychopathology can be demonstrated almost intuitively by noting a frequently cited example. Consider the statement, "My sleep is fitful and disturbed." When an individual responds "false" to such an item, it is unclear whether the response indicates the presence of a social desirability response set or the genuine absence of the symptom queried.

To eliminate this condfounding of social desirability and psychopathology, the Marlowe–Crowne Social Desirability Scale (1960) was constructed entirely of non-MMPI items without apparent psychopathological content. Two types of items were employed. The first was items in which the keyed response was socially desirable but improbable of occurrence (e.g., "I always practice what I preach"). The second type consisted of items in which the keyed response was socially undesirable but probable of occurrence (e.g., "I like to gossip at times").

A set of 50 items was then selected and submitted to 10 judges for social desirability ratings. Unanimous agreement as to the social desirability value was obtained for 36 items and 90 percent agreement was obtained on an additional 11 items. These 47 items were then submitted to 10 additional judges who rated them concerning the degree of maladjustment implied by socially undesirable responses. The ratings ranged from extremely well adjusted (1) to extremely maladjusted (5). The mean rating for all the items was 2.8, which is slightly below the neutral point of the scale.

The initial 47-item version of the Marlowe–Crowne Scale was then administered to 76 students. An item analysis indicated that 33 of the statements discriminated between high and low scorers at the 0.05 level or better. Of these, 18 were keyed in the "true" direction and 15 in the "false" direction. These items became the final version of the scale and are shown in Table 9–2.

The method of scale construction employed by Marlowe and Crowne used procedures standard for that time although by contemporary standards they may appear to lack rigor. However, several methodological problems must be noted. First, the test items were rated dichotomously as socially desirable or undesirable. Consequently, the *degree* of social desirability or undesirability was not controlled in item selection. Second, although the ratings indicated that the scale's general content was unrelated to the pathology dimension, individual items had ratings that departed from this standard. Third, the final selection of test items was determined on the basis of the responses of 76 introductory psychology students. The use of a broader and larger sample would have been more likely to produce an instrument that would have held up more adequately in cross validations with different subject groups.

Crowne and Marlowe (1964) reported a test–retest correlation of 0.88 and an internal consistency coefficient of 0.88 for the final form of the scale. Using college students also, Miklich (1966) obtained a similarly high Kuder-–Richardson reliability estimate of 0.74 for M–CSD scores. Fisher (1967) reported a one-week test–retest reliability of 0.84 for Peace Corps volunteers. Since these values are acceptable, the reliability or internal consistency of the scale has never been seriously questioned. The M–CSD Scale items may also be classified on an additional dimension, one that has posed difficulties with regard to the problem of reliability. One type of item present in the scale consists of those in which a socially desirable characteristic is attributed to the self; the second consists in denying socially undesirabile characteristics. If the scale is to have reliability and internal coherence, summing across both types of items to

Table 9-2   The Marlowe-Crowne Social Desirability Scale

Personal Reaction Inventory

Listed below are a number of statements concerning personal attitudes and traits. Read each item and decide whether the statement is true or false as it pertains to you personally.

1. Before voting I thoroughly investigate the qualifications of all the candidates. (T)
2. I never hesitate to go out of my way to help someone in trouble. (T)
3. It is sometimes hard for me to go on with my work if I am not encouraged. (F)
4. I have never intensely disliked anyone. (T)
5. On occasion I have had doubts about my ability to succeed in life. (F)
6. I sometimes feel resentful when I don't get my way. (F)
7. I am always careful about my manner of dress. (T)
8. My table manners at home are as good as when I eat out in a restaurant. (T)
9. If I could get into a movie without paying and be sure I was not seen, I would probably do it. (F)
10. On a few occasions, I have given up doing something because I thought too little of my ability. (F)
11. I like to gossip at times. (F)
12. There have been times when I felt like rebelling against people in authority even though I knew they were right. (F)
13. No matter who I'm talking to, I'm always a good listener. (T)
14. I can remember "playing sick" to get out of something. (F)
15. There have been occasions when I took advantage of someone. (F)
16. I'm always willing to admit it when I make a mistake. (T)
17. I always try to practice what I preach. (T)
18. I don't find it particularly difficult to get along with loud-mouthed, obnoxious people. (T)
19. I sometimes try to get even, rather than forgive and forget. (F)
20. When I don't know something, I don't at all mind admitting it. (T)
21. I am always courteous, even to people who are disagreeable. (T)
22. At times I have really insisted on having things my own way. (F)
23. There have been occasions when I felt like smashing things. (F)
24. I would never think of letting someone else be punished for my wrongdoings. (T)
25. I never resent being asked to return a favor. (T)
26. I have never been irked when people expressed ideas very different from my own. (T)
27. I never make a long trip without checking the safety of my car. (T)
28. There have been times when I was quite jealous of the good fortune of others. (F)
29. I have almost never felt the urge to tell someone off. (T)
30. I am sometimes irritated by people who ask favors of me. (F)
31. I have never felt that I was punished without cause. (T)
32. I sometimes think when people have a misfortune they only got what they deserved. (F)
33. I have never deliberately said something that hurt someone's feelings. (T)

Source: Crown and Marlowe, 1960. Copyright 1960 by The American Psychological Association. Reprinted by permission.

obtain a total score requires the assumption that both categories be equivalent with respect to the construct measured.

There is evidence, however, that denying undesirable characteristics and endorsing desirable traits are not equivalent. Diers (1964) developed 10 40-item personality scales that differed with respect to content (socially desirable or undesirable) and direction of scoring (keyed true or false). The scales were administered to 146 male and 81 female undergraduates. The correlation between social desirability scores for an inventory containing socially desirable items and an inventory containing socially undesirable characteristics was 0.38. Although this correlation is significent at the 0.01 level, it indicates also that only 14 percent of the social desirability variance could be attributed to the joint tendency to deny what is undesirable and to attribute to oneself what is desirable.

A number of additional studies bear on this problem. Kogan and Boe (1964) selected 32 items with socially undesirable scale values from the Interpersonal Checklist and administered them to 52 psychiatric patients and 65 college students. For neither group could they demonstrate a significant relationship between endorsing socially desirable and denying undesirable characteristics. Only when they selected the items with the most extreme social desirability scale values and corrected for attenuation were they able to obtain significant correlations. For the psychiatric population, the correlation between endorsing desirable items and rejecting undesirable items was 0.50, and for the college students the correlation was 0.62.

Greenwald and Clausen (1970) administered the M–CSD Scale in Likert format to 36 male and 24 female undergraduates. They found scores obtained from positively and negatively keyed items to be moderately correlated (0.45). Ford (1964) obtained correlations for keyed true and keyed false items of 0.57 for 192 college students and of 0.50 for 124 high school students.

Further evidence against the equivalence assumption is provided by Rump and Court (1971), who found that the manner of responding to items on the Neuroticism Scale of the Eysenck Personality Inventory had a higher correlation with denying undesirable traits on the M–CSD Scale than to total score or to the tendency to attribute to oneself desirable traits.

Theoretically, if denying undesirable characteristics and endorsing desirable characteristics are equivalent aspects of the social desirability dimension as reflected in total M–CSD score, then the magnitude of the correlation between scores derived from the socially desirable items and scores derived from the socially undesirable items should approach the reliability coefficients for the total score. However, the correlations between the positively and negatively keyed items of the M–CSD Scale are very far from these reliability coefficients. It may be concluded that, although denying undesirable and endorsing desirable personality statements are significantly related response tendencies, they are not entirely equivalent. The lack of equivalence between these response tendencies was demonstrated further in a recent study in which they were individually related to censure-avoidant behavior (Millham, 1974). For men, denying undesirable behaviors only was associated with cheating to avoid negative evaluation, whereas for women, both response tendencies were related to censure-avoidant behavior. The small number of items in these subscales and the consequent restriction in range make the Marlowe–Crown Scale a poor choice for further investigation of the attribution and denial components of social desirability responding. A longer, more recently developed scale of approval motivation has been constructed to measure specifically the tendency to deny undesirable and to endorse desirabile personality statements (Jacobson & Kellogg, 1976). Initial patterns of intercorrelations among the instrument's subscales are supportive of their independent contribution to approval motivation.

In sum, the M–CSD score is comprised of two significantly but only partially related response tendencies. The first is the tendency to attribute socially desirable but improbable characteristics to oneself; the second is the tendency to deny undesirable but highly probable characteristics. There is evidence that these tendencies may be differentially related to other response modes as well. It is likely that conflicting results obtained in relating M–CSD scores to other behaviors may be influenced by the practice of summing across the attribution and denial components of the M–CSD Scale in order to obtain the total score.

A further word about sex differences. The early reliability studies—and many of the later validity studies—never evaluated adequately the operation of sex differences. In many instances sex differences were simply assumed not to be operative. The risks inherent in this assumption have since been demonstrated. Goldfried (1964) found that for 108 male and 110 female college students 17 items from the M–CSD Scale discriminated between high and low scores for men and 15 discriminated for women. However, only eight of these items were common to both samples.

Millham's (1974) finding that the censure-avoidant dimension of approval motivation includes different self-presentation modes for men (denying undesirable M–C items) and for women (endorsing desirable *and* denying undesirable M–C items) adds to the suspicion that such sex differences in discriminating power of M–C items may have been present and inadequately appreciated as far back as the scale construction phase of research in this area.

FROM SOCIAL DESIRABILITY TO NEED FOR SOCIAL APPROVAL

Crowne and Marlowe (1960) initially presented their measure as "a new scale of social desirability independent of psychopathology." This statement has never been well supported. In their 1964 publication, the authors presented a comparison of the correlations of the ESD and M–CSD Scales with various MMPI

Scales. In most instances the correlations of the M–CSD with the scales of the MMPI were lower than those obtained for the ESD. However, in a number of cases the correlations of the M–CSD and the MMPI Scales were both substantial and significant. In other instances, significant relationships would have been obtained if the samples employed had been larger.

The situation may best be illustrated by viewing the correlations of the Sc scale of the MMPI—an excellent indicator of psychotic psychopathology—with the SD scales. The correlation of the ESD with Sc is $-.73$; the correlation of the M–CSD with Sc is $-.40$. It may be that M–CSD and Sc are not identical, but by the same token they are hardly independent of each other.

An MMPI Scale that correlated more highly with M–CSD than ESD was the L scale. This measure, sometimes referred to as a lie scale, has been traditionally thought of as a "faking good" scale or as an indicator of one's motivation to look good. This type of response was viewed by Crowne and Marlowe as indicating the operation of a need for social approval. From this point on, investigators spoke of approval motivation rather than of a social desirability factor. This "need" for social approval was conceptualized as a reliance on the evaluative judgment of others. The reliance was hypothesized to result from two factors: a motive to obtain approval ("approach" behavior) and a motive to avoid disapproval ("avoidance" behavior).

Approval motivated individuals were expected to be more conforming, persuasible, and amenable to social influence. Their behavior was assumed to be normatively anchored with respect to social customs and sanctions. Individuals attempting to avoid disapproval were viewed as demonstrating defensive behavior in situations that might result in social censure.

Both motives were treated as different aspects of a single factor. The attempt to view two related but dissimilar motivational systems as aspects of a unitary construct created numerous difficulties and ambiguities both in the formulation of hypotheses and in the interpretation of data.

EVALUATIVELY DEPENDENT BEHAVIOR AND THE M–C

A wide variety of paradigms have been employed in delineating the high M–C scorers' reliance on external evaluative cues as guides and organizers of their behavior. These paradigms comprise two broad categories. The first examines the effect of the general social and evaluative environment on performance tasks such as rotary pursuit, groove steadiness, short-term memory and perceptual judgments. Behavioral instances of evaluative dependence are seen as behavior shifts occurring as a function of changes in the evaluative context, and the behavior of high M–C scorers is expected to be more influenced by such changes than that of the low scorers. The second major grouping of studies examines the differential effectiveness of social reinforcement for high and low M–C scorers. Heightened responsiveness to evaluative contingencies is viewed as an instance of evaluative dependence, and high M–C scorers are expected to show this greater conditionability and social compliance under contingent social reinforcement.

Social and Evaluative Context

In two studies relating the M–C and evaluative context to behavior (Strickland & Jenkins, 1964; Strickland, 1965), the facilitative and disruptive effects of evaluative feedback on motor performance tasks were investigated. On tasks requiring moving a stylus down increasingly narrow sides of a groove, persons scoring high on the M–C were found to show improvement following positive evaluation of their performance whereas low scorers were unaffected by positive feedback. Similarly, negative evaluation resulted in disruption and poorer performance on the task for high scorers but did not influence low-scoring persons. The investigators found also that this interaction of M–C level with type of feedback occurred only when the evaluation was specific to the task being performed and not when it referred to a related but different motor performance task. In contrast to these findings, Milburn, Bell and Koeske (1970) reported that performance on a verbal recall task was facilitated for high M–C scorers under conditions of both subtle praise and subtle censure. It would appear that high M–C scorers are more responsive to situations and interventions that modify the overall evaluative nature of the task, and that increases in evaluative relevance increase their motivation to perform well on the tasks. However, high M–C scorers do not seem particularly sensitive in discriminating positive and negative evaluative cues, and their performance is disrupted by negative evaluation only when it is obvious and specific to the performance task.

Concern over and dependence on personal evaluation by others is expected to manifest itself also in greater social compliance and conformity to the others' expressed opinions and judgments. Therefore, high M–C scorers are expected to maximize congruence between their own behavior and that of others in their immediate social and evaluative environment. In a study examining such congruence Strickland and Crowne (1962) investigated the relationship of M–C scores to conformity to an oppositional majority. In this task subjects listened to a series of taped "knocks" presented at a rate that could be readily and accurately perceived. The subject's task was to state the number of "knocks" he had heard on each trial. The subject was instructed to state his response into a microphone so that it could be recorded along with the previous subject's responses. On each trial the subject heard the responses of three previous subjects before his own response was recorded. In fact, the responses of these previous "subjects" were deceptions, and on 12 of the 18 trials the accomplice's judgments were inaccurate. The relationship of M–C score and yielding to the inaccurate group opinion was analyzed. High-scoring subjects were found to conform significantly more often than the low-scoring subjects. In a similar experiment employing a "live" rather than a taped oppositional majority, Marlowe, Stifler, and Davis (1962) found that high M–C scorers conformed more to the judgment of an incorrect majority than did low M–C scorers when the task was to identify the larger of two tachistoscopically presented clusters of dots. Since high M–C scorers are hypothesized to be more sensitive than low scorers to contextual cues indicating evaluative relevance, such tendencies to conform to the expressed opinions of others might be expected to vary more with differences in the evaluative relevance of the situation for high than for low M–C scorers. Miller, Doob, Butler, and Marlowe (1965) confirmed that whereas both high and low M–C scorers tend to agree with inaccurate statements experts make about them, only high M–C scorers show differential agreement as a function of variation in the status of the judges and consequences of the evaluation.

The evidence from these studies indicates that the behavior of high M–C scorers is in fact more influenced by overall evaluative and social context than that of low scorers. However, although they tend to be particularly sensitive to indicators of evaluative relevance, high M–C scorers seem to differentiate poorly between the positive and negative meanings of such cues.

Responsiveness to Evaluative Contingencies

The heightened responsiveness to evaluative contingencies expected of evaluatively dependent subjects has been investigated primarily within verbal conditioning paradigms. The social nature of the response class, of the reinforcement, and of the experimental situation have rendered such paradigms particularly useful for examining the effects of evaluative contingencies on high and low M–C scoring persons.

Crowne and Strickland (1961) asked subjects to say all the words they could think of without counting or using sentences or phrases as responses. In the positive reinforcement condition, the experimenter said, "mm-hmmm" each time the subject emitted a plural noun; in the punishment condition the experimenter said "uh-uh" each time a plural noun was given on a response. There was also a nonreinforced, nonpunished control condition in which no feedback was given to the subject. The proportion of plural nouns given as responses in each of the five-minute trial blocks was measured.

In the positive reinforcement condition the only group that demonstrarated an increase over trials in the proportion of plural nouns were the high M–C scorers. Furthermore, they were the only group that differed from the nonreinforced controls.

In the punishment condition no group displayed a decrease in the proportion of plural nouns over trials. However, the high M–C punished group did give fewer plural nouns for each five-minute period than did any other punished or control group. The failure to obtain a learning curve could be owing to the lack of a baseline period. If conditioning occurred early in the first five minutes, then no learning curve would be obtained with the five-minute trial blocks employed. If this were the case, then the lower proportion of plural nouns emitted by high M–C punished subjects for all trials could indicate response suppression in this group.

In a study examining the effectiveness of vicarious social reinforcement on the conditioning of first person pronouns as subjects of a stimulus verb (Marlowe, Beecher, Cook & Doob, 1964), only high M–C scoring subjects demonstrated conditioning. In a similar study employing direct reinforcement, Strickland (1970) found a significant biserial correlation between M–C score and conditioning when individual subjects were divided on the basis of their response to reinforcement into conditioned and nonconditioned groups.

Buckhout (1965) reported that when he used ''good'' as a reinforcer of verbal statements that were counter to their previously expressed attitudes, only high M–C scoring subjects demonstrated conditioning. Dixon (1970) found that high M–C scorers were as easily conditioned to emit positive as negative self-references whereas low scorers demonstrated no conditioning at all. These results indicate that the intrinsic meaning of their behavior is not as important to high M–C scorers as is the evaluation (social reinforcement) of the experimenter. Furthermore, evaluation by the experimenter seems to have little effect on the behavior of low M–C scorers.

Spielberger, Berger, and Howard (1963) conditioned subjects to use first person pronouns and were one of the few sets of investigators not to find conditionability differences between high and low M–C scorers. In other studies (Bryan & Lichtenstein, 1966; Krasner, Knowles, & Ullman, 1965), the investigators failed to support the greater conditionability of high M–C scorers, but the designs contained additional and possibly confounding elements that make direct comparison difficult.

The evidence from these studies provides support for the hypothesis that high M–C scorers are more responsive to contingent social approval and disapproval than are low M–C scorers. The ease with which high M–C scorers are conditioned to emit even negative self-references indicates their behavior is more dependent on the immediate evaluation of another than on their strong disposition toward positive self-description. The evidence suggests also that low M–C scorers resist direct and blatant attempts at social control of their behavior. Although confirming the evaluatively dependent nature of high M–C scorers, the studies do little to elucidate the motivational properties of the construct. The particular characteristics of social approval and disapproval as reinforcers may reflect two very different reinforcement operations. It may indicate that evaluatively dependent persons place a high value on the informational properties of social stimuli, especially when it comes from a high status source. McDavid (1962) has referred to this as the cognitive function of social reinforcement and has related it to Festinger's (1954) and Schachter's (1959) conceptualization of gregariousness and affiliation motivation. Such motivation would be characterized by a sensitization to evaluative cues and an active approach toward situations that could provide social evaluative information as a guide to behavior and understanding. On the other hand, sensitivity to social approval and censure may be construed as indicating an interpersonal need for maintaining the acceptance of others and the reinforcing function of social approval as operating affectively rather than cognitively. Such sensitivity to rejection is characterized by social conformity and compliance (Mehrabian, 1970a, 1970b) and by an avoidance of situations that are heavily evaluative. As indicated previously, early conceptualization of evaluative dependence failed to differentiate between the approach and avoidance dimensions of the construct. However, as the literature on the behavioral concomitants of M–C score has increased, the issue has become better clarified.

Evaluative Dependence: to Approach or to Avoid?

Research on the risk-taking behavior of high and low M–C scoring subjects has been particularly influential in resolving the alternative approach and avoidance conceptualizations of evaluative dependence. The relevance of the risk-taking paradigm lies in the ability to construct designs in which a conflict can be generated between the desire to obtain social evaluation and approval (high risk) and the desire to avoid social evaluation and disapproval (low risk). Differences in such high and low risk behavior might be expected to shed some light on the motivational characteristics of evaluatively dependent persons.

Kanfer and Marston (1964) studied preferences for different types of interaction in a psychotherapy analogue. Subjects would express their opinions on a topic and then request comments from one of two experimenters. Experimenter 1 (low risk) limited his comments to reflective rephrasing of what the subject said. Experimenter 2 (high risk) was directive and speculative about possible dynamic relationships between the subject's comments and his early experiences. Subjects were classified according to their preferences for either reflective (low risk) or interpretive (high risk) comments. Subjects who chose to receive the reflective experimenter's comments could be classified as preferring low risk comments; subjects who selected the interpretive experimenter could be classified as preferring high risk comments. In the original experiment and in a replication, subjects choosing low risk comments had higher M–C scores than subjects choosing high risk interpretations.

Efran and Boylin (1967) investigated a subject's willingness to volunteer as a participant in a group discussion in which he and the psychologist could learn something about the way the two of them interacted. Subjects could increase their chances of obtaining approval by agreeing to participate in such an experimenter-sanctioned group (approach–approval). On the other hand, subjects could avoid the possibility of unfavorable evaluation by choosing instead to be an observer rather than a group participant (avoidance–censure). The point biserial correlation coefficient between M–C score and volunteering to be a group participant was found to be −0.39. In addition, the mean M–C score for subjects volunteering to participate was significantly lower than for subjects choosing to observe the group. Thus, when confronted with the choice of approaching a situation in which approval could be gained or avoiding the possibility of negative evaluation, high M–C scorers tend to avoid rather than approach evaluative situations.

Thaw and Efran (1967) investigated the relationship of M–C score to willingness to take risks in a dart-throwing task. They reasoned, as had Barthel (1961) in an earlier study, that the defensive and self-protective tendencies of high M–C scorers would result in a restriction of risks (high difficulty throws) that they would choose to take on the dart-throwing task. Distance from target was marked off in one-foot intervals from one to 20 feet. The score obtained on the dart board was multiplied by the distance the subject was from the board on each trial. Subjects were free to choose the distance from which they threw on each trial. High M–C scorers were found both to restrict the range of their choices and to stand closer to the target than low M–C scorers. Such low risk behavior is similar to the defensiveness of failure-avoidant subjects reported in the dart-throwing experiments of Atkinson, Bastian, Earl, and Litwin (1960). High M–C scorers demonstrate a preference for the safe low risk goal-setting that will prevent failure, even when such low risk behavior will deprive them of the opportunity for outstanding success and approval.

These studies taken together offer strong support for the proposition that high M–C subjects set low goals and avoid taking risks. In the Efran and Boylin study, high M–C scorers chose to avoid potential evaluative situations; they sought to avoid rather than to obtain the evaluation of others, even when there was the possibility of positive as well as of negative evaluation. These findings are in accord with a censure-avoidant interpretation of need for approval.

In a series of studies relating M–C scores to cheating behavior (Berger, 1971; Jacobson, Berger, & Millham, 1970; Millham, 1974), it was found that the opportunity to avoid negative evaluation was a sufficient motivation for high M–C scoring subjects to cheat following failure but that the opportunity to achieve recognition of outstanding success by the experimenter was not sufficient motivation for high M–C scoring subjects to engage in such decidedly socially undesirable behavior. In addition, when amount of cheating was analyzed, highly evaluative dependent subjects were found to cheat only enough to avoid dismal failure, which emphasizes further the avoidant nature of evaluative dependence.

In sum, the high M–C scorers' conformity and social compliance, their responsiveness to socially evaluative stimuli, and their low risk, defensive behavior may be viewed as an avoidance response designed to forestall rejection and to be uncorrelated with expectations of approval. No study provides clear-cut evidence for M–C score to be measuring the strength of an approach–approval motive and in no circumstance where a subject was faced with a choice of approaching evaluation or avoiding it did a subject choose to approach.

Evaluative Dependence and Aggression

The need of evaluatively dependent persons to avoid negative evaluation and forestall rejection has led to a number of studies examining the relationship of M–C score to inhibition of aggression. It has been expected that high M–C scorers would inhibit direct physical or verbal attacks on another, since, in addition to being socially undesirable, it invites negative evaluation and attack from the other party.

In two studies (Altrocchi, Palmer, Hellmann, & Davis, 1968; Palmer & Altrocchi, 1967) M–C score was related to the tendency of subjects to rate the overt hostile behavior of others as deliberate or as unconscious. The categorization of an individual's behavior as intentionally hostile represents a negative evaluation and consequently may be considered a form of aggression. The subjects in these studies viewed a 15-minute sequence from the film *Twelve Angry Men*. This film segment included portions of a jury's deliberation. Three of the jurors were strongly and overtly hostile to the defendant. The subjects were asked to rate the degree of hostility each of the jurors expressed toward the defendant and to what extent these jurors were aware and deliberately hostile. The degree to which a subject was unwilling to categorize an overtly hostile juror's behavior as intentional could be viewed as hesitance to evaluate others negatively. In the Palmer and Altrocchi study (1967) the M–C scores of male college students were found to be related to subject ratings of unconscious hostile intent for only one of the hostile jurors. In the Altrocchi et al. (1968) study, the M–C scores of college men and of college women were found to be unrelated to attributions of hostile intent when no special instructions were given beyond those necessary to ensure completion of the rating scale. When the subjects were instructed further to be objective and inhibit their own hostile feelings, there were again no relationships of M–C scores to the hostility ratings. However, when the subjects were instructed to complete their ratings on the basis of their own "gut reactions," the M–C scores of the male subjects were found to be positively related to their categorization of hostile behavior as unconscious. Thus, in the absence of specific instructions to focus on one's own emotional arousal, there is no strong evidence for any relationship between M–C score and the tendency to rate as hostile another's behavior. When subjects are instructed to focus on their own emotional arousal, however, high M–C men have a tendency to rate the overt hostility of the jurors as being less deliberate than do the low M–C scorers. It might be speculated that inhibited perception of aggressive responses by high M–C scorers occurs only when their own aggressive feelings have been heightened to a level causing them anxiety.

In accord with this hypothesis are the data from the control groups in several studies relating aggression to M–C scores. These control groups represent the aggressive behavior of high and low M–C subjects in a variety of situations that included no experimenter manipulation designed to augment or precipitate aggression. Fishman (1965) reported no difference between high and low M–C scorers in the amount of aggression (negative evaluation) expressed toward an experimenter following a task in which the subject was required to count backward from 100 to one by threes. Fishman also found no differences between high and low M–C scorers in emotional arousal as measured by systolic blood pressure before and after the counting task. Conn and Crowne (1964) reported no difference between high and low M–C scores in the negative evaluation or in negative personality descriptions of a subject confederate with whom they interacted. During this interaction, the subject confederate told abysmally bad jokes at which he laughed uproariously, slapping his legs and doubling over with mirth. The confederate crumpled up papers and shot baskets; he flew frisbees across the room and made and flew paper airplanes. All the while the subject confederate attempted to involve the subject in these games. Conn and Crowne also found no difference between high and low M–C scorers in the extent to which they involved themselves in this "euphoric" behavior. Taylor (1970) investigated the level of shock which a subject selected for his "partner" to receive if the "partner's" reaction time was slower than his own. On the initial trial there were no differences in level of shock as a function of M–C score.

Thus, there is no evidence that high and low M–C scorers are differentially aggressive in situations that are not arranged to frustrate or anger them.

In the experimental conditions of the studies just discussed there is considerable evidence that high M–C scorers do inhibit aggressive behavior when frustrated or attacked.

In the Fishman "counting backward" task two groups of subjects were confronted with failure and frustration. These subjects were informed that 95 percent of the subjects would be expected to complete the task within the time limit. They were further instructed that they would receive a bonus if they successfully completed the task within the time limit. In the arbitrary frustration group the subjects were informed that although they had successfully completed the task, the experimenter felt that they were unmotivated and did not do their best. Therefore, they would not receive the $2.00 bonus. In the nonarbitrary frustration group the subjects were informed that they did not successfully complete the task—probably as a function of their lack of motivation and of their not trying to do their best. Since they failed, they would not receive the $2.00 bonus. In both conditions the experimenter attacked the motivation and good faith of the subject; in the arbitrary condition the experimenter also broke his contract with the subject. Following the procedure, subjects were given the opportunity to aggress against the experimenter by means of an experimenter evaluation rating form that was supposed to significantly affect the experimenter's grade in a research course. High M–C scorers evaluated the experimenter significantly less negatively than low M–C scorers in both frustration conditions. For 11 out of the 18 low M–C scorers who strongly aggressed against the experimenter, there was a significant decrease in emotional arousal (decrease in systolic blood pressure) following aggression. However, only one of the 13 high M–C scorers who strongly aggressed against the experimenter demonstrated any decrease in emotional arousal. It seems that for low M–C scorers aggression against an attacker reduces the arousal. However, aggression does not appear to reduce arousal in high M–C scorers, and that may be one reason why they tend to inhibit such responses.

Prior to the "euphoric" interaction in the Conn and Crowne study, one group of subjects played a nonzero sum game in which they were taken advantage of by the confederate. If both players pressed a black button, they each got $3.00; if both players pressed a red button, they each got $0.10; if one pressed red and one pressed black, red got $5.00 and black got nothing. The confederate convinced the subject that they were goin to collaborate and press black all the time so that each of them would get $3.00 on each trial. When the time came, however, the confederate played red on every trial. During the subsequent interaction between subject and confederate, high M–C scorers who had been duped rated the confederate as *more* positive than high scorers who had not been duped by the confederate. Low M–C scorers, however, were significantly less positive in their ratings of the confederate when they had been duped than were low M–C scorers who had not been duped. In addition, high M–C scorers who had been duped did not express more hostility toward their confederate during a post-experimental interview than did high scorers who had not been tricked. Low M–C scorers, however, expressed much more hostility toward a confederate who had taken advantage of them than did low scorers did toward a confederate who had not deceived them. Thus, when taken advantage of, high M–C scorers tend to refrain from expressions of hostility whereas low M–C scorers express much more hostility toward the aggressor.

In the Taylor (1970) study, mentioned above, subjects chose shock levels to be delivered to their "partner" if their "partner" was slower than they in a reaction time experiment. In actuality there was no "partner" and the subject was programmed to "win" and "lose" an equal number of trials. As was reported earlier, there was no difference between high and low M–C scorers in the initial level of shock selected for delivery to their partner. However, after receiving a few low intensity shocks from their partner, low M–C scorers rapidly increased the level of shock to be delivered to their partner. High M–C scorers, however, did not increase their attack so long as their partner kept the shock to a minimum. As the shocks they were receiving from their partner increased to the unpleasantness threshold, high M–C scorers gradually increased the amount of shock they delivered. Thus, under no or minimal attack, high M–C scorers did ot aggress appreciably against their opponents. Low M–C scores strongly aggressed against their opponents as soon as they were attacked. High M–C scorers inhibited such aggression responses and only slowly increased their negative response as the attacks on them became more powerful.

From these studies it appears that there are no differences between high and low M–C scorers in the amount of unprovoked aggression in which they engage. However, when provoked and aroused, low M–C scorers openly aggress against an opponent and seem to experience some tension reduction as a result. High M–C scorers tend to inhibit much of their aggressive behavior, and when they do behave in a hostile manner they appear to experience little tension reduction as a result.

EVALUATIVE DEPENDENCE AND PERSONALITY CORRELATES

Defensiveness, Dissimulation, and Psychopathology

Items comprising the M–C scale were constructed in such a way that responding in a socially desirable direction requires dissimulation as well as positive self-description. The unrealistically positive presentation of self and unwillingness to admit even very common social transgressions have been seen as indicative of test-taking defensiveness as well as part of a more pervasive defensive behavioral style.

Consistently moderate to high correlations have been reported between the M–C and the K and L scales of the MMPI (Crowne & Marlowe, 1964; Fisher & Parsons, 1962; Katkin, 1964; Stone, 1965). The L scale contains test items so worded that denial reflects a rather pollyanna-ish self-evaluation. The K scale is an empirically devised defensiveness scale containing items generally endorsed by clinical populations whose self-reports show a greater tendency toward mental health than would be expected, given their deviant behavior. These results indicate that there is a significant tendency for subjects denying mundane and common social transgressions on the M–C to deny also probabilistically accurate statements concerning their psychiatrically deviant behaviors. Thus, negative relationships between evaluative dependence and self-report measures of psychopathology must be interpreted with great caution. It is highly probable that stylistic tendencies to respond in a socially desirable fashion may result in misleading negative correlations between indices of psychopathology and dissimilation-type social desirability measures. In fact, as evaluative dependence scores increase beyond the normative range, it may be hypothesized that they represent an increasingly pathological state of vulnerable, low self-esteem. Such an interpretation would be consistent with the characterization of M–C score as indicative of intense concern with evaluation by others and as associated with defensive maneuvers to avoid such evaluation. Further support for the interpretation that high M–C scores are vulnerable in their low self-esteem comes from a recent study by Hewitt and Goldman (1974), who found that subjects classified as having high self-esteem on a self-report inventory behaved similarly to low self-esteem subjects if their M–C score was high.

The increasing departure from reality in self-presentation inherent in high M–C scores has not been systematically or fully investigated with respect to its implications for personality functioning. As an instance of ''deception of the other'' such high scores can be seen as attempts at impression management motivated by an unusually intense and perhaps neurotic fear of disapproval. Nevertheless, the individual's reality testing would not necessarily be further constricted with respect to self-evaluation. In regard to self deception, however, defenses would operate to constrict reality more drastically and with more generally negative consequences.

In an early study, Jacobson and Ford (1966) found that high evaluatively dependent persons were less sensitive to evaluatively laden perceptual cues than were low scorers. Furthermore, in examining the effects of negative evaluation on motor performance, high M–C scorers demonstrated differential effects only when the evaluation was obvious and specific to the performance task (Milburn, Bell, & Koeske, 1970; Strickland, 1965; Strickland & Jenkins, 1964). These studies provide limited support for a model in which high evaluatively dependent persons filter out information concerning their experience that would lead to a reduction in self-valuation. Berger (1971) reported that high M–C scoring subjects distorted the evaluative meaning of their behavior following failure even when they believed that no one but themselves would know the results of their performance. It would appear that for at least some high evaluatively dependent persons, their censure avoidance and defensiveness represent ego protective mechanisms designed to guard a vulnerable self-esteem. The relative importance of ''self'' versus ''other'' deceptive components of evaluative dependence in particular situations and for particular individuals remains, however, largely uncharted territory.

Field Dependence

Evaluatively dependent persons' reliance on others' behavior (evaluations) as guides to their own actions and the generally context-bound nature of their behavior have led several investigators to propose a relationship between evaluative dependence and a dependence on external cues more generally (field dependence).

Rosenfeld (1967) employed male college students as subjects, with two measures of field dependence and a delayed auditory feedback task. The two measures of field dependence utilized were the Rod and Frame Test and Thurstone's Embedded Figures Test. The Rod and Frame Test required a subject to adjust a rod so that it appeared to be vertical. The rod, however, was surrounded by a frame that the experimenter tilted. The extent to which a subject relied on cues from the frame rather than on his bodily cues and sensations was taken as an indication of field dependence. The other field dependent measure, Thurstone's Embedded Figures Test, required a subject to locate a design concealed in a larger and more complex design. To perform adequately, the subject had overcome the effect of the embedding context (field). The greater difficulty a subject experienced in this task, the greater his field dependence was taken to be. The delayed auditory feedback task required a subject to read a 250-word textbook passage while his reading was fed back to him through earphones 0.05 of a second later. Efficient performance under these conditions required a subject to rely on his own proprioceptive cues rather than on the disruptive auditory feedback. The time required to read the passage under the delayed feedback condition was compared to the subject's performance under a no-feedback condition. The greater the disruption was under delayed feedback, the greater the subject's dependence on external cues was taken to be.

On the Rod and Frame Test high M–C scorers were found to be more field dependent than low M–C scorers. That is, high M–C scorers tended to adjust the rod so that it was vertical with respect to the frame rather than with reference to themselves. Rosenfled (1967) replicated this finding in a second experiment published in the same paper using the same methods.

On the delayed auditory feedback task, the performance of high M–C scorers was more disrupted by the feedback than was the performance of low M–C scorers. Thus, external cues do appear to have a greater effect on high M–C scorers than on low scorers.

On the embedded figures task there were no differences between high and low M–C scorers. The author conjectured that the negative results might be due to the inadequacy of the Thurstone test. However, a more fundamental difference between the embedded figure task and the other tasks under investigation might provide the most plausible explanation for the conflicting results. On the Rod and

Frame Test and on the delayed auditory feedback task the subject's perception was tested as being heavily dependent on either external (field) cues or on internal, self-referential cues. The results indicated that high M–C scorers are less self-referential and more field dependent in their perceptions than low M–C scorers. The Embedded Figures Test, however, measures a different type of field dependence, namely, an ability to separate figure from ground when all cues are external. It would appear that M–C score is unrelated to this latter aspect of field dependence. High M–C score appears to be related to reliance on external rather than internal perceptual cues but is not associated with differential ability to distinguish figure from ground when all cues are external.

Rotter and Tinkleman (1970) examined the field dependent behavior of high M–C scorers when the task was the rating of behaviors as either adjusted or maladjusted. The critical items to be rated were behavior descriptions that were neutral as indicators of adjustment. These items were then intermixed with other behavior descriptions that were either adjusted or maladjusted and served as contexts for the neutral descriptions. It was hypothesized that the judgments of the neutral behavior descriptions by high M–C scorers would be more influenced by the context than those by the low M–C scorers. It was found that high M–C scorers did rate neutral descriptions more in the direction of the external context than low M–C scorers. In fact, low M–C scorers did not demonstrate a context effect at all. It would appear that in making judgments concerning maladjustment and adjustment, high M–C scorers rely more on external cues than on any internalized standards and norms.

In these studies high M–C scorers demonstrated greater field dependence than low scorers when field dependence was taken to mean reliance on external as opposed to self-referential cues. Thus, the "evaluative" dependence of M–C scorers seems also to generalize to a dependence on situational cues even when these cues are not themselves evaluative.

Locus of Control

The heightened conditionability of evaluatively dependent persons and, in particular, their systematic efforts at influencing situations and individuals to avoid negative evaluation parallels in many important respects the behavior of persons with an "internal" locus of control (Rotter, 1966). Individuals with internal locus of control are characterized by a belief that situations and events are amenable to their influence and control. In other words, they expect a contingent relationship between their behavior and significant events in their environment. Persons with external locus of control are not characterized by systematic efforts to influence their social milieu, and consequently their behavior is less responsive to external and social contingencies.

Rotter's Internal-External Locus of Control Inventory is a 29-item forced-choice questionnaire designed to measure a person's expectancy that events in the world are under his control (internal) or outside of his control (external). In two studies employing undergraduates, the relationship of M–C scorers and I–E scores was investigated. High scores on the Locus of Control Scale indicate an external orientation, and thus a negative correlation between the M–C and I–E reflects a tendency for high M–C to be associated with internal locus of control. In one study (Altrocchi et al., 1968), there was a significant but low negative correlation for males between M–C and I–E scores but no significant correlation for females. In the second study (Gold, 1968) the pattern was reversed, and females obtained a significant low negative correlation between M–C and I–E but males did not.

Recently, Vuchinich and Bass (1974) reported a moderate negative relationship between M–C and I–E at both extremes of the I–E scale but a near zero correlation in the middle range. In addition, they reported that subjects with an internal locus of control score had higher M–C scores than subjects with moderate or external locus of control. It may be that previous attempts at establishing a relationship between evaluative dependence and locus of control have been inconsistent owing to their failure to consider the complex nature of the relationship. It is possible also that a defensive tendency by high evaluatively dependent persons to shift personal responsibility from self (internal) to external forces may attenuate the covariance between locus of control and evaluative dependence.

SUMMARY AND CONCLUSIONS

Edwards demonstrated that individuals could be reliably classified according to their tendency to attribute to themselves socially desirable characteristics and to deny socially undesirable characteristics. In addition, such individual differences in social desirability responding appeared to account for a major portion of the variance in responding on personality tests. One difficulty with Edward's measure of SD was that it sampled from self-reports of behavior that were heavily symptomological in nature. Marlowe and Crowne constructed a different scale that did not sample from items indicative of psychopathology. The M–C was constructed in a lie-type format, which meant that to score high on the scale a subject was required to attribute to himself desirable but highly unlikely characteristics and to deny about himself undesirable but highly likely behavior.

The M–C scale was found to have high test–retest reliability and generally high internal consistency. However, two potentially important formal characteristics of the scale have been largely overlooked. First, there is some evidence that the two components of total score, although significantly related, are somewhat unique response tendencies: the tendency to attribute socially desirable but improbable characteristics to oneself and the tendency to deny undesirable but highly probable characteristics. Future research should examine the extent to which these components are differentially predictive. The second problem is that different M–C items appear to be of significance for men and for women. It might be wise to establish firmly which items discriminate high and low M–C scoring men and women and to employ different sets of items for the two sexes.

There is no evidence that M–C score is biased by any yea-saying response tendency nor that M–C score is related to acquiescence measures when the social desirability of the acquiescence items is controlled.

Scores on the M–C have been interpreted as reflecting a motive that has been called "need for approval." Individual differences in the tendency to describe oneself in improbably favorable terms has been seen as indicating the strength of a motive to maintain a positive self-image and to obtain the positive evaluations of others. Soon after the development of the M–C scale, a second aspect of the approval motive was added to account for the defensive behaviors of high M–C scorers. This component was conceptualized as a need to avert negative evaluations. In its final form the approval motive was conceptualized as a need to obtain positive evaluations (approach component) and as a need to avert negative evaluations (avoidance component).

Subjects with a high need for approval are expected to behave in interpersonal situations in such a manner as to avoid the disapproval and obtain the approval of others. This evaluative dependence is hypothesized to manifest itself in increased motivation to do what is expected and desired by others. Consequently, high M–C scorers are expected to do better than low scorers in performance and learning tasks involving social approval. They are also expected to refrain from antisocial behavior that could bring about the disapproval of others.

In studies of motor performance there has been general evidence to support the notion that high M–C scorers are more influenced than low scorers by the positive and negative evaluations of others and that high M–C scorers have heightened motivation to make a good appearance, and consequently they do better than low scorers.

There is considerable evidence from verbal conditioning studies that high M–C subjects more readily conform to task demands than do low M–C scorers when these demands are communicated through direct approval–disapproval of subject behavior (social reinforcement). Furthermore, high M–C scorers will as readily conform to such task demands when reversals of established patterns of responding are required. In verbal conditioning and in reinforced conformity research, there has also been evidence that direct approval–disapproval of subject behavior has little effect on low M–C scorers. When task demands are communicated less directly to the subject by means of "opinions" or "judgments" of others, high M–C scorers also tend to conform more than low scorers as long as the communication comes from an expert source or from a person to whom the subject's conformity is important. Low M–C scorers give evidence of conforming to task demands when such demands are communicated indirectly, as in the nonreinforced conformity reserach.

These results support the hypothesis that high M–C scorers are more amenable to social influence than are low M–C scorers. They also suggest that low M–C scorers resist direct and blatant attempts at social control of their behavior.

In studies relating M–C score to field dependence, high M–C scorers have been found to demonstrate greater field dependence than low scorers when field dependence is taken to mean reliance on external as opposed to self-referential cues. Thus, the evaluative dependence of M–C scorers seems also to generalize to a dependence on situational cues even when these cues are not themselves evaluative.

In studies investigating the relationship of need–approval to risk-taking and goal-setting behavior, high M–C scorers have been found to prefer low risk behavior and to avoid rather than approach the evaluations of others, even when there is as much possibility for positive as for negative evaluation. Such findings are in accord with a censure-avoidant interpretation of need for approval.

The relationship of M–C score to aggressive behavior has been investigated in a number of studies. From these studies it appears that there are no differences between high and low M–C scorers in the amount of unprovoked aggression in which they engage. However, when provoked and aroused, low M–C scorers openly aggress against an opponent and seem to experience some tension reduction as a result. High M–C scorers tend to inhibit much of their aggressive behavior, and when they do behave in a hostile manner, they appear to experience little tension reduction as a result.

As already mentioned, in its final form the approval motive has been conceptualized as indicating a need to obtain positive evaluations (approach component) and as a need to avoid negative evaluations (avoidance component). However, it does not seem to make much theoretical sense to estimate the strength of two separate drive vectors (approach and avoidance) with a single score on a personality scale.

Careful analysis of the research evidence supports then, a censure-avoidant interpretation of the M–C score. No study provides clear-cut evidence that M–C score is measuring the strength of an approach–approval motive, and in no circumstance where a subject was faced with a choice of approaching evaluation or avoiding it did a subject choose to approach. To continue to view evaluative dependence as reflecting approach–approval as well as censure-avoidant vectors seems unnecessary and most probably inaccurate.

There is some tentative evidence that increases beyond the normative mid-range of the M–C score may represent increasingly pathological levels of vulnerable self-esteem. At least for some high evaluatively dependent persons and in some evaluatively laden situations, ego defense mechanisms operate to restrict reality testing and distort information threatening to self-valuation.

Finally, it should be pointed out that "self" versus "other" deceptive components of evaluative dependence remain largely unexplored and open for future research.

REFERENCES

Altrocchi, J., Palmer, J., Hellman, R., & Davis, H. The Marlowe–Crowne, Repressor–Sensitizer, and Internal–External Scales and attribution of unconscious hostile intent. *Psychological Reports,* 1968, *23,* 1229–1230.

Atkinson, J. W., Bastian, J. R., Earl, R. W., & Litwin, G. H. The achievement motive, goal setting, and probability preferences. *Journal of Abnormal and Social Psychology,* 1960, *60,* 27–36.

Barthel, C. E. *The need for approval and goal-setting behavior.* Unpublished research, The Ohio State University, 1961.

Berger, S. E. *The self-deceptive personality.* Unpublished doctoral dissertation, University of Miami, 1971.

Bryan, J. H., & Lichtenstein, E. Effects of subject and experienter attitudes in verbal conditioning. *Journal of Personality and Social Psychology,* 1966, *3,* 182–189.

Buckhout, R. Need for social approval and attitude change. *Journal of Psychology,* 1965, *60,* 123–128.

Conn. L. K., & Crowne, D. P. Instigation to aggression, emotional arousal, and defensive emulation. *Journal of Personality,* 1964, *32,* 163–179.

Crowne, D. P., & Marlowe, D. A new scale of social desirability independent of psychopathology. *Journal of Consulting Psychology,* 1960, *24,* 349–354.

Crowne, D. P., & Marlowe, D. *The approval motive.* New York: John Wiley, 1964.

Crowne, D. P., & Strickland, B. The conditioning of verbal behavior as a function of the need for social approval. *Journal of Abnormal and Social Psychology,* 1961, *63,* 395–401.

Dicken, C., & Wiggins, J. S. The social desirability scale is not a short form of the MMPI: A reply to Edwards and Walker. *Psychological Reports,* 1964, *14,* 711–714.

Diers, C. J. Social desirability and acquiescence in response to personality items. *Journal of Consulting Psychology,* 1964, *28,* 71–77.

Dixon, T. Experimenter approval, social desirability, and statements of self-reference. *Journal of Consulting and Clinical Psychology,* 1970, *35,* 400–405.

Edwards, A. L. The relationship between judged desirability of a trait and the probability that the trait will be endorsed. *Journal of Applied Psychology,* 1953, *37,* 90–93.

Edwards, A. L. *The social desirability variable in personality assessment and research.* New York: Dryden, 1957.

Edwards, A. L. *The measurement of personality traits by scales and inventories.* New York: Holt, Rinehart & Winston, 1970.

Edwards, A. L., & Walker, J. N. A short form of the MMPI: the SD scale. *Psychological Reports,* 1961, *8,* 485–486.

Efran, J. S., & Boylin, E. R. Social desirability and willingness to participate in a group discussion. *Psychological Reports,* 1967, *20,* 402.

Festinger, L. A theory of social comparison processes. *Human Relations,* 1954, *7,* 117–140.

Fisher, G. M. Normative and reliability data for the standard and the cross-validated Marlowe–Crowne Social Desirability Scale. *Psychological Reports,* 1967, *20,* 174.

Fisher, G. M., & Parsons, T. H. The performance of male prisoners on the Marlowe–Crowne Social Desirability Scale. *Journal of Clinical Psychology*, 1962, *18*, 140–141.

Fishman, C. G. Need for approval and the expression of aggression under varying conditions of frustration. *Journal of Personality and Social Psychology*, 1965, *2*, 809–816.

Ford, L. H. Acquiescence and the true-false consistency of three social desirability scales. *Educational and Psychological Measurement*, 1964, *24*, 301–308.

Fordyce, W. E. Social desirability in the MMPI. *Journal of Consulting Psychology*, 1956, *20*, 171–175.

Gold, D. Some correlation coefficients: relationships among I–E scores and other personality variables. *Psychological Reports*, 1968, *22*, 983–984.

Goldfriend, M. R. A cross-validation of the Marlowe–Crowne Social Desirability Scale items. *Journal of Social Psychology*, 1964, *64*, 137–145.

Greenwald, H. J., & Clausen, J. D. Test of relationship between yeasaying and social desirability. *Psychological Reports*, 1970, *27*, 139–141.

Heilbrun, A. B. Social-learning theory, social desirability, and the MMPI. *Psychological Bulletin*, 1964, *61*, 377–387.

Hewitt, J., & Goldman, N. Self-esteem, need for approval, and reactions to evaluations. *Journals of Experimental Social Psychology*, 1974, *10*, 201–210.

Jacobson, L. I., Berger, S. E., & Millham, J. Individual differences in cheating during a temptation period when confronting failure. *Journal of Personality and Social Psychology*, 1970, *15*, 48–56.

Jacobson, L. E., & Ford, L. H. Need for approval, defensive denial, and sensitivity to cultural stereotypes. *Journal of Personality*, 1966, *34*, 596–609.

Jacobson, L. I., & Kellogg, R. W. A multidimensional scale of social desirability. *Bulletin of the Psychonomic Society*, 1976.

Kanfer, F. H., & Marston, A. R. Characteristics of interactional behavior in a psychotherapy analogue. *Journal of Consulting Psychology*, 1964, *28*, 456–467.

Katkin, E. S. The Marlowe–Crowne Social Desirability Scale: Independent of psychopathology? *Psychological Reports*, 1964, *15*, 703–706.

Kogan, W. S., & Boe, E. E. Differential responding to items with high and low social desirability scale values. *Psychological Reports*, 1964, *15*, 586.

Krasner, L., Knowles, J. B., & Ullmann, L. P. Effect of verbal conditioning of attitudes on subsequent motor performance. *Journal of Personality and Social Psychology*, 1965, *1*, 407–412.

Marlowe, D., Beecher, R. S., Cook, J. B., & Doob, A. N. The approval motive, vicarious reinforcement and verbal conditioning. *Perceptual and Motor Skills*, 1964, *19*, 523–530.

Marlowe, D., Stifler, L., & Davis, M. *Personality correlates of primary and secondary suggestibility*. Unpublished research, Dartmouth College, 1962.

McDavid, J. The incentive and reward values of social approval and disapproval. ONR Contract: ONR840 (22), Technical Report No. 2. Coral Gables: University of Miami, 1962.

Mehrabian, A. The development and validation of measures of affiliative tendency and sensitivity to rejection. *Educational and Psychological Measurement*, 1970, *30*, 417–428. (a)

Mehrabian, A. Some determinants of affiliation and conformity. *Psychological Reports*, 1970, *27*, 19–29. (b)

Merrill, R. M., & Heather, L. B. The relation of the MMPI to the Edwards Personal Preference Schedule on a college counseling center sample. *Journal of Consulting Psychology*, 1956, *20*, 310–314.

Miklich, D. R. Social desirability and "acquiescence response set." *Psychological Reports*, 1966, *19*, 887–890.

Milburn, T. W., Bell, N., & Koeske, G. F. Effect of censure or praise and evaluative dependence on performance in a free-learning task. *Journal of Personality and Social Psychology*, 1970, *15*, 43–47.

Miller N., Doob, A. N., Butler, D. C., & Marlowe, D. The tendency to agree: Situational determinants and social desirability. *Journal of Experimental Research in Personality*, 1965, *1*, 78–83.

Millham, J. Two components of need for approval score and their relationship to cheating following success and failure *Journal of Research in Personality*, 1974, *8*, 378–392.

Palmer, J., & Altrocchi, J. Attribution of hostile intent as unconscious. *Journal of Personality*, 1967, *35*, 164–177.

Rosenfeld, J. M. Some perceptual and cognitive correlates of strong approval motivation. *Journal of Consulting Psychology*. 1967, *31*(5), 507–512.

Rotter, G. S., & Tinkleman, V. Anchor effects in the development of behavior rating scales. *Educational and Psychological Measurement*, 1970, *30*(2), 311–318.

Rotter, J. B. Generalized expectancies of internal versus external control of reinforcement. *Psychological Monographs*, 1966, *80*, (Whole No. 609).

Rump, E. E., & Court, J. The Eysenck Personality Inventory and social desirability response set with student and clinical groups. *British Journal of Social and Clinical Psychology*, 1971, *10*, 42–54.

Schachter, S. *The psychology of affiliation*. Stanford, Cal. Stanford University Press, 1959.

Spielberger, C., & Berger, A., & Howard, K. Conditioning of verbal behavior as a function of awareness, need for social approval, and motivation to receive reinforcement. *Journal of Abnormal and Social Psychology*, 1963, *67*, 241–246.

Stone, L. A. Relationships between response to the Marlowe–Crowne social desirability scale and MMPI scales. *Psychological Reports*, 1965, *17*, 179–182.

Strickland, B. R. Need approval and motor steadiness under positive and negative approval conditions. *Perceptual and Motor Skills*, 1965, *20*, 667–668.

Strickland, B. R. Individual differences in verbal conditioning, extinction, and awareness. *Journal of Personality*, 1970, *38*, 364–378.

Strickland, B. R., & Crowne, D. P. Conformity under conditions of simulated group pressure as a function of the need for social approval. *Journal of Social Psychology*, 1962, *58*, 171–181.

Strickland, B. R., & Jenkins, O. Simple motor performance under positive and negative approval motivation. *Perceptual and Motor Skills*, 1964, *19*, 599–605.

Taylor, S. Aggressive behavior as a function of approval motivation and physical attack. *Psychonomic Science*, 1970, *18*, 195–196.

Thaw, J., & Efran, J. S. The relationship of need for approval to defensiveness and goal setting behavior: A partial replication. *Journal of Psychology*, 1967, *65*, 41.

Vuchinich, R. E., & Bass, B. A. Social desirability in Rotter's Locus of Control Scale. *Psychological Reports*, 1974, *34*, 1124–1126.

CHAPTER 10

The Power Motive

DAVID G. WINTER,
Wesleyan University

and

ABIGAIL J. STEWART,
Boston University

Western civilization, as it has developed out of the Middle Ages, is perhaps most consistently characterized by its quest for power. From the beginnings of recorded history, of course, men have fought wars and dreamed of controlling vast domains; but with the rise of imperialism in the New World and India in the sixteenth century, the Western nations actually realized these dreams. Through the empire abroad and the nation-state at home, Western civilization greatly expanded the scope and range of social power, or the control of human behavior. Power in the sense of capability or capacity also seems characteristically Western, as least in its material aspects. Western nations have been driven to extend the capabilities of humanity: to overcome gravity and fly to the moon, to transform the earth and construct mighty towers, and to create machines that calculate literally with the speed of light. Finally, power as energy is a hallmark of the West, which created a civilization based on the profligate use of energy, expanded the imperial quest in search of more energy, and is now threatened by the loss of sources of supply of this energy.

Thus, the very power that so characterizes Western civilization may be leading to its collapse or radical change, as empires revolt, as the large nation-state becomes too complex to govern, and as technology threatens to destroy the delicate natural balances of life.

It is, then, not surprising that the most popular literary character in the West should be a character who seeks power: Don Juan, seducer of women, killer of men, and challenger of death itself with a bravado that brings about his destruction. More than 1700 authors have tried to depict Don Juan, from an obscure

391

Spanish monk writing at the time when Spanish imperial power began to crumble, through Molière, Mozart, Byron, Shaw, and down to one of the most recent versions by Robert Gardner (1974). Molière made clear how this typically Western fantasy of endless conquests through seduction was related to the other kind of conquest:

> There is no pleasure to compare with the conquest of beauty, and my ambition is that of all the great conquerors who could never find it in them to set bounds to their ambitions, but must go on for ever from conquest to conquest. Nothing can restrain my impetuous desires. I feel it is in me to love the whole world, and like Alexander still wish for new worlds to conquer. (*Don Juan,* Act I, scene 2)

Since both the actual history of the West and its literary imagination are so saturated with the quest for power, that quest should be a worthy and important object for psychological scrutiny.

Nevertheless, we must also remember that power always carries with itself something of irony: for the mighty are brought low by their overreaching ambition, their hubris or arrogance. One of the lessons of history is that power leads to its own destruction. Over 2400 years ago, the poet Aeschylus wrote these defiant words for the character Prometheus in *Prometheus Bound:*

> Worship, adore, and fawn upon whoever is thy lord. But for Zeus I care less than naught. Let him do his will, let him hold his power for his little day—since not for long shall he bear sway over the gods. (937–940)*

The words could be a judgment of today on the power-obsessed West, uttered by modern critics such as Sampson (1965), Rubinoff (1968), or Van Duyn (1969). Criticism of contemporary society is largely a criticism of power and the quest for power.

It is important, then, to understand both the quest for power and the distrust of such quests. In this chapter, we hope to consider a variable, assessed at both the individual and the national levels, that measures both the pursuit and the distrust of power. In following the history of the correlates of *power motivation,* we may gain an understanding of the conqueror (Don Juan) and the critic (Prometheus). Before we may hope for such an understanding, however, we need a technique for defining, measuring, and studying the power motive. After presenting such a technique, we will then trace out the ramifications of the power motive for both the individual and the social group, from the dyad to the nation–state.

---

* This and all subsequent quotations from "Prometheus Bound" are from the translation by Herbert Weir Smyth in the Loeb Classical Library. Used with permission of the Harvard University Press.

THE POWER MOTIVE AND OTHER POWER-RELATED VARIABLES

Psychologists have devised many different concepts for describing and measuring power. Since this chapter discusses the quest for power and surveys research about the power motive, it is important to distinguish power as a motive from these other concepts and variables. Table 10–1 lists six concepts of power, or variables concerning power, that have been drawn from recent psychological and sociological theory and research. Although we sometimes feel that two or more of these variables ought to go together, there is no logical reason that they do so, and when they are measured empirically they often do not correlate very highly with each other. First, the *power motive* means the quest for power, the desire for power, or the seeking of power (or the subjective feelings associated with power). This motive is not necessarily conscious, nor does it always lead to a single behavior or set of behaviors—for the reason that the behaviors that lead to power depend on the situation, and for the further reason that people's skill in getting what they want varies. In other words, the ways in which the power motive is expressed in action will depend on the other variables in Table 10–1. Moreover, the power motive may be in conflict with other motives such as affiliation, play, autonomy, or being taken care of.

The other variables listed in Table 10–1 can be contrasted with the power motive. Sociologists often think of power as an *attribute of certain roles* or positions (Concept No. 1)—elected leadership offices, informal positions of influence, and even occupation of certain key locations in a communications network (Collins & Raven, 1969, pp. 141–145). Yet whether the role permits or encourages power is not the same thing as the power motive, since we can readily think of different occupants of the same role position—for example, the American presidency—who differed in the extent to which they sought to expand the power of the role (Barber, 1972; Hargrove, 1966; Winter & Stewart, 1977a; and later in this chapter). *Power behavior* itself (Concept No. 2), or the actions of one person in affecting the behavior and emotions of another person, may be derived from power roles and increased by power motives, but it is not the same thing. The behavior could occur as the result of other motives (see Winter, 1973, Chaps. 1 and 2). Moreover, as suggested by Table 10–1, whether an action is labeled "power" may depend on the point of view of the observer (Winter, 1973, Chap. 1; Duijker, 1961). People differ in their *skill at using power* (Concept No. 3), but of course skills and motives do not always coincide. For example, according to legend, the Roman farmer Lucius Quinctius Cincinnatus (519–439 B.C.) was given absolute power, which he used with skill to defeat the Aequi and Volscians. After the battle, however, he resigned the dictatorship and went home to his farm.

From a more psychological point of view, people differ in their *feelings of being powerful* (Concept No. 4), of controlling the reinforcements of their be-

Table 10-1. Psychological Variables Involving Power

Focus	Concept No.	Variables	Measurement Procedures	References
Sociology	1. Roles permitting power	Role description	Sociological analysis; use of informants; study of legal system and history; experimental observation and manipulation.	Hunter (1953) Collins & Raven (1969) Gibb (1969)
	2. Power behavior	Occurence of power "Dominance" scales of CPI, EPPS, etc.	Observation; self-report questionnaire; judges' ratings; attributions	Merei (1949) Lippitt et al. (1952)
	3. Skill at using power	Winning/losing a power contest	Elections; sociometric procedures	Lasswell (1936)
	THE QUEST FOR POWER	*The power motive*	*Thematic Apperception Test*	Winter (1973)
	4. Feeling powerful	Internal-External Locus of control "Potency" Semantic Differential Scale Personal causation (origin–pawn)	Self-report questionnaire; Semantic Differential; TAT	Minton (1967) Osgood et al. (1957) deCharms (1968)
	5. Valuing power	Political Scale of Allport-Vernon-Lindzey	Allport-Vernon-Lindzey "Study of Values"	
Psychology	6. Beliefs about power	F–Scale Machiavellianism	Self-report questionnaire	Adorno et al. (1950) Christie & Geis (1970)

havior (Minton, 1967), or of being "origins" rather than "pawns" (deCharms, 1968). They may *value power* (Concept No. 5) as something good or as something bad, and again these values may or may not coincide with action. After leading the capture from the French of the fortress of Quebec City in 1759, General Wolfe is reputed to have said that he would rather have written Gray's "Elegy"; but the fact remains that whatever his values, his actions (as well as his role, skills, and possibly motives) involved power rather than poetry. Finally, we all have complicated *beliefs about power* (Concept No. 6): convictions regarding when, how, over whom, for what goals and with what constraints it should be exercised. Two clusters of such beliefs have become familiar personality variables—*authoritarianism,* typified by agreement with the statement, "People can be divided into two distinct classes: the weak and the strong"; and *Machiavellianism,* expressed most clearly in the belief that "the ends justify the means." In less formal psychological terms, idealism is a construct that is often involved in beliefs about power. For example, Woodrow Wilson's idealism led him to state of the American forces in World War I:

[They] were crusaders. They were not going forth to prove the might of the United States. They were going forth to prove the might of justice and right, and all the world accepted them as crusaders.[1]

Equally, Gandhi's idealism led him to prescribe a complex set of conditions for the use of power: it must be nonviolent, in a just cause, used only by the weaker party, without embarassing the stronger party, and to the ultimate benefit of all parties.

Many theories have suggested relationships among two or more of these variables. For example, feeling that one lacks power or control over reinforcement (Concept No. 4) is often thought to increase power motivation (Minton, 1967). The Yerkes–Dodson law suggests that power motivation should have an inverted U-shaped relationship to power skills (Concept No. 3) or actual success at getting power (Concept No. 2). Before we can test these theories, we must first have a clearly defined and well-developed way of measuring our concepts, especially the concept of the power motive. As we conceive of this variable, it is not the same as any of the other six variables involving power. Over time, with other things held constant, it should lead people to seek either real power (Concept No. 2) or some other state that produces the same kinds of feelings as does real power—feelings of "potency." The ways in which people high in power motivation seek these outcomes will vary enormously, depending on the circumstances in which they find themselves. Thus, the power motive does not refer to particular actions or behaviors; rather, it refers to the general class of goals, outcomes, or trends in the course of their behavior over time. It may be thought of as a gyroscopic setting that monitors and directs the long-term course of behavior through a flexible and variable series of intermediate and instrumental acts. (See Winter, 1973, pp. 20–30 for an extended discussion of the concept of "motive.")

MEASURING THE POWER MOTIVE

As we have seen, the research reported in this chapter is based on and guided by a special conception of what a motive is. This conception has important implications for the way in which the power motive is measured. As we have seen above, the most characteristic thing about a motive is not its particular associated actions but rather its *enduring, recurring, and retrievable associated cognitive clusters*. A motive involves cognitive "maps" of the goal state or goal feelings, cognitions of relevant instrumental actions, anticipations, memories, and very likely some way of activating special methods of processing perceptual information that is relevant to the motive (Erdelyi, 1974). These cognitions are in addition saturated with the positive and/or negative affects (or feelings) associated with the goal itself. In other words, the most continuous aspect of a motive, the thing that is most likely to be active (or arousable to activity) at any time is not its action(s) but rather its *affectively toned cognitive cluster*.

Our technique of measuring motives is derived directly from the insights of Freud and Jung about these affectively toned cognitive clusters or complexes.[2] These clusters precipitate fantasy and fantasy-like products of the mind: dreams, daydreams, myth, art, religion. They influence the content and speed of associations. They affect the ways in which ordinary, everyday stimuli and events are elaborated and given meaning (i.e., apperception). These fantasies and fantasy-like products are, in turn, less constrained by outer reality or inner censorship than are actions or conscious, reflective answers to questions. Even though fantasy, associations, or apperception can sometimes be distorted by inhibition or dissimulation, the distorted manifestations of the motive are still present; they can be recorded and interpreted or "decoded," whereas actions or responses to questionnaires can usually be completely controlled. For these reasons, then, the interpretation of fantasy, association, and apperception is, in Freud's words about dreams, the "royal road" to a knowledge of motives. The principal problems are to bring the production of fantasy under systematic experimental control and to work out the rules for interpreting, decoding, or scoring any particular motive.

Murray's development of the Thematic Apperception Test (TAT) and other techniques for a systematic investigation of fantasy (1937, 1938) solved the first of these problems. Presenting a person with a standard series of ambiguous pictures and asking him to make up stories about the pictures brought many of the heretofore random elements of fantasy behavior under the control of the investigator. In this way, Murray standardized the stimuli used to elicit fantasy, while at the same time preserving the necessary freedom for complexes or motives to affect the product. There remained, however, the problem of interpreting these products. How can we decide what to count as evidence of the power motive? Here the research strategy originally devised by McClelland, Atkinson, Clark, and Lowell (1953) for studying the achievement motive provides an answer. The TAT is known to be quite sensitive to variations in the testing situation and the mood in which it is taken. Indeed, this has been one of the biggest problems with its use. McClelland and his colleagues, therefore, intentionally manipulated the experimental situation in order to arouse the motive in question and thereby to study the effects of that motive on TAT story content. By noting which aspects of fantasy change under the experimental arousal of a motive, the researcher can construct a scoring system for measuring that motive in ordinary fantasy which is produced under ordinary, nonarousing conditions. Thus, a motive is operationally defined as the fantasy content (associative imagery, story themes, etc.) that change under one or more carefully defined types of experimental manipulation.

The important part of this research strategy is the design of the arousal conditions, since the operational definition of a motive is only as good (and as accurate) as the nature of the experimental manipulation. The scoring system for the power motive was developed through studying the effects on fantasy of several different power-arousal conditions, each in comparison with a neutral control condition in which power was not aroused, as shown in Table 10–2. The final measure of the power motive (or *n* Power, a convention of name first adopted by Murray and McClelland et al.) successfully differentiated aroused and neutral stories from each experiment when applied blindly and without knowledge of which stories came from which conditions. Thus, although one could argue that any single experiment did not really arouse power, or aroused something else besides power, the convergence or common features of all six experiments do seem indubitably to involve power. Thus, the common features of fantasy that shift in all the experiments, as outlined in Table 10–3, are the *n* Power scoring system.[3] This scoring system was used in all the research reported in this chapter. The complete scoring system, together with instructions for learning and using it, and a discussion of its psychometric properties can be found in *The Power Motive* (Winter, 1973).[4]

Before turning to the research on *n* Power, we note briefly the distinction between *Hope of Power* and *Fear of Power* at the bottom of Table 10–3. Like many other goals, power is something that people can dislike or fear, as well as like or want. The words of Prometheus, as we have seen, suggest that he felt a strong dislike of power, tinged with irony, mistrust, and perhaps fear. In the earlier discussion of motive, we noted that motives were affectively toned cognitions; the affect can obviously be either positive (pleasure, positive anticipation)

Table 10-2.   N Power Arousal Experiments

Experimental condition in which power was aroused	Neutral control condition in which power was not aroused	Reference
1. Candidates for student government offices awaiting the results of voting.	Students in an introductory psychology class.	Veroff (1957)
2. Subjects about to enact the role of "psychological experimenter."	Subjects about to participate in a psychological experiment.	Uleman (1972)
3. Students who have just observed a demonstration of hypnosis.	Students before observing hypnosis demonstration and unaware of it.	Uleman (1966); Stewart & Winter 1976
4. Students who had seen a film of John F. Kennedy's inauguration.	Students who had seen a film about science demonstration equipment.	Winter (1973)
5. Black students after improvising roles as members of a Black Action Group whose leader has been arrested.	Black students before improvising these roles.	Watson (1969)
6. Students after experiencing a multimedia presentation of inspirational speeches (Churchill on Dunkirk, excerpts from *Henry V,* etc.)	Students after experiencing a multimedia presentation of a travelogue	Steele (1973, 1977); Stewart & Winter (1976)

or negative (pain, negative anticipation). Thus, power is something that can be hoped for or sought and something that can be feared, mistrusted, or avoided. These are, then, two different power-related motives, or a way of partitioning the overall power motive score into an approach component and an avoidance component.[5] Strictly speaking, when we refer to the "power motive," we could mean any one of the following three different concepts: (1) the overall n Power score, which reflects the salience or motivational importance of power and is the sum of (2) Hope of Power, the approach motive and (3) Fear of Power, the avoidance motive.[6] In fact, however, research on power motivation is both simpler and less precise than this. Hope of Power is usually so highly correlated with overall n Power (range of r's = .70 to .90) and predicts so many of the same things, that the two variables are often not distinguished. Indeed, much of the research reported in this chapter simply used n Power as the measure and did not involve the Hope/Fear distinction. In such cases, n Power and Hope of Power can more or less be taken as synonymous. This is a confusing and unfortunate

Table 10-3.   A Brief Version of the *N* Power Scoring System[a]

Power Imagery: Scored if some person or group of persons in the story is concerned about establishing, maintaining, or restoring power − that is, impact, control, or influence over another person, group, or the world at large. Examples: (1) Someone shows power concern through actions that in themselves express power. (2) Someone does something that arouses strong positive or negative emotions in others. (3) Someone is described as having a concern for reputation or position.

Subcategories, to be scored only if Power Imagery is scored

Prestige: The characters are described in ways that increase or decrease their prestige. Settings, titles, adjectives of status, reputation, alliance with some prestigeful person or institution are all examples of prestige.

Stated Need for Power: An explicit statement that the character wants to attain a power goal. *Not* inferrable from mere instrumental activity.

Instrumental Act: Overt or mental activity by a character indicating that he or she is doing something about attaining a power goal.

Block in the World: An explicit obstacle or disruption to the attempt to reach a power goal.

Goal Anticipation: Some character is thinking about the power goal, with either positive or negative anticipations.

Goal States: Affective or feeling states associated with attaining or not attaining the power goal.

Effect: A distinct response by someone to the power actions of someone else in the story, or indication of widespread effect on the world at large.

Hope/Fear Distinction:

All stories are scored Hope of Power unless one or more of the following occurs in the story, in which case it is scored Fear of Power: (1) The power goal is for the direct or indirect benefit of someone else; (2) the actor has doubt about his ability to influence, control, or impress others; (3) the writer of the story suggests that power is deceptive or has a flaw, as by the use of contrast, irony, or explicit statement. Included are cases in which characters feel happy after power failures and sad after power successes.

[a]This brief version is intended for illustrative purposes only. It is not adequate for actual scoring purposes. A complete version of the *n* Power manual, together with practice stories and procedures for learning the system, is available in Winter (1973, Appendix 1). Scoring system Copyright © David G. Winter, 1968 and 1973.

situation, and in the course of this chapter we will try to clarify the difference between the two concepts.

The third concept, Fear of Power, is much less highly correlated with overall *n* Power (range of r's = .28 to .58), is uncorrelated with Hope of Power and often predicts quite different actions. It clearly involves power but in an ambivalent way as an "attractive aversion to power" (Winter, 1973, p. 144). We will discuss it in a separate section.

POWER-MOTIVATED ACTIONS IN EVERYDAY LIFE

At the beginning of this chapter we argued that the quest for power has been uniquely characteristic of Western civilization since the Middle Ages. We have traced how an objective psychological measure of the quest for power was developed and defined as the power motive, or n Power. We must now ask whether we have actually isolated one key motivational base of the rise of the West and whether we have succeeded in defining and quantifying the power motive. In other words, does the n Power scoring system predict the kinds of actions—conquest, organization, and profligate dissipation—that have been both the glory and the despair of the West? There is no easy way to go back in time to discover whether a Cortez, a Napoleon, or a Disraeli scores high in n Power, or whether General Wolfe had fantasies that were saturated with power imagery just before the victorious assault on Quebec (although later in this chapter we will explore a technique for measuring the motives of historical figures). As a first step, then, we must turn to the popular part of personality research carried out with two groups of subjects: college undergraduate males (largely white and middle class) and adult males (largely white). Within these groups we can study those actions that are typical of individuals high in power motivation. The behaviors we have argued to be characteristic of power in Western civilization—organization, conquest, and dissipation—can be roughly translated into variables such as holding office, frequency of aggressive acts, and alcohol consumption. When we have converted the grand sweep of history into personality research variables in this way, it seems at first as though we have left the high road on which we started and have become mired in the familiar, somewhat mundane road of psychological research. Rest assured, however, that there is a lot to be learned on that mundane road and that we will return in due course to the higher road of society and history.

Organization: Formal Social Power

The essence of power is the ability to make the material world and the social world conform to one's own image or plan for it.[7] This is a complicated process, involving steps such as forming a plan, articulating it, rallying support and amassing resources, convincing others, checking the implementation, using positive and negative sanctions, and so forth. In social units that have grown beyond the simplest stages, seeking and getting power takes place within the framework of rules and procedures for each step of the process: Power is said to be institutionalized in leadership roles or *offices*. Therefore, we would expect that the power motive should predict office seeking and office holding. Winter (1973, Chap. 4) found that officers in university student organizations did in fact score higher in n Power than nonofficers. Power motivation also predicted holding office in organizations among working class adults, a result that has been replicated by McClelland, Wanner, and Vanneman (1972, p. 180) and Boyatzis (1973). Winter found in addition that students high in *n* Power became dormitory counselors, members of important faculty–student committees, and staff workers on the university newspaper and radio station. Perhaps even more than offices in clubs and organizations, these latter positions seem to involve power as it is institutionalized in the present-day American university.

Yet among middle class and upper middle class adult males, the power motive does not predict, or correlate at significant levels with, holding office in voluntary organizations. A likely explanation for this fact emerges when we consider the occupations associated with power motivation among (upper middle class) college graduates: business executive, teacher or professor, psychologist, clergyman, and journalist. Longitudinal studies of English and American college graduates, as well as occupational preference studies of college students, confirmed that these are the careers pursued by men in *n* Power. What is common to each of these careers is the opportunity or duty to *direct in an immediate way the behavior of individual other persons in accordance with some preconceived plan and to use positive and negative sanctions on that behavior*. In each case, the directing and sanctioning takes place within a legitimate institutional structure. Thus, the business executive within the capitalist or socialist structure of industrial and economic organization directs and controls the behavior of subordinate workers.[8] Within formal institutions of education, teachers direct and sanction the learning behavior of students. Similarly, the clergy exhort and sanction within the framework of organized religion. Psychologists operate within the loose structure of "mental health" or the "helping professions" at a minimum (often within the structure of a university, clinic, or hospital), directing and sanctioning the behavior of their clients.[9] (Physicians, who are not especially high in power motivation, have a similar role, but their concern involves the anatomy, physiology, and biochemistry of the client more than his behavior.) Journalists operate within the structure of the communications industry; their task is not only to sanction others' behavior in an editorial way but to transmit significant information to all of us—which is the very essence of power.

Thus, power motivation predicts careers that involve direct and legitimate *interpersonal* power. Notice that careers such as science, law, and even politics, where power is probably involved but often in an indirect and abstract way, are not associated with the power motive. Thus, a scientist, by inventing the transistor, may revolutionize the lives of millions of people; but his power is not nearly so direct and interpersonal as the executive of the transistor manufacturing company who sets weekly production goals and overrules a subordinate's decision about the production process. As a result of the Watergate scandal, we have seen how a lawyer can challenge the president of the United States and, through the courts, force him to reveal damaging information and thereby resign. However, for every heroic special prosecutor or eminent defense attorney, there are thousands of lawyers who work out their clients' wishes in fields of corporate organization, real estate and taxes, and personal life (divorce, custody, and wills). Although we might expect that people high in power motivation would be more likely to *use* lawyers, the lawyers themselves are often hired experts and would not necessarily have the motive themselves. Finally, in the case of politics, we find a field that is so broad as to include a wide variety of roles and motives. That is, the politician who is a legislator may differ greatly from the executive; the level of the political office (local, state, federal) also may be a relevant variable. In short, politics is no single career; it is, however, intuitively reasonable to expect the power motive to help us understand many aspects of political behavior. Therefore, further on, we will devote and entire section of this chapter to politics.

In any case, the findings discussed above suggest that middle class men who are high in power motivation may not seek offices in voluntary organizations because they have power, or the sense of having power, through their careers. For the working class man, on the other hand, educational and social barriers make it unlikely that he will become an executive, teacher, psychologist, or clergyman (if he did, he would be labeled middle class). Most of the occupations available to him offer little chance for power, and they often involve being directed and sanctioned by someone higher up than he. This is particularly true of factory work. Since working class power motivation cannot seek expression in work, it is therefore likely to find an outlet in organizations outside of work. In this sense college students are in the position of the working class: Power is available through office holding rather than through their primary "career" of student, and so power motivation predicts office holding. All these disparate findings can be summarized in one conclusion: *The power motive predicts seeking and getting formal institutionalized social power by whatever means is most available to the person or most likely to be successful and within whatever situational constraints are operative.* For many American males, occupation is such an important part of life (Parsons, 1942) that it is the likely arena for power motivation; but if the power occupations are not available, then voluntary organizations become important.[10] In more formal terms, we could express the probability of any particular power behavior as the product (or sum) of the power motive and the likelihood that the behavior will be available or effective.

The Strategies of Power

Formal social power, whether it comes from the executive suite or from being president of a fraternity, is not bestowed by accident. Many factors in the situation, such as the nature of the group and the task at hand, determine who attains the position of power (Gibb, 1969). On the other hand, there are many ways in which an individual person can increase his power; these are part of the lore of politics (Lasswell, 1936) and the study of leadership (Haley, 1969). The tactics are so ancient that they find their roots in animal social organization, and they have been codified at least since the time of Machiavelli's famous manual of advice to the would-be prince. By examining some of these tactics as they are exemplified in the characteristic behaviors displayed by people high in power motivation, we can see why in the long run such people are successful at getting formal institutionalized power.

Visibility

To attain power, one must be visible above all. The plan that is to be the basis for the material and social world must be made public. Winter (1973) shows that college students high in the power motive make themselves visible in a variety of ways. They are more likely to write letters to the university newspaper. They imagine themselves hostilely attacking prominent and high-status people. They tend to gravitate toward positions and locations that are inherently powerful. One of their favorite techniques to achieve public visibility appears to involve taking extreme risks (McClelland & Watson, 1973; McClelland & Teague, 1975).

Building Alliances

By itself, mere visibility might lead a person to be labeled as a deviant or a crank rather than powerful. What seems to make the difference between these two outcomes is whether the person can build an alliance or organization—a power base. Winter (1973) found power-motivated college students doing just that: they chose friends who were relatively not well known by other students (i.e., friends who were more likely to be "loyal") and who had tastes similar to themselves. They spent relatively more time in bull sessions and were concerned to maintain smooth relationships and avoid disruption with friends. Finally, they were able to use whatever opportunity was available for expanding their "network" of social contacts.

Functioning in a Group

So far, we have shown how the power-motivated person achieves a position of power. Studies by Jones (1969) and Watson (1974) illustrate how such a person actually exercises power and why he is able to hang onto it. In both cases, previously unacquainted students were invited to participate in brief experimental discussions in ad hoc groups. Jones found that after the discussion, those group members high in n Power were voted by the others as having "most clearly defined the problems," "most encouraged the others to participate," and "most influenced the other participants." They also talked more. However, they were *not* voted as having "offered the best solutions to the problem," as having "worked hardest to get the job done and come to a good conclusion," or as being "best-liked." Watson found that when the group members were asked to "evaluate" other group members by means of pressing "positive" and "negative" evaluation buttons not visible to the others, men high in Hope of Power gave more and longer negative evaluations, particularly to other men and to an experimental confederate who tried to disrupt the discussion.

Thus, we see the power-motivated person seeking and wielding power and thereby distinguishing himself from three other roles: (1) the technical specialist who is concerned with the quality of performance on the task itself and who thinks up good solutions,[11] (2) the conscientious hard worker, and (3) the popular, well-liked social-emotional leader (Bales, 1958). For wielding power, the rules seem to be: speak up, define the problem (but encourage others to offer solutions), participate, and do not neglect negative evaluations of others in an attempt to be liked. These look as though they are good rules for the power game, and so it is not surprising that in following them, people high in the power motive are likely to wind up with formal institutionalized social power.

A Note on Conquest and Aggression

As we suggested in the beginning of this chapter, imperial conquest is perhaps the most striking characteristic of modern Western civilization. It is hard to translate this into behavior that can be studied at the individual level, and so we chose to begin this section with institutionalized power behavior. In almost all human (and animal) social situations, power generally flows through established, relatively stable, institutionalized channels. Direct aggressive attempts at conquest occur only in unusual circumstances: when a social unit is initially formed before a relatively stable dominance hierarchy is established, when two or more unacquainted social units encounter each other, and when an established and stable hierarchy is threatened or disintegrating. Examples of such circumstances in the history of the West would be, respectively, the establishment of the nation state (as in England under Henry VII or Spain under Isabella and Ferdinand); the discovery of "lesser breeds without the law" in the New World, Africa and Asia; and the political collapses after World War I and in the Depression.

Perhaps the most that we can hope to demonstrate with the kinds of subjects readily available are vestiges, hints of aggressive conquest motivated by the search for power. Athletic competition is often viewed as a vestige of aggression or a substitute for it. Winter (1973) did find that power-motivated men more often participated in directly competitive college sports, and Boyatzis (1973) confirmed this for older working class men. Power motivation is also related to vicarious athletic participation, whether by attendance, watching on television, or reading sports magazines. McClelland (1975) found that in a sample of working class men power motivation was correlated with the frequency of arguments reported, and Winter (1973) and Boyatzis (1973) both found that working class n

Power was related to the frequency of carrying out aggressive acts such as yelling in traffic, destroying furniture or glassware, and insulting clerks in stores.

Although all these findings are consistent with the view that aggression and conquest are manifestations of the power motive, it must be admitted that the evidence is rather slim. Some progress could be made by studying how different levels of power motivation affect behavior in some of the standard experimental paradigms used by social psychologists to study aggression (Berkowitz, 1970). Do power-motivated people have lower response thresholds to the cues that influence aggressive behavior? Are they more likely to imitate aggression or respond to frustration with aggression? Are they more aggressive in games? Yet aggression and conquest are very difficult to simulate realistically in the social psychological laboratory. Considerable ingenuity in selecting subjects and measuring motives will be necessary to shed light on this question. For example, later sections of this chapter discuss how the motives of major political actors and of nations as a whole can be assessed and related to outcomes such as war. Studies of power motivation at the individual level with aggressive criminals, gang leaders, and members of collapsing or threatened social systems would be a great contribution to our knowledge.

Prestige and Display

If power usually operates in its stable, institutionalized form, then there must be some means by which information about power—who has it, who does not have it, when it is being brought to bear—can be transmitted and perceived. That is, the change from aggressive conquest to stable organization depends on the existence or creation of a set of power symbols. There will be symbols indicating gradations in the amount of power a person has, and there will be symbolic gestures that stand for power behavior (dominating, leading, suggesting) and for acknowledging the power behavior of others (submitting, being loyal, agreeing). The concept of "rank" is a convenient term for this domain of power symbolism, for as Brown and Herrnstein (1975, pp. 221–242) point out, the symbols and gestures of rank extend from the most complex human behavior back to the orders of rank or "pecking orders" that occur in some form in all classes of vertebrate animals. Related to rank is the concept of prestige, which can be thought of as the effect of rank on the beholder—dazzlement, awe, and a little intimidation. Over 300 years ago, Hobbes (1651) pointed out that "Reputation of power is power . . . what quality soever maketh a man beloved, or feared of many; or the reputation of such a quality, is Power." (p. 70).

If rank and prestige are the means by which aggressive power is tempered and transformed into a stable social system, then we would expect that the power motive would be intimately involved with the symbols, gestures, and behaviors that indicate prestige. For if prestige is the usual way in which power is secured and demonstrated, then the person who seeks power will certainly seek prestige. If power is prestige, the acquiring prestige is one way to acquire power. Indeed, power can often be simulated by acquiring prestige without the trouble of securing the means of backing it up—the strategy of the "operator." As we would predict from Hobbes's maxim, the strategy will often work, at least until the bluff is called and the prestige of empty symbols collapses. Thus, prestige has an instrumental value to the quest for power. In addition, prestige often operates as the end satisfaction of the power quest. By a kind of reflexive self-perception or taking the role of the other, a person can perceive his own prestige and thus acknowledge his own power. Then in the role of ego he can perceive himself acknowledging his own prestige and power. If the feeling of power—the goal of the power motive—is ultimately dependent on the deference or submission of others, then prestige and the symbols of prestige enable us to enjoy that feeling by ourselves, without actually bothering with formal or aggressive social power. It is a kind of auto-erotic short-cut to the goal of the power motive. In its extreme form, this reflexive self-perception of prestige leads to an autistic or delusional perception of one's own power. One suspects that people whose prestige bluff has been called in real life are the most vulnerable to this delusion, for in their own imagination they can continue to build castles of prestige that give more satisfaction than does painful reality. Albert Speer relates that the last days of World War II brought Hitler to this kind of delusion, as in the midst of the total defeat of the Third Reich Hitler discussed and encouraged the architectural planning of vast state buildings, monuments, and cities (1970). No doubt he believed in those hours that he continued as the mighty *Führer* of an invincible *Reich*. This is an extreme form of the expressive function of prestige; at a more ordinary and poignant level, Willy Loman in *Death of a Salesman* and Walter Mitty are examples of "plain folks" deluding themselves about their power by means of fantasied prestige. There are, then, good reasons to expect the power motive to predict the acquisition of prestige symbols.

Winter (1973, pp. 127–133) reports studies of college students showing that although n Power is not related to social class or spending money, it does predict having prestigious possessions such as a television set, tape recorder, carpet or rug on the floor, and framed pictures or posters. Students high in the power motive are even more likely to put their name on the outer door of their room—in a small way marking out their "territory." They are more likely to hand in course papers in neat plastic bindings. They have a quicker response to fashion trends, so that as beards and mustaches became popular among college men in the late 1960s, such students were more likely to have them sooner.

One amusing example from the Wesleyan University 1971 Commencement illustrates the connection between the power motive and display. In those days every function, procedure, and ritual of the university was being challenged. Many graduating seniors argued that the traditional cap-and-gown commencement garb was not "relevant" to their lives, and so wore other clothes such as ordinary suits, dresses, or shirts and trousers. A few students, however, chose to express themselves by displaying themselves in what can only be described as "costume," walking up to get their degree tied to a cross, or dressed in "jailbird" clothing, dragging a ball and chain. There were 27 graduating seniors on whom prior motive scores were available, and the five who wore such costumes were significantly higher in n Power than the other 22 who wore gowns or just ordinary clothes.

One finding that has been replicated with college students, working class adult men, and middle class male executives is that the power motive is related to the number of credit cards that one regularly carries (Winter, 1973, p. 129; McClelland, Davis, Kalin & Wanner, 1972, pp. 179–180; Boyatzis, 1973). The credit card provides an excellent illustration of the reasons why power and the power motive are linked to prestigious possessions. First, many cards are in themselves symbols of prestige: you must have a certain level of income to qualify for them, and they have annual dues. Second, credit cards make you independent of the need for having money and the money system. In addition, the more cards you have, the more independent you are and the less likely to be embarrassed when an expensive restaurant refuses to accept a "mere" bank credit card. Third, the sheer act of paying with a credit card involves the clerk or waiter in much more activity and paperwork than does paying with cash: you have the pleasure of "seeing 'em jump" (a phrase of the writer Tom Wolfe). Finally, the ability to gratify any whim by the mere act of signing one's name probably brings to mind the effortless way in which royalty, presidents, and the very rich shop. So it is not surprising that high n Power people of both middle and working class carry more credit cards.

The relationship between the power motive and prestige requires one caution. What counts as prestige varies over time and across groups and cultures. What gave status to college students in 1970 was different from what worked with upper middle class executives, who at that time did not wear beards or mustaches. Interestingly enough, in both groups the power motive was associated with a preference for automobiles that had a certain kind of prestige: cars that were foreign and cars that were highly maneuverable (a high track-to-wheelbase ratio). The image of the highly maneuverable machine that responds "instantly to your slightest whim" (in the words of an automobile advertisement) and thereby multiplies and extends your capacity, speed, and power is a recurring symbol of power in Western civilization. As Canetti (1962) puts it, "*Smoothness* and *order* . . . have entered into the very nature of power. They are inseparable from it and, in every manifestation of power, they are the first things to be established" (p. 208). Ibsen's character John Gabriel Borkman adds a glittering, metallic cast to this "smoothly-maneuverable machine" imagery in his grandiose ramblings after his terrible fall from power:

Down there the metal sings. . . . when it's loosened. The blows of the hammer that loosen it—they're the midnight bell striking to set it free. And so the metal sings—for joy—in its own way.

. . .

And listen, down there by the river! The factories are at work! *My* factories! All those I would have built! Listen to them at work. It's the night shift. So, they work night and day. Listen, listen! The wheels whirling and the cylinders flashing—round and round. . . . I feel the veins of metal that stretch out their curved, branching, luring arms to me. I saw them before me like shadows brought to life.[12]

Again we see how the expressive function of prestige can lead, through autism, to madness, as in Borkman's final collapse.

The Expansive Profligate Impulse

Much of the attractiveness of prestigious possessions to the power-motivated person lies in their expressive value: by reflexive self-perception, the person observes himself and perceives that because he possesses the symbols of power, he therefore has power and so feels powerful. And in fact people high in Hope of Power do rate the concept of "myself" as more potent on the Semantic Differential scales (Winter, 1973, p. 141). Prestige and positions of formal social power are thus obvious ways of reaching the desired goal state of the power motive, namely *feeling powerful*. What makes the power motive so interesting and so complicated is that it also predicts a variety of behaviors that superficially have nothing to do with "real" power, ye that create the same inner feeling of power: alcohol consumption, possibly drug use, risk taking, and pitting one's self against physical challenges.

Several studies show that Hope of Power predicts drinking liquor. Winter (1973) reported significant correlations between Hope of Power and reported liquor consumption among male college students and middle class executives. McClelland, Davis, Kalin and Wanner (1972, p. 151–156) found that in samples of working class men, *n* Power in combination with low self-restraint (Activity Inhibition) was correlated with a reported history of heavy drinking and with the amount actually consumed in a bar social situation under experimental conditions. In a study of 54 working class male alcoholics who had attended a didactic two-week program designed to influence them to stop drinking, Brown (1975) found that those who were unremitted one year later were higher in Hope of Power than those who had stopped drinking. There is some evidence, moreover, that alcoholism treatment programs designed specifically to help alcoholics understand their power motives are more effective than standard treatment programs in fostering the desire to work and therefore social rehabilitation (Boyatzis, 1975). In numerous studies of the effects of male social drinking on fantasy,

McClelland et al. (1972, Chap. 7) were able to demonstrate that drinking itself increased levels of the power motive.

These findings will serve to emphasize the distinction between the power *motive* and power *behavior*. Objectively, a person does not possess more power just because he has taken a few drinks. Indeed, as his drinking leads him to the point of collapse, he rapidly becomes less powerful. Subjectively, however, he *feels* more powerful (perhaps because of increased secretion of adrenalin; see McClelland et al., 1972, pp. 281–282), so that drinking, as a means to the goal state of the power motive, feeling powerful, is associated with that motive. Is drinking then a power-related behavior? In the subjective sense it certainly is, and with these findings the concept of the power motive begins to diverge from power as defined only in a political or sociological sense. The value of the concept of a power *motive* is that it brings together many different actions that are themselves unrelated but that are related to a common underlying disposition (Murray, 1938, pp. 54–66).

The evidence is less clear with respect to other mind-altering drugs. McClelland and Steele (1972) found no relation between n Power and the use of marijuana among college males,[13] although Steele (1973) found a modest correlation of .35 ($p < .01$) in a subsequent study. Boyatzis (1973) also found a small but significant correlation between n Power and the number of different "drugs" taken in the sample of 144 working class men ($r = .17, p < .05$). Research in this area is especially difficult because the behavior at stake has been illegal and therefore is a somewhat underground phenomenon.

McClelland and Watson (1973) and McClelland and Teague (1975) found that the power motive was related to taking extreme risks in a public gambling situation and to choosing relatively less popular positions to defend in a hypothetical discussion of social issues. Interestingly enough, in the latter study high n Power men also tended to choose either stronger or weaker opponents in an arm-wrestling tournament (instead of choosing opponents of about equal strength). Fersch (1972) found that n Power predicted completing participation (versus dropping out) in an Outward Bound program among working class high school boys. Outward Bound programs stress the personal mastery of physical risks, challenges, hardship and "raw experience," and are thought to increase responsibility and confidence. This ideology, so reminiscent of the past times of President Kennedy's "New Frontier," is also the basis of competitive sports. What is similar about all three things is the incentive of expansive risk, and this is a key aspect of the feeling of power. This element is even attractive in a vicarious form to the power-motivated person, as shown by the relationships mentioned above of the power motive to reading about sports and watching sports events.

Taking all these studies together, it appears that the power motive leads people to emphasize expansiveness and extremes; to create inequalities, contrasts, and disparities; to exaggerate and intensify the ordinary course of experience. With the seeking of power comes what can best be described as an expansive release of energy. This release can be seen in many of the actions associated with the power motive and in the history of modern Western civilization; it has certainly been a counterpoint to aggressive conquest and the sudden expansion of human capability. Often this energetic release has been so far in excess of any instrumental purpose that it seems profligate, wasteful, and (in a world of finite resources) disastrous. In this connection, we come to the figure of Don Juan—the reckless seducer seeking ever-greater impact, and the most consistently popular literary character in the West.

Exploitation of Women

Don Juan sought power by seducing an endless series of women, deceiving and killing, where necessary, to reach this goal. In the lines from Molière's version of the legend quoted at the beginning of this chapter, we can see that Don Juan viewed the conquest of women as similar to the military conquest of cities. The portrayal of a besieged city as a bride, whom the attacking general would seduce (or ravish), has ancient roots in Western literature and in some of its earlier Eastern sources (Rank, 1913). The linkage of aggressive military conquest and sexuality viewed as a "conquest" of women is a major theme in Western culture; one indication of this is the widespread and continuing interest in the Don Juan figure. As Winter (1973, pp. 190–196) has shown, new versions of the Don Juan legend usually appear in great profusion shortly after a nation fights a war or gains (or loses) territory of its empire. When men are motivated to seek power in the political and military world, it appears that their sexual fantasies are precipitated around this same motive.

Does the power motive affect the actual behavior of men in their relationships with women? Winter (1973, Chap. 6) drew together several findings that suggested that power-motivated men did indeed act like minor-league Don Juans. Such men have a relatively more precocious and extensive sexual experience, and they prefer wives who are dependent and not independent. McClelland (1975, p. 48) found that power-motivated men also disclose (boast about?) the details of their sex life more readily. They act like the literary Don Juan in other ways too, although these actions may be related to sex only indirectly if at all. When it seems necessary, they disguise information about themselves, and they tend to be oblivious about important future events and threats. They are relatively resistant to perceptual illusions and do not like to be confined. There is even some evidence that they prefer red and black—the two colors that are cross-culturally associated with power (Adams & Osgood, 1973) and that were so popular for male dress in Spain at the time of writing of the first version of the Don Juan legend!

Perhaps by interpreting and understanding the Don Juan legend we can understand the origin and roots of the power motive itself. The most significant discussion of the legend is by Rank (1924/1975), who at that time was Freud's most brilliant pupil and a master at the psychoanalytic interpretation of literature. Rank argued that in an obvious way, Don Juan's actions derive from the Oedipus complex: The many seduced women represent the one unconquerable mother, and the many hostile murdered rivals the one rival father. Yet the transformations, displacements, and transvaluations that are presumed by this equation suggest earlier, pre-Oedipal roots. On the one hand, Don Juan's challenge to the statue of the slain father of one of his victims, and to death itself, represents the struggle against his split-off conscience or superego; but at the same time Don Juan is thereby seeking death as the only completely satisfying way to return to the unattainable mother. Don Juan thus treats women with brutal contempt because his wish for fusion with his mother is frustrated, the more so as she is distant and reserved.

How does this interpretation apply to the power motive? Winter (1973) argued that the analogous figure to the distant and reserved mother of Don Juan in today's society would likely be the upper middle class schoolteacher, and he found that schoolteacher mothers did indeed have sons with relatively higher n Power. Further research carried out after Winter's *The Power Motive* lends additional support to this line of discussion. In a sample of college undergraduate men, Slavin (1972) found that n Power had a moderate relationship ($r = .26$, $N = 90$, $p < .05$) to a pattern of fantasy called "Themes of Feminine Evil"—the tendency to write stories in which women are harmful to men, directly or indirectly: by exploiting them, rejecting them, or triumphing over them. Among men who were unambiguously pre-Oedipal in their basic pattern of identification, however, the correlation was substantially increased ($r = .61$, $N = 32$, $p < .001$).[14] Among these pre-Oedipal men, moreover, n Power predicted a pattern of behaviors toward women that is as conflicted as it is defensive: it predicted having attitudes of male dominance (about the ideal type of wife, about feminism, and about female work roles), withdrawal from women (dating less frequently and disclosing less), and being directly aggressive toward women (having hit women or tried to hurt a girl who hurt them). Where the identification with the mother is strong and the attraction to her less modified by the world, therefore, it appears that the power motive does indeed produce a donjuanesque brutal contempt for women.

Some recent unpublished research by the present authors gives a further clue. When male college students were asked to draw a female, n Power was associated with both emphasis on the female breasts (an exaggeration of the nurturant maternal aspects of the female form) *and* drawing bizarre, distorted figures. N Power was not associated with drawing exaggerated sexual characteristics, or bizarre figures, in drawings of a male. So these drawings of females seem the result of a view of women rather than of an artistic style.

Stewart and Rubin (1976) studied dating couples over a two-year period and found that male n Power was associated with relative dissatisfaction of both partners and perceived problems in the area of intimacy. Moreover, male n Power negatively predicted marriage and positively predicted the breakup of the relationship over the period of the study. (Nonmarriage and break-up are empirically distinct: Many couples simply continued to date. Moreover, avoiding marriage as a legal commitment and breaking up as a termination are also conceptually distinct.) McClelland, Davis, Kalin, and Wanner (1972, p. 357), found that in a sample of working class men, power motivation was associated with marital instability. Winter, Stewart, and McClelland (1977) have also found that, in a longitudinal study of college graduates of the class of 1964, Hope of Power as measured in their freshman year negatively predicted whether their wives would have a career and the professional level of that career 14 years later. Finally, Winter (1977) demonstrated in a cross-national sample that, under certain conditions, national levels of power motivation are associated with the social, educational, and economic suppression of women. Overall there is, then, a good deal of evidence linking the power motive to exploitation of and aggression toward women. To the man who strives for power, sex is apparently just another conquest.

Thus, all the major themes that, we have argued, are so characteristic of Western civilization—conquest, organization, prestige, dissipation, and exploitative sex—can be seen as manifestations of a single motive to acquire power. In addition, there are at least hints of evidence that the power motive in turn may originate in certain features of the prototypical relationships between the sexes—that of mother and son, and perhaps that of father and daughter.

POWER MOTIVATION IN WOMEN

As this chapter is being written, little research has been carried out on power motivation in women. In this section we will draw together what has been done, although we will also refer to studies of female subjects in the discussion of Fear of Power below. One of the most elementary rules of personality research is to analyze data for men and women separately before analyzing them together. In the case of the power motive, two kinds of questions need to be answered with respect to women. First, is the power motive aroused by the same experimental procedures that work for men? (A variant on this question is whether these arousal procedures also arouse something else in women, something that does not appear in men's TAT stories.) Second, does power motivation predict the same behaviors for women as it does for men? A more precise version of this second question is: Does the power motive predict the same behaviors for women as it does for men, when other conditions and moderator variables are constant?

In other words, does the motive relate to behavior in the same way for the two sexes? A glance at the complicated history of achievement motive research with women (French & Lesser, 1964; Lesser, 1973) suggests that these questions are important and that their answers are not obvious.

Two of the usual n Power arousal experiments have been carried out with women by Stewart and Winter (1976)—the demonstration of hypnosis and the famous speeches multimedia presentation (Nos. 3 and 6 in Table 10–2). In both cases, the results for women are the same as those for men—the arousal procedure significantly increased power motivation in the experimental group as compared with the control group. A further replication of his "famous speeches" study by Steele (1977) also showed that power motivation was significantly higher for both men and women after the arousal experience. Finally, Stewart (1975b) reports that in an analysis of the protocols used by Winter (1969) in a study of the effects on fantasy of nursing a baby, power motivation was not higher in the nursing than in the control group. In short, there is every reason to date to believe that n Power is aroused in women by the same experiences as in men. Moreover, Stewart (1975b) examined TAT protocols from the hypnosis and famous speeches arousal studies and found no *other* themes in the stories of women and not of men. Thus, there are good grounds for a preliminary affirmative answer to our first question and a negative answer to its variant.

The relationships between power motivation and behavior in women involve more extensive research, only some of which has been carried out to date (Winter, 1975). In studies of college women, the power motive has predicted some of the same actions as it does for men: holding offices, having prestigious possessions, and even a preference for red and black. In a longitudinal study of women college graduates of the class of 1964 tested in their freshman year, Stewart (1975a) found that among those women who had full-time careers and were middle class (versus upper class), the power motive predicted pursuit of the same careers as it did for men, with the exception of university professor. Stewart and Rubin (1976), however, found no evidence of any effect of female power motivation on satisfaction, problems, or duration of a couple's relationship. Wilsnack (1974) found that women's n Power scores did not increase after social drinking, although for women the power motive was related to reported drinking history and to amount consumed in a simulated social drinking setting in ways similar to those found with men. There is some evidence from research in progress that the power motive interacts with sex-role conceptions or style of Self-definition (Stewart & Winter, 1974) and other social roles. Among women who are self-defining, it predicts behavior in ways closer to the male pattern, whereas among socially defined women, the style traditionally associated with the female role, power motivation predicts power behaviors that are congruent with (and constrained by) that role.

McClelland (1975, Chaps. 2 and 3) presents data that suggest that the traditional female role accentuates the power-motivated woman's concern with building up her resources in order to *be* powerful (rather than to act powerfully), a concern focused particularly on the body and its discipline. McClelland (1975, Chap. 4) further argues, however, that such a concern is not intrinsic only to women (or to the traditional female role) but is rather a component of power motivation that is neglected in Western psychological research but is highly salient in other cultures—India, for example.

POWER MOTIVATION IN POLITICAL LIFE

The research that has been reviewed above gives some sense of the nature and possible origins of the power motive. Our claim at the outset was that this personality variable is uniquely significant in understanding the peculiar nature of modern Western society. At this point it is appropriate to broaden the inquiry to study directly the motives of political actors and other significant leaders. We will review studies of the motives of local politicians and civic leaders, state government bureaucrats, and American presidents. Although we have not as yet measured the *n* Power scores of Napoleon or Disraeli, we will discuss the scores of Woodrow Wilson and Franklin Roosevelt. In that discussion we will introduce a technique for studying the motives of major political actors at a distance.

Local Politicians and Leaders

Browning collected TATs from samples of politicians, civic leaders, and businessmen inactive in politics or civic affairs but carefully matched in other characteristics, in "Eastport," a city of about 150,000 population in the northeastern United States (Browning, 1968; Browning & Jacob, 1964). Two groups had power motive scores significantly higher than the appropriate control group: (1) urban renewal leaders who worked, largely outside the ordinary political party apparatus, on a massive renewal and reconstruction program that radically transformed the central city and had great effect on the lives of its residents, and (2) party politicians who were candidates for offices of real power potential and who initiated their own candidacy (versus being recruited by the party or having fathers active in politics) (Winter, 1973, pp. 102–105). These results suggest that mere involvement in politics, for any reason and at any level, is not necessarily the result of power motivation. Other incentives appealing to other motives (such as affiliation or deference) may be involved, and other pressures such as party pressure or the role model of a political parent may operate. Often these factors override the effects of any single motive, but within the political arena the power motive does appear to direct local leaders toward certain positions (the ones with high power potential) and activities (urban renewal) where the power satisfactions are likely to be enhanced.

State Bureaucrats

Grupp (1975) mailed a questionnaire and a one-picture TAT to appointed officals in state executive agencies in 10 different states, and obtained 588 replies. Despite the hazards of administering the TAT by mail (uncertain and variable arousal conditions) and the fact that motive scores are based on only one story, Grupp's results are of great interest in showing the power-motivated style of political and bureaucratic behavior. Those officials whose TAT story had any score for Hope of Power had the following characteristics: They had risen in their careers more rapidly (i.e., had higher incomes) than others of the same age, yet they were less satisfied with their job (using a measure based on the Cantril Self-Anchored Striving Scale; Cantril, 1965), felt that state executives had relatively less public prestige or esteem, and were less inclined to recommend state government service to young people as a career. Although they had no special views about their superiors or subordinates, they were less likely to consider their colleagues competent. Although limitations of the data make these results tentative, they do suggest that in political bureaucracies as in everyday life, the power motive leads to concern with prestige and public esteem and to negative evaluation of colleagues and coworkers.

American Presidents, 1905–1974

We now know something about how the power motive works in political life, but studies of local and state officials can only make us wonder how the power motive works at the national level—with respect to the major political figures who make decisions about war and peace, economic policy, and international relations. Such persons will probably always be unavailable for testing by personality researchers, and in any case some of the most interesting and important figures are dead. Rather than rely only on extrapolation from studies of lower-level officials or on clinical case studies that lack comparative quantitative data, Donley and Winter (1970) developed a method of scoring motives of public officials from their speeches. This technique has been applied to the inaugural speeches of the American presidents from 1905 through 1975 by Donley and Winter (1970), Winter (1973, pp. 212–220), Stewart (1974), and Winter and Stewart (1977a).[15] Scores of the presidents for the power, achievement, and affiliation motives are presented in Table 10–4. In this chapter we will limit ourselves to a discussion of the relationships between the power motive and selected presidential "behaviors": others' view of the president, his choice of advisers, and whether the United States entered a war during his administration. Since the three motives are intercorrelated in this sample, all results will be reported in terms of partial correlations in which the influence of the achievement and affiliation motives is removed.

Table 10-4.   Motive Scores of Presidential Inaugural Speeches, 1905-1974

President	N Power	Images per 1000 Words N Achievement	N Affiliation
T. Roosevelt (1905)	8.25	6.19	2.06
Taft (1909)	1.97	0.90	0.72
Wilson (1st—1913)	5.39	3.00	1.20
Harding (1921)	3.67	2.26	2.82
Coolidge (1925)	3.10	1.67	1.43
Hoover (1929)	3.03	4.04	2.02
F. D. Roosevelt (1st—1933)	6.32	5.26	1.05
Truman (1949)	7.32	4.07	3.66
Eisenhower (1st—1953)	4.07	2.85	4.47
Kennedy (1961)	8.33	6.82	5.30
Johnson (1965)	6.85	7.53	2.05
Nixon (1st—1969)	5.16	8.45	5.16
Ford (1974)	4.72	2.36	10.61
Carter (1977)	5.71	8.16	4.08
Means	5.28	4.54	3.33
Standard deviations	1.98	2.53	2.60

Source: Parts of this table are taken from Donley and Winter (1970). Reprinted from *Behavioral Science,* Volume 15, Number 3, 1970, by permission of James G. Miller, M. D., Ph.D., Editor.

Others' View of the President

Table 10-5 reports the correlation between power motivation and the ratings of the presidents by 500 historians along a number of dimensions. The power motive is strongly associated with high ratings for prestige, strength of action, activity, and accomplishments, but is not related to idealism or to flexibility. Thus, among presidents, as among more ordinary individuals, the power motive predicts prestige, display, and strong, decisive action, but it is not related to any particular ideological orientation or to rigidity or flexibility.

This general pattern is also confirmed by considering the classification of presidents by political scientist Barber (1972). Power motivation is positively correlated with Barber's classification as "active," but interestingly it is also positively correlated with Barber's judgment that the president liked his job (positive affect). Thus, it appears that power-motivated presidents give the impression not only of strength and activity but also of being happy with what they are doing.

All of this might be taken to indicate that presidents high in power motivation are "good" presidents, especially in light of the relationship with accomplishments, presented above. Such a conclusion does not square with the ratings on the overall contributions as president collected by Schlesinger (1962), which are

Table 10-5. Presidential Motives and Historians' Ratings

	Partial correlations[a] with:		
	N Power	N Achievement	N Affiliation
Maranell (1970) dimensions:			
General prestige	$.63^c$	$-.17$	$-.52^b$
Strength of action	$.74^d$	$.05$	$-.72^c$
Activeness versus passivity	$.68^c$	$.19$	$-.65^c$
Accomplishments	$.66^c$	$-.13$	$-.63^c$
Idealism vs. practicality	$.19$	$-.20$	$-.04$
Flexibility vs. inflexibility	$-.01$	$.03$	$.53^b$
Barber (1972) categories:			
Activity versus passivity	$.44^b$	$.57^b$	$-.44^b$
Positive affect (enjoyment of the office)	$.46^b$	$-.44^b$	$.03$
Schlesinger (1962) ratings on overall contribution	$.02$	$.41$	$-.49$

Source: Parts of this table are taken from Winter and Stewart (1977a). Reprinted from *A psychological examination of political leaders*, M. G. Hermann (Ed.). Copyright © 1977 by The Free Press, a Division of Macmillan Publishing Co., Inc.
[a]Correlations for each motive with each variable are with the effects of the other two motives partialled out.
[b]p < .13 (1-tailed)
[c]p < .05 (1-tailed)
[d]p < .01 (1-tailed)

uncorrelated with power motivation. Power motivation does predict making a strong public impact, taking strong, decisive actions, and perhaps even liking the job, but it is equivocal whether it predicts how "good" a president the person will be.

It is interesting that presidents high in power motivation are significantly more likely than other presidents to be the objects of successful or unsuccessful assassination attempts. This may happen because such presidents have a characteristic fondness for "display," which may tend to irritate or enrage the disaffected members of the political community; or it may be owing to their tendency for strong, decisive actions, which leave no room for hope of a change of heart among those who disagree. It may be owing simply to the greater activity of these presidents, which leads them to "rub shoulders" more often with precisely those individuals who are least satisfied with the presidents' performance in office. In any event, although the sample is small, the relationship is strong and must be considered in the evaluation of the relationship between power motivation and presidential performance. Perhaps the power motive causes presidents to arouse more positive feelings (among historians) *and* more negative feelings (among the disaffected)—in short, to generate more emotional response.

Choice of Advisers

One of the most discussed aspects of a president's administration is his choice and treatment of advisers. Particularly since Watergate, political scientist and layman alike have recognized the significance of the people around the president in determining the kind of administration. Interestingly, as shown in Table 10–6, power-motivated presidents tend to choose cabinet officers who are dissimilar from them in their personal lives. Choosing somewhat dissimilar people may give the president room for forming alliances and setting one member or faction against another. Alternatively, it may be a strategy for guaranteeing that no one can be too closely (and favorably) compared with the person who holds the office! Power motivation also predicts choosing people who have been lawyers or who have had legislative experience for cabinet positions, rather than people with previous experience or expertise in the field of appointment (e.g., housing, transportation, etc.). This suggests that what the power-motivated president values most in choosing subordinates is in fact power experience, a record of skillful and successful power maneuvering.

Table 10–6.   Presidential Motives and Characteristics of First Cabinet Appointees[a]

	Partial correlations[b] with:		
	N Power	N Achievement	N Affiliation
Discrepancy from president in age	$.66^d$	$.42^c$	$-.42^c$
Discrepancy from president in number of children	$.46^c$	$-.19$	$-.29$
Proportion who were lawyers	$.60^d$	$-.26$	$-.54^c$
Proportion with previous experience in the department of their appointment	$-.20$	$.35$	$-.15$
Proportion with previous experience in Congress or state legislature	$.69^e$	$-.85^e$	$.20$

Source: Parts of this table are taken from Winter and Stewart (1977a). Reprinted from *A psychological examination of political leaders*, M. G. Hermann (Ed.). Copyright © 1977 by The Free Press, a Division of Macmillan Publishing Co., Inc.
[a]First cabinet appointees includes the first cabinet picked. In the case of vice presidents assuming office on the death of the president, their own first appointee is counted, unless the "holdover" continued in office beyond that vice president's inauguration in his own right, in which case the holdover is counted as a first appointee. N = 12 presidents.
[b]Correlations for each motive are with the effect of the other two motives partialled out.
[c]$p < .13$ (1-tailed)
[d]$p < .05$ (1-tailed)
[e]$p < .01$ (1-tailed)

War and Peace

Probably the most important power decision a president ever makes is the decision to enter war. Certainly we would not maintain that this decision is determined only by a president's power motive; the complex world situation, public opinion, actions of other nations' leaders, and many other factors all enter significantly into the decision to wage or not to wage war. Nevertheless, there is some indefinable moment at which the president must himself make the final decision. Since that decision is so important, it is worthwhile to consider whatever effect—however small—the motives of the man making it have on the outcome. In fact, presidential n Power is correlated .62 ($p < .05$) with entry of the United States into a war (defined as onset of American participation in fatal international quarrels with more than 316 casualties) (Winter & Stewart, 1977a).

Of course, these presidents do not "make wars," but for whatever combinations of reasons, they do finally make the decision to take the country into war. Perhaps more disturbingly, they also tend not to make great efforts to prevent wars. The correlation between a president's power motivation and the conclusion of an international agreement to limit arms development (such as the Washington Naval Treaty of 1922 and the SALT talks agreements) is strongly negative ($r = -.63, p < .05$).

In summary, the power-motivated president makes a strong impact on people and on the nation. He takes strong, decisive action as president, and he likes his job. He chooses cabinet officers who have considerable experience and expertise with power but not necessarily with experience in the areas for which they are responsible. During his administration the nation enters war and does not conclude international arms limitation agreements. Overall these behaviors are quite consistent with those discovered in the psychological laboratory and in the university setting and suggest that power motivation predicts the same behaviors in a variety of different arenas. A person's power motive score may, then, not predict his choice of a context for behavior (e.g., the presidency), but it does predict what he will do once he has chosen a context.

The findings with twentieth century American presidents certainly suggest that the power-motivated person, in control of the political apparatus of the state, would indeed pursue the policies of activity, strength, and violence that seem to be at the root of the history of the West in modern times. The data so far are only suggestive, but the method of studying motives at a distance that was devised by Donley and Winter can certainly be adapted for the study of motives of other national leaders and statesmen of both the present-day world and of history.

THE POWER MOTIVE IN NATIONS AND IN HISTORY

The idea that there are differences in national character or in the personalities of people of different nations is one of the oldest and most elusive psychocultural theories, an idea widely believed and studied by professional psychologist and layman alike. Any reader who has traveled much in other countries has formed some idea of which nations are high in the power motive. In this section we will review the findings on power motivation across nations and over time. Be warned that there are problems of inference and difficulties of method ahead, but be assured that the results are most interesting and relevant to our central claim at the beginning of the chapter.

From 1930 until the middle 1950s, psychologists interested in other cultures and anthropologists trained in psychoanalysis pursued studies such as these under the heading of "Culture and Personality." Yet that movement seemed suddenly to lose its vitality and come to a halt. At the time, Inkeles and Levinson (1969; first version published 1954) made several critical and cautionary points about the study of national character, arguing for systematic and objective rigor in the description and measurement of personality in such research, lest the confirming evidence turn out to be little more than sophisticated stereotypes and casual impressions.

One such systematic procedure for the study of national differences in personality is the *coding of systematic samples of cultural documents*. McClelland (1961, 1975) devised such a technique to measure national levels of achievement motivation, which he then related to subsequent economic performance. He argued that the stories in children's readers (designed for use at about age eight) "tell us what is on the minds of significant elites in a country," (1962, p. 153), in part because "educational authorities everywhere seem concerned to make sure that children read what is considered normal, right and proper" (1961, p. 71). Such stories are very much like the brief imaginative stories that are produced when individuals take the TAT, so motive-scoring systems can readily be applied to them, and McClelland's research has produced impressive evidence that the scores do represent national motive levels in the sense that they correlate with national "behavior."

The sample of stories from children's readers of more than forty nations that McClelland used in *The Achieving Society* has been scored for power motivation. Winter (1972) found that n Power scores from the 1950 readers predicted relatively more rapid growth in technology between 1950 and 1968 among poor nations but not among rich nations (r's $= +.61, p < .05$, and $+.15$, respectively). Although n Achievement (the achievement motive, or a concern for excellence) (McClelland et al., 1953) is thought to be the motive force behind economic growth, it appears that the first stages of development, or "take off," are also facilitated by the power motive.

The most interesting results are to be found when we consider the pattern of high power motivation coupled with low affiliation motivation.[16] The affiliation motive, or n Affiliation, is a concern with establishing, maintaining, or restoring friendly relationships. It predicts friendly, sociable behavior if the situation is familiar and not threatening. Thus, *n* Affiliation would appear to be a natural check or constraint on the power motive. McClelland (1961, pp. 167–170) and Winter (1972) found that the high *n* Power and low *n* Affiliation pattern characterized nations with a totalitarian political organization. Winter also found that the opposite pattern—high affiliation and low power—was characteristic of nations that took the lead in innovating programs to reduce environmental pollution and establish resources planning. This latter finding suggests that the exploitation of human beings and the exploitation of the environment arise from the same motive base.[17] In more recent work, McClelland (1975, Chap. 9) calls this (high power/low affiliation) the "imperial" motive pattern and reports that the pattern predicts political violence as well as totalitarian organization in modern nations. He also scored samples of popular literature from different time periods: in England from 1500 through 1800 (plays and street ballads) and in the United States from 1780 through 1965 (children's readers, novels, and hymns). In both studies, whenever motive levels approached the imperial pattern, as defined above, the country was likely to become involved in a war or imperial expansion within the next decade.

Winter (1977) has also found that national Hope of Power is associated with the suppression of women under circumstances where women are particularly vulnerable targets for male power (i.e., when they marry at an earlier age than men); and when women are not such vulnerable targets, national Hope of Power predicts violence (war and homicide) and divorce.

The evidence, then, on power motivation in modern nations and in history is congruent with the findings from individuals and American presidents: The power motive leads to active, strong, imperial organization; under certain conditions it can also produce aggressive violence and exploitative suppression of women. In several different kinds of studies, then, the power motive manifests itself in actions and outcomes that have been so characteristic of the West in modern times.

FEAR OF POWER

So far we have considered only the approach aspect of the power motive—the positive desire to have power, or the quest for power. Yet as we suggested in the words of Prometheus at the outset of this chapter, many thinkers in the West view power with irony, suspicion, and criticism. We believe that this alternative view of power may be reflected in the construct Fear of Power—the avoidance aspect of the power motive, which Winter called "an aversive attraction to power" (1973, p. 144).[18] This aversive attraction involves an unusual sensitivity to power and awareness of power relationships in the world, coupled with a negative feeling about them. That is, an individual high in Fear of Power is interested in power in order to avoid it, to avoid the power of others and to avoid the appearance of having power one's self. There has been somewhat less research reported to date on Fear of Power than on overall n Power or Hope of Power. Perhaps this lack reflects the positive evaluation of power by psychologists and their lack of interest in studying people who have negative thoughts and feelings about it. Nevertheless, Fear of Power does have some interesting behavioral correlates, and it may be useful to think of these correlates as they occur in relation to the mythical character of Prometheus.

The Mythic Embodiment of Fear of Power

Prometheus, who described himself as "an ill-fated god" (119), was punished by Zeus (the god of gods) for having defied him by giving fire to mankind. This gift of fire enabled mankind to begin to develop civilization, and it enraged Zeus, who cared nothing for the merely mortal lives of men. As punishment for this act of defiance, Zeus ordered that Prometheus be bound to a rock, totally immobilized and forced to remain thus constrained "forever." In his account of this story in *Prometheus Bound,* Aeschylus offers a view of the character of Prometheus in the thoughts and words that Prometheus expresses while bound to the rock and enduring his punishment. We will use these thoughts and words to illustrate the ways in which the Prometheus figure may be taken as an archetype of the individual high in Fear of Power.

The Development of Fear of Power

Prometheus himself tells us that his struggle with Zeus began when he had no choice but to support Zeus in his "coup" to overthrow the god Kronos, although he was dubious about it: "The best choice seemed to be that I, joining my mother with me, should range myself, a willing volunteer, on the side of Zeus . . ." 218–220). Because he had no alternative, Prometheus sided with Zeus in his deadly battle with Kronos, although he did not trust Zeus to rule wisely and believed that the coup was unjust. Indeed, when Prometheus discovers that Zeus *does* rule unjustly, he thenceforth becomes suspicious and distrustful of authority. When the issue is important enough, he even defies authority. This defiance, however, is clearly born not of a conviction of strength but rather an experience of weakness. Having himself experienced the sense of being without a choice, of being compelled to do what is not natural or desirable, Prometheus thenceforth always sympathizes with the powerless and distrusts the powerful. Yet he is punished because in this process he has pitted his own power against that of Zeus. The Prometheus character certainly involves an "aversive attraction to power."

In less dramatic form, research evidence suggests that Fear of Power derives from the experience of powerlessness. Winter (1973, pp. 156–159) reported that Fear of Power is highest in men who were the youngest in a relatively large family. Being the youngest presumably entails both a large number of people more powerful than one's self and a large number of situations in which one is forced to experience one's helplessness against "injustice." For ordinary mortals as for Prometheus, then, it appears that the tendency to feel an aversive attraction to power (to be high in Fear of Power) derives from an early experience of others' power over one's self and relatively little freedom to maneuver around that power. Power is experienced as both outside the self and inescapable.

Suspicion of Power or Authority

The experience of the inescapability of power engenders in Prometheus a far-reaching disposition to distrust those who have real power. He distrusts both the methods of absolute power ["not by brute strength and not through violence, but by guile that those who should gain the upper hand were destined to prevail" (214–215)] and the individuals who possess it ["In one word, I hate all the gods that received good at my hands" (975–976)]. There is ample evidence of this mistrust of those with power or authority among individuals high in Fear of Power. In a recent study by the present authors, 62 male and female undergraduates in an introductory psychology course were shown a multimedia presentation of Zimbardo's "Stanford Prison Experiment" (Zimbardo, Haney, Banks, & Jaffe, 1972, 1973). After viewing the presentation, students were asked to indicate whether they would prefer to play the role of guard or the role of prisoner if asked to be in such an experiment. Those students who chose the "prisoner" role were significantly higher in Fear of Power than those who chose the "guard" role. Thus, it seems that people high in Fear of Power wish to avoid identifying themselves with traditional institutional power or authority, even at the cost of preferring (experimental) imprisonment. In a small way they make the choice that Prometheus made.

In another small study of general attitudes, college students high in Fear of Power more often endorsed items from a "Distrust" scale (Gold, Christie, & Friedman, 1976) than did other students.[19] In a more extreme form, Winter (1973, pp. 143–148) found that among male schizophrenics paranoia is significantly related to Fear of Power. Thus, it appears that, just as among normal individuals, Fear of Power is related to a somewhat exaggerated disposition to view all power or authority with suspicion and distrust; among individuals classified as schizophrenic this distrust too becomes pathological or paranoid.

Drawing from the psychoanalytic interpretation of paranoia as based on anxiety about repressed homosexual impulses, Winter suggested that at the root of Fear of Power was a fear of penetration by others of the same sex. It may well be that for the person high in Fear of Power this anxiety about homosexuality is a symbolic expression of a more general fear—a fear that other persons of the same sex will control him, or symbolically "penetrate" him (Wolowitz, 1965). The struggle of Prometheus with Zeus is certainly a head-on clash between two members of the same sex, in which the victory of Zeus is symbolized by the binding of Prometheus to a rock, binding not only with chains but with "rivets" (56) and "wedges" (65). All of this suggests that for the person high in Fear of Power, penetration and constraint are the active metaphors for power, just as in the case of Hope of Power the metaphor is conquest. Penetration and constraint are, moreover, most feared when they come from the same sex rather than the opposite sex. For Don Juan, the power object is of the opposite sex and the goal is conquest. For Prometheus, the struggle is with another male, and the goal is freedom from constraint.

Research evidence for this interpretation of the dynamics of Fear of Power comes from two quite different studies. Winter (1973, pp. 154–156) showed that men high in Fear of Power more often use profanity based on penetration, and especially homosexual penetration, than do other men. This kind of everyday behavior is especially important for understanding a construct such as Fear of Power because such ordinary behaviors are both spontaneous and habitually gratifying to the particular individual. The second study is a laboratory experiment conducted by Watson (1974), who found that whereas Hope of Power predicted the overall tendency to evaluate others negatively (as discussed above), Fear of Power predicted negative evaluation of others of the *same sex*. This result was true for both male and female subjects.

Protecting Autonomy and Independence

The crime of Prometheus, for which his freedom was constrained, was a crime of independence and not a crime of betrayal or direct confrontation. Prometheus did not start a revolution, nor did he oppose the kingship of Zeus; instead, he "saved mortals" (237). He would not let his free action to help others, to do what he thought was right, be controlled by Zeus. When he submitted to his punishment, he made no acknowledgement that he was wrong: "[I] am thus mercifully disciplined, a spectacle that shames the fate of Zeus" (242–243). For Prometheus, the important thing was to do what he wished, to do what he believed it his right to do:

Of my own will, aye, of my own will I erred—gainsay it I cannot. In succouring mortals I found suffering for myself. (265–269)

In the full knowledge of the probability of punishment by Zeus, Prometheus chose to exercise his free will rather than be constrained by the will of another. In addition, Prometheus also asserts his autonomy and independence from Zeus's attempts at persuasion once his punishment is carried out:

Not by persuasion's honied enchantments shall he charm me; and never will I, cowering before his dire threats, divulge this secret, until he shall release me from my cruel bonds and desire to proffer satisfaction for this outrage. (173–179)

Even in his bondage, Prometheus asserts that his will to independence remains: He will preserve his autonomy even while a slave.

This characteristic unbending commitment to one's own independence and autonomy is perhaps the most fully documented trait of individuals high in Fear of Power. For example, Winter (1973) showed that among college students, Fear of Power is associated with spending time alone rather than with others, and with a preference for those aspects of academic life involving the greatest independence or freedom from structure—seminars rather than lectures, papers rather than exams, essay questions rather than objective tests, and freedom of choice in courses rather than rigid requirements. Finally, students high in Fear of Power tend to disregard academic deadlines and simply hand in papers or take exams late.

In another study of 118 college students, Fear of Power measured in the freshman year negatively predicted senior year satisfaction with college. On a follow-up questionnaire sent 10 years after college graduation, these persons with high Fear of Power more often valued their theses, seminars, and field work, and less often valued lecture courses as making important contributions to what they had learned in college.

Finally, in a study of 173 female college students, Fear of Power was positively related to leaving school before graduation (transferring, dropping out, etc.) and to refusing to return a follow-up questionnaire 10 years after graduation (Stewart, 1975a). Among those who did return the questionnaire, moreover, Fear of Power was negatively associated with reporting that "peers" had had a great influence on one's life. Instead, high Fear of Power women tended to report significantly more often only that "public events" had had an influence on the course of their lives.

Among both men and women, then, there is evidence that people high in Fear of Power preserve their autonomy in three ways: (1) they avoid highly structured situations such as lectures, objective tests, and so on, (2) they disregard structure when faced with it (handing in papers late, transferring or dropping out, not returning a questionnaire), prefer things that involve autonomy (writing a thesis), and dislike things that do not (lectures), and finally, (3) they deny the influence of other people over them, which would be an admission of their own lack of independence, and admit only to the influence of inescapable social and political events. This positive feeling about things done by one's self and negative feeling about other things suggests a further important aspect of Fear of Power.

Valuation of Inner Self and not Things

In his unwillingness to renounce the action that brought down the wrath of Zeus upon him, Prometheus catalogs the aspects of his action on behalf of mankind that were of value: (1) his own cleverness, (2) his gift of knowledge to mankind, and (3) his teaching men to do useful work. Thus he says:

> They were witless erst and I made them to have sense and be endowed with reason. (443–444)

To Prometheus, knowledge either of his own or of others is of the highest value:

> Though they had eyes to see, they saw to no avail; they had ears, but understood not . . . without purpose they wrought all things in confusion. (447–448)

He is proud because:

> I taught them to discern the risings of the stars and their settings, ere this ill distinguishable. Aye, and numbers, too, chiefest of sciences, I invented for them, and the combining of letters, creative mother of the Muses' arts, wherewith to hold all things in memory. (457–461)

Above all else, then, Prometheus values the mind and the exercise of the mind, both in himself and in those he teaches. Next to the value of mind only, Prometheus values the ability to perform useful work: "how to mix soothing remedies" (482), the "ways whereby they might read the future" (484), and the craft techniques for making tools and instruments.

Prometheus is most profoundly a teacher, a giver of knowledge, one who values the gift of knowledge so much that he needs to give it to others. If he is interested in display at all, Prometheus is interested in the display of ideas rather than the display of things. He is impressed with the power of ideas and words, the products of the inner self, and not with the power of material objects. For "the chariot . . . an adornment of wealth and luxury" (465–466) he has only scorn.

In a similar way, individuals high in Fear of Power are not interested in possessions and objects. Instead of desiring and displaying their fancy, maneuverable cars, they have more traffic accidents that presumably damage their cars (Winter, 1973, p. 151)! Instead of collecting prestige objects, they tend to lend their possessions to others significantly more often (see below). In addition to this evidence of disinterest in possessions, there is also direct evidence that people high in Fear of Power *are* interested in ideas and the products of the mind. As mentioned above, in the college context they value their own work more than merely receiving the ideas of others. In addition, when asked to draw a picture of a human being (the Draw-a-Person test), people high in Fear of Power tend to draw figures with proportionately larger heads than do other people, which suggests that they see the head as relatively more important than other parts of the body, a valuation that affects either their perception or at least their drawing.

Because people high in Fear of Power value information, ideas, and their autonomy, we would expect that they would be quite careful to whom they communicate their inner thoughts. Indeed, in a sample of 58 college women, Fear of Power was negatively correlated with self-disclosure to others ($r = -.32, p < .05$) and was also positively related to lying to others ($r = .29, p < .05$) (disclosure and lying measured by the procedure described in Jourard, 1964). Guarding information about themselves even to the point of lying about it is a fusion of several aspects of Fear of Power: belief in the power of words and knowledge, suspiciousness and mistrust, and a desire to maintain autonomy.

Finally, although most of the research on career outcomes and power motivation did not consider Fear of Power as a separate variable, Stewart (1975a) found in a recent study of working women that Fear of Power predicted becoming a teacher ($r = .47, p < .001$). Future studies of career outcomes and motives should help to confirm that this particular "power career" is in fact a "Fear of Power career," involving as it does the transfer of knowledge to others. Not only are knowledge and the communication of knowledge important to the person high in Fear of Power, but teaching is also a special case of the pleasure he takes in helping others.

Performance in the Service of Others' Weakness

As we have seen, Prometheus took great pride in the fact that he helped mankind, that he served those who were weaker than the gods. Indeed, he is disgusted by the other gods' indifference to the poor and helpless:

> Soon as ever [Zeus] had seated himself upon his father's throne, he forthwith assigned to the deities their several privileges and apportioned unto them their proper powers. But of wretched mortals he took no heed, but desired to bring the whole race to nothingness and to create another, a new one, in its stead. Against this purpose none dared make stand save I myself—I only had the courage; I saved mortals. . . . (230–237)

Zeus's preoccupation with the trappings of power, with "ordering his kingdom," is both incomprehensible and revolting to Prometheus, who is filled with sorrow for ignorant mankind, suffering and about to perish. In the service of the ignorant and suffering poor, Prometheus dares to defy Zeus. He exercises power—not for his own good but for that of the weak and powerless.

Research studies of individuals high in Fear of Power seem to show this same pattern. In a sample of 80 college freshmen, Fear of Power predicted self-description as "responsible" some 14 years later ($r = .23, p < .05$). In a sample of 40 college students, Fear of Power was associated with lending expensive possessions such as cars, stereos, and clothing to others ($r = .44, p < .05$). Thus, it seems that people high in Fear of Power can act to help others (teaching, lending) but not to triumph over them. Indeed, these helping actions often have the effect of *equalizing* the difference between the helper with the high Fear of Power and those helped—teachers give knowledge, lenders give objects, and so on. The apparent outcome of the power action of the person high in Fear of Power is therefore not more power but less, since the other person—the "object" of the power action—gains rather than loses in the transaction.

A further pilot study supports this interpretation of the quality of actions of people high in Fear of Power. Ward, Olson, and Hammond (1975) conducted a power arousal experiment in which high school students who were members of a religious organization wrote TAT stories after listening to a sermon about the duty of the church to help other people and to solve social problems. The control group wrote stories without hearing the sermon and without knowledge of it. The aroused group's stories were significantly *higher* in Fear of Power and significantly *lower* in Hope of Power than the control stories. Not only does Fear of Power predict helping others, but appeals to help others arouse Fear of Power. Thus, it appears that the person high in Fear of Power feels that a power action is legitimate and acceptable *if it is in the service of equalizing a situation of power inequality or, more generally, resource inequality.* For this reason, Winter (1973, p. 220–222) suggested that Fear of Power is the motive of the charismatic leader. Such a leader typically appeals to the poor, attempts to lead them in an effort to equalize their power relationship with the rich and the powerful, and often renounces power, prestige, and reward for himself.

Finally, in a laboratory study, Fleming (1974) reported that among lower class black men who competed with middle class white men at a timed achievement task, Fear of Power predicted performance. Fear of Power did not predict performance for the middle class black men who competed with middle class white men. For the lower class black men, as compared with those from the middle class, success in this sort of competition is more likely to mean "power equalization" rather than self-aggrandizement. Since the power resources of race and class were more unequally distributed for the lower class group, it was more acceptable for them to act powerfully (to win) if they were high in Fear of Power, so that Fear of Power predicted power performance.

Although no further evidence for this formulation of the meaning of power actions on behalf of the weak exists as yet at the individual level, we do have some further evidence at the national level. First, using scores from the children's readers (as discussed above), we find a strong negative relationship between Fear of Power and national wealth (as measured by Gross Domestic Product in United States dollars per capita ($r = -.57$, $N = 36$ noncommunist countries, $p < .001$). That is, poor countries are significantly higher in Fear of Power than are rich countries. At the national level as well as at the individual level, then, *inequality* of power arouses Fear of Power. Is this Fear of Power also directed toward the restoration of power equality? If among nations Fear of Power leads to power actions only when in the service of equalizing power relationships that are perceived as unequal, then Fear of Power should predict war among poor countries but not among rich ones. Although the sample sizes are small, this is exactly the case. Of 24 countries with available data, the correlation between Fear of Power and months at war from 1932 to 1965 is $+ .85$ for the seven poor countries, whereas for the 17 rich ones the correlation is $- .09$ (p of difference between these correlations $< .01$). This finding at the national level suggests that although Fear of Power does not lead to power actions in a situation of power balance, it *does* lead to such actions (e.g., war) in a situation of (perceived) power imbalance. Put another way, Fear of Power does not predict power actions under most conditions; but when one group is weak and powerless and another is powerful and strong, then Fear of Power may well lead to power action in order to equalize the relations between the groups, to bring about a power balance. This seems intuitively reasonable when we recall that the fear behind Fear of Power is, as we have seen, the fear of inescapable and overwhelming power. If power in the external world is distributed relatively equally, then it is less likely to overwhelm, so that there is less to fear. If it is not equally distributed, then action must be taken to recreate a safer situation.

Unsuccessful Performance in the Service of Strength

To the extent that his defiance of Zeus served a personal goal of achieving more power for himself, Prometheus failed. Indeed, he refers to himself as "an ill-fated god" and he resents this fall from grace:

> Nay, impute it not to pride nor yet to wilfulness that I am silent. Painful thoughts devour my heart as I behold myself maltreated thus. (436–438)

Though outwardly silent, Prometheus inwardly storms with resentment and anguish. Interestingly, we learn from some of those who pass by in front of Prometheus that in part he has only himself to blame for his troubles. He is described as hurling forth "words so harsh and of such whetted edge"

(313–314), as needing "to put away thy wrathful mood" (317), and as having "too vaunting speech" (320–321). Perhaps Prometheus has not so skillfully managed his campaign to save mankind; perhaps he has not conducted himself as a leader so as to maximize his victory. We now turn to these aspects of Fear of Power: the tendency to experience internal anguish or anxiety, to disorganize, and to become ineffective in the course of power behavior or power situations. Let us remember the case of Prometheus: His action in some sense succeeded (he did help the race of men), but it failed in that as a god he was immobilized and degraded, forced silently and helplessly to bear his humiliation.

Winter (1973, p. 151) reported that among college students Fear of Power was positively related to "general activation," often taken as a measure of physiological arousal or anxiety. Similarly, in a study of 235 male college students, Fear of Power was significantly positively related to systolic blood pressure ($r = .15, p < .05$). In this case, blood pressure is probably a measure of anxiety, particularly in a sample so young as to rule out the effect of arteriosclerosis in elevating blood pressure. Last, in a sample of 55 female college students, Fear of Power was significantly positively associated with the number of cigarettes reported smoked per day. Although there are many postulated causes of cigarette smoking, it is certainly possible that high levels of anxiety might lead to compulsive smoking on the part of women high in Fear of Power. There is, then, both direct and indirect evidence for the notion that men and women high in Fear of Power may experience relatively high levels of anxiety or physiological arousal.

Winter suggests that this high "base-rate" arousal level may lead to great difficulties when the individual high in Fear of Power is faced with an unusually anxiety-provoking situation. One possibility is that he leaves the field or tries to escape the situation (and the anguish); this may be reflected, for example, in the previously mentioned findings that women high in Fear of Power transfer and drop out of college more often than other people, and that people with Fear of Power simply disregard deadlines.

What does this kind of person do, though, when faced with a situation that is anxiety provoking but that he cannot leave? Prometheus behaved acceptably until he felt it was his duty to help mankind. Then, apparently he blustered, raged, and was rude and irritating! Similarly, when forced to remain in a power situation, people high in Fear of Power fall apart. Winter reports that Fear of Power predicts traffic accidents. Possibly this is because driving a car is an activity that takes place in a highly structured context, in which low-to-moderate anxiety is adaptive. High levels of anxiety, however, may delay reaction times or lead to irrational, counter-productive actions, either of which could lead to a higher accident rate.

To test the theory that Fear of Power involves high levels of maladaptive arousal or anxiety, which then leads to poor performance under some conditions,

Winter (1973) devised an experiment in which such performance could be monitored. Briefly, subjects played a card game called "Auction Pitch," and their performance was assessed as to both playing efficiency and overall skill. As predicted, under conditions of playing the game competitively, to win for one's own sake, Fear of Power was significantly negatively associated with both measures of performance. It would be interesting to establish whether the performance of people high in Fear of Power could be improved by having players play on behalf of someone else. If our understanding of Fear of Power is correct, performance will only disorganize under conditions of playing for one's own exclusive benefit; if the situation can be structured so that the individual is working for someone else or to equalize an unequal power relationship, then Fear of Power may even facilitate performance, as in the Fleming study of lower class black men discussed above.

There is, then, a curious variation in the effect of Fear of Power on performance. For Fear of Power to motivate effective and reasonable power behavior, it must be or appear to be in the service of weakness, of leveling a power differential. When the goal is to increase strength or personal aggrandizement, Fear of Power leads to maladaptively high levels of anxiety and a consequent disorganization of behavior. Perhaps the awareness of increasing anxiety, which is experienced by people high in Fear of Power in competitive interpersonal situations, leads to their characteristic flight and retreat into autonomy. The "aversive" characteristic of power situations may thus be the capacity of these situations to arouse overwhelming anxiety.

Summary

We may conclude, then, that early experiences of powerlessness lead to high Fear of Power, which involves high anxiety in power situations, a devaluation of power and the trappings of power, and a high valuation of the self and its products (thoughts, words, ideas). In action, Fear of Power seems to express itself as avoidance of interpersonal power situations by "leaving the field" or by protecting personal autonomy. When inescapably engaged in an interpersonal power situation, Fear of Power may lead to effective power actions on behalf of others, or in the service of leveling power differentials, but it leads to ineffective actions in the service of making the strong even stronger.

This analysis suggests that futre research should focus on specifying the conditions under which Fear of Power may actually facilitate effective performance, as well as those under which it will lead to flight or poor performance. Put another way, we need better to understand the conditions under which Fear of Power *will* lead to effective power actions, and those under which it may lead to disorganized ineffective behavior.

THE POWER MOTIVE DISTINGUISHED FROM OTHER "POWER" VARIABLES

Having concluded a review of the correlates of both aspects of the power motive (Hope and Fear), only one major task remains. We must consider how the power motive is similar to and different from other personality variables that have to do with power. Does the power motive correlate highly with other variables purported to measure something similar? Does the power motive predict to the same behaviors as these other measures? A large number of variables purport to measure something like a "power drive." For example, there is a "dominance" scale in most personality inventories. Winter (1973) reports that the power motive measures (n Power, Hope and Fear) are not highly correlated with these measures or a number of other measures to which power motivation might appear conceptually related.

One possibility is that the power motive does not measure anything related to power at all. Another, more likely possibility is that these different measures are in fact measuring different aspects of power concern than is the power motive. We have suggested that power motivation measures the disposition to view power as a goal, either a positive (Hope) or a negative (Fear) goal. Briefly, we will show here that the lack of correlation of power motivation with other power-related variables is owing to conceptual differences and perhaps to measurement differences in the variable. That is, we will demonstrate that the power motive is empirically independent of other measures of power, that it predicts different behaviors than do other measures of power, and that it possesses these characteristics *for sound conceptual reasons*. Having done that, we may safely conclude that the power motive has substantial demonstrable discriminant validity.

We will consider below only a few variables with which power motivation is uncorrelated: competence or mastery, authoritarianism, Machiavellianism, and internal versus external Locus of Control. These few will have to serve as examples from the large domain of power-related variables existing in the literature.

Competence or Mastery

White's theory (1959, 1963) of competence (or mastery) motivation sometimes sounds like a theory of power motivation:

> It springs rather from what one can make the environment do by crying, by signaling, or by co-ordinated acts of competence. Fantasies of omnipotence can be based upon the infant's experience of commanding the environment to serve him (the master who rings for his servants) or upon his experience of mastering it by his own efforts (Robinson Crusoe, Superman). (White, 1963, p. 192)

Thus, competence seems to arise out of attempts to control or influence behavior. In addition, although White suggests (especially in the 1959 version) that competence motivation is universal, he does specify alternative outcomes for this universal motive, that is, a variable salience of mastery as an issue, depending on early experience. Relevant early experiences consist largely in a thwarting of the competence motive and lead to lower "ego strength" and "the inhibition of effectance" (White, 1963, pp. 84–92).

Ego strength is, thus, the power-related variable. White offers no measure of ego strength, but various researchers have constructed measures based on White's ideas (Costa, as presented in McClelland, 1972; Ezekial, 1968; Pizer, as reported in McClelland & Winter, 1969). Ezekial (1968) found that Peace Corps volunteers who score high on his measure of "ego strength" were more likely to be successful (as measured by their supervisors), to plan for the future, and to be satisfied with the present. Costa (reported in McClelland, 1972) found that his measure of ego strength predicted academic performance among school children. None of these findings seems related to those for power motivation, either conceptually or empirically. The first set sounds like some of the findings for the achievement motive (especially the concern for the future) (McClelland, 1961), and the second sounds like what McClelland had originally *hoped* the achievement motive would predict (McClelland, 1972). Pizer's scale differentiated those people who changed from those who did not in an achievement motivation training course, and therefore it is conceptually and empirically related to the achievement motive (McClelland & Winter, 1969, pp. 271–272). None of these findings is related to power; overall, one must conclude that White's concept of competence does not *clearly* relate to power (although mastery in some sense may be related to "achievement") and that the research generated *by* the theory is unrelated to power.

Authoritarianism

Authoritarianism as measured by the F–Scale (Adorno et al., 1950) is often thought of as a power-related trait. Greenstein (1969) describes the authoritarian as seeing "power relations where they do not exist" (p. 108), a view that seems to derive from those F–Scale items concerned with "power and toughness" (Brown, 1965, p. 488). A look at examples of these items, however, and at the behavior correlates of the F–Scale suggests that there is an important difference between the "authoritarian" and the "power-motivated" individual. Items concerning power on the F–Scale include, for example, the following:

People can be divided into two distinct classes: the weak and the strong.
Most people don't realize how much our lives are controlled by plots hatched in secret places.

These items appear to have a fairly strong paranoid overtone; given Winter's discovery that Fear of Power is related to paranoia, it might be plausible to consider authoritarianism as possibly related to Fear of Power (although Winter found no such relationship).

More important, however, than item composition are the correlates of authoritarianism. It is strongly related to conformity (i.e., to yielding) under conditions of group pressure in an experimental situation (Barron, 1953; Crutchfield, 1955; Lindgren, 1962; Nadler, 1959; Wells, Weinert, & Rubel, 1956). In addition, Elms and Milgram (1966) found that high authoritarianism predicted more yielding in the Milgram obedience experiment (i.e., administering the punishment). Finally, Haythorn, Couch, Haefner, Langham, and Carter (1956) and Haythorn, Haefner, Langham, Couch and Carter (1956) found that, in two small groups, high authoritarians were rated by others as autocratically telling others what to do and as being insensitive to others.

These findings seem inconsistent with those for both Hope and Fear of Power. As we have seen, Fear of Power predicts avoidance of interpersonal power arenas, a concern for autonomy, and deterioration of performance under conditions of interpersonal competition. Hope of Power, on the other hand, predicts dominance in groups, pursuit of interpersonal power arenas, and a concern for prestige and status. The correlates of authoritarianism are inconsistent with Winter's findings for group members high in *n* Power (that they are rated as asking others to participate, etc.); they suggest instead that authoritarians are more concerned with their particular opinions than with power per se. Equally, individuals high in Fear of Power should tend to *avoid* the power of others rather than *submit* to it. They may "disorganize" in competition, but they do not seem likely to give up—their autonomy is far too important to them. There seems to be no evidence, then, that the authoritarian tends to orient himself toward the goal of power, as does the power-motivated individual, by definition as well as empirically. This analysis suggests, then, that the conventional morality of authoritarians may be the more salient predictor of authoritarians' behavior. They may search the field for power cues but only so they can fit into their appropriate position in the power hierarchy, and not so they can pursue power over others or avoid others' power over them.

Machiavellianism

Machiavellianism is another variable that seems superficially related to power, both from a reading of the items and from the range of behavior it predicts. Christie and Geis (1970) and their coworkers have found that high Machiavellianism predicts highly successful competitive behavior, ability to persuade (especially Braginsky's study of child Machiavellianism, 1966), and willingness to cheat and lie. The also found that high Machs perform better in face-to-face interaction. Many of these findings seem consistent with Winter's findings for power motivation, as does Christie's only reported career preference (among medical students)—psychiatry. There is, however, an important distinction. High Machs' major concern appears to be with *winning over* or *beating* another person. The importance of an interpersonal setting for them appears to be that only then are they obviously beating someone else. The power-motivated person, according to Winter's gambling study (1973, p. 153), McClelland and Teague (1975), and McClelland and Watson (1973) does *not* win more, although he may like to gamble. In the language of motives, the Machs' incentive (goal) is beating another, whereas the incentive for high n Power people is controlling or influencing others and being recognized by others as powerful.

Although there are no data on persuasion and n Power, it may be that high n Power individuals would be no more successful at persuasion than they are in competition—partly because an attempt to persuade might well involve a failure and consequent loss of status. It is more rational for a person whose goal is power (not winning) either to encourage (as in the groups) or to "dazzle" others with display (extreme risks, prestigious possessions, etc.). To engage in a direct confrontation over an *issue* might be highly unrewarding in terms of the goal of power. Similarly, high Machs lie and cheat in order to *win*, whereas high n Power individuals lie in the service of presenting a better *image,* or controlling information. Power-motivated individuals might not be willing to risk a lie merely to win; it would be worthwhile only if it will make them more prestigious and respected.

A definitive answer to these questions could best be achieved by studies in which both n Power and Machiavellianism are variables. For example, power-motivated individuals seem systematically to select certain careers. High Machs, on the other hand, may randomly select careers, but they may choose particular specialities within them according to their goals (e.g., psychiatry within medicine). On the other hand, perhaps high Machs (unlike high n Power individuals) pursue careers such as politics, in which *winning* is a highly salient goal. There seems, then, a plausible explanation for the lack of relationship between n Power and Machiavellianism, but only further research can clearly delineate the differences. Such research might help us to differentiate what looks like "power," in the common-sense definition, into important subcategories determined by different goals (winning versus influencing and controlling, etc.).

Internal versus External Locus of Control

Finally, internal versus external Locus of Control (Rotter, 1966) has been considered by some (e.g., Minton, 1967) as a power-related measure. This may derive from the way people talk about the variable:

In Rotter's theory, the control construct is considered a generalized expectancy, operating across a large number of situations, which relates to *whether or not the individual possesses or lacks power over what happens to him* (Lefcourt, 1966, p. 207 [emphasis ours]).

However, the true definition of the variable (Lefcourt, 1966, p. 207) sounds rather less like power motivation:

As a general principle, internal control refers to the perception of positive and/or negative events as being a consequence of one's own actions and thereby under personal control; external control refers to the perception of positive and/or negative events as being unrelated to one's own behaviors in certain situations and therefore beyond personal control.

The behavior correlates of the I–E Scale (see Chapter 7) do not look much like those of power motivation either. Externals tend to conform (Crowne & Liverant, 1963; Odell, 1959) although the behavior of "internals" is known only to be "less conforming." Low externals (i.e., internals) tend to be more responsive to objective probabilities in gambling situations (Liverant & Scodel, 1960), as do people high in *n* Achievement but not in *n* Power.

Perhaps the correlates most important, however, for understanding the lack of relationship between *n* Power and Locus of Control are those with ethnicity (Battle & Rotter, 1963; Gore & Rotter, 1963; Graves, 1961; Lefcourt & Ladwig, 1966; Strickland, 1965).

In all of the reported ethnic studies, groups whose social position is one of minimal power either by class or race tend to score higher in the external-control direction. Within the racial groupings, class interacts so that the double handicap of lower-class and "lower-caste" seems to produce persons with the highest expectancy of external control. (Lefcourt, 1966, p. 212)

Thus, in one model frequently used by researchers in the area of motives (see, for example, Atkinson & Feather, 1966), where behavior is considered a joint function of motive, expectancy, and incentive, I–E is literally measuring expectancy or perceived (estimated) probability of success. Power, on the other hand, is measuring motive or a disposition to strive for a goal. Both are necessary for the prediction of behavior; but they cannot be (or measure, or predict) the same thing.

Summary

As we have seen, these measures that appear superficially to be measuring aspects of power are all measuring things nevertheless conceptually distinct from power *motivation*. Authoritarianism and Machiavellianism appear to measure attitudes or "sentiments about the nature of power, or power as an aspect of man's nature" (Winter, 1973, p. 18). The I–E scale seems to measure expectancies about one's ability to control events in one's life, and competence seems to be more closely related to the need for achievement than for power. Power motivation, in contrast to all of these, is an attempt to assess the disposition to strive for (or away from) power as a goal, and thus it differs conceptually from the other variables we have considered. In addition, the correlates of all the measures, as we have discussed, differ to varying degrees from those of power motivation. Each may be a valid measure of some aspect of power thinking and action, but power motivation is neither empirically related to, nor predicts the same behaviors as, the other measures. Thus it possesses discriminant validity.

Finally, it is important to note the fact that in some cases an important difference exists among these measures in the ways the variables are assessed. At least the last three variables (Machiavellianism, authoritarianism, Locus of Control) are all measured by questionnaires. Endorsement of items on these questionnaires represents "respondent" behavior—answers are partly determined by the fact that the question has been asked. Power motivation, in contrast, is measured with the TAT, an instrument far more open to "shaping" by the subject (see McClelland, 1966, on this distinction). The TAT may in fact be the more appropriate measure of the tendency to view power as a goal. Operant expression of an "interest" in power, as by means of the TAT, may be the best predictor of operant real-world power behavior, whereas respondent measures may be adequate predictors of other aspects of power in the real world.

RESEARCH UNDERWAY AND FUTURE TRENDS

In this chapter we have tried to draw together the research that has been done on the power motive and to put it in the context of one of the major psychological forces that has been active in modern Western civilization. We have suggested Don Juan and Prometheus as literary archetypes of the Hope of Power and the Fear of Power, respectively. Mythic figures have not only served as a way of organizing the research findings, but also suggested future research hypotheses. It would be repetitious to summarize the contents of this chapter again, and it would be premature to claim that we now know most of the important things about a personality variable as new as *n* Power. Therefore, we propose here to conclude with a survey of research that is currently underway and some suggestions about research that should be done. These are likely future trends in power-motivation research.

Combinations of the Power Motive and Other Variables

Several researchers have included the power motive in combination with other variables. Partly this strategy increases the precision of our understanding, but it must be admitted that much of this effort is intended to raise the magnitude of correlation coefficients from the usual ± 0.30 that Mischel (1968) has termed "personality coefficient[s]".

Stewart (1975a) devoted great effort to examining and specifying the subsample within which a particular relationship between personality and action holds. She argued that it was both unreasonable and contrary to the spirit of the definition of "personality" to expect that a given variable will always predict in the same way, regardless of the influence of other personality variables or of the constraints and opportunities of the real world. The introduction of such basic moderator variables as social class, current family and marital status, and differences in adult socialization experiences greatly increased the usual magnitude of correlation coefficients between motive scores and life outcomes.

McClelland (1975, Chap. 2) has combined measures of the power motive with a TAT measure of psychosocial stage of maturity devised by Stewart (1977). The theory and measurement of "stages" comes from the work of Freud (1908a, 1923) and Abraham (1927). McClelland then works out the correlates of the power motive at or in combination with the (oral) Stage I, at or in combination with the (anal) Stage II, and so on. In principle, a motive is a class of goals, and within each such class there may be goals representing transformations and sublimations of each of the zone-related components of the libido. Moreover, McClelland argues that motives often predict to clusters of behavior alternatives that are themselves uncorrelated or negatively correlated. He discusses a technique for identifying such clusters and calculating the correlation between the power motive and the entire cluster taken together. McClelland's results are interesting and should encourage future research.

Another nonmotive measure of style that can fruitfully be combined with the power motive is Self-definition (Stewart & Winter, 1974). This variable reflects rational, instrumental thinking, and it should be particularly useful as a moderator variable for the power motive in women, where sex-role conceptions about power and instrumentality may be expected to have especially important effects.

Finally, McClelland (1975) has also created clusters or configurations of motives by combining[20] motive scores and a variable called Activity Inhibition which is measured by the amount of *negation* in the story (frequency of the use of the word "not") (McClelland et al., 1972). Using the relationship between the power and affiliation motives, and Activity Inhibition, McClelland suggests the following four quadrants, each of which can be scored in a binary (yes or no) fashion (1975, Chap. 8):

(1) *Imperial pattern:* Power motivation higher than affiliation, and Activity Inhibition above the median. Persons showing this pattern seek institutional authority and show disciplined self-control. They make excellent managers because they create high morale in their subordinates. They are, however, subject

to stress and its long-term cumulative manifestations such as hypertension and heart disease (McClelland, 1976). At the national level, this pattern is associated with mobilization for defense, restriction of private consumption, and war.

(2) *"Don Juan" or conquistador pattern.* Power motivation higher than affiliation, and Activity Inhibition below the median. Persons showing this pattern act in a phallic, assertive way. They reject institutional responsibility. Wormley (1976) studied a group of mutual fund portfolio managers with responsibilities for between $10 million and $1.3 billion investments. Those showing the Don Juan pattern chose securities with a significantly higher index of volatility than the market as a whole (went up more than the market and went down more than the market) over five years of management. In other words, managers from this quadrant took greater risks with other people's money. This quadrant, then, seems to be the locus of the risky, expansive, and profligate impulsivity so characteristic of power in the Western world.

(3) *Bureaucratic pattern:* Affiliation motivation higher than power, and Activity Inhibition high.

(4) *Personal enclave pattern:* Affiliation motivation higher than power and Activity Inhibition low. Persons showing this pattern seek security in close personal ties, a "familistic" alternative to institutional power.

The concept of motive configurations seems especially important in the case of the power motive, for it is obvious that which of the many power behaviors a person chooses will depend on his other motives.

Continuing Research

There are several lines of research on the power motive that look both interesting and promising at this point. The innovation of McClelland in studying nations through coding contents of their cultural documents, and of Donley and Winter for studying the motives of past and present leaders should lead to further historical and cross-cultural studies of the power motive. In the case of speeches (and protocols of interviews, press conferences, etc.) there are several methodological problems that have to be worked out. We do not know precisely how the topic of a speech or the intended audience may affect its motive imagery; for that reason Donley and Winter used only inaugural speeches. It is both important and often difficult to establish a group of comparable speeches of comparable leaders, which is necessary given the ordinal or interval scaling of the motive measure. No doubt these problems can be solved with further research.

Although we know that the power motive leads to power in a general way, we need to know more about the process by which this happens. How do power-motivated people manage to get power? How do they act to establish their position in a social situation that is at first unstructured? In this connection we need to know more about the relationship of *n* Power to rank and gesture (Brown & Herrnstein, 1975, pp. 221–253). Such problems offer the chance to develop interesting nonreactive measures of the dependent variables.

Finally, the construct of Fear of Power especially needs further research. The idea that power can be both salient and aversive to a person may seem intuitively obvious to some and contradictory to others. The interpretation that we have offered in this chapter is consistent with the research evidence to date and makes sense in the light of the Prometheus myth, but the interpretation needs further empirical support.

Researchers interested in power motivation should consult *The Power Motive* (Winter, 1973), which contains the scoring systems (for *n* Power, Hope and Fear) and instructions for learning and using them. The edited volume by Atkinson (1958) contains an introduction to the general method, while the recent monograph by McClelland (1975) suggests some interesting new research lines.

NOTES

1   Speech at Pueblo, Colorado on September 25, 1919.

2   See Freud (1900, 1907, 1908b) and Jung (1918).

3   See Winter (1973, Chap. 3) and Veroff and Veroff (1972) for a discussion of the Veroff scoring system; see Winter (1973, Chap. 3) and Uleman (1972) for a discussion of the Uleman measure, since renamed "*n* Influence"; and see Hunt (1972) for a comparison of the Veroff and Uleman measures.

4   Briefly, the power motive as measured here does not correlate with any of the usual self-report scales for measuring power (California Personality Inventory, Edwards Personal Preference Schedule, Adjective Check List, etc.).

    The researcher who wants to know more about the details of measuring motives with the TAT should consult the handbook edited by Atkinson (1958, especially the appendices). Many different sets of pictures have been used as stimuli to elicit stories scored for motives. There is no one "best" set, and any picture that elicits a *variety* of stories is usable. However, the pictures reproduced in McClelland, Davis, Kalin and Wanner (1972, pp. 360–367) and by McClelland (1975, pp. 385–388) are examples of balanced sets that could be used for measuring the power, achievement, and affiliation motives.

    Since Weiner (Chap. 1) has raised the issue of the reliability of TAT motive scores, some discussion of *n* Power reliability is appropriate here. The usual test–retest correlation coefficient for *n* Power ranges from .30 to .50. However, there are many reasons why this may be a serious underestimate of the true reliability of the instrument (see Winter, 1973, pp. 86–92). Persons who take a second TAT may try consciously to tell different stories from the first TAT—or indeed to tell the same stories! When this random self-instruction is brought under experimental control, as was done by Winter and Stewart (1977b), then people who are told to try to tell the *same* story show test–retest correlation coefficients around .60 to .70, whereas people told to tell *different* stories show coefficients around .10 to .20. Thus, there appear to be reasons for the usual low TAT test–retest correlations *that do not affect the validity* of the TAT.

5   This distinction arises from the studies of conflict carried out by Hullian theorists (Miller, 1944) and can give rise to elaborate mathematical theory (cf. Atkinson & Birch, 1970); but the Hope of Power/Fear of Power distinction does not necessarily entail either the Hull–Miller theory or the particular mathematical models of Atkinson and Birch. These variables may be taken to be simple personality variables, unconnected with any particular motivational theory; alternatively, they can be taken to be based loosely on the broad distinction between pleasurable and painful affects: we like, want, and hope for some things; and we dislike, avoid, and fear others. Many goals, power among them, can arouse both tendencies. (see Bindra & Stewart, 1971, pp. 17–20, 139–147, 191–204).

6   One could also construct a measure of "net approach to power" (Hope minus Fear), following Miller's analysis of conflict and Heckhausen's (1963) procedure with achievement motivation. So far, such a measure has not been used in research on the power motive.

7   Constructing a definition of power is a complicated task. For a discussion of the issues and different points of view, see Winter (1973, Chap. 1 and associated references).

8   See Engels (1874) for a discussion of the necessity of power or authority even in a socialist or communistic economy.

9   In each of these careers, there is an official ideology that directs our gaze away from the power aspects of that career. Thus, businessmen "coordinate" rather than "direct," teachers "facilitate students' own learning," psychologists "assist" the patient's self-directed personal growth, and the clergy deal with Divine Will rather than their own. Such claims seem largely to be a reaction to the negative stereotype of "power" (see McClelland, 1970; Guggenbühl-Craig, 1971), or even a denial of inherent "power" (May, 1972). For public consumption and perhaps for private belief, these professions avoid the "authoritarian" connotations of power; but as suggested above, these are beliefs about the exercise of power rather than about power itself. Stripped of such negative connotations, power is obviously involved in all these occupations.

10 The situation of the many and varied "alternative" groups that reject traditional occupations and voluntary organizations is interesting in this respect. For the members of such groups, the two most common sources of power are thus unavailable. One would predict that in such cases, power-motivated people will seek some other forms of power such as: religious or secular proselytizing (Kanter, 1972), fantasies of alternative realities (Slack, 1974), or even anomic violence as in the case of the Manson family (Bugliosi, 1974).

11 This point suggests several parallel distinctions: that between excellence and control, between the technical specialist and the leader, and that between n Achievement and n Power (see Winter, 1973, pp. 93–95). Related to this distinction is a finding by McClelland (1975) that men high in n Power are more likely to endorse the following statements: "Good will is more important than reason"; "Action is more important than knowing the truth."

12 "John Gabriel Borkman," Acts 2 and 4. In *The Master Builder and Other Plays,* translated by U. Ellis-Fermor. Baltimore: Penguin Books, 1958.

13 They did find that marijuana use was related to a relatively personal versus social *orientation* of power motivation.

14 To be classified pre-Oedipal, a subject had both to report that he resembled his mother more than his father and not to view death as castration (i.e., to choose metaphors for death other than "a grinning butcher," etc.).

15 The reader is referred to Winter and Stewart (1977a) for details about the application of the motive scoring systems to speeches, for detailed definitions of the dependent variables, and for a general discussion of methodological issues and problems in scoring speeches.

16 Measured as standard-scored n Power minus standard-scored n Affiliation.

17   In studies of individuals, Kolb and Boyatzis (1970) found that people with this pattern tended to be rated by their peers as ineffective helpers.

18   See Winter (1973, Chaps. 3 and 5 and Appendix 1) for an account of the development and characteristics of the Fear of Power measure.

19   We are grateful to Bruce Johnston for designing and executing this study.

20   Standard-scored before combining.

REFERENCES

Abraham, K. *Selected papers*. London: Institute of Psychoanalysis and Hogarth Press, 1927.

Adams, F. M., & Osgood, C. E. A cross-cultural study of the affective meaning of color. *Journal of cross-cultural Psychology*, 1973, *4*, 135–156.

Adorno, T. W., Frenkel-Brunswik, E., Levinson, D. J., & Sanford, R. N. *The authoritarian personality*. New York: Harper, 1950.

Atkinson, J. W. (Ed.). *Motives in fantasy, action and society*. Princeton, N. J.: Van Nostrand, 1958.

Atkinson, J. W., & Birch, D. *The dynamics of action*. New York: John Wiley, 1970.

Atkinson, J. W., & Feather, N. T. *A theory of achievement motivation*. New York: John Wiley, 1966.

Bales, R. F. Task roles and social roles in problem-solving groups. In E. E. Maccoby, T. M. Newcomb, and E. L. Hartley (Eds.). *Readings in social psychology* (3rd ed.) New York: Holt, Rinehart and Winston, 1958.

Barber, J. D. *The presidential character: predicting performance in the White House*. Englewood Cliffs, N. J.: Prentice-Hall, 1972.

Barron, F. Some personality correlates of independence of judgment. *Journal of Personality*, 1953, *21*, 287–297.

Battle, E., & Rotter, J. B. Children's feelings of personal control as related to social class and ethnic group. *Journal of Personality*, 1963, *31*, 482–490.

Berkowitz, L. The contagion of violence: An S–R mediational analysis of some effects of observed aggression. In W. J. Arnold and M. M. Page (Eds.), *Nebraska Symposium on Motivation*. Lincoln: University of Nebraska Press, 1970.

Bindra, D., & Stewart, J. *Motivation* (2nd ed.) Harmondsworth, Mddx.: Penguin Books, 1971.

Boyatzis, R. E. *Alcohol and aggression: A study of the interaction*. Report to the National Institute of Alcohol Abuse and Alcoholism. Boston: McBer and Company, 1973.

Boyatzis, R. E. Power motivation training: A new treatment modality. *Proceedings*, the clinical/scientific conference of the National Conference on Alcoholism, 1975.

Braginsky, D. *Machiavellian and manipulative behavior in children: Two studies*. Unpublished doctoral thesis, University of Connecticut, 1966.

Brown, M. D. *The effectiveness of the personality dimensions of dependency, power, and Internal-External locus of control in differentiating among unremitted and remitted alcoholics and non-alcoholic controls*. Unpublished doctoral thesis, University of Windsor, 1975.

Brown, R. W. *Social psychology*. New York: Free Press, 1965.

Brown, R. W., & Herrnstein, R. J. *Psychology*. Boston: Little, Brown, 1975.

Browning, R. P. The interaction of personality and political system in decisions to run for office: Some data and a simulation technique. *Journal of Social Issues*, 1968, *24*, 3, 93–109.

Browning, R. P., & Jacob, H. Power motivation and the political personality. *Public Opinion Quarterly*, 1964, *28*, 75–90.

Bugliosi, V. *Helter Skelter: The true story of the Manson murders.* New York: W. W. Norton, 1974.

Canetti, E. *Crowds and power.* New York: Viking Press, 1962.

Cantril, H. *The pattern of human concerns.* New Brunswick, N. J.: Rutgers University Press, 1965.

Christie, R., & Geis, F. *Studies in Machiavellianism.* New York and London: Academic Press, 1970.

Collins, B. E., & Raven, H. H. Group structure: Attraction, coalitions, communication, and power. In G. Lindzey and E. Aronson (Eds.), *Handbook of social psychology* (Rev. ed.). Vol. 4. Reading, Mass.: Addison-Wesley, 1969.

Crowne, D. P., & Liverant, S. Conformity under varying conditions of personal commitment. *Journal of Abnormal and Social Psychology*, 1963, *66*, 547–555.

Crutchfield, R. S. Conformity and character. *American Psychologist*, 1955, *10*, 191–198.

deCharms, R. C. *Personal causation.* New York and London: Academic Press, 1968.

Donley, R. E., & Winter, D. G. Measuring the motives of public officials at a distance: An exploratory study of American presidents. *Behavioral Science*, 1970, *15*, 227–236.

Duijker, H. C. J. Het streven naar macht [The striving for power]. *Gawein—Tijdsschrift van de psychologische kring aan de Nijmeegse Universiteit*, 1961, *9*, 125–133.

Elms, A. C., & Milgram, S. Personality characteristics associated with obedience and defiance toward authoritative command. *Journal of Experimental Research in Personality*, 1966, *1*, 282–289.

Engels, F. On authority. In *Karl Marx and Frederick Engels: Selected works* (Vol. 1). Moscow: Foreign Languages Publishing House, 1951, pp. 575–579. (Originally published, 1874.)

Erdelyi, M. H. A new look at the New Look: Perceptual defense and vigilance. *Psychological Review*, 1974, *81*, 1–25.

Ezekial, R. S. The personal future and Peace Corps competence. *Journal of Personality and Social Psychology Monograph Supplement*, 1968, *8*, 1–26.

Fersch, E. *Inward bound: The motivational impact of a combined Outward Bound–Upward Bound program on adolescents from poverty families.* Unpublished doctoral thesis, Harvard University, 1972.

Fleming, J. Approach and avoidance motivation in interpersonal competition: A study of black male and female college students. Unpublished doctoral thesis, Harvard University, 1974.

French, E. G., & Lesser, G. S. Some characteristics of the achievement motive in women. *Journal of Abnormal and Social Psychology*, 1964, *68*, 118–128.

Freud, S. *The interpretation of dreams.* In J. Strachey (Ed.), The standard edition of the complete psychological works of Sigmund Freud (Vol. 9). London: Hogarth Press, 1953–1974. (Originally published, 1900.)

Freud, S. *The interpretation of dreams.* In J. Strachey (Ed.), *The standard edition of the complete psychological works of Sigmund Freud* (Vol. 9). London: Hogarth Press, 1953–1974. (Originally published, 1900.)

Freud, S. Character and anal erotism. In J. Strachey (Ed.), *The standard edition of the complete psychological works of Sigmund Freud* (vol. 9). London: Hogarth Press, 1953–1974. (Originally published, 1908.)(a)

Freud, S. Creative writers and day-dreaming. In J. Strachey (Ed.), *The standard edition of the complete psychological works of Sigmund Freud* (vol. 9). London: Hogarth Press, 1953–1974. (Originally published, 1908.)(b)

Freud, S. The infant genital organization. In J. Strachey (ED.), *The standard edition of the complete psychological works of Sigmund Freud* (vol. 19). London: Hogarth Press, 1953–1974. (Originally published, 1923.)

Gardner, R. *The adventures of Don Juan.* New York: Viking Press, 1974.

Gibb, C. A. Leadership. In G. Lindzey and E. Aronson (Eds.) *Handbook of social psychology* (Rev. ed.) (Vol. 4). Reading, Mass.: Addison-Wesley, 1969.

Gold, A. R., Christie, R., & Friedman, L. N. *Fists and flowers.* New York and London: Academic Press, 1976.

Gore, P. M., & Rotter, J. B. A personality correlate of social action. *Journal of Personality,* 1963, *31,* 58–64.

Graves, T. D. *Time perspective and the deferred gratification pattern in a tri-ethnic community.* Research Report 5, Tri-Ethnic Research Program, University of Colorado, Institute of Behavioral Science, 1961.

Greenstein, F. I. *Personality and politics.* Chicago: Markham, 1969.

Grupp, F. *The power motive with the American state bureaucracy.* Paper read at the Yale University Conference on Psychology and Politics, March, 1975.

Guggenbühl-Craig, A. *Power in the helping professions.* Zurich: Spring Publications, 1971.

Haley, J. *The power tactics of Jesus Christ and other essays.* New York: Grossman, 1969.

Hargrove, E. C. *Presidential leadership: Personality and political style.* New York: Macmillan, 1966.

Haythorn, W., Couch, A. S., Haefner, D., Langham, P., & Carter, L. F. The behavior of authoritarian and equalitarian personalities in groups. *Human Relations,* 1956, *9,* 57–74.

Haythorn, W., Langham, P., Couch, A. S., & Carter, L. F. The effects of varying combinations of authoritarian and equalitarian leaders and followers. *Journal of Abnormal and Social Psychology,* 1956, *53,* 210–219.

Heckhausen, H. *Hoffnung und Furcht in der Leistungsmotivation [Hope and fear in achievement motivation].* Meisenheim am Glan: Verlag Anton Hain, 1963.

Hobbes, T. *Leviathan.* New York: E. P. Dutton & Company, 1950. (Originally published, 1651.)

Hunt, S. M., Jr. *A comparison and validation of two thematic apperceptive measures of the need for power.* Unpublished doctoral thesis, University of Michigan, 1972.

Hunter, F. *Community power structure.* Chapel Hill: University of North Carolina Press, 1953.

Inkeles, A., & Levinson, D. J. National character: The study of modal personality and sociocultural systems. In G. Lindzey and E. Aronson (Eds.), *Handbook of social psychology* (Rev. ed.) (Vol. 4). Reading, Mass.: Addison-Wesley, 1969, pp. 418–506.

Jones, D. F. *The need for power as a predictor of leadership and exploitation in a variety of small group settings.* Unpublished honors thesis, Wesleyan University, 1969.

Jourard, S. *The transparent self.* Princeton, N. J.: Van Nostrand, 1964. Insight Books.

Jung, C. J. *Studies in word association.* London: Heineman, 1918.

Kanter, R. M. *Commitment and community: Communes and utopias in sociological perspective.* Cambridge, Mass.: Harvard University Press, 1972.

Kolb, D. A., & Boyatzis, R. E. On the dynamics of the helping relationship. *Journal of Applied Behavioral Science,* 1970, *6,* 267–289.

Lasswell, H. *Politics: Who gets what, when, and how.* New York: McGraw-Hill, 1936.

Lefcourt, M. H. Internal vs. external control of reinforcement: A review. *Psychological Bulletin,* 1966, *65,* 206–220.

Lefcourt, H. M., & Ladwig, G. W. Alienation in Negro and white reformatory inmates. *Journal of Social Psychology*, 1966, *68*, 153–157.

Lesser, G. S. Achievement motivation in women. In D. C. McClelland and R. S. Steele (Eds.), *Human motivation: a book of readings*. Morristown, N. J.: General Learning Press, 1973.

Lindgren, H. C. Authoritarian, independent, and child-centered practices in education: A study of attitudes. *Psychological Reports*, 1962, *10*, 747–750.

Lippitt, R., Polansky, N., Redl, F., & Rosen, S. The dynamics of power. *Human Relations*, 1952, *5*, 37–64.

Liverant, S., & Scodel, A. Internal and external control as determinants of decision-making under conditions of risk. *Psychological Reports*, 1960, *7*, 59–67.

Maranell, G. M. The evaluation of presidents: An extension of the Schlesinger poll. *Journal of American History*, 1970, *57*, 104–113.

May, R. *Power and innocence*. New York: Norton, 1972.

McClelland, D. C. *The achieving society*. Princeton, N. J.: Van Nostrand, 1961.

McClelland, D. C. National character and economic growth in Turkey and Iran. In L. W. Pye (Ed.), *Communication and political development*. Princeton, N. J.: Princeton University Press, 1962.

McClelland, D. C. Longitudinal trends in the relation of thought to action. *Journal of Consulting Psychology*, 1966, *30*, 479–483.

McClelland, D. C. The two faces of power. *Journal of International Affairs*, 1970, *24*, 29–47.

McClelland, D. C. *Education and competence*. Unpublished paper, Harvard University, 1972.

McClelland, D. C. *Power: The inner experience*. New York: Irvington Press, 1975.

McClelland, D. C. *Sources of hypertension in the drive for power*. Unpublished paper, Harvard University, 1976.

McClelland, D. C., Atkinson, J. W., Clark, R. A., & Lowell, E. L. *The achievement motive*. New York: Appleton-Century-Crofts, 1953.

McClelland, D. C., Davis, W. N., Kalin, R., & Wanner, E. *The drinking man*. New York: Free press, 1972.

McClelland, D. C., & Steele, R. S. Motives for drug taking among college men. In D. C. McClelland, W. N. Davis, R. Kalin, and E. Wanner, *The drinking man*. New York: Free Press, 1972.

McClelland, D. C., & Teague, G. Predicting risk preferences among power-related acts. *Journal of Personality*, 1975, *43*, 266–285.

McClelland, D. C., Wanner, E., & Vanneman, R. Drinking in the wider context of restrained and unrestrained assertive thoughts and acts. In D. C. McClelland, W. N. Davis, R. Kalin, & E. Wanner, *The drinking man*. New York: Free Press, 1972.

McClelland, D. C., & Watson, R. I., Jr. Power motivation and risk-taking behavior. *Journal of Personality*, 1973, *41*, 121–139.

McClelland, D. C., & Winter, D. G. *Motivating economic achievement*. New York: Free Press, 1969.

Merei, F. Group leadership and institutionalization. *Human Relations*, 1949, *2*, 23–39.

Miller, N. Experimental studies of conflict. In J. McV. Hunt (Ed.), *Personality and the behavior disorders* (Vol. 1). New York: Ronald Press, 1944.

Minton, H. L. Power as a personality construct. In B. Maher (Ed.), *Progress in experimental personality research* (Vol. 4). New York and London: Academic Press, 1967.

Mischel, W. *Personality and assessment*. New York: John Wiley, 1968.

Murray, H. A. Techniques for a systematic investigation of fantasy. *Journal of Psychology*, 1937, *3*, 115–143.

446 The Power Motive

Murray, H. A. *Explorations in personality*. New York: Oxford University Press, 1938.

Nadler, E. B. Yielding, authoritarianism, and authoritarian ideology regarding groups. *Journal of Abnormal and Social Psychology*, 1959, *58*, 408–410.

Odell, M. *Personality correlates of independence and conformity*. Unpublished master's thesis, Ohio State University, 1959.

Osgood, E. C., Suci, G. J., & Tannenbaum, P. H. *The measurement of meaning*. Urbana: University of Illinois Press, 1957.

Parsons, T. Age and sex in the social structure of the United States. *American Sociological Review.*, 1942, *7*, 604–616.

Rank, O. "Um Städte werben" ["Conquest" of cities]. *Internationale Zeitschrift für Psychoanalyse*, 1913, *1*, 50–58.

Rank, O. *The Don Juan legend*. Princeton, N. J.: Princeton University Press, 1975. (Originally published, 1924.)

Rotter, J. B. Generalized expectancies for internal vs. external control of reinforcement. *Psychological Monographs*, 1966, *80*, 1, (Whole number 609).

Rubinoff, L. *The pornography of power*. New York: Ballantine Books, 1968.

Sampson, R. V. *The psychology of power*. London: Heineman, 1965.

Schlesinger, A. M., Sr. Our Presidents: A rating by seventy-five historians. *New York Times Magazine*, July 29, 1962, pp. 12–14.

Slack, C. W. *Timothy Leary, the madness of the sixties and me*. New York: Peter H. Wyden, 1974.

Slavin, M. O. *The theme of feminine evil: The image of woman in male fantasy and its effects on attitudes and behavior*. Unpublished doctoral thesis, Harvard University, 1972.

Speer, A. *Inside the Third Reich*. New York: Macmillan, 1970.

Steele, R. S. *The physiological concomitants of psychogenic motive arousal in college males*. Unpublished doctoral thesis, Harvard University, 1973.

Steele, R. S. Power motivation, activation, and inspirational speeches. *Journal of Personality*, 1977, *45*, 53–64.

Stewart, A. J. *Presidential motives and presidential behavior*. Paper presented at the New England Psychological Association Convention, Boston, 1974.

Stewart, A. J. *Longitudinal prediction from personality to life outcomes among college-educated women*. Unpublished doctoral thesis, Harvard University, 1975. (a)

Stewart, A. J. *Power arousal and thematic apperception in women*. Paper presented at the American Psychological Association Convention, Chicago, 1975. (b)

Stewart, A. J. *Scoring system for Stages of Psychological Adaptation to the Environment*. Unpublished paper, Boston University, 1977.

Stewart, A. J., & Rubin, Z. Power motivation in the dating couple. *Journal of Personality and Social Psychology*, 1976, *34*, 305–309.

Stewart, A. J., & Winter, D. G. Self-definition and social definition in women. *Journal of Personality*, 1974, *42*, 238–259.

Stewart, A. J., & Winter, D. G. Arousal of the power motive in women. *Journal of Consulting and Clinical Psychology*, 1976, *44*, 495–496.

Strickland, B. The prediction of social action from a dimension of internal-external control. *Journal of Social Psychology*, 1965, *66*, 353–358.

Uleman, J. S. *A new TAT measure of the need for power*. Unpublished doctoral thesis, Harvard University, 1966.

Uleman, J. S. The need for influence: Development and validation of a measure, and comparison with the need for power. *Genetic Psychology Monographs*, 1972, *85*, 157–214.

Van Duyn, R. *Message of a wise Kabouter*. London: Duckworth, 1972. (Originally published, 1969.)

Veroff, J. Development and validation of a projective measure of power motivation. *Journal of Abnormal and Social Psychology*, 1957, *54*, 1–8.

Veroff, J., & Veroff, J. P. B. Reconsideration of a measure of power motivation. *Psychological Bulletin*, 1972, *78*, 279–291.

Ward F., Olson S. E., & Hammond, J. M. Personal communication, 1975.

Watson, R. I., Jr. *Motivation and role induction*. Unpublished honors thesis, Wesleyan University, 1969.

Watson, R. I., Jr. *Motivational and sex differences in aggressive behavior*. Unpublished doctoral thesis, Harvard University, 1974.

Wells, W. D., Weinert, G., & Rubel, M. Conformity pressure and authoritarian personality. *Journal of Psychology*, 1956, *42*, 133–136.

White, R. W. Motivation reconsidered: The concept of competence. *Psychological Review*, 1959, *66*, 297–333.

White, R. W. Ego and reality in psychoanalytic theory. *Psychological Issues*, 1963, *3*, 1–210.

Wilsnack, S. The effects of social drinking on women's fantasy. *Journal of Personality*, 1974, *42*, 243–261.

Winter, D. G. *Human motives and the no-growth society*. Unpublished paper, Wesleyan University, 1972.

Winter, D. G. *The power motive*. New York: Free Press, 1973.

Winter, D. G. *Power motives and power behavior in women*. Paper presented at the American Psychological Association Convention, Chicago, 1975.

Winter, D. G. Make power motivation and the status of women. In D. V. Hiller & R. Sheets (Eds.), *Women & men: The consequences of power*. Cincinnati: University of Cincinnati, Office of Women's Studies, 1977.

Winter, D. G, & Stewart, A. J. Content analysis as a technique for assessing political leaders. In M. G. Hermann (Ed.), *A psychological examination of political leaders*. New York: Free Press, 1977. (a)

Winter, D. G., & Stewart, A. G. Power motive reliability as a function of experimental instructions. *Journal of Consulting and Clinical Psychology*, 1977, *45*, 436–440. (b)

Winter, D. G., Stewart, A. J., & McClelland, D. C. Husband's motives and wife's career level. *Journal of Personality and Social Psychology*, 1977, *35*, 159–166.

Winter, S. K. Characteristics of fantasy while nursing. *Journal of Personality*, 1969, *37*, 58–72.

Wolowitz, H. M. Attraction and aversion to power: A psychoanalytic conflict theory of homosexuality in male paranoia. *Journal of Abnormal Psychology*, 1965, *70*, 360–370.

Wormley, E. P. *Portfolio manager preference in an investment decision making situation: A psychophysical study*. Unpublished doctoral thesis, Harvard University, 1976.

Zimbardo, P. G., Haney, C., Banks, W. C., & Jaffe, D. *Stanford prison experiment*. Stanford, Cal.: Philip G. Zimbardo, Inc., 1972. (Tape recording and slide set)

Zimbardo, P. G., Haney, C., Banks, W. C., & Jaffe, D. A Pirandellian prison: The mind is a formidable jailer. *New York Times Magazine*, April 8, 1973, pp. 38–60.

CHAPTER 11

Repression–Sensitization

PAUL A. BELL

Colorado State University

and

DONN BYRNE

Purdue University

In the Freudian tradition, personality psychologists have long assumed that individuals utilize various types of ego defense mechanisms. These characteristic modes of dealing with threatening, anxiety-evoking cues can be conceptualized as dimensions of personality. One cluster of defensive strategies consists of repression and denial as ways of escaping anxiety by way of avoidance. When confronted by threat, the individual attempts to deny or to minimize its existence, fails to verbalize feelings of anxiety, and avoids thinking about the consequences of the threat. At the opposite extreme are defenses that consist of the tendency to approach the threat by way of intellectualization and obsessive and ruminative worrying. The individual is acutely attuned to the presence of threatening stimuli, freely verbalizes feelings of anxiety and fear, and tries to control the danger by dwelling on its potential consequences. These two very different behavior patterns have been designated as repression and sensitization (Gordon, 1957).

At about the time the represser and sensitizer labels were first being applied, efforts were underway to tie the two constructs together by conceptualizing such defenses as lying along a unidimensional repression-sensitization continuum. This idea led to several attempts to construct measures of the dimension, and the development of measuring instruments led to a rapidly growing body of research in the area. We will first examine the scientific milieu in which this work began and then will attempt to summarize what has been learned about repression--sensitization in the last decade and a half.

Work on this project was supported in part by a grant from the National Science Foundation (SOC 74-15254) to Donn Byrne.

BACKGROUND

Perceptual Defense

In an experiemnt concerned with individual differences in perceptual behavior (the "new look" in perception, as it was called), Bruner and Postman (1947b) first attempted to assess the threat value of various words for a small group of undergraduates. They asked each subject to give his associations to each word, and reaction times were recorded. The list included anxiety-related words such as "death," "penis," and "blush." It was assumed that the longer it took a subject to make a response to a word, the more threatening that word was to the individual. For each subject, the six most threatening and six least threatening words were chosen for the perceptual task in addition to six words of intermediate threat. These 18 words were projected one at a time by means of a tachistoscope; each stimulus was first flashed very rapidly and then at increasingly slower exposure speeds. The process continued until the word was recognized. The exposure speed at which recognition occurred was assumed to represent the subject's perceptual threshold for the word. Interestingly enough, subjects tended to fall into one of two groups with respect to the way they responded. For some, the greater the threat associated with a word, the harder it was to perceive it. For others, the opposite relationship was found—greater threat led to faster recognition. These patterns were designated as perceptual defense and perceptual vigilance.

Based on the literature of ego defenses, the interpretation of the two perceptual patterns was in terms of adaptive processes developed by the individual to deal with threat (Bruner & Postman, 1947a). Research on perceptual defense expanded rapidly during the 1950s, and it utilized many visual and auditory stimuli representing various types of psychological threat. Recognition was made difficult by rapid exposure speeds, dim illumination, masking noise, and other perceptual interference. In these studies, individual differences in percpetual defense frequently were found to be associated with personality characteristics assessed by projective and objective tests.

The voluminous literature on perceptual defense is too extensive to be covered here in detail, but reviews are available by Blum (1955), Eriksen (1954), and Goldiamond (1958). There were numerous methodological and interpretive problems with the assessment of thresholds, and the resulting rather intense criticisms probably hastened the demise of this research method. Furthermore, if perceptual tasks were to be used as personality tests to measure defensiveness, flashy though the idea may have been, it was found that the tasks were inadequate in terms of such mundane criteria as reliability (Byrne & Holcomb, 1962). Nevertheless, research on perceptual defense was important to subsequent research on repression–sensitization, as has previously been suggested by Byrne (1964b):

An examination of the perceptual studies and the subsequent work suggests rather strongly the presence of an approach-avoidance sort of dimension with respect to response to threatening stimuli. It should also be noted that these behavior tendencies appear to be fairly pervasive ones in that they are identifiable in perceptual responses, responses given to projective tests, behavior in learning and memory tasks, and in symptoms of maladjustment. Such relational fertility is a convincing argument for the value of pursuing this variable in further research. (p. 173)

Repression-Sensitization

The existence of adequate measuring instruments is an obvious necessity in any research endeavor and, perhaps less obviously, such instruments tend to instigate research. That is, scientific activity sometimes occurs *because* of the availability of usable techniques. With respect to repression–sensitization, the development of a reliable test was needed in order to pursue a number of ideas about the behavioral consequences of defensive style. As with several other personality dimensions, a convenient place to seek a measuring device was the Minnesota Multiphasic Personality Inventory or MMPI (Hathaway & McKinley, 1951). The various scales of this inventory, taken individually or in combination, proved to be a happy hunting ground for those seeking operations to define approach and avoidance defensive tendencies.

Among the more promising MMPI-based measures of such behavior were those developed by Ullmann (1958) and by Altrocchi, Parsons, and Dickoff (1960). Ullmann extracted 44 MMPI items that discriminated a sample of facilitators and inhibitors (Shannon, 1962) who had been identified by analysis of their psychiatric case histories. A very different approach was used by Altrocchi et al. who added scores on three MMPI scales that could be seen as involving sensitization (depression, psychasthenia, and Welsh anxiety) and subtracted from that total the sum of scores on three other scales that seemed to involve repression (lie, defensive self-presentation, and hysteria-denial). Although this scoring system was relatively successful in differentiating individuals along a dimension of defensiveness, there were psychometric problems that needed resolution.

It was noted, for example, that in the Altrocchi et al. measure, some MMPI items contributed to more than one scale. Arbitrarily, then, these items were being differentially weighted in comparison to other items. In addition, some items were contained in both the sensitizing and repressing subscales, so they were simultaneously scored in opposite directions and hence nullified. Byrne (1961) modified this sytem so that all items were scored only once, and all items that were inconsistently scored were eliminated entirely. The resulting 156-item instrument was christened the Repression–Sensitization (R–S) Scale, with high scores indicating sensitization and low scores repression. Reliability was found to be reasonably high with a coefficient of .88 for both internal consistency and stability over a six-week period.

In subsequent work by Byrne, Barry, and Nelson (1963), this scale underwent an internal consistency item analysis. In order to be retained in the final scale, an item had to correlate with the total score at the .001 level of probability or better in two independent student samples. The resulting 127-item inventory was identified as the Revised R–S Scale. Reliability was again found to be substantial with a .94 coefficient of internal consistency and a .82 coefficient of stability over a three-month period. This R–S Scale is presented in Table 11–1, giving the MMPI item numbers and the scoring key. Normative data from Byrne et al. are provided in Table 11–2. It might be noted that although sex differences in repression–sensitization are absent among college students, female patients at the Mayo Clinic are found to be more sensitizing than males at every age level (Schwartz, 1972).

As will be seen in the remainder of this chapter, this scale has been used in a great deal of research attempting to link repression–sensitization with a variety of other personality characteristics and with assorted behaviors. Frankly, the scale's popularity suggests a cardinal rule in our field: Personality research is strongly influenced by the accessibility of a reliable, easily administered, objectively scored test that claims to measure a psychodynamically interesting characteristic.

Validating the R–S Scale: Clinical Judgments and Perceptual Defense

The notion of validation with any personality test is something of a misnomer. There is no single criterion by which one can determine how well this type of test measures what it purports to measure. In fact, every investigation that includes a personality scale is, at least in part, a validational study. Each positive and negative finding adds to our knowledge of the meaning of a personality measure and hence to its construct validity. Some investigations are, nevertheless, more directly validational than others. For example, if you developed a new measure of intelligence, your initial concern would likely be its ability to predict school grades rather than any esoteric excursions into the unknown.

With respect to repression–sensitization, preliminary confirmation of its validity would seem to require that it be related empirically to the types of behavior out of which the concept was derived. That is, scores on the R–S Scale should reflect differences in clinically observed defensive behavior, and they should be associated with differences in perceptual response to threat.

Tempone (1964b) described repressing and sensitizing defenses to nine clinicians and asked them to fill out a copy of the R–S Scale as they believed a represser would do. These judges reached above-chance agreement on 90 percent of the items (on the revised scale), in each instance in a direction consistent with the scoring key. In a follow-up study, R–S scores of patients (based on items on which there was clinical agreement) were significantly correlated with independent psychiatric ratings of repressive–sensitizing defenses. Thus, there is evidence that the scale measures the types of verbal responses that clinical practitioners define as ego defensive and that these responses are associated with the observable defensive behavior of psychiatric patients. Differences in verbal elaborations about unpleasant visual stimuli are also consistent with expectations; sensitizers literally have more to say about such material than repressers (Carroll, 1972).

The other important conceptual link is with the perceptual defense procedures. Once again, Tempone (1964a) provided the first basic evidence of this relationship. He selected extreme groups of repressers and sensitizers and subjected them to a success or failure experience on an anagrams task. The solutions to these anagrams then served as the critical words in the perceptual recognition portion of the experiment. With a tachistoscope, the experimenter presented subjects with both critical words from the anagrams and neutral words in a series of trials. As hypothesized, in the threatening failure condition, in response to the critical words, recognition thresholds increased for repressers and decreased for sensitizers. Similar results have been reported by Hutt (1965) using nonsense syllables paired with threatening words and by Schill and Althoff (1968) in an auditory perception task. Interestingly enough, represser–sensitizer differences occur even if the subjects only *believe* the stimulus is threatening. White and Wilkins (1973) presented neutral pictures tachistoscopically but gave some of the subjects false feedback that indicated they were "physiologically aroused." Under these conditions, recognition thresholds increased for repressers and decreased for sensitizers. Despite this body of rather consistent findings, it must be noted that in one perceptual recognition experiment there was no R–S Scale effect (Van Egeren, 1968). In a study related to perceptual defense, Haley (1974) found that repressers tend to avoid looking at the stressful content of an industrial accident film, whereas sensitizers do not engage in such visual avoidance.

Altogether, then, these studies provide evidence that the R–S Scale measures a personality variable that is consistent with what clinicians define as defense mechanisms and with individual differences in perceptual defense. The remainder of this chapter is devoted to a selective review of research that has attempted to relate repression–sensitization to a variety of other personality dimensions and to various behaviors that logically should be associated with such a variable.

PERSONALITY CORRELATES OF REPRESSION-SENSITIZATION

Following Mischel's (1968) dictum that the magnitude of the correlation between two personality dimensions is a positive function of the similarity of the measuring devices, it is not surprising to find many studies reporting significant relation-

Table 11-1. Scoring Key for the Revised R–S Scale

R-S Item No.	MMPI Item No.	Scoring Key	R-S Item No.	MMPI Item No.	Scoring Key
1	2	*	50	106	T
2	3	F	51	107	F
3	5	*	52	109	T
4	6	*	53	114	T
5	7	F	54	120	*
6	8	F	55	122	F
7	9	*	56	124	T
8	10	T	57	128	*
9	12	*	58	129	T
10	15	T	59	130	*
11	18	*	60	131	F
12	22	T	61	134	*
13	23	*	62	135	*
14	26	T	63	136	T
15	30	*	64	137	*
16	32	T	65	138	T
17	36	F	66	141	T
18	39	*	67	142	T
19	41	T	68	145	T
20	43	T	69	147	T
21	44	T	70	148	T
22	45	*	71	150	*
23	46	*	72	152	F
24	47	*	73	153	*
25	51	F	74	154	*
26	52	T	75	155	*
27	55	F	76	158	T
28	57	F	77	159	T
29	58	*	78	160	F
30	60	*	79	162	T
31	64	*	80	163	F
32	67	T	81	164	F
33	71	*	82	165	T
34	75	*	83	170	*
35	76	T	84	171	T
36	80	*	85	172	T
37	86	T	86	174	*
38	88	F	87	175	F
39	89	T	88	178	F
40	90	*	89	179	T
41	93	T	90	180	T
42	94	T	91	182	T
43	95	*	92	183	*
44	96	F	93	186	T
45	98	*	94	188	F
46	102	T	95	189	T
47	103	F	96	190	F
48	104	T	97	191	T
49	105	*	98	192	F

Table 11–1. *(continued)*

R-S Item No.	MMPI Item No.	Scoring Key	R-S Item No.	MMPI Item No.	Scoring Key
99	193	*	141	336	T
100	195	*	142	337	T
101	201	T	143	340	T
102	207	F	144	342	T
103	208	*	145	343	T
104	213	T	146	344	T
105	217	T	147	345	T
106	225	*	148	346	T
107	230	F	149	349	T
108	233	*	150	351	*
109	234	T	151	352	T
110	236	T	152	353	F
111	238	T	153	356	T
112	241	T	154	357	T
113	242	F	155	358	T
114	243	F	156	359	T
115	248	*	157	360	T
116	253	*	158	361	T
117	255	*	159	362	T
118	259	T	160	374	T
119	263	*	161	379	F
120	265	T	162	382	T
121	266	T	163	383	T
122	267	T	164	384	T
123	270	F	165	389	T
124	271	*	166	396	T
125	272	*	167	397	T
126	274	*	168	398	T
127	278	T	169	406	*
128	279	T	170	411	T
129	285	*	171	414	T
130	289	T	172	418	T
131	290	T	173	431	T
132	292	T	174	443	T
133	296	*	175	461	*
134	301	T	176	465	T
135	304	T	177	499	*
136	305	T	178	502	*
137	316	T	179	511	T
138	321	T	180	518	T
139	322	T	181	544	T
140	329	*	182	555	T

*Unscored buffer item.
Source: Reprinted with permission of publisher from:

Byrne, D., Barry, J., and Nelson, D. Relation of the revised Repression-Sensitization Scale to measures of self-description. *Psychological Reports,* 1963, 13, 323-334.

Table 11-2.   Normative Data for the Revised R-S Scale

R-S Score	Males		Females	
	Number	%	Number	%
100–109	1	0.1	2	0.4
90–99	11	1.5	3	0.5
80–89	26	3.6	14	2.4
70–79	45	6.1	31	5.4
60–69	59	8.0	56	9.8
50–59	96	13.1	89	15.6
40–49	131	17.9	107	18.7
30–39	149	20.3	120	21.0
20–29	128	17.5	93	16.3
10–19	74	10.1	49	8.6
0– 9	13	1.8	7	1.2
Mean Score	42.2		42.7	
Standard Deviation	20.1		18.7	
Number of Subjects	733		571	

Source: Reprinted with permission of publisher from:

Byrne, D., Barry, J., and Nelson, D. Relation of the revised Repression-Sensitization Scale to measures of self-description. *Psychological Reports,* 1963, 13, 323-334.

ships between scores on the R–S Scale and scores on other objective tests using a true–false or agree–disagree format.

MMPI Correlates

The MMPI studies go Mischel one better by examining the relationship between subscales contained in the same test and consisting of overlapping item content. It should not come as a surprise to find substantial correlations between repression–sensitization and many other MMPI dimensions. For example, R–S Scale scores correlate positively with depression, psychasthenia, social introversion, and neuroticism; negative correlations are found with hysteria, the lie scale, defensiveness, and ego strength (Joy, 1963). In a point we shall raise again shortly, one interpretation of such findings is that sensitizers exhibit more pathological symptoms than is true for repressers.

One of the most widely used of the special MMPI subscales is Taylor's (1953) Manifest Anxiety Scale (MAS). On the basis of the underlying assumptions about repression–sensitization, one might logically expect differences between repressers and sensitizers in their handling of anxiety. Given any sort of threat, repressers should deny the existence of anxious feelings whereas sensitizers should admit them openly. Despite the expectation of a relationship, the obtained correlations are so high that they raise doubts about their meaning. The reported coefficients range from .87 (Abbott, 1972; Golin, Herron, Lakota, & Reineck, 1967) to .91 (Joy, 1963). The fact that the two scales contain 29 overlapping items would seem to explain (or explain away) the findings. Sullivan and Roberts (1969) correlated the two scales with and without the common items included. With all items considered, the correlation was .91, but even with the common items omitted the correlation was still a remarkably high .76. Although other existing data verify the proposed defensiveness–anxiety relationship (e.g., Lomont, 1965; Phares, 1961; Ullmann & McReynolds, 1963; Worchel, 1955), the very high correlation between R–S and MAS may represent, in part, a measurement artifact.

Another widely used special MMPI subscale is Edwards' (1957) Social Desirability (SD) Scale. The SD Scale was designed to measure the extent to which individuals tend to respond to the social desirability of test item content. If someone is high in the tendency to give socially desirable answers, he or she is unlikely to endorse items with any kind of personally negative content. Since many MMPI items involve such content, it is not surprising that the SD Scale correlates substantially with most of its subscales (Edwards, 1959; Hanley, 1961; Wiggins, 1959). The R–S Scale is no exception, and it has been found to correlate with SD with a magnitude of −.90 and greater (Abbott, 1972; Joy, 1963).

Actually, the R–S Scale, the MAS, and the SD Scale are highly interrelated, and factor analyses indicate that all three tests load at a magnitude of .90 and above on the same factor (Abbott, 1972; Liberty, Lunneborg, & Atkinson, 1964). The relationship between social desirability and the R–S Scale can be examined best by turning from Edwards' MMPI test to the Marlowe-Crowne SD Scale, which contains fewer psychopathological, less stigmatized items (Crowne & Marlowe, 1960). This scale correlates with the R–S Scale, but the coefficients are between −.37 and −.49, which suggests that repression–sensitization is partly but not entirely a function of this response style (Cosentino & Kahn, 1967; Feder, 1967). An experiment by Merbaum (1972) also suggests some independence of repression–sensitization and the tendency to give socially desirable responses. Three months after taking the R–S Scale, extreme sensitizers and repressers were asked to retake the test but to respond in a way that would make them look as good as possible. As might be expected, the scores of both groups shifted in a represser direction, but, even under these instructions to dissemble, the original sensitizers still obtained higher scores than did the original repressers.

California Psychological Inventory (CPI) Correlates

Whereas the MMPI measures a series of primarily psychiatrically oriented dimensions, the California Psychological Inventory (CPI) (Gough, 1957) is concerned with individual differences with respect to comparatively normal aspects of behavior. Almost all these scales correlate negatively with the R–S Scale. The most substantial coefficients indicate that as sensitization increases, individuals are lower in sociability, social presence, sense of well-being, self-control, tolerance, making a good impression, achievement through conformance, and intellectual efficiency (Byrne, Golightly, & Sheffield, 1965). As on the MMPI, this pattern of relationships suggests better adjustment for the repressers than for the sensitizers.

Self-Concept Correlates

Because repressers are much less likely than sensitizers to admit embarrassing or negative personal attributes, one would expect R–S scores to be positively related to measures of self-ideal discrepancy and negatively related to measures of self-esteem. With Worchel's (1957) Self-activity Inventory as the measure of self-concept, these expected correlations with repression–sensitization are found to be in the .60s (Byrne, 1961; Byrne et al., 1963). On an adjective check list, sensitizers give more deviantly self-critical responses than do repressers (Lucky & Grigg, 1964). More recent research confirms these findings (Feder, 1968).

An inventory that is intended to measure self-actualization is the Personal Orientation Inventory (Shostrom, 1964, 1966). The correlations, shown in Table 11–3, between the subscales of this instrument and the R–S Scale are all nega-

Table 11–3. Correlations Between R–S Scale Scores and
Personal Orientation Inventory Subscales

	Correlation Coefficients		
	Males	Females	Total
Time Competence	−.71[c]	−.71[c]	−.71[c]
Inner Direction	−.75[c]	−.73[c]	−.74[c]
Self-actualizing Values	−.52[c]	−.57[c]	−.56[c]
Existentiality	−.44[c]	−.55[c]	−.50[c]
Feeling Reactivity	−.42[c]	−.44[c]	−.45[c]
Spontaneity	−.50[c]	−.63[c]	−.57[c]
Self-regard	−.81[c]	−.68[c]	−.75[c]
Self-acceptance	−.54[c]	−.51[c]	−.54[c]
Nature of Man	−.43[c]	−.64[c]	−.54[c]
Synergy	−.47[c]	−.54[c]	−.52[c]
Acceptance of Aggression	−.32[a]	−.36[b]	−.36[c]
Capacity for Intimate Contact	−.62[c]	−.63[c]	−.64[c]

Source: Foulds & Warehime, 1971. Copyright 1971 by the American Psychological Association. Reprinted by permission.
[a]$p < .05$
[b]$p < .01$
[c]$p < .001$

tive, indicating greater self-actualization toward the repressing end of the R–S continuum (Foulds & Warehime, 1971). The sensitizers lose again.

Other Personality Correlates

In the original formulation of the authoritarian personality, repressive defenses were considered to constitute a basic characteristic (Adorno, Frenkel-Brunswik, Levinson, & Sanford, 1950). Authoritarians were described as being aversive to introspection and were said to repress their own sexual and aggressive impulses. Support for this characterization was provided by Kogan (1956) in a perceptual recognition experiment. Accuracy in recognizing recorded sexual and aggressive sentences decreased as authoritarianism scores (California F Scale) increased. Thus, there was a tendency for those high in authoritarianism to display the type of perceptual defense ascribed to repressers. Unfortunately, studies seeking correlations between the R–S Scale and the California F Scale have failed to substantiate this relationship (Byrne, 1964b). In a possibly relevant unpublished study conducted during the 1964 presidential campaign, Byrne found that repression–sensitization was related to political preference. Goldwater supporters had a mean R–S Scale of 26.5; Johnson supporters had a mean of 36.8. Since other investigators reported that Goldwater supporters were more authoritarian than Johnson supporters (Milton & Waite, 1964), the R–S findings are at least of suggestive interest.

Correlations between repression–sensitization and scores on Rokeach's (1960) Dogmatism Scale, which is intended to measure rigidity of both the political left and right, have been found to be in the range of .32 to .44 in three independent samples of college students (Byrne, Blaylock, & Goldberg, 1966; Swindell & L'Abate, 1970). That is, sensitizers are found to be more dogmatic and closed-minded than repressers.

Finally, repression–sensitization has been found to be positively related to scores on Rotter's (1966) Locus of Control Scale (Tolor & Reznikoff, 1967) and to a measure of cognitive complexity (Wilkins, Epting, & Van de Riet, 1972). That is, sensitizers tend to anticipate external control of their behavior and to be more cognitively complex than repressers. Finally, the R–S Scale is unrelated to measures of intelligence (Byrne, 1964b; Fisher, 1969; Lomont, 1965), field dependence–independence (Ihilevich & Gleser, 1971), or religiosity (Swindell & L'Abate, 1970).

In summary, this array of findings does not fit any preconceived notions of the personality characteristics associated with defensive behavior. Relative to sensitizers, repressing individuals are found to be better adjusted, to express more positive self-concepts that are closer to their ideals, and to be more self-actualizing, open-minded, internalizing, and cognitively simple. What cannot be definitely concluded, however, is whether repression as measured by the R–S

Scale is an adaptive mechanism or whether the results all represent the obscuring effects of such inherent measurement problems as the operation of a social desirability response set and the unwillingness and/or inability of repressing individuals to verbalize their problems. One could speculate that the repressers are not only bad off but so bad off that they are utilizing massive ego defenses to deny the fact. That is, their positive characteristics could actually be taken as an indication of the extent of their psychopathology! Rather than finding ourselves eternally hoist by our own measurement petards in this way, it is clear that we must seek behavioral evidence beyond the confines of personality test intercorrelations. We will now turn to such research that has been conducted in several behavioral domains.

BEHAVIORAL CONSEQUENCES OF INDIVIDUAL DIFFERENCES IN REPRESSION–SENSITIZATION

Physiological Reactivity

Although the search for differential physiological indicators of specific emotional states has not been notably successful, it is well established that general emotional arousal is expressed in characteristic bodily reactions. When confronted by threat, for example, human subjects respond with increased heart and respiratory rates, elevated blood pressure, and higher levels of skin conductance. With respect to individual differences, it would seem logical to assume that those persons who are anxious and overtly responsive to threat would show more autonomic reactivity than would those who are seemingly unaware of or undisturbed by such situations. Specifically, sensitizers might be expected to respond with greater physiological arousal than repressers.

Research on repression–sensitization and related personality dimensions indicates that just the opposite relationship holds—excessive physiological arousal to threat is more characteristic of avoidance orientations than of approach orientations. For example, Schachter and Latane (1964) noted that relatively unemotional subjects had higher heart rates under arousing experimental conditions than did relatively emotional subjects. Valins (1967) reported similar findings for subjects exposed to shock during an experiment. Lazarus and Alfert (1964) presented males with a stressful film depicting a primitive subincision rite in which the penis is split open and flattened somewhat like a butterfly shrimp. Those subjects high in denial tendencies produced greater galvanic skin response (GSR) conductance while watching the movie than did the low-denial individuals.

Studies dealing specifically with repression–sensitization and autonomic reactivity have for the most part been consistent with such findings. In one experiment, Hare (1966) placed subjects in a situation in which they were informed that each time the sweep second hand on a clock passed the 30-second mark, they would receive an electric shock by means of electrodes attached to their fingers. GSR activity was measured throughout the experiment. The higher the R–S Scale scores of the subjects, the lower their GSR responses. The same experimenter obtained impressive evidence of the way in which defenses operate in an ongoing situation of threat. During a postexperimental inquiry, some subjects reported that they had tried to avoid thinking about the shocks, usually by imagining something else that was more pleasant. Those who engaged in such avoidance behavior the most had a mean R–S score of 22.7, whereas those who were least avoidant had a mean score of 38.3. Thus, the more repressive the subject, the more he or she actively tried not to think about the unpleasant shocks.

In a similar experiment, Scarpetti (1973) also exposed subjects to the clock and shock stress situation. On a measure of verbalized state anxiety, sensitizers indicated that they were more anxious than the repressers. On the physiological level, however, repressers once again showed greater GSR reactivity, and it also took them longer to extinguish these reactions after the shock was no longer administered. Thus, the verbalization of anxiety and the physiological indications of anxiety appear to be inversely related, and the Repression–Sensitization Scale predicts which response tendency is more likely to occur.

In an experiment involving five-person discussion groups, skin conductance responses were recorded throughout the session. As in the research just described, repressers gave evidence of more physiological arousal than sensitizers (Parsons, Fulgenzi, & Edelberg, 1969).

In the event that these findings seem unduly neat and incisive, it must be noted that others have reported the defensiveness–physiological relationship for females only (Lewisohn, Bergquist, & Brelje, 1972), some find no relationship between repression–sensitization and physiological responses (Baldwin, 1972; Pagano, 1973; Simal & Herr, 1970), and still others have reported a reverse relationship (Snortum & Wilding, 1971). A possible explanation for these inconsistencies lies in the degree of threat posed by the stimulus conditions. There is evidence that under the most threatening experimental conditions, autonomic reactivity is greater for repressers than for sensitizers, but that under mild threat the relationship may disappear or reverse (Epstein & Fenz, 1967; Stein, 1971).

Learning and Memory

Since repressers theoretically avoid threatening stimuli and sensitizers approach such stimuli, one might expect the Repression–Sensitization Scale to differentiate ability to learn and recall anxiety-evoking material. Those who repress and thus pay relatively little attention to threatening aspects of their environment would be expected to resist attending to and thinking about such stimulus elements and hence to perform less well in acquiring or remembering anxiety-linked material. Consistent with this expectation, differential recall of threatening material as a function of repression was reported in a study of Luborsky, Blinder, and Schimek (1965). With projective measures of repression, recall of the sexual content of pictures was found to be negatively correlated with repressive tendencies. The more subjects tended to use repressive defenses, the more difficulty they had in recalling sexual details. Analogous research using the R–S Scale has not been consistently supportive of such a relationship.

The expected represser–sensitizer differences seem to be most likely to occur when it is not obvious to the subject that the experimenter is expecting the threatening stimuli to be learned—that is, incidental learning. Markowitz (1969) instructed subjects to learn a list of 12 nonsense syllables. Each syllable was printed in the center of a card on which, incidentally, an actual word happened to appear in the corner ("for use in another experiment"). The words in the corner were either affectively positive (e.g., hope, peace), negative (fail, dead), or neutral (e.g., sigh, very). Half of the subjects were given neutral instructions and told that the experiment was trying to find out the average performance of college students. Half were given threatening instructions and told that the task was a measure of intelligence and would be checked against each subject's past academic performance. It was expected that there would be an interaction between repression–sensitization and the threatening instructions. As anticipated, threat resulted in poorer recall on the peripheral words for repressers and in improved recall for sensitizers. The only effect of word content, however, was that positive words were learned better than the others.

In other research, R–S Scale scores have been found to be unrelated to recall of threatening words when the subjects were directly instructed to learn them (Bergquist, Lewinsohn, Sue, & Flippo, 1968). Such findings suggest that if there are differences in learning and memory attributable to defensive style, these differences are rather easily overcome by specific elements of the experimental situation. It seems that the proposed avoidant behavior of repressers is operative only in situations in which learning is an incidental process. Selective attention to central versus peripheral stimuli in the environment may be an important aspect of the role of defense mechanisms in learning (Goldin, 1964; Holmes, 1974).

Sleeping and Dreaming

In classical Freudian theory, repression is strongest during the waking hours, but during sleep, the ego is less effective in maintaining the repressing process. As a result, repressed material comes to the surface in the form of dreams. This conceptualization leads us to expect differences in dream content and dream recall as a function of differences in the use of repression as a defense mechanism. Specifically, since repressers theoretically have a larger reservoir of repressed material, one might predict more dreaming, more threatening dream content, and less ability to recall dreams by repressers than by sensitizers.

Much of the relevant research has been based on the assumption that dreaming is associated with rapid eye movements or REM (Dement & Kleitman, 1957). Although not based on studies of the R–S Scale, several investigations suggest that REM is correlated with low dream recall and indicates an attempt to avoid perceiving an object or event (Antrobus, Antrobus, & Singer, 1964; Antrobus, Dement, & Fisher, 1964; Lachmann, Lapkin, & Handelman, 1962). If so, one might expect REM activity for repressers. Furthermore, interruption of this activity might have more serious consequences for repressers than for sensitizers.

To study the effects of defense mechanisms on REM processes, Pivik and Foulkes (1966) monitored the sleep of repressers and sensitizers on two consecutive nights. On one night each subject was awakened during REM sleep periods to deprive him of some of the normal opportunity to dream, and on the other night each subject was awakened during periods of nondreaming. When allowed to dream normally, sensitizers reported more intense dream content than repressers and had briefer REM periods. With REM deprivation, repressers reported more intense, fantasy-like dreaming, whereas sensitizers did not change in the type of dreams they had. Such deprivation also led to an increased frequency of REM for repressers but not for sensitizers. These very interesting and intriguing findings have, unfortunately, not been consistently confirmed in subsequent research (Foulkes, Pivik, Ahrens, & Swanson, 1968; Pivik & Foulkes, 1968).

Dream content has been found to be related to repression–sensitization with sensitizers associating more real-life incidents with their dreams and also more sexual and aggressive associations (Robbins & Tanck, 1970). Handal and Rychlak (1971), however, found no relationship between repression–sensitization and the death content of dreams. In a different type of study (Tebbs & Foulkes, 1966), the grip strength of subjects on a dynamometer was determined following awakening during dreaming or nondreaming. Sensitizers showed a decrease in grip strength on successive awakenings during both types of sleep, but repressers did not, indicating that differences in sleeping and dreaming patterns of repressers and sensitizers may differentially affect their physical performance.

The Similarity–Attraction Relationship

Attraction toward another individual requires that we perceive and analyze various attributes of that individual and arrive at a summary evaluation. Furthermore, most theories of attraction and person perception characterize these personal attributes in terms of positive–negative, pleasant–unpleasant, or rewarding–punishing properties (e. g., Anderson, 1968; Byrne, 1971; Newcomb, 1961). Much of the research on this behavior has involved the effect of similarity on attraction. Briefly, similarity with respect to many characteristics such as attitudes and personality attributes is found to have a positive effect on attraction. Similar attributes are found to function as rewards and dissimilar attributes as punishments (Golightly & Byrne, 1964). In addition, dissimilarity is found to elicit GSR reactivity indicative of anxiety in response to threat (Gormly, 1971).

Differential perception of interpersonal characteristics by repressers and sensitizers might be expected as a consequence of their differential response to negative cues. Most theories of attraction propose that liking is some function of the relative strength of the positive and negative cues. Thus, if repressers avoid or misperceive or ignore any portion of the negative cues, their subsequent attraction responses should be more positive than those of sensitizers exposed to the same initial cues. Furthermore if sensitizers seek out or exaggerate negative cues, the differential attraction responses of the two groups would be magnified.

Consistent with such a prediction, Kaplan (1968) asked repressers, neutrals, and sensitizers to interview a neutral target person and then to predict a number of personality traits of that person. Compared to sensitizers, repressers and neutrals tended to overestimate the positive traits and underestimate the negative ones. Gordon (1957) reported that repressers assumed personality similarity and sensitizers assumed personality dissimilarity between themselves and experimental partners. Nevertheless, the differential attraction responses that should accompany these differential perceptions were not found. Altrocchi (1961) reported comparable results. Similarly Byrne, Griffitt, and Stefaniak (1967) found that repressers and sensitizers did not differ in attraction toward strangers differing in either personality similarity (on the R–S Scale) or in attitude similarity. Byrne and Griffitt (1969) also found no represser–sensitizer differences in attraction responses. It should be noted that subjects did respond to the similarity variable and responded more positively to those like themselves in either repression–sensitization or attitudes; it is only the expected represser–sensitizer differences in such responses that are absent.

The effects of R–S Scale similarity on attraction are not limited to the laboratory, by the way. Over the years, a great many attitudinal and personality variables have been studied in real-life situations in relation to friendship formation, courtship, and marriage. In general, those who like each other enough to form a relationship tend to be similar. This generalization also holds true for repression–sensitization. Husbands and wives are found to have a greater-than-chance similarity in their repression–sensitization scores (Tolor, Rice, & Lanctot, 1975). Presumably, similarity in defensive style contributes to interpersonal attraction and hence to the likelihood of two individuals deciding to marry.

The failure to find the expected personality differences in attraction is nevertheless disappointing. Two explanations of this failure seem plausible. First, it may be that the negative stimuli employed (dissimilarity of response on items in attitude and personality scales) are not sufficiently threatening to elicit represser–sensitizer differences. The use of more potent stimuli, such as verbal insults, might possibly yield the expected results. A second explanation involves a basic assumption of the reinforcement–affect model of attraction (Clore & Byrne, 1974). According to that formulation, positive and negative stimuli influence the internal affective state of the perceiver, and this affective state (which varies along a pleasant–unpleasant dimension) mediates the attraction response. It may be that ego defenses do not modify this affective state and, if so, would not be expected to influence the attraction response.

Hostility and Aggression

The general characteristics of repressers and sensitizers also lead to the expectation of personality differences in perceiving hostility and in making overt aggressive responses. Repressers would be expected to avoid acknowledging hostile and aggressive impulses and to be relatively passive in response to verbal or physical attacks.

Perceived Hostility

One line of reserach has been concerned with the extent to which repressers and sensitizers attribute hostile feelings to themselves and to others. With subject samples as diverse as nursing students, undergraduates, and unwed mothers, it has been found that sensitizers attribute more hostility to self and others than do repressers (Altrocchi & Perlitsh, 1963; Altrocchi, Shrauger, & McLeod, 1964; McDonald, 1965, 1967). It might be noted that sensitizers are not rated as especially hostile by their peers; they simply see themselves in that way.

A related type of experimental evidence was reported by Palmer and Altrocchi (1967). They asked subjects to view jury deliberation scenes from the film *Twelve Angry Men* and then to judge the extent to which individual jurors were aware of their own hostile intentions. Repressers considered the jurors to be more unaware of their hostility than did sensitizers, regardless of the absolute level of juror hostility. Thus, repressers not only perceive themselves as relatively nonhostile, they feel that others are more hostile than they realize.

In a group discussion experiment, repressers rated themselves as less aggressive than either sensitizers or neutrals, but observers rated them as the most aggressive (Parsons et al., 1969). These experimenters pointed out the similarity between these experimental subjects and repressive patients in psychotherapy who "frequently manifest signs of anger, hostility, and aggressiveness but do not admit to the subjective experience of these states."

Overt Aggression

With respect to the overt expression of aggression and its physiological consequences, very interesting findings have been reported by Scarpetti (1974). An aggressive attack by another individual produces a state of arousal in the victim (e.g., Hokanson & Shetler, 1961), and the counterresponse of the victim then functions to reduce this state of arousal. When arousal reduction occurs, the victim has, in effect, been reinforced for responding in that particular way. Since either approach (attack) or avoidance (withdrawal or propitiation) counterresponses have been found to have such cathartic arousal-reducing properties (Hokanson & Megargee, 1970), persons predisposed to use either tactic would ordinarily be reinforced for their response to attack.

This line of reasoning led Scarpetti to predict that sensitizers would respond to attack with counteraggression, whereas repressers would respond with avoidance. Of equal importance was the prediction that such very different counterresponses would be equally effective for the respective personality types in reducing the arousal elicited by an aggressive adversary. To test these predictions, male repressers and sensitizers were placed in a situation in which there was a series of interchanges with a confederate. In the initial series of interactions, each subject received a prearranged number of electric shocks from the confederate, and the subject could respond each time with a counterattack (shocking the confederate) or a peaceful, rewarding response (illuminating a signal light). The sensitizers, as expected, tended to deliver shock to their attacker whereas the repressers delivered peaceful rewards. The physiological consequences of these different responses were also as expected. Using vasoconstriction and GSR as indicators, Scarpetti found that shock counterresponses were most effective in reducing arousal for sensitizers whereas reward counterresponses were most effective in reducing arousal for repressers.

This same experimenter was also able to show that it is possible to reverse these response tendencies by differentially rewarding the way in which repressers and sensitizers respond to attack. On another series of trials, Scarpetti reinforced repressers for making a shock counterresponse and reinforced sensitizers for peaceful counterresponses. This procedure was successful in creating aggressive repressers and passive sensitizers. When the differential reinforcement was discontinued, the two groups returned to their characteristic mode of responding to interpersonal attack. The physiological effects of the counterresponse also changed accordingly as the subjects learned new ways of responding to attack and then reverted to their usual response tendencies.

These findings by Scarpetti are not only important in demonstrating represser–sensitizer differences in aggression, they are also of theoretical importance in suggesting the way in which a characteristic interpersonal behavior is changed through reinforcement.

Sexual Responses

It is an interesting comment on our societal hang-ups that in much of the research on perceptual defense, threatening stimuli were operationally defined as words denoting sexual anatomy and sexual acts. The vigilant and defensive responses to such words appear to confirm the assumption that sexuality may easily become associated with anxiety and hence serve as a cue for defensive measures. Once again, approach and avoidance strategies are evident in several aspects of response to sexual stimuli.

One aspect of an individual's orientation to sexual matters is the extent to which he perceives the sexual versus the nonsexual meanings of various words. Word association tests have been constructed in which terms with double meanings are inserted periodically through the list. What comes to mind when you read the following words?

TABLE ROCK SCREW GREEN CAR CHERRY PENCIL LEAF BALLS

If your first association to words three, six, and nine were "driver," "pie," and "tennis," it might be that you were avoiding the sexual connotations of these double entendre words. Galbraith and Lieberman (1972) hypothesized that sexual meanings would be more likely to occur to sensitizers than to repressers. As predicted, under both neutral and sexual arousing conditions, sensitizers gave more sexual associations than did repressers.

Besides simply approaching or avoiding sexual meanings, how else might defense mechanisms influence sexual responses? Byrne and Sheffield (1965) asked male undergraduates to read erotic passages from books such as *Peyton Place* and *Lady Chatterly's Lover*. Afterward, the subjects rated their own feelings with respect to sexual arousal, disgust, entertainment, anxiety, boredom, and anger. Repressers and sensitizers were not differentially aroused in response to the descriptions of sexual behavior. The correlates of arousal were quite different for the two groups, though. For sensitizers, sexual arousal was associated with positive emotional states; for repressers, arousal was associated with negative emotional states. Thus, sensitizers were excited and entertained by the passages, but the repressers were excited and disgusted by them. Comparable results were reported by Wolff (1966), who asked subjects to read neutral or sexual passages aloud, but Paris and Goodstein (1966) found no represser––sensitizer differences in subjects' responses to erotica.

Sex differences in the effects of defensiveness were reported by Byrne and Lamberth (1971). Married couples were exposed to a series of erotic themes and assessed with respect to a series of dependent variables. Once again, repression–sensitization was not differentially related to arousal among male subjects. For females, however, sensitization was very strongly related to sexual arousal ($r = .59$). Furthermore, these females showed a pattern of emotional correlates such that as sensitization tendencies increased, feelings of sexual excitement, entertainment, and anxiety increased. Since the R–S relationship with emotions is nonexistent for married males, it may be the case that sexuality is less of a threat to them than to their wives. In responding to erotica, negative emotions play a greater role for females than for males (Byrne, Fisher, Lamberth, & Mitchell, 1974) and hence one might expect defense mechanisms to mediate their emotional responses more than is true for males. Strangely enough, male sexual behavior in the week following the experiment was related to repression–sensitization in that sensitizers were more likely to report thinking about sexual matters and engaging in sexual activity than were repressers; these patterns did not hold for females (Byrne & Lamberth, 1971).

As in other research with the R–S Scale, there are also some negative findings. For example, Good and Levin (1970) reported no represser–sensitizer differences in pupil dilation following exposure to erotic pictures. Clark and Neuringer (1971) found that represser–sensitizer differences in sex knowledge were attributable to incidental differences in verbal ability in their sample.

Medical Disorders

It has become commonly accepted in the medical profession and among the general public (see Ann Landers) that psychological factors play an important role in determining susceptibility to illness, the type of disorder that develops, and recovery rate. We might reasonably expect personality dimensions such as repression–sensitization to aid in predicting individual differences in response to disease.

In one such investigation, Byrne, Steinberg, and Schwartz (1968) administered the R–S Scale to two large samples of undergraduates. These students were also asked to complete a health survey dealing with the frequency of occurrence of a series of psychosomatic and somatic disorders and to indicate how often they were ill, took medicine, became involved in accidents, and visited a physician. Those items which were significantly related to repression–sensitization *in both samples* are given in Table 11–4. Note that all of the correlations are positive; sensitizers consistently report more medical problems than repressers.

Because that study utilized the survey method, it might be argued that sensitizers are simply more willing than repressers to *report* physical disabilities, possibly because they represent socially undesirable admissions. To explore that possibility, Byrne et al. (1968) obtained university health center records for a portion of the students in the second sample and examined the relationship between R–S Scale scores and the overt behavior of visiting the health center. For males, this index of medical disorders was consistent with the self-report data; sensitizers visited the health center more frequently than repressers. For females, the pattern was actually reversed although not significantly so, and the females as a group tended to visit the center less frequently than the males. Reasons for this surprising sex difference are not readily available, but an interesting possibility for future research is suggested by a study of pain tolerance by Merbaum and Badia (1967). Subjects were asked to judge a series of electric shocks as moderately painful, very painful, and so on. Shocks judged to be

Table 11-4.   Correlations Between R-S Scale Scores and Variables Related
to Physical Disorders for Two Independent Samples

Variable	Correlation with Repression-Sensitization	
	Group I	Group II
Tension Headaches		
Frequency	$.30^c$	$.18^b$
Colds		
Frequency	$.20^b$	$.18^b$
Nausea Before or After Eating		
Frequency	$.18^a$	$.12^a$
Severity	$.17^a$	$.11^a$
Emotional Difficulties or Problems		
Frequency	$.42^c$	$.18^b$
Severity	$.35^c$	$.12^a$
Heart Palpitations		
Frequency	$.23^b$	$.15^b$
Frequency of Illness	$.35^c$	$.11^a$
Frequency of Accidents	$.34^c$	$.16^b$
Frequency of Visiting Doctor	$.21^b$	$.13^a$
Total Number of Psychosomatic Complaints	$.37^c$	$.11^a$
Total Number of Complaints	$.38^c$	$.12^a$

Source: Byrne, Steinberg, & Schwartz, 1968. Copyright 1968 by the American Psychological Association. Reprinted by permission.
$^a p < .05$
$^b p < .01$
$^c p < .001$

highly painful were actually more intense for male repressers than for male
sensitizers, with male neutrals falling in between. For females, both repressers
and sensitizers could tolerate less pain than neutrals. It should be noted that
Barton and Buckhout (1969) found no sex differences in estimating the intensity
of an electric shock, but sensitizers made consistently higher estimates than
repressers. It seems very important to attempt to tie together possible sex differences in pain tolerance and sex differences in seeking medical aid.

Going beyond the campus samples, a large-scale study at the Mayo Clinic
revealed that when repressers do become ill, it is likely to be a purely organic
diagnosis. Sensitizers, on the other hand, tend to develop disorders with
psychological components (Schwartz, Krupp, & Byrne, 1971).

Among the more exciting lines of medical research are those that suggest a
relationship between indisputably organic disorders and personality variables.
The recent work on the type of individuals who are the most likely candidates for

cardiovascular disease is an obvious case in point. Less intuitively apparent are the personality correlates of incidence of a disorder such as cancer. Evidence has existed for some time that cancer patients are overly prone to use avoidance defenses, especially denial and repression, rather than approach defenses (e.g., Bahnson & Bahnson, 1966). Because the personality assessment usually occurs after the disease has been diagnosed, it is quite possible that avoidant defenses are a consequence of learning that one has cancer rather than a determinant of the disease. Nevertheless, many medical practitioners speculate that repression plus increased physiological activity in response to threat play a crucial role in the development of cancer. The connections with repression–sensitization are clear, and the practical implications of research directed at such questions would be enormously important. The possibility of identifying cancer-prone individuals and the further possibility of altering the predisposing personality characteristics would seem to be crucial research goals.

ANTECEDENTS AND CONSEQUENCES OF REPRESSION–SENSITIZATION: STEPS TOWARD A THEORY OF DEFENSIVE BEHAVIOR

It must be admitted that much of the theorizing about repression–sensitization has been at a relatively simple level. In fact, the predictive basis of most of the research discussed in this chapter so far is encompassed by the proposition: Repressers avoid, sensitizers approach. Despite occasional failures or inconsistencies, there is still a substantial body of data demonstrating that avoidance--approach behaviors occur in a variety of modes in response to a wide array of stimuli and that these differential behaviors may be predicted on the basis of scores on the R–S Scale.

Once that basic proposition has been accepted, it is time to look beyond these concerns and to consider the meaning of individual differences in defensiveness in more general terms. Such theory building has not yet been seriously undertaken with respect to repression–sensitization, but two types of research may be seen as representing relevant first steps: the child-rearing antecedents of defensive style and the effects of different defensive styles on psychological adjustment.

Although it is just an impression, and perhaps an incorrect one, two not perfectly compatible assumptions appear to underly much of the conceptual work in these areas. First, there is the *let-it-all-hang-out assumption* that it is better to verbalize, intellectualize, and agonize than to deny and repress. For that reason, it is, therefore, probably better to be a sensitizer than to be a represser. Isn't it true that most clinical and personality psychologists seem to be sensitizers? What better evidence could there be? Second, there is the *golden mean assumption* that too much of anything is probably bad. For that reason, it must be healthier to be a neutral than to be an extreme represser or an extreme sensitizer. Data to support such assumptions have not been as convincing as we might wish.

Antecedents of Repression–Sensitization

It has been proposed that the development of repression and denial defenses is the result of strict discipline and restrictiveness practiced by the child's parents. Sensitizing defenses, in contrast, develop in a family atmosphere of permissiveness toward the expression of impulses and emotions (Byrne, 1961; Miller & Swanson, 1960). In a laboratory analogue of such child-rearing techniques, Dulaney (1957) was able to develop perceptually repressive subjects by administering electric shock when they responded to threatening stimuli; perceptual sensitizers resulted when the experimenter permitted responses to threatening stimuli but punished competing responses. Thus both theory and laboratory data point to the etiology of repression–sensitization, but the research to date indicates that the direction of these differences is the opposite of our expectations.

In a study of the relationship of family environment to the development of defense mechanisms, Weinstock (1967) analyzed interviews of male subjects and their parents taken over a three-year period. This research found that repression and denial are primarily associated with a warm, relaxed, even-tempered, friendly family atmosphere.

In another type of investigation, Byrne (1964a) obtained the attitudes of subjects' mothers, subjects' own child-rearing attitudes, and subjects' perceptions of their mothers' child-rearing attitudes. The results are summarized in Table 11–5 and it can be seen that, once again, repressers appear to be raised in affectionate, accepting, warm interpersonal environments. The homes of sensitizers seem to be characterized by suppression, rejection, punitiveness, and unhappiness.

Interviews with repressing and sensitizing college sophomores yield similar results (Merbaum & Kazaoka, 1967). Sensitizers described their family relationships as involving stress, unhappiness, anger, criticism, and affective distance. Repressers described their families in close, affectionate terms.

Such findings threaten to upset some of our basic notions about the origins of defensive styles and about their meaning in terms of psychological health. It is still possible, of course, that the repressing defenses utilized by repressers and their families are responsible for an unrealistically positive and socially acceptable retrospective view of home life. Analogously, sensitizing defenses used in other families could be responsible for an unrealistically negative retrospective view in which any problems are magnified and overly emphasized.

It is a truism that "more research is needed," but in this instance the statement is more than cliché. We badly need detailed observational studies of parent–child interactions in which to document the parental behaviors that facilitate differential defensiveness. In the absence of such developmental data, our present findings and our current theorizing make somewhat strange bedfellows.

Table 11-5.   Child-rearing Attitudes Associated with Repression–Sensitization

Repressers	Sensitizers
Males	
1. Mother permissive about sexual behavior.	1. Mother suppressive about sexual behavior.
2. Mother perceived as having high self-esteem.	2. Mother perceived as having low self-esteem.
3. Mother perceived as having high expectations of son achieving masculine role.	3. Mother perceived as *not* having high expectations of son achieving masculine role.
Females	
1. Mother strict.	1. Mother permissive.
2. Mother does not expect deification of parents.	2. Mother expects deification of parents.
3. Mother feels confident in parental role.	3. Mother does not feel confident in parental role.
4. Mother perceived as accepting.	4. Mother perceived as rejecting.
5. Mother perceived as nonpunitive and not using physical punishment.	5. Mother perceived as punitive and as using physical punishment.
6. Mother perceived as having high self-esteem.	6. Mother perceived as having low self-esteem.
7. Father-mother relationship perceived as positive.	7. Father-mother relationship perceived as negative.
8. Mother perceived as consistent.	8. Mother perceived as inconsistent.

Source: Byrne, 1964a.

Maladjustment: Curvilinearity Revisited

One of the initial reasons for seeking to measure repression–sensitization was to be able to identify two very different but equally maladaptive types of defensive orientation (Byrne, 1961; Shannon, 1962; Ullmann, 1958, 1962). Conceptually, then, the relationship between adjustment and repression–sensitization was assumed to be curvilinear—individuals scoring toward the center of the R–S Scale should be better adjusted than those falling at either extreme. It is interesting to note that repressers and sensitizers make different assumptions about what is being measured by the R–S Scale (Lefcourt, 1966). Repressers think it is a measure of mental illness (on which they do well), whereas sensitizers believe it is a measure of honesty about oneself (on which they do well).

In an earlier review of this area (Byrne, 1964b), only two bits of evidence supported the general notion of curvilinearity. First, Ullmann (1962) found that psychiatric patients have a much higher standard deviation than college students on a measure of defensiveness (which corrleates in the .90s with the R–S Scale). Thus, comparatively normal college students cluster toward the center of the scale while severely disturbed mental patients have more representatives at the two extremes. The other supporting evidence comes from work on the overcontrolled personality (Megargee, 1966; Megargee, Cook, & Mendelsohn, 1967) that indicates that extreme repressers in the criminal population tend to commit sudden, violent acts of aggression, a finding that suggests that extreme repressers may be as maladjusted as extreme sensitizers.

The bulk of the remaining evidence at that time favored the idea of a linear relationship in that as sensitization increased, adjustment decreased. Much of the subsequent research is consistent with the proposition that repressers are relatively well-adjusted individuals and that sensitizing defenses are associated with maladjustment. During an interview, for example, repressers indicate that affectively positive material is more meaningful to them whereas sensitizers indicate that negative material is more meaningful (Merbaum & Kazaoka, 1967). You have seen in the present chapter that, time after time, the sensitizing defenses appear to be maladaptive in comparison with repressing defenses as shown in research on the MMPI, CPI, self-concept, dogmatism, perceived hostility, aggressiveness, and medical disorders. The family background of repressers also suggests a more psychologically facilitative home environment than does that of sensitizers. Other research confirms this general picture in that mental health clinic outpatients who are attending college are decidedly more sensitizing than ordinary college students (Tempone & Lamb, 1967). In the same study, R–S Scale scores were positively related to measures of conflict.

Detection of any chinks in the armor built of repression and denial is made difficult by the very nature of such defenses. Nevertheless, there continue to be tantalizing bits of evidence that suggest that all may not be as rosy with repressers as they keep telling us it is. We know, for example, that repressers have difficulty in perceiving threatening elements in their environment, that they are physiologically overreactive to stress even though they verbally discount their own feelings, that their learning of peripheral threatening cues is restricted, that they are more aggressive than they realize, that they associate negative feelings with sexual arousal, and that there is the possibility that one of the long-term consequences of repression is the development of organic diseases such as cancer. Also, it has been found that repressers are socially insensitive in that feedback has no effect on the duration of their verbalizations (Axtell & Cole, 1971).

In addition, there are scattered bits of evidence that neutrals function better than either repressers or sensitizers with respect to some behaviors. In a study of the relationship between humor appreciation and the R–S dimension, O'Connell and Peterson (1964) found that those who are least appreciative of humor tend to be repressers, followed closely by sensitizers. The most appreciative are neutrals. The authors interpret the finding as support for a curvilinear relationship between R–S and adjustment, with the middle-scoring group being the most mature and well adjusted. In a very different realm, Kaplan (1967) found that relative to neutrals, both repressers and sensitizers became less accurate in predicting the responses of a neutral target person as more and more information was given to them.

Altogether, then, the question of adjustment and defense mechanisms is obviously not a simple one, and the answer is multifaceted. Depending on the behavior in question and how it is measured, maladjustment can be found at all levels of repression–sensitization. Future research will need to focus less on a generic concept of "adjustment" and more on such specific questions as differential defensive styles in relation to their long- and short-range consequences, the intra- and interpersonal difficulties they cause, and their effects on behavioral efficiency in various situations. There just may not be any good guys and bad guys, or sick guys and well guys, with respect to an ideal way to defend oneself.

SOME METHODOLOGICAL ISSUES

Research in the area of repression–sensitization, as is true of any research, tends to proceed pell-mell as independent investigators pursue the problems they choose. Questions are asked and answered. A given phenomenon may be the subject of passing interest in a one-shot study or the subject of continued probing in years of paradigmatic research. As the fruits of such undirected labor accumulate, however, it is inevitable that certain general issues arise that are common to the entire basket. We will examine a few of these.

Methodological Problems

Chabot (1973) has pointed out several procedural difficulties with research on the R–S Scale. For example, Simmons (1966) showed that repression–sensitization scores tend to be 10 or more points lower when subjects are given the entire MMPI than when they are given the separate 127-item "Health and Opinion Survey" (the items of the R–S Scale per se, presented in Table 1 of this chapter). Differences of that magnitude create problems in generalizing results across experiments, and no convincing explanation for such differences has been proposed. To complicate matters further, when subjects were given the R–S Scale in both separate and embedded forms in counterbalanced order, higher scores were obtained on whichever form was taken first (Fisher, 1969). In any event, it appears that a given score varies in part as a function of the way in which the test is administered.

Another problem discussed by Chabot (1973) is the fact that there is no consistent or agreed-upon method of designating how subjects will be classified as "sensitizers," "neutrals," and "repressers." Some investigators have used the upper and lower quartiles of their subject sample, others use quite different percentile cutoffs, some divide the distribution into thirds, others use arbitrarily chosen score values, and still others do not report their method of selection. Such variations obviously interfere with the meaningful generalization of findings from experiment to experiment. For reasons of clarity of exposition, we have spoken rather facilely of sensitizers and repressers in this chapter on the basis of the way the terms were used in published research, but it should be noted that one experimenter's sensitizers may be another's neutrals, and so forth. At least some of the "inconsistent" results we have discussed are in part inconsistent because apples and peaches have been dumped into the same container. Conversely, when there are consistent findings despite methodological inconsistency, we can feel comforted by the generality and the robustness of the phenomenona.

The way to correct methodological inconsistency would seem to be simple and obvious. Those conducting research in this area could adopt standard procedures for administering the test and for subdividing the distribution. Before anyone embraces such imposed uniformity (whether it be decreed or decided by democratic vote), let a word be said in favor of the traditional creative anarchy of scientific research. Besides the practical impossibility of arriving at such rules or enforcing them, there is the very real possibility that they would be the "wrong" ones. To take an unlikely example, if we had decided at the beginning to divide all distributions at the median into repressers and sensitizers, we would never have learned about neutrals. A better solution to the problem of diversity would seem to be the universal adoption of full disclosure in our published research. That is, so long as it is clear how the test is given and who the subjects are, and so long as the means, standard deviations, and cutting points are presented in detail, it will be possible to evaluate the way in which divergent studies fit together procedurally.

Sex Differences

Another issue is the existence of potential sex differences in repression--sensitization research. In a survey of published work on the R–S Scale, Chabot (1973) noted that 50 percent of the studies used both sexes, 31 percent used only males, 11 percent used only females, and 8 percent did not report the sexual composition of the sample. Of the 58 investigations in which both sexes were included, 23 did not mention statistical analyses for sex differences, 18 found differences, and 17 indicated nonsignificant male–female comparisons.

The potential importance of sex differences was noted in the present chapter—in the material on medical disorders and on response to erotica, for example. Because of the obvious dangers of obscuring important findings by ignoring the sex of the subject and because of the intrinsic importance of knowledge about similarities and differences in the behavior of males and females, the least that should be asked of investigators is to report the gender of their subjects and, when both sexes are involved, to include that variable in their statistical tests.

Validity Redux: Does the R–S Scale Really Measure Repression–Sensitization?

In a sense, such a question is meaningless. One is tempted to reply, "If you believe in the R–S Scale, clap your hands!" Or, "Yes, Virginia, there really are defense mechanisms."

A better way of asking the same question is something like, "Is the R–S Scale a useful measure of something and is the best name for that something 'repression–sensitization'?" The first part of that rephrased question has been answered to our satisfaction by several years of research as documented by the material sampled in the present chapter. Scores on the R–S Scale provide a reliable basis on which to predict individual differences in a wide variety of verbal and nonverbal behaviors in realms as diverse as adjustment, perception, learning, physiological reactivity, sexuality, aggressivity, physical illness, and humor appreciation.

The second part of the question is one that should always be asked of every personality test each time it is used in research and that should never be considered to have been definitively answered (Byrne, 1974). With respect to the R–S Scale, we can say that research to date indicates that scores on that test predict a number of behavioral differences that are consistent with the fairly imprecise notions of what repression–sensitization should mean in terms of approach and avoidance behaviors. It is also true that some expected relationships have failed to materialize (e.g., a negative association with authoritarianism) and others are the opposite of that which was expected (e.g., child-rearing antecedents). Such a mixed bag of findings is not unusual, and it leaves sufficient latitude for different investigators to reach different conclusions as to the most appropriate label for the dimension in question. For the present authors at the present time (before Watergate, we might have said "at this point in time"), repression–sensitization seems as appropriate a designation as any alternative we could suggest.

This brings us back to the operational indistinguishability of the R–S Scale, the MAS, and Edwards' SD Scale. If these instruments correlate as highly as their respective reliabilities permit and if they are therefore empirically identical, why apply different names to the constructs they purport to measure? The answer is that a construct by any other name does not predict as sweetly. That is, research with a given personality variable is generated in part on the basis of its name, the surplus meaning attached to that name, and the theoretical underpinnings that led to that name. For example, it is highly unlikely that the

Repression–Sensitization Scale would have been used to predict differential conditionability of eye blinks (Spence, 1964) or that the Manifest Anxiety Scale would have been used to predict perceptual thresholds (Tempone, 1964b). Thus, operational identity is not the same as theoretical identity, and it is theory that leads us down particular research pathways (sometimes lined with primroses). Even if we are partially deluding ourselves and even if a very different explanatory system will eventually be needed to tie such seemingly unrelated research into a single neat package, the utility of our delusional systems should not be overlooked. The notion of individual differences in repression–sensitization has been an interesting one, and an imperfect measure of that construct has led us into many interesting areas of research. For the moment, that is as reasonable an answer to the validity question as any.

SUMMARY

The characteristic tendencies to respond to threat either with a pattern of avoidance defenses or a pattern of approach defenses have been labeled, respectively, repression and sensitization. It is assumed that these defensive styles represent the endpoints of a unidimensional repression–sensitization continuum.

Leading up to this conception was work on perceptual defense and the identification of those who were defensive and those who were vigilant in response to anxiety-arousing stimuli. There were several efforts to build a reliable measure of this defensive continuum, and one of the MMPI-derived instruments, the Repression–Sensitization Scale, has been used in much of the subsequent research in this area. The test is scored in such a way that high scores indicate sensitization and low scores repression. The most direct validational studies with the R–S Scale indicated that the test items are perceived by clinicians as measuring ego defenses, that test responses are associated with the expected behavioral differences of psychiatric patients, and that test scores predict the expected perceptual differences in response to threatening words.

The personality correlates of repression–sensitization have been established in a number of studies. In general, scores on the R–S Scale are positively related to most of the diagnostic scales of the MMPI, the Manifest Anxiety Scale, and negatively related to Edwards' Social Desirability Scale and the Marlowe-Crowne SD Scale. Almost all the scales of the California Personality Inventory correlate negatively with repression–sensitization. In other research, the R–S Scale seems to be negatively related to measures of self-esteem, unrelated to authoritarianism or intelligence, and positively related to dogmatism, cognitive complexity, and Rotter's I–E Scale.

Studies of the behavioral consequences of individual differences in repression–sensitization get away from the problems of test intercorrelations and the possible artifacts introduced by response set biases and variance attributable to measurement methodology. Such research has indicated that repressers show greater physiological reactivity to threat than do sensitizers and that in incidental learning situations repressers have greater difficulty in recalling threatening material than do sensitizers. Results from studies of dreaming suggest that sensitizers report more intense dream content than repressers and that repressers are more disturbed when deprived of REM sleep. Defense mechanisms appear to be unrelated to individual differences in attraction responses, but similarity of defense mechanisms has a positive effect on interpersonal attraction. Compared to repressers, sensitizers attribute more hostility to themselves and to others, but repressers are perceived as more aggressive than they believe themselves to be. In response to attack, sensitizers respond with counteraggression whereas repressers respond with avoidance, and these different overt responses are equally effective in reducing physiological arousal for their respective users. Compared to repressers, sensitizers are more likely to perceive the sexual meaning of double entendre words, to associate positive feelings with sexual arousal, and (for females) to be aroused by erotica or (for males) to report increased sexual activity after exposure to erotica. Sensitizers report more medical problems than repressers, and they are more likely to develop disorders with psychological components. Only among males are sensitizers more likely to visit a physician, perhaps because of sex differences in the relationship between pain tolerance and repression–sensitization.

Much of the theorizing about the R–S dimension has been limited to predictions of differential approach and avoidance tendencies in response to threat. Studies of child-rearing antecedents and adjustment consequences have tried to go beyond that. Speculation about the child-rearing antecedents of these personality styles appears to be wrong in that the available data suggest a positive, warm, accepting family background for repressers and a punitive, unhappy, rejecting background for sensitizers. Studies of maladjustment also present problems in that most of the data indicate that as sensitization tendencies increase, symptoms of maladjustment increase. There are bits of evidence, however, providing support for the original idea that repressers have many adjustment problems that are difficult to assess directly and that those with intermediate scores (neutrals) represent optimal adjustment.

Methodological considerations emphasize the importance of detailed reporting of procedural aspects of test administration and indications of the frequency distribution of test scores of one's sample in each published article. Sex differences should also be examined and reported whenever both sexes are represented. Validity questions never lead to a final answer with personality tests, but the R–S Scale is clearly a predictively useful measure for which the label "repression–sensitization" appears to be appropriate.

REFERENCES

Abbott, R. D. On confounding of the Repression-Sensitization and Manifest Anxiety Scales. *Psychological Reports, 1972, 30,* 392–394.

Adorno, T. W., Frenkel-Brunswik, E., Levinson, D. J., & Sanford, R. N. *The authoritarian personality.* New York: Harper, 1950.

Altrocchi, J. Interpersonal perception of repressors and sensitizers and component analysis of assumed dissimilarity scores. *Journal of Abnormal and Social Psychology, 1961, 62,* 528–534.

Altrocchi, J., Parsons, O. A., & Dickoff, H. Changes in self-ideal discrepancy in repressors and sensitizers. *Journal of Abnormal and Social Psychology, 1960, 61,* 67–72.

Altrocchi, J., & Perlitsh, H. D. Ego control patterns and attributions of hostility. *Psychological Reports, 1963, 12,* 811–818.

Altrocchi, J., Shrauger, S., & McLeod, M. A. Attribution of hostility to self and others by expressors, sensitizers, and repressors. *Journal of Clinical Psychology, 1964, 20,* 233.

Anderson, N. H. A simple model for information integration. In R. P. Abelson, E. Aronson, W. J. McGuire, T. M. Newcomb, M. T. Rosenberg, & P. H. Tannenbaum (Eds.), *Theories of cognitive consistency: A sourcebook.* Chicago: Rand McNally, 1968.

Antrobus, J. S., Antrobus, J. S., & Singer, J. L. Eye movements accompanying daydreaming, visual imagery, and thought suppression. *Journal of Abnormal and Social Psychology. 1964, 69,* 244–252.

Antrobus, J. S., Dement, W., & Fisher, C. Patterns of dreaming and dream recall: An EEG study. *Journal of Abnormal and Social Psychology, 1964, 69,* 341–344.

Axtell, B., & Cole, C. W. Repression–sensitization response mode and verbal avoidance. *Journal of Personality and Social Psychology, 1971, 18,* 133–137.

Bahnson, C. B., & Bahnson, M. B. Role of the ego defenses: Denial and repression in the etiology of malignant neoplasm. *Annals of the New York Academy of Sciences, 1966, 125,* 827–845.

Baldwin, B. A. Autonomic stress resolution in repressors and sensitizers following microcounseling. *Psychological Reports, 1972, 31,* 743–749.

Barton, M., & Buckhout, R. Effects of objective threat and ego threat on repressors and sensitizers in the estimation of shock intensity. *Journal of Experimental Research in Personality, 1969, 3,* 197–205.

Bergquist, W. H., Lewinsohn, P. M., Sue, D. W., & Flippo, J. R. Short and long term memory for various types of stimuli as a function of repression–sensitization. *Journal of Experimental Research in Personality, 1968, 3,* 28–38.

Blum, G. S. Perceptual defense revisited. *Journal of Abnormal and Social Psychology, 1955, 51,* 24–29.

Bruner, J. S., & Postman, L. Tension and tension release as organizing factors in perception. *Journal of Personality, 1947, 15,* 300–308. (a)

Bruner, J. S., & Postman, L. Emotional selectivity in perception and reaction. *Journal of Personality, 1947, 16,* 69–77. (b)

Byrne, D. The Repression–Sensitization Scale: Rationale, reliability, and validity. *Journal of Personality, 1961, 29,* 334–349.

Byrne, D. Childrearing antecedents of repression–sensitization. *Child Development, 1964, 35,* 1033–1039. (a)

Byrne, D. Repression–sensitization as a dimension of personality. In B. A. Maher (Ed.), *Progress in experimental personality research* (Vol. 1), New York: Academic Press, 1964. (b)

Byrne, D. *The attraction paradigm.* New York: Academic Press, 1971.

Byrne, D. *An introduction to personality: Research, theory, and applications.* Englewood Cliffs, N. J.: Prentice-Hall, 1974.

Byrne, D., Barry, J., & Nelson, D. Relation of the revised Repression–Sensitization Scale to measures of self-description. *Psychological Reports,* 1963, *13,* 323–334.

Byrne, D., Blaylock, B., & Goldberg, J. Dogmatism and defense mechanisms. *Psychological Reports,* 1966, *18,* 739–742.

Byrne, D., Fisher, J. D., Lamberth, J., & Mitchell, H. E. Evaluations of erotica: Facts or feelings? *Journal of Personality and Social Psychology,* 1974, *29,* 111–116.

Byrne, D., Golightly, C., & Sheffield, J. The Repression–Sensitization Scale as a measure of adjustment: Relationship with the CPI. *Journal of Consulting Psychology,* 1965, *29,* 586–589.

Byrne, D., & Griffitt, W. Similarity and awareness of similarity of personality characteristics. *Journal of Experimental Research in Personality,* 1969, *3,* 179–186.

Byrne, D., Griffitt, W., & Stefaniak, D. Attraction and similarity of personality characteristics. *Journal of Personality and Social Psychology,* 1967, *5,* 82–90.

Byrne, D., & Holcomb, J. The reliability of a response measure: Differential recognition-threshold scores. *Psychological Bulletin,* 1962, *59,* 70–73.

Byrne, D., & Lamberth. J. The effect of erotic stimuli on sex arousal, evaluative responses, and subsequent behavior. In *Technical report of the Commission on Obscenity and Pornography* (Vol. VIII). Washington, D.C.: U.S. Government Printing Office, 1971.

Byrne, D., & Sheffield, J. Response to sexually arousing stimuli as a function of repressing and sensitizing defenses. *Journal of Abnormal Psychology,* 1965, *70,* 114–118.

Byrne, D., Steinberg, M. A., & Schwartz, M. S. The relationship between repression–sensitization and physical illness. *Journal of Abnormal Psychology,* 1968, *73,* 154–155.

Carroll, D. Repression–sensitization and the verbal elaboration of experience. *Journal of Consulting and Clinical Psychology,* 1972, *38,* 147.

Chabot, J. A. Repression–sensitization: A critique of some neglected variables in the literature. *Psychological Bulletin,* 1973, *80,* 122–129.

Clark, L. F., & Neuringer, C. Repressor–sensitizer personality styles and associated levels of verbal ability, social intelligence, sex knowledge, and quantitative ability. *Journal of Consulting and Clinical Psychology,* 1971, *36,* 183–188.

Clore, G. L., & Byrne, D. A reinforcement–affect model of attraction. In T. L. Huston (Ed.), *Foundations of interpersonal attraction.* New York: Academic Press, 1974.

Consentino, F., & Kahn, M. Further normative and comparative data on the Repression– Sensitization and Social Desirability Scales. *Psychological Reports,* 1967, *20,* 959–962.

Crowne, D. P., & Marlowe, D. A. A new scale of social desirability independent of psychopathology. *Journal of Consulting Psychology,* 1960, *24,* 349–354.

Dement, W., & Kleitman, N. The relation of eye movements during sleep to dream activity: An objective method for the study of dreaming. *Journal of Experimental Psychology,* 1957, *53,* 339–346.

Dulaney, D. E., Jr. Avoidance learning of perceptual defense and vigilance. *Journal of Abnormal and Social Psychology,* 1957, *55,* 333–338.

Edwards, A. L. *The social desirability variable in personality assessment and research.* New York: Dryden, 1957.

Edwards, A. L. Social desirability and personality test construction. In B. M. Bass and I. A. Berg (Eds.), *Objective approaches to personality assessment.* Princeton, N. J.: Van Nostrand, 1959.

Epstein, S., & Fenz, W. D. The detection of areas of stress through variations in perceptual threshold, physiological arousal, and cognitive deficit. *Journal of Experimental Research in Personality*, 1967, *2*, 191–199.

Eriksen, C. W. The case for perceptual defense. *Psychological Review*, 1954, *61*, 175–182.

Feder, C. Z. Relationship of repression–sensitization to adjustment status, social desirability, and acquiescence response set. *Journal of Consulting Psychology*, 1967, *31*, 401–406.

Feder, C. Z. Relationship between self-acceptance and adjustment, repression–sensitization and social competence. *Journal of Abnormal Psychology*, 1968, *73*, 317–322.

Fisher, G. The Repression–Sensitization Scale: Effects of several variables and two methods of obtaining scores. *Journal of General Psychology*, 1969, *80*, 183–187.

Foulds, M. L., & Warehime, R. G. Relationship between repression–sensitization and a measure of self-actualization. *Journal of Consulting and Clinical Psychology*, 1971, *36*, 257–259.

Foulkes, D., Pivik, T., Ahrens, J. B., & Swanson, E. M. Effects of "dream deprivation" on dream content: An attempted cross-night replication. *Journal of Abnormal Psychology*, 1968, *73*, 403–415.

Galbraith, G. G., & Lieberman, H. Associative responses to double entendre words as a function of repression–sensitization and sexual stimulation. *Journal of Consulting and Clinical Psychology*, 1972, *39*, 322–327.

Goldiamond, I. Indicators of perception: I. Subliminal perception, subception, unconscious perception: An analysis in terms of psychophysical indicator methodology. *Psychological Bulletin*, 1958, *55*, 373–411.

Goldin, P. C. Experimental investigation of selective memory and the concept of repression and defense: A theoretical synthesis. *Journal of Abnormal and Social Psychology*, 1964, *69*, 365–380.

Golightly, C., & Byrne, D. Attitude statements as positive and negative reinforcements. *Science*, 1964, *146*, 798–799.

Golin, S., Herron, E. W., Lakota, R., & Reineck, L. Factor analytic study of the Manifest Anxiety, Extraversion, and Repression–Sensitization Scales. *Journal of Consulting Psychology*, 1967, *31*, 564–569.

Good, L. R., & Levine, R. H. Pupillary responses of repressors and sensitizers to sexual and aversive stimuli. *Perceptual and Motor Skills*, 1970, *30*, 631–634.

Gordon, J. E. Interpersonal prediction of repressors and sensitizers. *Journal of Personality*, 1957, *25*, 686–698.

Gormly, J. Sociobehavioral and physiological responses to interpersonal disagreement. *Journal of Experimental Research in Personality*, 1971, *5*, 216–222.

Gough, H. G. *Manual for the California Psychological Inventory*. Palo Alto, Cal.: Consulting Psychologists Press, 1957.

Haley, G. A. Eye movement responses of repressors and sensitizers to a stressful film. *Journal of Research in Personality*, 1974, *8*, 88–94.

Handal, P. J., & Rychlak, J. F. Curvilinearity between dream content and death anxiety and the relationship of death anxiety to repression–sensitization. *Journal of Abnormal Psychology*, 1971, *77*, 11–16.

Hanley, C. Social desirability and response bias in the MMPI. *Journal of Consulting Psychology*, 1961, *25*, 13–20.

Hare, R. D. Denial of threat and emotional response to impending painful stimulation. *Journal of Consulting Psychology*, 1966, *30*, 359–361.

Hathaway, S. R., & McKinley, J. C. *Manual for the Minnesota Multiphasic Personality Inventory*. New York: Psychological Corporation, 1951.

Hokanson, J. E., & Megargee, E. I. *The dynamics of aggression*. New York: Harper & Row, 1970.

Hokanson, J. E., & Shetler, S. The effect of overt aggression on physiological arousal. *Journal of Abnormal and Social Psychology*, 1961, *63*, 446–448.

Holmes, D. S. Investigations of repression: Differential recall of material experimentally or naturally associated with ego threat. *Psychological Bulletin*, 1974, *81*, 632–653.

Hutt, L. D. *An experimental investigation of perceptual defense and vigilance: Prediction from the Byrne scale of repression*–sensitization. Paper presented at the meeting of the Southwestern Psychological Association, Oklahoma City, April, 1965.

Ihilevich, D., & Gleser, G. C. Relationship of defense mechanisms to field dependence– independence. *Journal of Abnormal Psychology*, 1971, *77*, 296–302.

Joy, V. L. *Repression–sensitization and interpersonal behavior*. Paper presented at the meeting of the American Psychological Association, Philadelphia, August, 1963.

Kaplan, M. F. Repression–sensitization and prediction of self-descriptive behavior: Response versus situational cue variables. *Journal of Abnormal Psychology*, 1967, *72*, 354–361.

Kaplan, M. F. Elicitation of information and response biases of repressors, sensitizers and neutrals in behavior prediction. *Journal of Personality*, 1968, *36*, 84–91.

Kogan, N. Authoritarianism and repression. *Journal of Abnormal and Social Psychology*, 1956, *53*, 34–37.

Lachman, F. M., Lapkin, B., & Handelman, N. S. The recall of dreams: Its relation to repression and cognitive control. *Journal of Abnormal and Social Psychology*, 1962, *64*, 160–162.

Lazarus, R. S., & Alfert, E. Short-circuiting of threat by experimentally altering cognitive appraisal. *Journal of Abnormal and Social Psychology*, 1964, *69*, 195–205.

Lefcourt, H. M. Repression–sensitization: A measure of the evaluation of emotional expression. *Journal of Consulting Psychology*, 1966, *30*, 444–449.

Lewinsohn, P. M., Bergquist, W. H., & Brelje, T. The repression–sensitization dimension and emotional response to stimuli. *Psychological Reports*, 1972, *31*, 707–716.

Liberty, P. G., Lunneberg, C. E., & Atkinson, G. C. Perceptual defense, dissimulation, and response styles. *Journal of Consulting Psychology*, 1964, *28*, 529–537.

Lomont, J. F. The repression–sensitization dimension in relation to anxiety responses. *Journal of Consulting Psychology*, 1965, *29*, 84–86.

Luborsky, L., Blinder, B., & Schimek, J. Looking, recalling, and GSR as a function of defense. *Journal of Abnormal Psychology*, 1965, *70*, 270–280.

Lucky, A. W., & Grigg, A. E. Repression–sensitization as a variable in deviant responding. *Journal of Clinical Psychology*, 1964, *20*, 92–93.

Markowitz, A. Influence of the repression–sensitization dimension, affect value, and ego threat on incidental learning. *Journal of Personality and Social Psychology*, 1969, *11*, 374–380.

McDonald, R. L. Ego control patterns and attribution of hostility to self and others. *Journal of Personality and Social Psychology*, 1965, *2*, 273–277.

McDonald, R. L. The effects of stress on self attribution of hostility among ego control patterns. *Journal of Personality*, 1967, *35*, 234–245.

Megargee, E. I. Undercontrolled and overcontrolled personality types in extreme antisocial aggression. *Psychological Monographs*, 1966, *80*, (Whole No. 611).

Megargee, E. I., Cook, P. E., & Mendelsohn, G. A. The development and validation of an MMPI Scale of assaultiveness in overcontrolled individuals. *Journal of Abnormal Psychology*, 1967, *72*, 519–528.

Merbaum, M. The simulation of normal and MMPI profiles by repressors and sensitizers. *Journal of Consulting and Clinical Psychology,* 1972, *39,* 171.

Merbaum, M., & Badia, P. Tolerance of repressors and sensitizers to noxious stimulation. *Journal of Abnormal Psychology,* 1967, *72,* 349–353.

Merbaum, M., & Kazaoka, K. Reports of emotional experience by sensitizers and repressors during an interview transaction. *Journal of Abnormal Psychology,* 1967, *72,* 101–105.

Miller, D. R., & Swanson, G. E. *Inner conflict and defense.* New York: Holt, Rinehart & Winston, 1960.

Mischel, W. *Personality and assessment,* New York: John Wiley, 1968.

Milton, W., & Waite, B. Presidential preference and traditional family values. *American Psychologist,* 1964, *19,* 844–845.

Newcomb, T. M. *The acquaintance process.* New York: Holt, Rinehart, and Winston, 1961.

O'Connell, W., & Peterson, P. Humor and repression. *Journal of Existential Psychiatry,* 1964, *4,* 309–316.

Pagano, D. F. Effects of task familiarity on stress responses of repressors and sensitizers. *Journal of Consulting and Clinical Psychology,* 1973, *40,* 22–26.

Palmer, J., & Altrocchi, J. Attribution of hostile intent as unconscious. *Journal of Personality,* 1967, *35,* 164–176.

Paris, J., & Goodstein, L. D. Responses to death and sex stimulus materials as a function of repression–sensitization. *Psychological Reports,* 1966, *19,* 1283–1291.

Parsons, O. A., Fulgenzi, L. B., & Edelberg, R. Aggressiveness and psychophysiological responsivity in groups of repressors and sensitizers. *Journal of Personality and Social Psychology,* 1969, *12,* 235–244.

Phares, E. J. TAT performance as a function of anxiety and coping-avoiding behavior. *Journal of Consulting Psychology,* 1961, *25,* 257–259.

Pivik, T., & Foulkes, D. "Dream deprivation:" Effects of dream content. *Science,* 1966, *153,* 1282–1284.

Pivik, T., & Foulkes, D. NREM mentation: Relation to personality, orientation time, and time of night. *Journal of Consulting and Clinical Psychology,* 1968, *32,* 144–151.

Robbins, P. R., & Tanck, R. H. The Repression–Sensitization Scale, dreams, and dream associations. *Journal of Clinical Psychology,* 1970, *26,* 219–221.

Rokeach, M. *The open and closed mind.* New York: Basic Books, 1960.

Rotter, J. B. Generalized expectancies for internal versus external control of reinforcement. *Psychological Monographs,* 1966, *80* (Whole No. 609).

Scarpetti, W. L. The repression–sensitization dimension in relation to impending painful stimulation. *Journal of Consulting and Clinical Psychology,* 1973, *40,* 377–382.

Scarpetti, W. L. Autonomic concomitant of aggressive behavior in repressors and sensitizers: A social learning approach. *Journal of Personality and Social Psychology,* 1974, *30,* 772–781.

Schachter, S., & Latane, B. Crime, cognition, and the autonomic nervous system. In D. Levine (Ed.), *Nebraska Symposium on Motivation.* Lincoln: University of Nebraska Press, 1964.

Schill, T., & Althoff, M. Auditory perceptual thresholds for sensitizers, defensive and nondefensive repressors. *Perceptual and Motor Skills,* 1968, *27,* 935–938.

Schwartz, M. S. The Repression–Sensitization Scale: Normative age and sex data on 30,000 medical patients. *Journal of Clinical Psychology,* 1972, *28,* 72–73.

Schwartz, M. S., Krupp, N. E., & Byrne, D. Repression–sensitization and medical diagnosis. *Journal of Abnormal Psychology,* 1971, *78,* 286–291.

Shannon, D. T. Clinical patterns of defense as revealed in visual recognition thresholds. *Journal of Abnormal and Social Psychology*, 1962, *64*, 370–377.

Shostrom, E. L. A test for the measurement of self-actualization. *Educational and Psychological Measurement*, 1964, *24*, 207–218.

Shostrom, E. L. *Manual, Personal Orientation Inventory*. San Diego: Educational and Industrial Testing Service, 1966.

Simal, F. J., & Herr, V. V. Autonomic responses to threatening stimuli in relation to the repression–sensitization dimension. *Journal of Abnormal Psychology*, 1970, *76*, 106–109.

Simmons, A. D. A comparison of repression–sensitization scores obtained by two different methods. *Journal of Clinical Psychology*, 1966, *22*, 465.

Snortum, J. R., & Wilding, F. W. Temporal estimation and heart rate as a function of repression–sensitization score and probabilty of shock. *Journal of Consulting and Clinical Psychology*, 1971, *37*, 417–422.

Spence, K. W. Anxiety (drive) level and performance in eyelid conditioning. *Psychological Bulletin*, 1964, *61*, 129–139.

Stein, S. H. Arousal level in repressors and sensitizers as a function of response context. *Journal of Consulting and Clinical Psychology*, 1971, *36*, 386–394.

Sullivan, P. F., & Roberts, L. K. The relationship of manifest anxiety to repression–sensitization on the MMPI. *Journal of Consulting and Clinical Psychology*, 1969, *33*, 763–764.

Swindell, D. H., & L'Abate, L. Religiosity, dogmatism, and repression–sensitization. *Scientific Study of Religion*, 1970, *9*, 249–251.

Taylor, J. A. A personality scale of manifest anxiety. *Journal of Abnormal and Social Psychology*, 1953, *48*, 285–290.

Tebbs, R. B., & Foulkes, D. Strength of grip following different stages of sleep. *Perceptual and Motor Skills*, 1966, *23*, 827–834.

Tempone, V. J. Extension of the repression–sensitization hypothesis to success and failure experience. *Psychological Reports*, 1964, *15*, 39–45. (a)

Tempone, V. J. Some clinical correlates of repression–sensitization. *Journal of Clinical Psychology*, 1964, *20*, 440–442. (b)

Tempone, V. J., & Lamb, W. Repression–sensitization and its relation to measures of adjustment and conflict. *Journal of Consulting Psychology*, 1967, *31*, 131–136.

Tolor, A., & Reznikoff, M. Relation between insight, repression–sensitization, internal-external control, and death anxiety. *Journal of Abnormal Psychology*, 1967, *72*, 426–430.

Tolor, A., Rice, F. J., & Lanctot, C. A. Personality patterns of couples practicing the temperature–rhythm method of birth control. *Journal of Sex Research*, 1975, *11*, 119–133.

Ullmann, L. P. Clinical correlates of facilitation and inhibition of response to emotional stimuli. *Journal of Projective Techniques*, 1958, *22*, 341–347.

Ullmann, L. P. An empirically derived MMPI scale which measures facilitation–inhibition of recognition of threatening stimuli. *Journal of Clinical Psychology*, 1962, *18*, 127–132.

Ullmann, L. P., & McReynolds, P. *Differential perceptual recognition in psychiatric patients: Empirical findings and theoretical formulation*. Paper presented at the meeting of the American Psychological Association, Philadelphia, August, 1963.

Valins, S. Emotionality and autonomic reactivity. *Journal of Experimental Research in Personality*, 1967, *2*, 41–48.

Van Egeren, L. Repression and sensitization: Sensitivity and recognition criteria. *Journal of Experimental Research in Personality*, 1968, *3*, 1–8.

Weinstock, A. R. Family environment and the development of defense and coping mechanisms. *Journal of Personality and Social Psychology,* 1967, *5,* 67–75.

White, M. D., & Wilkins, W. Bogus physiological feedback and response thresholds of repressors and sensitizers. *Journal of Research in Personality,* 1973, *7,* 78–87.

Wiggins, J. S. Interrelationships among MMPI measures of dissimulation under standard and social desirability instructions. *Journal of Consulting Psychology,* 1959, *23,* 419–427.

Wilkins, G., Epting, F., & Van de Riet, H. Relationship between repression–sensitization and interpersonal cognitive complexity. *Journal of Consulting and Clinical Psychology,* 1972, *39,* 448–450.

Wolff, D. R. *The effects of stress on speech characteristics and perceived emotions of repressors and sensitizers.* Unpublished doctoral dissertation, Washington University, 1966.

Worchel, P. Anxiety and repression. *Journal of Abnormal and Social Psychology,* 1955, *50,* 201–205.

Worchel, P. Adaptability screening of flying personnel: Development of a self-concept: Inventory for predicting maladjustment. SAM, USAF, Randolph AFB, Texas, No. 56–62, 1957.

CHAPTER 12

Sensation Seeking

MARVIN ZUCKERMAN
University of Delaware

THEORETICAL AND EXPERIMENTAL BACKGROUND

The evolution of the Sensation Seeking Scale (SSS) from my earlier work in the area of sensory deprivation has been described in a chapter in another volume (Zuckerman, 1974) and will be more briefly recounted here. It is sometimes useful to know the developmental history of a test as well as its current status.

When the first SSS was designed, we had no grandiose plans to assess a fundamental "dimension of personality." In 1958 I became interested in the area of sensory deprivation because it seemed that we had a situation in which phenomena, ordinarily seen only in psychiatric patients, could be produced in a laboratory without ingestion of chemicals. Early reports of reactions in this "walk-in inkblot" situation (as Leo Goldberger has aptly dubbed it) suggested that the situation elicited first boredom, then anxiety, and finally hallucinations, delusions, body-image changes, and a peculiar vulnerability to suggestion. The first research, conducted in the laboratories of D. O. Hebb at McGill University, was stimulated by the government's interest in "brainwashing" as a consequence of the Korean war.

Whatever the original purpose of the study, the first results (Bexton, Heron, & Scott, 1954), showing dramatic intellectual, perceptual, affective, motor, and cortical changes, reinforced the growing feeling that something was lacking in the drive reduction theories of motivation holding sway at that time. Hebb (1949) had been trying to change the view of psychologists that motives were all "in the gut," that the cortex was a mere switchboard and memory storage bin, and that all men or women need is a good bed, a full stomach, and an occasional orgasm to keep them happy. With the possible exception of the latter need (because of social inhibitions or the gloves and cuffs worn?) subjects in sensory deprivation experiments should have been happy, but few actually were.

The drive or tension reduction nature of motivation is illustrated by Freud's

(1915) concept of the central nervous system (CNS): "The nervous system is an apparatus having the function of abolishing stimuli which reach it, or of reducing excitation to the lowest possible level: an apparatus which would even, if this were feasible, maintain itself in an altogether unstimulated condition" (p. 72, Freud, 1957).

Hebb (1958), looking at the knowledge of the CNS in the 43 years since Freud had made the above statement, said: "There appears to be a good case for thinking of a general drive state related to the nonspecific projection system of the brain stem, and of motivation tending to produce an optimal level of 'arousal' in this system, not as an adequate explanation, even of the facts now known, but as one that is both more adequate than existing theories and more capable of development" (p. 459).

The concepts of optimal level of stimulation (Leuba, 1955) and of optimal level of arousal (Hebb, 1955) and the idea of an inverted-U shaped relationship between stimulation and arousal on the one hand and learning and performance, approach–withdrawal (Schneirla, 1959), and affective reaction (Berlyne, 1960; McClelland, Atkinson, Clark, & Lowell, 1953; Wundt, 1874; Young, 1959) on the other, seemed to apply to the results from the sensory deprivation experiments.

Animal experiments (e. g., Butler & Harlow, 1954; Kish, 1955) had already shown that visual, auditory, or tactual stimulation had reinforcing properties, even when not associated with primary reinforcement. Butler and Alexander (1955) showed that monkeys confined in stimulation deprivation boxes would work hard for the reinforcement of looking out of their box into the lab. The animals worked to maintain some "relatively fixed amount of daily visual experience."

Similar results were found when humans in sensory deprivation were allowed to work for exteroceptive reinforcement (Bexton, 1953; Jones & McGill, 1967; Jones, Wilkinson, & Braden, 1961; Lambert & Levy, 1972; Vernon & McGill, 1960; Zuckerman & Haber, 1965). Jones (1969) summarized the work on humans to that date and postulated the existence of a homeostatic "information" drive, or a need for varied and unpredictable stimulus input.

The need for varied stimulation seemed to be important for an understanding of individual differences in response to sensory deprivation. Smith, Myers, and Johnson (1967) and Vernon and McGill (1960) showed that the amount of time spent looking at, or listening to, boring materials early in sensory deprivation predicted subsequent tolerance for or quitting the experiment. Zuckerman and Haber (1965) found that subjects who showed greater electrodermal arousal in a sensory deprivation experiment showed more responding for stimulation reinforcement in a subsequent experiment.

In 1961 it occurred to me that if we could develop a questionnaire measure of this need for stimulation or optimal levels of stimulation and arousal, we might be able to use it to predict responses to sensory deprivation. We began writing items reflecting the idea of a need for novel stimulation or arousal, often thinking of people we knew who seemed to exemplify the trait we were conceptualizing. Form I, consisting of 54 forced-choice items, was given to 268 male and 277 female undergraduates at Brooklyn College. The item intercorrelations were factor analyzed separately for the sexes. At that time we were looking only for a general factor, and we did find one accounting for about 30 percent of the variance. The factor we obtained was reliable across the sexes: Factor loadings for males and females correlated .91. The 22 items that loaded over .30 on this factor in both males and females constituted the General scale, which has been carried over into subsequent forms of the SSS. Separate male and female scales were also developed for this form II using 12 additional items that loaded for either males or females but not for both. Most of the research done with form II used the common item General scale.

Form II of the SSS was published (Zuckerman, Kolin, Price, & Zoob, 1964), and we began to use it in our research on sensory deprivation. In the mid-1960s a group of investigators who were still heavily involved in research on sensory deprivation flew up to Manitoba on a cold day in November (40 below zero) to plan a book on sensory deprivation. The late John Zubek organized this effort, which was finally published in 1969 (Zubek, 1969). Sensory deprivation had proven to be a very complex area. After the initial "Wow!" stage (1954 to 1961), investigators began to do some better controlled studies to isolate the variables producing the phenomena. Personality, set, expectation, sensory restriction, social isolation, movement restriction, duration of the experiment, and other variables were implicated in various ways (Zuckerman, 1969a). Given the task of writing one of the two theoretical chapters, I reviewed the physiological, perceptual style, and psychoanalytic theories and decided that, although each had some merits, a new type of theory was needed to explain the data.

The new theory (Zuckerman, 1969b) was based on the importance of individual differences in optimal levels of stimulation (OLS) and arousal (OLA). The first two postulates dealt with the stimulus determinants of arousability as well as the influence of habituation and tonic levels of arousal. The third postulate was the individual difference proposition suggesting that the OLS and OLA are reasonably stable and general traits of persons related to certain suggested constitutional factors, age, prior experience, recent levels of stimulation, task demand, and the diurnal cycle. Postulates IV to X were an attempt to apply the theory to explain the findings from the 15 years of sensory deprivation research. The theory is a psychophysiological one pointing to an interaction between environmental stimulation and characteristics of the CNS.

The chapter signified my commitment to the OLS–OLA idea. Now it became even more important to develop the SSS because it was our hope of making postulate III operational. It was becoming increasingly evident that sensory deprivation was a clumsy and expensive way to explore the theory. Too many other influences, such as set and experimental demand, influenced subjects in the "walk-in inkblot." Another factor, not exactly an inconsequential one, was that NIMH funds for sensory deprivation research were no longer available. However, much to my amazement, other investigators seemed interested in sensation seeking as a personality trait in its own right, apart from its predictive power in sensory deprivation experiments. So partly from financial exigency and partly from the obligation one feels to his own theory, I turned more of my efforts to the development of the SSS and the demonstration of its construct, rather than criterion validity (criterion validity being the prediction of sensory deprivation reactions).

Building a personality theory around a test is a risky venture. The risk is that failures in validity attempts may represent defects in the test instrument or the theory on which the test is based. Spence was once asked what would have happened if the results, using the Taylor Manifest Anxiety Scale as a measure of drive in his theory, had been negative. Without hesitation he replied that the TMAS, not the theory, would have gone into the garbage can. But Spence was working from a theory that was fairly well grounded in empirical research before the test was devised. Most personality theories do not have this advantage. In the case of a new personality theory such as the OLS–OLA one, development of the test validity must go hand-in-hand with developing and shaping the theory. There is a danger of circularity in the initial stages but no more so than in the Skinnerian construct of reinforcement. At some stage of validity we must decide that the test is the most adequate way we have of defining the construct and that failures of prediction in studies require alterations in our construct or theory rather than in a new test. I believe we have reached this stage with the SSS and offer the contents of this chapter to support my case.

DEVELOPMENT OF FACTOR SCALES (SSS IV)

Although the initial factor analysis yielded a broad sensation-seeking dimension cutting across diverse kinds of items, the first factor accounted for only a third of the variance. Farley (1967) suggested, from his analysis, that the SSS might contain more than a single factor. Zuckerman and Link (1968) rotated the factors in the original analysis and found evidence that there might indeed be additional factors but there were not enough items to define them. Using these factor analyses of forms I and II as a guide, items were written for a new experimental form (III).

The 113 items in form III were factor analyzed separately for 160 male and 172 female undergraduates from Temple University. Orthogonal and oblique rotations were used, yielding similar results. Orthogonal results were used to select items loading on four definable rotated factors. The results, described in Zuckerman (1971), were used to construct four new scales for form IV. Almost all the items loading on the first unrotated factor in the first factor analysis (Zuckerman et al., 1964) also loaded most highly on this factor in the last analysis (Zuckerman, 1971). The 22-item General scale was carried over intact into form IV to provide continuity with prior reserach and as a good overall measure of the broad SS tendency. It should be noted that the General scale has six items in common with the Thrill and Adventure Seeking Scale (TAS), five items with the Experience Seeking Scale (ES), and three items with the Boredom Susceptibility (BS) scale, and therefore it is not an independent scale. There is no item overlap among the four factor scales, TAS, ES, BS, and Dis (to be discussed below), except for one item in common between the ES and BS scales.

Zuckerman, Bone, Neary, Mangelsdorff, and Brustman (1972) present the correlations among the four factor scales in several samples. Despite the attempt to derive independent scales it is apparent that the factor scales are intercorrelated, as high as .5 for males and .6 for females. The Thrill and Adventure Seeking scale is the most independent but it is correlated with the ES scale. The dimensions of sensation seeking are not independent but, as we shall see, they sometimes have common correlates and sometimes exhibit discriminant validity.

The first factor was expected on the basis of prior analyses by Farley (1967) and Zuckerman and Link (1968) and has been labeled *Thrill and Adventure Seeking* (TAS). The items express a desire to engage in outdoor noncompetitive sports or activities involving elements of risk such as flying, scuba diving, parachute jumping, motorcycle riding, deep sea sailing, skiing, mountain climbing, and so on. The key item is 21: "I sometimes like to do things that are a little frightening" (high SS) versus "A sensible persons avoids activities that are dangerous" (low SS).

The second factor was called *Experience Seeking* (ES), and the items describe the seeking of new experiences through the mind and senses and an unconventional, nonconforming style of life. The philosophy is summed up in item 47: "I like to have new and exciting experiences and sensations even if they are a little frightening, unconventional or illegal" (high SS) versus "I am not interested in experience for its own sake" (low SS).

The third factor was called *Disinhibition* (Dis) because it described the use of alcohol for social disinhibition and an interest in "wild" parties, gambling, and the need for sexual variety. It could have been called the "Swinger" scale. The philosophy is expressed in item 64: "Almost everything enjoyable is illegal or immoral" (high SS) versus "The most enjoyable things are perfectly legal and moral' (low SS).

The fourth factor, called *Boredom Susceptibility* (BS), was better defined in males than in females. The items express a dislike of any repetition of experience, routine work, predictable, dull, or boring people, and a restlessness when things are unchanging. The social expression is illustrated by item 12: "I get bored seeing the same old faces" (high SS) versus "I like the comfortable familiarity of everyday friends" (low SS).

The 72-item form IV of the SSS, which contains these four factor scales, the General scale, and some filler items, is contained in Appendix A at the end of this chapter. Standard score (Appendix B) and percentile conversions (Appendix C), and a scoring key (Appendix D) are also included.

Reliabilities of the Scales

Factor reliabilities were computed by correlating the factor loadings of males with those of females across the items comprising each of the scales. The coefficients were: Gen .95, TAS .75, ES .83, Dis .81, and BS .37. With the exception of BS, the factor structures of the scales were quite similar for males and females. The BS factor was derived only from male loadings because it was not clearly defined in females. However, the scale is scored in the same way for females as for males.

Odd-Even split-half reliabilities were calculated and corrected by the Spearman–Brown formula in two samples: the Temple University sample used for the factor analysis, and samples of 41 males and 51 females from the University of North Carolina. With the exception of the BS scale all internal reliabilities were adequate ranging from .68 to .88. The BS reliabilities in males were .75 and .58; in females they were .56 and .38. Because the BS factor was not well defined in females, the BS scale is not a homogeneous one for them.

In regard to retest reliabilities following one hour of sensory bombardment (LoGuidice, 1974), 139 male undergraduates showed marked trait stability in the face of a drastic procedure; coefficients were Gen .87, TAS .80, ES .93, Dis .89 and BS .87. For 21 females undergoing the same conditions the coefficients were Gen .71, TAS .92, ES .77, and Dis .93. Zuckerman et al. (1972) found one-week retest reliabilities in a group of 38 males and females: Gen .89, TAS .94, ES .92, Dis .91, and BS .82. Murtaugh (1971) examined the retest reliability of the General Scale over a three-month interval in prisoners. The first test was given in a maximum security and social isolation period, whereas the second test was given in the regular prison setting. The reliability coefficient was .72. The SS scales show good stability over time in the face of radically different conditions.

Cultural Similarities and Differences

Farley (1967) factor analyzed the items in form II of the SSS using a sample of British apprentice and civil service males. Ohkubo (1972) translated the SSS form II into Japanese and factor analyzed the items of the translated form. Naturally one would expect a translated test administered in a different country to have a different factor structure, not only for linguistic reasons but also because of cultural differences. The differences between working-class British males and American college students would be due more to cultural differences than to language differences, although differences in idioms might also affect meanings. I correlated the first unrotated factor loadings from these two studies with those found in the first study at Brooklyn College (Zuckerman et al., 1964). The correlation between the first factor in the American and English groups was .64. Although not as high as the factor reliability between American males and females (r = .91), the results are encouraging for the cross-cultural validity of the general sensation-seeking factor. The Japanese group's loadings, however, correlated only .35 with both the American and English groups' loadings. Although significant, the low factor reliability suggests that we must be wary in making cross-cultural generalizations on the basis of the questionnaire measure.

With this caution in mind, we can compare the means for American and Australian high school and college students and Japanese and Thai college students tested with translated versions of the SSS (Table 12–1). There is a high degree of similarity in the means of United States male college students. The freshmen, tested when they entered the University of Delaware, were significantly lower than the sophomores and juniors, who largely constituted the introductory psychology classes. The entering freshmen were similar to the high school students. The freshwomen were also lower than their counterparts in the sophomore and junior classes and similar to high school students tested by Farley and Cox (1971). In this latter study there were no sex or age differences. The students in the high school had been tested at each age from 14 to 17 with no apparent trend in SSS scores.

Table 12–1.   Mean SS–General Scores of Students from Different Schools and Cultures; Sex Differences

	N		SS Means		"t"
	Male	Female	Male	Female	M vs F
Farley & Cox, U.S. suburban					
HS Students	64	64	13.1	12.3	1.22
Forer, Australian HS Seniors	86	–	12.2	–	–
Zuckerman, U.S., U. of Del. Freshmen	296	280	12.8	12.0	2.2[a]
Zuckerman, U.S., U. of Del. Sophs. & Jrs.	686	850	13.4	12.6	4.56[b]
Bone & Cowling, U.S. W.Va.					
Wesleyan Col.	86	90	13.5	11.8	3.00[b]
Wolfe, U. S., Geneseo College	98	260	13.9	12.9	2.29[a]
Ohkubo, Japanese College Students	640	590	11.1	10.3	3.79[b]
Berkowitz, Thai College Students	329	196	11.1	9.9	3.21[b]

[a]p < .05.
[b]p < .01.

The Japanese and Thai students did not differ from each other, but both were lower on the SS General Scale than American college students. Although these differences could be interpreted as evidence of cultural differences in sensation seeking, Eastern cultures being presumably more inner looking and contemplative, we must remember that the items may suffer some change of meaning in translation.

Sex Differences

Every group in Table 12–1 except Farley and Cox's high school students showed a significant sex difference with males scoring higher in sensation seeking. The lack of significance in Farley and Cox's sample is primarily due to the size of their N's since the same differences were significant in the larger samples and the standard deviation is about the same in all samples (3.4 to 3.8).

Table 12–2 shows the sex differences on all the SS scales in form IV in the freshman and sophomore and junior samples at the University of Delaware. Significant differences are found on all scales, but the largest differences are found on the Disinhibition scale. This is probably a function of the difference in male and female attitudes toward casual or impersonal sex. Zuckerman, Tushup, and Finner (1976) found equally large differences between male and female undergraduates in attitudes toward heterosexual experience, with females setting more criteria for the social and emotional relationship as a prerequisite to sexual behavior. These differences in attitude did not affect female levels of sexual experience, but they did affect the number of partners with whom women had that experience.

Relationships with Education, Social Class, and Race

Kish and Busse (1968) found mean SSS General scores of 9.8, 11.0, and 13.0 for adult male subjects with grade school, high school, and college educations respectively. Only the difference between grade school and college education groups was significant. Farley and Farley's (1967) sample, composed primarily of English apprentices (working class), had a mean SSS score almost identical to that of college students at Adelphi University (Zuckerman et al., 1964), but somewhat lower than the mean obtained at the University of Delaware. Since these latter comparisons involve both social class and cultural differences, it is surprising that the means are so close.

Both Carrol and Zuckerman (1977) and English and Jones (1972) reported that black drug addicts score lower on the SSS than white addicts. Carrol found significant differences on every scale except Disinhibition. Most of the blacks were from lower socioeconomic groups, so it is not certain if this is a racial, socioeconomic, or a difference peculiar to drug addicts. Certainly a scale, such

Table 12-2. Means on SSS IV for Males and Females at University of Delaware; Sex Differences

	Entering Freshmen							Intro. Psych. Classes						
	Males N = 296		Females N = 280					Males N = 686		Females N = 850			
SS Scales	$\overline{X}$	SD	$\overline{X}$	SD	t			$\overline{X}$	SD	$\overline{X}$	SD	t
Gen	12.8	3.7	12.0	3.8	2.2[a]			13.4	3.6	12.6	3.8	4.6
TAS	10.6	2.7	9.8	3.0	3.4			11.1	2.6	9.9	3.0	8.6
ES	9.2	3.9	7.9	3.7	4.1			9.6	3.9	8.5	3.9	5.4
Dis	6.4	3.2	3.9	2.5	10.4			6.7	3.3	4.6	3.9	13.5
BS	7.7	3.2	6.8	2.9	3.4			7.9	3.1	7.3	3.2	3.2

[a]p less than .05; all other ts in table are significant below .001 level.

as the Thrill and Adventure Seeking one, which speaks of seeking thrills through sports such as scuba diving, sailing, and so on, might not be appropriate to the kind of thrill and adventure seeking that characterizes lower socioeconomic groups. The fact that no racial differences are found on the Disinhibition scale suggests that this type of sensation seeking is common to all classes in Western society.

Age Differences

In Postulate IIIB of the optimal level theory I have proposed (Zuckerman, 1969b) that the sensation-seeking trait increases with age until some time in adolescence and then falls with increasing age. This postulate is based on the assumption that sensation seeking is a function of the arousability of the CNS, and on the observations of curiosity and play in animals: "It also appears that the propensity for playful manipulation in chimpanzees, as apparently in man, reaches its maximum between infancy and adulthood" (Berlyne, 1960, p. 150). Kish (1966) also noted that the animal data on exploratory behavior showed an increase up to certain ages, usually adolescence, and then a decline with age.

Farley and Cox (1971) found no increase from ages 14 to 17 in their high school sample, although the data mentioned previously showed an increase between entering freshpersons and sophomores and juniors. The abruptness of the latter change suggests that it is owing to the influence of the change of environment from high school to college rather than to age alone. Considering the vocabulary level and content of the SSS it would probably not be feasible to use it below the age range tested by Farley, so that some other method would have to be used to test the SS increase part of the postulate.

A number of studies have correlated SSS scores with age. These are summarized in the SS manual and research report (Zuckerman, 1975). Within the limited age ranges of the younger college sample (17 to 21) and Carrol's (1977) drug addict sample (20 to 29), there is no correlation with age; but in older normal, prisoner, and patient samples with more extended age ranges, high negative correlations have been found between age and sensation seeking, ranging from $-.30$ to $-.64$. The highest negative correlations are found with Experience Seeking. These relationships make it essential that age be covaried in any comparisons between samples that differ in age. There is a great need for age group norms for the SSS so that older and younger subjects can be compared directly.

DEVELOPMENT OF A STATE SENSATION SEEKING SCALE

Before plunging into the validity literature on the trait SSS, I would like to describe the recent development of a new state SSS. The development of this measure opens up new possibilities for research and has allowed us to predict specific sensation-seeking behavior in two situations.

The distinction between traits, or relatively enduring dispositions, and states, or more time-delimited arousal of affects or motives, can be traced back to Murray (1938), although he was primarily concerned with devising trait measures. Zuckerman (1960) devised a trait and state measure for anxiety called the Affect Adjective Check List (AACL). Using the AACL in his first studies, Spielberger (1966) developed a trait–state theory of anxiety. More recently, Spielberger, Gorsuch, and Lushene (1970) developed their own State–Trait Anxiety Inventory (STAI).

Patrick, Zuckerman, and Masterson (1974), have suggested that the trait–state approach might be applied to other kinds of motive or need measures such as those contained in the Gough–Heilbrun (1965) Adjective Check List (ACL). Some of the need measures contained in this test (e.g., Change), as well as adjectives from other lists such as Nowlis' (1965) ACL, offered the possibility of developing a state measure of sensation seeking. Such a measure would allow us to measure the strength of sensation seeking at a given point in time rather than inferring it from a general trait measure. A former student of mine, Neary (1975), undertook this task.

The initial pool of 156 adjectives was drawn from the ACL (Gough & Heilbrun, 1965), the SSS trait form, the state form of the Zuckerman Inventory of Personal Reactions (Zuckerman, 1976), and the AACL anxiety scale (Zuckerman, 1960). The items from the anxiety scale were included on the assumption that anxiety might be a factor in sensation seeking (Kish, 1973). Using an empirical technique of item selection employed by Spielberger et al. (1970), subjects were asked to imagine being in certain situations that might arouse sensation-seeking feelings and to describe how they would feel by responding to the 156 items of the checklist. The procedure was repeated for each of the situations.

Three of the four hypothetical situations used were drawn from the items of the trait SSS. The four situations included a hypnosis experience, a parachute jumping situation, an experimental drug-taking situation, and a boring lecture situation (the last to assess boredom susceptibility). Item analyses were carried out contrasting the reactions of high and low trait sensation seekers to the hypothetical situations. Adjectives checked significantly more often by high or low trait sensation seekers, for at least two of the situations and for both males and females, were retained for the next experimental form. The only items checked more frequently by the low sensation seekers were items from the AACL anxiety scale.

At this point we decided it would be better to keep the anxiety and sensation-seeking factors separate since these are probably two independent states that are only negatively correlated in certain types of risk situations. The separation of the factors was accomplished by a factor analysis.

The 15 adjectives selected as characteristic of the response of high trait sensation seekers were combined with the 21 items from the anxiety scales of the AACL in a new form. The new form used a rating scale of from 1 (not at all) to 5 (very much) for each item to provide more variance in scores.

The responses of a new sample of 293 students to the new form were correlated and factor analyzed using a principal components solution with a varimax rotation that maximized the orthogonality of the factors. A two-factor solution was used. The criterion for retention of an item was that it have a substantially greater loading on the factor it was supposed to measure than on the other factor.

All 15 of the adjectives that were in the original state sensation-seeking scale were found to load positively on the sensation-seeking factor. These items were interested, elated, adventurous, pleased, lucky, daring, enthusiastic, amused, imaginative, confident, zany, curious, cooperative, mischievous, and playful. The affect aroused in high sensation seekers by the hypothetical situations seems to be a mixture of elation and surgency. All are positive affect words. Some of the other adjectives from the original AACL anxiety scale were eliminated because they loaded higher on the sensation-seeking factor. The remaining adjectives constitute the shortened anxiety state scale. Items followed by a plus are scored in the positive direction, and items followed by a minus are scored in the negative direction for anxiety: afraid +, secure −, desperate +, steady −, upset +, contented −, nervous +, frightened +, tense +, shaky +, calm −, fearful +, terrified +, panicky +, and worried +.

The new test, which we call the Sensation Seeking and Anxiety States Test (SSAST), is shown in Appendix E. SSAST contains a 15-item state sensation seeking (SS) scale and a 15-item state anxiety (A) scale. The remaining six items are the items from the anxiety scale that did not meet the factor analysis criteria. The keyed items are indicated on the form with the scale to be scored and a plus or minus indicating the direction of scoring.

Reliabilities of the State Scales

Neary (1975) tested the reliability and validity of the new state scales in a study in which students were tested on baseline occasions a week apart and in which a subgroup took the SSAST on two other occasions: (1) while deciding if they would take a new "experimental" drug that "might produce hallucinations," and (2) while waiting to start a group hypnosis induction for which they had not specifically volunteered. The validity aspect of the study will be discussed later in this chapter.

The trait–state model I have proposed (Zuckerman, 1976) states that both trait and state tests should have high internal consistency but that state tests, in contrast to trait tests, should have low retest reliabilities. States are assumed to be fluctuating over time and influenced by immediate external conditions. The trait communality between states that defines individual differences should be expressed in low, but significant, correlations between states on different occasions (Patrick et al., 1974).

Table 12–3 shows the internal consistency and retest reliabilities of the SSAST SS and A scales. The reliability pattern is what is expected for state scales: high internal consistency and low, but significant, retest reliability. The trait scales of the SSS (Zuckerman, 1971; 1975) have been shown to have high internal and retest reliability as described earlier in this chapter.

Correlations between Trait and States

Another part of the Zuckerman (1976) trait–state model suggests that traits should show only low correlations with single states on any nonaroused occasion but higher correlations with the mean of states over a number of nonaroused occasions, and (again) higher correlations with the relevant state in an aroused condition. Table 12–4 shows correlations between the trait SSS General Scale and the SSAST SS and A state scales on baseline and experimental occasions in the Neary (1975) study. The mean of states is the mean on five weekly administered tests.

The results show low positive correlations between the trait SSS and state SSS but only insignificant correlations with the State A on the baseline-1 occasion. The correlations between the trait and mean of state SS scores are much higher and typical of correlations between similar concepts assessed by different methods. The correlations between the trait and state SS in the drug-taking condition are higher than on the baseline occasions, but this is not true for the hypnosis condition. Trait SS did not correlate with state anxiety except in the drug condition in which the negative correlations were significant for females and for the total group but not for males.

The results confirm the model, except for the failure of correlations between trait and state in the hypnosis condition. In contrast to the drug condition, the hypnosis condition did not elicit anxiety arousal; the lack of appraised risk may have resulted in the failure of high and low trait sensation seekers to behave differently.

RELATIONSHIPS BETWEEN SENSATION SEEKING AND OTHER TRAITS

When one comes up with a new "dimension of personality" there is some obligation to locate this dimension in the space already crowded by other test dimensions. What the psychometric world does not need is another trait measuring neuroticism–anxiety or extroversion. In the terms of Campbell and Fiske (1959), it is just as important to establish the "discriminant validity" of a test

Table 12-3. Internal Consistency and Retest Reliabilities[a] of State Sensation Seeking (SS) and Anxiety (A) Scales

	Internal Consistency				Retest Reliability			
	State SS Scale		State A Scale		State SS Scale		State A Scale	
	Males	Females	Males	Females	Males	Females	Males	Females
Week 1	.88	.87	.87	.92				
Wk. 1 vs. Wk. 2[c]					.48	.38	.39	.32
Drug Exp.	.93	.93	.93	.95				
Drug vs. Hyp. Exp.[d]					.48	.57	.48	.41
Hypnosis Exp.	.93	.91	.92	.92				

[a] all correlations significant, $p < .01$.
[b] based on interitem correlations.
[c] for entire class N males = 86, N females = 102.
[d] for experimental group only. N males = 55, N females = 58.

Source: Neary, 1975.

Table 12-4.   Predictions of SS and A States
from Trait SSS

	Trait SSS (General)		
	Male	Female	All
State SS-baseline 1	$.23^a$	$.39^b$	$.32^b$
State A-baseline 1	.17	−.17	−.05
x̄ baseline SS	$.50^b$	$.45^b$	$.48^b$
x̄ baseline A	.03	−.12	−.08
State SS (drug cond.)	$.44^b$	$.36^b$	$.41^b$
State A (drug cond.)	−.04	$-.37^b$	$-.25^b$
State SS (hyp. cond.)	.25	.15	$.21^a$
State A (hyp. cond.)	−.07	−.13	−.11

$^a p < .05.$
$^b p < .01.$
Source: Neary, 1975.

(what it is not) as the "convergent validity" (what it is or is like). Of course, major dimensions of personality have been marked out by pioneers like Eysenck (1953) and Cattell (1957), and more recently by Norman (1963). Even though there is some disagreement on the number of dimensions (3, 5, or 16) it is not difficult to organize more specific factors under broader factors in a hierarchical model using second-order factor analysis. However, it is possible to draw axes anywhere through the n dimensional space and attempt to define a dimension that may have been neglected by former test constructors. It is as if the coast lands and river banks of a new continent have been mapped while possibly more fertile hinterlands have gone unexplored.

The question of which are the "fundamental" dimensions of personality is unanswerable except in one sense. Rather than which dimension is more fundamental, one may ask the question of which trait dimensions yield the best relationships with behavior and general experience and which seem most closely related to the physiological genotypes that may underlie basic temperaments.

Freud and Jung focused attention on neuroticism–anxiety and introversion –extroversion, but "normal" dimensions such as Cattell's "Surgency" have been relatively neglected by trait researchers. Perhaps it is time to give the axes another spin.

The Manual for the SSS (Zuckerman, 1975) and my chapter (Zuckerman, 1974) give many tables of correlations between the SSS and other multivariate personality tests, and I will reproduce only a few in this chapter and summarize the rest. I believe we have reached the point where further correlations of the SSS with established tests is redundant since we now have a fairly good idea what the SSS measures in common with other trait tests.

Convergent Validity with Similar Scales

At the same time the SSS was developed (Zuckerman et al., 1964), Garlington and Shimona (1964) independently developed another test based on the same construct called the Change Seeker Index (CSI). Although not much research was done with the CSI, several authors (Acker & McReynolds, 1967; Looft & Baranowski, 1971; McReynolds, 1971) published studies of correlations between this test and the SSS form II. These correlations range from .62 to .68, indicating fairly good correspondence between the CSI and the General scale of the SSS.

Pearson (1970) developed a set of Novelty Experiencing Scales (NES) on a rational (a priori) rather than factor analytic (empirical) basis. The four scales describe novelty experiencing through:

1. *External Sensation,* or active participation in physical activities.
2. *Internal Sensation,* or unusual dreams, fantasies, and feelings.
3. *External Cognitive,* or unusual cognitive processes focused on mechanical, crafts, or games problems.
4. *Internal Cognitive,* or unusual cognitive processes focused on explanatory principles.

In her first study Pearson (1970) found that the General SSS in form II correlated highly ($r = .68$) with the External Sensation scale but negligibly with the other three. Bone and Belcher (1974) correlated form IV of the SSS with the NES; their results are shown in Table 12–5.

The males showed a specific pattern of correlation between the SSS factor scales and the NES rational scales. The SS Thrill and Adventure Seeking scale was related to the NES External Sensation scale, the SS Experience Seeking was correlated specifically with the NES Internal Sensation scale, and the SS Disinhibition was related (negatively) to the External Cognitive scale.

The neat pattern of convergent and discriminant validity seen in males was not apparent in females. Although the NES External Sensation was most highly correlated with the SS Thrill and Adventure Seeking scale, it also correlated with the General Scale, the Experience Seeking Scale, and the Boredom Susceptibility Scale. The NES Internal Sensation scale correlated significantly with Experience Seeking, but it correlated just as highly with all the other SS scales. External Cognitive correlated only with the SS General scale, and Internal Cognition correlated with the General, Experience Seeking and Boredom Susceptibility scales. For females, the dimensions of the sensation seeking scale do not line up with the dimensions of the Novelty Experiencing Scale. Except for the high correlation in females between Thrill and Adventure Seeking and External Sensation, the two tests do not correlate highly enough to regard them as measures of the same constructs.

Table 12-5. Correlations[a] of SSS IV with Novelty Experiencing Scale (Pearson)

| | Pearson Novelty Experiencing Scales | | | | | | | |
| | Males (N = 56) | | | | Females (N = 65) | | | |
SS Scales	E-Sen	I-Sen	E-Cog	I-Cog	E-Sen	I-Sen	E-Cog	I-Cog
Gen	25	16	−15	−06	60^c	35^c	32^b	43^c
TAS	41^c	09	06	−02	68^c	35^c	14	20
ES	15	31^c	−10	02	42^c	35^c	21	26^b
Dis	10	−03	−35^b	−09	16	38^c	12	04
BS	14	02	−10	−03	30^b	35^c	14	34^c

[a] Decimals omitted.
[b] $p < .05$.
[c] $p < .01$.
Source: Bone and Belcher (1974).

Another similar construct is Murray's (1938) Need for Change. Both the SS and the Change constructs emphasize the need for variety of experience and the dislike of routine. Acker and McReynolds (1967), Pearson (1970), and Zuckerman (1975) correlated the SSS General scale with the Change scale of Jackson's Personality Research Form (1967) in samples of males and females. The six correlations ranged from .29 to .60; the median r was .46. Zuckerman and Link (1968) correlated the Need for Change in the Gough–Heilbrun (1965) ACL and in the Edwards (1959) PPS with the SS General scale and found correlations of .43 and .46 respectively. As with the measure of novelty experiencing, the measures of need for change have some communality with the SSS but the two are nowhere near redundant.

Discriminant Validity: Social Desirability (SD)

Because Edwards (1957) has shown SD to be a major confounding factor in personality questionnaires, a new test constructor feels constrained to demonstrate the lack of influence in his test. Farley (1967) factor analyzed the SSS items from form II along with the Edwards (1957) and the Crowne–Marlowe (1960) SD scales, and the Eysenck and Eysenck (1964) Lie scale and reported that no appreciable amount of variance in the SSS was accounted for by the social desirability factor.

Thorne (1971) correlated the SSS II with the Edwards (1957) SD scale and Wolfe (1971) correlated it with the Crowne–Marlowe SD scale. None of the correlations was significant in the former study, and although the correlation for males was significant in the latter study, it was only $-.185$ ($p < .05$).

Zuckerman et al. (1972) correlated the MMPI L and K scales, which may be considered measures of social desirability, with form IV of the SSS. Since only 1 of 20 correlations for males and females was significant, it seems that SD, as measured by these scales, plays no role in the SSS.

Farley and Hallbrich (1974) gave the SSS IV to 90 undergraduates asking 30 subjects to create the worst impression they could on the test, 30 to create the best impression they could, whereas the remaining subjects took the test under normal instructions that request an "honest appraisal of yourself." No differences were found between these groups on any of the scales, reinforcing the conclusion from the other studies that social desirability, or the desire to create a good impression, has little influence in responding to the SS.

Minnesota Multiphasic Personality Inventory (MMPI)

The MMPI (Hathaway & McKinley, 1951) is perhaps the most widely used objective test of psychopathology. It has been correlated with the SSS IV in normals (Zuckerman et al., 1972) and in schizophrenic psychiatric patients in Veterans Administration hospitals (Daitzman & Tumilty, 1972). The SSS II

General Scale has been correlated with the MMPI in normals (Zuckerman & Link, 1968), in male psychiatric offenders (Blackburn, 1969), in male and female felons (Thorne, 1971), and in male alcoholics (Kish & Busse, 1969). The MMPI scale most consistently correlated with all the SS scales is Hypomania (Ma), a measure of impulsivity, energy, and activity. Although the Ma scale was developed using a criterion group of clinical hypomanics, it is the most frequent peak in normal profiles and probably measures cyclothymic, or impulsive, extroverted tendencies. A significant correlation between Ma and the SSS General scale has been found in every clinical and prisoner sample except the alcoholic sample of Kish and Busse (1969).

Two other MMPI scales showing a general pattern of correlation with the SS scales in students are the F and Psychopathic Deviate (Pd) scale. The F-Scale is a measure of atypical responding to the test, and the Pd scale measures nonconformity to social mores and antisocial tendencies. The relation between the SSS and clinically diagnosed psychopathy will be examined in a later section. The Pd scale is most consistently correlated with the Experience Seeking and Disinhibition scales, which represent the more nonconforming forms of sensation seeking.

Experience Seeking was the only scale showing any consistent pattern of low positive correlation with neurotic (Hypochondriasis) or psychotic (Schizophrenia) MMPI scales in college students, but, interestingly enough, the correlations of ES with neurotic scales (Depression and Hysteria) were negative in hospitalized schizophrenics (Daitzman & Tumilty, 1972).

Psychological Screening Inventory (PSI)

Lanyon's (1970) PSI is a test developed as a short screening device for the major dimensions of psychopathology and normal personality. *Alienation* measures that which is characteristic of hospitalized schizophrenics; *Social Nonconformity* measures the asocial or impulsive tendencies found in prisoners; *Discomfort* measures neurotic tendencies; *Expression* is an extroversion scale; and *Defensiveness* measures the tendency to attempt to make a good impression on the test. Bone (1972) correlated the PSI and SSS IV in college student samples of males and females. The primary pattern of correlation was: (1) between Social Nonconformity and all SS scales in males and between Social Nonconformity and Experience Seeking, Disinhibition, and Boredom Susceptibility in both sexes; (2) between Expression and all SS scales in males, and between Expression and Thrill and Adventure Seeking in both males and females; (3) a limited pattern of low positive correlation between Discomfort and Experience Seeking in both sexes.

Eysenck Personality Inventory (EPI) and PEN Test

Eysenck has designed several tests to measure the basic personality dimensions of extroversion, neuroticism, and psychoticism. The SSS manual reports nine samples in which the General scale of the SSS II was correlated with the Extraversion (E) scale of the EPI. Eight of the nine correlations were significant, but the median correlation was only .29. This low pattern of correlation was typical of E correlations with the SSS IV in 12 other samples. In this latter group of samples the only scale of the SSS showing a consistent pattern of significant correlation (9 of 12 samples) with E was Disinhibition, and the median correlation with this scale was only .31.

Eysenck (1967) has suggested that sensation seeking is an aspect of extroversion. Apparently (as indicated by the studies cited above) a low but significant order of relationship does exist between the constructs, as defined by the EPI's E and SSS Disinhibition and General scales, but it is a *low* order of relationship accounting for only 10 percent of the variance in the two scales.

The second major dimension of Eysenck's test is neuroticism, or emotional stability–instability. In 10 samples, the greatest number of significant correlations between the Neuroticism scale and any of the five SS scales was two. Apparently there is no strong or consistent relationship between sensation seeking and neuroticism, a conclusion also reached in studies using the MMPI and PSI inventories.

Eysenck's third major dimension is Psychoticism. This dimension is assessed in his PEN test only. Only three samples, one female and two male undergraduate ones, have been used to examine the relationship with the SSS. The SS Experience Seeking scale correlated with psychoticism in one male sample, and the SS Boredom Susceptibility scale correlated with psychoticism in one male and one female sample. Eysenck (1971) has indicated that SS items tend to fall in the extroversion–psychoticism quadrant of his factor space, but it would seem that insufficient data exist at present to establish a relationship with psychoticism.

Sixteen Personality Factor Test (16 PF)

Cattell, Saunders, and Stice's (1950) 16 PF test is a questionnaire representing the outcome of many years of research on the factors Cattell considers to be the main dimensions of personality. Zuckerman et al. (1972) correlated the 16 PF with the SSS IV, using male and female undergraduates. Both males and females showed a similar pattern: *positive* correlations between the SSS and Dominance, Surgency, Adventurous, Bohemian, and Radicalism scales, and *negative* correlation with the Superego and Control scales. Gorman (1970) also correlated the two tests and, although the pattern of correlation was similar, most of his correlations were not significant because of his low Ns.

California Psychological Inventory (CPI)

Gough (1957) designed the CPI as a measure of ''folk'' traits or those traits people commonly use in describing one another. Kish (1971) reported correlations of the SS II General scale with the 18 scales of the CPI in a sample of 100 hospitalized male alcoholics. The SSS correlated positively and significantly with five of the six scales in the group called "Class I" by Gough. This group of scales was designed to measure poise, ascendance, and self-assurance in social relationships. Class II variables were designed to measure socialization, self-control, and good impression. The SSS correlated negatively and significantly with three of these scales. The SSS also correlated positively with scales of Flexibility and Masculinity.

As in the 16 PF, the pattern of correlation in the CPI suggests that sensation seeking is related to an impulsive type of extroversion, and the high sensation seeker is characterized by nonconformity, unconventionality, and little concern with social mores, responsibility, or self-control. Of course, another way of understanding the correlates of sensation seeking is by saying that the low sensation seeker is overly conforming, conventional, and controlled.

Tests of Murray's Needs

Murray's (1938) inventory of "needs," or traits, has served as a taxonomic guide for several objective measures of personality including Edwards' (1959) Personal Preference Schedule (PPS), Gough and Heilbrun's (1965) Adjective Check List (ACL), and Jackson's (1967) Personality Research Form (PRF). Zuckerman and Link (1968) correlated the SSS II General scale with the PPS and ACL in a group of 40 undergraduate and graduate males. In both tests, the SSS correlated *positively* with scales of Autonomy, Change, and Exhibitionism, and *negatively* with scales of Deference, Nurturance, Orderliness, and Affiliation.

Zuckerman (1975) correlated the PRF with the SSS IV in groups of male and female undergraduates, and Daitzman and Tumilty (1972) correlated these tests in a sample of male VA schizophrenics. The pattern of results in both groups was similar. The Harm Avoidance scale of PRF showed the highest *negative* correlations with SSS variables, particularly with the General and Thrill and Adventure Seeking scales. The reason for these high negative correlations is clear in view of Jackson's (1967) definition of a high scorer on Harm Avoidance: "Does *not* enjoy exciting activities, especially if danger is involved: avoids risk of bodily harm; seeks to maximize personal safety." (p. 7).

The Cognitive Structure scale showed consistent *negative* correlations with all the SS scales. A high scorer on the Cognitive Structure scales is described as one who "does not like ambiguity or uncertainty in information, wants all questions answered completely; desires to make decisions based upon definite knowledge, rather than upon guesses or probabilities" (p. 6).

The highest *positive* correlations in these two studies were between the SSS scales and the Change, Play, and Impulsivity scales of the PRF. The Change construct is defined as doing things just for fun, including games, sports, social activities, enjoyment of jokes, and having an easygoing attitude toward life. The highest correlations of Play are with the SS Disinhibition scale.

The Impulsivity scale correlated significantly with every SSS scale in all the samples and constituted the highest correlations in the VA group. Jackson has defined a high scorer on this scale as one who "tends to act on the 'spur of the moment' and without deliberation; gives vent readily to feelings and wishes, speaks freely; may be volatile in emotional expression" (p. 7).

Other patterns found were positive correlations of the SSS with the Autonomy scale and negative correlations with the Orderliness scale in the undergraduate groups, and positive correlations with Aggression, Exhibitionism, and Dominance scales, particularly in females.

Test of Emotional Styles (TES) and The Monitoring of Emotion

Allen and Hamsher (1974) developed a test of emotional styles. Allen (1974) correlated the three scales of the TES with the SSS IV. None of the correlations was significant in females. The TES orientation scale, a measure of the tendency to seek emotional experience, correlated positively and significantly with all the SS scales except Boredom Susceptibility. This finding tends to support the notion that sensation seeking has to do with the optimal level of arousal. The TES Expressiveness and Responsiveness scales, which are said to measure the frequency of situations in which emotions are expressed and the intensity with which they are expressed, correlated significantly with the Experience Seeking and Disinhibition scales only.

Gorman and Wessman (1974) actually measured emotions daily over a four-week period. A factor defined by the SSS and Pearson's (1970) External Sensation scale was strongly associated with high levels of positive emotion over the entire period during which emotions were assessed.

Internal-External Locus of Control (I–E)

Rotter (1966) designed the I–E scale to measure the extent to which persons regard locus of control of reinforcement to be internal (self-generated) or external (dependent on chance or others). The correlational results in eight samples are reported in the SSS Manual (Zuckerman, 1975). Disinhibition showed the most consistent relationship with I–E, correlating positively with a belief in external control in four of the eight samples, and four of the six male samples.

Experience Inventory (EI)

Fitzgerald (1966) developed the EI to measure the constructs "openness to experience" and "regression in the service of the ego." Zuckerman et al. (1972) correlated the EI and SSS IV, after excluding eight items from the EI that sounded like paraphrases of SSS items. The EI correlated significantly with all scales except Boredom Susceptibility in both undergraduate males and females.

As we might expect, the highest correlations ($r = .40$ and $r = .51$) were with the SSS Experience Seeking scale.

Personal Orientation Inventory (POI)

The POI is a test devised by Shostrom (1966) to assess various aspects of the construct of Self-Actualization. Zuckerman (1975) correlated the SSS and POI in an undergraduate sample. The POI scales most consistently and significantly correlated with the SSS in both males and females were Inner Directedness, Existentiality (flexibility in application of values), Spontaneity (freely expressing feelings behaviorally), Acceptance of Aggression (feelings of anger), and Capacity for Intimate Contact (warm interpersonal relationships). In males, the General, Thrill and Adventure Seeking, and Experience Seeking scales related most highly to the POI, whereas in females all SS scales related equally to the POI.

Anxiety Scales

As we saw in prior sections, the SSS correlates minimally with tests of neuroticism; such tests are known to correlate high enough with general anxiety trait measures so that they can be assumed to be measuring the same thing. It is not surprising therefore that studies by Bone, Montgomery, Sundstrom, Cowling, and Caleb (1972), McReynolds (1971), Zuckerman and Link (1968), and Zuckerman, Schultz, and Hopkins (1967) found no correlation between the SSS and the Taylor (1953) Manifest Anxiety Scale. Bone et al. (1972) also correlated the SSS with Sarason and Mandler's (1952) Test Anxiety Questionnaire, Cattell and Scheier's (1963) overt and covert IPAT anxiety scales, and Spielberger et al.'s (1970) State and Trait Anxiety Inventory (STAI). Only the trait scale of the STAI correlated significantly, but low ($r = -.23$), with the SSS.

Spielberger (1966) has noted that the kind of general anxiety scales listed above predict response to social situations involving threat to the ego, or failure, but cannot predict response to threats of pain or bodily harm. Since a high sensation seeker, particularly one of the Thrill and Adventure Seeking type, seems to relish activities where there is some minor threat of physical harm, we would expect the SSS to correlate with anxiety measures involving threat of pain rather than with general trait anxiety.

Segal (1973) correlated the SSS IV with Endler, Hunt, and Rosenstein's (1962) Stimulus–Response Inventory of Anxiousness. The three situations in this anxiety test correlating most consistently with the SSS were those described by Endler et al. (1962) as containing elements of personal danger from inanimate forces.

Kilpatrick, Sutker, and Smith (1976) used a number of anxiety measures of general and specific types and the SSS IV in a study of drug users and alcoholics in a VA hospital population. Besides the Spielberger et al. (1970) State–Trait

Anxiety Inventory, they used the Wolpe and Lang (1964) Fear Survey Schedule III, a test of specific fears grouped into categories. None of the SS scales correlated with the STAI scales. The General and Thrill and Adventure Seeking scales of the SSS both correlated negatively with fears of animals, fears of tissue damage, and classical phobias, but they did not correlate with social-interpersonal fears or fears of failure or loss of self-esteem. None of the other SSS scales correlated with any of the anxiety scales.

Mellstrom et al. (1976) correlated the SSS Thrill and Adventure Seeking scale with general trait measures, such as the Taylor MAS and the Spielberger STAI trait scale, and with inventories of specific fears, such as the Geer (1965) Fear Survey Schedule and the Zuckerman Inventory of Personal Reactions (1976). The SSS TAS scale was not highly correlated with the general trait anxiety measures but correlated negatively with the sum of specific fears on the GFSS and ZIPERS.

Although the SSS is not related to general neurotic, or ego-threat, anxiety, the Thrill and Adventure Seeking scale is negatively related to specific fears of physical harm or common phobias. The low sensation seeker tends to be harm avoidant and phobic. The lack of fear of harm in high sensation seekers is related to their tendency to volunteer for unusual experiments and to engage in risky occupations, as we will see in later sections.

SENSATION SEEKING AND THE SEARCH FOR NEW EXPERIENCE

Sex Experience

The sensation seeker is conceived of as a person who continually searches for novel experience in order to reach optimal levels of arousal. Although Freud felt that the aim of the sexual ''instinct'' is tension reduction, or orgasm, he did not explain why the building up of tension is pleasurable, and why one form of tension reduction, such as coitus, is preferred to another, such as masturbation. He regarded sensation seeking in the exteroceptive senses as displacements or sublimations of libidinal instincts localized in the genitals, mouth, and anus, as well as the general somesthetic senses of the body. If the aim of the sexual ''instinct'' is tension reduction, why does man seek such complicated variations in his sexual experience, both in partners and modes of expression?

I would suggest that Freud put the cart before the horse. The infant is born with a general sensation-seeking motive, and sex differentiates as a specific kind of sensation seeking from the more general need for stimulation from all the senses. The young infant seems to spend as much or more time playing with his fingers and toes as with his genitals. The infant explores with his eyes and ears, as well as with his mouth, and moves toward moderately novel stimulation rather than away from it.

Although there were no sexual items in form II of the SSS, a number of items indicating a need for sexual variety were included in form IV. Most of these items ended up in the Disinhibition scale. If sex is a specific motive, we would expect that the correlation between sexual experience and sensation seeking would be limited to the Disinhibition scale. We would also not expect to find correlations between sexual experiences and other kinds of experience seeking, such as drug experimentation.

Our first study of sex (Zuckerman, Neary, & Brustman, 1970) contrasted high and low scorers on the General SSS scale on a scale of sexual experience devised by Zuckerman (1973). The sex experience scale is a Guttman-type scale containing heterosexual activities starting with various forms of kissing, and moving on to forms of petting, genital stimulation, coitus in various positions, and oral-genital activities. Other scales were devised for homosexual activities and number of partners with whom activities were engaged. High sensation seekers of both sexes on the General SS scale (which contains no specifically sexual items) reported a greater variety of heterosexual activities with a greater number of partners than did the lows.

These findings were extended in new samples covering the entire distribution of SSS scores (Zuckerman et al., 1972; Zuckerman, Tushup, & Finner, 1976), enabling us to compute correlations between sex experience and SSS scores. Table 12–6 shows the correlations obtained between the SS scales and the sex experience scale in undergraduate samples. Sexual experience correlated with all the SS scales for the males in both samples, and the correlations with several of the SS scales were higher than were those with Disinhibition. Sexual experience correlated with three of the five SS scales in one female sample and four of the five in the other. The number of partners with whom the subjects had heterosexual intercourse also correlated with all the SS scales for the males and with the Experience Seeking and Disinhibition scales for the females. Homosexual and masturbation experience scales did not show much correlation with sensation seeking except for some low relationship with the Experience Seeking scale in males.

These results indicate that variety in heterosexual activity and partners is related to a broad sensation-seeking motive that goes beyond the specific sexual sensation seeking contained in some of the items in the Disinhibition scale.

Fisher (1973a) used the SSS II General scale in his study of sexual responsiveness in young married women. In all three samples in which it was used, the SSS correlated with masturbation. Masturbation was used by most of these young women as a supplement to their normal sexual outlet in coitus, rather than as a substitute for coitus. The SSS also correlated with self-ratings of sexual responsiveness in two of three samples, although it did not correlate with consistency in reaching orgasm. In the Zuckerman et al. (1976) study only the Experience Seeking scale correlated with orgasmic experience in females.

Table 12-6. Correlations between the SSS IV and Sexual Experience[a]

| | Zuckerman et al. 1972 | | Zuckerman et al. 1976 | | | | | | | |
| | Heterosexual Activities | | Heterosexual Activities | | Homosexual Activities | | N Het. Partners | | N Hom. Partners | |
SS Scales	Male	Female	Male	Female	Male	Female	Male	Female	Male	Female
Gen	51^c	15	39^c	29^b	15	10	40^c	27	11	00
TAS	44^c	16	42^c	35^c	06	15	47^c	20	01	-16
ES	37^b	32^b	45^c	37^c	23^b	16	35^c	28^b	21	17
Dis	33^b	43^c	39^c	33^c	20	-11	42^c	29^b	.11	-10
BS	36^b	29^c	23^b	20	-02	01	25^b	20	-04	02

[a] Decimals omitted. Ns: 1972 study M = 38, F = 60; 1974 study M = 82, F = 71.
[b] $p < .05$.
[c] $p < .01$.

Other data not in his book but reported by Fisher in a personal communication (1973b) include the findings that high sensation seeking women:

1. Preferred a high frequency of intercourse.
2. Maintained their interest in sex during pregnancy.
3. Believed that sexual freedom should be increased in society.
4. Frequently had multiple orgasms.
5. Had copious vaginal lubrication during intercourse.
6. Frequently slept in the nude.
7. Became sexually excited during a lab session.
8. Had a low number of sexual responses on the Holtzman inkblot test.

With the exception of the last finding, all the data suggest that the high sensation seeking woman is sexually hyperarousable. Fisher discreetly did not report data on extramarital activity, but our prediction is that a positive relationship would be found with sensation seeking. The data also support the experience of one of my former research assistants who used the SSS to select females he dated. He reported a high validity for the Disinhibition scale. He, himself, achieved the maximum score on this scale. As it turns out, he could have used any of several other scales as well.

Zuckerman et al. (1976) also included sexual attitude scales in their study. All the SS scales except Boredom Susceptibility correlated with permissive parental attitudes toward manifestations of sexuality in children and toward heterosexuality in adults. The high sensation seekers set less strict social and emotional relationship criteria for engaging in heterosexual activity. This last finding would account for the fact that high sensation seekers had experience with a greater number of partners. Experience Seeking and Disinhibition scales were correlated with an interest in viewing erotic films in both males and females.

Drug and Alcohol Experience

Although some popular theories of drug abuse and alcoholism suggest that these maladaptive habits are maintained by reduction of aversive conditions produced by physiological addiction, many drug abusers and alcoholics report that they simply crave the ''high'' euphoric feelings produced by the drug. The sensation-seeking aspects are clearer in the young drug experimenter, or ''garbage head,'' who tries any drug that comes along whether ''upper'' or ''downer'' or ''tripper.'' Drugs and alcohol provide quick means of changing one's level of arousal, of producing new kinds of experience (particularly by hallucinogens), and of disinhibiting the lower brain centers by dampening cortical inhibitory centers. It is the latter mechanism that accounts for the paradoxical feeling of being ''high'' on physiologically depressant drugs such as barbiturates or alcohol. Drugs and alcohol are ways of dealing with boredom, or a sameness of environment and work. The user of drugs is a nonconformist to the mores and laws that approve of alcohol but disapprove of other drugs. The drug user runs the risk of going to jail, at the maximum, and of incurring the wrath of parents and authorities, at the minimum. He also risks encountering adverse effects from the drugs, since he rarely knows the dosage or adulterants in the drugs he buys. I see drug usage as a form of sensation seeking with the aim of changing the level of arousal in order to experience novel feelings or euphoria.

The Experience Seeking scale contains two items referring to an interest in drugs, and the Disinhibition scale contains some items expressing an interest in social drinking. As with sexual experience, we except drug and alcohol experience to be related to other scales than the ones containing relevant items if the experience is truly based on a broad sensation-seeking motive.

Our first study (Zuckerman et al., 1970) used an undergraduate sample given a drug questionnaire. High sensation seekers, defined by the SS General scale, reported more use of drugs and alcohol than lows of both sexes. In our second study (Zuckerman et al., 1972) subjects from the entire range of sensation seeking were used, and the five SS scales were correlated with a score consisting of the number of drugs ever used. Another one-item scale established the typical weekly frequency of alcohol drinking. Table 12–7 shows the correlations obtained between variety of drug use, alcohol use, and the SS scales. Also shown in the table are the correlations between sex experience and use of drugs and alcohol.

Table 12–7.   Correlations between SSS IV and Use of Drugs and Alcohol

| | Experience Scales | | | |
| | Drugs | | Alcohol | |
SS Scales:	M	F	M	F
Gen	42^c	36^c	27	18
TAS	42^c	28^b	39^b	15
ES	47^c	55^c	10	26^b
Dis	08	43^c	47^c	43^c
BS	34^b	32^b	−09	12
Experience				
Sex	41^c	51^c	25	30^b
Drugs			−14	46^c

^{a} Decimals omitted, Males N = 38, Females N = 60.
$^b p < .05.$
$^c p < .01.$
Source: Zuckerman et al., 1972.

Variety of drug experience correlated significantly with every SS scale in males and females except Disinhibition in the males. Although the highest correlations were found with the Experience Seeking scale, they were not much higher than the correlations with the other scales. Alcohol use, on the other hand, was more specifically correlated with the Disinhibition scale, which contains drinking items, although there was some secondary correlation between alcohol use and the Thrill and Adventure Seeking scale in males and the Experience Seeking scale in females. Sex, drug, and alcohol experience were all intercorrelated in females. Sex and drug experience were correlated in males, but alcohol use did not correlate with either of the other two kinds of experience.

Experimentation with a variety of drugs seems to be a manifestation of a general sensation-seeking trait in college students. Apparently males do not use drugs for disinhibitory purposes whereas females do. Alcohol use seems to be a more specific type of sensation seeking, more closely tied to disinhibition. In the college males studied, alcohol use was not correlated with drug use, although it was for females.

In a later article (Zuckerman, 1972a) we examined the differences in drug use among low, medium, and high sensation seekers in the studies discussed above. In the case of every drug except barbiturates and tranquilizers, the high sensation-seeking group contained the greatest proportions of users. Significant differences among high, medium, and low SS subjects were found in the use of marijuana, hashish, amphetamines, and LSD. In other words, there seems to be some preference for psychedelic and stimulant drugs, rather than "downers" in high sensation seekers. Heroin use was very rare in this population. The use of cocaine (a stimulant) was limited to six subjects, all of whom were in the high sensation-seeking group.

The difference in sensation seeking between marijuana users and nonusers was not found in a second sample (Zuckerman, 1972a), which was composed of more juniors and seniors than the first sample (Zuckerman et al., 1970). The reason for the lack of difference in the older subjects seems to be that by the last years of college even low sensation seekers use marijuana, at least occasionally. Yesterday's sensation seeking can become tomorrow's social habit.

Brill, Crumpton, and Grayson (1971) compared marijuana nonusers, one-time users, and groups ranging in use from less than once a month to every day. These subjects, consisting of 18- and 19-year-old freshpersons and sophomores at UCLA, were fairly equivalent to our younger sample. The groups were compared on the SSS II General scale and on the Psychopathic Deviate (Pd), Manifest Anxiety, and Ego Strength scales from the MMPI. The only scales significantly differentiating the groups were the SSS and Pd scales.

Pursuing the suggestion of a relationship between sensation seeking and choice of drugs, Murtaugh (1971) compared three groups of subjects from a male prison population. Using a drug history to classify the prisoners, he formed a suppressant drug group (men who had used mainly heroin and opiate derivatives), a stimulant drug group (men who had used mainly amphetamine), and a nonuser group (men who had never used anything but alcohol or marijuana). The groups were matched for age, education, and I.Q. The stimulant users had significantly higher SS General scores than nonusers, and the suppressant drug users had significantly lower scores than nonusers. The results suggest that drugs are chosen in terms of optimal level of arousal; high sensation seekers prefer a high level of arousal and low sensation seekers prefer a low level.

Carrol and Zuckerman (1977) took the hypothesis a step further. Since most drug users have a mixed history of drug use, they used an index consisting of the proportionate time of the total drug history during which drug abusers were using drugs in three classes: stimulants, depressants, and hallucinogens. The subjects were male residents of three inpatient drug rehabilitation centers in the Wilmington, Delaware area. All were between 20 and 29 years of age and currently drug free. Age, education, race, and I.Q. were all controlled through partial correlation methods.

The results showed a low but significant relationship between the indices of drug preference and the SSS. Depressant drug use correlated negatively with Experience Seeking, stimulant and hallucinogenic drug use correlated positively with Disinhibition, and stimulant use also correlated positively with Boredom Susceptibility. Intelligence correlated negatively with depressant drug use and positively with stimulant drug use, suggesting that cognitive ability may also be related to optimal level of arousal and therefore to drug preference. Stimulants keep the brain in an aroused state and are therefore better for cognitive activity than depressants.

A recent study by Platt (1975) is not compatible with the hypothesis that heroin users are relatively low on sensation seeking. Comparing heroin addicts and nonaddicts, all of whom were admitted to a youth correction center, and covarying several variables including age and I.Q, Platt found that the heroin addicts scored significantly higher on the General and Experience Seeking subscales of the SSS.

In all the inpatient studies described above, alcohol was not considered a drug or directly compared to drug use of other types. Actually, alcohol is the first drug used by most drug abusers, and many return to it after they give up other types of drugs. Kilpatrick, et al. (1976) compared regular drug users (mostly polydrug users), problem drinkers (mostly alcoholics), occasional drug and alcohol users (the modal group in this population), and nonusers in a VA medical hospital population. The groups were not different in age. Although occasional users were significantly higher than nonusers on every SS scale, the problem drinkers were higher than the occasional users on the Boredom Susceptibility scale only. The drug users were higher than the problem drinkers and all other groups on every SS scale except Boredom Susceptibility.

Overall, the results suggest that heavy drug use is related to a general sensation-seeking trait but that heavy drinkers cannot be characterized as high general sensation seekers. Previously, Brownfield (1966) had reported that hospitalized alcoholics scored lower than normal controls on an overall SS score, but his controls differed in age and education from his alcoholics. Kish (1970a) found no differences between alcoholic patients and others, and Pare (1973) found no differences between VA alcoholic patients and hospital employees after age differences were covaried. These studies underline the importance of controlling age in any comparisons using the SSS.

Why should drug use but not alcohol use be related to general sensation seeking? One distinction is that drugs are illegal but alcohol is not. To use drugs heavily means involvement in a high-risk criminal game. Many former drug users candidly admit that the sensation-seeking activities involved in getting the drugs were a part of the excitement that added to the satisfaction of their former lives. Making drugs legal would probably reduce this sensation-seeking gratification. Prior to the laws passed in the 1920s making opiates illegal, the main users were respectable middle class women, probably low sensation seekers.

Cigarette Smoking

Cigarette smoking is a milder drug habit but one with serious long-term consequences. If sensation seeking is involved in the need for cigarettes, then knowledge of the cancer risk may not be a deterrent and may conceivably add to the appeal of the activity. Schubert (1964) first hypothesized that cigarette smoking may be related to a trait he called "arousal seeking." Although nicotine is a stimulant and smoking elevates heart rate, smoking sometimes has a paradoxical relaxing effect. The relaxation one gets from a cigarette when one is fatigued and trying to sustain an optimal level of arousal for work or social activity is a good example of the optimal level concept.

Zuckerman (1974) compared 26 regular smokers with the SSS norm group (which also includes regular smokers and therefore provides a conservative comparison). The smokers of both sexes were significantly higher than the norm group on the General SS scale and tended to be higher on Boredom Susceptibility as well. Male smokers were also higher on Experience Seeking and Disinhibition, and female smokers were higher on Thrill and Adventure Seeking. Daitzman and Tumilty (1972) also found correlations between smoking and Thrill and Adventure Seeking and Experience Seeking scales in their VA psychiatric patients. The data appear to support Schubert's hypothesis that the smoker is at least in part an "arousal seeker."

Food Preferences

The Food Preference Inventory (FPI) is supposed to measure "oral passivity," as expressed in food preferences. Actually, it measures the preference for bland, sweet, and soft foods, as opposed to a preference for spicy, sour, and crunchy foods. Both Kish and Donnenwerth (1972) and Buchsbaum and Murphy (1974) correlated the SSS General scale with the FPI and found significant negative correlations. Although this could be interpreted in the sense of the FPI construct (i.e., low sensation seekers are oral-passive types), it would probably be more correct to say that high sensation seekers prefer spicy, sour, and crunchy foods because they provide more gustatory stimulation.

SENSATION SEEKING AND RISK TAKING

The fact that some men seek out risky experiences that others avoid has always puzzled theorists operating within a drive reduction theory and has led some analysts to postulate such dubious concepts as "counterphobic" tendencies, "unconscious need for punishment," or the "unconscious equation of fear and sexual excitement." The tendency to gamble and take risks seems to be endemic to our species, and some men never need to be forced to go to war.

Gambling

Gambling is a minor form of risk taking since the usual wager is only money. But if the gambler is an "arousal seeker" whose thrill is the risk and the building up of arousal prior to the outcome, we would expect him to bet larger sums at longer odds.

Waters and Kirk (1968), using undergraduate volunteers, examined the relationship between the General SSS and preferred odds in betting on the outcome of the draw of a card. In three experiments, significant correlations were found between the SSS and the proportions of subjects' bets made at the highest risk options (or the longest odds).

Kuhlman (1975) attempted to relate sensation seeking to the gambling behavior of undergraduate male students in a simulated casino set up in a classroom at the University of Delaware. The students were not actually gambling with their own money (although there was a financial incentive), and therefore the risk element was not great. Two kinds of responses were examined: the responses to hypothetical gambles in a questionnaire and actual responses when betting scrip money at three games—blackjack ("21"), roulette, and craps. Only the Disinhibition scale of the SSS showed any kind of consistent relationship with betting behavior, correlating significantly with average bet size in both the hypothetical situation and the blackjack game. The high disinhibitor tends to be a big bettor. The SSS was the only personality scale used that correlated with betting behavior.

Physical Risk Taking

Hymbaugh and Garrett (1974) gave the SSS II to 21 skydivers and 21 controls matched for age, sex, and socioeconomic status. The skydivers were significantly higher on the General scale, as expected. The mean difference between groups was eight points, therefore the group difference could not be accounted for by the single SSS item that indicates a desire to try parachuting.

Kusyszyn, Steinberg, and Elliot (1973) compared a heterogeneous group of risk takers, including firemen, riot squad police (volunteers), race car drivers, parachutists, and snowmobilers, with a control group composed of civil servants and college students. The risk-taking group scored significantly higher than the control group on the General and Thrill and Adventure Seeking scales.

Levin and Brown (1975) compared the SS scores of a group of patrolmen and sheriff's deputies with a group of jailors. Levin (1974) reported comparisons made without age correction showing that the patrolmen scored significantly higher on Thrill and Adventure Seeking and the General scale. The published article reports that, in groups matched for age, the patrolmen scored lower on Boredom Susceptibility but does not report whether the General and TAS scores were still significantly higher in the age-controlled samples.

Bacon (1974) examined SSS IV differences among three groups: (1) a volunteer group of divers who engaged in risky underwater rescue and salvage work with no monetary compensation, (2) members of a volunteer fire department who also took risks without being paid for it, (3) students at an institute of technology. The student control group (3) was matched with the other two groups in age and socioeconomic background. This study, carried out by an undergraduate student at Widener College, provides a good comparison of risk takers with others because the risky activities were not part of the paid vocations of the participants and thus represented more "pure" risk taking.

Table 12–8 shows the mean scores in the three groups and the "t" tests between them. Both the divers and the firemen were significantly higher than the students on the General, Disinhibition, and Boredom Susceptibility scales. The divers, but not the firemen, were significantly higher than the students on Thrill and Adventure Seeking. Neither experimental group was higher than the students on Experience Seeking.

Irey (1974) compared professional and paraprofessional volunteers working in crisis intervention centers with professionals working in more traditional academic and clinical roles. The crisis intervention workers scored significantly higher on all the SS scales. Traditional physicians were a particularly low-scoring group.

The final study concerns a faddish kind of risk taking that swept through the United States for a brief period in the spring of 1974, namely, "streaking." For the benefit of future readers who may not remember, "streaking" consisted of

Table 12-8.   Means and Differences between Means (t's)
of Risk Taking and Control Groups

SS Scales	Means			t's	
	Divers	Firemen	Students (Controls)	Divers vs. Students	Firemen vs. Students
Gen	15.2	16.6	13.2	2.56^a	5.15^b
TAS	11.7	10.5	9.7	3.27^b	1.37
ES	10.3	12.7	11.4	1.50	1.56
Dis	10.2	8.8	6.4	5.67^b	4.13^b
BS	8.1	10.0	6.3	4.73^b	6.49^b

$^a p < .05.$
$^b p < .01.$
Source: Bacon, 1974.

taking off one's clothes and running (or walking, or bicycling, etc.) through a public place. Although most streakers ran little risk, beyond catching a cold, some were arrested and exposed (sic). Bone (1974) asked 90 psychology students to respond to the following five-point scale: 1 = have no desire to streak; 2 = have thought of streaking but probably would not; 3 = have thought of streaking and probably will in the future; 4 = have streaked before. The means on the scale were 3 for males and 2 for females. The correlation between the "streaking" scale and the SS scales are given in Table 12–9.

The streaking scale correlated significantly with all the SS scales except Experience Seeking. The highest correlations were with the General and Thrill and Adventure Seeking scales. Although many explanations were offered for the streaking phenomenon, the following quotation from the *New York Times* of March 10, 1974, illustrates the arousal and sensation seeking reinforcements of the activity.

Table 12-9.   Correlation between SSS IV and the
"Streaking" Scale

SS Scales	Streaking Desire, Intent, & Experience	
	Males (N = 55)	Females (N = 35)
Gen	.47^b	.47^b
TAS	.47^b	.39^b
ES	.24	.20
Dis	.28^a	.28^a
BS	.33^a	.37^a

$^a p < .05.$
$^b p < .01.$
Source: Bone, 1974.

Like other participants they discovered the heady exhilaration that is said to accompany streaking; first the sense of daring, then the nervous anticipation as you undress, the last fleeting moment of fear before you start, the wet grass underfoot, the pounding heart during the dash, the smiles of spectators flashing by, the wind brushing against your cheeks and the warm sense of accomplishment as you dress—uncaptured—at your goal.

VOLUNTEERING FOR EXPERIMENTS AND UNUSUAL ACTIVITIES

During my period at Albert Einstein Medical Center in Philadelphia, we conducted experiments in sensory deprivation and used hypnosis to study emotions. We obtained our volunteers by placing advertisements in student newspapers in the Philadelphia area. Even though we offered payment, it struck us that the volunteers arriving for these studies did not look like a random sample of the student population. Even for that period of the 1960s, when long hair and unusual modes of dress were on the increase, we seemed to get more than the usual number of odd-appearing individuals who often carried motorcycle helmets. We decided to investigate our subject selection, so Zuckerman, Schultz, and Hopkins (1967) gave the SSS II to subjects at three universities and afterward asked if they would volunteer for the two types of experiments we were doing: sensory deprivation and hypnosis.

Both male and female undergraduates who volunteered for hypnosis experiments were found to be higher on the SS General scale than nonvolunteers. The same differences were found for sensory deprivation volunteers except that the differences were short of significance for one group of male subjects.

Bone, Cowling, and Choban (1974a) replicated and extended the Zuckerman et al. (1967) study by correlating the SSS IV with self-rated willingness to engage in a variety of experiments, including hypnosis and sensory deprivation experiments, but also including less unusual experiments. Table 12–10 shows their results.

Males high on the General SSS tended to volunteer for the more unusual experiments including sensory deprivation, ESP, hypnosis, and drug studies but not for learning studies, social psychology experiments, or sleep research. Females high in general sensation seeking volunteered for hypnosis and drug research and also for sleep research.

Thrill and Adventure Seeking was not generally related to volunteering for males, nor were there many other significant subscale correlations for males. For females, however, the Disinhibition, Boredom Susceptibility, and Experience Seeking scales were most related to volunteering, particularly for ESP, hypnosis, and drug experiments.

One winter session at the University of Delaware a number of unusual projects were run by members of the faculty including: (1) a gambling group in which

Table 12-10.   Correlations between the Sensation-Seeking General
Scale and Willingness to Volunteer for Experiments

	Correlations SSS vs. Volunteering	
Type of Experiment	Males	Females
Learning Studies	.00	.09
Social Psychology	.19	.07
Sleep Research	.23	$.32^a$
Sensory Deprivation	$.38^b$	.20
ESP	$.26^a$	.19
Hypnosis	$.40^b$	$.35^a$
Drug Research	$.31^a$	$.40^b$

$^a p < .05.$
$^b p < .01.$
Source: Bone, Cowling, and Choban, 1974a.

participants could learn principles of probability and test them in an improvised gambling casino with contests in roulette, poker, blackjack, and craps; (2) a sensitivity training group with training exercises of the verbal and nonverbal types; (3) an alpha training group for those who wished to learn to control their brain waves in order to produce altered states of consciousness, (4) a group for smokers who wanted to quit smoking through the use of an aversive conditioning technique. All participants in these projects were given the SSS IV. The results are described in more detail in the SSS manual (Zuckerman 1975). One characteristic of male and female volunteers for most of the groups was their higher scores (compared to the SSS norm group) on the Experience Seeking scale. Both male and female volunteers for gambling were also higher on Disinhibition. Boredom Susceptibility was higher in males and females volunteering for Alpha training. Female volunteers for gambling, T-groups, and alpha training were significantly higher on the General SS scale, but only the male volunteers for the smoking group were higher on this scale (which may be a function of the fact that heavy smokers generally are higher on this scale).

Myers and Eisner (1974) carried out a study on groups from a community college who were asked to volunteer for free courses in either karate or transcendental meditation (TM). About a third of their initial subject pool volunteered for each of the activities. Beyond the comparisons of volunteers and nonvolunteers, the authors compared those who showed up for training versus the no shows, the quitters versus the stayers in the activity, and frequent versus infrequent meditators in the TM group.

No differences were found between volunteers and nonvolunteers for karate training. However, volunteers for TM were significantly higher than nonvolunteers on the General, Experience Seeking, and Boredom Susceptibility scales. Although high sensation seekers did tend to volunteer for TM, they were also the most likely not to show up for training, to quit before finishing the course, and to be infrequent meditators. Although high sensation seekers seem drawn to TM as a novel kind of cognitive experience, they do not follow through, or do not seem to find what they are looking for in it. Considering the monotonous nature of the activity, their reactions are not unexpected.

Sensation seekers are prone to volunteer for unusual kinds of experiments that promise new kinds of cognitive or sensory experience. Experience Seekers seem particularly drawn to unusual training activities, but the search for new experience does not seem to be sustained if the new experiences are not immediately forthcoming. The Boredom Susceptibility aspect of sensation seeking seems to reassert itself and sensation seekers "split." This sequence can be seen in the sensory deprivation experiments that will be described in a subsequent section.

PREDICTION OF RESPONSES TO SELECTED SITUATIONS

Hypnotizability

As noted above, the SS scale predicts volunteering for hypnosis experiments. Since persons who are eager to be hypnotized usually prove to be good hypnotic subjects, we would expect the trait of sensation seeking to predict hypnotizability. The high sensation seeker is open to new experiences (Zuckerman et al., 1972), which is a trait associated with hypnotizability (Hilgard, 1965). However, as Barber (1964) has pointed out, hypnotizability may be in large part related to attitudes and sets generated by the immediate situation rather than by any general personality trait. Zuckerman, Persky, and Link (1967) found that states of hostility and depression, measured just prior to hypnosis, predicted subsequent hypnotizability whereas trait measures of the same affects were unable to do so. The results suggest that Barber's viewpoint is correct and that only state measures will predict hypnotizability.

Zuckerman et al. (1972) attempted to predict hypnotizability using the trait SSS. Significant positive correlations in one sample were undone by significant negative correlations in the other. This kind of result is familiar in the long history of personality–hypnosis research in which significant results usually fail to replicate in subsequent samples.

Neary (1975) applied his newly developed state measure of sensation seeking (which also measures state anxiety) to the prediction of hypnotizability. As in the Zuckerman et al. (1972) study, a trait measure did not predict hypnotic suscepti-bility. However, the state measure of sensation seeking, taken just prior to hypnosis, correlated significantly with hypnotizability in males ($r = .28, p < .01$), females ($r = .46, p < .01$), and the total sample ($r = .37, p < .01$). This finding is one of many studies (Zuckerman, 1976) showing superiority of concurrent state measures to trait measures in the prediction of specific responses to specific situations.

Drug Taking

The SSS has shown significant correlations with overall drug experience. However, taking a drug in a specific situation may not be as readily predictable.

Neary (1975) tested both trait and state sensation seeking as predictors of the decision to take or not to take a new drug. Subjects who reported for an experiment were told that they would be asked to take a pill (shown to them) that could "produce some strange effects, possibly hallucinations." Before being allowed to ask questions they were given the SSS and the state sensation seeking and anxiety test. As soon as they filled out the tests, they were told they could decline to take the drug or agree to take it. The trait and state measures were correlated with their decision using point biserial correlations. The trait measure did not correlate with the decision to take the drug. The state SS measure correlated positively with the decision in males ($r = .28, p < .05$), females ($r = .26, p < .05$), and the total group ($r = .30, p < .01$). The state anxiety measure correlated negatively with the decision in males ($r - .33, p < .05$), females ($r = - .33, p < .05$), and the total group ($r = - .36, p < .01$). Whereas hypnotizability was predictable from the single factor of state sensation seeking, the decision to take a hallucinogenic drug was related to both state sensation seeking and state anxiety.

Fear Responses in Phobic Situations

Mellstrom et al. (1976) used the SSS Thrill and Adventure Seeking scale along with various general and specific trait anxiety scales to predict responses in three types of potentially phobic situations: looking down from an open balcony at a great height, exposure to a live snake, and temporary isolation in total darkness. Four types of fear measures were used in each situation (anxiety state, fear thermometer, observers ratings, and behavioral indices. The SSS TAS scale correlated negatively and significantly ($p < .01$) with behavioral and self-report indices of fear in the situation in 75 percent of the comparisons (4 in each situation, or 12 in all), in contrast to significant positive correlations of a composite score based on the general anxiety trait measures in 25 percent of the comparisons. The specific anxiety trait measures were even more successful, predicting the response measures in 92 percent of the comparisons. The findings indicate that the SSS TAS scale can predict phobic responses in specific situations with an effectiveness exceeding that of general trait anxiety based on a composite variable made up of the Taylor MAS, the Spielberger STAI scale, and the Eysenck Neuroticism scale. Persons low on the SSS TAS tend to be phobic in these situations, refusing to move into them, terminating the situation quickly, manifesting observable fear, and reporting considerable anxiety.

Responses to Sensory Deprivation and Confinement

The studies using the SSS in sensory deprivation experiments have been described in greater detail in a previous chapter (Zuckerman, 1974) of another book. It will be recalled that the SSS II was designed as a possible predictor of stress response to sensory deprivation. We were surprised to find that the volunteers for our sensory deprivation experiments were high sensation seekers (Zuckerman et al., 1967). The situation seemed to attract sensation seekers who expected to experience unusual cognitive and hallucinatory effects and regarded the experience as a challenge. In our first study (Zuckerman, Persky, Hopkins, Murtaugh, Basu, & Schilling, 1966), the highest scorers on the SSS either terminated the experiment prematurely or showed great restlessness (measured body movement) in both the sensory deprivation and a boring social isolation situation. However, the SSS General scale did not correlate with any of the self-report measures of stress response to these confinement situations.

Similarly, in the second study (Zuckerman, Persky, Link, & Basu, 1968) the SSS did not predict self-report stress measures in the sensory deprivation or social isolation situations. In a third situation, involving confinement with another person with varied visual and auditory stimulation available, the SSS correlated negatively with stress measures, that is, low scorers experienced stress whereas high scorers adapted well. This situation of close confinement with a stranger may have been overstimulation for low sensation seekers.

Zubek (1968) found that high scorers on the SSS General scale were more likely to quit an immobilization experiment (not sensory deprivation) than were those with low SS scores. In subsequent studies of sensory deprivation the SSS failed to predict endurance. Myers (1967) also found no relation between the SSS and endurance in sensory deprivation in his earlier work, but in a later study he found a curious curvilinear relationship with reactions to sensory deprivation (1972).

In the 1972 study, Myers addressed himself specifically to the personality prediction of responses of 64 Navy volunteers to seven days of sensory deprivation. He used an extensive battery of tests, selected from prior research findings, including the SSS II. There were four stages of endurance used as criteria: (1) early quitters who quit within 2 days; (2) late quitters who quit between two and seven days; (3) one-time, seven-day subjects who stayed to the end but would not revolunteer for future sensory deprivation studies; (4) seven-day subjects who revolunteered for future sensory deprivation studies. There were significant differences between the groups. The means on the SS General scale were as follows: (1) early quitters 15.6; (2) late quitters 13.1; (3) one-time seven-day completers 14.1; (4) seven-day revolunteers 18.8. Most of the difference was produced by the high sensation-seeking scores of the seven-day revolunteers. The next highest group was the early quitters. Apparently, many high sensation seekers find some interesting kinds of experience in a long sensory deprivation experiment. Obviously, external stimulation was not rewarding but, rather, certain kinds of cognitive or internal imagery experiences were. These results show clearly that sensation seeking cannot be identified simply with the need for exteroceptive stimulation. This may be why we had such difficulty in the next group of experiments to be described.

In one of our early sensory deprivation experiments (Zuckerman & Haber, 1965) we found that subjects who showed a high electrodermal reaction (increase in skin conductance) to one sensory deprivation experience showed a large response for simple visual and auditory stimulation in a second sensory deprivation experiment. If bar pressing for stimulation could be conceived of as a measure of stimulation seeking, it seemed plausible that our SSS scale would predict such responding. Therefore, Zuckerman and Hopkins (1965) subjected high and low scorers on the SSS General scale to six hours of sensory deprivation followed by a one-hour period in which they could press a button to see slides or listen to music. Neither the number of slides viewed, the rate of slide viewing, nor the amount of music listened to differentiated high and low SSS subjects. In retrospect, perhaps we should not have shifted from meaningless to meaningful stimulation.

Further failures to find a relation between the SSS and the stimulation-seeking response in sensory deprivation situations have appeared in the literature. Smith and Myers (1966) found no prediction of auditory stimulation seeking. Kish and Busse (1969) and Landon and Suedfeld (1969) found no correlation with visual stimulation seeking. Hocking and Robertson (1969) gave their subjects a choice of button pressing for visual, auditory, or kinesthetic (movement on or off the bed in the experimental room) stimulation. Low SSS scorers responded more for visual stimulation whereas high scorers exhibited a preference for kinesthetic stimulation. This last finding suggests that restriction of movement might be the most stressful part of the sensory deprivation experience for high sensation seekers. Restless movement was the most characteristic response to sensory deprivation of high sensation seekers in Zuckerman et al.'s 1966 experiment, and it was in a body immobilization study that Zubek (1968) found the SSS predicting quitting.

Lambert and Levy (1972) carried out a study that was a more direct followup of the Zuckerman and Haber (1965) experiment mentioned above, especially in regard to the crucial point of letting subjects respond from the time that they were put into isolation. A significant interaction was found between sensation seeking and time in sensory deprivation. During the first hour the high and low sensation seekers did not differ much in rate of responding but, as time in the experiment increased, the high sensation seekers increased their rate of responding more than did the lows. Skin conductance was related to rate of response (as could be predicted from the Zuckerman and Haber study) but not to the sensation-seeking trait.

It appears from the studies outlined above that when high sensation seekers have no external stimulus-seeking option in the first hours of sensory deprivation, they find other, mostly internal, ways (cognition, imagery, movement) to stimulate themselves so that when external stimulation is finally offered, they do not utilize it more than low sensation seekers. However, if external stimulation is provided from the outset, high sensation seekers gradually come to rely on the external stimulation and finally exceed the lows in response.

Leadership Behavior in Social Groups

Ozeran (1973) related the SSS to behavior in leaderless, task-oriented groups. High SSS subjects more frequently began conversations, spoke more, and tended to be selected more often as leaders of the group by other group members. These findings are consistent with the correlations between the SSS and traits of Dominance and Surgency noted earlier.

Responses of Delinquents and Addicts to Confinement

Farley and Farley (1972) used the SSS II to study a group of incarcerated female delinquents ranging in age from 14 to 17. High scorers on the General SSS made more escape attempts, were punished more often for disobeying supervisors, and engaged in fighting more than low scorers. Farley (1973) has reported that similar results were found with incarcerated male delinquents. English and Jones (1972) found that narcotic addicts "eloping" from a rehabilitation center were higher on the SSS than stayers. At our rehabilitation center in Wilmington we found no relation between quitting and SSS scores, although high scorers on the SSS were more likely to return to drugs and crime after leaving the center.

PERCEPTUAL STYLES AND PREFERENCES

Field Dependence

In the first article on the SSS (Zuckerman et al., 1964) it was postulated that high sensation seekers should be field independent and lows should be field dependent. It was argued that high sensation seekers find states of high arousal more palatable than do lows, and might therefore be considered "tuned in" to their internal sensations more than to the external field.

Zuckerman et al. (1964) found the predicted relationship in males but not in females, using Thurstone's form of the Embedded Figures Test. Subsequently, Zuckerman and Link (1968) found significant correlations with Witkin's Embedded Figures Test and with the Rod and Frame Test. However, Bone and Choban (1972) failed to find a significant relationship between the SSS and the Rod and Frame test, and Buchsbaum and Murphy (1974) found a significant correlation of field independence with only one of the five SS scales: Experience Seeking.

Bone, Montgomery, and Cowling (1974) used an Identical Figures Task, another measure of field dependence, and found significant correlations with three of the five SS scales, including the General, in females but not in males. Farley (1974) did not find any relationship between the SSS and a Hidden Figures Test, another index of field dependence.

The evidence is mixed and at present we must conclude that the hypothesis of a relationship between sensation seeking and field independence is not supported.

Preference for Complexity

Zuckerman et al. (1970) found that high sensation seekers score higher than lows on the Barron–Welsh Art Scale, a measure of the preference for complexity, asymmetry and movement in designs. The Barron–Welsh test seems to reflect the predilections of artists and creative persons in other fields. Zuckerman et al. (1972) attempted to develop a more specific preference-for-designs test by using the most discriminating items from the Welsh test. The resulting scale correlated significantly with the SS scale. The designs differentiating low and high sensation seekers, illustrated in the 1972 article, show the dramatic difference between their preferences. Every design preferred by lows is simple, symmetrical, and static; the reverse is true for the designs preferred by the highs.

Looft and Baranowski (1971) and Griffin (1972) reported significant correlations between preferences for complexity in polygons and the SS General scale. Osborne and Farley (1970) have been the only investigators to fail to find a relationship between preference for complexity and sensation seeking, but they used paintings as their stimuli and thus confounded the preference for complexity with learned attitudes toward styles of art.

Color Preferences

A preference for blue in clothing seems to have something to do with sensation seeking. For instance, Berkowitz (1967) found that high sensation seekers among Thais preferred blue (and green as well), whereas the lows preferred reds, oranges, and yellows, the colors of the robes of villagers and monks. Furthermore, a pilot study carried out at the University of Delaware found that those college students who scored high on sensation seeking preferred blue in clothing.

COGNITIVE ABILITIES AND STYLES

Intelligence

Of the studies carried out, only Lamb (1972) and Blackburn (1969) did not find significant correlations between the full scale WAIS I.Q. and the SSS, although Blackburn's correlation of .19, found in male psychiatric patients, approaches that found in other studies.

Buchsbaum and Murphy (1974) correlated the WAIS I.Q. with the SSS in a group of high school students, and Carrol (1977) calculated the same correlation in a group of former drug abusers in therapeutic communities. The correlations are shown in Table 12–11 along with Pemberton's (1971) correlations between the SSS and the Scholastic Aptitude Test (SAT) total score in male and female freshpersons at the University of Delaware.

The SS General scale correlated low but significantly with measures of intelligence in all four samples. Experience Seeking and Boredom Susceptibility correlated with intelligence in three of the four samples. Despite the positive correlation of Experience Seeking with Pemberton's SAT measure of intelligence in males, ES correlated negatively with men's scholastic achievement (Grade Point Index) in the same study. Anderson (1973) found that the Disinhibition scale correlated negatively with grade achievement in high school students, while Bone and Cowling (1974a) found negative correlations between Disinhibition and an Achievement Motivation Questionnaire. Anderson also found that Experience Seeking was positively correlated with class absences. One can interpret the above evidence by suggesting male experience seekers find the classroom somewhat less stimulating than their other activities, which seem to center around sex, drugs, music, and parties. Female Thrill and Adventure Seeking seems to be related to intelligence, but Disinhibition in women is negatively correlated with the SAT. High disinhibitors among females also did poorly in grade achievement.

Table 12-11.   Correlations between SSS and measures of Intelligence and "Scholastic Aptitude"

SS Scales	WAIS FS-I.Q. Buchsbaum & Murphy (1974)	Carrol (1977)	SAT Pemberton (1971) Males	Females
Gen	$.22^a$	$.29^b$	$.19^b$	$.19^b$
TAS	.11	$.38^b$	.13	$.16^a$
ES	$.34^b$	$.21^a$	$.18^b$	.02
Dis	$.19^a$	.11	$-.07$	$-.14^a$
BS	$.21^a$	$.23^a$	$.20^b$	.10

[a] $p < .05$.
[b] $p < .01$.

Although these and other data (Kish & Busse, 1968; Kish & Leahy, 1970; Kish & Donnenwerth, 1972) suggest a low positive relationship between General sensation seeking and intelligence and aptitudes, the abilities of high sensation seekers are not reflected in their classroom achievements. Pemberton (1971) found that the SSS correlated negatively with a scale of "Academic Potential" and positively with a scale of "Creative Potential," suggesting that the nonconforming style of the sensation seeker is not adapted to a routinized classroom situation.

Originality and Creativity

The Obscure Figures Test (OFT) (Acker & McReynolds, 1965) was designed to measure "cognitive innovation." Acker and McReynolds (1967) found a significant positive correlation between the OFT and the SSS in undergraduates, and Kish (1970b) reported a similar finding in psychiatric patients.

Farley (1971) reported correlations between the SSS and two measures of cognitive innovation: Pearson and Maddis' (1966) Similes Preference Inventory, and a word completion test designed by Farley. Bone, Cowling, and Belcher (1974) found an unusually high correlation ($r = .60, p < .0001$) between the SSS and the Similes Preference Inventory.

Taylor and Levitt (1967), Farley, Peterson, and Whalen (1974), and Buchsbaum and Murphy (1974) reported positive correlations between the SS General scale and Pettigrew's (1958) Category Width Scale in males, although the correlations were not significant for females in the first two studies. The Category Width Scale is a measure of cognitive expansiveness, rather than cognitive innovation, and seems to tap some of the manic quality of high sensation-seeking males.

Lamb (1966) found a relationship between the SSS and original responses on the Rorschach Inkblot test. Bone and Cowling (1974b) reported a positive relationship of the SSS Mednick and Mednick's (1967) Remote Associates Test (RAT), but we were unable to replicate this finding at the University of Delaware. We did find a relationship with Guilford's (1967) Uses Test, which requires subjects to give unusual uses for common objects.

Davis, Peterson, and Farley (1973) gave the SSS II to a class in creativity in which students were required to turn in creative writing and arts projects or ideas for inventions or original teaching methods. Each person's projects were rated for creativity on a 1 to 7 scale. The SSS General scale correlated significantly with the project ratings in both males ($r = .66, p < .001$) and females ($r = .37, p < .01$), and, furthermore, correlated more highly with creativity performance ratings than two other personality tests specifically designed to measure creativity.

These studies show, with fair consistency, that sensation seeking is associated with creativity. The abilities of the high sensation seekers, not expressed in grades, can find an expression in original thinking. Unfortunately, this kind of originality is not always recognized or rewarded in the large university.

Rigidity-Flexibility

Bone, Cowling, and Choban (1974b) found a specific pattern of negative correlation between Breskin's (1968) test of Rigidity and the SS Experience Seeking scale in both males ($r = -.50, p < .01$) and females ($r = -.32, p < .05$). In females the measure also correlated negatively with every other scale except Disinhibition. Gorman and Wesman (1974) also report a negative association between Breskin's test of Rigidity and a factor defined by the SSS and Pearson's (1970) External Sensation scale.

Rote Learning

On the basis of Maltzman and Raskin's (1965) finding relating paired associate learning to the strength of the Orienting Reflex, Kish (1967) suggested that high sensation seekers would be good at this kind of learning. He predicted that high sensation seekers would have strong orienting reflexes (a prediction we have confirmed in studies to be discussed later) and good attention to incoming stimuli, making for good retention in paired associate learning. Kish (1967) and Kish and Ball (1968) confirmed Kish's prediction in samples of alcoholics and schizophrenics but could not confirm it in a sample of college students (Kish, 1971). Bone and Cowling (1974c) report no correlation between a free recall measure of learning and the SSS General scale in a sample of college students. It is possible that the intermediate process of attention varies more and therefore is more crucial in individual differences in learning in the clinical groups than in college groups.

Dreams, Daydreams, and Hallucinatory Experiences

On the basis of my previous discussion of why high sensation seekers volunteer for sensory deprivation experiments and use drugs, particularly stimulant and hallucinogenic ones, we would expect sensation seekers to have vivid daydreams, nightdreams, and waking intense imagery, bordering on hallucination. These phenomena are sometimes lumped together under the Freudian label of "primary process" thinking. Myers (1972) and Zuckerman et al. (1972) found a correlation between the SSS II and Fitzgerald's EI test (designed around the construct 'regression in the service of the ego''). Myers also found a moderately high correlation between the SSS and Goldberger's (1961) Inkblot measure of "tolerance for primary process."

Zuckerman et al. (1970) compared low and high scorers on the General SSS in regard to their responses to a questionnaire designed by Jackson and Pollard (1966) to measure primary process types of experience in everyday life. The four scales of the questionnaire assess such experience in visual, auditory, body sensation, and cognitive spheres. The high sensation-seeking females scored significantly higher than the lows on three of the four scales (auditory, body, and cognitive) and were higher on the visual scale but not significantly so. The high sensation-seeking males scored higher on three of the four scales but not significantly so.

Windholz (1970) postulated that daydreaming is an attempt to maintain an optimal level of stimulation in the face of a boring or dissatisfying life experience. He found a significant but low correlation ($r = .37, p < .01$) between the General SSS and the General Daydreaming Scale of Singer and Antrobus' (1972) Imaginal Process Inventory but no correlation between the SSS and a dissatisfaction measure based on a Self-Ideal discrepancy test.

Belcher, Bone, and Walker (1972) presented findings showing that vividness of fantasy in recalled nightdreams is associated with the General SSS and Thrill and Adventure Seeking scales in both sexes. All the data tend to support the idea that the sensation seeker is prone to seek both internal and external types of stimulation to reach optimal levels of arousal and is not frightened by his "primary process" or "regression in the service of the ego."

ABNORMAL POPULATIONS

Drug abusers and alcoholics have been discussed in a prior section. Theories of abnormal behavior suggest that sensation seeking may be an important variable in other types of disorders. Quay (1965) suggested that the sociopathic personality is a pathological sensation seeker, driven by the need to compensate for a low level of arousal or arousability by seeking intense and varied stimulation. The input–dysfunction theory of schizophrenia (Venables, 1964) postulates that the schizophrenic is unable to screen out irrelevant stimuli or focus attention on relevant stimuli. Because he is subjected to such a confusing sensory bombardment, the schizophrenic should tend to seek out simple and low levels of stimulation. Meehl (1962) has suggested that anhedonia is a characteristic of a certain kind of schizophrenia. Since the high sensation seeker seems a hedonist, we would again expect the schizophrenic to be low in sensation seeking, that is, not looking for pleasure through his senses.

Sociopathy

Many studies in this area do not differentiate between the primary (or true) sociopath and the secondary sociopath, the latter having some of the characteristics of neurotics. Blackburn (1969) found no differences on the SSS II between male prisoners clinically diagnosed as psychopaths and nonpsychopathic controls, and matched for age. Similarly, Thorne (1971), after making age adjustments in his data, found no differences on the SS General scale among male felons, delinquents, and mentally ill patients. However, he found that female felons and delinquents scored higher than mentally ill females. Le Blanc and Tolor (1972) compared male prison inmates with staff on the SSS IV, controlling for I.Q. He found that the prisoners scored higher on the Experience Seeking scale only.

Emmons and Webb (1974) classified their prisoners on some objective criteria. They compared male prisoners classified as psychopathic, "acting out neurotic," and normal controls on the SSS IV. They used the social anxiety index from Lykken and Katzenmeyer's (1968) Activity Preference Questionnaire and the Pd (sociopathy) scale from the MMPI to make their classifications. All groups were matched for age, I.Q., education, and race.

The groups did not differ on the General and Thrill and Adventure Seeking scales, but the psychopathic group scored significantly higher than the neurotic and control prisoner groups on the Experience Seeking, Disinhibition, and Boredom Susceptibility scales. The Experience Seeking and Disinhibition scales are the only ones correlating with the Pd scale in college students (Zuckerman et al., 1972) and reflect the more nonconforming types of sensation seeking.

Blackburn (in press) also classified prisoners into primary psychopaths, secondary psychopaths, and nonpsychopaths, using the Pd scale and factor scales for impulsivity and sociability. Both psychopathic groups scored significantly higher than the nonpsychopathic group on all the SS scales, but the primary psychopaths scored significantly higher than the secondary psychopaths on the Thrill and Adventure Seeking and the Disinhibition scales. Taken together, the last two studies support Quay's hypothesis, especially for the primary psychopath.

Schizophrenia

Brownfield (1966) reported that schizophrenics scored lower on sensation seeking than normals but not lower than alcoholics. However, Kish (1970), in a study that controlled for age and education, found that male schizophrenics scored significantly lower than controls (attendants), alcoholic patients, and nonschizophrenic patient groups. Schizophrenics who were the lowest scorers on the SSS were compared with those scoring higher. The low scorers on the SSS were rated as significantly more behaviorally retarded on a nurse's observation scale. Kish summarizes these results:

The lowered SSS score appears to reflect the apathy of these schizophrenics as a group. Individually, the SSS appears to measure a trait related to alertness and interest in the environment, which is reflected in degree of ward activity. (p. 173)

PSYCHOPHYSIOLOGICAL AND BIOCHEMICAL CORRELATES OF SENSATION SEEKING

Orienting Reflex

Kish's (1967) suggestion that sensation seekers might be characterized by strong orienting reflexes, as well as other hypotheses about the biological basis for sensation seeking, led us to research on the orienting reflex (OR). Pavlov conceived of the OR as the basis for "curiosity" or the "what is it?" reaction. Although the OR is measured in terms of behavioral and autonomic measures in animals, it usually refers to autonomic or EEG responses in humans. The relationship between stimulation and arousal is not clear. Is the sensation seeker one who is hypoaroused (in a state of low tonic arousal), or is he hypoarousable (requiring novel or high intensity stimulation to reach optimal levels)? A third possibility is that he is hyperarousable to novel stimulation but normally arousable to repeated stimulation. His optimal level of arousal might be set by the high levels of response to novel stimulation. A fourth possibility is that he has normal levels of arousal and arousability but has strong inhibitory tendencies that result in rapid habituation when stimulation is repetitive. The OR experiment offers a convenient way to examine these hypotheses.

The electrodermal (GSR) reactions of high and low sensation seekers (on the General SSS) to novel and repeated stimulation was examined in experiments by Zuckerman (1972b) and Neary and Zuckerman (1976). In the first study, subjects selected from the upper and lower 15 percent of scores on the General SSS were exposed to 10 presentations of a simple visual stimulus, followed by 10 presentations of a complex visual stimulus. Prior to stimulus presentations, a 10-minute recording was obtained to establish baseline levels of arousal.

High sensation seekers did not differ from lows on baseline or on experimental levels of tonic arousal. The high sensation seekers showed significantly greater skin conductance response than the lows to the first, or novel, presentation of both simple and complex stimuli; but on the second and subsequent presentations their responses were at the same magnitude as those of lows. Habituation was calculated as the slope on trials 2 to 10 as is standard in the field. Although the highs showed a tendency to habituate more rapidly on these trials, the difference was not quite significant ($p < .10$).

In the second experiment (Neary and Zuckerman, 1976), subjects were again selected from extremes of the distribution of sensation seeking. Auditory as well as visual stimuli were used, and novel stimuli of both types were presented as the eleventh trial after a habituation series of 10 trials.

Generally, the results were similar to those of the first study with the high sensation seekers making greater skin conductance responses than lows to novel stimulus presentations but not to repeated stimuli. The responses to auditory stimuli in the second study were quite like the responses to visual stimulation in the first. As in the first experiment, there were no significant differences in tonic levels of arousal or habituation slopes.

The results support the idea that the sensation seeker's optimal level of arousal (or arousability) is set by the high level of arousal characteristically produced by novel stimulation. The high sensation seeker does have a strong OR, which may indicate an excitable CNS (defined below) and which may provide the basis for his curiosity and risk-taking propensities.

Russian investigators have interpreted the strength of the OR as a measure of a psychophysiological trait called "equilibrium," or the balance between excitatory and inhibitory processes in the CNS (Nebylitsyn, 1972). The OR data presented above suggest that sensation seeking may be related to an "excitatory" type of CNS. Another primary trait, according to the Russians, is "strength of the nervous system." This trait is defined in terms of levels of sensory thresholds and levels of tolerance for stimulation. Persons with weak nervous systems are more sensitive to stimuli at lower intensities but less able to tolerate stimulation at higher intensities, and the reverse is true for persons with strong nervous systems. Investigators have examined the relation of this strength-of-nervous system dimension to sensation seeking by means of sensory thresholds and pain and sound tolerance.

Sensory Thresholds and Stimulation Tolerance

Neary and Zuckerman (1976) found no relation between absolute auditory and visual thresholds and the SSS. Similarly, Bone, Choban and Cowling (1974) found no correlations between the SSS and tactual sensitivity, using the Von Frey hairs to measure volar forearm sensitivity. Kuhlman (1974) found no relationship between the SSS and the lower sensing thresholds for electric shock.

With respect to tolerance of high intensity stimulation, Buchsbaum and Molino (1974) found a significant positive correlation ($r = .47$) between sound tolerance and the Boredom Susceptibility scale of the SSS. The other SS scales correlated positively but not significantly with sound tolerance. Farley and Kline (1972) also reported that high sensation seekers are able to tolerate greater noise intensities. Kuhlman (1974) found significant positive correlations between electric shock tolerance and the General, Experience Seeking, and Boredom Susceptibility scales of the SSS.

The results of these various studies show a predicted relationship between sensation seeking and tolerance for high intensities of stimulation, but do not show a relationship between sensation seeking and sensory sensitivity at low intensities of stimulation.

Sleeping and Insomnia

Sleeping is a psychophysiological phenomenon that may have some relevance to the construct of a weak or strong nervous system. A weak nervous system would presumably be sensitized to minor external stimuli brought into the foreground during the general quiet of the night and would also be disturbed by "primary process" mental activity, which often accompanies states of drowsiness. Coursey, Buchsbaum and Frankel (1975) compared a group of insomniacs to matched controls in psychophysiological laboratory sleep experiments. Evoked potential responses to stimulation of varying intensities and personality characteristics were studied. The authors predicted that the insomniacs would be reducers of high intensity stimulation (defined by cortical averaged evoked response procedures to be described in the next section), low in sensation seeking on the SSS, and neurotic.

The authors' predictions were confirmed for sensation seeking, stimulus reducing, and neuroticism. The correlation between the General SSS and sleep efficiency (percentage of the time in bed spent sleeping, defined by EEG patterns) was .68, higher than for any of the other measures used. A step-wise regression showed that sensation seeking accounted for the most variance and, when it was partialed out, none of the other variables were significantly related to the sleep criterion.

Cortical Augmenting–Reducing

Augmenting–reducing is a hypothetical psychophysiological personality dimension introduced by Petrie (1960) who used pain thresholds and the kinesthetic aftereffect (KAE) to define it. Reducers are postulated to be persons who characteristically dampen or inhibit incoming stimulation and who therefore have high pain tolerance but poor tolerance for low input stimulation (i.e., sensory deprivation). Augmenters are persons who augment incoming stimulation. Sales (1971) found a significant correlation of +.28 between the KAE and the SSS in one sample but could not replicate the finding in another.

Many persons have found the KAE technique unreliable and difficult to standardize. As a voluntary response measure to peripheral stimulation, it is a questionable way to measure brain response characteristics. Buchsbaum (1971) has devised a method to measure augmenting–reducing directly from the cortex using the Averaged Evoked Response (AER). The technique consists of presenting different intensities of visual stimulation to subjects and measuring the magnitude of response at each stimulus intensity. The slope of the relationship between stimulus intensity and AER amplitude defines augmenting or reducing for each subject, high positive slopes indicating augmenting and low, zero, or negative slopes indicating reducing. One interesting clinical finding is that manic depressive bipolar types characteristically show an augmenting pattern, even when not in the symptomatic state. Lithium, which reduces manic swings, changes augmenting to reducing patterns. Buchsbaum's measure seems to be a reliable and valid measure of cortical excitability (augmenting) versus inhibition (reducing) and may correspond to what the Russians call the dimension of strong versus weak nervous system.

Buchsbaum (1971) predicted a relationship between the AER measure of augmenting–reducing and sensation seeking. He reported pilot data from a factor analysis of the SSS items with the slope measure showing some relationship in the positive direction.

Zuckerman, Murtaugh, and Siegel (1974) attempted to test the relationship further and correlated the AER-to-visual-stimulation with each of the SS scales in a sample of 49 male undergraduates. The correlations obtained are shown in Table 12–12 along with correlations obtained in other studies with the MMPI Hypomania scale and with certain biochemical variables to be discussed in the next section.

The only scale that correlated significantly with augmenting was Disinhibition, but this correlation was quite high and significant. The nature of the relationship between Disinhibition and augmenting–reducing was further elucidated by dividing the group at the median into high and low disinhibitors and excluding subjects falling exactly at the median. The two groups were compared on AER amplitudes across intensities of stimulation. Analysis of variance indicated a significant group by intensities interaction. As can be seen in Figure 12–1, the high disinhibitors showed a characteristic augmenting pattern and the lows showed a reducing pattern.

In view of Buchbaum's finding that augmenting is characteristic of manics, it is interesting that augmenting correlates significantly with Disinhibition. As Table 12–12 shows, Disinhibition was the SS scale most highly correlated with the MMPI Hypomania (Ma) scale in one sample of male undergraduates. The pattern of correlation between augmenting and the SSS is quite similar to the pattern of correlation between the MMPI Ma scale and the SSS.

Biochemical Correlates of Sensation Seeking

Monoamine Oxidase (MAO)

In the brain, MAO catalyzes the oxidative deamination of many biogenic amines including the neurotransmitters norepinephrine and dopamine. Although the relationship between brain MAO and platelet MAO is not known, *low* platelet MAO levels have been found in bipolar manic-depressives. If we assume that MAO has something to do with dampening neural reactivity in the cortex, as in reducers, then we would expect MAO to correlate negatively with sensation seeking, particularly of the Disinhibition type.

Murphy et al. (1977) and Schooler et al. (in press) correlated platelet MAO levels and the SSS in two samples containing male college students. The results are shown in Table 12–12. Disinhibition correlated significantly and negatively with MAO in one sample. The General SSS showed negative correlations of

Table 12-12. Hypomania and Physiological Correlates of the SSS IV

SSS	MMPI Ma[c]	Aug-Red Slope[d]	MAO		Androgens		Estrogens
			I[e]	II[f]	g	II[h]	II[h]
Gen	.30[a]	.23	-.52[b]	-.45[b]	-.11	.15	.33[a]
TAS	.04	.08	-.08	-.16	-.08	.02	.09
ES	.26[a]	.23	-.43[b]	-.26	-.01	.13	.33[a]
Dis	.43[b]	.59[b]	-.27	-.51[b]	.56[b]	.41[b]	.38[b]
BS	.18	.16	-.48[b]	-.34	.06	-.07	.02

a $p < .05$.
b $p < .01$.
c 60 male undergraduates, Zuckerman et al. 1972
d 49 male undergraduates, Zuckerman et al. 1974
e 46 male undergraduates, Schooler et al. in press
f 30 male undergraduates, Murphy et al. 1977
g 25 male undergraduates, Daitzman, 1976.
h 51 male undergraduates, Daitzman, 1976.

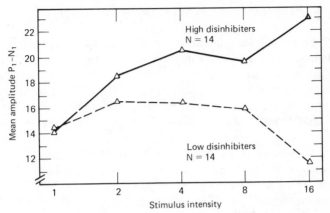

Figure 12–1. Amplitudes of averaged evoked potentials to visual stili of varying intensities in high and low sensation seekers (Disinhibition Scale). (Copyright © 1974, The Society for Psychophysiological Research. Reprinted with permission of the publisher from "Sensation Seeking and Cortical Augmenting-Reducing," by Marvin Zuckerman; Thomas Murtaugh, and Jerome Siegel, PSYCHOPHYSIOLOGY, 1974, *11*, 535–542.)

significance in both samples. The ES and BS scales correlated negatively and significantly with MAO in one of the samples.

Gonadal Hormones

Daitzman (1976) investigated the correlations between androgens and the SSS in a pilot sample of 25 male subjects, and between androgens and estrogens and the SSS in a second sample of 51 male subjects. The results are shown in Table 12–12.

In both the pilot and experimental samples a significant positive correlation was found between androgens and Disinhibition. In the experimental sample a significant correlation was also found between estrogens and Disinhibition. All these correlations remained significant after partialing out all extraneous variables including height, weight, age, and recency of orgasm. The correlations between estrogens and the General and Experience Seeking scales did not remain significant after extraneous variables were partialed out.

As indicated above, Disinhibition was significantly correlated with the levels of both types of gonadal hormones in males. A small sample of seven females showed the same relationships between sex hormones and Disinhibition. These relationships were significant despite the small N.

Since the gonadal hormones are thought to increase the concentration of catecholamines, these findings, like those on the AER and MAO, as well as the finding that Disinhibition correlates with traits of hypomania and Extroversion, suggest that the Disinhibition type of sensation seeking is a result of a hyperexcitable CNS.

Genetic and Environmental Sources of Sensation Seeking

If some of the SS scales are indeed related to CNS response characteristics, it is conceivable that sensation seeking might be to some degree genetically transmitted. Kish and Donnenwerth (1972) correlated the SS scores obtained from parents of students with those of the students themselves. All the correlations were positive, but only one of the correlations, father with daughter, was significant.

Parent–child correlations confound not only age, shown to be an influence in the SSS, but also environment. Twin comparisons are a better method of getting at genetic transmission. Buchsbaum (1973) has used the SSS along with a variety of other personality, cognitive, and psychophysiological variables in a study of monozygotic (MZ) and dyzygotic (DZ) twins of both sexes. Table 12–13 shows the obtained correlations for MZ and DZ twins in regard to the SS scales and two other measures (the MMPI social introversion scale and WAIS I.Q.) for comparison. I computed the h^2 values from the intraclass correlations as a measure of the variance produced by heredity.

The genetic influence in the SS scales does not seem as high as in introversion or intelligence scales however, all the scales except Experience Seeking show some genetic influence, ranging from 27 percent to 40 percent of the variance.

Virtually no studies have been done of the family background of sensation seekers. We might expect that parents will provide an environmental contribution to a sensation-seeking trait by providing a highly stimulating environment for the child and encouraging exploration and autonomy.

In a study carried out by Bacon (1974), male risk takers (divers and volunteer firemen) and controls were given a family background survey in which they described their parents and their relations to them. More than the controls, the risk takers indicated that their fathers had been active and forceful and that they

Table 12–13.   Intraclass Correlations of Monozygotic and Dyzygotic Twins on the SSS, S_i, WAIS I.Q.

SSS	Intraclass r's		
	MZ	DZ	h^2_a
Gen	.59	.43	.28
TAS	.75	.58	.40
ES	.54	.55	−.02
Dis	.54	.37	.27
BS	.41	.08	.36
MMPI S_i	.83	.10	.81
WAIS IQ	.79	.17	.75

[a] based on Holzinger's formula.

Source: Buchsbaum, 1973.

had been disobedient and unafraid in standing up to their parents. There was also some indication of greater economic instability in the families of risk takers, but this could be a bias of sampling since the controls were all in a technical college.

SUMMARY

This review of research on the SSS has not included some areas such as vocational interests and attitudes, which can be found in Zuckerman, 1974. In this chapter, I have tried to deal with the more fundamental issues of trait definition, experience, behavior, and physiological bases of sensation seeking.

We have seen that sensation seeking is related to the impulsive aspect of extroversion but not to sociability, neuroticism, or psychoticism. Sensation seeking has proven to be an important variable in food preference and in sex, drug, and smoking experience, but only specific types of sensation seeking are related to drinking behavior. Sensation seeking is related to gambling and to volunteering for dangerous activities. Sensation seekers also tend to volunteer for the more unusual type of psychology experiments such as those on sensory deprivation and hypnosis. A newly developed state sensation-seeking scale predicts hypnotizability and the readiness to take a drug. Sensation seekers volunteer for meditation training but tend to lose patience with it. They volunteer for sensory deprivation studies and get restless in short-term experiments, but they sometimes find interesting experiences in long-term ones. Low sensation seekers tend to be phobic in regard to certain types of unusual situations with low objective risk elements.

Sensation seekers prefer complexity in designs, and some studies have suggested that they are field independent, although some failure in replication has occurred here. Sensation seeking has low positive correlation with intellectual potential, and although high sensation seekers tend to think creatively, they tend to do poorly in academic work.

Sociopathy seems to be associated with certain types of sensation seeking, whereas schizophrenics are low sensation seekers.

Involved in the genotype of sensation seeking is an excitable CNS as expressed in strong orienting reflexes to novel stimuli and an augmenting reaction to increasing intensities of stimulation. The excitability of the CNS seems to be related to biochemical characteristics of the sensation seeker including low MAO levels and high levels of gonadal hormones. Heredity seems to be a moderately important determinant of the trait. More definite genetic studies of twins have been conducted at the Institute of Psychiatry of the Maudsley Hospital in collaboration with Sybil and Hans Eysenck and David Fulker. These studies, using large samples of twins, have shown a substantial heritability of 58% for total sensation seeking scores.

REFERENCES

Acker, M., & McReynolds, P. The Obscure Figures Test: An instrument for measuring "cognitive innovation". *Perceptual and Motor Skills,* 1965, *21,* 815–821.

Acker, M., & McReynolds, P. The need for novelty: A comparison of 6 instruments. *The Psychological Record,* 1967, *17,* 177–182.

Allen, J. G. Personal communication, 1974.

Allen, J. G., & Hamsher, J. H. The development and validation of a test of emotional styles. *Journal of Consulting and Clinical Psychology,* 1974, *42,* 663–668.

Anderson, R. E. *Relationship between sensation seeking and academic achievement, school attendance, academic ability and alcohol use.* Unpublished master's thesis, University of Alberta, 1973.

Bacon, J. *Sensation seeking levels for members of high risk volunteer organizations.* Unpublished manuscript, 1974.

Barber, T. X. Hypnotizability, suggestibility and personality: V. A critical view of research findings. *Psychological Reports,* 1964, *14,* 299–320.

Belcher, M. M., Bone, R. N., & Walker, T. D. *The relationship of various components of Zuckerman's Sensation-Seeking Scale to dream report ratings.* Paper presented at Association for the Psychophysiological Study of Sleep, New York, April 1972.

Berkowitz, W. R. Use of the Sensation-Seeking Scale with Thai subjects. *Psychological Reports,* 1967, *20,* 635–641.

Berlyne, D. E. *Conflict, arousal and curiosity.* New York: McGraw-Hill, 1960.

Bexton, W. H. *Some effects of perceptual isolation in human subjects.* Unpublished doctoral dissertation, McGill University, 1953.

Bexton, W. H., Heron W., & Scott, T. H. Effects of decreased variation in the sensory environment. *Canadian Journal of Psychology,* 1954, *8,* 70–76.

Blackburn, R. Sensation seeking, impulsivity and psychopathic personality. *Journal of Consulting and Clinical Psychology,* 1969, *33,* 571–574.

Blackburn, R. *Psychopathy, arousal, and the need for stimulation.* In R. Hare & D. Schaling (Eds.), *Psychopathic Behavior.* London: Wiley, in press.

Bone, R. N. PSI correlations with the MPI and Zuckerman's Sensation Seeking Scale. In R. I. Lanyon, *Psychological Screening Inventory Research and Development Notes,* No. 3, May, 1972.

Bone, R. N. Is the streaker a sensation seeker? Personal communication, 1974.

Bone, R. N., & Belcher, M. M. *Sensation seeking and the tendency toward novelty seeking.* Personal communication, 1974.

Bone, R. N., & Choban, R. C. Sensation seeking scale Form IV, and field independence. *Perceptual and Motor Skills,* 1972, *34,* 634.

Bone, R. N., Choban, M. C., & Cowling, L. W. *Sensation seeking and Von Frey Hairs.* Personal communication, 1974.

Bone, R. N., & Cowling, L. W. *Sensation seeking and achievement motivation.* Personal communication, 1974. (a)

Bone, R. N., & Cowling, L. W. *Sensation seeking and category width.* Personal communication, 1974. (b)

Bone, R. N., & Cowling, L. W. *Sensation-seeking and free recall learning.* Personal communication, 1974. (c)

Bone, R. N., Cowling, L. W., & Belcher, M. M. *Sensation seeking and the Similes Preference Inventory*. Personal communication, 1974.

Bone, R. N., Cowling, L. W., & Choban, M. C. *Sensation seeking and volunteering for experiments*. Personal communication, 1974 (a)

Bone, R. N., Cowling, L. W., & Choban, M. C. *Sensation seeking and rigidity*. Personal communication, 1974. (b)

Bone, R. N., Montgomery, D. D., & Cowling, L. W. *Sensation seeking and the Identical Figures Task*. Personal communication, 1974.

Bone, R. N., Montgomery, D. D., Sundstrom, P. E., Cowling, L. W., & Caleb, R. S. Relationship of sensation seeking and anxiety; IPAT, State and Trait, TAS and MAS. *Psychological Reports*, 1972, *30*, 874.

Breskin, S. Measurement of rigidity, a non-verbal test. *Perceptual and Motor Skills*, 1968, *27*, 1203–1206.

Brill, N. Q., Crumpton, E., & Grayson, H. M. Personality Factors in marihuana use. *Archives of General Psychiatry*, 1971, *24*, 163–165.

Brownfield, C. A. Optimal stimulation levels of normal and disturbed subjects in sensory deprivation. *Psychologia*, 1966, *9*, 27–38.

Buchsbaum, M. Neural events and the psychophysical law. *Science*, 1971, *172*, 502.

Buchsbaum, M. Personal communication, 1973.

Buchsbaum, M., & Molino, J. Personal communication, 1974.

Butler, R. A., & Alexander, H. M. Daily patterns of visual exploratory behavior in monkeys. *Journal of Comparative and Physiological Psychology*, 1955, *48*, 247–249.

Butler, R. A., & Harlow, H. Persistence of visual exploration in monkeys. *Journal of Comparative and Physiological Psychology*, 1954, *47*, 258–263.

Campbell, D. T., & Fiske, D. W. Convergent and discriminant validation by the multitrait –multimethod matrix. *Psychological Bulletin*, 1959, *56*, 81–105.

Carrol, E. N., & Zuckerman, M. Psychopathology and sensation seeking in 'downers,' 'speeders,' and 'trippers': A study of the relationship between personality and drug choice. *International Journal of Addictions*, 1977, *12*, 591–601.

Cattell, R. B. *Personality and motivation structure and measurement*. New York: Harcourt, Brace & World, 1957.

Cattell, R. B., Saunders, D. R., & Stice, G. F. *The 16 personality factor questionnaire*. Champaign, Ill.: Institute for Personality and Ability Testing, 1950.

Cattell, R. B., & Scheier, I. H. *Handbook for the I.P.A.T. Anxiety Scale* (2nd ed.) Champaign, Ill.: Institute for Personality and Ability Testing, 1963.

Coursey, R. D., Buchsbaum, M., & Frankel, B. L. Personality measures and evoked responses in chronic insomniacs. *Journal of Abnormal Psychology*, 1975, *84*, 239–249.

Crowne, I. P., and Marlowe, D. A new scale of social desirabilty independent of psychopathology. *Journal of Consulting Psychology*, 1960, *24*, 349–354.

Daitzman, R. *Personality and behavioral correlates of androgens and estrogens*. Unpublished doctoral dissertation, University of Delaware, 1976.

Daitzman, R., & Tumilty, T. N. *Personality and behavioral correlates of sensation seeking among male schizophrenics*. Unpublished manuscript, 1972.

Davis, G. A., Peterson, J. M., & Farley, F. H. Attitudes, motivation, sensation seeking and belief in ESP as predictors of real creative behavior. *Journal of Creative Behavior*, 1973, *8*, 31–39.

Edwards, A. L. *The social desirability variable in personality assessment and research*. New York: Dryden, 1957.

Edwards, A. L. *Manual for the Edwards Personal Preference Schedule*. New York: Psychological Corp., 1959.

Emmons, T. D., & Webb, W. W. Subjective correlates of emotional responsivity and stimulation seeking in psychopaths, normals, and acting-out neurotics. *Journal of Consulting and Clinical Psychology*, 1974, *42*, 620–625.

English, G. E., & Jones, R. E. *Sensation seeking in hospitalized drug addicts*. Paper presented at Southeastern Psychological Association, Atlanta, Georgia, April, 1972.

Eysenck, H. J. *The structure of human personality*. New York: John Wiley, 1953.

Eysenck, H. J. *The biological basis of personality*. Springfield: Thomas, 1967.

Eysenck, H. J. Personal communication, 1971.

Eysenck, H. J., & Eysenck, S. B. G. *Eysenck Personality Inventory*. San Diego: Educational and Industrial Testing Service, 1964.

Farley, F. H. Social desirability and dimensionality in the Sensation-Seeking Scale. *Acta Psychologia*, 1967, *26*, 89–96.

Farley, F. H. Measures of individual differences in stimulation seeking and the tendency toward variety. *Journal of Consulting and Clinical Psychology*, 1971, *37*, 394–396.

Farley, F. H. Personal communication, 1973.

Farley, F. H. Sensation seeking motive and field independence. *Perceptual and Motor Skills*, 1974, *38*, 330.

Farley, F. H., & Cox, S. O. Stimulus-seeking motivation in adolescents as a function of age and sex. *Adolescence*, 1971, *6*, 207–218.

Farley, F. H., & Farley, S. V. Extroversion and stimulus seeking motivation. *Journal of Consulting Psychology*, 1967, *31*, 215–216.

Farley, F. H., & Farley, S. V. Stimulus-seeking motivation and delinquent behavior among institutionalized delinquent girls. *Journal of Consulting and Clinical Psychology*, 1972, *39*, 140–147.

Farley, F. and Hallbrick A. S. Personal communication, 1974

Farley, F. H., & Kline, K. *Noise and light tolerance thresholds and the stimulation seeking motive*. Unpublished study, University of Wisconsin, Madison, 1972. Cited in Farley, Peterson & Whalen, 1974.

Farley, F. H.. Peterson, J. M., & Whalen, T. J. The stimulation-seeking motive: Relationship to conceptual category breadth. *Bulletin of the Psychonomic Society*, 1974, *3*, 449–451.

Fisher, S. *The female orgasm*. New York: Basic Books, 1973. (a)

Fisher, S. Personal communication, 1973. (b)

Fitzgerald, E. T. Measurement of openness to experience: A study of regression in the service of the ego. *Journal of Personality and Social Psychology*, 1966, *4*, 655–663.

Freud, S. Instincts and their vicissitudes. In J. Rickman (Ed.), *A general selection from the works of Sigmund Freud*. New York: Doubleday Anchor Books, 1957. (Originally published, 1915.)

Garlington, W. K., & Shimona, H. E. The Change Seeker Index: A measure of the need for variable sensory input. *Psychological Reports*, 1964, *14*, 919–924.

Geer, J. H. The development of a scale to measure fear. *Behavior Research and Therapy*, 1965, *3*, 45–53.

Goldberger, L. Reactions to perceptual isolation and Rorschach manifestations of the primary process. *Journal of Projective Techniques*, 1961, *25*, 287–302.

Gorman, B. S. 16 PF correlates of sensation-seeking. *Psychological Reports,* 1970, *26,* 741–742.

Gorman, B. S., & Wesman, A. E. The relationships of cognitive styles and moods. *Journal of Clincal Psychology,* 1974, *30,* 18–36.

Gough, H. G. *Manual for the California Psychological Inventory* Palo Alto, Cal.: Consulting Psychologists Press, 1957.

Gough, H. G., & Heilbrun, A. B. *The Adjective Check List Manual* Palo Alto, Cal.: Consulting Psychologists Press, 1965.

Griffin, S. R. Personal communication, 1972.

Guilford, J. P. *The nature of human intelligence.* New York: McGraw-Hill, 1967.

Hathaway, S. R., & McKinley, J. C. *The Minnesota Multiphasic Personality Inventory Manual* (Rev. ed.). New York: Psychological Corp., 1951.

Hebb, D. O. *The organization of behavior.* New York: John Wiley, 1949.

Hebb, D. O. Drives and the CNS (conceptual nervous system). *Psychological Review,* 1955, *62,* 243–254.

Hebb, D. O. Alice in Wonderland or psychology among the biological sciences. In H. Harlow & C. N. Woolsey (Eds.), *Biological and biochemical bases of behavior.* Madison: University of Wisconsin Press, 1958.

Hilgard, E. R. *Hypnotic susceptibility.* New York: Harcourt, Brace & World, 1965.

Hocking, J., & Robertson, M. The Sensation-Seeking Scale as a predictor of need for stimulation during sensory restriction. *Journal of Consulting and Clinical Psychology,* 1969, *33,* 367–369.

Hymbaugh, K., & Garrett, J. Sensation seeking among skydivers. *Perceptual and Motor Skills,* 1974, *38,* 118.

Irey, P. A. *Personality dimensions of crisis interveners vs. academic psychologists, traditional clinicians and paraprofessionals.* Unpublished doctoral dissertation, Southern Illinois University, 1974.

Jackson, D. N. *Personality research form manual.* Goshen, N.Y.: Research Psychologists Press, 1967.

Jackson, C. W., & Pollard, J. C. Some nondeprivation variables which influence the "effects" of experimental sensory deprivation. *Journal of Abnormal Psychology,* 1966, *71,* 383–388.

Jones, A. Stimulus-seeking behavior. In J. P. Zubek (Ed.), *Sensory deprivation: Fifteen years of research.* New York: Appleton-Century-Crofts, 1969.

Jones, A., & McGill, D. W. The homeostatic character of information drive in humans. *Journal of Experimental Research in Personality,* 1967, *2,* 25–31.

Jones, A., Wilkinson, H. J., & Braden, I. Information deprivation as a motivational variable. *Journal of Experimental Psychology,* 1961, *62,* 126–137.

Kilpatrick, D. G., Sutker, P. B., & Smith, A. D. Deviant drug and alcohol use: The role of anxiety, sensation seeking and other personality variables. In M. Zuckerman and C. D. Spielberger (Eds.), *Emotions and anxiety: New concepts, methods and applications.* Hillsdale, N. J.: Lawrence Erlbaum, 1976.

Kish, G. B. Learning when the onset of illumination is used as a reinforcing stimulus. *Journal of Comparative and Physiological Psychology,* 1955, *48,* 261–264.

Kish, G. B. Studies of sensory reinforcement. In W. K. Honig (Ed.), *Operant behavior.* New York: Appleton-Century-Crofts, 1966.

Kish, G. B. *Stimulus seeking and learning.* Unpublished manuscript, 1967.

Kish, G. B. Cognitive innovation and stimulus seeking: A study of the correlates of the Obscure Figures Test. *Perceptual and Motor Skills,* 1970, *30,* 95–101. (a)

Kish, G. B. Reduced cognitive innovation and stimulus-seeking in chronic schizophrenia. *Journal of Clinical Psychology*, 1970, *26*, 170–174. (b)

Kish, G. B. CPI correlates of stimulus-seeking in male alcoholics. *Journal of Clinical Psychology*, 1971, *27*, 251–253. (a)

Kish, G. B. Personal communication, 1971. (b)

Kish, G. B. A two-factor theory of sensation seeking. A paper presented at a symposium: the sensation-seeking motive. Meeting of the American Psychological Association, Montreal, Canada, August, 1973.

Kish, G. B., & Ball, M. E. *Effects of individual differences in stimulus-seeking upon learning rate in schizophrenics*. Unpublished manuscript, 1968.

Kish, G. B., & Busse, W. Correlates of stimulus seeking: Age, education, intelligence, and aptitudes. *Journal of Consulting and Clinical Psychology*, 1968, *32*, 633–637.

Kish, G. B., & Busse, W. MMPI correlates of sensation-seeking in male alcoholics: A test of Quay's hypothesis applied to alcoholism. *Journal of Clinical Psychology*, 1969, *25*, 60–62.

Kish, G. B., & Donnenwerth, G. V. Sex differences in the correlates of stimulus seeking. *Journal of Consulting and Clinical Psychology*, 1972, *38*, 42–49.

Kish, G. B., & Leahy, L. Stimulus-seeking, age, interests, and aptitudes: An amplification. *Perceptual and Motor Skills*, 1970, *30*, 670.

Kuhlman, D. M. Personal communication, 1974.

Kuhlman, D. M. Individual differences in casino gambling? In W. R. Eadington (Ed.), *Gambling and society*. Springfield, Ill.: Thomas, 1975.

Kusyszyn, I., Steinberg, P., & Elliot, B. *Arousal seeking, physical risk taking, and personality*. Unpublished manuscript, 1973.

Lamb, C. W. *Forms of need for variety: Differential expression following arousal and boredom*. Unpublished doctoral dissertation, Ohio State University, 1966.

Lamb, C. W. Personal communication, 1972.

Lambert, W., & Levy, L. H. Sensation-seeking and short term sensory isolation. *Journal of Personality and Social Psychology*, 1972, *24*, 46–52.

Landon, B. K. & Suedfeld, P. Information and meaningfulness needs in sensory deprivation. *Psychonomic Science*, 1969, *17*, 248.

Lanyon, R. I. Development and validation of a psychological screening inventory. *Journal of Consulting and Clinical Psychology Monograph*, 1970, *35*, No. 1, Part 2.

LeBlanc, R. F., & Tolor, A. Alienation, distancing, externalizing and sensation-seeking in prison inmates. *Journal of Consulting and Clinical Psychology*, 1972, *39*, 514.

Leuba, C. Toward some integration of learning theories: The concept of optimal stimulation. *Psychological Reports*, 1955, *1*, 27–33.

Levin, B. H. Personal communication, 1974.

Levin, B. H., & Brown, W. E. Susceptibility to boredom of jailers and law enforcement officers. *Psychological Reports*, 1975, *36*, 190.

Lo Guidice, J. Personal communication, 1974.

Looft, W. R., & Baranowski, M. D. An analysis of five measures of sensation seeking and preference for complexity. *Journal of General Psychology*, 1971, *85*, 307–313.

Lykken, D. T., & Katzenmeyer, C. G. Manual for the Activity Preference Questionnaire (APQ), University of Minnesota Research Laboratories, 1968.

McClelland, D. C., Atkinson, J. W., Clark, R. A., & Lowell, E. L. *The achievement motive*. New York: Appleton-Century-Crofts, 1953.

McReynolds, P. Behavioral choice as a function of novelty-seeking and anxiety-avoidance motivations. *Psychological Reports*, 1971, *29*, 3–6.

Maltzman, I., & Raskin, D. C. Effects of individual differences in the orienting reflex on conditioning and complex processes. *Journal of Experimental Research in Personality*, 1965, *1*, 1–16.

Mednick, S. A., & Mednick, M. T. *Examiners manual remote associates test*. Boston: Houghton Mifflin, 1967.

Meehl, P. E. Schizotaxia, schizotypy, schizophrenia. *American Psychologist*, 1962, *17*, 827–838.

Mellstrom, M., Cicala, G. A., & Zuckerman, M. General versus specific trait anxiety measures in the prediction of fear of snakes, heights, and darkness. *Journal of Consulting and Clinical Psychology*, 1976, *44*, 83–91.

Murphy, D. L., Belmaker, R. H., Buchsbaum, M., Martin, N. F., Ciaranello, R., & Wyatt, R. J. Biogenic amine-related enzymes and personality variations in normals. *Psychological Medicine*, 1977, *7*, 149–157.

Murray, H. A. *Explorations in personality*. London & New York: Oxford University Press, 1938.

Murtaugh, T. L. *Perceptual isolation, drug addition and adaptation phenomena*. Unpublished master's thesis, Temple University, 1971.

Myers, T. I. Personal communication, 1967.

Myers, T. I. *Psychobiological factors associated with monotony tolerance*. Report No. 197-015, July, 1972. American Institutes for Research, Institute for Research in Psychobiology, Washington, D.C.

Myers, T. I., & Eisner, E. J. *An experimental evaluation of the effects of karate and meditation*. Report No. 42800 (P-391X-1-29) of the American Institutes for Research, October 31, 1974, Washington, D.C.

Neary, R. S. The development and validation of a state measure of sensation seeking. Unpublished doctoral dissertation, University of Delaware, 1975.

Neary, R. S., & Zuckerman, M. Sensation seeking trait and state anxiety, and the electrodermal orienting reflex. *Psychophysiology*, 1976, *13*, 205–211.

Nebylitsyn, V. D. *Fundamental properties of the nervous system*. New York: Plenum Press, 1972.

Norman, W. T. Toward an adequate taxonomy of personal attributes: Replicated factor structure in peer nomination personality ratings. *Journal of Abnormal and Social Psychology*, 1963, *66*, 574–583.

Nowlis, V. Research with the Mood Adjective Check List. In S. S. Tompkins & C. E. Izard (Eds.), *Affect, cognition and personality*. New York: Springer, 1965.

Ohkubo, Y. Personal communication, 1972.

Osborne, J. W., & Farley, F. H. The relationship between aesthetic preference and visual complexity in abstract art. *Psychonomic Science*, 1970, *19*, 69–70.

Ozeran, B. J. *Sensation-seeking as a predictor of leadership in leaderless, task oriented groups*. Unpublished master's thesis, University of Hawaii, 1973.

Palmer, R. D. Visual acuity and stimulus-seeking behavior. *Psychosomatic Medicine*, 1970, *32*, 277–284.

Pare, W. P. *Sensation seeking and extraversion in hospitalized alcoholics*. Unpublished manuscript, 1973.

Patrick, A. W., Zuckerman, M., & Masterson, F. A. An extension of trait–state distinction from affects to motive measures. *Psychological Reports*, 1974, *34*, 1251–1258.

Pearson, P. H. Relationships between global and specified measures of novelty seeking. *Journal of Consulting and Clinical Psychology*, 1970, *34*, 199–204.

Pearson, P. H., & Maddi, S. R. The Similes Preference Inventory: Development of a structured measure of the preference toward variety. *Journal of Consulting and Clinical Psychology*, 1966, *30*, 301–308.

Pemberton, W. A. *Further dimensions of sensation seeking.* Paper presented at meeting of the Delaware Psychological Association, May, 1971.

Peterson, D. M. Relations among sensation seeking and simulated and behavioral personal space. *Journal of Psychology*, 1973, *83*, 79–88.

Penney, R. K., & Reinehr, R. C. Development of a stimulus–variation seeking scale for adults. *Psychological Reports*, 1966, *18*, 631–638.

Petrie, A. Some psychological aspects of pain and the relief of suffering. *Annals of the New York Academy of Science*, 1960, *86*, 13–27.

Pettigrew, T. F. The measurement and correlates of category width as a cognitive variable. *Journal of Personality*, 1958, *26*, 532–544.

Platt, J. J. "Addiction proneness" and personality in heroin addicts. *Journal of Abnormal Psychology*, 1975, *84*, 303–306.

Quay, H. C. Psychopathic personality as pathological stimulation seeking. *American Journal of Psychiatry*, 1965, *122*, 180–183.

Rotter, J. B. Generalized expectancies for internal vs. external control of reinforcement. *Psychological Monographs*, 1966, *80*, (Whole No. 609).

Sales, S. Personal communication, 1971.

Sarason, S. B., & Mandler, G. Some correlates of test anxiety. *Journal of Abnormal Psychology*, 1952, *47*, 810–817.

Schneirla, T. C. An evolutionary and developmental theory of biphasic processes underlying approach and withdrawal. In M. R. Jones (Ed.), *Nebraska Symposium on Motivation*. Lincoln: University of Nebraska Press, 1959.

Schooler, C., Zahn, T. P., Murphy, D. L. & Buchsbaum, M. S. Psychological correlates of monoamine oxidase in normals. *Journal of Nervous and Mental Diseases*, in press.

Schubert, D. S. P. Arousal seeking as a motivation for volunteering. MMPI scores and central nervous system stimulant use as suggestive of a trait. *Journal of Projective Techniques and Personality Assessment*, 1964, *28*, 337–340.

Segal, B. Sensation seeking and anxiety assessment of responses to specific situations. *Journal of Consulting and Clinical Psychology*, 1973, *41*, 135–138.

Shostrom, E. L. *Manual for the Personal Orientation Inventory*. San Diego, Cal.: Educational and Industrial Testing Service, 1966.

Singer, J. L., & Antrobus, J. S. Dimensions of daydreaming: A factor analysis of imaginal process and personality scales. In P. Sheehan (Ed.), *The function and nature of imagery*. New York: Academic Press, 1972.

Smith, S., & Meyers, T. I. Stimulation seeking during sensory deprivation. *Perceptual and Motor Skills*, 1966, *23*, 1151–1163.

Smith, S., Meyers, T. I., & Johnson, E. Stimulation seeking throughout seven days of sensory deprivation. *Perceptual and Motor Skills*, 1967, *25*, 261–271.

Spielberger, C. D. Theory and research on anxiety. In C. D. Spielberger (Ed.), *Anxiety and behavior*. New York: Academic Press, 1966.

Spielberger, C. D., Gorsuch, R. L., & Lushene, R. E. *Manual for the State–Trait Anxiety Inventory (STAI)*. Palo Alto, Cal.: Consulting Psychologists Press, 1970.

Taylor, J. A. A personality scale of manifest anxiety. *Journal of Abnormal and Social Psychology*, 1953, *48*, 285–290.

Taylor, R. L., & Levitt, E. E. Category breadth and the search for variety of experience. *Psychological Record*, 1967, *17*, 349–352.

Thorne, G. L. The Sensation-Seeking Scale with deviant populations. *Journal of Consulting and Clinical Psychology*, 1971, *37*, 106–110.

Venables, P. H. Input dysfunction in schizophrenia. In B. A. Maher (Ed.), *Progress in experimental personality research* (Vol. I). New York: Academic Press, 1964.

Vernon, J., & McGill, T. E. Utilization of visual stimulation during sensory deprivation. *Perceptual and Motor Skills*, 1960, *11*, 214.

Waters, L. K., & Kirk, W. E. Stimulus-seeking motivation and risk taking behavior in a gambling situation. *Education and Psychological Measurement*, 1968, *28*, 549–550.

Windholz, G. Dissatisfaction and sensation-seeking as related to frequency of daydreaming reported by male subjects. *Perceptual and Motor Skills*, 1970, *30*, 892–894.

Wolfe, R. Personal communication, 1971.

Wolpe, J., & Lang, P. J. A fear survey schedule for use in behavior therapy. *Behavior Research and Therapy*, 1964, *2*, 27–30.

Wundt, W. M. *Grundzuge der physiologischen psychologie*. Leipzig: Engleman, 1874.

Young, P. T. The role of affective processes in learning and motivation. *Psychological Review*, 1959, *66*, 104–125.

Zubek, J. Personal communication, 1968.

Zubek, J. (Ed.). *Sensory deprivation: Fifteen years of research*. New York: Appleton-Century-Crofts, 1969.

Zuckerman, M. The development of an Affect Adjective Check List for the measurement of anxiety. *Journal of Consulting and Clinical Psychology*, 1960, *24*, 457–462.

Zuckerman, M. Variables affecting deprivation results. In J. P. Zubek (Ed.), *Sensory deprivation: Fifteen years of research*. New York: Appleton-Century-Crofts, 1969. (a).

Zuckerman, M. Theoretical formulations: I. In J. P. Zubek (Ed.), *Sensory deprivation: Fifteen years of research*. New York: Appleton-Century-Crofts, 1969. (b)

Zuckerman, M. Dimensions of sensation seeking. *Journal of Consulting and Clinical Psychology*, 1971, *36*, 45–52.

Zuckerman, M. Drug usage as one manifestation of a "sensation seeking" trait. In W. Keup (Ed.), *Drug abuse. Current concepts and research*. Springfield, Ill.: Thomas, 1972. (a)

Zuckerman, M. Sensation seeking and habituation of the electrodermal orienting response. *Psychophysiology*, 1972, *9*, 267–268. (Abstract) (b)

Zuckerman, M. Scales for sex experience for males and females. *Journal of Consulting and Clinical Psychology*, 1973, *41*, 27–29.

Zuckerman, M. The sensation seeking motive. In B. A. Maher (Ed.), *Progress in experimental personality research* (Vol. 7). New York: Academic Press, 1974.

Zuckerman, M. *Manual and research report for the sensation seeking scale*. Unpublished manuscript, March 1975.

Zuckerman, M. General and situation specific traits and states: New approaches to assessment. In M. Zuckerman & C. D. Spielberger (Eds.), *Emotions and anxiety: New concepts, methods and applications*. Hillsdale, N.J.: Erlbaum, 1976.

Zuckerman, M., Bone, R. N., Neary, R., Mangelsdorff, D., & Brustman, B. What is the sensation seeker? Personaltiy trait and experience correlates of the Sensation Seeking Scales. *Journal of Consulting and Clinical Psychology*, 1972, *39*, 308–321.

Zuckerman, M., & Haber, M. M. Need for stimulation as a source of stress response to perceptual isolation. *Journal of Abnormal Psychology*, 1965, *70*, 371–377.

Zuckerman, M., & Hopkins, T. R. Unpublished study, 1965.

Zuckerman, M., Kolin, E. A., Price, L., & Zoob, I. Development of a Sensation-Seeking Scale. *Journal of Consulting Psychology*, 1964, *28*, 477–482.

Zuckerman, M., & Link, K. Construct validity for the Sensation-Seeking Scale. *Journal of Consulting and Clinical Psychology*, 1968, *32*, 420–426.

Zuckerman, M., Murtaugh, T. M., & Siegel, J. Sensation seeking and cortical augmenting –reducing. *Psychophysiology*, 1974, *11*, 535–542.

Zuckerman, M., Neary, R. S., & Brustman, B. A. Sensation-Seeking Scale correlates in experience (smoking, drugs, alcohol, "hallucinations" and sex) and preference for complexity (designs). *Proceedings*, 78th Annual Convention, APA, 1970.

Zuckerman, M., Persky, H., Hopkins, T. R., Murtaugh, T., Basu, G. K., & Schilling, M. Comparison of stress effects of perceptual and social isolation. *Archives of General Psychiatry*, 1966, *14*, 356–365.

Zuckerman, M., Persky, H., & Link, K. Relation of mood and hypnotizability: An illustration of the state vs. trait distinction. *Journal of Consulting Psychology*, 1967, *31*, 464–471.

Zuckerman, M., Persky, H., Link, K. E., & Basu, G. K. Experimental and subject factors determining responses to sensory deprivation, social isolation and confinement. *Journal of Abnormal Psychology*, 1968, *73*, 183–194.

Zuckerman, M., Schultz, D. P., & Hopkins, T. R. Sensation seeking and volunteering for sensory deprivation and hypnosis experiments. *Journal of Consulting Psychology*, 1967, *31*, 358–363.

Zuckerman, M., Tushup, R., & Finner, S. Sexual attitudes and experience: Attitude and personality correlates and changes produced by a course in sexuality. *Journal of Consulting and Clinical Psychology*, 1976, *44*, 7–19.

APPENDIX A

INTEREST AND PREFERENCE TEST (FORM IV SSS)

DIRECTIONS: Each of the items below contains two choices, A and B. Please indicate *on your answer sheet* which of the choices most describes *your likes* or *the way you feel.* In some cases you may find items in which both choices describe your likes or feelings. Please choose the one which *better* describes your likes or feelings. In some cases you may find items in which you do not like either choice. In these cases mark the choice you dislike *least.* Do not leave any items blank.

It is important you respond to *all items* with only *one choice,* A or B. We are interested only in *your likes or feelings,* not in how others feel about these things or how one is supposed to feel. There are no right or wrong answers as in other kinds of tests. Be frank and give your honest appraisal of yourself.

1. A. I dislike the sensations one gets when flying.
   B. I enjoy many of the rides in amusement parks.
2. A. I would like a job which would require a lot of traveling.
   B. I would prefer a job in one location.
3. A. I would like to hitchhike across the country.
   B. Hitchhiking is too dangerous a way to travel.
4. A. I do not find gambling worth the risk.
   B. I like to gamble for money.
5. A. I can't wait to get into the indoors on a cold day.
   B. I am invigorated by a brisk, cold day.
6. A. I like "wild" uninhibited parties.
   B. I prefer quiet parties with good conversation.
7. A. I can't stand watching a movie that I've seen before.
   B. There are some movies I enjoy seeing a second or even a third time.
8. A. Using "four letter words" in public is vulgar and inconsiderate of the feelings of others.
   B. I sometimes use "four letter words" to express my feelings or to shock someone.
9. A. I find a certain pleasure in routine kinds of work.
   B. Although it is sometimes necessary, I usually dislike routine kinds of work.
10. A. I often wish I could be a mountain climber.
    B. I can't understand people who risk their necks climbing mountains.
11. A. I dislike all body odors.
    B. I like some of the earthy body smells.
12. A. I get bored seeing the same old faces.
    B. I like the comfortable familiarity of everyday friends.
13. A. I like to dress in unusual styles.
    B. I tend to dress conservatively.
14. A. I am only interested in traveling in civilized parts of the world.
    B. I would like to travel to strange, out of the way places like the upper Amazon or Antarctica.
15. A. I like to explore a strange city or section of town by myself, even if it means getting lost.
    B. I prefer a guide when I am in a place I don't know well.
16. A. I dislike people who do or say things just to shock or upset others.
    B. When you can predict almost everything a person will do and say he or she must be a bore.
17. A. I usually don't enjoy a movie or play where I can predict what will happen in advance.
    B. I don't mind watching a movie or play where I can predict what will happen in advance.

18. A.   I have tried marijuana or would like to.
    B.   I would never smoke marijuana.
19. A.   I would not like to try any drug which might produce strange and dangerous effects on me.
    B.   I would like to try some of the new drugs that produce hallucinations.
20. A.   I would prefer living in an ideal society where everyone is safe, secure and happy.
    B.   I would have preferred living in the unsettled days of our history.
21. A.   A sensible person avoids activities that are dangerous.
    B.   I sometimes like to do things that are a little frightening.
22. A.   I dislike "swingers".
    B.   I enjoy the company of real "swingers".
23. A.   I find that stimulants make me uncomfortable.
    B.   I often like to get high (drinking liquor or smoking marijuana).
24. A.   A person should change jobs from time to time simply to avoid getting into a rut.
    B.   A person should find a job which is fairly satisfying to him and stick with it.
25. A.   I order the dishes with which I am familiar, so as to avoid disappointment and unpleasantness.
    B.   I like to try new foods that I have never tasted before.
26. A.   In a good sexual relationship people never get bored with each other.
    B.   It's normal to get bored after a time with the same sexual partner.
27. A.   I enjoy looking at home movies or travel slides.
    B.   Looking at someone's home movies or travel slides bores me tremendously.
28. A.   I like to try new brands on the chance of finding something different or better.
    B.   I stick to the brands I know are reliable.
29. A.   I would like to take up the sport of water-skiing.
    B.   I would not like to take up water-skiing.
30. A.   Most adultery happens because of sheer boredom.
    B.   Adultery is almost always the sign of a sick marriage.
31. A.   I would like to try surf-board riding.
    B.   I would not like to try surf-board riding.
32. A.   I find people who disagree with my beliefs more stimulating than people who agree with me.
    B.   I don't like to argue with people whose beliefs are sharply divergent from mine, since such arguments are never resolved.
33. A.   I would like to take off on a trip with no pre-planned or definite routes, or timetable.

    B.   When I go on a trip I like to plan my route and timetable fairly
         carefully.
34. A.   I prefer the "down-to-earth" kinds of people as friends.
    B.   I would like to make friends in some of the "far-out" groups like
         artists or "hippies".
35. A.   I would not like to learn to fly an airplane.
    B.   I would like to learn to fly an airplane.
36. A.   Most beards are unsightly.
    B.   I like to see men wearing beards.
37. A.   I would like to go scuba diving.
    B.   I prefer the surface of the water to the depths.
38. A.   I would like to meet some persons who are homosexual (men or
         women).
    B.   I stay away from anyone I suspect of being "queer".
39. A.   I prefer modern jazz or classical music to more popular or light clas-
         sical music.
    B.   I prefer popular or light classical music to modern jazz or classical
         music.
40. A.   I like to drive in open convertibles.
    B.   I do not like to drive in open convertibles.
41. A.   I would like to have the experience of being hypnotized.
    B.   I would not like to be hypnotized.
42. A.   The most important goal of life is to live it to the fullest and experi-
         ence as much of it as you can.
    B.   The most important goal of life is to find peace and happiness.
43. A.   I would like to try parachute jumping.
    B.   I would never want to try jumping out of a plane with or without a
         parachute.
44. A.   I enter cold water gradually giving myself time to get used to it.
    B.   I like to dive or jump right into the ocean or a cold pool.
45. A.   I do not like the irregularity and discord of most modern music.
    B.   I like to listen to new and unusual kinds of music.
46. A.   I prefer friends who are excitingly unpredictable.
    B.   I prefer friends who are reliable and predictable.
47. A.   I am not interested in experience for its own sake.
    B.   I like to have new and exciting experiences and sensations even if
         they are a little frightening, unconventional or illegal.
48. A.   When I go on a vacation I prefer the comfort of a good room and bed.
    B.   When I go on a vacation I would prefer the change of camping out.
49. A.   When I go in an ocean or lake I like to stay close to shore.
    B.   Sometimes I like to swim far out from the shore.

50. A.   I often enjoy flouting irrational authority.
    B.   I am generally respectful of lawful authority.
51. A.   The essence of good art is in its clarity, symmetry of form and harmony of colors.
    B.   I often find beauty in the "clashing" colors and irregular forms of modern paintings.
52. A.   I enjoy spending time in the familiar surroundings of home.
    B.   I get very restless if I have to stay around home for any length of time.
53. A.   I like to dive off the high board.
    B.   I don't like the feeling I get standing on the high board (or I don't go near it at all).
54. A.   I like to date members of the opposite sex who are physically exciting.
    B.   I like to date members of the opposite sex who share my values.
55. A.   Heavy drinking usually ruins a party because some people get loud and boisterous.
    B.   Keeping the drinks full is the key to a good party.
56. A.   I sometimes like to do "crazy" things just to see the effects on others.
    B.   I almost always behave in a normal way. I am not interested in shocking or upsetting others.
57. A.   The worst social sin is to be rude.
    B.   The worst social sin is to be a bore.
58. A.   I look forward to a good night of rest after a long day.
    B.   I wish I didn't have to waste so much of a day sleeping.
59. A.   A person should have considerable sexual experience before marriage.
    B.   It's better if two married persons begin their sexual experience with each other.
60. A.   Even if I had the money I would not care to associate with flighty persons like those in the "jet set".
    B.   I could conceive of myself seeking pleasures around the world with the "jet set".
61. A.   I like people who are sharp and witty even if they do sometimes insult others.
    B.   I dislike people who have their fun at the expense of hurting the feelings of others.
62. A.   Almost everything enjoyable is illegal or immoral.
    B.   The most enjoyable things are perfectly legal and moral.
63. A.   A good painting should shock or jolt the senses.
    B.   A good painting should give one a feeling of peace and security.

64. A. There is altogether too much portrayal of sex in movies.
    B. I enjoy watching many of the "sexy" scenes in movies.
65. A. I do not enjoy discussions where people get so "heated up" they end up insulting each other.
    B. I enjoy a heated intellectual argument even if people sometimes get upset.
66. A. I feel best after taking a couple of drinks.
    B. Something is wrong with people who need liquor to feel good.
67. A. People who ride motorcycles must have some kind of an unconscious need to hurt themselves.
    B. I would like to drive or ride on a motorcycle.
68. A. People should dress according to some standards of taste, neatness and style.
    B. People should dress in individual ways even if the effects are sometimes strange.
69. A. Sailing long distances in small sailing crafts is foolhardy.
    B. I would like to sail a long distance in a small but seaworthy sailing craft.
70. A. I have no patience with dull or boring persons.
    B. I find something interesting in almost every person I talk with.
71. A. Skiing fast down a high mountain slope is a good way to end up on crutches.
    B. I think I would enjoy the sensations of skiing very fast down a high mountain slope.
72. A. I prefer people who are calm and even tempered.
    B. I prefer people who are emotionally expressive even if they are a bit unstable.

APPENDIX B[a]

STANDARD (T) SCORE FOR MALES (M) AND FEMALES (F)

Raw Scores	General M	General F	TAS M	TAS F	ES M	ES F	Dis M	Dis F	BS M	BS F	Raw Scores
0	12	17	7	17	25	28	29	33	25	27	0
1	15	20	11	20	28	31	33	37	28	30	1
2	18	22	15	23	31	33	36	41	31	33	2
3	21	25	19	27	33	36	39	44	34	36	3
4	24	28	23	30	36	38	42	48	38	40	4
5	26	30	27	34	38	41	45	52	41	43	5
6	29	33	30	37	41	44	48	55	44	46	6
7	32	35	34	40	43	46	51	59	47	49	7
8	35	38	38	44	46	49	54	62	50	52	8
9	38	41	42	47	49	51	57	66	54	55	9
10	40	43	46	50	51	54	60	70	57	58	10
11	43	46	50	54	54	56	63	73	60	62	11
12	46	48	53	57	56	59	66	77	63	65	12
13	49	51	57	60	59	62	69	81	66	68	13
14	52	54	61	64	61	64	73	84	70	71	14
15	54	56			64	67			73	74	15
16	57	59			67	69			76	77	16
17	60	61			69	72			79	80	17
18	63	64			72	75			82	83	18
19	66	66									19
20	68	69									20
21	71	72									21
22	74	75									22

[a] Based on University of Delaware Introductory Psychology Students

Males N = 686 Females N = 850

APPENDIX C[a]

PERCENTILE SCORES FOR MALES (M) AND FEMALES (F)

Raw Scores	General M	General F	TAS M	TAS F	ES M	ES F	Dis M	Dis F	BS M	BS F	Raw Scores
0	0	0	0	0	0	0	0	0	0	0	0
1	0	0	0	0	0	0	1	5	0	0	1
2	0	0	1	1	1	2	7	17	0	2	2
3	0	1	1	1	4	6	13	28	4	5	3
4	1	1	1	3	7	11	21	39	8	11	4
5	1	2	2	5	11	19	28	51	15	20	5
6	2	4	4	9	16	26	35	64	22	31	6
7	3	7	6	13	23	34	44	75	35	42	7
8	5	11	10	20	31	42	59	84	48	55	8
9	8	15	16	28	38	51	69	91	58	66	9
10	12	20	23	38	50	60	79	96	71	75	10
11	20	28	34	51	61	69	87	98	80	82	11
12	28	37	45	64	70	76	93	99	86	88	12
13	38	47	61	79	75	82	98	99	92	92	13
14	51	57	82	91	82	89	99	99	96	97	14
15	62	66			88	93			99	99	15
16	72	75			94	96			99	99	16
17	79	84			97	98			99	99	17
18	87	91			99	99			99	99	18
19	93	95									19
20	96	98									20
21	99	99									21
22	99	99									22

[a] Based on University of Delaware Introductory Psychology Students
Males N = 686   Females N = 850

APPENDIX D

SCORING KEY FOR SENSATION SEEKING SCALE (SSS)

Form IV

I. *General SSS* (Males and Females) 22 items
  Score: 2A, 5B, 10A, 11B, 12A, 15A, 19B, 20B, 21B, 29A, 33A, 35B, 41A, 42A, 43A, 44B, 46A, 48B, 51B, 63A, 67B, 72B.

II. *Thrill and Adventure Seeking* (TA) (Males and Females) 14 items
  Score: 1B, 10A, 21B, 29A, 31A, 35B, 37A, 40A, 43A, 49B, 53A, 67B, 69B, 71B.

III. *Experience Seeking* (ES) (Males and Females) 18 items
  Score: 3A, 8B, 13A, 14B, 18A, 19B, 33A, 34B, 36B, 38A, 39A, 45B, 46A, 47B, 50A, 51B, 56A, 68B.

IV. *Disinhibition* (Dis) (Males and Females) 14 items
  Score: 4B, 6A, 22B, 23B, 26B, 30A, 54A, 55B, 59A, 60B, 61A, 62A, 64B, 66A.

V. *Boredom Susceptibility* (BS) (Males and Females) 18 items
  Score: 7A, 9B, 12A, 16B, 17A, 20B, 24A, 25B, 27B, 28A, 32A, 46A, 52B, 57B, 58B, 63A, 65B, 70A.

APPENDIX E

SCORING FOR NEARY—ZUCKERMAN SSAST[a]

Directions

The following statements describe various moods and feelings. Please read each statement and indicate on the 1 to 5 scale the degree to which the statement describes how you feel *NOW*, at this time.

Answer the statements on your answer sheet.

Use the following scale in answering each item:

(1) Not at all (2) Slightly (3) Somewhat (4) Definitely (5) Very much

SS 1.	I feel interested.	SS19.	I feel imaginative.
A 2.	I feel afraid.	A20.	I feel tense.
3.	I feel thoughtful.	SS21.	I feel confident.
SS 4.	I feel elated.	A22.	I feel shaky.
A 5.	I feel secure. R	23.	I feel pleasant.
A 6.	I feel desperate.	SS24.	I feel zany.
SS 7.	I feel adventurous.	A25.	I feel calm. R
SS 8.	I feel pleased.	SS26.	I feel curious.
A 9.	I feel steady. R	A27.	I feel fearful.
SS10.	I feel lucky.	SS28.	I feel cooperative.
A11.	I feel upset.	29.	I feel cheerful.
12.	I feel loving.	A30.	I feel terrified.
13.	I feel daring.	31.	I feel mischievous.
14.	I feel contented. R	SS32.	I feel joyful.
A15.	I feel nervous.	A33.	I feel panicky.
SS16.	I feel enthusiastic.	SS34.	I feel playful.
SS17.	I feel amused.	35.	I feel happy.
A18.	I feel frightened.	A36.	I feel worried.

[a] Sensation Seeking and Anxiety States Test

KEY—SS=Sensation Seeking State (15 items) weighted score 1 to 5 each item.

Total score=Sum of weighted score on each item (range=15 to 75)

Neutral occasion, 86 males, 102 females (undergrads), Males $\overline{X}$=39.5, SD=10.7; Females $\overline{X}$=39.6, SD=10.2.

A=Anxiety State Test (15 items) weighted score as above except that items marked R are scored in the reverse direction, i.e., 5=1, 4=2, 3=3, 2=4, 1=5 (range=15 to 75)

Neutral occasion 86 males, 102 females (undergrads), Males $\overline{X}$=25.3, SD=7.3; Females $\overline{X}$=25.9, SD=9.3.

CHAPTER 13

TRUST

LOIS C. STACK

Hutchings Psychiatric Center
Syracuse, New York

"Trust everybody—but cut the cards." This maxim, drawn from *Mr. Dooley's Philosophy* (Dunne, 1900/1970), illustrates two different types of trust. "Trust everybody" recognizes the vital necessity of human interdependence. Valuing such interdependence, we place ourselves in a precarious situation every time we extend trust. Hence, Mr. Dooley's secondary message: just to make sure, "cut the cards." Whether in poker, love, business, or war, we constantly risk our very being. We are doomed if we trust all and equally doomed if we trust none. To protect ourselves, we are forced to take each situation as it comes: judging intentions, sizing up risks, weighing and evaluating expected outcomes, and —just in case all else fails—instituting protective measures such as card cutting or signing legal contracts.

Although most people agree on the importance of trusting others, they have found it necessary to assess each situation before investing their trust. The degree of risk, the personal characteristics and intentions of the partner, and the potential rewards are some of the considerations that go into a decision either to trust or mistrust. Individual perceptions of situational characteristics vary, so that in any given situation some people would insist that the cards be cut whereas others would not. In addition, individuals differ in their feelings about the trustworthiness of people in general: the degree to which they subscribe to Mr. Dooley's admonition to "trust everybody."

Trust, an assured reliance on another person, is necessary for human survival. George Eliot recognized the isolation that accompanies the complete lack of it: "What loneliness is more lonely than distrust?" We need to be able to trust others not only for our own personal sense of well-being but also for the smooth functioning of society. Some segments of the world's population tend crops and cattle, others prepare them for food consumption, still others make them directly available to us. We have come to depend on these and other complicated processes to fulfill our own needs. Every day we trust our money to banks, our security to various government agencies, our well-being to a network of law enforcement

561

and other agencies. We even have enough trust in human nature not to worry about being hit by a car passing us on the street.

The best known general theory of trust is that of Erikson (1963), who has been concerned with the development of personality early in life. Erikson has emphasized that within the first two years of life each individual must learn to trust at least one other person. Trust is considered basic to all other aspects of personality development, especially the growing sense of personal identity. Erikson also has pointed out the situational aspects of trust: There is a dynamic process of balancing between trust and mistrust. The balance changes constantly from situation to situation and develops continuously throughout the lifespan. Questionnaire data indicate that people demonstrate individual differences in levels of trust, and these levels have been systematically related to behavioral as well as cultural differences. What is needed is to demonstrate that trust, as Erikson defines it, is indeed basic to the unfolding sense of identity and to psychologically healthy personality development. Can a person go through life constantly expecting the worst from his colleagues, friends, and family, and still be considered psychologically well adjusted? Conversely, is it possible for someone to trust other people without trusting himself?

We have only anecdotal evidence that a sense of trust might be considered basic to a healthy personality. Many educational and interpersonal problems seem to stem from a lack of basic trust. Educational researchers have devised numerous enrichment programs for socially disadvantaged children, but these programs have produced few lasting effects on intellectual achievement (Hellmuth, 1967). Such disappointing results are often blamed on the children's basic mistrust, which mitigates the effectiveness of social reinforcers and prevents the sort of mutual interpersonal interaction on which true education depends. The same problem has been noted with emotionally disturbed children. Such children exhibit faulty peer and adult relationships, and the more enlightened treatment programs usually emphasize the need to develop a sense of basic trust (Hobbs, 1966). In the treatment of adults, too, most schools of psychotherapeutic treatment recognize a common goal: the restoration of a sense of trust. Trust might be construed also as one of the underlying factors in job success. A person who lacks the trust of his coworkers undermines effectiveness and fosters strained professional relationships. Because of this, he may not get the promotion he feels he deserves, thus reinforcing in his mind a mistrust of his environment.

In addition to the personal and interpersonal realms, the fields of commerce, politics, and international relations are also affected by trust and mistrust. For example, a syndicated newspaper columnist recently offered her own rule of thumb for assessing a used-car dealer's trustworthiness: "Make sure he sings in your church choir, has a son running for political office, a wife who is a homeroom mother, and doesn't flinch when you suggest taping the entire sales pitch" (Bombeck, 1975). Trust is basic to our entire financial system: Witness the bank failures of 1929, when virtually everyone withdrew funds in a simultaneous display of lost confidence. Conversely, when some years ago the banks in Ireland closed for several months owing to a strike, sheer optimism kept the commercial system alive. The Irish people wrote checks on all sorts of odd pieces of paper, drawn against funds that were inaccessible for several months, and these "checks" were exchanged and cashed with little difficulty. People displayed very high levels of trust, first in accepting IOUs for goods and services payable whenever the strike could be settled (provided the person actually had the funds he purported to have), and second in believing that the banking system would eventually get the whole mess straightened out and resume normal operations. Breakdown of the entire Irish economy may well have been averted by this massive demonstration of trust.

Governments may rise or fall according to the degree of popular trust they inspire. Confidence in the United States government was shaken severely by the Watergate scandal. Each day brought new revelations of previously undetected instances of deception in high government office, and the reverberations were felt across the nation. Redevelopment of a sense of trust was widely cited as the first order of business for a nation struggling to recover from the depths of trauma. Incoming President Gerald Ford publicly proclaimed a restoration of faith as his first duty, since government cannot function without the people's trust. Such a concept is built into all democratic governments; many depend on a parliamentary vote of confidence to decide whether the leadership will continue or change.

In this section we have noted that trust is believed to affect many arenas of interpersonal exchange: educational, social, commercial, and political. The following section examines generalized trust—that is, the feelings people have about the general trustworthiness of others. The study of trust as it varies over transactions—that is, its situational determinants—will be discussed in the remaining sections of the chapter.

GENERALIZED TRUST

From the moment of birth, each individual encounters a variety of others who treat him positively or negatively, who keep their promises or do not. Each person generalizes from these past experiences in the process of developing expectancies about how the next person will treat him. These expectancies about the trustworthiness of people in general are what is meant in this chapter by *generalized trust*. Some individuals tend to give most people the benefit of the doubt, trusting loved ones and strangers alike until experience shows it is not warranted. Others expect only the worst of everyone around them. These people have developed differing levels of generalized trust based on their past interpersonal experiences.

These levels in themselves do not determine whether a person will trust or mistrust another in any specific situation. One reason, of course, is the difficulty of relating any internal, inferred characteristic such as a trait to some observable behavior (Mischel, 1968). This reason has led to the current trend in personality research of investigating situational determinants of behavior. The trend is of great importance in the study of trust, because trusting behavior always depends on the situation and the other person's behavior.

Identical situations may be perceived differently by different persons, however; and one of the determinants of this perception is the individual's level of generalized trust. People who trust few others respond differently to situations than those who trust nearly everyone. The study of both situational characteristics and generalized trust is necessary for full understanding of the construct.

To study a dimension of personality, we must first define what is to be studied. From a broad, general definition we proceed to a specific, operational definition that states exactly what we are measuring in terms of the measuring instrument itself. A major problem in the study of trust has been that although all words carry multiple meanings to various listeners, abstract words such as *trust* have even more associative meanings than most. *Confidence, reliance,* and *faith* are often used interchangeably with the word *trust;* each of these words is also fraught with abstract associations. Webster defines *trust* in the sense of a belief: an assured reliance on some person or thing; a confidence dependent on the character, ability, strength, or truth of someone or something. The distinguishing feature of trust, according to Webster, is that it may rest on blended *evidence of experience* and on more *subjective grounds,* such as knowledge, affection, admiration, respect, or reverence. These dual sources of trust (objective and subjective) seem to differentiate it from related concepts.

Provided with a definition of trust, we still encounter the problem of deciding how to measure it. The first attempts to measure generalized trust proceeded from broad, abstract definitions as found in Webster; a more recent line of research has narrowed the focus to a belief in the credibility of others.

Trust Measures

Philosophies of Human Nature Scale (PHN)

In the early 1960s Wrightsman (1964, 1974) became interested in people's assumptions about human nature that appeared to be pervasive and influential forces in guiding behavior. He reasoned that we all seek to understand, simplify, and predict the behavior of those around us since their behavior can have such a great influence on our success in life. One of the substantive areas Wrightsman investigated was beliefs about the trustworthiness of people in general. He postulated several other dimensions of belief about human nature as well: man's strength of will and rationality, altruism, independence from group pressures, and two others concerning the complexity and variability of persons. For each dimension, 20 statements were prepared, using as sources writings of philosophers and social scientists, essays of college students on the topic of human nature, and expressions of assumptions about human nature found in the mass media. In the final version, called the Philosophies of Human Nature (PHN) Scale, 14 items for each dimension were rated on six-point scales measuring the extent of agreement or disagreement with each statement. Wrightsman (1974) described the problems of item selection in this way:

> The formation and selection of this pool of statements were, of course, critically important; no final, revised, purified scale could succeed if the initial pool of items were weak. The process of selecting items, although thorough, was hampered because there was no classification of situations from which to select representative statements. For example, the dimension of trustworthiness of human nature has been defined as the extent to which people are seen as moral, honest, and reliable—but moral in *what*? There are many diverse activities and relationships in which a person can be trustworthy and untrustworthy—with money, with secrets, with responsibilities to perform, with someone else's wife. In a very thorough and self-disciplined way, an employee of the Committee to Re-Elect the President carries out his assigned duties to bug the Democratic Party headquarters—although he knows his actions are illegal. The butcher who owns a small meat market always resists the temptation to cheat on his income tax but routinely overweighs the meat that he sells to his customers. Are such people untrustworthy? . . . For those who set forth to measure beliefs about trustworthiness, this problem will remain unsolvable until situations in which people can be considered trustworthy or untrustworthy are classified. We selected statements for the trustworthiness scale that tapped attitudes about a variety of situations, including monetary activities, cheating on exams, and tasks that involve individual responsibility. (pp. 49–50)

Wrightsman thought that beliefs about trustworthiness would be unrelated conceptually to those concerning altruism, that is, that these dimensions would be independent. It now appears that these two beliefs cannot be separated; people who are considered unreliable and dishonest are also perceived as selfish and uncooperative (Walker & Mosher, 1970). The strong relationship between the two subscales is demonstrated by correlations ranging from 0.66 to 0.71 in five samples of test scores totaling 1101 subjects (Wrightsman, 1974). Thus, although the version of the PHN that has been used for the past 10 years contains 14 items for each of two theoretically independent dimensions, the latest version recognizes that the items tap different aspects of the same dimension.

An empirical definition of trust has resulted from two separate factor analyses of item responses to the PHN scale by 1059 subjects. By statistically examining the intercorrelations of test items over a very large pool of subjects, such analyses can identify the items that cluster together empirically. Although the two analyses differed technically (Wrightsman, 1974), results were essentially similar. If individuals tended to have one set of opinions about people's trustworthiness and another about their altruism, as Wrightsman originally hypothesized, responses to the two sets of PHN items should have sorted themselves into two statistical factors. Instead, all the items clustered together. However, rather than form one main trust factor, they separated into two components—negative beliefs and positive beliefs. A few of the items loading on the new factors came from still other PHN dimensions. Appendix A presents the revised PHN subscales. Ten negatively worded statements comprise the first factor, Cynicism, and ten positively worded ones the other, which Wrightsman terms Beliefs That People Are Conventionally Good. The separation of these concepts is interesting. The original PHN dimensions were originally conceptualized as bipolar. People's beliefs about trustworthiness and altruism were expected to vary from negative to positive with cynical beliefs opposed by trusting beliefs. The factor analyses indicate, however, that negative beliefs coexist with positive ones. People can be pessimistic about others' honesty and morality, yet simultaneously believe that they can be relied on in a pinch.

The two dimensions of beliefs about human nature appear to be significantly related, yet so different from each other as to form separate, independently measurable aspects of trust–mistrust. Correlations between the two dimensions in three samples of college students were -0.27, -0.33, and -0.61 (Wrightsman, 1974). This set of correlations indicates that a person's responses to negative statements about human nature cannot be predicted accurately from his responses to positive statements about human nature, although there is a tendency toward an inverse relationship. Each dimension of PHN trust is concerned with whether people can be relied on to help and care for one another, to tell the truth as they see it, and to behave according to ethical standards. One contains beliefs that people, by and large, are good and can be trusted, whereas the second notes that, on the other hand, people have been known to lie, cheat, and steal. The fact that two factors are necessary to account for the construct supports the balancing process proposed by Erikson: Each person is continually weighing trust against mistrust.

Perceptions of unselfishness and reliability are accompanied by social evaluation. The degree of trustworthiness we attribute to others is affected by how much we like them. Webster referred to a subjective as well as an objective basis for trust. At times this subjective basis may override objective considerations, as Charlie Brown has found in his annual football place-kicking episode in the *Peanuts* comic strip. Every year Lucy graciously offers to hold the ball for his place-kick, and every year she deftly withdraws the ball just after Charlie Brown's leg gains momentum in its inevitable path out from under him. Yet every year Charlie, after some initial distrust based on his objective assessment of past experience, yields to his subjective feelings, including his liking for Lucy. His "undying faith in human nature" holds sway, to his great regret as history repeats itself. A subjective, social evaluation of human nature can indeed be one of the bases for generalized trust, but an objective assessment of the situation is equally important.

The relationship between social evaluation and trust has been considered by Tedeschi (1973) in a theory of interpersonal attraction. He believes that attraction plays a central role in interpersonal relations because of the ultimate helplessness of people and the fact that they must depend on others for reinforcement. This necessary reliance on others for help implies both trust and altruism. Tedeschi's theory attempts to unravel three overlapping constructs—trust, altruism, and interpersonal attraction: "Trust mediates liking because reliable communications are helpful to the person and enable him to gain rewards and/or avoid punishments" (p. 208).

Trust, altruism, and attraction are closely related. According to Tedeschi, a person who appears helpful will be liked and trusted. On the other hand, if his intentions are self-serving, he may still be liked but not trusted. Tedeschi does not believe that like and dislike of others are polar opposite attitudes. Instead, he assumes they are independent, much in the same manner that Wrightsman found PHN trust and mistrust to be separate but moderately related. Testing this hypothesis, Nacci, Stapleton, and Tedeschi (1973) found that individuals' attraction to their partners (the expectancy that partners would provide benefits) in an experimental game was unrelated to the individuals' disattraction (the expectancy that partners would do harm). This finding of independence suggests that it is possible to expect both benefits and harm from others simultaneously in differing degrees. These expectancies also have an affective component, the degree to which the partner is liked or disliked. Tedeschi's theory fits well with Wrightsman's definition of trust as a combination of positive and negative beliefs about the trustworthiness and unselfishness of people in general. Experimental evidence thus supports Freud's concept of *ambivalence:* It is possible simultaneously to like and dislike, to trust and distrust other people.

Interpersonal Trust Scale

The study of trust depends on how one defines it; ultimately, it takes its definition from the instrument developed to measure it. Rotter (1967) chose to measure the expectancy that the word, promise, or verbal or written statement of an individual or group can be relied on. Such a definition, termed *interpersonal trust,* attempts to exclude subjective elements such as attraction and to focus on two more objective aspects of trust. First, only credibility is to be considered, not morality. That is, will a person do what he says he will do? Second, the word *expectancy* implies an estimate of the probability of occurrence of an act, based on past experience. This conception of trust derives from principles of a social learning theory (Rotter, 1954) in which a person is seen to develop expectancies for a given behavior to lead to a particular positive or negative outcome. Each individual has different expectancies for reinforcement in interactions involving trust: He is not as likely to be reinforced for believing a stranger as for believing his best friend. (Whether he chooses to believe will depend also on his personal valuation of the reinforcement.) After many experiences with different agents in varying situations, an individual builds up generalized expectancies. The Interpersonal Trust Scale (IT) attempts to measure these expectancies.

Since expectancies differ across situations, Rotter (1971) devised what he called an additive test, "one whose purpose is to sample a broad range of situations of more or less equivalent strengths with the effectiveness of the instrument dependent upon the adequacy of the sampling of the situation" (p. 445). The IT scale samples a wide variety of social objects: parents, classmates, teachers, politicians, physicians, and so forth. A high score shows trust across objects. In addition to the specific items, a few "were stated in broader terms presumed to measure a more general optimism regarding society" (Rotter, 1967, p. 653). This appears to be a recognition that a subjective aspect cannot entirely be excluded in measuring trust. Stability and internal consistency of the scale are adequate (Rotter, 1967) and comparable to those of the PHN (Wrightsman, 1964, 1974). For research purposes, the scale may be obtained from Dr. J. B. Rotter at the University of Connecticut, Storrs, Conn. 06268. Most of the items appear also in the Hochreich and Rotter (1970) study.

Items in the two trust questionnaires are remarkably similar. For example, compare the IT's, "It is safe to believe that in spite of what people say, most people are primarily interested in their own welfare" with the PHN's "Most people inwardly dislike putting themselves out to help other people." IT: "Fear of social disgrace or punishment rather than conscience prevents most people from breaking the law." PHN: "Most people are not really honest for a desirable reason; they are afraid of getting caught." IT: "Hypocrisy is on the increase in our society." PHN: "Most people will speak out for what they believe in." At least seven of the 25 IT items refer to a generalized social object and are directly comparable to PHN items.

However, the diversity of social objects in the IT scale allows differential assessment of dimensions of trust. Factor-analytic studies can be useful not only to clarify the construct of trust but also to increase the measure's utility for predicting behavior. For example, Rotter (1975) reports that two replicated factors of the IT have been found to be more closely related than the total IT score to certain behaviors. One factor is trust of peers or other familiar social agents. Items that reflect this are: "Parents usually can be relied upon to keep their promises," and "Using the Honor System of not having a teacher present during exams would probably result in increased cheating." In a current study under Rotter's supervision, students who score low on this dimension of peer trust appear to cheat fellow students more than do those who trust familiar agents. The second IT factor is institutional or political trust, or trust in those with whom people have little direct contact; for example, "The judiciary is a place where we can all get unbiased treatment.'' Roberts (1972) found political trust to be significantly related to high levels of social activism by students. Chun and Campbell (1974) also have investigated dimensions of the IT scale but have not related them to behaviors.

Trust Scale Relationships

Given these two major measures, what is the difference between trust conceived as a set of positive and negative attitudes toward people and trust as a generalized expectancy about what they will do? Although the two instruments measure somewhat different aspects, the significant positive relationship between the two scales suggests that they are both measuring the same underlying construct of trust. Investigators report correlations of 0.62 (O'Connor, 1970) and 0.76 (Chun & Campbell, 1974) for N's of 30 and 187 college students.

The strongest area of overlap is in attitudes toward people and society in general. The PHN score reflects a more evaluative attitude toward others (attraction–disattraction), whereas the IT score reflects expectancies about specific interpersonal agents. Both have demonstrated similar and adequate levels of stability and internal consistency. Conceived as an expectancy about the actions of specific agents, trust (IT) has been tied somewhat more successfully to actual behaviors and other validating evidence than has trust (PHN). Validation of the latter has consisted in attempting to demonstrate different levels of trust for various subgroupings of people. Validating results for these measures are presented in the next sections.

Before we turn to such results, however, several other trust instruments should be mentioned. One is a five-item Faith-in-People/Misanthropy scale (Rosenberg, 1956); another (Constantinople, 1970) requires 10 self-ratings, with items derived from Eriksonian theory. Three instruments have been developed for use with children as young as the fourth grade (Hochreich, 1973; Imber, 1973; Wrightsman, 1974). Current information about trust as a personality dimension depends mainly on work using the IT and PHN. The exploration of relationships among trust scores, other personality dimensions, and trusting behaviors not only helps to define generalized trust but provides validating evidence for the measuring instruments. The following sections present that evidence.

Construct Validity

Similarities and differences have been noted between the two major measures of trust. Each has defined the construct somewhat differently; in both cases the original definition has been refined by subsequent research, particularly factor analyses.

This chapter has presented the PHN in a form substantially revised from that which was used in most of the research already completed. Although the form of the IT has not been altered, subsets of items comprising dimensions of trust have been identified. Thus, refinement of the construct definition and measurement has been one of the major achievements of trust research to this point. In the sections that follow, trust refers to scores on the Trustworthiness subscale of the PHN or to the total IT score. Although no data are yet available for the revised PHN or the IT dimensions, it is expected that their use will result in a much clearer picture of generalized trust.

Group Differences

One of the most pervasive group differences found in the study of personality is that between the sexes. A first consideration for any measure, then, is whether males and females achieve different scores. Erikson's theory of basic trust offers no grounds for expecting sex differences in trust. Although women commonly are stereotyped as being more trusting than men (Hochreich, 1975), no differences have been observed in using the IT (Rotter, 1967; Sawyer, Pasewark, Davis, & Fitzgerald, 1973). However, Roberts (1972) has found that women score significantly higher than men in the IT dimension Trust of Peers and men significantly higher in Political Trust. Differential scores on the two dimensions possibly cancel each other, accounting for the similarity of total IT scores for the two sexes.

Women consistently score higher than men on the PHN (Wrightsman, 1974). Maccoby and Jacklin (1974), in a review of research on sex differences, state that women are more likely than men to report that they like people with whom they interact. Since the PHN carries an evaluative aspect of trust, sex differences in these scores probably indicate that females like people in general somewhat better than do males. In other words they may be just as careful to "cut the cards," as IT total scores would indicate, but they may believe more strongly that people (especially peers and those whom they contact directly) are good and *should* be trusted.

In his theory of psychosocial development, Erikson (1963) emphasizes that interpersonal caretaker behaviors are not the only determinants of trust. The caretaker needs the support of the family, and the family in turn is ultimately supported by the society around it. Schools, churches, culture, and traditions all contribute to the societal support that sustains caretakers in their role of teaching trust to children. Given this theory, we would expect to find differences in measured trust between groups that differ in the degree of societal support available. Both trust instruments have demonstrated such differences. It is generally conceded that black people have fewer financial supports, a higher degree of interference with their culture and traditions, and less contact with dominant United States institutions. It is no surprise, then, that they consistently respond less trustingly on both scales than do whites (Switkin & Gynther, 1974; Wrightsman, 1974).

Evidence for socioeconomic group differences, however, is conflicting. Using fathers' occupations as indices of socioeconomic status, Rotter (1967) found that college students from the more affluent levels of society scored significantly higher in IT trust ($p < 0.01$; N = 547) than did those from the lower levels, but others have found nonsignificant differences for 959 high school students similarly categorized (Sawyer et al., 1973). No PHN differences have been reported.

Religious support, too, can be expected to result in higher levels of trust according to Erikson's theory. The IT scale significantly ($p < 0.001$) differentiated among religious groups of respondents, with Jewish college students scoring highest and those listing none, agnostic, or atheist, lowest (Rotter, 1967). Furthermore, those students whose parents were of differing religions were significantly less trusting ($p < 0.001$) than those who had the presumably stronger moral support of parents belonging to the same faith. Religious differences have not been related directly to PHN scores, although it has been shown that students at strict, fundamentalist colleges score lower than do others (Wrightsman, 1974), which has been attributed to strong fundamentalist teachings about the sinfulness of man.

Another indication that trusters and mistrusters may have different family backgrounds comes from an investigation of their parents' trust (Katz & Rotter, 1969). Fathers of highly trusting sons scored significantly above fathers of low trusters on the IT scale. However, no significant effects were found for daughters, nor did mothers appear to exert the differential effect shown for fathers.

Early socialization can be assumed to affect not only trust–mistrust but the establishment of delinquent behavior patterns. It often has been speculated that juvenile delinquents are less trusting than nondelinquent adolescents. Testing this hypothesis has been difficult because of the dearth of trust scales written simply enough for full comprehension by younger groups. When the PHN was used to test three groups (N = 142) of 12- to 18-year-old boys and girls in state correctional schools or detention homes, only those able to read and understand the statements were tested, and they were found to be more mistrusting than controls (Richards, Mates, & Whitten, 1967). A less complexly worded form of the IT (correlation with adult form, 0.89) was constructed and administered to 92 male and female incarcerated delinquents ages 14 to 18 years (Fitzgerald, Pasewark, & Noah, 1970). No differences were found between delinquents and normals on trust measured by this revision, nor were scores much different from college students' means. Reasons for the discrepancy in results are unknown; but the development of trust measures more suitable for a younger, less literate population may enable clarification of the relationship between delinquent behavior and mistrust.

We might expect high and low trusters to differ in their choice of occupation. Although there is no theoretical basis for such a supposition, it seems logical that those who choose to work with people in one of the helping professions or in teaching would like people and be more optimistic about society than would persons who choose occupations with little human contact. Wrightsman (1974) has provided extensive data on PHN scores in various occupational groups. In general, guidance counselors and teachers demonstrated the most trusting, favorable views of others. Graduate students in clinical and counseling psychology were similar to psychotherapists in showing a moderate degree of trust, whereas experimental psychology graduate students scored significantly as less trusting than those in other areas of psychology.

One thing known about college students is that "they ain't what they used to be"—at least as regards trust. Each trust instrument has been administered annually to similarly constituted groups of incoming students, the IT to 4605 elementary psychology students during the years 1964 to 1969 and the PHN to 2117 freshmen during the years 1962 to 1971. The colleges probably drew different samples, since the first was a state university in Connecticut and the second a private teachers' college in Tennessee. Nevertheless, both found that the successive groups of students tested were increasingly mistrusting over the years. A linear trend analysis of the PHN data showed the decline in trust between 1962 and 1968 to be highly significant ($p < 0.0001$); after 1968, scores varied inconsistently around the low 1968 mean (Baker & Wrightsman, 1974). IT scores dropped to the point that a student of average trust (72.4) in 1964 would be considered highly trusting in 1969, when the mean dropped to 66.6 (Hochreich & Rotter, 1970). Mean scores on the PHN trustworthiness subscale dropped about 10 points from 1962 to 1968, almost a whole standard deviation. (To illustrate the size of the difference, take an example from the field of intelligence testing: If a person earned an I.Q. score of 78, he would have been classified as "borderline mentally retarded" in 1962 and "normal" in 1968.) It is not known whether this decline in trust scores was owing to students' increased willingness to admit feelings of distrust (the increased social desirability of a cynical stance) or to real feelings of increased despair about others and society. The latter interpretation is supported by increased Taylor Manifest Anxiety scores—again a significant trend ($p < 0.0001$). An item analysis of the IT scale showed no change in trust of direct contact agents but significant changes in 14 items dealing with politics, peacekeeping, and communications. Roberts (1972) found that subscale scores of the IT for political but not peer trust had changed significantly. Research on such trends needs to be brought up to date with additional work on trends in the social desirability of answering items in a cynical, mistrusting fashion. In addition, it should be pointed out that the published norms for the two instruments should be revised, since the original data were gathered in the early 1960s.

Relationship with Other Constructs

Establishing validity for the two trust measures requires a consideration of their relationships with other constructs. Evidence will be presented that persons who score high on trust measures also tend to demonstrate a moderate need for social approval (social desirability) and feelings of personal control over their own lives (internal locus of control) *and* are not Machiavellian.

Social desirability has already been mentioned in regard to trends toward increased mistrust in college students. Persons who demonstrate a need for social approval also tend to respond in a more trusting fashion, as indicated by correlations of about 0.30 between the Marlowe–Crowne social desirability scale (Crowne & Marlowe, 1964) and both major trust instruments. The relationship is considerably stronger for females than for males (Pearson's $r = 0.38$ versus 0.21; Rotter, 1967). Although many instruments are constructed to minimize such a correlation, developers of both trust instruments thought it unwise to eliminate items that were related to the motive for social approval. The degree to which an individual subscribes to the social norm to "trust everybody" is a component of trust.

Feelings of trust are related to feelings of control over one's own life and interpersonal affairs, judging from correlations in the 0.30s between the Internal-External Locus of Control Scale (Rotter, 1966) and both of the trust instruments. A person who feels powerless probably is also less able to trust others than one who can predict and control events around him. People who feel themselves controlled by outside forces score significantly lower on the two trust instruments.

Machiavellianism is probably the personality dimension most closely related to trust. Its -0.67 correlation with PHN trustworthiness indicates that trust is almost the polar opposite of Machiavellianism. Examination of items in the three factors found for the Machiavellian (Mach) scale (Christie & Geis, 1970, p. 387) shows that two deal with diffuse negativistic beliefs about society and the goodness or evil of man and are close to the realm of cynicism and mistrust. The third deals with Machiavellian tactics (e.g., "It is wise to flatter important people") and is not discussed in either of the trust scales. The high negative correlation between the two scales indicates that mistrusting persons are very likely to subscribe to Machiavellian beliefs.

One way of understanding a construct is to measure it in different ways and relate it to a variety of other constructs also measured in several ways. This multitrait, multimethod approach (Campbell & Fiske, 1959) allows the proportions of variance owing to methods and constructs to be partialed out. Such a matrix has never been completed for the construct of trust. One of the problems is the scarcity of measuring methods other than self-report questionnaires. As we will see later in this chapter, devising alternate ways to measure trust has been one of the stumbling blocks in the area. Rather than use questionnaire scores, trust can be rated by another person, either a trained judge or one of the subject's peers. The latter procedure was used by Rotter (1967) to assess the validity of the IT scale in a multimethod approach. Members of two fraternities ($N = 73$) and two sororities ($N = 83$) completed the IT scale, a self-rating of trust, and a set of sociometric ratings. For the self-rating, students compared their own trust to that of ''the average college student'' on a four-point scale: *much more, more, less, much less*. Each of the seven sociometric scales consisted of two narrative descriptions of persons at the ends of the scale for that personality trait. To avoid stereotyping, scales were not labeled. For example, trust was described (Rotter, 1967) this way:

> This person expects others to be honest. She is not suspicious of other people's intentions, she expects others to be open and that they can be relied upon to do what they say they will do.
> This person is cynical. She thinks other people are out to get as much as they can for themselves. She has little faith in human nature and in the promises or statements of other people.[1]

Respondents were to nominate three persons who fit each of the trust and mistrust descriptions and to do the same for bipolar descriptions of dependency, humor, gullibility, trustworthiness, popularity, and friendship. The study thus provided a comparison of three methods of measuring trust: questionnaire, self-rating and sociometric rating.

Table 13–1 shows highly significant ($p < 0.01$) correlations among the three. These represent the strongest relationships found for the IT scale. None of the trust measures correlated more highly with sociometric ratings of other constructs than they did with each other (one of the validity criteria suggested by Campbell and Fiske, 1959), except in the case of sociometric trustworthiness, which related to the IT about as well as the trust self-rating. The lower, but still significant, correlations of IT scores with other constructs measured sociometrically indicate that trusters were considered less dependent on others, more popular, and better friends than were mistrusters. These relationships were borne out for the sociometric measure of trust as well, although not for the self-rating. Gullibility, defined as ''naïve and easily fooled in contrast to sophisticated, experienced, etc.'' (Rotter, 1967, p. 663) is difficult to separate from trust. If we didn't know of Charlie Brown's battle between mistrust and his ''deep, abiding faith in human nature,'' we might consider his approach to Lucy's football a gullible one. It is difficult to know where trust ends and naïveté begins, but students in this study evidently perceived the distinction, as indicated by the nonsignificant relationship with the three trust measures.

Behavioral Correlates of Trust

Scores on the two trust measures differentiate various groups and discriminate the trust construct from other related constructs, but do these scores bear any relation to actual behaviors? If the paper-and-pencil indicators are valid, then high scorers ought to behave differently from low scorers. Investigation has

Table 13-1. Intercorrelations of Three Trust Measures and Other Personality Variables

Variable	1	2	3	4	5	6	7	8
1. Interpersonal Trust Scale								
2. Trust (sociometric rating)[a]	.37[b]							
3. Trust (self-rating)	.29	.39						
4. Trustworthiness[a]	.31	.62	.24					
5. Dependency[a]	-.23	-.07	-.06	-.45				
6. Humor[a]	.09	.34	.14	.26	-.36			
7. Gullibility[a]	-.03	.13	.01	-.24	.78	-.33		
8. Popularity[a]	.20	.43	.05	.57	-.46	.61	-.43	
9. Friendship[a]	.19	.42	.09	.50	-.53	.66	-.60	.83

Source: From "A New Scale for the Measurement of Interpersonal Trust" by J. B. Rotter, *Journal of Personality*, 1967, *35*, 651–665. Copyright 1967 by Duke University Press. Reprinted by permission. "The correlations . . . were obtained by calculating separate correlations for each [of four] group[s], transforming to z scores, finding the average z score, and then transforming to an r for the entire group" (Rotter, 1967, p. 661).

[a]Sociometric ratings.

[b]$r = .21$ for $p < .01$; $r = .16$ for $p < .05$; N = 156.

575

taken two different tacks: an interest in behavioral correlates of trust and a search for behavioral trust measures. Results from these two lines of research will be presented in the next sections.

One consistent finding is that mistrusters behave in a less trustworthy fashion than trusters. An empirical basis for La Rochefoucauld's observation that "our want of trust justifies the deceit of others" was noted in Rotter's (1967) sociometric study, which found that mistrusting fraternity and sorority members were also nominated as untrustworthy persons. In experimental games trusters take less advantage of partners than do mistrusters (Schlenker, Helm, & Tedeschi, 1973). They signal partners clearly, behave in accordance with their signals, and generally act in a more trustworthy fashion than do mistrusters.

These experimental games usually permit no face-to-face contact among partners, and the laboratory set-ups bear little resemblance to everyday situations. Hamsher (1968) devised a simulated stock market game in an attempt to achieve more realism in the experimental investigation of trust. Of the six players in each group, at least one had knowledge of the winning company. Hamsher hoped this arrangement would focus players' attention on reliability of the messages, rather than on competitive or chance aspects of the game situation. Players passed anonymous messages to each other in which they could either help others through "tips" or hinder through false information. Verity of the messages had to be evaluated in order to choose the companies in which to invest. In spite of the attempt to devise a more natural setting for the observation of trust and mistrust, results were approximately the same as in other game experiments. People responded to the competitive demands of a game situation, resulting in a lack of correlation between questionnaire (IT) and behavioral trust. High trusters (IT) were no more likely to believe others than were low trusters. However, they told fewer lies. Those who trusted their partners' communications in the course of the stock market game also transmitted more truthful and responsible messages.

Suppose that you have been ushered into the office of a prospective employer, who sits reviewing information in a file folder marked with your name. Just after your interview begins, the executive is called from the room unexpectedly. Would you peek at the folder or not? Rotter (1971) reports that Boroto (1970) studied resistance to temptation in a situation very like that one. Students did not believe they were coming for a job interview, however, but for a psychology experiment. After entering the interview room, the experimenter was suddenly called to the telephone, leaving the student alone with a folder of personal information. Since the study also focused on sex guilt, some pornographic pictures were dropped, then hastily raked up and replaced in their folder as the experimenter rushed out of the room. While he was "on the phone," participants were observed surreptitiously. Certainly the temptation to look at either of these folders must have been very great. Indeed, our right to review files of personal information about us (as in credit bureaus, school records, and so forth) has now been upheld by law as has our right to see pornography. Most people looked at one or both folders; and it is not surprising that their mean IT trust score was 66, close to the population mean. Those subjects who did not look at either folder, however, had a mean score of 80, almost one and one-half standard deviations above the mean. These extremely trusting subjects acted in a notably trustworthy fashion in not invading the experimenter's private papers.

Other investigations bear not only on the behavioral relationship between trust and trustworthiness but also have implications for the validity of psychological research in general. Geller (1967) asked male high and low IT scorers to perform a task designed to arouse their suspicion and thus measure degrees of behavioral trust. (This task will be described fully in the section on behavioral measures of trust.) Before the task, these people participated in a variation of the Asch (1956) conformity experiment, which involved deceiving a person into believing he was participating with others in an experiment when, in fact, the "others" were tape recorded. Between the Asch experimental procedure and administration of the trust scale, half of the participants were told about the deception by a confederate and the others were not. As expected, members of the deception-revealed group, regardless of trust scores, were judged suspicious by the blind judges who rated them in the task. When they were interviewed after the experiment, the mistrusters (low IT scores) denied their suspicions, but the trusters admitted them. Much psychological research (unfortunately and incongruously including that in the area of trust) involves deception. Rotter (1971) notes that in such studies post-experimental interviews are relied on

. . . to demonstrate the success of the deception. What these results indicate is that low trusters, the people who might be expected to be most suspicious, are the ones who will deny suspicion. While these results may not be generalizeable to all deception studies, they are true for this study under conditions where the subject has good reason to feel that he has already been tricked by the experimenter. (p. 448)

Whether trusters may volunteer in disproportionate numbers to mistrusters for psychological experiments is unclear. After an experiment that included undergraduate women with high, moderate, and low PHN trust scores, Nottingham (1972) mailed questionnaires to all participants, ostensibly asking for reasons for their participation. Twelve of 18 subjects in the low-trusting group failed to return their questionnaires, a significant contrast to the four defaults in each of the high and moderate trust groups. (Nottingham's curiosity had been aroused when he noticed that of the group of 54 originally requested to participate, the only four refusals came in the low trust group.) However, the authors of another study (Cash, Stack, & Luna, 1975; N = 44) found no significant differences in IT scores among groups who either participated, refused, or simply failed to appear for the behavioral task. These latter results fit better with Christie and Geis's (1970) observation that highly Machiavellian persons (probably low trust) are most likely to volunteer and show up for experiments. Probably the difference in the observations lies in the descriptions of projected experiments. Low trusters (high Machs) may relish a chance to play a game that would enable them to use their competitive skills and Machiavellian tactics (as Christie has found) or even to perform a task; but they may shy away from the interpersonal probing of questionnaires, surveys, and attitude testing (as Nottingham has found). Trust may interact with the type of research conducted, each type biased in terms of volunteers recruited.

Basic communication patterns of trusters and mistrusters appear to differ in important ways. For example, trusters covertly may offer their partners more help and positive regard, as well as more trustworthy verbal messages (Wrightsman, 1974). Since they communicate more truthfully to others, is it reasonable to expect that they demand truth in return? Because the IT scale is based on a conceptualization of trust as a belief in others' credibility, validation of that scale would rest specifically on the demonstration that trusters are more prone to believe others than are mistrusters. Political events during the 1960s and 1970s led to the much-cited "credibility gap" between the American public and its government. Is it possible that such a gap is wider for mistrusters than for trusters? Two investigations lend support to that interpretation. The first (Hamsher, Geller, & Rotter, 1968) centered on the report of the Warren Commission, which was formed to investigate the 1963 assassination of President John F. Kennedy. Even though members of the commission appeared to have been chosen with regard to their strong credibility and integrity, their word was doubted by students who earlier had responded mistrustingly on the IT scale. A significant negative relationship was exhibited between trust scale scores and the belief that the Warren Commission knew there was a conspiracy and was concealing it.

In 1968 the American public suffered another shock: The Democratic convention in Chicago was disrupted by thoroughly televised violent encounters between protesters and the city police. Again, a prestigious commission was formed to investigate the disorders, presenting an opportunity to replicate the earlier study. Again, a significant tendency ($p < 0.01$) was found for students who believed the report to be more trusting than those who did not (Lotsof & Grot, 1973). In contrast to the first investigation, most of the significance this time was owing to females; male believers had higher mean trust scores than disbelievers, but the difference was not significant.

Behavioral Trust Measures

Trusters, then, behave differently from mistrusters in their acknowledgement of attitudes. They are more likely to believe government pronouncements; they also communicate in a more trustworthy fashion. Do they also demonstrate more actual trust in the course of their interpersonal dealings? What is actual trust, and how is it demonstrated? The study of trust is still foundering on these questions, which boil down to a search for ways to measure behavioral trust—the criterion behavior that should relate to paper-and-pencil-measured trust. We are brought back to Wrightsman's original concern over the classification of situations in which a trust–mistrust dimension may be applied appropriately. Narrowing the construct to a belief in others' promises helps in the selection of situations, but we then face the problem of arranging for its scientific measurement within those situations. The degree of a person's belief may be solicited in questionnaire or interview form (in which there may be a tendency for mistrusters to misrepresent themselves), or it may be measured by examining his behavior after something has been promised him. Although the latter method is probably the more difficult, three investigators have attempted it with interesting results.

Hamsher (1968), using the stock market game mentioned earlier, attempted to find a behavioral criterion for IT scale scores. Participants, however, failed to perceive the possibility of establishing mutual trust relationships within the situation and behaved as if it were a competitive game (which it probably was). This finding shows that the dimension of generalized trust is overlaid and obscured by the norms appropriate to certain situations: "Cut the cards."

In Geller's (1967) study, trust was measured by judges' ratings. Students were recruited for an auditory discrimination experiment and asked to indicate as quickly as possible whether two pretested and easily identifiable musical chords were the same or different. As the experimenter demonstrated the use of a laboratory apparatus bearing two brass knobs labeled *same* and *different,* he pulled out the latter and received an apparently unexpected shock (complete with noise and a blue flame). After dramatized histrionics, the experimenter muttered that he thought he had fixed that, retreated behind the apparatus, and 10 seconds later came out with assurances that it was repaired so it would not shock the participant. The discrimination procedure (using the first four chords, all different) represented the criterion situation for trust. A subject's belief in the experimenter's assurances was measured by noting the time delay until the subject pulled the knob (if he ever did) and his spontaneous comments or other behavioral indications of distrust. Trust measured in this situation correlated significantly (0.38) with IT scores but only for those persons who had not participated in another deceptive experiment immediately prior to the discrimination task.

Two other groups had just participated in the Asch-type conformity experiment, sitting alone in booths, believing they were interacting with others (actually they were responding to tape-recorded partners). Trust scores of these previously deceived subjects were not significantly related to their trust in the discrimination procedure described above. The distinction between trust and gullibility, noted in the sociometric study of trust, is supported by these findings. High trusters will not continue to trust when they have been previously tricked. In the group who knew they had been tricked in the Asch experiment, the relationship between behavioral and questionnaire trust was nil ($-$ 0.04). For a second group in which the deception was concealed, it was slightly higher (0.14). The Asch procedure raises suspicions, as suggested by the comparison of the lower, nonsignificant correlation coefficients with the significant relationship (0.38) between the two types of trust for the group who participated only in the trust task.

Another behavioral measure of trust has been suggested by proponents of sensitivity training groups (Schutz, 1967). In these groups, persons are asked to demonstrate their trust by closing their eyes and falling backwards into the arms of another person who promises to catch them. The backwards direction of the fall precludes any possibility of saving oneself should the catcher renege. Refusal of the offer could be based on an estimate of the catcher's strength and size. If he looks large enough to prevent injury, a decision to cooperate may indeed indicate generalized trust. Cash and his coworkers (1975) decided to test that hypothesis using a male catcher who inspired confidence (6 ft., 10 in. tall, 230 lbs.) Two independent observers recorded the time it took each of the 34 participants to start their fall after the signal had been given. Partialing out a strong correlation (0.51) between age and seconds taken to fall (attributed to normal ravages of time), results showed that high trusters (as measured by the IT) took less time to fall than did low trusters ($-0.39, p < 0.05$).

Measuring Trust in Experimental Games

The search for ways to measure trust has led to the suggestion that cooperation might be a valid indicator. Although it is tempting to assume that one cooperates because he trusts, common sense tells us this is not always the case. Many international treaties pledging cooperation probably are based more often on mutual distrust than on trust. Sometimes cooperation or lack of it stems from factors entirely unrelated to trust. A student may expend more effort on an individual class project than he would working with several others—not because he mistrusts them and believes that the others would not contribute equally to the work or share their information with him but simply because he has a job that does not permit him to attend a group session.

As in the real world, motives behind cooperative and noncooperative behaviors in laboratory situations are also confusing. Cooperation has been studied most often in two-person games in which the gains or losses incurred by each person are a function of partners' joint choices. Many of these games are modeled after the now-classic dilemma (Luce & Raiffa, 1957) faced when two persons are arrested on suspicion of a certain crime but without adequate evidence for conviction. The district attorney tries to get that evidence by separating the two prisoners and trying to induce at least one to confess. Here is what he says: If neither confesses, each will be booked for a minor charge with a minimum jail term (e.g., one year). However, if one confesses and turns state's evidence and the other does not, the confessor will go free while the nonconfessor will serve the maximum time for the crime (10 years). If both confess, the D.A. will recommend a light sentence for both (five years). Each suspect perceives that he can go free if he confesses and turns state's evidence; however, if both attempt this, they will both be prosecuted and serve five years instead of none. Clearly, the most advantageous joint outcome is the minor one-year sentence resulting from mutual nonconfession. Making such a choice, however, requires each partner to trust the other not to confess; each must be willing to serve one year in order to achieve the best joint outcome. If one trusts whereas the other does not, the truster will get 10 years rather than the one year he expected. Such is the prisoners' dilemma (PD), the model for experimental mixed-motive games in which two noncommunicating players each chooses one of two strategies resulting in four joint outcomes. In the laboratory the outcomes are not freedom versus prison sentences but usually game points or small sums of money. If both players choose cooperatively, each gains a moderate amount of points (e.g., $+9$). If one decides not to cooperate, he can gain even more ($+10$), and the other will lose points (-10). However, if both try to maximize either their own gain or their partner's loss, instead of gaining they will both lose equal amounts (-9), much as the two prisoners faced the five-year sentence if they both confessed. The paradigm can be varied almost infinitely by changing the payoffs, making them real or imaginary, having players choose simultaneously or consecutively, having them play preprogrammed electronic partners versus real ones, and so forth. Games of this sort permit the abstract study of influences on cooperation, but in their usual form they appear to contribute little to an understanding of generalized trust. Cooperation depends on a variety of factors (e.g., risk-taking behavior, perceptions of the partner, partner's strategy, etc.); it is no wonder that generalized trust seems to play no role. Players evidently do not perceive the PD game as a situation relevant to trust or mistrust, because no consistent relationships have been found between game cooperation and trust questionnaire scores (Wrightsman, 1974).

It is possible to modify the PD game situation for the study of trust, however. When trust is redefined as a cooperative response observed under specified conditions, significant relationships with trust scale scores begin to emerge. Such a measure of trust is a cooperative response in conjunction with an expectation for cooperation from the partner. This measure rules out people as trusting who play cooperatively but actually expect competition. A second refined measure is a person's cooperation after he has received his partner's promise to cooperate. Whether he then cooperates seems to be a function of how much he believes the partner.

The first measure—an expectancy for partner cooperation in conjunction with a cooperative game choice—was used by Wrightsman (1966) to assess trust in a one-trial game. Those scored as trusting not only expected their partners to cooperate and cooperated themselves; they even gave the reason for their choice as trust, fairness, or cooperation. In two experiments, 49 students classified as behaviorally trusting had significantly higher ($p < 0.05$) PHN trust scores than did 33 classified as distrusting and 68 as neutral.

That trust can be assessed only in a situation in which information is passed from one person to another has been emphasized in a recent mixed-motive investigation (Schlenker et al., 1973) which used the second refined measure mentioned above. Defining interpersonal trust as "a reliance upon information received from another person about uncertain environmental states and their accompanying outcomes in a risky situation" (p. 419), the authors inserted promises into the traditional PD game. If participants believed a promise to cooperate on the next trial, it was theorized, they would cooperate. To do otherwise would possibly start a conflict spiral in a game with an indeterminate end point (players were not told how long the game would last). Competition was considered to be a signal of disbelief, since those who did not believe were faced with the choice of cooperating and being exploited or competing in order to protect themselves against exploitation. Forty women played 50 trials of the PD game. Twice during each block of 10 trials, a signal was received that the partner would cooperate on the next trial. A player's cooperation subsequent to the promise was significantly related ($p < 0.05$) to her IT score; trusters believed 71 percent of the promises, compared to 56 percent for mistrusters. Trust scores were unrelated to cooperation when no message was sent. These results fit well with Rotter's definition of trust as a belief in the credibility of others. Contrary to the findings of most other studies, these results show that generalized trust is related to cooperation over a series of PD trials—but only to those in which the individual has something on which to base his decision for trust or mistrust. (A much stronger predictor of cooperation after the message was whether the promiser had kept his promise in the past. Promisers who kept 90 percent of their promises elicited significantly [$p < 0.001$] more cooperation than those who kept only 10 percent.)

Trusters and mistrusters, as measured by questionnaires, cooperate and compete similarly in standard mixed-motive games; both respond similarly to the gamelike qualities of the situation. On the initial trial, however, trusters cooperate and expect reciprocal cooperation more than do mistrusters. Longer games that offer players clearly trust-relevant information such as promises also show differential responses for high and low trust scorers.

To summarize, individuals develop characteristic levels of generalized trust as a result of many separate trustworthiness judgments demanded by a continuing series of interpersonal interactions. The Interpersonal Trust Scale and the Philosophies of Human Nature Scale have been developed to measure this generalized trust. Mistrusters tend to believe that their reinforcements in life are controlled by external rather than internal (self) forces, and they subscribe to a Machiavellian orientation. Scale scores have been related to a number of behaviors, but such behaviors generally are importantly influenced by situational factors. The remainder of this chapter examines situational determinants.

SITUATIONAL TRUST

"Trust everybody—but cut the cards," says Mr. Dooley. Part of being human is being able to trust, if not everybody, at least someone now and then. Earlier we have been concerned with the degree to which individuals have developed generalized trust. Yet generalized trust forms only the basis for perceptions of individual situations. Each person within each situation has to be evaluated separately; sometimes the cards need to be cut, sometimes not.

Although situations that evoke trust–mistrust decisions can vary from two-person games to international treaties, two elements must be present for the situation to involve interpersonal trust. First, there must be some communication, even if it is only one-way. This follows from a definition of trust as a belief in others' credibility; even a broader definition of trust would necessitate some sort of information on which to base subsequent reliance. Second, there must be some risk involved. The outcome of a transaction must depend on some uncertainty over which another person exerts some control. Naturally, both partners must be aware to some extent of this inherent risk and the consequences of interdependence versus independence.

Both of these elements are provided by a form of the PD game that includes promises. Modifying the PD game in this way, several investigators have produced a body of research on the credibility of promises that has intriguing implications for understanding the development of trust. The next two sections will examine the determinants of credibility and the effects on it of various risks. The third section will explore a number of attitudes that have been related to credibility and noncredibility, and the last will suggest a direction for future research.

Credibility of Promises

Imagine yourself about to play one of the PD-type games. The other participant (same sex) has been designated the message "sender" and is in the next cubicle. Since you arrived second, you will be the message "receiver." On a desk in your cubicle is an electronic control panel, the top of which contains a two-by-two matrix with payoffs to each person displayed for the four cooperative-competitive response combinations (Table 13–2). Cumulative counters automatically total points, and you are to try to get as many as you can. You are told that at preselected times the sender will have the option of sending the promise displayed on the panel: "I will make Choice A on the next trial." If he exercises his option, you must respond by pushing one of three buttons, signaling either "I will make Choice A on the next trial," "I will make Choice B on the next trial," or "I don't wish to say what I will do on the next trial." You play 50 or 100 trials of the game, and in two or three out of every 10, you receive a message and respond. The sender sometimes keeps his promise and sometimes double-crosses you. At the end of the experiment you are asked to record your impressions of your partner, whom you could not have met because his moves were simulated by the experimenter. Debriefing to explain the purpose of this deception follows, and you are asked to refrain from spreading the word. How do you feel about the experimenter? About psychology in general? About yourself, now that you have been deceived?

Most scientific information about responses to promises is based on laboratory experiments like the one just described. The measure of credibility is whether people cooperate after the simulated partner has promised to do the same. We have already seen that trusters tend to believe these promises more than do mistrusters. Rotter has conceptualized trust as a generalized expectancy developed from a person's past history of reinforcement. If this is so, manipulation of reinforcement variables should affect situational trust (i.e., the extent to which one attributes credibility to another). The more a person has been rewarded for believing promises and the greater the value of the reward to him, the more likely he should be to believe promises.

The literature on the credibility of promises generally confirms these hypotheses. Those whose belief of promises is usually rewarded are more willing to believe than those infrequently rewarded for believing (Ayers, Nacci, & Tedeschi, 1973; Gahagan & Tedeschi, 1968; Schlenker et al., 1973). But trust is a

Table 13–2.   Sample Matrix Display of Payoff Values
for Prisoner's Dilemma Game

Opponent's Choice	Player's Choice	
	A	B
A	+4, +4[a]	+5, −5
B	−5, +5	−4, −4

[a]First figure of each pair is subject's payoff, second figure is opponent's payoff. For example, if both select Choice A, each player earns 4 points.

function not only of reinforcement level. It is also a function of degree of risk, as indicated by the fact that when the outcome is virtually certain because the partner invariably has kept his word, the situation is exploited and cooperation ceases (Lindskold & Bennett, 1973).

The decision to trust or mistrust is also a function of the relative power of the two participants. When power is equal, belief of promises is based on past credibility—the more often promises have been honored, the more the partner is trusted. Those with less power than their partners can become exploitative when partners' promises to cooperate are highly credible. The more powerful particip- ant tends to ignore partners' promises and to be uncooperative throughout the game (Tedeschi, Lindskold, Horai, & Gahagan, 1969). Another example of the interrelationship between credibility and power is that people are more likely to believe threats as the punishment magnitude and status of the threatener increase (Bonoma, Schlenker, Smith, & Tedeschi, 1970; Faley & Tedeschi, 1971).

Credibility of Threats

If you believe a threat, can you be said to trust the threatner? The outcome of trust is generally expected to be beneficial, as in Erikson's hypothesized concept (1963) that trust develops from affectively positive experiences with other peo- ple. On the other hand, Rotter conceptualizes trust as a belief in the credibility of either a positive or a negative statement. If this is so, threateners who have carried out their threats in the past would be considered more credible or trust- worthy than threateners who rarely administer the promised punishment. Several experiments have supported this hypothesis (Faley & Tedeschi, 1971; Horai & Tedeschi, 1969; Nacci & Tedeschi, 1973). When noncompliant behavior in response to a threat is punished more than half the time, individuals are more likely ($p < 0.001$) to believe subsequent threats. However, when a threatener acts in a cooperative fashion toward his partner at the same time as he threatens to penalize the partner's noncooperations, credibility of the threats no longer appears to mediate behavior. Bonoma and Tedeschi (1973) have shown that responses in such situations depend more on deeds than on words. Players cooperate to the degree that the threatener actually cooperates. Reinforcement theory would predict such results since the cooperative action of the threatener positively reinforces his partner's cooperation, whereas the punishment of an actualized threat is less effective.

Consider the relationship between trust and credibility at this point. Principles of learning (including reinforcement histories and reward values) have been shown in these sections on credibility to mediate situational trust—the belief in verbal promises or threats. The generalization of credibility situations across time and persons results in the sort of generalized trust discussed in the first part of this chapter.

Interpersonal Impressions

Does a person who is the target of highly credible threats develop the same sort of generalized trust as one who receives highly credible promises or of one who experiences both promises and threats? Although trust can be defined as a belief that either promises or threats can be relied on, can a consistently punished person be called trusting? Probably not, for two reasons: (1) learning theory notes that punishment is not only a less effective teaching method but also produces unwanted, often unspecified, side effects, and (2) experiments in promise and threat credibility show that the two modes of influence result in differential impressions of promisers and threateners. To make a trusting decision, people evaluate available information and form an impression of the situational partner. Even if the information is only a pattern of responses in a mixed-motive game, significant relationships obtain between those patterns and peoples' perceptions of the simulated partners. As generalized expectancies for credibility develop, the differential effects produced by negative or positive credibility experiences probably result in different sorts of generalized trust, depending on the generalization of perceptions of the other. The result of such generalization of impressions may be the positive and negative attitudes toward others that Wrightsman includes in his concept of trust.

What are the interpersonal impressions generated in the modified PD games we have been discussing? For one thing, the more credible the promises of a simulated partner, the more he is liked (e.g., Schlenker et al., 1973). However, no systematic relationship has been discovered between the level of credibility and partners' evaluations of threateners (e.g., Faley & Tedeschi, 1971). People who keep their promises are considered weaker (but nicer) than those who do not, and threateners who carry out their threats are considered stronger than those who do not. These results derive from participants' ratings of partners on seven-point continua between bipolar adjective pairs, such as *good–bad* and *strong–weak*.

Another investigation of interpersonal impressions related to promises and threats used a similar technique. Heilman (1974) set out to discover whether a person who had been a credible promiser would be believed as a threatener and whether the promise of a previous threatener was equally credible. First, 88 high school girls were given messages describing a fictitious partner who had either promised or threatened in a previous interaction. On the basis of that information alone, the girls were asked their impressions of the person. Threateners were evaluated significantly more negatively ($p < 0.001$) and considered less likely to keep their word ($p < 0.05$) than promisers. The credibility of these threateners and promisers was then manipulated by telling half of each group that the threat or promise was fulfilled or not fulfilled. Impressions of the partner collected at this point indicated that credibility interacted significantly ($p < 0.001$) with the mode of promise. Credible promisers were most positively evaluated, whereas those who "welshed" were seen as mean and selfish, sometimes even worse than threateners who fulfilled their threats. Views of nonfulfilling threateners became less negative; although they were never considered truly positive, they were perceived as being second only to promisers who kept their word. Regardless of whether the initial act was a threat or a promise, perceived trustworthiness was related only to whether the commitment was fulfilled: Those who fulfilled their promises or threats were seen as more likely to keep their word ($p < 0.001$) than were those who did not. Finally, subjects were either promised or threatened by the same fictitious partner and asked to judge the probability of the fulfillment. Heilman discovered in this final step that credibility seems to transfer from promises to threats but not the other way around. Promisers who had kept their word in the past were rated credible and evaluated positively, no matter whether they promised or threatened the second time. Nonfulfilling threateners the first time around were judged only minimally credible the second time in regard to either threats or promises. On the other hand, for threateners who had kept their word, only their threats were believed—not their promises. If past credibility experience were the sole determinant of trust, these actualized threateners should have been believed in both instances. Neither did past credibility experience uniformly influence reactions to promisers who had reneged: Their promises were doubted, but their threats were believed. In this study the subjective aspect of trust noted by Webster's dictionary appears to have outweighed the objective one.

Credibility of Speakers and Writers

Judgment of others' credibility and impressions of their personal characteristics are formed not only on the basis of promises and threats but also on verbal communication in general. Giffin (1967) has reviewed the source credibility literature and concluded that perceptions of writers' and speakers' credibility depend on five variables: expertness, reliability (trustworthiness), intentions, activity level, and personal attractiveness. Although the last three variables appear to lack generality across studies, the first two are well supported by a variety of experiments. The two variables, then, determining whether a speaker is believed are impressions of (1) his authoritativeness, expertise, or intelligence, and (2) his trustworthiness. Studies in the areas of speech, communication, and attitude change have shown that it is possible to manipulate introductions of speakers so as to induce credibility. Speakers' actual behaviors and communications that induce belief or nonbelief in listeners also need to be investigated, as does the linkage between listeners' attributions of credibility and generalized trust. Because more variables are involved, these two kinds of investigations may be more difficult tasks than the investigation of the credibility of promises.

Suggestions for Future Research

Earlier it was pointed out that the study of trust has been hampered by the lack of available theory to guide research. As a first step toward the development of such a theory, Kee and Knox (1970) have proposed a model (Figure 13–1) that can be used to pinpoint areas of current knowledge and those yet to be investigated. The figure shows three classes of independent variables involved in any trust-related situation: (a) the person's previous experiences, (b) structural and situational factors, and (c) dispositional factors, such as willingness to take risks and generalized trust. Most of this chapter has been devoted to evidence that these three classes of variables are related to behavioral trust or suspicion. Kee and Knox, however, suggest that research results would be clarified if trust were viewed as having two aspects: the observable behavior and a subjective state underlying that behavior. A measure of subjective probability about a partner's trustworthiness may relate more consistently to the three independent variables than do behavioral trust or suspicion. For example, a person may be only 20 percent certain of his partner's trustworthiness but still *act* as if he trusted. A judgment of trust or mistrust is often based on the performance or nonperformance of one behavior, but measurement of subjective probabilities would allow finer discrimination. Heilman (1974) used a dichotomous measure of subjective probability—whether people believed that their partners would invoke a penalty. This technique allows groups to be placed along a range of probability from 0.01 to 1.00 according to the resultant group means. A second class of variables

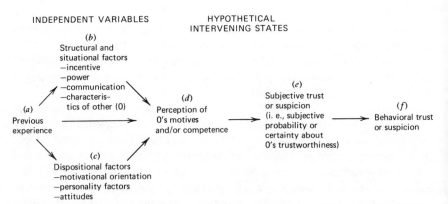

Figure 13-1.   A Conceptual Model for the Study of Trust (This figure, drawn from "Conceptual and Methodological Considerations in the Study of Trust and Suspicion," by H. W. Kee and R. E. Knox, is reprinted from the *Journal of Conflict Resolution,* Vol. XIV, No. 3 (Sept. 1970), p. 361 by permission of the publisher, Sage Publications, Inc.)

hypothesized to intervene between person/situation and trust is the person's perceptions of his partner: intentions, competence, and so forth. These are the variables examined by studies on the credibility of speakers and include the evaluative perceptions found to develop as a result of PD game strategies. The proposed Kee and Knox model suggests that the groups of independent variables should directly influence trust-relevant perceptions of the partner and that these perceptions are the basis for the subjective and objective aspects of trust. Of the five classes of variables relating to behavioral trust and suspicion, *a, b, c,* and *d* have been linked to some extent with some type of behavioral trust. Kee and Knox suggest the importance of studying the linkage with subjective rather than objective trust; subsequently the relationship between the two aspects of trust could be investigated. In addition, relationships among dispositional and situational variables and trust need to be explored. For example, to what degree do persons of high and low generalized trust respond differently to situational factors? How does this response affect perceptions of their partners and subjective or objective trust? How does willingness to take risks interact with trust? Are there sex differences in either generalized trust or reactions to situational factors?

Some methodological problems in the study of trust are (1) observing and measuring trust and suspicion in their natural habitats, (2) finding measures that generalize from the laboratory to real-life situations, and (3) developing methods to study trust among more than two partners.

Finally, as more is learned about trust-engendering actions and situations, particular attention must be paid to methods capable of fostering trust in the initially wary or cynical.

To summarize, situational trust has been studied mainly in variations of the PD game in which subjects receive messages from partners. The credibility of the messages is mediated by the proportion of promises or threats the partner has carried out in the past, as well as by other reinforcement variables. After a fulfilled promise, partners' threats are believed; but a promise that follows an actualized threat is not believed. Impressions of partners are systematically related to promises and threats. Promisers are more highly regarded than threateners. Promisers who keep their word and threateners who do not are evaluated more favorably than promisers who renege and threateners who fulfill their threats. Trusters are more likely than mistrusters to believe promisers but are not more likely to believe threateners. A person's perceived competence or expertness is another determinant of his credibility.

The study of situational trust may be facilitated by measuring the subjective aspect of trust in addition to or instead of observable behaviors assumed to indicate trust. Future research needs to link both the subjective and objective to generalized trust and to other dispositional and situational variables.

DETERMINANTS OF SITUATIONAL TRUST

Whether in international affairs, business dealings, teacher–student situations, or family relationships, the outcome of almost any interpersonal interaction will be affected by one person's trust or mistrust of the other. In the search for determinants of situational trust, several principles have emerged that have implications for improving interpersonal relationships.

Communication

A major determinant of trust seems to be communication—the more the better (Deutsch, 1962; Loomis, 1959). Since credibility depends on past reliability and on the risks involved, it is clear that the more information available on these points, the more reliable will be the decision to trust or mistrust. Ambiguity invites a decision based jointly on generalized trust and misperceptions drawn from attention to random aspects of the situation. Information should be released gradually by people developing a trusting relationship as a series of sequential actions and reactions (Deutsch, 1960), for it is this sort of joint control that is essential for the development of trust. Each partner must understand fully that his own goal attainment depends to some extent on the actions of the other. Unless this is understood, there is no reason to rely on another.

Risk

Such joint control of goal attainment results in a certain amount of risk for each partner, a second determinant of trust. A trusting relationship begins with a commitment period, during which partners exchange signals of their intentions (Swinth, 1967). One of the clearest signals appears to be one partner's deliberate self-exposure to some level of risk; if the other partner does not exploit this vulnerability, future interactions will probably be trusting. Should the first overture be exploited, trust can still be achieved if the exploiter then exposes himself to risk (thus signaling a desire for interpersonal trust) and is accepted. In any case, partners need to act and react flexibly, suspicious of each other's behavior, yet tolerant of untrustworthiness and slow to retaliate during the initial stages of trust building. Such tolerance serves to demonstrate the good will that is an integral part of trust and also makes allowance for any initial misperceptions of risk, intentions, or other aspects of the situation. Trust usually depends on partners' perceptions of future interaction as well as past (Boyle & Bonacich, 1970; Conviser, 1973). Partners who expect to get along with each other in the future need to build a relationship of mutual trust; if they never expect to see each other again, they would be free to "take the money and run." Because of the long-term nature of trust relationships, flexibility of signals during the commitment period is very important (Bixenstine & Gaebelein, 1971). If a partner invariably accommodates himself to the other, he invites exploitation. If he appears suspicious of the other's moves and retaliates when the other takes advantage of him, he may set off a vicious cycle of exploitation and retaliation leading to a mistrusting relationship. PD game research indicates that it is very easy to get locked into such destructive interaction patterns. One way to avoid this appears to be to proceed cautiously, registering open disbelief when it seems warranted, retaining the ability to punish untrustworthiness but seldom using it.

Obviously, avoiding patterns of mistrust during the commitment process is different from undoing such patterns once they have become locked in, as any psychotherapist knows. In such cases, other determinants of situational trust may be manipulated to produce credibility where none has existed before. The salience of comparative risks, power, and rewards needs to be increased. Unfortunately, in situations already fraught with mistrust, both partners may be reluctant to take the first step toward trust. To get around this, perhaps the reward for trusting can be increased at the same time the risk for trusting is decreased so as to achieve the initial credibility experience on which others can be built. Suppose a teen-age boy mistrusts his father. The son might be unwilling to risk the embarrassment that would result if the father broke his promise to keep a family secret from the boy's girlfriend. On the other hand, a first step toward trust might be achieved if the boy were induced to risk something less. Although some would value money more highly than face-saving, this boy does not, and he is willing to trust his father's promise of $5.00 for washing the car. After all, if the father reneges, the son loses little but gains a clean car. If the father pays off, a basis for future credibility is established.

Changing the balance of power is another way to manipulate comparative risks. A nation that has recently acquired nuclear weapons can afford to sign a peace treaty that previously had appeared too risky. Regardless of the other country's past performance in fulfilling commitments, the country with nuclear weapons will be more likely to sign after it has acquired more power over joint decisions.

Credibility of Promises

A third determinant of trust is credibility based on both expectancies about people in general and about specific persons. Credibility is based on fulfillment of promises, probably in a linear fashion. The more promises kept, the greater the perceived credibility—up to a point of a qualitative shift in peoples' perceptions of situations. If every promise is consistently kept by some agent, subsequent promises no longer carry an element of risk. The situation perceived by the promisee appears to shift from the domain of trust–mistrust to another—often exploitation. Parents who consistently honor promises are probably in no danger of teaching their children to exploit them, however, for it is a rare parent who is never forced by circumstances to renege on a promise. Only one instance of this sort adds to future parental promises the uncertainty that demands either trust or mistrust. Exploitation may be invited in a shorter series of invariably honored promises, however, particularly within a potentially competitive framework, such as that of international relations. A country may be equally open to attack whether it rarely or invariably honors nonaggression pacts. Its commitments will be more likely believed the greater the proportion of honored promises in past dealings. However, complete reliability would result in a loss of the joint control over outcome, which is an essential aspect of a trust-relevant situation.

Joint control and uncertainty can be reintroduced into a situation if a partner has threat as well as promise capabilities. Even if no punishments are ever instituted, the fact that they might be makes promises more believable (Lindskold & Bennett, 1973). The deterrent striking force deemed necessary by United States power strategists appears to fit well within this theoretical conception of trust–mistrust. Morally committed to honoring its international agreements as a way of developing trusting relationships, the United States retains some control over joint outcomes in order to ensure that the relationship does in fact depend on trust rather than on exploitation.

A deterrent striking force may benefit parents as well as nations. In a study reported by Rotter (1971), Into found that low trusters were likely to report that their parents made no threats or made them and did not keep them but that high trusters' parents both made and kept threats. The study required college students to recall their childhoods and the behaviors of both their fathers and mothers. Such retrospective studies have problems of distorted perception and memory loss over extended time periods but provide a basis for later concurrent investigations of parental behaviors and children's trust. Into also found that parental modeling and direct teaching of trust and trustworthiness are related to the development of generalized trust, as is parental credibility. Children's mistrust was related to low threat credibility, whereas trust was built on a combination of credible threats and promises. Parents of trusters made trust a salient issue by providing a variety of information (threats as well as promises), underscoring the element of risk by the introduction of threats, and fulfilling commitments to both promises and threats.

It appears that threats alone will not build trust, although their use or even potential use in conjunction with honored promises seems to enhance future credibility. No information is available about the generalized trust of children whose parents threaten and punish reliably, yet never promise. One reason for the lack of information on this point is the difficulty of measuring trust in young children so that it can be related to concurrent parent behaviors. One study used a modified Eriksonian rating scale (Santrock, 1970) to relate children's trust scores to mothers' behaviors observed in their own homes (Stack, 1972). Mothers of children rated trusting were observed to interact more frequently and more positively in terms of affect, and more enthusiastically than mothers of mistrusters. The latter gave more negative commands (''Don't do that!'') and displayed more anger to their mistrusting offspring. Although threats as such were not part of this study, the generally negative attitudes displayed by mothers of mistrusters suggest that persistently negative messages, no matter how credible they may be, are related more strongly to mistrust than to trust.

Another issue needing clarification is the relationship between threat and promise credibility. It appears that a man who has threatened to withdraw his financial support from a proposed business deal will not be trusted when he promises to share the cost of the next transaction, whether or not he actually withdrew from the first deal. On the other hand, if he is a believable promiser who has offered his share in past deals and followed through with the money, people will believe him when he threatens to pull out of a transaction. Thus, because of the subjective aspects of trust, the order of threats and promises appears to make a difference.

Social Evaluation

A threatener is probably evaluated more negatively than a promiser, regardless of credibility. Threats are considered more unpleasant, hostile, inappropriate, bossy, and unfair than promises. This sort of social evaluation, then, which appears to mediate future interpersonal transactions, is another determinant of trust. To the degree that a person has kept his word in the past, he is rated kind, good, honest, and wise. Such evaluations may be strongly related to trust if little other information is available on which to base a decision but may be irrelevant when combined with other data. One evaluates the personal appearance of the stranger at the door to determine whether to let him in. An ''honest face'' may be the sole criterion, or we may demand more information by asking him his business. If it turns out that he has something to sell, the honest face probably will not suffice to determine his trustworthiness. His attractiveness does not change, but some indication of his own and his company's reliability and the risk involved for the potential customer will become factors relevant to trusting or mistrusting the salesman.

Generalized Trust

The relationship between credibility and social evaluation is particularly important in the consideration of generalized trust. As children learn whether most people do or do not honor their promises and threats, they also come to evaluate people in general. Presumably children who grow up in an atmosphere of broken promises will be more prone to view others as bad, cruel, dishonest, and foolish than those who experience fulfilled commitments. To the extent that no situational information is available for a trust decision (a man appears at the door), these generalized feelings will account for the decision. Thus, a mistruster will be unlikely to find an "honest face." He might require more information in order to trust the stranger, since his risk in trusting a person is subjectively greater than the risk experienced by a truster, who expects most people to be good. Furthermore, to reach the same level of subjective probability as the truster that the stranger could be trusted, the mistruster might require a higher criterion of credibility than the truster. To compensate for the greater perceived risk, he might not be willing to trust the other unless he knew somehow that the stranger honored 90 percent of his promises, whereas someone with more generalized trust would be willing to trust on the basis of 50 percent credibility. Other factors, such as rewards and power, may also be perceived differently by those with different levels of generalized trust.

Situational trust is determined by at least five factors. First is the degree of risk or uncertainty present. Second, communication provides data on which to base the trust–mistrust decision. Third, whether or not partners have kept their promises in the past is a strong influence on future credibility and trust. Fourth is social evaluation, based on past and present behavior, appearance, similarity to significant others, and so forth. A fifth determinant is the generalized trust or mistrust forged out of all previous interpersonal experiences; generalizing across persons and occasions, everyone develops his own unique attitude toward the reliability and credibility of people in general. These five determinants of trust, and perhaps others, interact as people decide whether or not to cut the cards.

SUMMARY

In the course of interpersonal transactions, individuals develop generalized levels of trust/mistrust. The Interpersonal Trust Scale and the Philosophies of Human Nature Scale measure these generalized levels or the degree to which people subscribe to the social norm to "trust everybody." The first part of this chapter discussed trust findings derived from use of these instruments. This generalized trust, however, is only one factor in an individual's decision either to trust or mistrust in any given situation. In the second part of the chapter, situational factors contributing to the decision were presented. The final section explored the interrelationships among generalized trust and situational determinants—all factors in the individual's decision whether or not to "cut the cards."

NOTES

1. J. B. Rotter (*Journal of Personality*, Volume 35, pp. 651-665, "A new scale for the measurement of interpersonal trust," Copyright, 1967, Duke University Press.

REFERENCES

Asch, S. E. Studies of independence and conformity: A minority of one against a unanimous majority. *Psychological Monographs*, 1956, *70* (9, Whole No. 416).

Ayers, L., Nacci, P., & Tedeschi, J. T. Attraction and reactions to noncontingent promises. *Bulletin of the Psychonomic Society*, 1973, *1*, 75–77.

Baker, N. J., & Wrightsman, L. S. The Zeitgeist and philosophies of human nature, or Where have all the idealistic, imperturbable freshmen gone? In L. S. Wrightsman, *Assumptions about human nature: A social-psychological approach*. Monterey, Cal.: Brooks/Cole, 1974.

Bixenstine, V. E., & Gaebelein, J. W. Strategies of real opponents in eliciting the cooperative choice in prisoner's dilemma game. *Journal of Conflict Resolution*, 1971, *15*, 157–166.

Bombeck, Erma. At Wit's End (syndicated column). *Syracuse Post-Standard*, Jan. 13, 1975, p. 20.

Bonoma, T. V., Schlenker, B. R., Smith, R. B., & Tedeschi, J. T. Source prestige and target reactions to threats. *Psychonomic Science*, 1970, *19*, 111–113.

Bonoma, T. V., & Tedeschi, J. T. Effects of source behavior on target's compliance to threats. *Behavioral Science*, 1973, *18*, 34–41.

Boroto, D. R. The Mosher forced choice inventory as a predictor of resistance to temptation. Unpublished master's thesis, University of Conn., 1970.

Boyle, R., & Bonacich, P. The development of trust and mistrust in mixed-motive games. *Sociometry*, 1970, *33*, 123–139.

Campbell, D. T., & Fiske, D. W. Convergent and discriminant validation by the multitrait–multimethod matrix. *Psychological Bulletin*, 1959, *56*, 81–105.

Cash, T. F., Stack, J. J., & Luna, G. C. Convergent and discriminant behavioral aspects of interpersonal trust. *Psychological Reports*, 1975, *37*, 983–986.

Christie, R., & Geis, F. L. *Studies in Machiavellianism*. New York: Academic Press, 1970.

Chun, K., & Campbell, J. B. Dimensionality of the Rotter Interpersonal Trust Scale. *Psychological Reports*, 1974, *35*, 1059–1070.

Constantinople, A. Some correlates of average level of happiness among college students. *Developmental Psychology*, 1970, *2*, 447.

Conviser, R. H. Towards a theory of interpersonal trust. *Pacific Sociological Review*, 1973, *16*, 377–399.

Crowne, D. P., & Marlowe, D. *The approval motive: Studies in evaluative dependence*. New York: John Wiley, 1964.

Deutsch, M. The effect of motivational orientation upon trust and suspicion. *Human Relations*, 1960, *13*, 123–139.

Deutsch, M. Cooperation and trust: some notes. In M. R. Jones (Ed.), *Nebraska Symposium on Motivation*. Lincoln: Un versity of Nebraska Press, 1962.

Dunne, F. P. *Mr. Dooley's Philosophy*. Boston: Gregg Press, 1970. (Originally published, 1900)

Erikson, E. H. *Childhood and Society* (2nd ed.). New York: Norton, 1963.

Faley, T., & Tedeschi, J. T. Status and reaction to threats. *Journal of Personality and Social Psychology*, 1971, *17*, 192–199.

Fitzgerald, B. J., Pasewark, R. A., & Noah, S. J. Validity of Rotter's IT scale: A study of delinquent adolescents. *Psychological Reports*, 1970, *26*, 163–166.

Gahagan, J. P., & Tedeschi, J. T. Strategy and the credibility of promises in the Prisoner's Dilemma game. *Journal of Conflict Resolution*, 1968, *12*, 224–234.

Geller, J. D. Some personal and situational determinants of interpersonal trust (Doctoral dissertation, University of Connecticut, 1967). *Dissertation Abstracts International*, 1968, *28*, 4755-B. (University Microfilms No. 68-1345)

Giffin, K. The contribution of studies of source credibility to a theory of interpersonal trust in the communication process. *Psychological Bulletin*, 1967, *68*, 104–120.

Hamsher, J. H. Validity of personality inventories as a function of disguise of purpose (Doctoral dissertation, University of Connecticut, 1968). *Dissertation Abstracts International*, 1969, *29*, 3086-B–3087-B. (University Microfilms No. 69-2139)

Hamsher, J. H., Geller, J. D., & Rotter, J. B. Interpersonal trust, internal-external control and the Warren Commission Report. *Journal of Personality and Social Psychology*, 1968, *9*, 210–215.

Heilman, M. E. Threats and promises: Reputational consequences and transfer of credibility. *Journal of Experimental Social Psychology*, 1974, *10*, 310–324.

Hellmuth, J. (Ed.). *Disadvantaged child* (Vol. 1). New York: Brunner/Mazel, 1967.

Hobbs, N. Helping disturbed children: Psychological and ecological strategies. *American Psychologist*, 1966, *21*, 1105–1115.

Hochreich, D. J. Children's scale to measure interpersonal trust. *Developmental Psychology*, 1973, *9*, 141.

Hochreich, D. J. Sex-role stereotypes for internal-external control and interpersonal trust. *Journal of Consulting and Clinical Psychology*, 1975, *43*, 273.

Hochreich, D. J., & Rotter, J. B. Have college students become less trusting? *Journal of Personality and Social Psychology*, 1970, *15*, 211–214.

Horai, J., & Tedeschi, J. T. Effects of credibility and magnitude of punishment on compliance to threats. *Journal of Personality and Social Psychology*, 1969, *12*, 164–169.

Imber, S. Relationship of trust to academic performance. *Journal of Personality and Social Psychology*, 1973, *28*, 145–150.

Into, E. C. Some possible child rearing antecedents of interpersonal trust. Unpublished master's thesis, University of Connecticut, 1969.

Katz, H. A., & Rotter, J. B. Interpersonal trust scores of college students and their parents. *Child Development*, 1969, *40*, 657–661.

Kee, H. W., & Knox, R. E. Conceptual and methodological considerations in the study of trust and suspicion. *Journal of Conflict Resolution*, 1970, *14*, 357–366.

Lindskold, S., & Bennett, R. Attributing trust and conciliatory intent from coercive power capability. *Journal of Personality and Social Psychology*, 1973, *28*, 180–186.

Loomis, J. L. Communication, the development of trust, and cooperative behavior. *Human Relations*, 1959, *12*, 305–315.

Lotsof, E. J., & Grot, J. S. Interpersonal trust, I–E control, and the Walker report on the Democratic convention disorders. *Psychological Reports*, 1973, *32*, 747–752.

Luce, R. D., & Raiffa, H. *Games and decisions*, New York: John Wiley, 1957.

Maccoby, E. E., & Jacklin, C. N. *The psychology of sex differences.* Stanford, Cal.: Stanford University Press, 1974.

Mischel, W. *Personality and assessment.* New York: John Wiley, 1968.

Nacci, P., Stapleton, R. E., & Tedeschi, J. T. Empirical restatement of reciprocity norms. *Journal of Social Psychology,* 1973, *91,* 263–271.

Nacci, P., & Tedeschi, J. T. Trust and reactions to threats. *Bulletin of the Psychonomic Society,* 1973, *1,* 421–422.

Nottingham, J. A. The *N* and the out: Additional information on participants in psychological experiments. *Journal of Social Psychology,* 1972, *88,* 299–300.

O'Connor, J. Personal communication, November, 1970.

Richard, W. C., Mates, C. B., & Whitten L. *Personality traits and attitudes of adolescent girls with behavior disorders.* Paper presented at the meeting of the Southeastern Psychological Association, Atlanta, April 1967.

Roberts, M. D. Changing patterns of college student trust (Doctoral dissertation, University of Connecticut, 1972). *Dissertation Abstracts International,* 1972, *32,* 5457-B–5458-B. (University Microfilms No. 72-8901)

Rosenberg, M. Misanthropy and political ideology. *American Sociological Review,* 1956, *21,* 690–695.

Rotter, J. B. *Social learning and clinical psychology.* Englewood Cliffs, N. J.: Prentice-Hall, 1954.

Rotter, J. B. Generalized expectancies for internal versus external control of reinforcement. *Psychological Monographs,* 1966, 80 (1, Whole No. 609).

Rotter, J. B. A new scale for the measurement of interpersonal trust. *Journal of Personality,* 1967, *35,* 651–665.

Rotter, J. B. Generalized expectancies for interpersonal trust. *American Psychologist,* 1971, *26,* 443–452.

Rotter, J. B. Personal communication, June, 1975.

Santrock, J. W. Influence of onset and type of paternal absences on the first four Eriksonian developmental crises. *Developmental Psychology,* 1970, *3,* 273–274.

Sawyer, R., Pasewark, R., Davis, F., & Fitzgerald, B. Relationship of Rotter's interpersonal trust scale and social class. *Psychological Reports,* 1973, *32,* 989–990.

Schlenker, B. R., Helm, B., & Tedeschi, J. T. The effects of personality and situational variables on behavioral trust. *Journal of Personality and Social Psychology,* 1973, *25,* 419–427.

Schutz, W. E. *Joy.* New York: Grove Press, 1967.

Stack, L. C. An empirical investigation of Erik Erikson's theory of the development of basic trust in three-year-old children (Doctoral dissertation, George Peabody College, 1972). *Dissertation Abstracts International,* 1972, *33,* 3294-B. (University Microfilms No. 72-34, 214, 271)

Swinth, R. L. The establishment of the trust relationship. *Journal of Conflict Resolution,* 1967, *11,* 335–344.

Switkin, L. R., & Gynther, M. D. Trust, activism, and interpersonal perception in black and white college students. *Journal of Social Psychology,* 1974, *94,* 153–154.

Tedeschi, J. T. Attributions, liking, and power. In T. Huston (Ed.), *Perspectives on interpersonal attraction.* New York: Academic Press, 1973.

Tedeschi, J. T., Lindskold, S., Horai, J., & Gahagan, J. P. Social power and credibility of promises. *Journal of Personality and Social Psychology,* 1969, *13,* 253–261.

Walker, D. N., & Mosher, D. L. Altruism in college women. *Psychological Reports,* 1970, *27,* 887–894.

Webster's Third New International Dictionary of the English Language, Unabridged. Springfield, Mass.: Merriam, 1971.

Wrightsman, L. S. Measurement of philosophies of human nature. *Psychological Reports,* 1964, *14,* 743–751.

Wrightsman, L. S. Personality and attitudinal correlates of trusting and trustworthy behaviors in a two-person game. *Journal of Personality and Social Psychology,* 1966, *4,* 328–332.

Wrightsman, L. S. *Assumptions about human nature: A social-psychological approach.* Monterey, Cal.: Brooks/Cole, 1974.

APPENDIX A

Revised Philosophies of Human Nature Scale[1]

This questionnaire is a series of attitude statements. Each represents a commonly held opinion, and there are no right or wrong answers. You will probably disagree with some items and agree with others. We are interested in the extent to which you agree or disagree with matters of opinion.

Read each statement carefully. Then, on the separate answer sheet, indicate the extent to which you agree or disagree by circling a number for each statement. The numbers and their meanings are as follows:

If you agree strongly, circle +3.
If you agree somewhat, circle +2.
If you agree slightly, circle +1.
If you disagree slightly, circle −1.
If you disagree somewhat, circle −2.
If you disagree strongly, circle −3.

First impressions are usually best in such matters. Read each statement, decide if you agree or disagree and determine the strength of your opinion, and then circle the appropriate number on the answer sheet. *Be sure to answer every statement.*

If you find that the numbers to be used in answering do not adequately indicate your opinion, use the one that is *closest* to the way you feel.

---

[1]From *Assumptions about Human Nature: A Social-Psychological Approach* by L. S. Wrightsman. Copyright © 1974 by Wadsworth Publishing Company. Reprinted by permission of the publisher, Brooks/Cole Publishing Company, Monterey, California.

1. If most people could get into a movie without paying and be sure that they would not be seen, they would do it. (C)[a]
2. Most people have the courage of their convictions. (T)
3. The average person is conceited. (C)
4. Most people try to apply the Golden Rule, even in today's complex society. (T)
5. Most people would stop and help a person whose car was disabled. (T)
6. The typical student will cheat on a test when everybody else does, even though he has a set of ethical standards. (C)
7. Most people do not hesitate to go out of their way to help someone in trouble. (T)
8. Most people would tell a lie if they could gain by it. (C)
9. It's pathetic to see an unselfish person in today's world, because so many people take advantage of him. (C)
10. "Do unto others as you would have them do unto you" is a motto that most people follow. (T)
11. People claim that they have ethical standards regarding honesty and morality, but few people stick to them when the chips are down. (C)
12. Most people will speak out for what they believe in. (T)
13. People pretend to care more about one another than they really do. (C)
14. People usually tell the truth, even when they know they would be better off by lying. (T)
15. Most people inwardly dislike putting themselves out to help other people. (C)
16. Most people would cheat on their income tax if they had the chance. (C)
17. The average person will stick to his opinion if he thinks he's right, even if others disagree. (T)
18. Most people will act as "Good Samaritans" if given the opportunity. (T)
19. Most people are not really honest for a desirable reason; they're afraid of getting caught. (C)
20. The typical person is sincerely concerned about the problems of others. (T)

---

[a] Letters in parentheses indicate subscales.
C = Cynicism, T = Trust.

Author Index

600

65, 66, 67, 70, 72, 74, 76, 77, 81, 82,
280, 298, 390, 497, 509, 548
Speisman, J. C., 46, 79, 82
Spence, J. T., 66, 72, 82
Spence, K. W., 38, 40, 41, 66, 82, 477, 484
Srole, L., 106, 127
Stack, J. J., 577, 592, 595
Stack, L. C., 597
Stagner, R., 87, 127
Stahelski, A. J., 117, 118, 119, 126
Steele, R. S., 28, 33, 398, 409, 445, 446
Stefaniek, D., 464, 480
Steffensmeier, D. J., 164
Stefflre, B., 155, 164
Stein, S. H., 461, 484
Steinberg, M. A., 468, 469, 480
Steinberg, P., 519, 546
Steinfeld, S. L., 190, 213
Steininger, M., 142, 155, 162
Stephens, M. W., 276, 302
Stern, H., 256, 261
Stern, W., x, xiv
Stewart, A. J., 393, 398, 412, 413, 414,
415, 416, 417, 418, 419, 426, 427, 438,
440, 441, 446
Stewart, J., 441, 442
Stice, G. F., 506, 543
Sticht, T., 143, 164
Stifler, L., 374, 389
Stokes, D. E., 123, 125
Stone, G. C., 105, 126
Stone, L. A., 381, 390
Stotland, E., 111, 126
Stoudenmire, J., 64, 82
Strahan, R., 64, 82
Straits, B. C., 277, 303
Strassberg, D. S., 285, 286, 289, 303
Strauss, P. S., 143, 149, 150, 153, 164
Strickland, B., 272, 273, 276, 277, 280,
281, 284, 285, 291, 300, 373, 374, 375,
382, 388, 446
Stroufe, L., 51, 52, 79
Stutler, D. L., 62, 82
Suci, G. J., 446
Suedfeld, P., 546
Sugerman, A. A., 176, 210
Sullivan, D. H., 457, 484
Sullivan, H. S., 38, 83
Sundstrom, P. E., 509, 543
Sutker, P. B., 509, 545
Swanson, E. M., 463, 471, 481
Swanson, G. E., 471, 483
Swartz, J. D., 192, 199, 211
Swindell, D. H., 459, 484
Swinth, R. L., 590, 597
Switkin, L. R., 597

Taft, R., 241, 261
Tanck, R. H., 463, 483
Tannenbaum, P. H., 446
Tatsuoka, M. M., 51, 75
Taulbee, E. S., 61, 82

Taylor, D. A., 55, 83, 156, 160
Taylor, F. R., 83
Taylor, J. A., 38, 40, 51, 456, 484, 509,
548
Taylor, R. L., 530, 549
Taylor, S., 379, 380, 390
Taynor, J., 35
Teaugue, G., 403, 409, 435, 445
Tebbs, R. B., 463, 484
Tedeschi, J. T., 567, 576, 586, 595, 596,
597
Telford, C. W., 155, 163
Tempone, V. J., 452, 453, 473, 477, 484
Tennyson, R. D., 60, 83
Terhune, K. W., 151, 164
Thackray, R. I., 224, 261
Thaw, J., 377, 390
Thibaut, J., 314, 356
Thomas, J. A., 155, 163
Thomas, L. E., 282, 303
Thorne, G. L., 504, 505, 533, 549
Thornton, C. L., 192, 208
Thorpe, J. S., 192, 211
Throop, W. F., 264, 303
Thurstone, L. L., 176, 213, 215
Titchener, E. B., 38, 83
Titus, H. E., 85, 124, 127
Tobias, S., 60, 83
Tolor, A., 272, 280, 303, 459, 464, 484,
533, 546
Tomkins, S. S., 42, 77
Tosi, D. J., 164
Touchstone, R. N., 224, 261
Travel, N., 236, 261
Tresemer, D., 29, 35
Trope, Y., 15, 35
Troth, W. A., 62, 78
Tseng, M. S., 278, 303
Tumilty, T. N., 504, 505, 507, 517, 543
Tunstall, O. A., 242, 261
Turk, D., 71, 72, 80
Tursky, B., 269, 302
Tushup, R., 494, 511, 550
Tyre, T. E., 293, 303

Uleman, J. S., 398, 440, 446, 447
Ullman, L. P., 375, 389, 451, 457, 472, 484

Vacchiano, R. B., 143, 149, 150, 153, 164
Valins, S., 460, 484
Vandenberg, S. G., 205, 214
Van de Rat, H., 459, 485
Van Duyn, 392, 447
Van Egeren, L., 453, 484
Vanik, V., 29, 32
Vanlehn, R., 52, 78
Van Meel, J., 198, 215
Vanneman, R., 401, 445
Venables, P. H., 532, 549
Vernon, J., 488, 549
Vernon, P. E., 181, 190, 214
Veroff, J., 6, 26, 35, 398, 440, 447

Subject Index

D